POP CULTURE
LATIN AMERICA!

Upcoming titles in ABC-CLIO's series

Popular Culture in the Contemporary World

Pop Culture Caribbean! Media, Arts, and Lifestyle, by Brenda F. Berrian

Pop Culture China! Media, Arts, and Lifestyle, by Kevin Latham

Pop Culture Germany! Media, Arts, and Lifestyle, by Catherine Fraser

Pop Culture India! Media, Arts, and Lifestyle, by Asha Kasbekar

Pop Culture Japan! Media, Arts, and Lifestyle, by William H. Kelly

Pop Culture Russia! Media, Arts, and Lifestyle, by Birgit Beumers

Pop Culture UK! Media, Arts, and Lifestyle, by Bill Osgerby

Pop Culture West Africa! Media, Arts, and Lifestyle, by Onookome Okome

POP CULTURE LATIN AMERICA!

Media, Arts, and Lifestyle

Lisa Shaw
Stephanie Dennison

ABC CLIO

Santa Barbara, California Denver, Colorado Oxford, England

Library of Congress Cataloging-in-Publication Data
Shaw, Lisa, 1966–
Pop culture Latin America! : media, arts, and lifestyle / Lisa Shaw, Stephanie Dennison.
p. cm. — (Popular culture in the contemporary world)
Includes bibliographical references and index.
ISBN 1-85109-504-7 (hardback : alk. paper) — ISBN 1-85109-509-8 (e-book)
1. Popular culture—Latin America—History—20th century. 2. Latin America—Civilization—1948–
I. Dennison, Stephanie. II. Title. III. Series: Contemporary world issues.
F1414.2.S495 2005
306'.098'09045—dc22

2004024669

07 06 05 10 9 8 7 6 5 4 3 2 1

This book is also available on the World Wide Web as an eBook.
Visit abc-clio.com for details.

ABC-CLIO, Inc.
130 Cremona Drive, P.O. Box 1911
Santa Barbara, California 93116-1911

Text design by Jane Raese

This book is printed on acid-free paper.
Manufactured in the United States of America

Contents

Preface

This book provides an overview of Latin American popular culture since the 1940s, focusing on the contemporary period. We have selected thematic chapters that reflect the most dynamic and often unique aspects of the region's popular cultural production, such as popular religion and festivals and popular music, ranging from Argentine tango to Brazilian and Mexican hip-hop. Our aim has also been to provide information on topics or people with whom the English-speaking world may already have come into contact, such as the internationally acclaimed authors Paulo Coelho and Gabriel García Márquez, whose works are available in translation all over the world, and recent movies from Latin America, such as the Mexican film *Amores perros* (*Love's a Bitch*, 2000) and the Brazilian block-buster *Cidade de Deus* (*City of God*, 2002). In addition, we have included the chapter "Cultural Icons," which looks at how Latin Americans have been portrayed and perceived abroad, a fascinating area that is overlooked in existing studies of the region. The coverage in a work of this size cannot possibly be exhaustive, but in overviews of a variety of popular cultural expressions we have tried to include references to cultural practices found in as wide a range as possible of Spanish- and Portuguese-speaking communities in Latin America. Thus, although large Latin American nations with significant and well-researched cultures such as Mexico and Brazil are afforded a good number of entries, smaller nations such as Costa Rica and the Dominican Republic are also included (see, for example, the chapter "Travel and Tourism").

All of our contributors have extensive academic knowledge of the region and its popular culture, but we have endeavored to combine scholarly rigor and accuracy with an engaging and accessible style of writing that we hope will appeal to a wide readership, particularly high school and college students but also the general public. In order to make our text accessible and user-friendly, we have included both a detailed index and numerous cross-references to related entries. After each entry we have included suggestions for further reading, citing, where possible, texts written in English.

We would like to thank the following individuals and institutions for their assistance and support in the writing of this book: our contributors, Thea Pitman, Keith Richards, and Claire Taylor; Andrea Noble (University of Durham, England); the University of Leeds, England; Carmen Caldeira de Barros; and Alex Nield and Fernando Barbosa.

Chronology

1492	Christopher Columbus, in the name of the Spanish Crown, arrives at the continental landmass that we now refer to as the Americas.
1500	Pedro Alvares Cabral, a Portuguese navigator, lands on the northeastern coast of what is now Brazil.
1519–1520	Hernán Cortés reaches and conquers Mexico in the name of Spain, overcoming the Aztec emperors.
1530	The Portuguese establish their colony in Brazil. Slaves imported from Africa replace indigenous forced labor on sugar plantations. An estimated four million Africans will have been brought to Brazil by the end of the international slave trade in 1850.
1532–1572	Francisco Pizarro begins the conquest of Peru in the name of Spain, establishing Lima as the capital and destroying the Inca state.
1595	The number of African slaves entering Spanish colonies increases hugely as a consequence of the Spanish Crown's use of Portuguese slave traders.
1750–1774	Brazil's borders are formally established.
1781–1811	Latin America undergoes a period of unrest and revolts by indigenous peoples, African slaves and their descendants, and republican movements.
1810	The fight for independence from Spanish or Portuguese colonial rule gains momentum. Brazil shakes off Portuguese rule in 1822 and most Spanish-speaking territories have become independent by 1828.
1823–1872	Slavery is gradually abolished country by country, except in Cuba and Brazil.
1845	The United States annexes Texas.

1850s	By this point the pattern of nations within Latin America is similar to the one we know today.
1886	Slavery is finally abolished in Cuba.
1888	Slavery is finally abolished in Brazil, and the first Republic of Brazil is created the following year.
1895–1902	This period sees the Cuban War of Independence, followed by the Hispano-Cuban-American War and the U.S. occupation of Cuba and Puerto Rico (the latter until 1952).
1910–1920	The Mexican Revolution brings to an end the *Porfiriato*, the long period of dictatorship of Porfirio Díaz.
1930	Getúlio Vargas becomes president of Brazil by a bloodless coup and remains in power until 1945. He returns to the presidency by democratic vote in 1950 and commits suicide in office in 1954.
1946	Juan Perón comes to power by a coup in Argentina and remains as dictator until 1955. In 1973 he returns to the presidency by democratic vote for a year.
1954	Alfredo Stroessner becomes dictator of Paraguay until 1989.
1956–1959	The Cuban Revolution brings socialist leader Fidel Castro to power, where he remains. Thousands of Cubans settle in Florida as a result.
1961	The United States and Cuba break off diplomatic relations.
1964	A military coup in Brazil gives rise to a period of dictatorship that lasts until 1985.
1965	The guerrilla group FARC (Revolutionary Armed Forces of Colombia) is formed.
1973	A bloody coup in Chile installs General Augusto Pinochet as military dictator until 1990.
1976–1983	This period of military rule and intense repression in Argentina is known as the *Guerra Sucia* (Dirty War).
1979	The Sandinista revolution occurs in Nicaragua, followed by the Contra war between 1981 and 1987.
1980	Civil war begins in El Salvador and lasts until 1992.

1980	Shining Path (Sendero Luminoso) begins terrorist activities in Ayacucho, Peru.
1982	Great Britain and Argentina fight the Falklands/Malvinas War.
1985	Argentina, Brazil, and Uruguay return to democracy.
1990	Chile returns to democracy. Alberto Fujimori is elected president of Peru and later stages an internal coup, dissolving Congress with the help of the military.
1991	Official celebrations commemorate the five-hundredth anniversary, or quincentenary, of the "discovery" of America.
1991	MERCOSUR (MERCOSUL in Portuguese), the Common Market of the South, is created, encompassing Brazil, Argentina, Uruguay, and Paraguay.
1994	The NAFTA agreement (North American Free Trade Agreement) is signed among Mexico, Canada, and the United States. The Zapatista revolts begin in the Chiapas region of Mexico.
1998	Controversial leader Hugo Chávez is elected president of Venezuela.
1998	Puerto Ricans vote in plebiscite not to become the fifty-first U.S. state.
2000	The Partido Revolucionario Institucional (PRI, Institutional Revolutionary Party) loses the presidential elections in Mexico for the first time, thus ending a period of sixty-eight years of absolute majority.
2000	Alberto Fujimori flees Peru in disgrace.
2001	A period of severe economic crisis begins in Argentina and worsens in 2002.
2002	Former trade union leader Lula (Luis Ignácio Lula da Silva) becomes the first Brazilian president of working-class origin.

2003 Outrage is caused among the international community and human rights organizations by Fidel Castro's decision to condemn to death three Cubans who hijacked a boat in an attempt to flee the country.

Bibliography

Swanson, Philip, ed. 2003. *The Companion to Latin American Studies.* London: Arnold.

1

Introduction

Defining the Popular in the Latin American Context

The notion of popular culture is not a straightforward one, and a single definition of the term "popular" has proved elusive. The term is often used simply to refer to cultural products enjoyed or experienced by large numbers of people, chiefly but not necessarily those on the lower rungs of the social hierarchy. Alongside this perhaps obvious numerical sense of the word, some people use "popular" to signify "low-brow" culture, diametrically opposed to "elite" culture in terms of sophistication, the received standards of good taste, and its presumed consumers. Others consider "popular culture" to refer solely to that which has origins in preindustrial traditions, and the term may often be synonymous with "folk" or "peasant culture" in certain Latin American contexts. In this book it is not our intention to try to establish a single understanding of the concept of popular culture; rather, we intend to familiarize readers with the main definitions and ideas that have been put forward. Leading scholars who have provided theories on what constitutes popular culture in the Latin American subcontinent include Jesús Martín-Barbero, Renato Ortiz, Fernando Ortiz, Angel Rama, Ricardo Gutiérrez Mouat, Néstor García Canclini, William Rowe, and Vivian Schelling.

Martín-Barbero has noted the tendency to classify the popular either as the romanticized notion of the "authentic" or as the negative idea of "vulgarized." He proposes that the popular in Latin America is instead a "dense space of interactions, interchanges and re-appropriations, the movement of *mestizaje* (cultural hybridity)" (1994, p. 92). Renato Ortiz has said that the notion of the "popular" as merely synonymous with numerical consumption arose in the Brazilian context as a consequence of the emergence of the culture industry and a market of symbolic national goods since the 1970s.

Mouat has further observed that "mass culture bridges the gap between marginal cultures (popular and regional) and consumer culture, whose mode of production and circulation is now perceived to be hegemonic" (1993, p. 163). He does not believe that popular culture and mass culture are one and the same thing; rather, he considers mass culture to be a form of mediation between popular and hegemonic culture. Canclini, meanwhile, believes that the traditional view of popular culture as existing in opposition to elite culture is invalid, since this binary is complicated by the existence of mass culture. However, he illustrates how the distinctions among these three categories are increasingly being blurred by the processes of modernization and globalization. Globalization is not, however, a purely negative force, bringing with it only the eradication or appropriation of popular culture; it also provides new openings for the reception and interpretation of cultural products. As William Rowe and Vivian Schelling note: "the vast increases in channels of communication which flow across cultural boundaries have the effect of dismantling old forms of marginalization and domination and making new forms of democratization and cultural multiplicity imaginable" (Rowe and Schelling 1991, p. 1).

In their study of popular culture in Latin America, Rowe and Schelling identify three different versions of popular culture in the subcontinent: first, popular culture seen as authentically rural, threatened by industrialization and the modern culture industry; second, popular culture as a variant of mass culture, trying to copy the cultural forms of advanced capitalist nations; third, popular culture as the culture of the oppressed, subaltern classes, in which their imaginary, ideal future is created. In Rowe and Schelling's view all these categories combine and intermingle in Latin America. They also draw a distinction between popular and mass culture: the former shares neither the audience nor the popularity (in raw numerical terms) of the latter, despite the fact that neither remains entirely distinct from the other. The traditional duality between "popular" (or "low") and "high" culture is dangerous, they argue, since it can lead to other assumed, symmetrically polarized oppositions that have highly pejorative implications for popular culture, such as "vulgar" versus "polite" and "impure" versus "pure."

As a result of these assumed oppositions, popular culture is often thought of as the domain of the uneducated and illiterate. Latin America has one of the lowest rates of school completion in the world, preschool education is barely available, and residents of rural areas are less likely to receive a decent education than their urban counterparts. At times the only access Latin Americans have to education is outside formal institutions (i.e., traditional schooling) in what has been termed popular education. The uneven patterns of literacy make it harder for large sections of the region's population to have access to some forms of popular culture (those using the written word, in particular) than to others. But in the context of Latin America the interlinking of literacy/popular education and popular culture is much more extensive. In fact, in many of its manifestations it is often difficult to separate Latin American popular culture from popular education. Perhaps the best-known and arguably the most effective popular educational method is that developed by Brazilian educator Paulo Freire (1921–1997) in the 1960s and 1970s. Freire's method differs from traditional teaching methods in that students are encouraged to learn first and foremost about their "oppression" and to develop the tools to "liberate" themselves. As Liam Kane explains, "politically, education could never remain neutral: traditional education promoted the values of the dominant classes, ignored the real-life knowledge and experience of the 'oppressed,' and maintained a social order in which the oppressed came to blame themselves, not the oppressors, for their destitution" (2000, p. 595). The kinds of materials used in Freire's method, which has been popularized throughout the third world, include *literatura de cordel* (chapbooks), murals, popular songs, films, theater, and so on. The consciousness-raising techniques that Freire espoused were partly inspired by Liberation Theology and are reminiscent of Brazilian dramatist Augusto Boal's Theater of the Oppressed, both of which, in turn, can be said to play a significant role in popular education in Latin America and beyond.

Much popular cultural production in Latin America, then, serves to liberate the individual or communities from oppression or can be adapted to that purpose. There are many examples of such "liberatory" cultural expressions discussed in this book, including the work of Mexican muralist Diego Rivera and the plays and songs written and performed under military dictatorships in Chile and Argentina. This in itself is one of the favored interpretations of popular culture—a culture of resistance. Analyses of culture using this perspective can be found in the work of Paraguay's Roa Bastos and Brazil's Marilena Chauí, for example. Thus, not only does popular culture have strong ties with popular education in Latin America, but it also frequently has links with left-wing politics. One significant example of this can be found in Chiapas, Mexico, in the form of the Zapatismo movement, and another in the form of the *Movimento dos Sem Terra*, or Landless People's Movement in Brazil: both successfully integrate the political and the cultural in their agendas.

Key Theoretical Perspectives

The theorists cited above tend to agree on certain key concepts and issues that inevitably crop up when the issue of popular culture in Latin America is discussed. Below we have summarized these central notions as they have been conceived in and applied to this particular regional context.

Modernity

Uneven processes of development characterized Latin American countries throughout the twentieth century and continue to do so in an increasingly globalized new millennium. Cultural theorists often refer to the "other" or "peripheral" experience of modernity in Latin America, where the modern and the premodern continue to coexist. Canclini, for example, has contrasted the advanced state of cultural modernity in the region with its relatively underdeveloped socioeconomic and political modernity. For this reason, Latin American popular culture embraces both elements of postmodern mass media, such as the ubiquitous telenovela (television soap opera), and vestiges of the cultural practices of colonial or even pre-Columbian civilizations, such as religions created by African slaves in Cuba (*Santería*) and Brazil (*Candomblé*) or food and dress of indigenous origin in Mexico and the Andean countries. The work of Mexican photographer Graciela Iturbide effectively portrays this coexistence of the indigenous/rural and the modern.

In the context of Latin American culture, *Santería* and *Candomblé* are often viewed as folkloric in the sense that their basic content predates industrialization. Folklore, then, is frequently thought of as being in opposition to modernity. It is generally associated with rural or indigenous populations and with communities rather than individuals; a certain naïveté of spirit is suggested by the term itself. Theorists of popular culture recognize, however, that it is increasingly difficult to talk of expressions of culture that are "authentically" indigenous, rural, and premodern given the extent of *mestizaje/mestiçagem* (racial mixing, in Spanish and Portuguese, respectively), the migration of rural populations en masse to urban areas, and the wide-reaching power of the media (consider, for example, the influence of the media conglomerates Televisa in Mexico and Globo in Brazil). That said, tourists in Latin America, both international and domestic, frequently seek out the "exotic," which more often than not in cultural terms means the folkloric. This preindustrial "other" is particularly attractive to Europeans, North Americans, and urban Latin Americans, who feel that modernity has forced upon them a globalized culture that is no different from that of the rest of the Western world. This pursuit of the "exotic" or folkloric in turn affects cultural production in the region, since many producers of traditional handicrafts, for example, depend on the tourist market for their economic survival. Some tourists are drawn to indigenous communities, in Peru and Mexico, for example, where they fully expect to see "Indians" dressed in traditional garb.

Hybridity

Latin American cultural forms have perennially been involved in complex negotiations with foreign models and the demands of Westernization, giving rise to what has been called cultural *mestizaje/mestiçagem*, or cultural hybridity. With the advent of modernity this process intensified, as exemplified by the development of cinema in Latin America. As Ana López says, "we could argue that the cinema was one of the principal tools through which the desire for and imitation of the foreign became paradoxically identified as a national characteristic shared by many Latin American nations" (2000, p. 167).

Canclini argues that the dependency theory model, which opposes cultural imperialism to national popular cultures, is inadequate to understand current power relations in Latin America. Latin American culture has often entered into a complex dialectical relationship with its European and North American counterparts, not least with regard to local film industries and the omnipotent and omnipresent Hollywood product. Latin American films, such as the Brazilian *chanchadas* or, more recently, Mexican horror films, have reappropriated Hollywood techniques and genres, often in the form of parody, in order to "dehierarchise," to use Canclini's terminology, the established asymmetry between the center (Hollywood) and the periphery (locally produced film) (Canclini 1989, p. 229).

Canclini's work on "deterritorialisation" and intercultural movements across the U.S.-Mexican border is particularly useful in the context of Latin American reworkings of Hollywood paradigms. He analyzes hybrid and simulated cultural products in border contexts, such as in cities like Tijuana, and argues that the homegrown version becomes a resource for defining identity, whereby the "authentic" becomes relativized. Tijuana-based periodicals, for example, rework definitions of identity and culture from the starting point of the border experience, becoming a voice for a generation who grew up exposed to both Mexican and U.S. culture (Canclini 1989,

p. 238). The work of Chicano performance artist Guillermo Gómez Peña focuses explicitly on this notion of border crossing. Chicanos, some but by no means all of whom inhabit the physical frontier land with the United States, experience two cultural worlds. Canclini argues that popular sectors in Latin America deal with ideological oppression today by "incorporating and positively valuing elements produced outside of their own group (criteria of prestige, hierarchies, designs, and functions of objects)" (p. 260).

Transculturation

Transculturation is an alternative and more positive term for acculturation. "Acculturation" suggests that one culture subsumes another, as colonial relations are frequently perceived. "Transculturation" suggests that two cultures in contact are both influenced in what is often a complex process of negotiation. It is thus similar to the notion of hybridity, discussed above, and it offers a more inclusive definition of national culture (that is, it does away with the need to define what is "authentic" and homegrown). The theory of transculturation is most often associated with Uruguayan critic Angel Rama (1926–1983), who borrowed the expression from the Cuban intellectual Fernando Ortiz (1881–1969). Ortiz, in *Cuban Counterpoint: Tobacco and Sugar* (1940), argued that the slave trade and agriculture in the Caribbean combined elements of African and Hispanic cultures, which influenced each other. Rama later picked up on the notion of transculturation "as a model for a nationalism capable of integrating the heterogeneous elements characteristic of many Latin American countries" (Gollnick 2003, pp. 110–111). Both Ortiz and Rama felt that discussing Latin American culture and politics as a unidirectional, center-periphery relationship (seen, for example, in the influential dependency theory of the 1960s, which ultimately blamed the region's backwardness on the growth of the nations of the "center") was inadequate. That criticism can also be found in the theories of a number of other cultural critics from Latin America. Renato Ortiz, for example, has argued that it is too simplistic to view Brazilian culture as unique and peripheral and that it makes more sense to consider it within the context of a globalized culture industry. The Brazilian writer Roberto Schwarz, in his theory of "misplaced ideas," which is beginning to gain popularity among scholars of Latin American cultural studies, holds that in Brazil ideas appropriated from Europe have always been negotiated first.

Cultural Imperialism and Globalization

Latin Americans themselves, however, do not always read the importing of ideas, cultural practices, and technologies from abroad in the same way. The notion of cultural imperialism continues to influence aspects of popular culture in Latin America. As Arturo Arias points out, "from the very first moment when present-day Latin American nations came into contact with the Western world, they were placed in a subordinate position and an asymmetrical relationship of power to the West, politically, economically and culturally" (2003, pp. 26–27). A consciousness of this subordinate position and of the threat (perceived or real) of cultural domination, particularly from the United States, was particularly strong in the region in the 1960s. Anti-imperialist messages can be found, for example, both in the protest music of this period and in the reaction to Latin American cultural expressions that dared to appropriate cultural forms from abroad, such as the Tropicália movement in Brazil. The famous text by Ariel Dorfman and Armand Mattelart on cultural imperialism in Disney cartoons was well known among the region's left-wing intelligentsia and students in the 1970s, and anti-U.S. feeling is present to this day in many grassroots social movements in Latin America. Notions of cultural imperialism are making a comeback in some quarters, in the face of the threat (again, perceived or otherwise) that globalization now poses to national cultures. Within the context of neoliberal globalization, the products, not least music CDs and movie DVDs, of Europe and all North America continue to swamp the Latin American market (Schelling 2000, p. 27).

That said, in recent years, creative possibilities have been opened up by economic and cultural globalization, a feature of late modernity that has given rise to new markets and increasingly important additional sources of income. In popular music, this process has produced such crossover music as that of Ricky Martin and Shakira. In cinema, it has led to international coproductions. As this book testifies, Latin Americans continue to enjoy a rich and distinctive popular culture, a fact that is recognized and appreciated by the hundreds of thousands of foreign tourists who visit the region annually. Equally, armchair travelers are today able to buy translations of the novels of so-called Boom and post-Boom writers Gabriel García Márquez and Isabel Allende or the New Age fiction of Paulo Coelho at their local bookstore, to purchase posters and greeting cards featuring images by Diego Rivera or Fernando Botero, or even to see a display of the Afro-Brazilian dance-fight *capoeira* performed by students at a nearby college. Images of Latin America created abroad can be found in chapter 8, "Cultural Icons"; such images reflect foreigners' perennial fascination with Latin America, often considered as the "exotic other."

Popular Culture in the Context of This Book

As discussed above, there is no one workable definition of popular culture, and for the purposes of this book we have taken the term to encompass aspects of all the main theoretical positions outlined above. Thus, we have included cultural products enjoyed by the mass market, such as commercial music and blockbuster movies. We have also considered culture produced by the poor masses, sometimes referred to as the "popular" classes, such as the architecture of shantytowns in Brazil and Peru. We have chosen to illustrate both "elite" culture designed to embrace those on the lower rungs of the social hierarchy, such as the murals of Diego Rivera and José Clemente Orozco, and "low-brow" culture that often sets out to undermine the pretensions of "high" or "hegemonic" art, such as the parodic *chanchada* musicals made by the Brazilian film industry and the films of Cantinflas in Mexico. Finally, we have included elements of folk or peasant culture, such as popular medicine and healing in Mexico and Central America, and we have included contemporary urban culture, such as street slang in Mexico and Argentina and rap and hip-hop music in Brazil. We thus hope to have covered all bases and to have avoided privileging any particular definition of popular culture.

Bibliography

Arias, Arturo. 2003. "Politics and Society." Pp. 26–46 in *The Companion to Latin American Studies*, edited by Philip Swanson. London: Arnold.

Canclini, Néstor García. 1989. *Culturas híbridas: Estrategias para entrar y salir de la modernidad.* Mexico City: Grijalbo.

Chauí, Marilena. 1986. *Conformismo e resistência: Aspectos da cultura popular no Brasil.* São Paulo: Brasiliense.

Dorfman, Ariel, and Armand Mattelart. 1984. *How to Read Donald Duck: Imperialist Ideology in the Disney Comic.* New York: International General.

Foster, David William. 1978. *Augusto Roa Bastos.* New York: Twayne.

Gollnick, Brian. 2003. "Approaches to Latin American Literature." Pp. 107–121 in *The Companion to Latin American Studies*, edited by Philip Swanson. London: Arnold.

Kane, Liam. 2000. "Freire, Paulo." Pp. 595–596 in *Encyclopedia of Contemporary Latin American and Caribbean Cultures*, vol. 2, edited by Daniel Balderstone, Mike Gonzalez, and Ana M. López. London: Routledge.

López, Ana M. 2000. "'A Train of Shadows': Early Cinema and Modernity in Latin America." Pp. 148–176 in *Through the Kaleidoscope: The Experience of Modernity in Latin America*, edited by Vivian Schelling. London and New York: Verso.

Martín-Barbero, Jesús. 1994. "Identidad, comunicación, y modernidad en América Latina." Pp. 83–110 in *Posmodernidad en la periferia: Enfoques latinoamericanos de la nueva teoría cultural*, edited by Herman Herlinghaus and Monika Walter. Berlin: Langer.

Mouat, Ricardo Gutiérrez. 1993. "Post-modernity and Postmodernism in Latin America: Carlos Fuentes's *Christopher Unborn.*" Pp. 153–179 in *Critical Theory, Cultural Politics, and Latin American Narrative*, edited by Steven M. Bell, Albert H. Le May, and Leonard Orr. Notre Dame, IN: University of Notre Dame Press.

Ortiz, Fernando. 1940. *Contrapunteo cubano del tabaco y el azúcar* (Cuban Counterpoint: Tobacco and Sugar). Havana: J. Montero. Reprint, 1995, Durham, NC: Duke University Press.

Ortiz, Renato. 2000. "Popular Culture, Modernity, and Nation." Pp. 147–167 in *Through the Kaleidoscope: The Experience of Modernity in Latin America*, edited by Vivian Schelling. London and New York: Verso.

Rama, Angel. 1984. *La ciudad letrada* (The Lettered City). Hanover, NH: Ediciones del Norte. Reprint, 1996, Durham, NC: Duke University Press.

Rowe, William, and Vivian Schelling. 1991. *Memory and Modernity: Popular Culture in Latin America.* London: Verso.

Schelling, Vivian. 2000. "Introduction: Reflections on the Experience of Modernity in Latin America." Pp. 1–33 in *Through the Kaleidoscope: The Experience of Modernity in Latin America*, edited by Vivian Schelling. London and New York: Verso.

Schwarz, Roberto. 1996. *Misplaced Ideas: Essays on Brazilian Culture.* London and New York: Verso.

Torres, Carlos Alberto, and Julie Thompson. 2000. "Education." Pp. 509–511 in *Encyclopedia of Contemporary Latin American and Caribbean Cultures*, vol. 2, edited by Daniel Balderstone, Mike Gonzalez, and Ana M. López. London: Routledge.

2
Popular Music

In an increasingly globalized world where popular culture transcends national and continental boundaries with relative ease, the catchall term "Latino music" is often used to classify a heterogeneous group of styles and artists that have become household names in the United States and Europe. The transnational popularity of such contemporary performers as Ricky Martin and Shakira has prompted renewed interest in the sociocultural origins of their music, not least so that die-hard fans can learn more about the early careers of their idols.

Of all the musical forms associated with Latin America today, salsa is perhaps the most familiar to international listeners. In both the United States and Europe, salsa is often seen as quintessentially Latino music, but the term "salsa" is in fact generic and describes a range of dance rhythms found in Spanish America. Currently, salsa crosses continental as well as Latin American boundaries. It is used in a variety of commercials and television soundtracks in the United States and the United Kingdom, and it has become a big hit in the unlikely form of the Orchesta de la Luz, a Japanese salsa band whose members do not speak Spanish, who sing the lyrics phonetically, and who have played to great acclaim both nationally and internationally.

The penetration of the international market by Latin American artists and musical genres is not, however, solely the consequence of globalization. Nor is it a recent phenomenon. Throughout the twentieth century a variety of styles made the journey from Latin America to the United States and Europe. From Brazil, for example, Carmen Miranda took samba to the New York World's Fair in 1939, then on to Broadway and subsequently to Hollywood. During the era of the Good Neighbor Policy, and particularly during World War II, President Franklin D. Roosevelt's administration courted Latin American nations by encouraging the dissemination of their music north of the border. Miranda and other Latin American musicians performed stylized versions of the music of their homelands for a cosmopolitan audience. In that era of ostensibly reciprocal cultural exchange between the two continents, even Walt Disney's cartoon feature films featured samba in their soundtracks. Likewise, in the 1930s and 1940s, bolero traveled from Cuba and Mexico to the United States, where it was recorded by the likes of Bing Crosby, Nat King Cole, and Frank Sinatra. Later, the 1960s saw the success of the Leonard Bernstein musical *West Side Story*, which raised the U.S. public's awareness of Latino culture and so paved the way for such diverse artists as Herb Alpert, Trini López, and Ritchie Valens.

Since then the ever-increasing dominance of transnational corporations within the record industry has intensified the global reach of Latin American rhythms. Within the United States the prodigious late twentieth-century growth of the Latino population, with its demand for cultural self-representation, has provided a vast market for music and musicians of Latin American origin. Within Latin America, musical styles move relatively unhindered across geographical borders, increasingly forming creative unions with new trends from abroad such as hip-hop and rap music. On a continent where song has often represented the primary vehicle for self-expression and even political dissent, popular music continues to innovate and stimulate.

—*Lisa Shaw*

See also: *Cultural Icons:* Latin Americans in Hollywood (Carmen Miranda)

Salsa

Salsa arose from music played by Latin immigrants in New York, beginning in the last half of the twentieth century. Whatever the precise origins of the term "salsa," the music itself has its roots in the music played by Puerto Ricans in 1950s New York, spearheaded principally by Tito Puente and Tito Rodríguez. Salsa drew from a variety of other musical styles, principally from jazz and Cuban *son*. The style spread rapidly and became popular across the whole of Latin America, especially in Venezuela, Panama, and Colombia.

There has been much written about the origins of the term "salsa," but it is principally a commercial rather than a musicological creation. Although the term had occurred in isolated instances in songs—for instance, in Ignacio Piñeiro's 1928 song "Échale salsita" ("Put Sauce on It") and in the name of the 1940s Cuban group Los Salseros, led by Cheo Marquetti—the widespread use of the term to denote a marketable musical style is generally attributed to the New York record company Fania, a major introducer of Latino sounds. Fania used the term as a catchall expression for the various Latino singers and groups on its books. Jerry Masucci, director of Fania Records, stated that "before the word salsa was coined, people who knew music used to say: son, guaracha, danzón, chachacha; but those who weren't musical experts found this hard to follow. In Fania we thought we needed a word as simple as 'yes,' 'rock and roll' or 'country music,' so we hit on 'salsa'" (quoted in Calvo Ospina 1995, p. 75).

Following the early innovations by Puentes and Rodríguez, the U.S.-based Fania All-Stars, a group of Puerto Rican, U.S., Dominican, and Cuban musicians, was also instrumental in increasing the popularity of salsa. *Nuestra Cosa Latina* (*Our Latin Thing*, 1971), a documentary film of a Fania All-Stars concert, boosted salsa's prominence. Among the figures in this group who have since gone on to become solo artists in their own right are Willie Colón and José Feliciano.

Reasons for the rise in salsa are varied, but the shape of the music itself is a significant factor. As José Matosantos argued, the developments in jazz from the 1950s onward were becoming increasingly technical and were therefore very difficult to dance to. Salsa emerged as a counterpart to jazz. It is an eclectic blend, in which the tumbadora, timbal, and bongo give the percussion section a Cuban flavor, and the brass section, heavy on the trumpets and trombones, shows clear influences of U.S. big-band musical styles. Thus, although some Cubans argue that salsa is merely a modern version of *son*, it in fact drew from a whole series of rhythms and is more an amalgam of styles than one particular style. Juan Carlos Quintero Herencia notes that salsa composers draw upon a variety of different types of music, including the cumbia, samba, bolero, and cha-cha-cha.

In Venezuela, some of the leading *salseros* (salsa composers and performers) include the group Federico y su Combo and José Luis Rodríguez, known as El Puma, a singer who came to the fore in the 1970s and is also famous for his boleros. One of the undisputed kings of contemporary Venezuelan salsa is Oscar D'Leon, whose 1999 album *El verdadero león* (*The Real Lion*) includes some of his best and most danceable salsa music.

Undeniably, however, it is Colombia that in recent years has become one of the hotbeds of salsa, with the city Cali declaring itself the unofficial "capital of salsa." Leading figures of Colombia's salsa boom include Joe Arroyo and Fruko. Fruko, who had originally made his name with cumbia, performed in the 1970s with his group Los Tesos, described by some as the first real Colombian salsa group. Fruko and Los Tesos developed some of the salsa sounds that were to make his name in this style; Fruko's salsa tends to give precedence to the voice of the lead singer, who is frequently backed by piano and a minimal instrumental setup. The album *Tesura* (the title is a play on the group's name, Los Tesos) launched his career in Colombia, and a concert at Madison Square Garden in 1976 spread Fruko's name internationally. Particularly outstanding of Fruko's recent work is *¡Esto sí es salsa de verdad!* (*This Really Is Salsa!* 1999), which provides an example of the clean, crisp sound that has made Fruko so popular.

At the same time, another key figure was emerging in Colombian salsa. Joe Arroyo, who began his career with the Discos Fuentes record label, started to develop his own original style of salsa. Arroyo started out with Fruko but formed his own band in 1981, La Verdad, and then went on to record under his own name. Although stylistically similar to Fruko in some respects, Arroyo's salsa has a more tropical sound and is often based around bass lines drawn from such traditional Colombian sounds as cumbia and vallenato. Arroyo is still very much a force today, and his prominence is further confirmed by his high profile in the media, illustrated by the use of one of his songs as the theme song of the popular 2002–2003 Colombian telenovela, *Siete veces amada* (*Seven Times Beloved*).

Another strand of salsa in Colombia is the big-band-style salsa, epitomized by bands such as Grupo Niche, founded in 1979, and Orchesta Guayacán. Grupo Niche's song "Cali, pachanguero" ("Lively Cali") has come to serve as an anthem for the city and for its status as one of the capitals—if not *the* capital—of contemporary salsa. Orchesta Guayacán came onto the scene later than Grupo Niche but continues the big-band sound and has reworked a variety of musical rhythms, some Colombian, some transnational, into a salsa style. This reworking is best illustrated by their 1996 CD *Como en un baile* (*Like at a Dance*), in which musical forms such as cumbia, vallenato, currulao, and paso doble, among others, are given a salsa-esque reworking.

—*Claire Taylor*

See also: *Popular Music:* Bolero; Cumbia; Samba; Vallenato; *Mass Media:* Telenovela

Bibliography

Aparicio, Frances R. 1998. *Listening to Salsa: Gender, Latin Popular Music, and Puerto Rican Cultures.* Hanover, NH: Wesleyan University Press.

Boggs, Vernon. 1992. *Salsiology: Afro-Cuban Music and the Evolution of Salsa in New York.* New York: Excelsior Music Publishing.

Calvo Ospina, Hernando. 1995. *¡Salsa! Havana Heat: Bronx Beat.* London: Latin America Bureau.

Duany, J. 1984. "Popular Music in Puerto Rico." *Latin American Music Review* 5: 186–216.

Lemarie, Isabelle. 2002. *Cuban Fire: The Story of Salsa and Latin Jazz.* London: Continuum.

Matosantos, José. 1996. "Between the Trumpet and the Bongo: A Puerto Rican Hybrid." *Massachusetts Review* 37, no. 3: 428–437.

Quintero Herencia, Juan Carlos. 1997. "Notes toward a Reading of Salsa." Pp. 189–222 in *Everynight Life: Culture and Dance in Latin/o America,* edited by Celeste Fraser Delgado and José Esteban Muñoz. Durham, NC: Duke University Press.

Waxer, Lise. 2001. "*Las caleñas son como las flores:* The Rise of All-Women Salsa Bands in Cali, Colombia." *Ethnomusicology* 45, no. 2: 228–259.

Tango

The musical style tango and its accompanying dance emerged among the urban poor of Buenos Aires in the 1890s and enjoyed their heyday between 1917 and 1935, when they captured the imaginations of Europeans and North Americans and subsequently gained respectability and acceptance among the Argentine elite. The most renowned singer of tango from this golden age was Carlos Gardel (1890–1935), who took the tango to Paris and New York and who still enjoys mythical status inside and outside Argentina. With Gardel's death in a plane crash in 1935, tango entered a period of decline, but its fortunes were revived during the populist regime of Juan Perón (1946–1955). Since then, *tango nuevo* (new tango) has been closely associated with the name of Astor Piazzolla (1921–1992), who incorporated elements of jazz and classical music into the genre.

The population of Buenos Aires ballooned from 100,000 in 1880 to a million in 1910 because of internal migration from rural areas and large-scale immigration from Europe, particularly Italy. The underclass included Italian-speaking, Spanish-speaking, and Afro-American populations, who inhabited the city's slums. They created a hybrid way of speaking called lunfardo in defiance of the elite, who in response dismissed this "slang language" as that of the criminal fraternity. Among these lunfardo speakers was born a musical dance style that brought together an eclectic mix of traditions of music and movement. Musically, it took influences from the Spanish-Cuban habanera, the Spanish contradanza, the African music played by ex-slaves in Buenos Aires, and the vulgar dance and music of the city's sprawling fringes, which were inhabited by rural migrants who brought with them their gaucho verse. The resulting folk dance style and the music associated with it were referred to using a variety of terms, including "milonga" and "tango." In the late 1800s and early 1900s this style became increasingly popular, not least as a consequence of the income generated locally by prostitution, with which this music and dance was closely linked by way of its shared social contexts.

Tango was originally played on a guitar, but between 1900 and 1917 musicians began to perform it on the bandoneon, a type of accordion, which was more suited to the larger venues that by now were also presenting tango performances. The lyrics of these songs were initially a vehicle for denouncing the living conditions of the urban poor, but as the music and its creators migrated toward the city center these social themes were replaced by a more personal, emotional content. Thus, from 1917 to 1935 the lyrics of tango became more important, not least since they began to be recorded on gramophone records. They focused on loneliness, betrayal, and unrequited love as experienced by the male protagonist, who is always the victim within a failed love affair. Female singers rarely performed tangos, and when they did sing professionally they rarely made their reputations in cabaret clubs, unlike their male counterparts. Instead, female performers appeared in theatrical performances or on the radio, which became an important medium for the genre's dissemination in the 1920s. Permeated with nostalgia for a disappearing way of life, this melancholy *tango-canción* (tango-song), as it was known, expressed the protagonist's anxieties and apprehensions. The macho, aggressive *compadrito* character, the peasant newly arrived in the city, who has much in common with the mythical *malandro* of Brazilian samba (the Brazilian equivalent of the zoot-suiter), disappeared from tango lyrics in this era, as did the references to prostitutes and violence. The *tango-canción* was forever associated with Gardel, who left Argentina in 1933 and popularized the tango among international audiences by starring in film musicals. However, after Gardel's death, the *tango-canción* gave way to the *tango-danza* (tango-dance), which placed more emphasis on the music and the dance steps than on the lyrics. In the United States a sanitized tango dance was promoted, whereas in Europe the avant-garde intelligentsia were captivated by the music's transgressive potency, and it was incorporated into the soundtrack of Luis Buñuel's and Salvador Dalí's surrealist film *Un chien andalou* (*An Andalusian Dog*, 1929).

With the untimely death of Carlos Gardel, tango entered a brief period of decline, largely due to the influx of foreign rhythms, such as the rumba and bolero. However, during the populist regime of Juan and Evita Perón this music experienced a surge in popularity and was transformed into a symbol of national identity. As was the case with samba in Brazil, the new media, chiefly the radio and the talking cinema in Argentina, brought tango into mass culture. Tango became caught up in the process of popular mobilization instigated by Perón, who sought to co-opt support for a capitalist path of development among the poor, and under his rule the cultural production of the lower classes, such as tango, was given increased exposure on a national stage. Since then tango has moved in and out of favor. It was marginalized by the military junta between 1976 and 1983 but subsequently reemerged with renewed vigor both within Argentina and abroad. Tango's renaissance is largely attributable to Piazzolla, who began his musical career in the 1930s playing in tango bands in Argentina and went on to study classical music. He drew on his varied musical background to revolutionize tango, bringing symphony orchestras and the traditional bandoneon together in a highly controversial move. His international fame and popularity peaked in the 1980s, when he performed his avant-garde tango all over the world. Today tango clubs, or *milongas*, are thriving in both Buenos Aires and the Uruguayan capital, Montevideo, and the music continues to inspire contemporary artists, such as the transnational pop icon Shakira.

—*Lisa Shaw*

See also: *Popular Music*: Bolero; Samba; Transnational Pop Icons; *Cultural Icons:* Political Icons (Evita); Legends of Popular Music and Flim (Carlos Gardel); Regional and Ethnic Types (The Gaucho in Argentina and Uruguay); *Language:* Lunfardo

Bibliography

Castro, Donald S. 1991. *The Argentine Tango as Social History, 1880–1955: The Soul of the People.* Lewiston Idaho/Queenston Ontario (Canada)/Lampeter UK: Edwin Mellen.

Collier, Simon. 1986. *The Life, Music, and Times of Carlos Gardel.* Pittsburgh, PA: University of Pittsburgh Press.

Guy, Donna J. 1991. *Sex and Danger in Buenos Aires: Prostitution, Family, and Nation in Argentina.* Lincoln and London: University of Nebraska Press.

Washabaugh, William, ed. 1998. *The Passion of Music and Dance: Body, Gender, and Sexuality.* Oxford and New York: Berg.

Samba

The samba, a Brazilian musical style and associated dance form, emerged in the first decades of the twentieth century in Rio de Janeiro and has become well known throughout the world because of its close association with the city's annual Carnival celebrations. The samba rhythm is Afro-Brazilian in origin and was the music of the Carnival celebrations of the poor blacks and mixed-race community of Brazil's then capital. Subsequently, thanks to the development of the radio and record industry in the 1920s and 1930s, samba was popularized among the white middle classes. The genre developed various offshoots, such as the slower, less rhythmic *samba-canção* (samba-song) with its melancholy lyrics (sometimes likened to U.S. blues), which predominated in the late 1940s and early 1950s. Samba went on to influence the bossa nova movement and the work of singer-songwriters such as Chico Buarque de Holanda in the late 1950s and beyond. Since then, many different varieties of samba have emerged, such as *samba-de-enredo* (theme-samba), which is played by the *escolas de samba* (samba schools, the large neighborhood organizations that perform in the Rio Carnival) and whose lyrics are based on the theme chosen for the celebrations in a given year. Samba has a 2/4 meter, an emphasis on the second beat, and a stanza-and-refrain structure.

The samba rhythm is widely believed to have descended from the batuque, a percussive accompaniment to the circle dance of the same name, performed by African slaves on Brazil's colonial plantations. The term "samba" is thought to have originated in present-day Angola, where the Kimbundu word *semba* referred to a batuque dance step. By the beginning of the nineteenth century, although slaves continued to participate in the batuque, free blacks developed a musical accompaniment to the dance played on the *viola*, a type of Portuguese guitar. Some experts argue that the true musical forefather of samba was the *lundu*, a music and dance form performed by slaves in the eighteenth century that had a religious significance and that was performed to bring good luck. With the abolition of slavery in 1888, many former slaves and their offspring settled in Rio de Janeiro, then the capital, and by the second decade of the twentieth century an Afro-Brazilian community existed near the port and the city center. Samba emerged within this community in the home of an Afro-Brazilian woman, Hilária Batista de Almeida, better known as Tia (Aunt) Ciata, a priestess of the Afro-Brazilian religion *Candomblé*. She hosted gatherings at her home, near the central Praça Onze square, where clandestine religious ceremonies were held and music was performed. Her home was a meeting place for a heterogeneous group of popular musicians and enthusiasts, both black and white, some semiliterate, others well educated, who brought together a wide range of musical styles, both homegrown and imported. It was from one such gathering that the first officially designated samba, "Pelo Telefone" ("On the Telephone"), emerged in 1916. The song was credited to the Afro-Brazilian Ernesto dos Santos, better known by his nickname, Donga, but in all likelihood it was a collective creation.

In the 1920s samba was associated with Rio's black and mixed-race inhabitants, who had been driven out of the center of the city as part of a savage urbanization program and who now inhabited the hillside shantytowns or *morros* (hills). The lyrics of the percussion-based *samba-de-morro* (shantytown samba) that they created centered on their marginal lifestyle and celebrated the local antihero, or *malandro*, who turned his back on manual labor—still closely linked to the exploitation of slavery—in favor of a lifestyle of womanizing, gambling, and carousing. This brand of samba, which in its almost purely percussive form was also referred to as *samba-de-batucada* (percussion-samba), and those who created it were marginalized by the authorities, unlike the more respectable type of samba that evolved directly from "Pelo Telefone" and its more eclectic mix of creators. Under President Getúlio Vargas (1930–1945) *sambistas* (samba composers and performers) were forced to abandon the figure of the *malandro* hustler and to espouse the work ethic of the political regime, which imposed censorship restrictions and actively co-opted popular musicians. As a consequence, a new variety of samba, known as the *samba-exaltação* (samba-exaltation), emerged in the late 1930s; its lyrics were highly patriotic, praising the beauty and riches of Brazil. A classic example is the samba "Aquarela do Brasil" ("Watercolor of Brazil"), written in 1939 by the white, middle-class songwriter Ari Barroso (1903–1964). Barroso was one of a group of white *sambistas* who emerged in the late 1920s and 1930s, together with the acclaimed lyricist Noel Rosa (1910–1937), whose careers were fueled by the development of the gramophone record, the radio, and the talking cinema.

Affairs of the heart had provided the exclusively male *sambistas* with an enduring source of inspiration for their lyrics since the 1920s, and this new generation of talented middle-class composers developed the sentimental, plaintive *samba-canção* by combining this theme with an emphasis on melody rather than rhythm, adding more complex harmonies to the increasingly sophisticated lyrics. This variety of samba popularized the genre among the middle class and dominated Brazilian music until the advent of bossa nova in the late 1950s.

Samba, specifically *samba-de-enredo*, is the music that accompanies the Rio Carnival processions today. The parades by the *escolas de samba* dance along to the *bateria*, that is, the drum-and-percussion section, which consists of *surdos* (bass drums), *caixas* (rattles), *tamborins* (small drums hit with sticks), *cuícas* (friction drums), *reco-recos* (scrapers), and *agogôs* (double bells). High-register plaintive harmonies are added by the *cavaquinho* (a kind of ukulele), and the *puxador* (lead singer) provides the melody.

Today musicians like Paulinho da Viola defend samba in its traditional form, following in the footsteps of the *sambistas* of the Estácio de Sá district of Rio, such as Ismael Silva, who created the first *escola de samba*, called Deixa Falar (Let Them Speak), in 1928. Although Paulinho da Viola does not accept samba mixed with other types of popular music, recent years have witnessed the emergence of various hybrids, such as *sambalanço*, heavily influenced by Brazilian soul music, and samba-reggae.

—*Lisa Shaw*

See also: *Popular Music:* Bossa Nova; *Popular Religion and Festivals: Candomblé;* Popular Festivals (Carnival in Brazil)

Bibliography

McGowan, Chris, and Ricardo Pessanha. 1998. *The Brazilian Sound: Samba, Bossa Nova, and the Popular Music of Brazil.* Philadelphia: Temple University Press.

Shaw, Lisa. 1999. *The Social History of the Brazilian Samba.* Aldershot, UK, and Brookfield, VT: Ashgate.

Vianna, Hermano. 1999. *The Mystery of Samba: Popular Music and National Identity in Brazil.* Chapel Hill: University of North Carolina Press.

Bossa Nova

Bossa nova, an internationally acclaimed Brazilian musical style, emerged in the mid-1950s in the upscale district of Copacabana in Rio de Janeiro. It was epitomized by Antônio Carlos (Tom) Jobim's and Vinícius de Moraes's hit song "Garota de Ipanema" ("The Girl from Ipanema"). Bossa nova took much of its inspiration from samba, but some examples of the genre also show influences from North American jazz. This new sound was taken far beyond the boundaries of the city of Rio thanks to multinational record companies and television, and it was particularly popular in the United States as a consequence of collaborations between Brazilian musicians and such musicians as the North American saxophonist Stan Getz, the jazz musician Charlie Byrd, and singer Frank Sinatra.

Bossa nova (literally, "new style/fashion") essentially slowed down and simplified the samba rhythm while incorporating unusual, rich harmonies and syncopations. It grew out of the improvised jam sessions held at small nightclubs in Copacabana and in the homes of young musicians and intellectuals in Rio de Janeiro's sophisticated, beachfront Southern Zone in the middle to late 1950s. Because of its creators' social origins, bossa nova is often referred to as the samba of the middle classes. Critics have also attributed the intimate, soft, con-

Tom Jobim sits at his piano and plays the flute in his home studio in Rio de Janeiro, Brazil, February 1985. (Stephanie Maze/Corbis)

trolled nature of this musical style to the enclosed physical spaces in which it emerged, namely, the bijou apartments of the modern high-rise blocks that lined Rio's most famous beaches. The singer Nara Leão, who played hostess at her apartment in Copacabana to gatherings that centered on musical improvisation, is often referred to as the muse of the movement, and she went on to record many of her friends' songs. Another key player in the creation and popularization of bossa nova was the guitarist João Gilberto, who hailed from Brazil's northeastern state of Bahia and whose wife, Astrud, recorded the original version of "The Girl from Ipanema." It was with the release of Gilberto's album *Chega de saudade* (*No More Longing*) in 1959 that bossa nova fever began in Brazil. The release in the same year of Marcel Camus's award-winning film *Orfeu Negro* (*Black Orpheus*), whose soundtrack included compositions in this "new style" by Jobim and Moraes, popularized bossa nova among an international audience. This was the first large-scale global exposure for Brazilian music. First performed in 1962, the archetypal bossa nova "The Girl from Ipanema" is the most internationally well known of Brazilian songs, and it has been rerecorded many times in Portuguese and in English.

Bossa nova emerged during a period of economic development and optimism in Brazil, during the presidency of Juscelino Kubitschek (1956–1961), who promised "fifty years' progress in five." The vitality and confidence of this era were symbolized

João Gilberto on guitar and Stan Getz on saxophone, playing at the Rockefeller Center, 1972. (Bettmann/Corbis)

by the building of a new, futuristic capital city, Brasília, inaugurated in 1960, largely as a result of Kubitschek's personal crusade. The lyrics of bossa nova clearly reflect the spirit of these times. Key examples of the style, such as Jobim's and Moraes's "Chega de saudade" ("No More Longing," 1958) and Jobim's "Corcovado" (1960), are love songs that evoke the carefree mood of middle-class youth in urban Brazil. "Corcovado," which celebrates music making itself, and "The Girl from Ipanema" both explicitly allude to the beauty of Rio de Janeiro, creating a romanticized vision of life. For this reason, bossa nova's lyrics have often been dismissed as bland and superficial, lacking in meaning and emotional depth. Nonetheless, other examples of the style display a self-conscious and even ironic dimension. João Gilberto's "Bim Bom" (1958), for example, with its seemingly nonsensical lyrics, can be interpreted as a parody of the meaningless, trite lyrics of the *samba-canção* of the early to middle 1950s. Similarly, two other well-known examples of bossa nova center on clever interplays of lyrics and melody. The lyrics of Tom Jobim's and Newton Mendonça's "Desafinado" ("Off-Key," 1958) refer to a romantic relationship that has gone "off key" or "out of tune," a theme that is mirrored in the musical accompaniment. Recorded by Gilberto in his characteristic whispering style, "Desafinado" was an ironic riposte to critics who disparagingly wrote that bossa nova was "music for off-key singers." The song became a playful yet defiant anthem for this nascent musical style. In the same vein, Jobim's and Mendonça's "Samba de uma nota só" ("One Note Samba") is entirely self-referential, and as the lyrics explain, the melody deliberately repeats a single note, ironically taking to extremes bossa nova's tendency to repeat a single melodic motif in different registers. Some critics have also argued that bossa nova cannot be simply dismissed as apolitical, since as the badge of the new, white, affluent, city-dwelling generation it represented a determination to break with an atmosphere of populist sentimentality that had been deliberately engendered by Brazil's political leaders over the previous two decades.

Many of the most famous songs of bossa nova have been overcommercialized outside Brazil, and in the form of recordings that emphasize the repetitive, almost monotonous nature of their melodies, they are used widely in Europe and North America to provide "easy listening," "Muzak," or "light music" for settings such as airport lounges and shopping centers. However, in Brazil bossa nova has not suffered the same fate, and it continues to be closely associated with a minimalist vocal delivery, usually by a solo voice, delicately accompanied by a simple guitar or piano and light percussion. Bossa nova enjoyed its heyday between 1958 and 1964, but this musical style had a profound impact on jazz and international music, and it also influenced the subsequent generation of Brazilian songwriters.

—Lisa Shaw

See also: *Popular Music:* Samba

Bibliography

Castro, Ruy. 2000. *Bossa Nova: The Story of the Brazilian Music That Seduced the World.* Chicago: A Cappella.

McGowan, Chris, and Ricardo Pessanha. 1998. *The Brazilian Sound: Samba, Bossa Nova, and the Popular Music of Brazil.* Philadelphia: Temple University Press.

Treece, David. 1992. "Between Bossa Nova and the Mambo Kings: The Internationalization of Latin American Popular Music." *Travesía: Journal of Latin American Cultural Studies* 1, no. 2: 54–85.

Mariachi, Ranchera, Norteña, Tex-Mex

These four closely related styles of music lie at the heart of popular music from Mexico and the border region with the United States. Although they do not represent the totality of Mexican popular music, they are of great importance to the contemporary Mexican popular music scene, and the first three styles have come to signify essential "Mexicanness" both to Mexicans and Chicanos themselves and to the rest of the world.

The Mariachi Del Rio performs at the Fiesta Nopalitos in Carrizo Springs, Texas, c. 1990. (David Seawell/Corbis)

Mariachi music had its heyday in the first half of the twentieth century. Its popularity was due to its prominent use in the movies of the golden age of Mexican filmmaking. It achieved worldwide fame at this point, but it has since been replaced in the public's favor by Tex-Mex and remains popular in Mexico and around the United States–Mexico border only. Scholars do not agree on the exact origins of mariachi music or of its name. Some trace it to the original contact between the indigenous peoples of Mesoamerica and the Spanish conquistadors (claiming that "mariachi" is an indigenous word for musician or possibly for the tree from which mariachi guitars are made); others trace it to mid-nineteenth-century Franco-Mexican contact (claiming that "mariachi" is a corruption of the French word *mariage* and refers to the music typically played at weddings); still others suggest that the name stems from a popular festival in honor of a virgin known as María H. (pronounced mah-ree-ah-chay) at which musicians played this type of music. None of the theories is completely convincing.

Mariachi music is based on the Mexican *son*, a musical form born of the fusion of Spanish, indigenous Mesoamerican, and (to a lesser extent) African cultures in the eighteenth century. (Note that the Mexican *son* is not the same as the Cuban *son*, although they have similar origins.) Mariachi music originated in the state of Jalisco, but it became popular throughout Mexico in the first half of the nineteenth century because its hybrid origins helped give different social groups a sense of belonging to a fledgling national community. Since the end of the nineteenth century it has branched out from its repertoire of *sones* to include waltzes and polkas as well as boleros (romantic ballads). The themes of the songs are extremely varied, ranging from love and betrayal to politics, revolutionary heroes, and even nonsense verse. There is a standard repertoire of mariachi songs—including such numbers as "Cielito lindo" ("Little Angel") and "Jalisco"—that all Mexicans recognize, but many mariachi musicians know up to 1,500 different songs and are able to improvise others for their clients (for a fee).

What makes mariachi music identifiable as such despite such a broad repertoire is partly the musical instruments used, partly the form of delivery of the songs, and partly the musicians' style of dress. The traditional instruments were the harp, violins, and several types of Mexican guitar, including the vihuela (a small guitar similar to a lute) and the guitarrón (a small double bass). These guitars gave the music its traditional sound. In more recent years, owing to the popularity of jazz and Cuban music, the harp has been abandoned and trumpets have been added. The style of delivery is also important: the songs are sung with a nasal voice and in a dispassionate manner. Finally, all mariachi band members wear *charro* clothing (the dress of the Mexican cowboy): ankle boots, a wide-brimmed sombrero, tight pants with lots of shiny buttons down the sides, and a fitted, decorated jacket.

In general, mariachi bands were exclusively male. Nevertheless, there have been exceptional all-women bands, such as Mariachi Las Coronelas (Mariachi Band the Colonels' Wives) of the 1940s. All-women bands have been more prevalent in the southwestern United States, where there have been several since the 1970s. Furthermore, in the 1980s Linda Ronstadt promoted new international interest in mariachi music with her album *Canciones de mi padre* (*My Father's Songs*). Mexican superstar, heartthrob, and transnational pop icon Juan Gabriel has also helped revitalize the tradition, both in Mexico and abroad, by blending mariachi music with soft rock and symphony orchestras.

Ranchera, from *la canción ranchera* (music from the ranches), is a derivative of mariachi music, and its singers are still identifiable by their *charro* costumes. Increasing urbanization in Mexico in the first decades of the twentieth century provoked a strong sense of nostalgia for rural idylls, hence the reference in the music's name to the countryside. The style of delivery tends to be much more melodramatic than that of traditional mariachi music, and the repertoire is almost exclusively made up of boleros. Although many film stars, such as Pedro Infante and Jorge Negrete, are remembered for their renditions of this kind of music, the most famous exponent of ranchera songs was singer-songwriter José Alfredo Jiménez. The style has also been adopted by a pantheon of female divas, including Lucha Reyes, Eugenia León, and Lola Beltrán. In recent years, in the songs of Alejandro Fernández, it has accommodated the influence of rock music. Furthermore, Lebanese-Mexican singer Astrid Hadad has given it a subversive review in her reworking of Lucha Reyes's repertoire, and Chicana singer Lila Downs has increased its inherent hybridity, blending it with indigenous music from the state of Oaxaca and also with norteña.

Whereas mariachi and ranchera music originate from the Mexican *son*, norteña, from *música norteña* (music from the North), has its roots in nineteenth-century *corridos*. These were epic ballads from northern Mexico that usually recounted stories of conflict between Mexicans and Anglos and that were hence important in the creation of a sense of popular Mexican national identity through resistance to Anglo imperialism. The *corridos* had their heyday in the 1920s, when they were reinvested with meaning by the events of the Mexican Revolution (1910–1920). The button accordion and such dances as the waltz and the polka, all introduced to Mexico from eastern Europe in the late nineteenth century, give norteña its typical sound and rhythm. Like mariachi, norteña music often has a deadpan style of delivery and a nasal style of singing. Despite the reference to regionalism in the music's name, norteña is popular throughout Mexico; there are whole TV channels and radio stations dedicated to it. Its popularity is still due to the theme of resistance of *el pueblo* (the common people) in the lyrics. The group Los Tigres del Norte (Tigers of the North) has become superstars in both Mexico and the United States, modernizing norteña with the introduction of saxophones and cumbia rhythms. Their success provoked a music boom in the 1990s known as banda, which combines norteña music with the brass band music typical of village fiestas all over Mexico.

Tex-Mex conjunto is the name given to norteña music north of the U.S.-Mexican border. It is indigenous to the region, since the southwestern United States formed part of Mexico until 1848, and it is also continually refreshed by contact with contemporary forms of Mexican popular music. Although it has distinctive characteristics that distinguish it from norteña and mariachi, it is primarily dance music that combines the repertoire of ranchera with the wider one of boleros and sets them to a polka tempo. The dance itself is often called the *quebradita* (break a leg). The dominant instrument is the accordion, and the style of delivery is generally less nasal than that of mariachi or norteña. In the early twentieth century, Tex-Mex was a disreputable, working-class form of entertainment; today the songs of people such as Lydia Mendoza and Chelo Silva are popular with all classes and with both Chicano and Anglo sectors of society. It has become the consummate expression of Texan identity. Furthermore, Tex-Mex has recently gained worldwide popularity through such figures as Flaco Jiménez and his work with major Anglo artists, and it has even started to exert its influence over Mexican popular music itself. Since the late 1950s, Tejano, a pop-oriented urban form of Tex-Mex, has evolved. The singer Selena is most renowned for her contribution to this style. The group Los Lobos has also gained an international following for their blend of Tex-Mex and rock music.

—*Thea Pitman*

See also: *Popular Music:* Bolero; Cumbia; Transnational Pop Icons; *Popular Theater and Performance:* Circus and Cabaret (Astrid Hadad); *Cultural Icons:* Legends of Popular Music and Film (Pedro Infante); *Popular Cinema:* Melodrama

Bibliography

Bensusan, Guy. 1985. "A Consideration of Norteña and Chicano Music." *Studies in Latin American Popular Culture* 4: 158–169.

Burr, Ramiro. 1999. *The Billboard Guide to Tejano and Regional Mexican Music.* New York: Watson-Guptill.

Farquharson, Mary. 2000. "Mexico: Much More Than Mariachi." Pp. 463–476 in *The Rough Guide to World Music*, vol. 2, *Latin and North America, Caribbean, India, Asia, and Pacific*, edited by Simon Broughton and Mark Ellingham. London: Rough Guides.

Gradante, William. 1983. "Mexican Popular Music at Mid-Century: The Role of José Alfredo Jiménez and the Canción Ranchera." *Studies in Latin American Popular Culture* 2: 99–114.

Peña, Manuel. 1999. *The Mexican-American Orquesta: Music, Culture, and the Dialectic of Conflict.* Austin: University of Texas Press.

Sobrina, Laura, and Leonor Xóchitl Pérez. 2002. "Unique Women in Mariachi Music." Mariachi Publishing Company. http://www.mariachipublishing.com (consulted 7 January 2003).

Cumbia

Panama was the original birthplace of what was to become cumbia music, but by the time Colombia and Panama separated at Panama's independence in 1903, cumbia had already become a Colombian national music. Cumbia is traditionally led by the accordion (and as such has certain links with vallenato) and was originally a type of folk music. It started as a slow dance that was practiced by the slaves and the indigenous Indians of Colombia's northern coastal region.

The cumbia still being played today stems from songs that appeared during the independence struggles in Colombia in the first two decades of the nineteenth century, when the group Los Gaiteros de San Jacinto played an early version of cumbia. Relying mostly on drums and traditional indigenous flutes made from bamboo or sugarcane, these cumbia songs frequently expressed the distress of the African slaves. Modern-day cumbia is characterized by its earthy lyrics, which use a rich colloquial language and frequent double entendres. The themes are often culturally specific, referring to Colombian customs and the concerns of everyday life in Colombia.

Some of the earlier versions of what can be termed "modern" cumbia arose in the 1950s. One song from that period, "La pollera colorá" ("The Colored Skirt"), sung at the time by Los Trovadores de Baru, a group from Cartagena, has become the unofficial national anthem of Colombia and has spawned a long list of adaptations since its first recording. Other groups and singers from this period include Los Cumbiamberos de Pacheco, who rely mostly on the accordion, and Los Guacharacas, who derive their name from the key instrument they play, the guacharaca (see the section on vallenato for more information on this instrument). Key players, whose influence is still felt in cumbia music today, were the group Los Corraleros de Majagual, originally formed in 1961. A number of its members have gone on to have solo careers. One such is Julio Estrada, better known as Fruko, who is generally considered to be one of Colombia's leading talents in the modern blend of cumbia with salsa rhythms.

In 1977 Fruko took the lead of the group La Sonora Dinamita. The Discos Fuentes record company had originally created a cumbia band called La Sonora Dinamita to perform música tropical, a combination of salsa and cumbia. The original group had split up in 1963, but their re-forming under Fruko led to a string of hits, including "Del montón" ("An Ordinary Girl"), one of their most popular songs. La Sonora Dinamita's skill lay in fusing the traditional cumbia music with a more popular sound. They gained popularity first throughout Colombia, then in Mexico, and finally across Latin America as a whole. A major innovation in 1981 was the introduction of a female vocalist, Mélida Yará Yanguma, better known as La India Meliyará, whose strong voice gave a new edge to La Sonora's sound.

La Sonora Dinamita still performs some of the most popular cumbias, including classics such as "Mi cucu" (a Colombian version of the song "My Toot Toot"), "Amor de mis amores" ("Love of My Loves"), "Escándalo" ("Scandal"), and "A mover la colita" ("Move Your Bum"), as well as new songs, with a notably contemporary and at times sarcastic twist, such as "La cumbia del Viagra" ("Viagra Cumbia"). The album *Éxitos tropicosos* (*Tropical Hits*, 1998) provides a good roundup of some of these hits, including "Mi cucu," "Mete y saca" ("In and Out"), and "Que te la pongo" ("I'll Put It on You"), and the compilation *32 Cañonazos* (*32 Greatest Hits*, 2002) combines both classic cumbias such as "Del montón," "Mi cucu," and "Amor de mis amores" with new ones such as "Cumbia del sida" ("AIDS Cumbia"). Nevertheless, although La Sonora Dinamita still performs and produces records today, the actual makeup of the group is unclear, and what was once a clearly defined ensemble has now fragmented into a variety of groups performing at different locations.

Even though the cumbia scene is dominated by La Sonora Dinamita in its various formations and offshoots, there are hundreds of cumbia bands in Colombia today. Many of these gain an audience at the annual Fiesta de Nuestra Señora de La Candelaria, held at the end of January and the beginning of February in Cartagena. A key feature of the celebration is the performance of cumbia. In addition to these performances, which may include smaller ensembles, cumbia has been incorporated into the big-band style of Colombian music, a leading exponent being the Orquesta Los Tupamaros, whose compilation *20 años* (*20 Years*, 1996) includes "Los amores de Petrona" ("Petrona's Loves"), and the Orquesta Guayacán. Moreover, cumbia has been given a further boost in recent years by its reworking into new and eclectic forms, most notably tecnocumbia and cumbia villera.

—*Claire Taylor*

See also: *Popular Music:* Salsa; Tecnocumbia; Vallenato

Bibliography

Burton, Kim. 2000. "Colombia: El sonido dorado." Pp. 372–385 in *The Rough Guide to World Music*, vol. 2, *Latin America and North America, Caribbean, India, Asia, and the Pacific*, edited by Simon Broughton and Mark Ellingham. London: Rough Guides.

Dorier-Apprill, Elisabeth. 2000. *Danses "latines" et identités, d'une rive a l'autre: Tango, cumbia, fado, samba, rumba, capoiera.* Paris: L'Harmattan.

Steward, Sue. 1999. "Colombia: Continental Connections." Pp. 128–137 in *Salsa: Musical Heartbeat of Latin America.* London: Thames and Hudson.

Bolero

Bolero is a balladic style of music, romantic in theme and slow in tempo, usually in 2/4 time. Whereas salsa and merengue are the current preferences for dance music in much of Latin America, the bolero remains the favorite romantic music for listening. The bolero's official golden age was the 1930s, 1940s, and 1950s, but it is still a flourishing musical genre today.

The bolero has its roots in an old Spanish dance, and it first emerged as a Latin American musical form in the nineteenth century. However, although its original sources were Hispanic, the bolero that has developed in Latin America is a cultural hybrid, with influences from African rhythms and inspiration from twentieth-century jazz. Most experts date the appearance of bolero to the late nineteenth century, most often to between 1885 and 1898. Geographically, the bolero song originated in Cuba and then spread rapidly around the Caribbean area, taking root in the surrounding islands and Mexico.

The heyday of Mexican bolero began in the 1930s with such key *bolerista* groups as Los Hermanos Martínez Gil and Trío Tarácuri, but soloists were increasingly coming to the fore. Perhaps the person who had the greatest impact on the development of the bolero was the now legendary Agustín Lara (1901–1970), whose sentimental boleros became popular in the dance halls of Mexico. The popularity of boleros from the 1930s onward led to the spread of this genre outside Latin America, with boleros being taken up by a variety of U.S. singers, including Bing Crosby, Nat King Cole, and Frank Sinatra. Perhaps the most famous of all boleros is "Bésame mucho" ("Kiss Me a Lot," 1941), composed by the Mexican Consuelo Velásquez, who was only sixteen at the time. This song has since been recorded by a wide range of singers (not all of them Latin American), including leading female exponents of bolero such as Mexico's Toña la Negra and Puerto Rico's Ruth Fernández and more recently Luis Miguel on his *Vivo* (*Live*, 2000) album. However, "Bésame mucho" arguably enjoyed its greatest worldwide recognition in the version by the Beatles, recorded in 1962, which appeared on their album *Beatles Live at the Star Club in Hamburg* (1962).

Although the bolero has altered over time in terms of its rhythms and influences—to encompass, among others, varieties such as the bolero son, bolero moruno, bolero mambo, bolero beguine, bolero feeling, and bolero ranchera—one constant is the theme of its lyrics: love and its associated seductions, secret meetings, forbidden passions, and lovers' quarrels.

The bolero has enjoyed a renaissance in recent years. The most striking of its current performers is the young Luis Miguel, who has gained popularity throughout Latin America and Spain and who has recorded a variety of boleros of yesteryear. Miguel's recent album, *Mis boleros favoritos* (*My Favorite Boleros*, 2002), includes his versions of such now classic boleros as "Perfidia" ("Treachery," originally by Alberto Domínguez) and "Solamente una vez" ("Only Once," by Agustín Lara). Other key figures in the revival of the bolero include the Venezuelan José Luis Rodríguez, better known as El Puma, who has brought out several albums of boleros and whose recent double CD entitled *Inolvidable* (*Unforgettable*, 1997–1999) reworks the songs of Los Panchos, one of the classic trios performing bolero music.

The Mexican transnational pop icon Juan Gabriel is another prominent figure to have continued the bolero tradition. Gabriel has brought out albums that include a variety of boleros such as "Frente a frente" ("Face to Face") and "No me vuelvo a enamorar" ("I Won't Fall in Love Again"). Similarly, figures such as the Puerto Rican José Feliciano have performed in the bolero genre, with the Grammy-nominated album *Señor bolero* (*Mr. Bolero*, 1998) including some of Feliciano's best work in this genre. Contemporary revivals of the bolero are dominated by male singers, but some female vocalists stand out, such as the Puerto Rican Lucecita Benítez, who has incorporated the bolero genre into albums such as *Mujer sin tiempo* (*Timeless Woman*, 1983). Even the recent phenomenon of the Buena Vista Social Club has engaged in the renaissance of the bolero, with Ibrahím Ferrer recently recording boleros.

—*Claire Taylor*

See also: *Popular Music:* Mariachi, Ranchera, Norteña, Tex-Mex; Merengue; Salsa; Transnational Pop Icons

Bibliography

Rico Salazar, Jaime. 1987. *Cien años de boleros: Su historia, sus compositores, sus intérpretes y 500 boleros inolvidables.* Bogota: Centro Editorial de Estudios Musicales.

Valdés Cantero, Alicia, ed. 2000. *Nosotros y el bolero.* Havana: Letras Cubanas.

Zavala, Iris M. 2000. *El bolero: Historia de un amor.* Madrid: Celeste.

Mambo

Mambo is based on an Afro-Cuban rhythm and is most frequently associated with the Cuban musician Dámaso Pérez Prado. The mambo came about as a development of the danzón, adding the conga drum to the charanga ensemble, which characteristically features a wooden Creole flute, piano, bass, violins, güiro (a type of scraper made from a hollowed-out gourd), and timbales (a set of drums). This music was first called *danzón de nuevo ritmo* (danzón of the new rhythm) and later came to be known as mambo.

Although there is no single inventor of this style, its early origins are usually associated with the musician Orestes "Macho" López, whose 1938 tune "Mambo" is seen by many as the earliest example of this type of music. However, the most prominent name in the history of mambo has to be the Cuban musician Dámaso Pérez Prado, who, from the 1940s onward, adopted the term "mambo" and recorded several songs of this style with his band. Pérez Prado, whose range as a musician stretched from pianist and organist to bandleader, arranger, and composer, is largely credited with popularizing the mambo musical form. He developed the mambo formula for his band with a brass and saxophone lineup, essentially uniting big, jazz-band sound with Latin rhythms. In 1948 he settled in Mexico, where he recorded several songs, many of them with fellow Cuban Benny Moré. After establishing himself in Mexico, he began to gain international fame in the mid-1950s as the mambo fad spread across the United States, fueled by the U.S. Latino population. Notably, his "Cereza Rosa" (1951), sung in English in 1955 as "Cherry Pink and Apple Blossom White," was a key crossover hit. It stayed at number one for ten weeks in the United States and for two weeks in the United Kingdom.

Aside from Pérez Prado, the three most important bands in the U.S. Latino community were Machito y sus Afro-Cubanos and the bands of Tito Puente and Tito Rodríguez. Tito Puente, one of the kings of mambo, famous above all for his hit song "Oye como va" ("Hear How It Goes"), has produced many albums of mambo over the years. Other leading players, such as Celia Cruz, have also sung mambo and have created fruitful crosscurrents between mambo and salsa.

The mambo craze proper was diminishing by the 1960s, but in recent years interest in mambo has resurfaced, partly owing to a variety of media crossovers. Oscar Hijuelos's novel *The Mambo Kings Play Songs of Love* (1989) won the Pulitzer Prize

Tito Puente drumming at Monterey Jazz Festival, Monterey, California. (Craig Lovell/Corbis)

in 1990 and was subsequently made into the film *Mambo Kings* (1992), a U.S.-French production directed by Arne Glimcher and starring, among others, Antonio Banderas. The film, about two Cuban brothers attempting to make their way on the New York music scene, was full of examples of mambo music and brought mambo back to the attention of U.S. audiences. It also featured appearances by some of the real-life mambo stars, such as Celia Cruz and Tito Puente, and the success of both novel and film revived interest in the mambo.

In addition to novels and feature films, mambo has come to the fore in the shape of rerecordings and commercial uses. Pérez Prado's 1949 hit "Mambo Number 5," one of his several numbered mambos, rose to fame again in 1999 owing to the cover version (a performance or recording of a work previously done by another performer) by the German-born Lou Bega, whose version was a number one hit in the United Kingdom and Germany and appears on his album *A Little Bit of Mambo*. Similarly, Pérez Prado's hit song "Guaglione" (1958) was revived for use in a Guinness commercial in 1994, leading to the song reaching the U.K. top ten in 1995.

—*Claire Taylor*

See also: *Popular Music:* Danzón; Salsa

Bibliography

Daniel, Yvonne. 1995. *Rumba: Dance and Social Change in Contemporary Cuba.* Bloomington: Indiana University Press.

Gerard, Charley, with Marty Sheller. 1989. *Salsa! The Rhythm of Latin Music.* Crown Point, IN: White Cliffs Media.

Giro, Radamés. 1993. *El mambo*. Havana: Letras Cubanas.

Merengue

Merengue originated in the Dominican Republic in the mid-nineteenth century and is arguably that country's most popular dance music. It has since spread throughout Latin America and the Caribbean. Thanks to a group of Dominican and Puerto Rican DJs working in New York, it has recently fused with house music to give rise to the music known as merenhouse.

The origins of the term "merengue" are obscure, although it is generally accepted that merengue as a musical genre derived from principally two distinct sources: the French minuet of the nineteenth century and the music of African slaves. The slaves of the Dominican Republic took up the dance from their colonial rulers but added new rhythms to it, including an upbeat. Thus, although early merengue had European origins, it soon acquired an Afro-Caribbean flavor and, indeed, remains an example of musical syncretism today.

The typical merengue ensemble consists of the guitar, the güiro (a type of scraper made from a hollowed-out gourd), the tambora (a two-headed drum), and the marimba. Although merengue is still performed by such traditional ensembles, variations on merengue—from the growing influence of big-band-style arrangements throughout the twentieth century to more recent house and hip-hop reworkings—have brought about changes in the makeup of merengue bands.

A key figure in the development of merengue is the Dominican-born musician Juan de Dios, who changed his name to the more marketable and U.S.-friendly Johnny Ventura—itself symbolic of his commercial skills. In the 1960s, Ventura heralded the emergence of a new style of merengue, transforming some of the now traditional big-band setups into smaller ensembles with fewer saxophones and horns. Key to this was Ventura's own weekly television show, *The Combo Show*, which featured merengue in a much more vibrant setting, complete with dance steps, and which launched the career of many other merengue greats. Among other innovations, Ventura sped up merengue, incorporated elements from rock and roll, and employed a much more aggressive marketing style, able to compete with U.S. imports.

By the 1970s, it was the turn of Wilfrido Vargas, trumpeter, composer, singer, and bandleader, to transform merengue. Vargas's 1978 album *Punto y aparte* (*Full Stop*) represented a defining moment in the development of this musical style. Vargas initiated a series of crossovers with other sounds, including elements from Haitian bands, from cumbia, and from vallenato, and introduced synthesizers in some of his later work.

By the 1980s merengue was gaining ground as the Dominican recording industry became stronger, and a new style of merengue evolved. Partly owing to the increased immigration of Dominicans to the United States and partly because of the relative simplicity of its two-step rhythm—an easier dance step than salsa—merengue grew in popularity, and for many Latino dancers it became the preferred dance style.

Perhaps the most significant figure in the contemporary merengue scene is Juan Luis Guerra. Guerra, educated both in Dominican music schools and in the United States, represents the internationalization of merengue, as well as other musical forms. On his return to Santo Domingo from the United States, Guerra formed the vocal quartet 4.40, reputedly named after the A 440. In the 1980s, Guerra developed a softer, slower, more poetic version of the merengue, exemplified by his 1987 hit "Ojalá que llueva café" ("Let It Rain Coffee"). This song, originally written for a television commercial for coffee, was adopted by coffee growers around the country and became their unofficial anthem. Guerra's skill lies in transforming merengue to include jazz and African influences while maintaining a Dominican focus in terms of lyrics.

Guerra is joined by the group Rikarena, made up of fellow Dominicans, on the contemporary merengue scene. Rikarena's albums, such as *Sin medir distancia* (*Measureless Distance*, 1997) and *Rikarena . . . con tó* (*Rikarena . . . with Everything*, 1998), are examples of the fast, danceable merengue that has become their trademark.

In addition to the Dominican brand of merengue, groups from other Latin American countries have sprung up in recent years. One long-standing player on the merengue scene is Jossie Esteban, who in 1979 founded the group Jossie Esteban y la Patrulla 15. Based in Puerto Rico, Esteban's group has continued to have a string of hits, with the CD *Hot, hot merengue* (1992) being of particular interest, especially for its reworking of the classic bolero "Perfidia" ("Treachery") into a merengue rhythm. Even more recent is the Puerto Rican group La Makina, whose best work includes *Para el bailador* (*For the Dancer*, 1999). Similarly, singer Elvis Crespo—born in New York but of Puerto Rican origin—has had a string of merengue hits, including his chart-topping single "Suavemente" ("Softly"). This song and the album of the same name to which it belongs are examples of some of the best combinations of merengue with a rock-pop sound.

A further development in the genesis of merengue, and one that will doubtless continue, is the emerging work of a group of new producers and DJs who are generating musical hybrids of merengue and house music. Such so-called merenhouse style is best exemplified by bands such as Proyecto Uno, a group founded in 1988, made up of two Dominicans and two Puerto Ricans, and based in New York. Proyecto Uno's albums include *In Da House* (1994), which remained on the charts for months, and their recent *Pura gozadera* (*Pure Pleasure*, 2002).

—*Claire Taylor*

See also: *Popular Music:* Bolero; Cumbia; Salsa; Vallenato

Bibliography

Austerlitz, Paul. 1997. *Merengue: Dominican Music and Dominican Identity.* Philadelphia: Temple University Press.

Manuel, Peter, with Kenneth Bilby and Michael Largey. 1995. *Caribbean Currents: Caribbean Music from Rumba to Reggae.* London: Latin American Bureau.

Steward, Sue. 1999. "Santo Domingo: The Merengue Capital." Pp. 105–117 in *Salsa: Musical Heartbeat of Latin America.* London: Thames and Hudson.

Vallenato

The musical form known as vallenato originated on the Caribbean coast of Colombia. More than most other popular musical forms in contemporary Latin America, vallenato maintains a close relationship with its particular geographical region of origin. Indeed, the term itself, "vallenato," comes from *valle* (valley), referring to the northern coastal region of Valledupar, and *nato* (born): as its name makes clear, this is music that was born in Valledupar.

Traditionally, the music is played on three main instruments: the guacharaca, the accordion, and the caja drum. The guacharaca, the original instrument of the trio, is a wooden instrument with ridges; sound is produced by scraping the surface with a hard instrument. The name "guacharaca" derives from a tropical forest bird whose cry the instrument is supposed to imitate. The next in the trio is the three-row button accordion, which nowadays has come to be the defining feature of vallenato. Legend has it that the accordion was brought to Colombia by German sailors in the nineteenth century. The final instrument, the caja, is a small, high-pitched, single-headed drum. Vallenato's musical trio represents the triple heritage of Colombia's northern region and the syncretism of this music: the guacharaca, of indigenous origin; the accordion, of European origin; and the caja, of African origin.

Vallenato in its early days was a type of folk music, one that was fundamentally a part of oral culture. Vallenato is part of oral culture in both its composition and its performance: vallenato songs have been preserved and transmitted in oral form, and some of the key masters of vallenato were unable to read written music. The oral quality of vallenato songs is closely linked to their original motivations. Vallenato is, principally, a storytelling device. It sprang up as a type of informal "news service" that passed on news in a pretechnological environment.

The orality of this music can be seen in several ways in the songs themselves: the abundance of proper names, for instance, is indicative of the fact that many of these songs described the deeds of local people or addressed them directly. An example is a classic vallenato composed by the now legendary Rafael Escalona, "Miguel Canales" (1944), which functions not only as a piece of music but as a way to convey a message from the composer, Escalona, to his friend, the eponymous Miguel. Another example is "Testamento" ("Testament," 1948), which Escalona composed to one of his girlfriends and which includes not only the personal story of the composer but also a description of a journey through Valledupar.

Orality also affects the structure of this music. Typically vallenato songs have repeated refrains at the beginning and at the end of each verse, which aids in the singing of the songs from memory rather than from sheet music. In addition to these refrains, which are individual to each song, vallenato has a "signature" feature: *ayombe* (from *ay hombre*, "hey man" in Spanish) is usually shouted at the beginning or end of a song or during a musical interlude between verses.

In recent years, these more traditional versions of vallenato have constantly been rerecorded. Their most outstanding performer is Jorge Oñate, whose style of singing maintains some of the oral and folkloric inflections. Oñate's album *Lo mejor de los mejores* (*The Best of the Best*, 1994) is, as the name suggests, a collection of some of the classic vallenato songs, including several by Escalona and by other leading exponents of the genre, such as Carlos Huertas. Another similar exponent of this "classic" vallenato style is the duo Los Hermanos Zuleta, a partnership between brothers Tomás Alfonso Zuleta and Emiliano Alcides Zuleta, with Tomás Alfonso, better known as Poncho, as the lead singer and Emiliano as the accordionist.

In addition, a variety of singers from the 1970s onward have played and composed more modern vallenato works. The most significant of these include Binomio de Oro, which originally started out in the mid-1970s as a duo, with Rafael Orozco and Israel Romero as singer and accordionist, respectively. However, after the death of Orozco in June 1992, the group became known as Binomio de Oro de América, with Jean Carlos Centeno replacing Orozco as lead singer. Some of Binomio's best work can be found on the albums *Clase Aparte* (*No Comparison*, 1980) and *Festival Vallenato* (1982). *A su gusto* (*To Your Taste*, 1996) provides a good example of the sound of the "new" Binomio lineup.

In addition to the large-group style of Binomio, there are a number of solo singers. The best is probably Diómedez Díaz, who began his musical career in the 1970s. Díaz has collaborated briefly with Cocha Molina and has teamed up over the years principally with three expert accordionists: Nicolás "Colacho" Mendoza, Juan Humberto Rois, and, most recently, Iván Zuleta, nephew of the aforementioned Zuleta brothers. The 1989 album *Grandes éxitos de Diómedez Díaz* (*Greatest Hits of Díomedez Díaz*) brings together some of Díaz's best work with a variety of accordionists, including the outstanding songs "Camino largo" ("The Long Path"), "Todo es para ti" ("Everything Is for You"), and "Cantando" ("Singing"), the last composed by Díaz himself. Of his later work with Zuleta, the 1995 album *Un canto celestial* (*A Heavenly Song*) stands out. It was produced shortly after the death of Díaz's previous accordionist, Rois, and the title song is dedicated to Rois's memory.

More recent groups include Los Chiches Vallenatos, founded around 1987, which specializes in what can be termed *vallenato romántico* (romantic vallenato). The group's 1994 album *Grandes éxitos de los Chiches Vallenatos* (*Greatest Hits of the Chiches Vallenatos*), produced by the ubiquitous Discos Fuentes record company, provides a compilation of some of its best work. Another key group in this strain of vallenato romántico is Los Diablitos, which began in the 1980s, led by the accordionist Omar Geles and singer Miguel Morales, although Morales later withdrew from the group and was replaced first by Jesús Manuel Estrada and finally by Alexander Manga. Examples of some of their best music include the early album *Diabluras vallenatas* (*Vallenato Mischief*, c. 1998) with the Geles-Morales lineup.

From the late 1980s and into the 1990s vallenato took a new route, developing a more modern, "pop" sound. The outstanding figure in this transformation is the singer and actor Carlos Vives, whose career was greatly aided by his performance in Caracol's 1991 telenovela *Escalona*, based on the life of Rafael Escalona. Vives brought out two albums derived from the soap opera, *Escalona, un canto a la vida* (*Escalona, a Song to Life*, 1994), and *Clásicos de la provincia* (*Classics of the Province*, 1994), which were generally faithful renderings of Escalona's originals, but he then swiftly went on to composing and singing his own work, amalgamating the vallenato style with other rhythms and bringing in a strong presence of other instruments, such as the electric guitar. Some of the best of Vives's original work includes his recent album *Déjame entrar* (*Let Me In*, 2000), which illustrates this fusion of vallenato elements with sounds and styles from rock and pop. Although vallenato purists may deny that Vives's latest compositions fall into the vallenato category at all, what cannot be denied is the force and originality of these works.

—*Claire Taylor*

See also: *Mass Media:* Telenovela

Bibliography

Abadía Morales, Guillermo. 1991. *Instrumentos musicales: Folklore colombiano.* Bogota: Banco Popular.

Araujo Noguera, Consuelo. 1998. *Escalona: El hombre y el mito.* Bogota: Planeta.

Llerena Villalobos, Rito. 1985. *Memoria cultural en el vallenato: Un modelo de textualidad en la canción folclórica colombiana.* Medellín: Centro de Investigaciones, Facultad de Ciencias Humanas, Universidad de Antioquia.

Posada, Consuelo. 1986. *Canción vallenata y tradición oral.* Medellín: Universidad de Antioquia.

Quiroz Otero, Ciro. 1983. *Vallenato: Hombre y canto.* Bogota: Icaro.

Tropicália

Tropicália, also sometimes referred to as tropicalismo, emerged at the end of the 1960s in Brazil, as part of a wider movement in the arts. Its creation was led by two singer-songwriters from the northeastern state of Bahia, Caetano Veloso and Gilberto Gil, and although the style was short-lived, it had a profound impact on attitudes and cultural production. The emergence of this musical style was heralded by Veloso's performance of his song "Alegria, Alegria" ("Joy, Joy") at a televised music festival in 1967. Tropicália coalesced as a movement in 1968, during a period of intense political and cultural upheaval that coincided with the hardening of Brazil's military dictatorship. Veloso's and Gil's irreverent performances had alarmed the military authorities, even though their critique of contemporary Brazil in song lyrics had for the most part evaded the censors. In December 1968 the regime placed them under house arrest, and they subsequently went into exile in London. Thus, by 1969 Tropicália, as a coherent musical movement, had ended, although both Veloso and Gil have gone on to enjoy widespread artistic and commercial success in their own right.

Veloso's performance of "Alegria, alegria" on the TV Record television station in 1967 met with the outrage of the general public, which considered his groundbreaking use of the electric guitar in this rock song as a sign that Brazilian popular music had sold out to North American and European styles. From then on, Tropicália became a fusion of Brazilian and foreign influences, taking much of its inspiration from the modernist poetry of Oswald de Andrade, who in the 1920s had advocated that Brazil devour and combine both homegrown cultural forms and those imported from abroad in order to create something new and representative of Brazilian sociocultural reality. Thus, the tropicalist musicians took their lead from contemporary European and North American artists, such as the Beatles and Bob Dylan.

In 1965 Veloso and Gil had moved from their home state of Bahia to São Paulo. There they teamed up with other popular musicians, such as Gal Costa, Júlio Medaglia, Torquato Neto, Tom Zé, José Carlos Capinan, and the rock group Os Mutantes (The Mutants). The so-called *grupo baiano* (Bahian group), consisting of Veloso, Gil, Costa, and Zé, developed a dynamic artistic relationship with the leaders of the avant-garde music scene in the city. The tropicalists' contact with rampant modernity and pervasive consumerism in the industrialized metropolis of São Paulo clearly molded their musical output. In May 1968 the core members of the group collaborated in the recording of the concept album *Tropicália, ou panis et circensis* (*Tropicalia, or Bread and Circuses*), the movement's musical manifesto, which also featured Nara Leão, the "muse" of bossa nova and Brazilian protest music, who had adhered to the tropicalist cause. The back of this album cover featured a film script written by Veloso, which opened with a chorus of international celebrities singing "Brazil is the country of the future," a tongue-in-cheek allusion to the exaggeratedly patriotic *samba-exaltação*, which Veloso undermines by simultaneously commenting that "this genre is out of fashion." This album was seen as Brazil's answer to the Beatles' *Sgt. Pepper's Lonely Hearts Club Band* (1967).

The name "Tropicália" was taken from the title of a piece of installation art created in 1967 by the experimental artist Hélio Oiticica, and it reflected the movement's deliberate invocation of stereotypical images of Brazil as a tropical paradise. The tropicalist musicians, however, subverted these clichéd images of the nation by alluding in their songs to the political violence and social misery under the military dictatorship in the late 1960s. Tropicália's two manifesto songs were "Tropicália," by Veloso, and "Geléia Geral" ("General Jelly"), by Gil and Neto, whose highly intelligent and ironic lyrics characterized the movement as a whole. "Tropicália" was a powerful allegory of the Brazilian nation in the aftermath of the 1964 military coup, and "General Jelly," which combined traditional folkloric music from the northern state of Maranhão with rock music played on electric instruments, mixed hackneyed images of Brazil, such as allusions to samba and mixed-race beauties, with references to the modern capitalist world. The main themes of tropicalist songs included urban migration, mass culture, third world marginality, and political violence, and the songwriters celebrated the kitsch aspects of Brazilian culture. The tropicalists delighted in cultural hybridity, mixing elements of high and low culture, the traditional and the modern, the national and the international. Thus, they made an important contribution to dismantling the barriers between erudite and popular music. Their songs articulated a critique of Brazilian modernity and challenged dominant representations of national culture. Tom Zé's first solo album of 1968, for example, can be interpreted as a satirical chronicle of his first impressions of the city of São Paulo, particularly its voracious capitalist culture. The tropicalists were not, however, protest musicians, and they were not considered to be radicals or leftists. It was Veloso's and Gil's visibility and notoriety, rather than any subversive message in their songs, that prompted their house arrest on 27 December 1968 and their subsequent voluntary exile in London, where they spent the next two and a half years.

Although their departure signaled the end of the movement, the shock waves of Tropicália have been felt in Brazil and beyond to this day. The North American musician Beck, for example, was inspired by the work of Os Mutantes to release an album in 1998 entitled *Mutations*, which included a track called "Tropicália."

—*Lisa Shaw*

See also: *Popular Music:* Bossa Nova; Brazilian Protest Music; Samba; *Sport and Leisure:* Consumerism (Brazil); *Visual Arts and Architecture:* Art (Hélio Oiticica)

Bibliography

Dunn, Christopher. 2001. *Brutality Garden: Tropicália and the Emergence of a Brazilian Counterculture.* Chapel Hill and London: University of North Carolina Press.
McGowan, Chris, and Ricardo Pessanha. 1998. *The Brazilian Sound: Samba, Bossa Nova, and the Popular Music of Brazil.* Philadelphia: Temple University Press.
Perrone, Charles. 1993. *Masters of Contemporary Brazilian Song: MPB 1965–1985.* Austin: University of Texas Press.

Andean Rock and Popular Music

Popular music in the Andean countries (for the purposes of this volume, Bolivia, Ecuador, and Peru) is inescapably influenced by the legacy of the Spanish conquest: in the highlands, an influx of mainly European musical forms combined with those of indigenous origin. Traditional Andean wind instruments such as the quena (a bamboo flute held vertically) remain but are now played alongside European instruments. Chief among these is the guitar, though violin, harp, and even saxophone have found their way into groups playing *mestizo* (culturally and ethnically mixed) forms of Andean music. In the latter half of the twentieth century, as a result of urban migration and of greater tolerance of indigenous culture on the part of urban whites and *mestizos*, Andean music has begun to fuse with rock and other global styles.

The European influx gave rise to various new hybrid musical idioms. The most prominent *mestizo* Andean song form by far has been the huayno (to use the most common term, though it is often called wayñu in Bolivia and sanjuanito in Ecuador). Huayno adapts native tonal structures and the pentatonic scale to a European format, allowing the incorporation of indigenous oral storytelling strategies, whether the song is in Quechua or Spanish (or, as is often the case, both at once). The form became more widely accepted as a result of the early twentieth-century *indigenista* movement in Cusco, which set out to rehabilitate native culture in the definition of a national identity. The most famous example of the genre is probably "El condor pasa" ("The Condor Passes"), derived from a classical piece by Daniel Alomías Robles in the Huánuco area of the central Peruvian highlands. The song has been covered (reperformed or rerecorded by other artists) and adapted countless times, most famously by Paul Simon in the 1970s. This very adaptability, as well as the expressive range of the form, may explain why huayno is still alive and important today. Andean "folklore" thrives in differing degrees of authenticity. For instance, artists like Ñanda Mañachi (Show Me the Way) from Ecuador have remained true to their indigenous roots, and the Bolivian band Los Kjarkas specializes in romantic ballads sung in the huayno style.

During the massive urban migration of the second half of the twentieth century, Andean music underwent a transformation. This was particularly true of Peru, due to the high degree of urban migrations and the consequent transformation of the music as it came into contact with rock, pop, and Peruvian tropicalismo.

The result was the style known as chicha (the term comes from the name of a popular maize-based drink), which is not simply a form of music but also a broad cultural expression belonging to displaced Andean peoples in their attempt to come to terms with city life. Chicha music uses melodic and structural patterns similar to those of the huayno, but its lineup of electric or amplified instruments (mostly guitar and drums) is designed to reach large audiences at open-air concerts and dances. Chicha's popularity among the urban migrants of Lima and other large coastal cities drew the contempt of middle-class Peruvians, who were ever eager to hear the latest rock and pop from the United States and the United Kingdom.

More recently Peru has witnessed the upsurge of tecnocumbia, which has largely superseded chicha as the musical expression of the urban migrant and has become a new target for the scorn of Lima sophisticates. Tecnocumbia bands—such as the successful Skándalo (misspelt Spanish for "scandal"), which was followed by Joven Sensación (Young Sensation) and several others—speak for a younger generation already established in the city and with no memories of the Andes. Hence, Andean tecnocumbia songs no longer have nostalgic lyrics of yearning for an abandoned rural idyll; rather, they express a will to address urban reality.

The Andean tradition has nonetheless been maintained, though in unavoidably altered form, among indigenous communities. At the same time, certain rock groups have shown an interest in indigenous culture and even in producing music in the native languages. Among these are the Peruvian rocker Miki González, who was particularly prominent in the 1980s, and an Andean group singing in Quechua, Uchpa (Ash). In Bolivia the rock band Octavia has used tapes or live performance of traditional native songs and built compositions around them.

An almost unique phenomenon in Andean music has been the career of Bolivian singer Luzmila Carpio, whose period of exile in Paris resulted in her becoming well known and respected as a musical ambassador for her people. Carpio still lives in France, although she is a regular visitor to her home in the province of Norte Potosí. On albums like *Warmi* (*Woman*, 1998) she contributes songs aimed at raising political consciousness and levels of education. Carpio has been taken up by one of the World Music labels in the United Kingdom, a move that has not noticeably compromised her authenticity. Other Andean artists belonging to this phenomenon, in recent years, are the Bolivians Jenny Cárdenas and Emma Junaro.

Andean musical forms also found their way into the nueva canción political song movement, most notably in Chile and Argentina during the periods of military dictatorship of the 1970s and 1980s.

—*Keith Richards*

See also: *Popular Music:* Contemporary Urban Music: (Tecnocumbia); Nueva Canción

Bibliography

Aretz, Isabel. 1980. *Síntesis de la etnomúsica en América Latina.* Caracas, Venezuela: Monte Avila Editores.

Olsen, Dale A., and Daniel E. Sheehy, eds. 1998. *Garland Handbook of Latin American Music: South America, Mexico, Central America, and the Caribbean.* New York: Garland.

Danzón

By today's standards, danzón is a rather old-fashioned, slow form of Latin ballroom dancing. Nevertheless, it is still very popular in its country of origin, Cuba, as well as in its adopted home, Mexico. It is based on a French courtly dance, the contredanse, and was taken to Cuba by Haitians fleeing revolution in their own country in the late eighteenth century. The contredanse then blended with traditional Cuban dance forms to create the danza and, by the late nineteenth century, the danzón. Danzón bands were originally known as *charangas francesas* (French orchestras)—a reference to the type of European instruments used and possibly also to the French women who ran the high-class brothels in Havana where the music was popular at the turn of the century. Nowadays they are simply known as charangas. *Charangas francesas* usually comprised a small rhythm section, a larger string section, and a wooden flute. It is this lack of emphasis on percussion and the addition of the flute that gives danzón its distinctive sweet, elegant, European sound. Nevertheless, syncopated rhythms and the use of some percussion instruments did betray some Afro-Cuban influence. Increasingly since the 1950s, other instruments, such as the piano or the conga drums, have been incorporated into the orchestras, and a vocal element, often a bolero (a romantic ballad), has been added to the music. There has also been evidence of influence from the more fully Afro-Cuban musical form, the *son*, and danzón is clearly one of the many roots of contemporary salsa music. Nevertheless, danzón still exists in its own right as a recognizable traditional form of dance.

The dance itself is characterized by modesty and reserve. The music of the danzón is split into a melody and a *paseo* (stroll). During the melody the pairs of dancers follow a strict, limited pattern of steps, maintaining an upright posture and holding each other at a distance. The woman is also required to avert her gaze from her partner out of modesty. During the *paseo*, as the name suggests, the couples either stroll arm in arm about the dance floor, greeting the other dancers, or stand still and talk together.

In Cuba the danzón became popular with both the working classes and the bourgeoisie, and from the 1870s to the 1930s it was considered the country's national dance. Indeed, in its heyday danzón was so popular that its influence reached as far as Mexico, primarily the Gulf Coast region (Veracruz) and Mexico City. In Mexico the dance remains a predominantly working-class leisure activity, although it has been given a recent boost in popularity on a national and international level by María Novaro's 1991 film *Danzón.*

—*Thea Pitman*

See also: *Popular Music:* Bolero; Salsa

Bibliography

Fairley, Jan. 2000. "Cuba—Son and Afro-Cuban Music: ¡Qué rico bailo yo!" Pp. 386–413 in *The Rough Guide to World Music*, vol. 2, *Latin and North America, Caribbean, India, Asia, and Pacific*, edited by Simon Broughton and Mark Ellingham. London: Rough Guides.

Manuel, Peter, Kenneth Bilby, and Michael Largey. 1995. *Caribbean Currents: Caribbean Music from Rumba to Reggae.* Philadelphia: Temple University Press.

Salon Mexico. 2003. "A Brief History of Danzón." http://www.salonmexico.20m.com/custom2.html (consulted 7 January 2003).

Nueva Canción

Nueva canción (new song) was a movement rather than a single musical style. It spread throughout Latin America between the 1950s and 1970s, and its aim was to express opposition to military dictatorships and foreign, particularly U.S., hegemony in the region. Like many such forms of cultural expression it found a catalyst in the triumph of the Cuban Revolution in 1959 and in the general atmosphere of resistance to authority in Europe, the United States, and elsewhere, and it drew inspiration from earlier anti-imperialist movements, such as that of Sandino in 1930s Nicaragua. In musical terms nueva canción, which usually featured acoustic instruments (mainly guitar, percussion instruments, and occasionally wind instruments), drew upon a variety of sources that depended largely upon local or national popular cultures. There were also strong foreign influences: the U.S. protest song movement, singer-songwriters in Europe, and some strands of rock music. Most of the musicians who survived this violent era found themselves in exile, and the importance in this movement of that exile cannot be underestimated, since it led the tone and content of many of the songs to lean toward expressions of nostalgia and alienation.

One of the countries most closely associated with nueva canción is Chile, where the outstanding exponents were Violeta Parra (1917–1967) and Víctor Jara (1932–1973). Both became almost synonymous with the Popular Unity government of Salvador Allende in the early 1970s, but their individual styles were different. Parra's strange, otherworldly voice and quasi-mystical lyric style were seldom overtly polemical, stressing instead the human spirit with its need for unity and potential for the celebration of life. Her most famous song, "Gracias a la vida" ("Thanks to Life"), became a nueva canción anthem despite the complete absence of social or political allusions. On the other hand, Jara's style was considerably more straightforward, rooted in folk tradition and emphasizing solidarity and political awareness with a talent for vivid metaphors that, in songs like "El arado" ("The Plough"), reached both unschooled and sophisticated audiences without descending into the facile or sentimental. After Jara's brutal murder at the hands of Augusto Pinochet's forces during the 1973 coup (Parra had already died by that time), it was left to exiled artists like the Andean folk group Inti-Illimani (the name invokes respectively the Inca sun god and Bolivia's highest mountain) to maintain opposition to the military regime.

Andean folk music also found its way into the political song movement in Argentina, where antiestablishment figures like Mercedes Sosa and Atahualpa Yupanqui (1908–1992) were able to adapt and reclaim folk traditions that had long been synonymous with rural conservatism. Sosa's potent voice covered (reperformed or rerecorded music by another performer) songs by artists as diverse as Charly García and Bola de Nieve (real name Ignacio Jacinto Villa, 1911–1971), memorably captured in *Mercedes Sosa en Argentina,* a live concert album marking her return from exile in 1983. The singer-songwriter Yupanqui, who, significantly, borrowed the name of the Inca lord executed by the Spanish conquistadors, was known mainly as an exponent of folklore, but it seems clear that his songs of hardship and persecution alluded largely to his own experiences as a political fugitive. The controlled anger with which he wrote and performed was expressed through stark, often ironic imagery that, despite many years spent abroad, constantly drew upon musical traditions of the Argentine interior. Songs like "Preguntitas sobre Dios" ("Little Questions about God") also showcase his mastery of local guitar styles and their adaptation to his brooding sensibility.

In Buenos Aires and Montevideo, with their inevitable and understandable use of European cultural models, the musical sources for nueva canción were found in diverse places: Spanish ballads, the Italian and French folk revivals, and British rock. The Argentine León Gieco's "Sólo le pido a Dios" ("I Just Pray to God"), which despite its title is rhetorically secular, became another nueva canción anthem. Gieco, who in the 1990s turned to making rock albums, distinguished himself through a terse yet impassioned vocal and lyrical style. The Uruguayan Daniel Viglietti, meanwhile, was widely admired for his whimsical political songs, sensitive cover versions of the works of other songwriters, and musical settings of poetry, graced with a powerful yet tender vocal delivery. The legendary rock composer and performer Charly García can also be attributed with some contribution to nueva canción in the form of songs such as "Dinosaurios" ("Dinosaurs"), a thinly veiled prophecy on the fate of the Argentine military junta that was allowed to escape censorship.

Another politically traumatized region in which nueva canción emerged as a voice of dissent was Central America, where the Nicaraguan brothers Carlos and Luis Enrique Mejía Godoy became its leading lights. Their opposition to the regime of Anastasio Somoza in Nicaragua was conducted from Costa Rica.

It is hardly surprising that the spirit of nueva canción was most strongly and confidently expressed in Cuba. Unmolested by political or military authority, the Nueva Trova Cubana (New Cuban Troupe) was a loose grouping of artists eager to voice the island's revolutionary zeal and exuberance. The very name of the group hinted at a break with the past, and such singers as Silvio Rodríguez and Pablo Milanés indeed dispensed with many elements of a Cuban musical heritage that was seen as outmoded and redolent of a past, steeped in inequality, racism, and ignorance, when Cuban nightclubs, brothels, and casinos were patronized by North American visitors. Ironically perhaps, the rehabilitation of *son*, cha-cha-cha, rumba, and other such genres began under Rodríguez's tenure as minister of culture in the mid-1990s. Nevertheless, the popularity of "Silvio y Pablo" (as they are invariably known in tandem), though past its 1980s heyday, remains high. The two men, despite their close association as figureheads, have quite distinct styles. Rodríguez constructs highly intricate melodic patterns with poetically audacious, optimistic lyrics accompanied by his virtuoso guitar playing. Among his most famous and popular albums are *Días y flores* (*Days and Flowers*, 1975) and *Unicornio* (*Unicorn*, 1985). He intersperses his more experimental songs, with their abstruse and whimsical imagery, with politically confrontational songs. Likewise, Milanés has always exercised a certain social responsibility in his craft despite his more wistful reflections on love, loss, and social responsibility.

The legacy of nueva canción is, to date, more ideological than musical; it can be seen primarily in Latin American rock music, particularly during the 1980s and 1990s. Explicit political content is unusual, but even some of those artists who refrain from even coded social comment often display their leanings through their actions or choice of material. One example is the Argentine band Divididos (Divided), with their blues-rock adaptations of songs like Atahualpa Yupanqui's "El arriero" ("The Muleteer"). Among other rock singers and composers whose sentiments and lyrics inherit something of nueva canción is singer-composer Fito Páez, who in 1990 made an unequivocal political statement with the album *Tercer mundo* (*Third World*), a musical travelogue based on his own experiences in Latin America. In 1994 Páez gave a concert in Havana at the invitation of Silvio Rodríguez. In 1997 Páez and several of the artists mentioned above, plus Mexican bands Café Tacuba, El Tri, and Maldita Vecindad (Damned Neighborhood); Paralamas do Sucesso (Mudguards of Success) from Brazil; and Los Tres (The Three of Them) from Chile, participated in the benefit album *Chiapas*, whose proceeds went to the Zapatismo movement in southern Mexico.

—*Keith Richards*

See also: *Popular Music:* Contemporary Urban Music (Rock Music); *Popular Social Movements and Politics:* Zapatismo

Bibliography

Jara, Joan. 1998. *Víctor: An Unfinished Song.* London: Bloomsbury.

Sairley, Jan. 1994. "Nueva Canción." Pp. 569–577 in *World Music: The Rough Guide,* edited by Simon Broughton, Mark Ellingham, and Richard Trillo. London: Penguin Books.

Schechter, John M., ed. 1999. *Music in Latin American Culture: Regional Traditions.* New York: Schirmer Books.

Brazilian Protest Music

Although protest music in Brazil did not constitute a movement as such, as it did in other Latin American countries under dictatorships, during the days of repression there emerged a number of singer-songwriters who both inspired a politically committed generation at the time and influenced the shape of popular music for future generations. The most significant of these singer-songwriters were Geraldo Vandré and Chico Buarque.

Geraldo Vandré (Geraldo Pedrosa de Araújo Dias) was born in 1935 in Paraíba in northeastern Brazil. His musical style has been defined as a mixture of bossa nova and the folkloric traditions of his native region. His songs, often interpreted by other performers, proved very successful at the televised music festivals of the mid-1960s, vehicles that revealed a wealth of songwriting talent. These music competitions eventually came to an end toward the close of the 1960s because many of the popular competitors had been forced into exile and because material was increasingly being censored. Geraldo Vandré became famous at the festivals for his fiery protest songs, especially "Prá não dizer que não falei de flores" ("So as Not to Say I Didn't Speak of Flowers"), also known simply as "Caminhando" ("Walking"). The song took second place at a festival in 1968 and was subsequently banned for ten years by the military government for its lyrics, which were deemed offensive to the armed forces, and for its capacity to provoke subversion, particularly among students. "Caminhando" quickly became a favorite anthem among political protesters during demonstrations, particularly during the difficult years of severe censorship and imprisonment of political adversaries (1968–1976). As a result of the song's prohibition, Vandré left Brazil for his own safety in 1969.

Another singer-songwriter to find fame on the music festival circuit was Chico Buarque (Francisco Buarque de Holanda), who has enjoyed a considerably longer professional life than Geraldo Vandré. Buarque did not write traditional protest songs as such; he wrote gentle sambas with very clever and often intricate lyrics that gradually, with the hardening of the Brazilian military regime in the late 1960s, came to challenge the political status quo. Eventually Buarque, like Vandré and the Tropicália musicians Caetano Veloso and Gilberto Gil, was forced to leave the country for fear of persecution. On his return in 1970, his songs were heavily censored (for example, only one song in three released by him in 1971 was approved). In songs such as "Construção" ("Construction") from 1971, Buarque's lyrics are so imaginative and deceptively simple that they are frequently included in poetry anthologies. "Construção" depicts the alienation and death of a faceless construction worker, representative of the hundreds and thousands of migrant workers who came to Rio de Janeiro and São Paulo in the 1960s and 1970s to work, in the most precarious of conditions, in the construction industry. The song thus criticizes the developmentalist policies of the military government, which showed little concern for the vast majority of Brazilians who experienced little or nothing of the supposed prosperity of the times. Occasionally, the censors were temporarily fooled by Buarque's intelligent and powerful lyrics, such as those contained in the ostensible love song "Apesar de você" ("In Spite of You"), whose refrain begins "In spite of you tomorrow will be another day"—a clear indictment of the military regime. The song was later banned. In 1973 he wrote with Gilberto Gil the song "Cálice" ("Chalice"), further expressing the bitterness felt toward the repressive government of the day. (In Portuguese the word *cálice*, in addition to meaning "chalice," is a homophone of the command *cale-se*, meaning "shut up," and thus acts as a comment on the silencing of dissent under the military dictatorship.) The first time Buarque and Gil attempted to perform this song, they were "shut up" by the authorities, who invaded the stage and turned off their microphones. The song was subsequently banned, and it then became, rather like Vandré's "Caminhando," an anthem against the dictatorship. Buarque had such difficulty with the censors that he released material under a pseudonym, Julinho de Adelaide. One such was the song "Acorda Amor" ("Wake Up, Love"), in which the singer, fearing for his safety at home one night, tells his partner to call a thief for help ("chame ladrão"), echoing a widely held belief at the time that the real criminals in society were the police. By 1984, with the end of the military regime in sight, Buarque's lyrics became more positive, as witnessed in the samba "Vai Passar," with its double meaning of "it's on its way past" (a reference to a Carnival parade mentioned in the song) and "it will soon be over" (a reference to the dictatorship). Buarque also wrote musicals and later, in the 1990s, best-selling novels. He continues to write songs and perform before live audiences, and his popularity shows no sign of waning.

—Stephanie Dennison

See also: *Popular Music:* Bossa Nova; Samba; Tropicália

Bibliography

Gonzalez, Mike, and David Treece. 1992. *The Gathering of Voices: The Twentieth-Century*

Poetry of Latin America. London and New York: Verso.
McGowan, Chris, and Ricardo Pessanha. 1998. *The Brazilian Sound: Samba, Bossa Nova, and the Popular Music of Brazil.* Philadelphia: Temple University Press.
Perrone, Charles. 1993. *Masters of Contemporary Brazilian Song: MPB 1965–1985.* Austin: University of Texas Press.

Contemporary Urban Music

Brazilian Rap and Hip-Hop

Among the most successful and politically committed urban music crazes to hit Brazil in the last ten years are rap and hip-hop, inspired by North American rap ("rhythm and poetry") music, which emerged in black ghettos of the United States in the 1980s. The most successful rap band in Brazil is Racionais MCs (The Rational MCs), one of many bands to appear since the late 1980s in the *periferia*, or poor suburbs that surround Brazil's megacity, São Paulo. In the late 1980s break dancers, DJs, graffiti artists, and rappers would meet at the Largo de São Bento and Rua 24 de Maio in the center of São Paulo on weekends, where Brazilian rap's distinctive sound (often incorporating roots, samba, and reggae) and lyrics began to be developed. In the 1990s, those interested in the hip-hop scene began to meet in the suburbs in "posses." There are around 30,000 of these posses in existence today. They were organized in 1989 into a movement with the founding of the Movimento Hip Hop Organizado (Organized Hip Hop Movement, MH2O). The movement's manifesto demanded "*poder para o povo preto*" (power for the black people), so although in the United States such posses are often synonymous with gangland violence, they are much more politically motivated in São Paulo. For example, posses would often hold discussion groups on racism, police violence, and black history, and these themes in turn would inform rap music's lyrics.

The first album by the Racionais MCs was released in 1992, entitled *Holocausto Urbano* (*Urban Holocaust*). Between 1992 and 1997 they gradually built up a following, both within the poor neighborhoods of the suburbs of São Paulo and Rio de Janeiro and among Brazil's middle-class youth. Their fourth album, *Sobrevivendo no inferno* (*Surviving in Hell*, 1997) is Brazil's most successful rap album to date: it sold over one million copies and was widely pirated. Like many other rap acts, such as O Rappa from the Baixada Fluminense (poor suburbs of Rio de Janeiro), the Racionais MCs express an antialcohol or antidrug attitude in their music, seeing drugs as destructive of their communities. An exception to this is the aptly named band Planet Hemp, whose sole reason for existence seems to be to rap about the virtues of cannabis. Both Racionais MCs and O Rappa sponsor charity projects, and in a conscious effort to "keep it real," many rappers tend to avoid big media vehicles and multinational music corporations. Most are signed to independent music labels, many of which are owned by rap performers themselves. The Racionais MCs own their own music label (Cosa Nostra). The Poder Para o Povo Preto (Power for Black People) enterprise (partly owned by K. L. Jay, the Racionais DJ) comprises a record label, two black music shops, and an Afro-hairdresser in São Paulo.

Not all Brazilian rap groups and performers are black or of mixed race. For exam-

Brazilian singers Afro-X (left) and Dexter, who together form the rap music duo 509-E, pause inside their uncharacteristically large cell in the Carandirú penal complex, where the two are inmates of Latin America's biggest prison, 21 June 2000. (Reuters/Corbis)

ple, Yuka, the front man of O Rappa, is white. In most cases white stars such as Yuka are also from the poor suburbs and can therefore relate to the common themes of rap music, such as the struggle for respect for their impoverished communities and the attempt to combat the proliferation of arms and police violence there. (Yuka was hit by a police bullet in 2002.) It is interesting, however, that O Rappa's Website complains about economic rather than racial segregation in Brazil. Another successful white rapper, in this case from a privileged background, is Gabriel o Pensador (Gabriel the Thinker—real name Gabriel Contino, born 1974), the white son of a successful television presenter, who represents the pop side to rap music in Brazil.

At the other end of the spectrum of acceptability are a number of popular rap acts that either met in prison or are still incarcerated, for example, 509-E and Detentos do Rap (both from Carandirú prison in São Paulo) and Escadinha, with a prison connection in Rio de Janeiro (Bangú). Needless to say, despite the politically motivated and socially aware lyrics and attitude of the hip-hop movement in general in Brazil, particularly when compared with hip-hop acts in the United States, rappers and their audience have been and continue to be the victims of scorn, suspicion, victimization, and even violence at the hands of the press and the police.

—Stephanie Dennison

See also: *Popular Music:* Samba

Bibliography

Caldeira, Teresa. 2000. *City of Walls: Crime, Segregation, and Citizenship in São Paulo.* Berkeley and Los Angeles: University of California Press.

Hanchard, Michael. 1994. *Orpheus and Power: the "Movimento Negro" of Rio de Janeiro and São Paulo.* Princeton: Princeton University Press.

Magaldi, Cristina. 1990. "Adopting Imports: New Images and Alliances in Brazilian Popular Music of the 1990s." *Popular Music* 18, no. 3: 309–330.

Michalas, Apostolos. 2001. "Rapping in the Periphery of São Paulo: Black Consciousness and Revolutionary Discourse in the Works of Racionais MCs." MA thesis, Institute of Latin American Studies (London).

Mexican Rap and Hip-Hop

Just as Mexican popular music has had an impact on the music scene in the United States with Tex-Mex and Tejano, such U.S.-born musical styles as rock, rap, and hip-hop have also influenced the development of new hybrid forms south of the border. The key factor that facilitates this cultural exchange is the existence of the Chicano (and more broadly Latino) community, which is conversant in both Anglo and Latin American cultural traditions and which eclectically blends elements from both in its own music.

Rap and hip-hop music in the United States is traditionally associated with black street culture and with urban youth in general. "Rap" refers to the performance of rhythmic, slang-inflected monologues supported by some musical backing; hip-hop is a slightly more danceable variant, frequently associated with the rise of break dancing in the 1980s. Although rap has generally been promoted as a black musical phenomenon, the 1980s also saw the development of Latino rap in the United States, as urban Latino youths quickly absorbed the musical styles of their black neighbors. Rock Steady Crew, The Terror Squad, Big Pun, and Fat Joe are some of the most successful of these Latino (often specifically Nuyorican) rap acts on the East Coast. On the West Coast, Latino (and more specifically Chicano) acts such as Mellow Man Ace and Kid Frost also became very popular in the late 1980s. In the 1990s the boom continued, with new Chicano rap acts such as Aztec Tribe, Darkroom Familia, and South Park Mexican. Shortly thereafter, full-fledged Mexican rap groups began to emerge, such as Control Machete (Machete Control), from Monterrey, and Molotov, from Mexico City. Inevitably, these Mexican rap groups have continued to blend U.S. rap with elements of Mexican popular music and to combine U.S. English slang with Mexican Spanish slang in a heady Chicano-inflected Spanglish. They have also produced lyrics that speak directly to Mexican youth about their own social and political situation. Control Machete, founded in 1995, is most accurately classified as hip-hop, blended with the distinctive sounds of traditional Mexican guitar harmonies and the rhythms of danzón, for example. One of their best-known tracks, "Danzón," combines the traditional music of danzón and a rap about the current state of the Mexican nation; a line in the chorus is taken from the work of popular black Cuban poet Nicolás Guillén. In general, Control Machete's lyrics are aggressively anti-imperialist and pro-*raza* (race, the common term that Mexicans and Chicanos use to indicate their ethnicity).

Molotov, founded in 1996 (not to be confused with New York City–based punk band Molotov Cocktail), produces a potent

Rapper Fat Joe (center) and the Terror Squad perform during the VH1 Hip Hop Honors show, 3 October 2004, in New York City. (Scott Gries/Getty Images)

mix of rap, hip-hop, and the already hybrid form that is Mexican rock. The group has stirred up a substantial amount of controversy, both for the political views expressed in its songs' lyrics, which rage against Mexican media conglomerates such as Televisa, and for the rather puerile, sexist, and homophobic nature of much of their material. The group claims that the humor it brings to its work should liberate it from the latter criticism.

Both Molotov and Control Machete have been immensely popular in Mexico, contributing songs to the soundtracks of a number of highly successful recent Mexican films, such as *Amores perros* (*Love's a Bitch*, 2000, with music by Control Machete) and *Y tu mamá también* (*And Your Mother Too*, 2001, with music by Molotov). Molotov also provided the title and title track for Fernando Sariñana's blockbuster film *Todo el poder* (*All the Power*, 1999). These best-selling Mexican rap and hip-hop bands have also garnered a substantial following in the United States; cultural exchange at the U.S.-Mexican border continues to flow in both directions. Molotov and Control Machete have both toured the United States and Europe, and Molotov has toured with bands such as REM and Metallica. A number of critics consider that the fusion of Latin American musical styles with rap and hip-hop seen in the work of these two groups is the way forward for popular music in general.

—*Thea Pitman*

See also: *Popular Music:* Mariachi, Ranchera, Norteña, Tex-Mex; *Language:* Chicano Spanish; *Popular Cinema:* The Mexican Film

Industry (Box-Office Successes and Contemporary Film in Mexico)

Bibliography

Cruz, Cesar A. 2003. "The Rage of the Young and the Restless." Digital Aztlan/Brownpride.com. http.//www.brownpride.com/latinrap/latinrap.asp?a=molotov/index (consulted 1 April 2003).

Montes, Richard. 2003. "Hip-hop/Rap." Digital Aztlan/Brownpride.com. http://www.brownpride.com/latinrap/default.asp (consulted 1 April 2003).

"Raperos mexicanos." n.d. Digital Aztlan/Brownpride.com. http://www.brownpride.com/latinrap/latinrap.asp?a=mexside/index (consulted 1 April 2003).

Smith, Geri. 2000. "Will Young Rockers Really Rock the Boat?" *Businessweek Online*, 26 June. http://www.businessweek.com/2000/00_26/c3687167.htm (consulted 8 May 2003).

Mangue Beat

Mangue beat is a new Brazilian musical form that appeared in the 1990s in the northeastern cities of Recife and Olinda. It was popularized by the talented Chico Science, who died in a car crash in 1996. Science (Francisco de Assis França, 1966–1996), brought up in the suburbs of Olinda, an old colonial town adjoining Recife, began experimenting with black music in the 1980s in a variety of bands, mixing 1960s rock with soul, funk, and hip-hop sounds. He took on the moniker "Chico Science" in order to sell himself as the "King of Musical Alchemy." In 1991 he made contact with a Bloco Afro (Afro-Brazilian) Carnival club called Lamento Negro (Black Lament) from the suburbs of Olinda. The club's regional percussion was mixed with Chico Science's black music, and a new band was formed: Nação Zumbi (Zumbi Nation). This new style of music was dubbed mangue (in a reference to the swampy land that surrounds Recife, where many people live in slums). Mangue beat has a hard, aggressive sound that cleverly blends heavy rock with northeastern folkloric music, including maracatu (an Afro-Brazilian slow processional dance form associated with Carnival in Recife) and embolada (an improvisational musical form with tongue-twisting lyrics, often with a set refrain and using alliterative words that are difficult to pronounce). The band's debut album, *De lama ao caos* (*From Mud to Chaos*), was released in 1994 to critical acclaim. Chico Science's second and final album, *Afrociberdelia* (1996), was influenced by ambient music, rap, funk, and psychedelic guitar as well as by the familiar rhythms of rock and maracatu and by northeastern baião (accordion-based folk music, popularized in the 1940s by Luiz Gonzaga and back in fashion with Brazil's urban middle class). The band's songs were used, to dramatic effect, in the 1997 film set in the backlands of the Northeast, *Baile perfumado* (*Perfumed Ball*). Despite Chico Science's untimely death, Nação Zumbi continues to produce music in its native state of Pernambuco, along with other mangue beat bands such as Fred Zero Quatro (Fred Zero Four).

—Stephanie Dennison

See also: *Popular Music:* Contemporary Urban Music: (Brazilian Rap and Hip-Hop); *Popular Cinema:* Youth Movies, Cinema, and Music; *Popular Religion and Festivals:* Popular Festivals (Carnival in Brazil)

Bibliography

McGowan, Chris, and Ricardo Pessanha. 1998. *The Brazilian Sound: Samba, Bossa Nova, and the Popular Music of Brazil.* Philadelphia: Temple University Press.

"Rádio Piratininga: Especial Chico Science." n.d. http://www.winf.com.br/piratininga/historiachico.htm (consulted 10 May 2004).

Rock Music

Although rock music is a musical style and broader cultural phenomenon born in the United States and practiced extensively in the English-speaking world, its influence can be felt throughout Latin America. In the first instance, in the 1950s and early 1960s, Anglo rock music, known either as *rocanrol* or *música rock*, became popular in its own right in the region. Subsequently, local English-language covers (a performance or recording of a work previously done by another performer) of Anglo rock songs were produced, followed by versions of these same songs in literal and then in much freer translations. Gathering impetus from the early 1970s onward, local musicians have chosen to blend elements of Anglo rock music, such as the electric guitar and the accentuated 4/4 beat, with elements taken from Latin American popular music (the immediately identifiable sounds of particular percussion instruments and the rhythms and harmonies of danzón or cumbia, for example). This music has come to be known throughout the Spanish-speaking world as *rock en español* (rock in Spanish).

Because this kind of rock music is able to blend elements of both Anglo and Latin American cultural traditions and thus to express, in both the music and the lyrics, a particular national cultural identity, it has also been called *rock nacional* (national rock music). The conduit for cultural influence has been the existence of the Latino (often Chicano) communities in the United States, which have themselves frequently blended U.S. rock music with elements of their cultures of origin to produce such key crossover figures and acts as Ritchie Valens, Santana, Jerry García (of the Grateful Dead) and Los Lobos.

Throughout its short history, rock music has been associated with youth culture and the urban environment, particularly with the more marginalized, such as the urban poor and the *chavos banda* (gangs). Rock music has sought to express the point of view of this group and has been key in the formation of an urban youth counterculture in such countries as Mexico and Argentina. It has had a difficult relationship with the establishment in both countries. In the first instance, the influence of Anglo-American music was seen by the establishment as a betrayal of local cultural values, even when songs were sung in Spanish. Nevertheless, at key moments both Mexico and Argentina have endorsed *rock en español* as a national cultural product, producing a complex relationship of both rejection and acceptance between the state and its organs of media diffusion, on the one hand, and the bands and artists themselves, on the other.

In Mexico, rock music with a substantial emphasis on Anglo culture and on hedonism became a notable middle-class youth phenomenon in the 1960s. The adherents of this trend were known as *jipitecas* (Mexican hippies). In contrast to the *jipitecas* were the more politically radical, and consequently less rock-oriented, participants in the student movement. These two opposing currents in Mexican youth culture eventually converged into the movement known as La Onda (The Wave), which was born as a result of the Mexican government's repression of all forms of youth culture, seen most clearly in the 1968 massacre of hundreds of young people at Tlatelolco Square in Mexico City. La Onda, although frequently condemned by critics for merely translating U.S. counterculture to a Mexican setting, sponsored the gradual change from Anglo rock to more socially aware Mexican *rock nacional* or *guacarock* (a humorous reference to the combination of the Mexican dip guacamole and rock).

Even though the Mexican government did its best to discourage the imperialist threat to national culture that was Anglo rock music and hippy culture, it was no less censorious of the growth of Mexican rock music proper, and after permitting the staging of the Avándaro rock concert in 1971 (the Mexican Woodstock) in order to gauge the strength of the countercultural movement, it clamped down even more heavily on manifestations of youth culture in the aftermath. Mexican rock music thus retreated to the working-class neighborhoods of the big cities, to the *hoyos fonquis* (the underground clubs), until guacarock was reborn in the 1980s, stimulated by the spontaneous mobilization of large sectors of the urban working classes after the devastating 1985 Mexico City earthquake. Groups and acts that date from this early period in Mexican rock are Rockdrigo, Botellita de Jerez, and Three Souls in My Mind (this last band is almost a national institution in present-day Mexico and is known affectionately as El Tri).

In recent years the massive and conservative media conglomerate Televisa, which has strong allegiances to the Mexican government, has tried to manipulate the popular appeal of rock music by sponsoring certain pop-rock bands and singers such as Los Timbirichi, Alejandra Guzmán, and transnational pop icons Thalía and Gloria Trevi. Nevertheless, some groups—such as Caifanes, Café Tacuba, Maldita Vecindad, Los de Abajo, and Plastilina Mosh—have managed to achieve massive success via such routes yet retain their countercultural edge. Evident, too, in the work of these groups is the radical blend of cultural influences: Caifanes had a big hit in the 1980s with "La negra Tomasa," a rock version of a traditional cumbia. Maldita Vecindad is known for blending mambo, danzón, ska, rap, and rhythm and blues within any one song. Most recently the combination of rap and hip-hop with Mexican *rock nacional* has become popular in the work of the band Molotov.

Argentine rock music has come to occupy the same (urban) space and to perform a social function (that of creating a sense of solidarity among the marginalized sectors of society) similar to that of Argentina's most identifiable popular musical form, the tango, in the first half of the twentieth century. It is no surprise, then, that the first key figure in Argentine rock music went by the name of Tanguito. Tanguito was a marginal, ephemeral figure who started translating Anglo rock songs into Spanish (and composing a few of his own) in the late 1960s. Under the military dictatorship (1976–1985), all forms of community and mass gatherings were repressed, and Argentine youth was specifically targeted for repression because it was considered innately subversive. Thus, rock music was censored and concerts were banned. Nevertheless, the rock magazine *Expreso imaginario* (*The Imaginary Express*) managed to keep up publication during the worst years of repression, and this helped rock music to survive and indeed to flourish as the vehicle for the expression of countercultural values and specific opposition to the regime.

During the Falklands/Malvinas War (1982), however, the Argentine government banned the dissemination of English-language music and hence favored Argentine *rock nacional* despite its oppositional stance. Although many musicians cautiously benefited from this increased dissemination of their work, their audiences were attentive to the relationship between artist and authority, and those thought to have compromised their integrity in this way were accused of being *transa* (sellouts). It is also for this reason that so many Argentine rock bands broke up once they started to achieve mass appeal, and the most important Argentine rock musicians are best identified by name rather than by the many bands in which they played. Key figures here are Charly García, León Gieco, and Luis Alberto Spinetta. The kind of rock favored by these musicians was progressive rock, with strong links to U.S. folk music (Bob Dylan, Pete Seeger, and so on) and to protest songs in general. The resultant music was rarely danceable and was appreciated more for its lyrics than for its upbeat tempo. Argentine rock music has continued to blend cultural currents, exploring its relationship with the tango (see, for example, García's albums *Tango*, 1985, and *Tango 4*, 1991) and with Argentina's other forms of popular music (see Gieco's work with Argentinean folk musicians on *De Ushuaia a La Quiaca, From Ushuaia to La Quiaca*, 1985).

Rock music has continued to be an important forum for youth culture in Argentina in the years since the end of the dictatorship. Many of the older artists, such as García, Spinetta, Fito Páez, and groups such as Virus and Patricio Rey y sus Redonditos de Ricota (Patricio Rey and His Chubby Friends from Ricota), have continued to produce interesting work. As have Mexican rock groups, other Argentine rock groups, such as Soda Stéreo and Los Enanitos Verdes (The Little Green Dwarves), have achieved mass appeal and international dissemination by media conglomerates; their reputations within the world of rock culture have subsequently suffered. Newcomers to the rock scene who have achieved critical acclaim include rappers Illya Kuryaki and The Valderramas.

In Brazil, *rock nacional* coexists comfortably alongside so-called Música Popular Brasileira (MPB, Brazilian Popular Music), foreign rock music (especially from the United States, Britain, and Ireland), and other popular forms such as hip-hop and samba-reggae. By far the most successful rock band to come out of Latin America was the Brazilian (but Phoenix, Arizona-based) "death metal" group Sepultura (Grave), which enjoyed considerable international success in the late 1980s and 1990s. Despite singing in English and thus identifying strongly with their international fan base, Sepultura's music was concerned with Brazilian history and culture. For example, the 1996 album *Roots*, with its Afro-Brazilian percussion, dealt with the decimation of Brazil's Amerindian populations and the horrors of the slave trade. The band's founder, Max Cavalera, left in 1997 to form Soulfly, a band with musical aspirations similar to those of Sepultura, which also delves into Brazilian themes and rhythms.

—Thea Pitman and Stephanie Dennison

See also: *Popular Music:* Contemporary Urban Music (Mexican Rap and Hip-Hop); Cumbia; Danzón; Mambo; Nueva Canción; Tango; Transnational Pop Icons

Bibliography

Agustín, José. 1996. "Rock mexicano." Pp. 111–116 in *La contracultura en México: La historia y el significado de los rebeldes sin causa, los jipitecas, los punks, y las bandas*. Mexico City: Grijalbo.

"Encyclopedia del rock argentino." n.d. Website del rock argentino. http://www.rock.com.ar (consulted 20 May 2003) [in Spanish].

"Historia del rock argentino" n.d. http://www.rockeros-argentinos.com.ar/paghistorock.htm (consulted 13 May 2003) [in Spanish].

Lipsitz, George. 1992. "Chicano Rock: Cruising around the Historical Bloc." Pp. 267–279 in *Rockin' the Boat: Mass Music and Mass Movements*, edited by Reebee Garofalo. Boston: South End.

Martínez, Rubén. 1993. "Corazón del rocanrol." Pp. 150–165 in *The Other Side: Notes from the New L.A., Mexico City, and Beyond.* New York: Vintage.

Monteleone, Jorge. 2002. "Figuras de la pasión rockera: Ensayo sobre rock argentino." *Everba.* http://www.everba.org/summer02/figuras_jorge.htm (consulted 13 May 2003) [in Spanish].

Morales, Ed. n.d. "Rock Is Dead and Living in Mexico: The Resurrection of La Nueva Onda." Rockeros Website. http://www.rockeros.com/tidbit/rockmex.htm (consulted 13 May 2003).

Vila, Pablo. 1992. "Rock Nacional and Dictatorship in Argentina." Pp. 209–229 in *Rockin' the Boat: Mass Music and Mass Movements*, edited by Reebee Garofalo. Boston: South End.

Zolov, Eric. 1999. *Refried Elvis: The Rise of Mexican Counterculture.* Berkeley and Los Angeles: University of California Press.

Tecnocumbia

"Tecnocumbia" refers to recent reworkings of the cumbia genre that combine this traditionally Colombian folk music, which expresses local and national themes, with other musical forms from countries such as Argentina and Peru to give rise to a variety of musical hybrids.

Young Argentinean groups such as Los Pibes Chorros (The Thieving Lads) and Yerba Brava (The Wild Weed) have adapted traditional formats, transforming the often romantic content of cumbia into a social protest and description of harsh reality. This new style of cumbia, known variously as cumbia gangsta, hard cumbia, or cumbia villera (slum cumbia), arose in the suburbs of Buenos Aires. It reworks both the content and style of traditional cumbia. In terms of content, the lyrics are peppered with street slang and focus on social issues, often dealt with in uncompromising terms. The changes to the style and sound of the music have come about through combining the cumbia rhythm with elements from reggae, rap, and hip-hop, among others. Such bands have gained fans in Chile, Paraguay, and Uruguay.

Modern urban versions of cumbia have also been developed extensively in Peru and have come to form what is now classified as tecnocumbia. This music draws on a variety of influences, including Tex-Mex music, the rhythms of Brazilian music (especially that of Manaus), Bolivian saya, merengue, and the so-called *música chicha*, itself a hybrid of Colombian cumbia and Andean music. This music mixes the more traditional sounds of Peruvian cumbia with synthesizers and keyboards, which have come to play a major role in the music. Tecnocumbia, which arose in the mid-1990s, is popular both in Lima and in the provinces, and its foremost exponent is Rosa Guerra Morales, or Rossy War, as she is better known. War has been called the "Queen of Tecnocumbia," and her first album, *Como la flor* (*Like a Flower*, 1995), brought her hits with the songs "Te acuerdas de mí" ("You Remember Me") and the title song "Como la flor." War is one of Peru's best-selling singers, and her music has also gained popularity outside Peru. She has played across much of Latin America, including Chile, Bolivia, Ecuador, Colombia, and Venezuela.

—*Claire Taylor*

See also: *Popular Music:* Contemporary Urban Music (Mexican Rap and Hip-Hop);

Cumbia; Mariachi, Ranchera, Norteña, Tex-Mex; Merengue

Bibliography

Moss, Chris. 2002. "The People Will Be Heard." *Guardian*, 4 October. http://www.guardian.co.uk/arts/fridayreview/story/0,12102,803625,00.html (consulted 7 October 2002).

Transnational Pop Icons

A number of contemporary Latin American singers and musicians have become household names outside their countries of origin, often even outside their cultural and linguistic borders. In some cases artists have adapted traditional musical styles, such as by smoothing stylistic raw edges, censoring content in order to become acceptable abroad, or incorporating musical styles already globally popular into new fusions. The linguistic aspect is also crucial, and several artists have recorded in English and other languages so as to penetrate wider markets.

Mexican-U.S. border culture has been very important in the emergence of transnational pop icons. The most prominent exponents of Tex-Mex music, the Mexican accordionist Flaco Jiménez and North American guitarist Ry Cooder, have in turn inspired other artists to experiment with new forms of cultural fusion, with ex–Talking Heads veteran David Byrne and Chicano rock band Los Lobos among those also dabbling in the genre. However, the most prominent artist springing from the U.S. Latino community, at least in terms of record sales, is surely Texas-born Selena (1971–1995), whose album *Amor prohibido* (*Forbidden Love*) achieved quadruple platinum in 1994. Selena helped Tejano music spread beyond the cultural and ethnic confines of the southeastern U.S. Latino community and rendered it marketable on a world scale. Selena is remarkable not only for her huge success and the near-deification that followed her murder in 1994 but also for bringing U.S. Latino culture into Mexico on a scale previously unimaginable and for breaking down the suspicion and scorn with which U.S.-based artists were often seen south of the border. Another crossover artist, Cuban-born Gloria Estefan, represents another U.S. Latino community. Her band, Miami Sound Machine, which came to prominence in the late 1970s, attracted Anglo audiences by tempering its original raw salsa with a romantic element. She has remained successful, recording in Spanish, Portuguese, and English with an eye to satisfying the full spectrum of her fan base without overly compromising her musical roots.

Cooder and Byrne, always with an eye to the World Music market, have separately explored Latin America's musical heritage. Some of the results have been collaborations, such as Cooder's foray into Cuba and his famous "rediscovery" of survivors from the pre-revolutionary nightclub scene. Wim Wenders's documentary *Buena Vista Social Club* (1999) famously records the musical and personal interactions between classic exponents of bolero, *son*, guaracha, and other Cuban genres, on the one hand, and their intrepid "savior," Cooder, on the other. This film's massive success relaunched the careers of such artists as Compay Segundo, Rubén González, Omara Portuondo, and Ibrahím Ferrer. Meanwhile, Byrne has produced numerous albums in collaboration with Latin American artists, most notably *Naked* (1988) and *Rei Momo* (1989), as

Cuban group Buena Vista Social Club (right to left): Amadito Valdés, Barbarito López, Ibrahím Ferrer, Eliades Ochoa, Omara Portuondo, Guajiro Maribal, Pio Leyva, and Cachaito López, during a press conference in Mexico City on 20 May 2002. (Henry Romero/Reuters/Corbis)

well as many compilations of music from Brazil, Cuba, and Peru.

A Peruvian artist who has benefited from exposure to an international audience is the singer Susana Baca, whose music follows the traditions of her African heritage. The coastal Afro-Peruvian landó song form, which draws upon both African and Spanish traditions, was made socially acceptable by the efforts of white singer Chabuca Granda in the 1960s and was subsequently popularized by such artists as Eva Ayllón, Andrés Soto, and Tania Libertad. Baca, who acted as Granda's personal assistant for some years, is notable for continuing these traditions while making careful innovations based on contact with Latin American and other musical forms. Her 2001 album *Espíritu vivo* (*Live Spirit*), recorded in New York, brings in a number of influences previously unseen in her work, including material by Caetano Veloso, Björk, and Cuban percussionist Mongo Santamaría.

An altogether more overtly commercial artist is Thalía, who made her name in telenovelas in her native Mexico but has since become a successful pop singer who commands the affection of a wide audience. Cheerfully deploying her sexuality and benefiting from a slick publicity machine, Thalía is nonetheless a respected and genuinely popular professional who has made a name across not only Latin America and the United States but also in Europe. Despite her recent moves toward crossover, she is seen as an essentially Mexican artist. Other Mexican stars having enjoyed similar success include Luis Miguel (born in Puerto Rico of an Italian mother and Spanish father), whose career has spanned more than two decades, during which he has moved from pop to

Peruvian singer Susana Baca performs during the OFF-Fest four-day music festival held in the Macedonian capital Skopje, 6 June 2004. (Robert Atanasovski/AFT/Getty Images)

boleros. The romantic image associated with this artist's good looks and impassioned delivery has been crucial to his enduring prominence and to his winning a string of international awards. Mexican singer-songwriter Juan Gabriel has also achieved international fame, without the childhood advantages Luis Miguel's show business upbringing brought him. Indeed, Juan Gabriel's troubled early life in Michoacán and Ciudad Juárez is legendary and has ultimately enhanced his image as an artist who, being the product of a disadvantaged background and true to his roots, embodies all senses of the word "popular."

A singer-songwriter who blends traditional forms with entirely modern sensibilities is Lila Downs. Her music proclaims her manifold cultural heritage, not just a Mexican-U.S. double heritage but a combination of her mother's indigenous roots and those of her white North American father. Her work reflects a life shared among rural Oaxaca (one of the Mexican states in which native culture is strongest), California, Mexico City, and Wisconsin. Downs is able to sing in Mixtec, Nahuatl, and Zapotec as well as in Spanish and English, and she does so as a declaration of pride and cultural affirmation. Her use of rural native dress invites comparisons with Frida Kahlo, comparisons that were strengthened by her appearance in the film *Frida* (2002). Of her two albums to date, *Árbol de la vida*

Singer Lila Downs participates in the American Civil Liberties Union's Freedom Concert at Avery Fisher Hall, 4 October 2004, in New York City. (Matthew Peyton/Getty Images)

Ricky Martin arrives at the premiere of *Cold Mountain* in Los Angeles, California, 7 December 2003. (Frank Trapper/Corbis)

(*Tree of Life*, 1999) is closer to indigenous tradition; *La línea* (*The Border*, 2001) is a collection of songs taken from all the above-mentioned traditions to make up a powerful statement on the problems of the Mexican-U.S. border.

The Puerto Rican singer Ricky Martin is credited with bringing Latin pop into the mainstream. Enrique Morales IV (known as Kiki to his close friends) was born in 1971 in San Juan, the capital of Puerto Rico. From an early age he took an interest in performing, trying out for Menudo, a kiddie-pop band based in Puerto Rico, and eventually being offered a place in the group two years later. Menudo went on to dominate the teen music market all over Latin America, including Brazil (where it released records in Portuguese and inadvertently caused riots at its live shows), as well as the Latino music market in the United States. After five years with the band, Ricky tried and failed to launch a solo career in New York. He then moved to Mexico, where he took part in musicals and telenovelas and secured a record deal with Sony. He released a self-titled album in 1992, followed by *Me amarás* (*You Will Love Me*, 1993), *A medio vivir* (*Half Alive*, 1995), and *Vuelve* (*Come Back*, 1998). His Spanish-language album sales reached a staggering thirty million. Meanwhile, he tried his luck again in 1994 in the United States, taking a role in the daytime soap opera *General Hospital* and singing on Broadway. By the release of his fourth album (*Vuelve*) in 1998, he was beginning to get noticed beyond the Latin American and Latino market (the single "Maria," for example, was a big summer hit in clubs in the United States and in the holiday resorts of Europe). Also taken from that album was "The Cup of Life," the signature tune to the 1998 football (soccer) World Cup finals held in France. As with most Latino singing stars, it was not until Ricky released his first English-language album (*Ricky Martin*) in 1999 and gave an electrifying performance at the 1999 Grammy Awards (his live shows are always dazzling affairs) that he broke into the U.S. market (his album went straight to number one on the Billboard Charts). He was on the cover of *Time* magazine in the same week that his album was released. Ricky Martin is six feet two inches tall, lean and chisel-jawed, with pale skin and blond-highlighted hair. On stage he is known for his sexy gyrating hips, but in fact he sticks to a very limited range of dance moves. His music is a straightforward blend of U.S. pop and non-specific Latin American rhythms, with the odd reference in Spanish thrown into the chorus (see, for example, the single "Livin' La Vida Loca," which made him a household name). His looks, moves, and songs thus offer a familiar, easily absorbed, and safe version of Latin American culture for Anglos in the United States and for middle-of-the-road music listeners elsewhere (Ricky has a huge following in Russia, for example). Ricky followed up the success of *Ricky Martin* with a second English-language album, *Sound Loaded* (2000), which included the hit single "She Bangs" and a duet performed with another singer of Latin American origin, Cristina Aguilera, entitled "Nobody Wants to Be Lonely."

Despite his high-profile on-off relationship with Mexican TV presenter Rebecca de Alba, the international press has delighted in debating Ricky's sexuality. Like pre-outed George Michael, Ricky refuses to be drawn on the subject. Keeping his fans guessing has helped ensure a large following of both teenage girls and gay men. He has not been quite so successful at avoiding controversy in other areas of his life, however. He was sued by his former manager in 2004 and was said to have alienated his one-time songwriter-producer Robi Draco Rosa by his participation in the opening ceremony of George W. Bush's presidential inauguration, which Rosa felt was a betrayal of what every Puerto Rican should stand for. He did, however, turn down the chance to star alongside Jennifer Lopez in a remake of *West Side Story*, fearing the film would promote negative stereotypes of Puerto Ricans.

The diminutive Colombian singer-songwriter Shakira (Shakira Isabel Mebarak Ripoll) is one of the most successful Latin American artists on the international stage in recent years. Born in 1977 in Barranquilla, an industrial city with a population of one million located on the Caribbean coast, to a Colombian mother and Lebanese father, her meteoric rise to fame outside of Colombia (she has been a superstar there since she was a teenager) coincided with a boom in interest in all things Latino in the U.S. entertainment industry. Like Ricky Martin, her musical style can be described as a mixture of Latin rhythms and stadium rock, but unlike Ricky, she has been able to garner a certain credibility with the international music press by writing her own material; playing

Colombian pop star Shakira performs at El Campin stadium in Bogota, 12 March 2003. Shakira sang songs from her English-language album *Laundry Service* for the first time in Colombia. (Daniel Munoz/Reuters/Corbis)

guitar, harmonica, and drums; and occasionally voicing controversial views, such as her antiwar stance during her U.S. and British tour of 2003. According to good friend, Boom writer, and fellow Colombian Gabriel García Márquez, her success is partly due to the fact that she is hardworking, very determined, and completely focused on her musical career. She had not even started secondary school when a record company signed her in her native Colombia, and she released her first album in 1990. Like Ricky Martin, before making it really big in the music industry, she made an incursion into the world of the telenovela, starring in 1992 in the Colombian production *El Oasis* (*The Oasis*).

Shakira moved to Miami, the mecca for all Latino performers seeking transnational success, in the mid-1990s. There she made contact with Gloria and Emilio Estefan. Gloria would be a significant influence on Shakira's songwriting from then on. Her fourth album, *Donde están los ladrones?* (*Where Are the Thieves?*, 1998), sold well in Latin America and in the Latino market in North America. The musical influences on the album are heavy rock, mariachi, and Lebanese music. After the album's success and on the eve of the launch of her international career, Shakira dyed her hair blonde and began to use thick eyeliner, eliciting the inevitable comparisons to other young starlets such as Britney Spears and Christina Aguilera (and alienating some of her homegrown fans). Her first album in English, *Laundry Service*, was recorded on a farm in Uruguay and released in 2001. It sold two million copies in the United States alone. The first single from the album, "Whenever, Wherever," went to number one in many countries. The song featured Andean panpipes and a pop-rock chorus, and the accompanying video included some obligatory belly dancing to remind fans of her Middle Eastern roots. On *Laundry Service*, the singer notably toned down the strident quality of her voice, which had until then sounded like a cross between ululating and the mock-Irish warbling of Dolores O'Riordan of The Cranberries.

As Shakira's international career was being carefully forged, she was conducting a very high-profile relationship with Antonio De La Rua, the lawyer son of ex–Argentine president Fernando De La Rua (the single "Underneath Your Clothes" from *Laundry Service* was written about her famous boyfriend). The jet-set Latin American couple faced considerable criticism for their flashy lifestyle after the economic crash in Argentina in 2001.

—Keith Richards and Stephanie Dennison

See also: *Popular Music:* Bolero; Mariachi, Ranchera, Norteña, Tex-Mex; Salsa; *Popular Literature:* The Boom; *Mass Media:* Telenovela; *Popular Cinema:* Youth Movies, Cinema, and Music; *Visual Arts and Architecture:* Art (Frida Kahlo)

Bibliography

Adams, Rachel. 2002. "Shakira." Ch. 3 in "Great Female Singers of Our Time and Place," MA thesis, University of Manchester.

Bethell, Leslie, ed. 1998. *A Cultural History of Latin America: Literature, Music, and the Visual Arts in the 19th and 20th Centuries.* Cambridge and New York: Cambridge University Press.

Clark, Walter Aaron, ed. 2002. *From Tejano to Tango: Latin American Popular Music.* New York: Routledge.

Furman, Elina. 1999. *Ricky Martin.* New York: St. Martin's.

García Márquez, Gabriel. 2002. "The Poet and the Princess." *Guardian Weekend,* 8 June, 16–19.

Patterson, John. 1999. "Spanglish Made Easy." *London Guardian,* 3 June.

Peña, Manuel H. 1999. *The Mexican American Orquesta: Music, Culture, and the Dialectic of Conflict.* Austin: University of Texas Press.

Ricky Martin Official Website. http://www.rickymartin.com (consulted 30 August 2003).

Roberts, John S. 1998. *The Latin Tinge: The Impact of Latin American Music on the United States.* 2nd ed. New York: Oxford University Press.

San Miguel, Guadalupe. 2002. *Tejano Proud: Tex-Mex Music in the Twentieth Century.* College Station: Texas A&M University Press.

3

Popular Social Movements and Politics

Popular movements in Latin America in the late twentieth century have generally been a response to two major phenomena: first, the wave of military dictatorships that overtook the region between the 1960s and 1970s, and second, the imposition of neoliberal economic policies from the mid-1980s to the present. Numerous other contributory factors and consequences have accompanied these phenomena, of course, such as the inroads made by foreign economic interests after most of the region achieved independence from Spanish rule in the 1820s. The emergence of vigorous indigenous movements in several countries must also be taken into account, as must the increasing role in the political process, both formal and otherwise, of women.

Spanish rule had ended in continental Latin America by the third decade of the nineteenth century. (The last colony to become independent, nominally at least, was Cuba in 1898.) The region then came under the influence of mostly British economic concerns. Argentine beef was one main British interest, and railways were built to bring the supply to the port of Buenos Aires, from which tinned meats were sent to the United Kingdom. The British exploited nitrates from the Pacific coast of Bolivia (a coastline later taken by Chile) and guano from the Peruvian coast for fertilizer. European governments and companies coveted oil deposits across the region, as did the new emerging power of the United States. For although the British hand could be seen behind such conflicts as the War of the Pacific (1879–1883), in which Bolivia and Peru both lost territory to Chile, and the Chaco War (1932–1935), in which Paraguay took over most of the oil deposits of southeastern Bolivia, Latin America's northern neighbor was to become far more influential in the twentieth century, taking a leading role in developing fruit-growing enterprises in the Caribbean region and moving aggressively into resources of raw materials elsewhere.

The legacy of Latin America's colonial past, and its correlate, its neocolonial and neoliberal present, is a social reality still bereft of the institutions and infrastructure necessary for formal democracy to attain any real meaning. Nation-states in the region were created out of the remains of the Spanish colonial system and conditioned by the urgency the "political" classes felt to comply with the new foreign powers. Three main elements of this legacy are transport networks existing only to move raw materials to the coast for export; hegemonic urban centers in Mexico City, Lima, and Buenos Aires; and limitation of education and health services mostly to a privileged minority decided by ethnic origin.

As the 1930s saw an influx of Marxist ideas and as the example set by the Soviet Union and China became clear, political parties began to adapt socialist ideas to the Latin American context. The American Popular Revolutionary Alliance (APRA), founded and led in 1930s Peru by Víctor Raúl Haya de la Torre, is one example of a party founded with social reformist aims: after enduring several decades of repression the APRA finally took power in 1985 with the election of Alan García, who proved to be one of the most corrupt and opportunistic leaders in even that country's unfortunate political history. Nonetheless García, who lived in exile in Colombia and France for much of the 1990s, only narrowly lost the presidential election of 2001. The APRA experience exemplifies two common occurrences by no means exclusive to Latin America: first, the ease with which political parties can betray their initial impulse, and second, the dogged loyalty of some voters to parties that have long ceased to represent their true interests, as well as the catastrophically short memory of the electorate when it comes to the return of disgraced politicians (another striking example being the election in 1997 of the Bolivian ex-dictator Hugo Banzer).

Unsurprisingly, many people see their only hope of political representation outside formal politics in direct action (guerrilla warfare, or "terrorism"), in protest of a less confrontational kind, or in the development of self-sufficient infrastructures that bypass central power. Resistance may be mounted along all manner of positions, concepts of difference, or stances that are morally or ethically unassailable. Las Madres de la Plaza de Mayo have learned to use motherhood itself as the basis for their indefatigable actions in search of justice, displaying a faith in fundamental decency that is finally being endorsed by the Argentine president Néstor Kirchner, with his pledge to address the grievances of those who lost family members in the military dictatorship of the late 1970s.

Elsewhere, the fundamental basis of protest is ethnicity: age-old wounds stemming from the abuse of racial difference and the assumption of racial superiority granting one group a divine right to enslave and oppress another. Examples of responses to these conditions can be seen in the rebellions linked to Zapatismo in southern Mexico, in the repeated standoffs with government forces in Bolivia, and to some extent in the Peruvian Shining Path guerrilla movement. The role of certain tendencies in the Catholic Church must also be acknowledged, for example, that of such leaders as El Salvador's martyr to social justice, Archbishop Óscar Arnulfo Romero.

Another indisputably justified position from which protest stems is the lack of provision of the most basic necessities, such as land, water, food, and the opportunity to learn and work. These fundamental needs have long occasioned protest movements of all kinds across the entire continent.

—Keith Richards

Bibliography

Eckstein, Susan. 1988. *Power and Popular Protest: Latin American Social Movements.* Berkeley and Los Angeles: University of California Press.

Garretón Merino, Manuel Antonio. 2003a. *Incomplete Democracy: Political Democratization in Chile and Latin America.* Chapel Hill: University of North Carolina Press.

———. 2003b. *Latin America in the Twenty-first Century: Toward a New Sociopolitical Matrix.* Coral Gables, FL: North-South Center.

Peloso, Vincent C. 2003. *Work, Protest, and Identity in Twentieth-Century Latin America.* Wilmington, DE: Scholarly Resources.

Pineo, Ronn F., and James A. Baer. 1998. *Cities of Hope: People, Protests, and Progress in Urbanizing Latin America.* Boulder, CO: Westview.

Peronismo

The political movement Peronismo takes its name from Juan Perón (1895–1974), president of Argentina from 1946 to 1955 and from November 1973 to July 1974. Peronismo, also known under the banner of the Partido Justicialista (Justicialist Party), is frequently described as nationalist and populist, and it is still strongly associated by many with the charismatic figure of Evita, Perón's first wife.

Juan Perón first came to prominence as part of the military government ruling in the mid-1940s in Argentina, when he served as secretary of labor. Considered a fairly minor post at the time, the Labor Department was transformed by Perón and gained in stature and in responsibilities. From 1944 onward Perón made a concerted effort to engage working-class support, and one of his important moves was negotiation with the unions. Perón granted legal standing to trade unions, allowing them to negotiate directly with the government, although, crucially, these negotiating powers were restricted only to those recognized by Perón, which led in effect to the government imposing settlements. At this time Perón began to promise a "new Argentina," one that would champion the rights of the *masas descamisadas* (shirtless masses).

Perón won the presidential elections of 1946 with a 54 percent majority. Shortly afterward he announced his five-year Economic Plan, which began with the declaration "in 1810 we were liberated politically: today we long for economic independence." The principal aims of the plan were to achieve economic independence for Argentina by reducing foreign influence on the economy, principally by nationalizing foreign-owned companies and by paying off Argentina's external debt. One of Perón's greatest triumphs was the nationalization of the railway in 1948, which up to then had been a British-owned company, and the cancellation of Argentina's foreign debt in 1947, which was celebrated with a mass ceremony named the "Declaration of Economic Independence."

Although Perón and the political movement he created stated that their aim was to find truly Argentine solutions while helping workers, Peronismo is far from communism. Despite some improvements in conditions for the urban working class and the introduction in the early years of such key legislation as that concerning pensions, the maximum working day, and paid holidays, Peronismo became increasingly autocratic over time. Frequently, although Peronismo is characterized by the use of working-class rhetoric in its declarations, its policies have often been conservative; as Thomas Skidmore and Peter Smith have noted, "as the economic policy became more orthodox, Peronist rhetoric became more strident" (1992, p. 91). Perón's rule grew steadily more draconian, and toward the end of his first term he had the Argentine constitution amended to allow himself to stand for reelection. In 1951 he was reelected with 67 percent of the vote. Over the years Perón's policies became more authoritarian, gagging the press, rigging the election of the judiciary, and purging the universities, among other repressive measures. Thus, Peronismo is a difficult movement to define.

By 1955 Perón had been forced into exile, and Peronismo had been outlawed, although support still continued and Peronist unionism remained strong within the Argentine working class. In 1962 Peronists were allowed to stand for election again, and Perón himself made a brief reappearance on the Argentine political stage in 1973, when he was once again elected president.

Nowadays, Peronismo is still in evidence in Argentine politics, although its outlook has changed from the early days of Perón's rule. As Steven Levitsky has noted, although Perón's party may have started off as a labor-based party, by the mid-1980s it had changed to a "clientelistic party" in which unions had a very minor role. Moreover, under the recent leadership of Carlos Menem, the Peronist president of Argentina from 1989 to 1999, the Peronist policy of reducing foreign interests in Argentina was reversed, as Menem embarked on a neoliberal policy and encouraged foreign investment. Thus, although Peronismo is still a political force in Argentina, its policies have changed over time.

—Claire Taylor

See also: *Cultural Icons:* Political Icons (Evita)

Bibliography

James, Daniel. 1988. *Resistance and Integration: Peronism and the Argentine Working Class, 1946–1976.* Cambridge: Cambridge University Press.

Levitsky, Steven. 2003. *Transforming Labor-Based Parties in Latin America: Argentine Peronism in Comparative Perspective.* Cambridge: Cambridge University Press.

McGuire, James W. 1999. *Peronism without Perón: Unions, Parties, and Democracy in Argentina.* Stanford: Stanford University Press.

Rock, David. 1987. *Argentina, 1516–1987: From Spanish Colonization to the Falklands War and Alfonsín.* London: Tauris.

Skidmore, Thomas E., and Peter H. Smith. 1992. "Argentina: From Prosperity to Deadlock." Pp. 68–113 in *Modern Latin America.* Oxford: Oxford University Press.

Castrismo

The Cuban political movement Castrismo is named after the high-profile socialist leader Fidel Castro. Fidel Castro Ruz is the most controversial politician of his generation in the Western world, provoking equally fierce passions on either side of the ideological divide, represented by Cubans based in Havana and Miami. The biographical details of his life are by now well known: born in 1926 into a wealthy family in Mayari in the underprivileged eastern Oriente province, Castro trained as a lawyer and in 1953 made his name by leading the famous if abortive attack on the Moncada barracks. The speech "History Will Absolve Me" with which Castro undertook his own defense marked him as a gifted orator and rhetorician. After spending two years in prison Castro was

Fidel Castro speaks to the crowd at the Hotel Antofagasto, c. 1950–1960, Antofagasto, Chile. (Bettmann/Corbis)

amnestied and sent into exile in Mexico, where he organized the 26 of July Movement (whose name was taken from the date of the Moncada attack). This rebel force landed in eastern Cuba in 1956 and eventually overthrew the dictatorship of Fulgencio Batista in 1959. The revolutionary government subsequently alienated the United States with a program of nationalization of foreign interests, and Castro became a symbol of courageous self-determination or Communist tyranny, depending upon one's political leanings in the polarized atmosphere of the Cold War.

Castro's status in the United States as a villain, as has been argued in several quarters, has largely served to enhance his image in Cuba and every other center of resistance to U.S. foreign policy. Debate over Castro's role in the island's politics generally focuses upon the nation's advances in social policy (particularly in education and health care), on the one hand, and its uncompromising attitude toward political dissent, on the other. Any discussion of Castro must, however, take into account his appeal to Cuban nationalism for a population that had hitherto known little more than repeated humiliation. Without this factor, it is difficult to explain his continued hold on power for well over four decades. Castro's legendary charisma is undeniable and, allied to his keen instinct for political survival, has certainly aided his position. Without considerable popular support, however, his longevity as a Cuban leader would surely have been curtailed. For many, this unofficial mandate counterbalances the more coercive elements of Cuban communism.

Thomas Paterson's *Contesting Castro* (1994) is an absorbing account of Washington's fixation with the Cuban leader, into whose hands U.S. foreign policy has played on countless occasions. All attempts to undermine the Castro regime by sabotage, invasion, economic embargo, and even assassination have further enhanced Castro's standing both within Cuba, where he is still widely regarded as an embodiment of national independence, and elsewhere in the so-called third world, where he is an example to be emulated.

Not surprisingly, depictions of Castro tend to be either hagiographic, typified perhaps by Herbert Matthews's 1969 book *Fidel Castro*, or demonizing, as represented by Alicia Castro's 1998 book *Castro's Daughter*. Fidel Castro has few natural allies, though these have increased considerably in the early twenty-first century with the election in South America of a series of presidents with socialist sympathies. Luis Inácio "Lula" da Silva in Brazil, Néstor Kirchner in Argentina, and Lucio Gutiérrez in Ecuador have all displayed a will to institute radical social reforms, but within a framework that makes U.S. intervention unlikely.

—Keith Richards

Bibliography

Bunck, Julie Marie. 1994. *Fidel Castro and the Quest for a Revolutionary Culture in Cuba.* University Park: Pennsylvania State University Press.

Castro, Alicia. 1998. *Castro's Daughter: An Exile's Memoir of Cuba.* New York: St. Martin's.

Coltman, Leycester. 2003. *The Real Fidel Castro.* New Haven, CT: Yale University Press.

Matthews, Herbert L. 1969. *Fidel Castro.* New York: Simon and Schuster.

Paterson, Thomas G. 1994. *Contesting Castro: The United States and the Triumph of the Cuban Revolution.* Oxford: Oxford University Press.

Quirk, Robert. 1995. *Fidel Castro.* New York: Norton.

Rice, Donald E. 1992. *The Rhetorical Uses of the Authorizing Figure: Fidel Castro and José Martí.* New York: Praeger.

Chavismo

The Venezuelan political movement Chavismo, named after long-term leader Hugo Chávez, is similar politically to Cuba's Castrismo. Hugo Chávez Frías, born in 1954 in Sabaneta in the state of Barinas, graduated with a degree in engineering from a military academy in 1975 and led a coup attempt against the government of Carlos Andrés Pérez in February 1992. Jailed for two years before receiving a pardon, Chávez has nonetheless constantly criticized the oligarchy that traditionally ruled Venezuela as corrupt and self-serving, content to monopolize the country's huge oil wealth for its own ends.

A critic too of the hegemony of the United States, Chávez is the closest of Latin America's leaders to Fidel Castro in more than merely geographical terms, and he occupies a similarly beleaguered position. Castro is a regular visitor to Caracas, and the bond between the two leaders has given rise to talk of an axis between their countries, both of which have Caribbean coastlines and thus share geopolitical interests. The two governments have reached accords on mutual support, featuring particularly the provision to Cuba of Venezuelan oil it desperately needs.

Constantly balked by opposition from an oligarchy indignant at his populist and socialist policies, Chávez has nonetheless managed to mobilize popular support against several attempts to oust him, maintaining the power base that brought him landslide election victories in both 1998 and 2000. The land redistribution policies he instituted have provoked the wrath of the landowning classes, which also own practically all the media. For this reason Chávez has had to work in constant opposition to the main shapers of public opinion in Venezuela. Despite this, he has managed to achieve two election victories, and although the probity of these elections has been called into question, Chávez's popularity remains indisputably high.

This also became evident in the wake of an attempted coup in April 2002, when Chávez, deposed by a junta transparently representing the oligarchy, was reinstated through direct action by the country's poorest sectors. The coup attempt, and the strike that accompanied it, were a response to the radicalization of the government's policies after Chávez's second election victory and its increased emphasis on reform and the restriction of private enterprise. Even though Chávez has yet to substantially improve the material condition of the lower classes, he appears still to enjoy their support in preference to those already tried and found wanting.

Chávez's personal style is a curious mix of authoritarianism and bonhomie, as can be seen in his television broadcasts, which have been known to exceed three hours. The president is at pains to identify himself with nineteenth-century revolutionary leader Simón Bolívar (1783–1830) and to bask in the reflected glory of a previous transformation. To this end he had his country's official name changed to the Bolivarian Republic of Venezuela, and he usually has photographs taken or televised discourses filmed in front of a portrait of the Liberator of South America. To follow the argument of Donald E. Rice, Chávez is employing the figure of Bolívar in much the same way as Castro has mobilized the Cuban national hero José Martí. The Venezuelan leader's television persona is chatty, recounting international conferences and meetings with heads of state in the manner of one describing a week's work at the *hacienda* or factory. However, behind this persona lies an astute political brain: Chávez has consolidated upon his election victory and has been careful to nurture the popular support that won him power. This was shown beyond doubt by his victory in the August 2004 referendum to decide whether he should continue in power.

—Keith Richards

See also: *Popular Social Movements and Politics:* Castrismo

Bibliography

Ellner, Steve. 2003. *Venezuelan Politics in the Chávez Era: Class, Polarization, and Conflict.* Boulder, CO: Lynne Rienner.

Gott, Richard. 2000. *In the Shadow of the Liberator: Hugo Chávez and the Transformation of Venezuela.* London: Verso.

Rice, Donald E. 1992. *The Rhetorical Uses of the Authorizing Figure: Fidel Castro and José Martí.* New York: Praeger.

MST

The Movimento dos Trabalhadores Rurais Sem Terra (Landless Rural Workers Movement, MST), an association set up in Brazil in 1984, is now one of the world's largest and most influential direct-action land-reform groups. The MST was founded officially in Cascavel, in the southern state of Paraná, but many people date the recent tradition of organized occupation of unproductive land from 1979 and the first occupation by the landless poor in Ronda Alta, Rio Grande do Sul.

The MST is among the nongovernmental groups that have proliferated in third world countries in the face of increased poverty and the undermining of local economies by trade liberalization. It also forms part of the Brazilian "redemocracy" movement of the late 1970s and early 1980s, which began as the dictatorship's hold on the country was gradually loosened. The perennially pressing issue of land reform has never been properly addressed in Brazil, where 45.1 percent of farmable land currently is owned by *latifundiários*, or large-scale landowners.

There have previously been few attempts to mobilize the rural poor: the Ligas Camponesas (Peasant Leagues) of the 1950s, which demanded land reform in the northeast of Brazil, were brutally crushed and were used by the Right as evidence of the infiltration of socialism in Brazil. That said, a Land Statute dating from 1964 (the beginning of the dictatorship) and reconfirmed in the postdictatorship Federal Constitution of 1988, guarantees access to land for people who wish to work it and live off it. Land thus has a social function, and the state has an obligation to promote access to it. The MST interprets this as meaning that unused and underused land can be appropriated. The purpose, then, of the MST is to organize rural workers and encourage them to occupy such land in order to speed up the redistribution of land rather than sitting back and waiting for government to reappropriate unproductive land and hand it over to the rural poor. (The legal system in Brazil is notoriously slow, and rural elites have always been a wealthy, politically powerful, well-organized, and often well-armed group for whom possession of land is and always has been an important investment and indicator of wealth.)

The MST is present in twenty-three of the twenty-seven Brazilian states, and 1.5 million people are associated with the movement. Around 350,000 families have been settled, and a further 80,000 live in camps awaiting formal settlement (known as *assentamento*). The MST regularly holds national congresses: more than 11,000 participants attended the congress in Brasília in 2000. It is hard to deny either the impact of the MST on bringing to light the issue of land reform or the success of its approach to the issue: three-quarters of today's *assentamentos* originated as land occupations.

Once unused, underused, and abandoned farms are occupied by families organized by the MST; cooperatives and credit unions are set up; and the land is farmed to grow fruit, dairy products, grains, coffee, meat, and so on. The families sell their produce to commercial food companies, farmers' markets, and the MST shop in São Paulo. The *assentamentos* run their own schools (1,800 at the last count); MST members are often sent to specially set up teacher-training programs at sympathetic institutions, including state-run universities, designed for MST members, where the methods of the internationally renowned Brazilian educator Paulo Freire are widely used. A large number of local and international charity organizations take an interest in the social and educational side of life on the *assentamentos*, and government support is offered for many educational and cultural initiatives.

The highly informative MST Website states: "our struggle is not only with the great estates; it is with the neoliberal economic model." It emphasizes the movement's links with the Cuban Revolution of 1959 and its support for Palestine. The

MST has successfully forged links with like-minded groups as far afield as South Africa, the Philippines, and throughout Asia. It is deeply suspicious of multinational corporations, genetically modified crops (it is hoped that all MST farms will soon be organic), and the Free Trade Area of the Americas (ALCA): the most important international campaign the MST is currently involved in is the Continental Campaign against ALCA. The movement has also demanded a plebiscite on Brazil's foreign debt, which currently stands at over 200 billion dollars.

The news media in Brazil, particularly the highly regarded weekly newsmagazine *Veja*, delight in sending up the MST for what they would define as misplaced political correctness and naïve socialist beliefs that seem to hark back to a different era (the highly politicized pre-dictatorship 1960s, for example). Others are suspicious of the militant nature of the organization: the term *militante* is freely used on the Website, and the *assentamentos* are said to be superseding Cuba as a training ground for future militants. But despite this the movement has plenty of support in Brazil in urban as well as rural areas. A more dangerous enemy is the unsympathetic landed elite, whose members are regarded as being behind the large number of deaths and shootings of MST members since the (unarmed) movement was set up. Between March 1987 and September 2003, 137 MST workers were murdered. The worst attack to date on landless protesters occurred in 1996 in Eldorado do Carajás, where 19 MST members were shot dead and 57 were severely wounded. A total of 155 policemen were subsequently accused of their murder, and over 100 were finally brought to court in 2002. In June of that year only two were convicted of any wrongdoing, and the rest were acquitted.

Sebastião Salgado's 1996 photographic project *Terra* (*Land*) brought the struggle and achievements of the MST to light abroad, as well as helping turn Salgado into an internationally acclaimed photojournalist. Salgado continues to support the movement, for example by being involved in setting up an MST Environment College.

—*Stephanie Dennison*

See also: *Visual Arts and Architecture:* Photography (Sebastião Salgado)

Bibliography

Branford, Sue, and Jan Rocha. 2002. *Cutting the Wire: The Story of the Landless Movement in Brazil.* London: Latin America Bureau.

Hopkinson, Amanda. 2002. "Of Human Grandeur." *London Guardian*, 27 July.

Movimento dos Trabalhadores Rurais Sem Terra—Brasil Website. http://www.mst.org.br (consulted 1 December 2003).

"People's Power." 2000. *London Guardian*, 28 June.

Zapatismo

The contemporary Mexican protest movement Zapatismo is named after the revolutionary leader Emiliano Zapata. In the early hours of 1 January 1994, the day that the North American Free Trade Agreement (NAFTA) among the United States, Canada, and Mexico was due to come into effect, a few hundred armed indigenous rebels calling themselves the Ejército Zapatista de Liberación Nacional (EZLN, The Zapatista Army for National Liberation) stormed seven towns in the southern Mexican state of Chiapas and laid siege to them for a number of days. Relatively little blood was shed, but the political impact of their move was massive and continues to affect Mexico. The Mexican government quickly deployed over half of its troops to the area (approximately 12,000 soldiers) and succeeded in retaking key urban sites, containing the rebels in the remote highland and jungle areas of the region. However, the government stopped short of taking out the rebels altogether (though it could have done so easily), opting to engage in a series of "dialogues" with the EZLN via government spokesman Manuel Camacho Solís, a veteran negotiator of the post-1985 earthquake protests. Clearly, the government did not want to jeopardize the new trade agreement by paying too much heed to a bit of insurrection in the farthest-flung parts of the country; nor did it want to attract national and international condemnation by perpetrating a massively visible act of genocide after all the media hype surrounding the *quincentenario*, the five-hundredth anniversary of the "discovery" of the Americas and its concomitant sense that issues of racial conflict had been resolved. After all, 1994 was the year for national elections in Mexico. To date, the dialogues between the Zapatistas and the Mexican government—the Partido Revolucionario Institucional (PRI, Institutional Revolutionary Party) or, since 2000, with the Partido de Acción Nacional (PAN, National Action Party)—have resolved relatively little. Yet perhaps the importance of the Zapatista movement has more to do with its novel organizational structure, its aims, and its means of achieving those aims than with demonstrable results.

Unlike previous left-wing guerrilla groups across Latin America, the Zapatistas have managed to unite and fight in a nonhierarchical and inclusive manner. That is to say, they are not directed from the top down, with troops taking orders from a leader who is perhaps somewhat divorced from the realities of the indigenous people's lives by dint of origin and education. Although their spokesperson, the charismatic, well-educated, and well-spoken Subcomandante Marcos is clearly not an indigenous Chiapanecan peasant; he is only their spokesperson, not their leader. Instead, indigenous *comandantes* (commanding officers) set the political agenda, and they in turn are dictated to by all members of the community they represent: men, women, and even children. Furthermore, the EZLN is inclusive in that it represents members of different ethnic groups (including poor *ladinos*, or nonindigenous Chiapanecans) and religions and of both sexes. The structure, then, is profoundly democratic and is much more likely to help broker lasting solutions agreeable to all parties and to cement grassroots community solidarity than any previous group has been.

Although the demands of the Zapatistas are fairly typical of an indigenous uprising, their ultimate aspirations are not. The EZLN has petitioned the government for restitution of land rights accorded by the revolutionary Mexican Constitution, which the government was in the process of rescinding; for improvements in living conditions and infrastructure (health, education, sanitation, roads, services, salaries); and for recognition of indigenous peoples' rights. This last point is one of the only areas where the dialogues have been successful, and some indigenous self-governance in accordance with traditional legal systems has been granted. Nevertheless, the EZLN has also petitioned for matters that affect more than just indigenous Chiapanecans. They

A Zapatista rebel stands guard near a news conference held by Subcomandante Marcos in the village of La Realidad in Chiapas on 22 February 2001. (Reuters/Corbis)

have protested against the Mexican government's neoliberal policies and willingness to sign agreements with the United States that will have detrimental effects on poor people throughout the nation, and they have protested against the antidemocratic, repressive, and corrupt tactics of the Mexican government, challenging its legitimacy to hold power. Yet the Zapatistas do not seek to claim that power for themselves. Rather, they define themselves as a movement that seeks to disappear once it has achieved its objective of revolutionizing Mexican society and its form of government.

Finally, the EZLN has been particularly innovative in the ways it has sought to achieve its objectives. Although the initial armed uprising was hardly original, since then they have fought for the hearts and minds of Mexican civil society and the international community via the media, particularly via media that the Mexican government cannot effectively silence, such as the Internet. They have continued to provide information so as not to fall out of the media's eye, and they have further involved national and international communities by inviting them to physically participate in their campaign, in peace camps set up to deter the Mexican military from attacking Zapatista settlements, in *aguascalientes* or ad hoc conventions held in jungle clearings, and in educational Zapaturs (tours of the Zapatista heartland). Furthermore, the communiqués issued by Subcomandante Marcos make great use of humor, allegory, symbolism, and even the techniques of magical realism. Indeed, his whole per-

Subcomandante Marcos waves to supporters in Tepoztlan during his seventeen-day march through Mexico to lobby Congress for the passage of an Indian rights bill. (Shaul Schwarz/Corbis Sygma)

sona—the gentle voice, the pipe, the balaclava (mask) that he never removes in public—has seduced a national and international audience eager for a new revolutionary icon who is also lovable (even sexy) and entertaining. Marcos has even been used as a source of inspiration for fashion. Yet even this last, rather facile, reappropriation of Zapatista iconography by Mexican popular culture should not be seen as proof that the EZLN's cause has been sanitized and reabsorbed by mainstream Mexican society. This kind of impact on the popular imagination can still be seen as an expression of the need for alternatives to mainstream politics in Mexico. Remarkably, this small group of revolutionaries has managed to have its voice heard all across Mexico (and beyond) for nearly ten years now, and it has stimulated debate over key issues that affect all Mexicans.

—*Thea Pitman*

See also: *Popular Social Movements and Politics:* Post-1985 Earthquake Movements in Mexico; *Sport and Leisure:* Fashion (Mexico); *Travel and Tourism:* Cultural Tourism; *Mass Media:* The Internet

Bibliography

Collier, George A., and Elizabeth Lowery Quaratiello. 1994. *BASTA! Land and the Zapatista Rebellion in Chiapas.* Oakland, CA: Food First Books.

Holloway, John, and Eloína Peláez, eds. 1998. *Zapatista! Reinventing Revolution in Mexico.* London: Pluto.

Katzenberger, Elaine, ed. 1995. *First World, Ha Ha Ha! The Zapatista Challenge.* San Francisco: City Lights.

Subcomandante Marcos. 1995. *Shadows of Tender Fury: The Letters and Communiques of Subcomandante Marcos and the Zapatista Army of National Liberation.* Introduction by John Ross. New York: Monthly Review.

Shining Path

The guerrilla movement Sendero Luminoso (Shining Path) began in the southern Peruvian Andes in 1980 and rocked Peruvian society during the late 1980s and early 1990s, causing considerable political and psychological impact. Springing from a Maoist branch of the Peruvian Communist Party in the city of Ayacucho under the leadership of the philosophy lecturer Abimael Guzmán, Shining Path established its emergence upon the Peruvian political landscape through a series of gestures aimed at imprinting images of violence upon the national consciousness. Carlos Degregori has pinpointed the beginning of the movement as 17 May 1980, when ballot boxes in the small Andean town of Chuschi were publicly burned and dead dogs, bearing labels identifying them with the then Chinese leader Deng Xiaoping (1904–1997), appeared hanging from lampposts in the capital, Lima.

The raw brutality associated with these images became Shining Path's stock-in-trade, as figures associated with the orthodox political process were threatened and, if the warnings were not heeded, eliminated. Such figures tended to be low-profile rural authorities, mayors in the small Andean towns and villages that were the guerrillas' power base. The southern Andes had witnessed sporadic indigenous rebellions throughout the history of colonial and particularly republican Peru. Shining Path sought to build on this legacy but using a strategy borrowed from Mao Zedong: mobilizing the countryside against the cities and preventing food supplies from reaching urban populations. In the Peruvian context this meant chiefly the people of Lima, capital of the Viceroyalty and a city long associated with the Spanish imperialism that built it, considered inimical to indigenous, particularly Andean, interests.

Despite the Marxist insistence upon class struggle, the campaign took on clear ethnic parameters, a form of millenarian vengeance exacted by the dispossessed Andean peasantry against their oppressors. Guzmán, under his nom de guerre Comandante Gonzalo, was proclaimed heir to the legacy of Marx, Lenin, and Mao as the Fourth Sword of Marxism. Shining Path developed a rhetoric that was at once chilling and unintentionally comical. An anonymous letter to the Communist Party Central Committee speaks of "Gonzalo Thought, all-powerful and infallible ideology that illuminates our path and arms our minds" (quoted in Starn et. al. 1995, p. 336). However, behind the apparent auto-satire was an unmistakable ruthlessness: neither the will of Shining Path nor the very real threat to established power that the group constituted by the early 1990s was ever seriously called into question.

What was certainly more open to doubt was the authenticity and sincerity of the organization's ideological position, particularly once it was established that a substantial source of its income was cocaine trafficking. Since the 1980s the coca-growing upper Huallaga Valley in northern Peru has been an arena in which Shining Path vies for influence with more orthodox traffickers and with the now almost defunct Tupac Amaru Revolutionary Movement

(MRTA). The MRTA, named after an eighteenth-century native rebel and often considered a more humane alternative to Shining Path, was decimated in April 1997 when its occupation of the Japanese ambassador's residence in Lima ended with an army raid that killed all fourteen participating members.

Shining Path's appeal to the indigenous peasantry exploited age-old resentments and drew upon the traditional rebelliousness of this sector of the population. The great uprising led by Tupac Amaru II in the 1780s, which narrowly failed to end Spanish rule, is still a part of indigenous political consciousness. Shining Path's rise in the countryside, though, was largely orchestrated from the outside through manipulation by Guzmán and others of the political theory of José Carlos Mariátegui (1894–1930). However, as several observers have pointed out, Mariátegui's ideas of the incorporation of Andean traditions of reciprocity into a Marxist framework are very distant from Guzmán's authoritarian stance and his organization's taste for intimidation. Rural populations found themselves caught between the guerrillas and the no-less-brutal Peruvian military, forbidden by both sides to aid the enemy and subject to vicious reprisals if they stepped out of line. In fact, early support for the rebellion faded as people in the countryside grew disillusioned, and *rondas campesinas* (armed peasant vigilante groups) were sponsored by the government to help stem the tide of insurgency.

In February 1992 Shining Path claimed one of its more high-profile victims, albeit one from humble origins: the grassroots shantytown leader and organizer María Elena Moyano (1958–1992), who commanded considerable respect and affection throughout the country, was savagely murdered and her body publicly mutilated. Moyano was killed because the revolutionaries saw her model of independent and non-ideologically based self-help, even though it was of an essentially socialist nature, as a threat to their own control over minds, if not hearts. Such actions heightened popular revulsion for the rebels' activities as well as fear of the consequences of opposing them. In September of the same year this aura was largely dispelled when Guzmán was captured during a raid on a suburban house in Lima. Notwithstanding Guzmán's messianic status as leader and his importance in coordinating the group's functions, Shining Path has not been entirely defeated.

James Rochlin has declared that "the rebels' extraordinary reliance on violence created a legacy whereby Peruvians generally associate the memory of SL [*Sendero Luminoso*] with unabashed carnage rather than with any positive achievements" (2003, p. 255). Nonetheless, it may be too early to speak in terms of a legacy when the group, albeit diminished in size and impact, is still far from extinct: Shining Path has seen a notable resurgence during the first years of the twenty-first century.

—Keith Richards

See also: *Popular Social Movements and Politics:* Base Communities in the Andes

Bibliography

Degregori, Carlos Iván. 1994. "The Origins and Logic of Shining Path: Two Views." Pp. 51–75 in *The Shining Path of Peru*, edited by David Scott Palmer. New York: St. Martin's.

Gorriti Ellenbogen, Gustavo. 1999. *The Shining Path: A History of the Millenarian War in*

Peru. Chapel Hill: University of North Carolina Press.

Poole, Deborah, and Gerardo Rénique. 1992. *Peru: Time of Fear*. London: Latin America Bureau.

Rochlin, James Francis. 2003. *Vanguard Revolutionaries in Latin America: Peru, Colombia, Mexico*. Boulder, CO: Lynne Rienner.

Starn, Orin, Carlos Iván Degregori, and Robin Kirk, eds. 1995. *The Peru Reader: History, Culture, Politics*. Durham, NC, and London: Duke University Press.

Stern, Peter A. 1995. *Sendero Luminoso: An Annotated Bibliography of the Shining Path Guerrilla Movement*. Albuquerque: SALALM Secretariat, University of New Mexico.

Base Communities in the Andes

In the poor districts of Andean capitals such as Lima, squatter settlements, known as base communities, have formed as a result of large-scale migration to cities. The massive urban migration that has taken place in Latin America, above all in the second half of the twentieth century, has thrown up a whole set of previously unknown social phenomena. Since the 1940s the Peruvian capital, Lima, has seen a particularly striking influx, mostly of people from the Andes. The influx of indigenous Quechua-speakers has never exactly been welcome in this proud "City of Kings," the hub of the Spanish Viceroyalty founded in 1535. But the newcomers have changed the nature of urban life in the region, bringing cultural elements first scorned but then gradually integrated, albeit in a diluted form as acculturation takes place. To the visitor entering or leaving this metropolis the sight of squatters' settlements stretching far out into central Peru's coastal deserts is extraordinary: the immediate question it raises is how communities can subsist in such an arid and inhospitable place.

Water is indeed of particular concern, and often a source of conflict, in the establishment of these communities. The river Rimac that flows through central Lima is already reduced to a trickle by the demands made upon it, and the flow of people into the area shows little sign of abating. Henry Dietz has written of some three hundred illegal settlements in the metropolitan area, and Lima's population has concomitantly exploded. Peter Lloyd's study shows that the area had some half a million inhabitants in the 1940s, rising to around three and a half million by 1975. According to current estimates that figure has again doubled: around one-third of Peruvians live in Lima, and it is estimated that the population will soon reach 10 million. The euphemistic Peruvian term *pueblos jóvenes* (young towns) is particularly apposite if one takes into account the number of children involved in these migrations, as the national average age continues to fall.

Of course, the effect upon the city has been more than simply demographic. The economic transformation has also been extraordinary, as was shown by Hernando de Soto's 1989 study *The Other Path*. Soto examined the growth of the "informal sector" (another Peruvian euphemism, this time alluding to the black market, unregistered commercial activity, transport, squatting, and street vending). He argued that the existence of this form of activity is a social fact that is not about to disappear and that social structures and institutions have to be amended to include people who have no alternative but to sidestep the law. To crack down on such activity would simply be to outlaw the majority of the population. Lima's mayor, Alberto Andrade, instigated a cleanup of the city's historic center that involved moving away street vendors as well as painting and planting flowers. This cosmetic measure has so far simply shifted the problem, even if it has made tourists more comfortable.

The experience of migration has had a considerable effect on women, bringing them into a new environment where they come into contact with new ideas, often for the first time. This has been true in the case of the many housemaids brought into urban middle-class households, some of whom are allowed the opportunity to study. It also applies to women in new settlements faced with extreme poverty, especially in the wake of the "Fujishock," Peruvian president Alberto Fujimori's policy of economic austerity in the early 1990s. This kind of hardship meant that communal kitchens were practically the only option for new settlers to cook, eat, and socialize in. The role of women as defenders of family well-being, in the absence of men, who were working long hours or indulging in irresponsible drinking, consequently became more demanding and militant.

The outstanding example of women from this environment was María Elena Moyano (1958–1992), an activist and representative of the Villa El Salvador settlement south of Lima. She became a living symbol of the dignity and human potential conceivable in even these surroundings. The transcendent nature of Moyano's persona is evident in the manner of her death, at the hands of Shining Path assassins and in the presence of her sons. Her body was blown up with dynamite in the crassly misguided hope of erasing her significance, but the three hundred or so mourners at her funeral confirmed the contrary. Moyano said that the communal kitchens were a matter of far more than mere nutrition. She argued that they also served as a venue for voicing grievances. Moyano was commemorated in the 1998 film about her life *Coraje* (*Courage*), written and directed by Alberto Durant.

—*Keith Richards*

See also: *Popular Social Movements and Politics:* Shining Path; *Visual Arts and Architecture:* Architecture and Landscape Design (*Pueblos Jóvenes*)

Bibliography

Chueca, Marta, and Javier Alva Gambini. 1989. *No sólo se cocina en los comedores.* Lima: Centro Latinoamericano de Trabajo Social (CELATS).

Dietz, Henry A. 1980. *Poverty and Problem-Solving under Military Rule: The Urban Poor in Lima, Peru.* Austin: University of Texas Press.

———. 1998. *Urban Poverty, Political Participation, and the State: Lima, 1970–1990.* Pittsburgh, PA: University of Pittsburgh Press.

Dobyns, Henry F. 1971. *Peasants, Power, and Applied Social Change: Vicos as a Model.* Beverly Hills, CA: Sage.

Lloyd, Peter. 1980. *The "Young Towns" of Lima: Aspects of Urbanization in Peru.* Cambridge: Cambridge University Press.

Moyano, María Elena, and Diana Miloslavich Túpac, eds. 2000. *The Autobiography of María Elena Moyano: The Life and Death of a Peruvian Activist.* Gainesville: University Presses of Florida.

Musset, Alain. 2002. *Villes nomades du nouveau monde.* Paris: Editions de l'Ecole des Hautes Etudes en Sciences Sociales.

Soto, Hernando de. 1989. *The Other Path: The Invisible Revolution in the Third World.* New York: Harper and Row.

Base Communities in Brazil

Comunidades de base, or shantytown community groups, emerged in Brazil in the 1960s and came to the fore in the late 1970s on the initiative of the progressive Catholic Church. The heyday of the communities coincided with the military dictatorship, when restrictions on personal freedoms meant that the church and the community were virtually the only spaces where people could come together. Since then, shantytown residents' associations in Brazil's major cities have continued to fight for improved conditions, such as running water and sewers, and for recognition of their land rights. The responsibility for providing answers to the huge housing shortage in Brazil has largely been left to the poor themselves. More recently, such communities have been working with such non-governmental organizations as local universities and have successfully embraced technology in order to improve the quality of the lives of their inhabitants.

Rocinha, in Rio de Janeiro, is the largest *favela*, or shantytown, in the world. With a population of some 200,000, it has a thriving sense of community that has given rise to various initiatives, including a Website and a television channel. Its so-called Tourist Workshop organizes training for local young people in English, geography, first aid, and tourism to enable them to work with tour operators involved in promoting visits to the neighborhood, which now refers to itself on its official Website as an "ex-*favela*." Rocinha has its own trade association that assists its approximately 2,500 commercial establishments, ranging from shops selling electrical goods to cybercafés, from branches of banks to radio stations. The Rocinha Vocational Center teaches local youngsters how to use the Internet and how to learn the information technology skills necessary for the world of work.

Base communities in São Paulo were part of the so-called Operation Periphery established in the 1970s by the city's archbishop, Cardinal Dom Paulo Evaristo Arns, a leading proponent of Liberation Theology. Priests and resources were directed to the outlying districts of the city, where impoverished migrants were erecting their makeshift homes. In these emerging neighborhoods, with unpaved streets and no amenities, priests and nuns worked alongside the inhabitants, encouraging them to hold community meetings where community members could apply the teachings of the Bible to the realities of their lives and where they could also deal with such practical issues as building schools, setting up health centers, and gaining access to electricity. As these practical goals were achieved, participation in these groups declined. The exhausting routine of the city, and especially the two-hour commute by bus each day to work, made it increasingly difficult for ordinary people to dedicate time and energy to these base communities.

Today universities collaborate with shantytown community projects, such as that of the Favela do Gato (Shantytown of Cats, "cat" being the slang term for a person who climbs up electric poles to illegally obtain power for his community), located in São Gonçalo, Rio de Janeiro State. With the help of the Department of Architecture and Urban Planning at the nearby Fluminense Federal University, Niterói, the resourceful inhabitants of this shantytown have developed the political and technical skills necessary to help them better their living environment. They successfully campaigned against a highway scheme that would have relocated the entire neighborhood, and they fought for the building of a new service road that would integrate the community into the surrounding area. In addition, the existing inhabitants were granted ownership of the land they occupied, in exchange for agreeing not to permit the shantytown to grow any further. The Catholic University of Rio de Janeiro (PUC-Rio) is currently involved in various projects to help educate children and teenagers in the shantytowns of Vidigal and Santa Maria.

—*Lisa Shaw*

See also: *Popular Religion and Festivals:* Popular Catholicism; *Visual Arts and Architecture:* Architecture and Landscape Design (*Favelas*)

Bibliography

Boff, Leonardo, and Clodvis Boff. 1987. *Introducing Liberation Theology.* Tunbridge Wells, UK: Burns and Oates.

Gay, Robert. 1994. *Popular Organization and Democracy in Rio de Janeiro: A Tale of Two Favelas.* Philadelphia: Temple University Press.

Nagle, Robin. 1999. "Liberation Theology's Rise and Fall." Pp. 462–467 in *The Brazil Reader: History, Culture, Politics,* edited by Robert M. Levine and John Crocitti. Durham, NC, and London: Duke University Press.

Pino, Júlio Cesar. 1997. *Family and Favela: The Reproduction of Poverty in Rio de Janeiro.* Westport, CT: Greenwood.

Rocinha Website. http://www.rocinha.com.br (consulted 20 November 2003).

Post-1985 Earthquake Movements in Mexico

In 1985 two earthquakes sparked a series of organized protests in Mexico. Mexico was hit by an earthquake measuring 8.1 on the Richter scale and lasting ninety seconds early in the morning of 19 September 1985. Another of slightly less intensity and duration struck the next evening.

Although the epicenters for both quakes were located in the Pacific Ocean just off the coast of the state of Michoacán, Mexico City, particularly the old downtown area, was the worst hit area in the whole country because the city is built on unstable ground (a dried-up lake). Significantly, it was not the centuries-old monuments that perished but the badly maintained old housing blocks in the city center, together with many more recent, often government-sponsored or owned, buildings (hospitals, ministry buildings, and housing complexes) that had not been built according to contemporary international guidelines on how to protect structures against earthquakes. The resultant damage caused by the two quakes was considerable: according to Paul Haber, conservative estimates suggest that around 10,000 people lost their lives and a further 250,000 were left homeless.

In the eighteen-month period that followed the earthquakes, the Mexican government was compelled to reconstruct or repair 80,000 homes, and plans were in place to accommodate a further 8,000 people who were not technically homeless but who were living in other people's homes. Furthermore, the new homes were built in the same location as the previous ones rather than in new settlements on the outskirts of the city, as the government had initially intended, and they were made available at highly subsidized prices. This reasonably prompt and ample response to a disaster of significant proportions would not have happened had those involved—the *damnificados* (injured, or in this case, homeless people)—not organized themselves and protested en masse to achieve their objectives.

Whether the mobilization of thousands of *damnificados* constitutes a fairly brief instance of successful urban protest or the creation of a popular social movement to achieve improvements in living conditions and radical social change on a more general level remains an issue that scholars dispute. To Alan Gilbert, the mass demonstrations of up to 30,000 protesters that took place on a number of occasions from late September to December 1985 were no more than an instance of successful urban protest. He has credited the protesters with good large-scale organization, but he also noted that they benefited from a fortuitous moment when international attention was directed at the country: the 1986 soccer World Cup was jeopardized by the protests. In the event, international aid, prompted by the will for the World Cup to go ahead in the planned location, allowed the Mexican government to respond to the protests in the way it did. Gilbert also noted that even though Mexico was in a period of recession for almost the entire 1980s, it was only the earthquakes that provoked such large-scale demonstrations. Thus, to Gilbert, the popular response to the earthquake was limited to solving the problems caused by that event. It did not then spread into a wider sense of popular mobilization against the government with a view to demanding ongoing improvements in living conditions for the lower classes or breaking down traditional and undemocratic political structures such as clientelism (the focusing of benefits on a political party's supporters rather than on society as a whole).

Other critics see the 1985 earthquakes as having had much more far-reaching consequences. Although Haber has conceded that the protesting organizations, such as the Unión de Vecinos y Damnificados—19 de septiembre (19 September Union of Earthquake Victims), did have to become less radical and in many cases had to accept affiliation with the ruling party to achieve their objectives, he has also noted that many of the popular organizations that formed as a result of the earthquake continued to exist long after the direct solution to their problems had been provided. Furthermore, with time, many expanded their remit precisely to pressure for general improvements in living conditions and urban infrastructure and even for more democratic government, consistent with definitions of what constitutes a popular social movement. A substantial number of important Mexican writers and intellectuals, such as Elena Poniatowska and Carlos Monsiváis, have also picked up on what Mexican society has gained from the experience of the earthquake protests. Monsiváis has noted that, given the government's initially reluctant response in the aftermath of the earthquake, Mexicans were forced to work together as never before, thus galvanizing a new sense of "civil society," of community solidarity and civic responsibility, and an ongoing critical stance toward the government. And both Monsiváis and Poniatowska have commented in some detail on the formation of specifically working-class women's organizations, such as the Promotora de Costureras en Lucha (the seamstresses' union), that owe their creation to the experience of the post-earthquake protests. Furthermore, such popular icons as Superbarrio—visually, a cross between a masked wrestler like El Santo and Superman—emerged from the protests to defend the homeless and the poor and inject a subversive dose of humor into popular protest.

—*Thea Pitman*

See also: *Sport and Leisure: Lucha Libre*; *Popular Literature:* Testimonio

Bibliography

Betancourt, Fernando, ed. 1995. *Imágenes y testimonios del 85: El despertar de la sociedad civil.* Mexico City: Unión de Vecinos y Damnificados—19 de septiembre.

Da Cruz, José. 1993. *Disaster and Society: The 1985 Mexican Earthquakes.* Lund, Sweden: Lund University Press.

Gilbert, Alan. 1998. *The Latin American City.* London: Latin America Bureau.

Haber, Paul Lawrence. 1997. "Earthquake of 1985." Pp. 423–427 in *Encyclopedia of Mexico,* vol. 1, edited by Michael S. Werner. Chicago: Fitzroy Dearborn.

Monsiváis, Carlos. 1987. "Los días del terremoto." Pp. 17–122 in *Entrada libre: Crónicas de la sociedad que se organiza.* Mexico City: Era.

Poniatowska, Elena. 1995. *Nothing, Nobody: The Voices of the Mexico City Earthquake.* Foreword by Aurora Camachom de Schmidt and Arthur Schmidt. Philadelphia: Temple University Press.

Las Madres de la Plaza de Mayo and Other Women's Movements

Las Madres de la Plaza de Mayo (the Mothers of the Plaza de Mayo) is the term used to describe a protest movement that supplied the clearest voice in Argentina opposing the vicious military dictatorship that terrorized the country between 1976 and 1982. The movement was made up of the mothers of those who had "disappeared." "Disappearance," the euphemism for the military's strategy of abduction, torture, and summary execution, became a source of despair for families who might otherwise have remained cowed by the violence erupting around them as the military sought to "restructure" society by eliminating anyone suspected of harboring left-wing sympathies. These women, wearing the white head scarves that have become their emblem and carrying placards bearing photos of their missing relatives, constitute an image by now familiar from news reports and documentaries. The impact of their action, however, was enormous. As Marguerite Guzmán Bouvard has pointed out, the regular demonstrations in the center of Buenos Aires registered utter rejection of the prevailing social and historical mood. "Against the military values of hierarchy, obedience and the unchecked use of physical force, the Mothers practiced pacifism, cooperation, and mutual love" (1994, p. 1). The demonstrations, moreover, directly and consciously flouted a law passed in the early days of the tyranny. That these middle-aged, unassuming women were such unlikely dissenters also added to their effect on sympathizers and enemies alike. Dismissed at first as *las locas* (madwomen), they became the form of opposition most uncomfortable for the military junta to face, one that embodied the very same Christian values that the military claimed to uphold. It was politically feasible to outlaw and violently repress trade unionism, radical theater, and other such activities; being seen as opposing motherhood was an entirely different prospect.

The women's courage, albeit born of desperation, was nevertheless extraordinary. As Jo Fisher's collection of testimonies reveals, these were usually mothers of families that had been shattered, financially as well as emotionally, by what had been done to them (the military would also steal from the homes of those they "visited"). Also remarkable is the Mothers' ingenuity in adversity. The head scarves were the most clearly visible examples of an entire system of visual codes and signals through which they initially managed to recognize one another and to organize despite a ruthless and ubiquitous secret police. Meetings would sometimes be held in the few churches that would allow them, or else they would be disguised as informal social occasions. The Grandmothers of the Plaza were another vital presence, active particularly in investigating another appalling practice: stealing the young children of murdered parents for illicit adoption by childless military couples. This question was memorably raised by Luis Puenzo's film *La historia oficial* (*The Official Version*, 1985); another fine cinematic version of these events is *La amiga*, directed by Jeanine Meerapfel in 1989. *La amiga* exemplifies what Diana Taylor has seen as exploitation by the Mothers and Grandmothers of theatrical devices in the expression of their grievances.

Demonstration by the Mothers of the Plaza de Mayo in Buenos Aires, 4 May 1995. (Carlos Carrion/Corbis Sygma)

Las Madres de la Plaza de Mayo are an example of women's potential to effect change through direct action. That potential can be seen in various other protests in Argentina and elsewhere in Latin America that may have little to do directly with gender but that provide a space in which women are able to affirm their political potency as representatives of a community. Two further Argentine examples are Laura Padilla, who successfully led protests against a fertilizer plant in the southern province of Neuquén in 1996, and Nana (no surname is provided), who took part in a huge demonstration, in the northwestern city of Santiago del Estero in December 1993, by state employees frustrated and angered at the authorities' failure to pay long-overdue wages. These two women and their roles are profiled by Javier Auyero, who examines "the ways in which these two women use (not necessarily in conscious ways) elements of their everyday lives to make sense, to experience, and to remember collective struggle" (2003, p. 206).

A fine example elsewhere is that of Domitila Barrios de Chungara, a Bolivian miner's wife who overcame prejudices against women in that environment to become a prominent figure in the struggle for improved living conditions and wages, as well as the mining town's very existence as a community. In some ways a conservative woman, distancing herself from feminism and emphasizing her Christian faith, Domitila Barrios de Chungara nonetheless adopted a radical stance against early manifestations of globalization in the late 1970s and provided an example of unrelenting willpower and remarkable courage.

The figurehead of Guatemalan Indian resistance is Rigoberta Menchú, whose autobiography remains a classic of *testimonio* literature, despite attempts to besmirch her credibility. Native women have taken up Rigoberta's example elsewhere in Central America, for instance in Chiapas in southern Mexico, where a generation of young women are active in a church that combines elements of Liberation Theology with traditional Catholicism and the indigenous cosmogony that incorporates worship of natural phenomena and defines the place of humanity as strictly within natural boundaries. The system of reciprocity and complementarity that characterizes many native American philosophies also posits an equitable and balanced relationship between the sexes as crucial for all forms of progress.

Cuba is still the only Latin American country where the emancipation of women has been set as a cornerstone of national development—although this policy is not without its contradictions, given the concomitant persecution of gays during the early years of the Revolution and the growth of sex tourism on the island.

—Keith Richards

See also: *Travel and Tourism:* Sex Tourism; *Popular Literature:* Testimonio; *Popular Cinema:* Melodrama; *Popular Religion and Festivals:* Popular Catholicism

Bibliography

Arditti, Rita. 1999. *Searching for Life: The Grandmothers of the Plaza de Mayo and the Disappeared Children of Argentina.* Berkeley and Los Angeles: University of California Press.

Auyero, Javier. 2003. *Contentious Lives: Two Argentine Women, Two Protests, and the Quest for Recognition.* Durham, NC, and London: Duke University Press.

Barrios de Chungara, Domitila, and Moema Viezzer. 1978. *Let Me Speak!* New York: Monthly Review.

Behar, Ruth. 2002. "Gender Que Pica un Poco." Preface to *Gender's Place: Feminist Anthropologies of Latin America* by Lezzie Jo Frazier, Janise Hurtig, and Rosario Montoya. New York: Palgrave Macmillan.

Fisher, Jo. 1989. *Mothers of the Disappeared.* Boston: South End.

Guzmán Bouvard, Marguerite. 1994. *Revolutionizing Motherhood: The Mothers of the Plaza de Mayo.* Wilmington, DE: Scholarly Resources.

Jetter, Alexis, Annelise Orleck, and Diana Taylor. 1997. *The Politics of Motherhood: Activist Voices from Left to Right.* Hanover, NH: University Press of New England.

Simonelli, Jeanne. 2001. "Complementaridad: Realities of Gender in Contemporary Mesoamerica." Paper presented at the annual meeting of the American Anthropological Association, Washington, DC, November.

Taylor, Diana. 1994. "Performing Gender: Las Madres de la Plaza de Mayo." Pp. 275–305 in *Negotiating Performance: Gender, Sexuality, and Theatricality in Latin/o America*, edited by Diana Taylor and Juan Villegas Morales. Durham, NC, and London: Duke University Press.

The Bolivian Gas War

The implications for Bolivia and for the rest of Latin America of the so-called Gas War, the *Guerra del Gas*, have yet to be fully understood. Between 8 and 19 October 2003, this major Bolivian political crisis curtailed the second presidency of Gonzalo Sánchez de Losada and forced politicians across the region to be wary of adopting neoliberal economic policies without consulting the electorate.

This type of action, involving popular mobilization in street demonstrations and other measures, has numerous precedents, which Álvaro García Linera and colleagues describe as being union, mass (or multitude), or community based. It is certainly true that trade unions have been of huge political importance in Bolivia in the twentieth century, and above all in the mining industry, which exerted considerable muscle until its decline in the early 1990s. As examples of mass-based action, García Linera sees the regrouping of the lower classes along new lines, often mobilized by just such issues as gas privatization. And "community" refers mainly to rural indigenous groups, which have also been abundantly evident in informal political action.

The earliest forms of popular protest in Bolivia, in fact, were based on indigenous demands for the restitution of lands and rights or even for the outright removal of European rule. In the 1780s a huge rebellion led by Tomás Tupac Katari laid prolonged siege to La Paz and posed a very real threat to the survival of the Spanish colony. In republican times, too, numerous rebellions arose, both in the countryside and in the mines, as frustrations periodically came to a head. The political classes have long known and feared the mining communities, such as Siglo Veinte (Twentieth Century) and Catavi, for the virulence and coherence of their political action. The miners' indigenous heritage was an element in their militancy even if they considered themselves distinct from (and often superior to) the peasantry. A movement called Katarismo that began in the 1970s gave a voice to indigenous peoples and suggested answers, often pragmatic, to their immediate problems.

The 1991 March for Land and Dignity (*Marcha por el Territorio y la Dignidad*) was a great success. During the thirty-four days it lasted, numerous indigenous groups were brought together for the first time. Native peoples from the tropical north and east of the country came into close contact with others from the Chaco, with the Aymara-speaking groups from the high plains around La Paz, and with the Quechua-speakers from the lower elevations around Cochabamba and Sucre. The march was the beginning of a new period of struggle in which indigenous groups were no longer isolated and intimidated. As a result of this action, native peoples were granted representation in parliament for the first time, and the constitution was rewritten to include the terms "pluriethnic" and "multicultural" to describe the nation. Nonetheless, the living conditions of native peoples still leave much to be desired.

In April 2000 the issue of water privatization (the so-called Guerra del Agua or Water War) rocked the Andean city of Cochabamba when the government of Hugo Banzer (1926–2002) announced plans to sell rights to local water administration to a British-Spanish-Bolivian consortium. Cochabamba has long been troubled by an insufficient water supply, and substantial urban migration has compounded the problem. The considerable price increases that would have occurred under privatization measures provoked such impassioned and insistent opposition that ultimately the government was forced to back down. As Willem Assies has shown, the protests were characterized by a shift in forms of organization: "The trade-union structures that since the 1952 Revolution had been a major vehicle of protest played only a marginal role, and territorial organizations such as neighborhood associations and potable-water committees emerged as the main carriers of protest activity" (2003, p. 15).

The issue that triggered the Gas War in 2003 was the proposed sale to the United States and Mexico of substantial reserves of natural gas from the southern region of Tarija. However, gas from landlocked Bolivia would have to be piped to the coast for delivery, and debate had been going on for some time about what route any gas pipeline should take. The suggestion of piping the gas through Chile was broached but encountered much opposition because Chile still occupied a coastline it had wrested from Bolivia in the nineteenth century. A route through Peru was less direct but less objectionable. However, a third possibility came to the fore: that of declining to sell the gas and of using it instead to improve the living conditions of Bolivia's own population. Ordinary people—by now tired of watching the country's natural resources be sold off as raw materials in transactions benefiting only the political and commercial sectors—began to agitate for implementation of this possibility. The seeds of this protest were already evident in the 2000 Water War, particularly middle-class mobilization into support for the poorer sectors and identification with their complaints.

The massacres of civilian demonstrators, who were almost always indigenous persons, provoked solidarity from intellectuals and professionals, who formed human chains, went on hunger strikes, and marched in the streets to demand that Gonzalo Sánchez de Losada resign from the presidency. However, the success of the protest must be seen in the context of a newly politicized indigenous peasantry, a group now largely urbanized and, with the vertiginous growth of the city of El Alto (once a mere satellite of La Paz huddled around the international airport), having its own distinct power base. Violent government reactions to the protest, far from quelling dissent, roused the urban middle classes to oppose a measure they might well otherwise have at least tacitly supported. The recent emergence of indigenous political leaders such as the Aymara representative Felipe Quispe and the former coca-growers' leader Evo Morales—however diminished their credibility in the eyes of the establishment—will render Bolivia's immediate political future of considerable interest.

—*Keith Richards*

See also: *Language:* Indigenous Languages; *Visual Arts and Architecture:* Architecture and Landscape Design (Popular Architecture in Bolivia)

Bibliography

Assies, Willem. 2003. "David versus Goliath in Cochabamba: Water Rights, Neoliberalism, and the Revival of Social Protest in Bolivia." *Latin American Perspectives* 130, no. 3: 14–36.

Contreras Baspineiro, Alex. 1991. *Etapa de una larga marcha.* La Paz: Asociación Aquí Avance/Educación Radiofónica de Bolivia.

García Linera, Álvaro, Raquel Gutiérrez, Raúl Prada, and Luis Tapia, eds. 2001. *Tiempos de rebelión.* La Paz: Comuna.

Prada Alcoreza, Raúl. 2003. "El gasto heroico." In *Clajadep*, 21 December. http://clajadep/ahaine.org/articulo.php?p=2294&more=/&c=1 (consulted 17 November 2003).

4
Sport and Leisure

Sport

Many of the popular sporting interests of Latin Americans will be familiar to North Americans and Europeans. These tend to be sports that, although initially the leisure pursuits of Europe's elite, are now frequently associated with poverty and the nations of the third world (that is, they are sports for which no expensive equipment is needed and for which quick-thinking savvy is an advantage). These sports include football (soccer), boxing, and athletics. It may come as a surprise to learn, then, that a number of sports still associated with the U.S. and European bourgeoisie are played in many Latin American countries. Argentina and Uruguay, for example, have an international profile in rugby football, a sport dominated by British Commonwealth nations. Cycling is very popular in Colombia, and Colombians regularly finish in the top ten of the prestigious Tour de France. Brazil has a very strong tradition in yachting and has produced a number of world-class swimmers, and Argentine tennis players compete regularly in Grand Slam tournaments. Motor sport has frequently been dominated by Latin American drivers, including the great Argentine Juan Manuel Fangio (1911–1995); Brazil's Emerson Fittipaldi (1946–), Nelson Piquet (1952–), and Ayrton Senna (1960–1994); and Colombia's Juan Pablo Montoya (1975–). Other sports at which Latin Americans excel include volleyball, basketball, beach volleyball, and track and field. In the 2004 Olympic Games in Athens, Greece, Latin American countries won gold medals in the following sports: track and field (three, by Cuba and the Dominican Republic), boxing (five, by Cuba), wrestling (Cuba), baseball (Cuba), soccer (Argentina), basketball (Argentina), beach volleyball (Brazil), volleyball (Brazil), yachting (two, by Brazil), and tennis (two, by Chile).

A number of homegrown sporting and leisure pursuits are found in Latin America. One of the most recognizable is *capoeira*, the trendy Brazilian martial art/dance that is now enjoying considerable success outside of Brazil. Wrestling is an international spectator sport, but wrestling in Mexico (*lucha libre*) has been transformed to such an extent that it is difficult to think of it as anything other than authentically Mexican. Jai alai, which originated in the Basque area of Spain and which is popular in Mexico and Central America, has made considerable inroads in Florida and elsewhere in the United States; many U.S. citizens follow the sport solely to bet on the outcome of matches. Latin Americans, when their governments allow them, also enjoy gambling (racecourses can be found throughout Latin America). Lotteries are popular in many countries throughout the world, but in Brazil the lottery, the *jogo do bicho*, is a national obsession.

—Stephanie Dennison

Soccer

Association football (soccer, in the United States) is by far the most popular sport in Latin America, surpassed only by baseball in some of the Caribbean countries. The game's enormous success must be attributed to its adaptability to manifold styles, temperaments, and philosophies as well as to its accessibility to those unable to afford expensive equipment: a piece of flat ground and a ball (or box, tin can, or the like) will suffice. In the nineteenth century Britain had deep economic and political interests in Latin America. The nineteenth-century British engineers who introduced the game left a readily visible legacy in the names of prominent clubs, including River Plate, Banfield, and Newell's Old Boys in Argentina; The Strongest in Bolivia; and Corinthians in Brazil. The introduction of the game by the English reflects the depth of British influence in Latin America at the time—Britain had economic interests in Argentine beef, Peruvian guano, Bolivian (later Chilean) nitrates, Bolivian (later Paraguayan) petroleum, and railroad building over much of the continent and was involved in the War of the Pacific (1879–1883) and the Chaco War (1932–1935). Soccer arguably has non-European precedents in Latin America. Some Brazilians will argue that soccer already existed in Brazil well before the English "invented" the game, and in most Central American pre-Columbian civilizations, a team game played with a hardened latex ball held great social and even religious importance.

Unfortunately, another import from England is soccer-related violence, which in Argentina resulted in thirty-seven deaths during the 1990s. A game between Chacarita and Boca Juniors in August 2003 led the authorities to suspend league games, dock three points from Chacarita's total, and revise procedures to deal with this problem. Soccer-related violence is also a problem in several other Latin American countries. Tamir Bar-On has examined the reactionary nature of most soccer clubs in Latin America and their contribution to the continuation of racism, male chauvinism, and the basest nationalism. It is certainly fair to say that soccer has aided repressive governments by providing an escape valve for social frustrations and sublimating possible class resentment. Collusion with authority has at times been conscious, but it has also simply been the result of manipulation of the game's popularity. An often-quoted example of this is Brazil's famous World Cup (Copa do Mundo) win in Mexico in 1970 at the height of the military dictatorship: the Brazilian national team's record-breaking third World Cup victory was hailed by the government as a kind of legitimization of the country's authoritarian regime.

The notorious Soccer War between Honduras and El Salvador in 1969 is another example of the sport's being manipulated for political ends, and it caused a great deal of international stereotyping about Latin American volatility, immaturity, and misdirected passion. Although the conflict was sparked by an international match between these two countries, it in fact had far more to do with a long-standing border dispute and whipped-up Honduran resentment at the presence of some 300,000 Salvadorian immigrants. The only clear outcome was electoral triumph for the Salvadorian military in 1970, followed by continued repression.

Latin Americans are proud of the fact that no European team has ever won a World Cup in Latin America. In fact, Brazil's is the only team to have won a World Cup outside its own continent (in Sweden in 1958 and in Japan in 2002). Three Latin American countries have won World Cup titles: Uruguay, Brazil, and Argentina. In 1930, Uruguay, playing at home, triumphed in the very first tournament, a win seen as an endorsement of the reforms then taking place under José Batlle's government. The Uruguayans prevailed again in 1950 in Brazil in one of the game's most famous victories: the decisive final match saw them overcome Brazil's team, which was willed on by a crowd of some 200,000 at the famous Maracanã stadium in Rio de Janeiro. The outstanding players from that legendary Uruguayan team were inside forward Juan Schiaffino and center-half Obdulio Varela, the self-effacing but highly influential captain.

Brazil has won the World Cup a record five times, making them *pentacampeões:* in Sweden in 1958, Chile in 1962, Mexico in 1970, the United States in 1994, and Japan/South Korea (joint hosts) in 2002. Ironically, however, the losing sides and their performances are often the best remembered. For example, the 1982 Brazilian team that came in a poor fifth in Spain is thought by many to be the best ever *seleção*, or national squad, boasting great players such as Zico, Socrates, and Falcão. Brazil has been runner-up twice, on both occasions to the utter disbelief of both domestic and international followers of soccer. Conspiracy theories still abound to explain Brazil's poor performance against France in the final of 1998, particularly the involvement of Nike, the team's chief sponsor, in the decision to allow a seemingly mentally unbalanced Ronaldo to play.

Argentina, like Uruguay, has won twice. As hosts in 1978 they prevailed in what was seen by many as a propaganda coup for the then military dictatorship. This victory was blighted by political implications and by the dubious circumstances in which Argentina defeated Peru in a second-stage group match, thereby going into the final at the expense of Brazil. Nonetheless, the team contained some wonderfully gifted players, such as the goal scorer Mario Kempes and midfielder Osvaldo Ardiles, and was arguably the best in the tournament even without home-field advantage or the shenanigans of which they were accused. In 1986 Argentina again prevailed, the controversy this time being provided by the genius and gamesmanship of Diego Armando Maradona.

Maradona, the Spanish-speaking world's most famous soccer player, inspired utter devotion in his fans and often loathing in his foes. His classic rise from the poverty of a Buenos Aires barrio to dizzying levels of fame and wealth was accompanied by scandal both on and off the pitch. Maradona made his league debut shortly before his sixteenth birthday, and by age twenty-one he was playing for the Argen-

Diego Maradona holds up the World Cup trophy as he is carried off the field after Argentina defeated West Germany 3–2 to win the World Cup soccer championship in Mexico City, 1986. (Reuters/Corbis)

tine capital's "people's team," the Boca Juniors, soon attaining near-divine status in the city's port districts (Boca, literally "mouth," refers to the River Plate estuary). Too young for his country's 1978 World Cup win, he made a brief appearance in the 1982 tournament in Spain at which Argentina was humbled and its star was "hacked" out of the game by Italy's so-called assassin, Claudio Gentile. It was at the Mexico finals in 1986 that Maradona emerged into genuine global fame with a string of sensational, match-winning performances culminating in victory over West Germany in the final. On the way, he removed England from the quarter-finals with two goals that epitomized his double-edged genius: the infamous "Hand of God" effort with which he deceived nobody but the referee (he pushed the ball into the net with his hand), followed by a devastating second goal achieved by dribbling through what seemed to be the entire English side.

In his club career, Maradona experienced extreme sporting highs and personal lows. His move to Barcelona in 1982 was by no means unsuccessful: altogether Maradona scored thirty-eight goals for the Catalans in only fifty-eight matches. But this period was also memorable for the injury he suffered in September 1983. Maradona had accumulated numerous enemies within the international league, envious of his status and possibly piqued by the Argentine's perceived arrogance as an upstart "Sudaca" (a disparaging term used by

Spaniards toward South Americans). The one who took ultimate satisfaction from this enmity was Athletic Bilbao's robust defender Andoni Goikoetxea, whose brutal tackle put Maradona in the hospital.

The Argentine player finally found a home in the European club in Napoli, whose fans were as starved of sporting success as they were deprived in material and social terms. The Neapolitans took the young Argentine to their hearts, and he repaid them by leading the team out of the doldrums and into the European Champions' Cup via Italian titles in 1987 and 1990. Nevertheless, the bad publicity arising from Maradona's drug habits and allegedly unprofessional lifestyle eventually caused him to leave Italy and return to Argentina. His international swan song in the 1994 World Cup was ruined by a positive test for performance-enhancing drugs—a result many viewers might have predicted after witnessing the frenzied celebration of his brilliant goal in a match against Greece.

Maradona has remained true to his socialist beliefs and has become a friend of Fidel Castro, whom he visits when Argentina becomes too hot, both meteorologically and metaphorically. In 1998 he was given a suspended prison sentence for firing an air rifle at reporters camped outside his home. His distrust of the press has made him something of a recluse in Buenos Aires. He hit the world headlines once again in April 2004 when he was rushed to the hospital after an alleged overdose.

But the worldwide fame of Maradona is an exception; for the most part, only Brazilian players achieve superstardom. The first soccer superstar, although by no means the first great Brazilian player, was Edson Arantes do Nascimento, otherwise known as Pelé, from the small town of Três Corações in the state of Minas Gerais. Other nicknames he has acquired over the years—Black Pearl, God, and the King—give an idea of the esteem in which he is held in Brazil. Now a registered brand worth millions, Pelé's fame began when he played for Brazilian club Santos in the 1950s. He was the star player of Brazil's long-overdue first World Cup victory in 1958. He was on the winning side four years later, and by 1970 and Brazil's third World Cup victory, he had scored twelve goals, a record only matched in 2002 by fellow Brazilian Ronaldo. He also played in the 1966 finals in England, where he was so mercilessly "hacked" by a number of unsporting players that he contemplated giving up soccer for good. Such was Pelé's fame at the height of his soccer career that he famously stopped a war: in 1967 the two sides in Nigeria's civil war called a forty-eight-hour cease-fire so Pelé could play an exhibition match in the capital, Lagos.

Pelé retired when he still had plenty to offer the sport in 1974. But a couple of years later a U.S. team, the New York Cosmos, made him an offer he could not refuse, and thus began a second and more financially fruitful phase of his career. Before moving to the United States, Pelé had made a series of poor investments and was practically bankrupt. It was only after the move that he seems to have acquired the business acumen for which, among other things, he is famous. Over the years he has made a number of guest appearances in films, usually playing himself, and he has published more than one autobiography. He currently makes his fortune from licensing the use of his name in advertising (although never for cigarettes or alcohol), from sports management (he played a crucial role in bringing the World Cup finals to

Pelé, Brazilian soccer player, 1963. (Hulton-Deutsch Collection/Corbis)

the United States in 1994), and from occasional soccer commentary.

The best-known Brazilian and one of the most familiar faces of African origin on the planet, Pelé has been careful not to be dragged into discussions of politics or, specifically, of race relations, for which he has not always been thanked. Despite this, in 1995 he accepted the role of special minister of culture and sport in Brazil. By the end of his career Pelé had scored a remarkable 1,281 goals in 1,363 matches. In 1999 he was voted Athlete of the Century by the International Olympic Committee, beating the likes of Muhammad Ali. Ironically, Pelé has never taken part in the Olympic Games.

Despite Pelé's veneration in Brazil and abroad, many Brazilians (particularly supporters of the Rio club Botafogo) argue that the greatest soccer player was Mané Garrincha (Manoel Francisco dos Santos, 1933–1982), the crooked-legged arch-dribbler, who was said to have been incredible at the club level in Brazil, where he was particularly dazzling as a player for Botafogo. At the international level, whenever Garrincha and Pelé played together, Brazil never lost a match. He was one of the stars of the 1958 World Cup victory, and he is remembered as almost single-handedly winning for Brazil its second consecutive World Cup in 1962, when Pelé was injured. Others argue that Pelé's title is under threat by a new wave of great players: Ronaldo (1976–), perhaps the best-known Brazilian player currently in action, and a multiple winner of the FIFA (International Federation of Football [Soccer] Associations) World Player of the Year award whose fame (like that of so many other international soccer stars such as English midfielder David Beckham) is sustained in part by lucrative advertising contracts with sportswear companies; Cafu (1970–), the only soccer player to have two World Cup medals and who is still playing; and two more of Ronaldo's teammates from the top-quality 2002 World Cup–winning side, Rivaldo (1972–) and Ronaldinho Gaucho (1980–). All five players currently play at club level in Europe.

In Latin American soccer, perhaps the greatest underachievers have been the Mexicans, who have hosted the World Cup twice but have still to do better than the quarter-final stage that they reached as hosts in 1970 and 1986. Peru reached that same stage in 1970 with a team inspired by the great forward Teófilo Cubillas, losing 4–2 to the eventual winner, Brazil. Ironically, one of Peru's best sporting performances coincided with the country's worst-ever earthquake, which killed some 70,000 people.

Brazil's Ronaldo celebrates after scoring the fourth goal with a penalty kick in the second half of a Group C match at the World Cup soccer championship in Sogwipo, South Korea, 8 June 2002. (Reuters/Corbis)

Latin America's premier club competition is the Copa Libertadores, inaugurated in 1960 and dominated by teams from Brazil, Uruguay, and Argentina. This domination was punctuated by triumphs for the Paraguayan team Olimpia on three occasions (1979, 1980, and 2002) as well as by Chilean club Colo Colo (1991) and Colombia's Nacional de Medellín (1989). The most frequent winners have been the Uruguayan clubs Peñarol and Nacional, with four triumphs each, and the Argentines of Independiente (seven wins, including four consecutive ones between 1972 and 1975), Boca Juniors with five wins, and Estudiantes de la Plata with three victories. Some of these clubs have gone on to win the World Club Championship against the winners of the European Cup (now Champions' League), Peñarol and Nacional leading the way with three victories apiece. Since 1998 teams from Mexico have been allowed to compete, surprising many observers with the impact they have made. The Cruz Azul club reached the final in 2001, losing to Boca Juniors only in a penalty shoot-out.

The Copa América, equivalent to the European Nations Cup but played at different intervals, has been won by the big three countries on most occasions. However, less fancied nations have triumphed: Peru and Paraguay have both won on two occasions, Bolivia and Colombia once each.

—Keith Richards and Stephanie Dennison

Bibliography

Arbena, Joseph, ed. 1988. *Sport and Society in Latin America: Diffusion, Dependency, and the Rise of Mass Culture.* New York: Greenwood.

Bar-On, Tamir. 1997. "The Ambiguities of Football, Politics, Culture, and Social Transformation in Latin America." *Sociological Research Online* 2, no. 4. http://www.socresonline.org.uk/socresonline/2/4/2.html (consulted 1 October 2003).

Bellos, Alex. 2002. *Futebol: The Brazilian Way of Life.* London: Bloomsbury.

Burns, Jimmy. 2002. *Hand of God: The Life of Diego Maradona.* London: Bloomsbury.

Galeano, Eduardo. 2003. *Soccer in Sun and Shadow.* London: Verso.

Kissinger, Henry. 1999. "Heroes and Icons: Pelé." *Time,* 14 June. http://www.time.com/time/time100/heroes/profile/pele03 (consulted 1 March 2004).

Parry, Chris. 1999. *The Beautiful Game: A Journey through Latin American Football.* London: Phoenix.

Sebreli, Juan José. 1998. *La era del fútbol.* Buenos Aires: Editorial Sudamérica.

Baseball

Ironically, perhaps, the favorite game of the United States has been taken up precisely in those countries with which the United States has experienced the deepest political problems. In addition to Japan, *béisbol,* as it is known in Spanish, is played at high or professional levels in Cuba, Nicaragua, Mexico, the Dominican Republic, Puerto Rico, Panama, and Venezuela. Other Latin American countries that have a keen interest in the game but that have so far made a modest impact are Argentina, Colombia, Honduras, and Belize.

It is argued that in the middle to late nineteenth-century "America's game" spread from its East Coast origins westward to California and south to the Caribbean. However, according to Peter C. Bjarkman, "ballplaying on American soil (that is, the mainland United States) was never all that far ahead of the game's evolution in other nations of the region. Canada and Cuba seem to share almost equally in the game's earliest history and prehistory" (1994, p. 235). The first recorded "baseball-like" game took place in Beechville, Ontario, in 1838, a year before the supposed "invention" of the game by Abner Doubleday. The first official game to be played in Latin America apparently took place in Cuba in 1874, and Cuban settlers introduced baseball to the Dominican Republic in the 1880s, to Venezuela in 1895, and to the Yucatan peninsula in the 1990s. Overall, the Cubans appear to have had as much influence in spreading the sport in their region as did the North Americans.

Professional leagues opened in Cuba in 1878 and in Mexico in 1925. Organized clubs were appearing elsewhere by the late nineteenth century, and by the late 1930s and early 1940s, Nicaragua, Venezuela, and Puerto Rico had all entered the World Amateur Championship.

Early Latino baseball players had to overcome the issue of segregation, which led to some farcical situations in which players of clearly African heritage were smuggled into whites-only leagues on the basis that they were not U.S. nationals and hence were not officially "colored." Nevertheless, clubs also encountered problems when they went to sign these players: in 1911, for instance, the Cincinnati Reds acquired two presumably mulatto Cubans and faced the wrath of their fans, who expressed severe misgivings. The removal of the ban on black players opened the gates for Latinos of African heritage to enter the league.

The impact of Latino players in U.S. Major League Baseball has long been significant, even though it has been downplayed as a result of the deep-seated prejudice that denied the existence of Latinos of traditional Anglo-Saxon sporting values. Attention was focused not on truly successful Latino athletes but on those Latino players whose actions reinforced the notion that Latinos were volatile, hot-headed, and generally unreliable. This bias diminished the importance of the careers of such players as the Cuban pitcher Adolfo Luque, who was a huge success with the Cincinnati Reds in the 1920s. The Mexican second baseman Bobby Ávila's fame grew out of controversy as much as out of the superb season he enjoyed in 1954 with the Cleveland Indians, when he won the batting crown on what some regarded as a technicality. The brilliant Puerto Rican Roberto Clemente, an outfielder with the Pittsburgh Pirates from 1955 until the early 1970s, was seen by many as the greatest Latin American player ever in the U.S. major leagues, but he complained that appreciation of his contribution came late because of his ethnic origins.

Such tales of injustice nonetheless opened the way for the far more generous recognition afforded the likes of the Los Angeles Dodgers' Mexican pitcher Fernando Valenzuela in the 1980s and the Dominican Sammy Sosa since the 1990s, players who have demonstrated the depth of talent in the Latin American game. This might be seen as another aspect of the cultural phenomenon known in the United States as the "Latin boom" that is visible in many other manifestations as well, from cooking to music.

Cuba is probably the Latin American country where baseball has become most popular and where it has become most embroiled in politics. The two putative "fathers" of Cuban baseball, Nemesio Guillot and Esteban Enrique Bellán, were both educated in the United States and brought equipment and tactical knowledge back to Cuba in the 1860s. Fidel Castro, a fairly talented pitcher in his younger days, nonetheless attempted in the early 1960s to remove baseball, with its inevitable associations with the United States, from the national sporting agenda. But his plan to impose soccer, which would have brought the island into line with the sporting preferences of most of the rest of Latin America, had to be abandoned because of popular outcry. Instead, revolutionary Cuba drew some of its greatest sporting kudos from baseball. Moreover, baseball has even been used as a diplomatic means of easing tension between Cuba and the United States.

—Keith Richards

See also: *Sport and Leisure:* Soccer

Bibliography

Arbena, Joseph L., ed. 1988. *Sport and Society in Latin America: Diffusion, Dependency, and the Rise of Mass Culture.* New York: Greenwood.

Beardsell, Peter R. 2000. *Europe and Latin America: Returning the Gaze.* Manchester, UK: Manchester University Press.

Bjarkman, Peter C. 1994. *Baseball with a Latin Beat: A History of the Latin American Game.* Jefferson, NC: McFarland.

Burgos, Adrian, Jr. 2000. "Learning America's Other Game: Baseball, Race, and the Study of Latinos." Pp. 225–239 in *Latino/a Popular Culture,* edited by Michelle Habell-Pallán and Mary Romero. New York and London: New York University Press.

Cockcroft, James D. 1996. *Latinos in Béisbol.* New York: F. Watts.

Dreifort, John E., ed. 2001. *Baseball History from Outside the Lines: A Reader.* Lincoln: University of Nebraska Press.

Figueredo, Jorge S. 2003. *Who's Who in Cuban Baseball.* Jefferson, NC: McFarland.

Regalado, Samuel O. 1998. *Viva Baseball! Latin Major Leaguers and Their Special Hunger.* Urbana: University of Illinois Press.

Boxing

Boxing, in Latin America as elsewhere, has provided an escape for young men from humble backgrounds. Mexico and Central America, Cuba, and Argentina have been the most successful regions, producing numerous world champions.

One of the finest middleweights of all time was the Argentine Carlos Monzón (1942–1995), who went undefeated in his last eighty-one fights, over a period of thirteen years up to 1977. Monzón lost only three of a total of 102 professional fights. Perhaps the most memorable world title fight involving an Argentine was the 1922 heavyweight bout in New York between Luis Angel Firpo and the then champion, Jack Dempsey. Dempsey was knocked out of the ring in the first round but returned (within ten seconds, according to the judges) to win with a knockout in the second. Another noteworthy Argentine boxer was Pascual Pérez, who won his country's first-ever world championship at flyweight in 1954 and remained undefeated for five years thereafter. José María "Mono" Gatica (1925–1963), whose nickname *Mono* (the monkey) conveyed popular affection despite his relative lack of success in the ring, was an Argentine lightweight whose career was blighted by events and circumstances only indirectly connected to boxing. Leonardo Favio's 1992 film *Gatica, el Mono* charts the rise and fall of this fighter, the love and hatred he inspired in equal measure, and his sometime role as a sporting flagship of Peronismo during the presidency of Juan Domingo Perón.

The Cuban Teófilo Stevenson (1952–) won gold medals as a heavyweight in three successive Olympic Games (1972, 1976, and 1980), but he never turned professional. Stevenson was a symbol for revolutionary Cuba and Castrismo, and his prodigious sporting feats have always provided welcome positive publicity for the island. Despite Cuba's boycotting the Olympic Games in 1984 and 1988, Cuban athletes have won a total of thirty Olympic gold medals in boxing, an extraordinary feat for a country with Cuba's resources.

The legendary Panamanian Roberto "Manos de Piedra" Durán (1951–) dominated the lightweight division of which he was champion between 1972 and 1979, when he moved into welterweight and had his best-remembered fights, the two epic encounters with Sugar Ray Leonard in 1980. After an ignominious defeat in his second battle with Leonard, Durán became one of only a few men to claim three separate titles when he won at junior middleweight in 1983. Another important fighter from the same era was the Nicaraguan Alexis Arguello (1952–), who won a remarkable three world titles in separate divisions (featherweight, junior lightweight, and lightweight) between 1974 and 1981.

Gregory Rodríguez has analyzed the role of boxing as a focal point for Los Angeles Mexican immigrant identity, concentrating on the career of welterweight world champion Oscar de la Hoya (1971–). This well-groomed, clean-living fighter has earned a living from the game well beyond normal expectations among his community. But the very absence of scandal and bad habits in his life has encouraged an image of aloofness, an image compounded by his moving away from the barrio and indulging in other activities, such as singing. His Grammy nomination and marriage to Puerto Rican singer Millie Corretjer, along with an elegant but deadly boxing style, have placed de la Hoya in an ambiguous position with regard to Mexican Americans, who identify far more closely with the attritional style and closeness to social roots of the Mexican Julio César Chávez (1962–), over whom he won a resounding victory to claim the WBC (World Boxing Council) Super Lightweight title in 1996.

—*Keith Richards*

See also: *Popular Social Movements and Politics:* Castrismo; Peronismo

Bibliography

Rodríguez, Gregory. 2002. *Boxing and Masculinity: The History and (Her)story of Oscar de la Hoya.* Pp. 252–268 in *Latino/a Popular Culture,* edited by Michelle Habell-Pallán and Mary Romero. New York and London: New York University.

Sugden, John Peter. 1996. *Boxing and Society: An International Analysis.* Manchester, UK: Manchester University Press.

Lucha Libre

Lucha libre, Mexican wrestling, is a sport characterized by stage names, elaborate masks, and highly staged routines. Wrestling first came to Mexico in the early twentieth century when Salvador Lutteroth González founded the Empresa Mexicana de Lucha Libre (Mexican Wrestling Company) at the start of the 1930s. The early matches held in Mexico featured foreign stars such as Bobby Sampson (United States) and Cyclone Mackey (Ireland) alongside Mexican talent, although Mexican lucha libre soon came into its own. The sport grew in popularity over the years and progressed from its initial humble origins to ever grander premises. In 1956 the Arena México was inaugurated, able to hold 20,000 spectators, and the wrestlers in the inaugural sessions included Médico Asesino (Doctor Death), Rolando Vera, and the legendary El Santo (The Saint).

As Heather Levi has noted, in Mexico *lucha libre* functions by assigning the roles of good guy and bad guy to opposing competitors or teams, known by the terms *técnico* (technical) and *rudo* (crude). Whereas the *técnico* aims to win by using superior technique and skill, the *rudo* uses illegal techniques, smuggles weapons into the ring, and tries to escape from the ring to avoid injury. Often, however, there is no clear audience identification with the good guys, and frequently it is the *rudos* that the spectators "love to hate." A key part of this performance/sport is the wearing of masks, themselves a traditional part of Mexican culture. Having one's mask removed by an opponent is seen as the ultimate shame, although the fighter who does the de-masking is immediately disqualified.

The popular appeal of the *lucha libre* hero was given a great boost by the series of "Santo" films that spanned three decades of popular cinema in Mexico. In these films the wrestling legend El Santo (the stage name for Rodolfo Guzmán

Huerta, 1917–1984) appeared in a variety of scenarios, although always playing himself, complete with mask and costume. El Santo was frequently pitted against a series of supernatural enemies, as can be seen in such movies as *Santo contra las mujeres vampiros* (*Santo against the Vampire Women*, 1962), *Santo contra la invasión de los marcianos* (*Santo against the Martian Invasion*, 1966), and *Santo contra la hija de Frankenstein* (*Santo against Frankenstein's Daughter*, 1971). The Santo film series became part of cult cinema in Mexico, and Santo grew to a figure of almost mythological proportions.

Lucha libre continues to be a popular spectator sport in Mexico, and films and videos of its heroes are still sought after. In 1992, El Santo's son, also a wrestling hero and performing under the name Hijo del Santo (Son of the Saint), brought to the screen the film *Santo, la leyenda del enmascarado de plata* (*Santo, the Legend of the Man in the Silver Mask*), in which he played his father. In 1991, the Museo de Culturas Populares (Museum of Popular Cultures) held an exhibition of *lucha libre*, an indication that this sport has been accepted into the realms of popular national culture.

—*Claire Taylor*

See also: *Popular Cinema:* Mexican Horror Films

Bibliography

Box y lucha (Boxing and Wrestling) Website. http://www.boxylucha.com.mx/revista.htm (consulted 2 January 2004).

González Ambriz, Marco. 2003. "Mad Mex: *Santo contra los zombies.*" In *Revista cinefagia*, 30 June. http://www.revistacinefagia.com/madmex001.htm (consulted 2 January 2004).

Levi, Heather. 1999. "On Mexican Pro Wrestling: Sport as Melodrama." *Cultural Politics* 16: 173–188.

Capoeira

Capoeira is a combination of martial art and dance created by African slaves in Brazil; it is often described as the only truly Brazilian sport. There are two main varieties of *capoeira*: *capoeira regional* (regional capoeira), a style perfected by a leading practitioner of the art, Mestre Bimba, in the 1930s, and *capoeira tradicional* or *capoeira (de) Angola* (literally, "traditional capoeira" or "Angolan capoeira"), associated with Mestre Pastinha and his *capoeira* school, established in 1941. The movements of the two varieties differ, but both tend to center on displays of physical strength such as handstands. The object of the game is to try to trip up or kick one's opponent, increasing one's own freedom of movement while restricting that of the other player.

Forbidden by their masters to fight, the African slaves were forced to hide behind what appeared to be a display of acrobatics, whose movements were inspired by those of wild animals. *Capoeira* served as an outlet for expressing the injustices of slavery, its freedom of movement liberating the slave's mind and body from bondage. It allowed the slaves to prepare themselves physically for possible insurrection against their owners or for combat with members of rival ethnic groups among the slave population, but perhaps more importantly, *capoeira* became a source of self-expression and ethnic identity. The famous Brazilian sociologist Gilberto Freyre argued that *capoeira* was tolerated by the white plantation owners because it provided a grisly form of entertainment, akin to the equally common practice of cockfighting.

Students dance *capoeira* during a demonstration for world peace in front of the Brazilian National Congress in Brasilia, 19 December 2003. (Jamil Bittar/Reuters/Corbis)

The musical accompaniment to a game of *capoeira* is provided by various instruments, most importantly the *berimbau*, a musical bow with a metal string and a gourd resonator; other instruments include the *atabaque* drums. The rhythm of the *berimbau* dictates the speed of the play within the *roda*, or ring of participants, known as *capoeiristas*. One by one the musicians, all of whom are practitioners of the sport, begin to play their instruments, beginning with the *berimbau*. As the music begins, two *capoeiristas* take their places within the *roda*, crouching down before the *berimbau*. Before the *jogo* (game) begins, one of the musicians, usually the person in charge of the roda, sings a song praising the *orixás* (deities) of the Afro-Brazilian religion *Candomblé*. This song also praises the *mestre* (master) of the given *capoeira* group, who has either directly or indirectly taught all the members their skills. Those forming the *roda* repeat the words of the song in a chorus. They then begin to clap their hands, and the two crouching within the *roda* touch the *berimbau*, cross themselves (usually asking for protection from the *orixás*), shake hands with each other, and then begin to *jogar* (literally, "play") *capoeira*. A soloist continues to sing, and all the other members of the *roda* join in the chorus throughout the game, each of which usually lasts between three and five minutes, and for a maximum of ten.

After the abolition of slavery in Brazil in 1888, free blacks migrated from the plantations of the northeast and the mines of the interior to the then capital, Rio de Janeiro. They took with them their cultural practices, and *capoeira* became associated with this marginalized underclass, who were forced to live in poverty in the emerging shantytowns and sprawling poor suburbs of the city. The *capoeirista* became synonymous in the minds of the white elite with the gangs of young unemployed and stigmatized Afro-Brazilians who roamed the streets of the city and were forced to turn to a life of crime. After the demise of the monarchy and the establishment of the Republic in 1889, rival political factions in the capital employed gangs (*maltas*) of *capoeiristas*. The largest and most powerful gangs were the Guaiamuns and Nagoas. Linked to republicans and monarchists, respectively, these gangs were used as violent and bloody troops to settle disputes, rivalries, and infighting. Confrontations between this criminal element of *capoeira* and the police were so frequent that such politically motivated attacks could be passed off as random occurrences, without incriminating any of the politicians involved. Gang members were not exclusively of African descent; gangs included poor white men, and capoeira also appealed to a bohemian element of elite society. Once firmly in power, the republican establishment no longer required the assistance of hired thugs to intimidate their monarchist rivals, and thus in 1890, in an effort to eliminate lawlessness and gang culture, a law was passed that prohibited the practice of *capoeira* and displays of physical agility and dexterity in public.

Capoeira was outlawed until the 1930s, when the regime of President Getúlio Vargas (1930–1945) began to embrace expressions of Afro-Brazilian culture in its drive to forge a sense of Brazilian national identity and to attenuate the power of ethnic practices. Mestre Bimba (Manoel dos Reis Machado, 1900–1974), a gifted black *capoeirista* from the state of Bahia, was the first to open a *capoeira* school, known as an *academia*, in 1932. He broke down the complex movements of the art form into a series of simple sequences, making it more accessible to those who wished to learn the skill and creating what is known as *capoeira regional*. His students included members of the lower classes as well as rich politicians, doctors, and former policemen. Mestre Bimba's aim was to clean up *capoeira's* image, to take it off the streets, and to distance it from *capoeira tradicional/capoeira (de) Angola* and its associations with violence and criminality. On 9 July 1937, Bimba's efforts were recognized when the first Vargas government granted him a permit and registered his school. When Vargas returned to the presidency in the early 1950s, he invited Mestre Bimba to the presidential palace and declared that *capoeira* was the only true Brazilian sport. Mestre Pastinha (Vicente Joaquim Ferreira Pastinha, 1889–1982) sought to preserve the more traditional form of *capoeira*, founding his Centro Esportivo de Capoeira Angola (Sporting Center for Angolan Capoeira) in the Pelourinho district of the city of Salvador, Bahia, in 1941.

Today *capoeira* is played by members of all sectors of Brazilian society and by men and women of all racial backgrounds, and increasingly *capoeira* schools are located in modern shopping malls and charge high enrollment fees. Schools in poorer neighborhoods are becoming less and less common. The popularity of *capoeira* extends far beyond Brazil, with groups of practitioners in the United States, Europe, and Japan. Street performances can be seen in London's Covent Garden plaza, as well as in *capoeira's* traditional home, the city of Salvador, Bahia, the heart of Afro-Brazilian culture. In 2003 the BBC used a short sequence of *capoeira* to entertain viewers in the brief time slot between its television programs.

—*Lisa Shaw*

See also: *Popular Religion and Festivals: Candomblé*

Bibliography

Almeida, Bira. 1986. *Capoeira, a Brazilian Art Form: History, Philosophy, and Practice.* Berkeley: North Atlantic Books.
Capoeira, Nestor. 2002. *Capoeira: Roots of the Dance-Fight-Game.* Berkeley: North Atlantic Books.
———. 2003. *The Little Capoeira Book.* Berkeley: North Atlantic Books.
Howell, Lloyd. 2000. *Capoeira: Martial Art of Brazil.* London: Warriors Dreams.
Lewis, John Lowell. 1992. *Ring of Liberation: Deceptive Discourse in Brazilian Capoeira.* Urbana: University of Chicago Press.

Jai Alai

The sport known in Mexico, Cuba, Florida, and other areas as *jai alai* is very similar to the game called *pelota* originally played in the Basque country. In fact the name "jai alai" means "merry festival" in Basque. Similar in principle to squash, *jai alai* involves propelling a small ball against a wall (known as a fronton) so that it will rebound within agreed lines but in a manner impossible for one's opponent to return. The difference, however, is in the manner of propulsion: in *jai alai* a curved basket, or *cesta*, is used to catch the ball and immediately whip it with a speed and force impossible in squash. Indeed, *jai alai* is claimed to be the world's fastest ball sport; the handmade rubber and goatskin projectile (*pelota*) travels as fast as 180 miles per hour. *Jai alai* was brought to Cuba from the Basque country at the end of the nineteenth century, and it spread to other countries from there. Minor differences from the original game have evolved, including the use of protective helmets and reviewed scoring methods. A variation using bare hands, called *frontón*, is played in other areas of Latin America.

—*Keith Richards*

Bibliography

Codden, Hal. 1978. *Jai Alai: Walls and Balls.* Amsterdam: Gamblers Book Club.
Taylor, Richard. 1987. *Jai Alai.* New York: Doubleday.

Jogo do Bicho

Jogo do bicho (literally, the "animal game") is a very popular illegal lottery in Brazil. The *jogo do bicho* dates from 1892, when Baron João Baptista Vianna Drummond (1835–1897), desperate to raise funds for his privately owned Zoological Gardens in Vila Isabel, Rio de Janeiro, dreamed up a scheme to attract visitors. With the overthrow of the Brazilian Empire and the proclamation of the Republic in 1889, financial support from the local government for the baron's enterprise had ended, since it would have been seen as favoritism. Instead, Drummond was given permission to boost revenue by promoting "legal gambling" at the zoo. The *jogo do bicho* was inspired in part by the *jogo das flores* (flower game), which a businessman in downtown Rio was running (without much success). In the *jogo das flores*, customers would guess which out of a list of twenty-five flowers would come up trumps each day. Drummond adapted the format to include twenty-five of the animals found at his zoo. When customers entered the zoo, they would receive a ticket with a picture of an animal, and they would win a prize if that animal was the one randomly chosen and placed on display at the end of the day. The first animal to be drawn was an ostrich. The twenty-five animals remain in the *jogo do bicho* as it is played in Rio de Janeiro today (there are some regional differences to the game), but now each animal is linked to four numbers, which in turn are linked to the official lottery results in a given week. The game has thus become more complicated over time, and there are a number of ways to bet and win.

Drummond's scheme caught on almost immediately. Within weeks local newspapers had gotten into the habit of reporting which animal had won the draw. And within a matter of days, Rio's chief of police had written to Drummond ordering him to stop the game because gambling was prohibited. This was the first in a long line of futile attempts to halt the popular lottery. The *jogo do bicho* in its original form did not constitute gambling because punters did not bet on animals as such: they were randomly assigned on entrance tickets. Soon the game was adapted so that punters could choose which animals to bet on, and therefore the act of attending the zoo became separated from the game itself. With this phase, it was only a matter of time before bookmakers began to appear, most of whom were organized by the wily baron himself. These bookmakers would stand in line at the zoo, buy up large quantities of tickets, and sell them elsewhere in the city. Rio's bourgeoisie could gamble from the comfort of their own homes (they always sent a servant out, thus avoiding direct dealings with the bookmakers and their runners). The game even caught on in other states, inspired by the original lottery but with localized results. Newsletters were soon published just on the subject of the game, containing tips on how to choose an animal and number on a given day. Today, a number of Websites offer similar betting tips, for example showing ways for punters to analyze their dreams in order to choose the right animal.

The authorities banned the *jogo do bicho* at the zoo in 1895: the federal lottery was suffering as a result of the game's popularity, so pressure was exerted on local police and the justice system to take action. At this point the prototype of the modern *banqueiros*, or lottery bankers, rapidly began to appear in order to keep the game going, albeit clandestinely. Most of the *banqueiros* came from Rio's very large immigrant population (Arabs, Spanish, Portuguese, and so on) because they had less to lose from brushes with the law.

Roberto DaMatta has argued that the reason gamblers have been and continue to be happy to hand over their money to rather shady characters who are ultimately part of a vast illegal network is that, since its inception, *jogo do bicho* has been associated with honesty, in the form of the nobleman Drummond and his insistence on displaying the result of the draw at the zoo for all to see. Another of Brazil's foremost sociologists, Gilberto Freyre, argued in 1933 that the game had caught the

Brazilian public's imagination because of its totemic nature, linking it to Brazil's indigenous population and lending it a certain cachet.

According to Robert Levine, the *jogo do bicho* turns over approximately 1.4 billion dollars annually and provides 100,000 jobs in Rio de Janeiro and São Paulo. In 1999 there were more than 3,000 *pontos*, or places (shops, homes, and the most popular place: street corners) where bets were taken on the game. Because the game is illegal, no tax is paid by punters or bookmakers, and state and federal governments lose an inordinate amount of revenue as a result.

By the mid-twentieth century the *jogo do bicho* had become an organized crime practice based on an unofficial partnership among police, bankers, and dealers of the game. The *jogo do bicho* falls into a gray zone between clearly legal and clearly illegal. It has been associated with money laundering, for example through support of Rio's samba schools and the annual Carnival parade. Over the last twenty years or so the game has developed a problematic connection to drug trafficking: *bicheiros*, as the organizers of the game are known, are blamed for establishing Brazil as a base for exportation of cocaine from Colombia to Europe. The extent to which *bicheiros* have access to powerful figures in Brazilian society was clear during a recent *jogo do bicho* scandal, involving impeached president Fernando Collor de Mello, the mayor of São Paulo, the governor of Rio, civil rights activist Herbert de Souza, police officers, and even João Havelange, ex-president of FIFA (International Federation of Football [Soccer] Associations).

Such has been the fascination with the lottery organizers, particularly before the 1980s and the arrival on scene of the notorious drugs barons, that the figure of the *bicheiro* has entered into Brazilian urban mythology, witnessed, for example, in Nelson Rodrigues's creation *Boca de Ouro* (Gold Mouth), in the famous and very popular 1959 play of the same name. Both the *bicheiros* and the *jogo do bicho* itself are examples of Brazil's flexible attitude to laws and official policy.

—*Stephanie Dennison*

See also: *Popular Religion and Festivals:* Popular Festivals (Carnival in Brazil)

Bibliography

DaMatta, Roberto, and Elena Soárez. 1999. *Aguias, burros, e borboletas: Um estudo antropológico do jogo do bicho.* Rio de Janeiro: Rocco.

Freyre, Gilberto. 1956. *The Masters and the Slaves: A Study in the Development of Brazilian Civilization.* Translated from the Portuguese by Samuel Putnam. New York and London: Knopf.

Levine, Robert M. 1997. *Brazilian Legacies.* Armonk, NY, and London: M. E. Sharpe.

O Jogo do Bicho Website. http://www.ojogodobicho.com (consulted 1 February 2004).

Consumerism and Fashion

Consumer behavior in the capitalist countries of Latin America is very similar to that of the United States: consumers throughout the continent desire the latest fashions and electronic equipment and have an unfortunate habit of spending on frivolous items beyond their means and occasionally at the expense of such basic goods as food. In Latin America anything imported—cars, whisky, sound systems, and so on—is traditionally seen as lending status to the consumer and as being of better quality. For those Latin Americans who can find the money to do so, a yearly shopping trip to Miami is de rigueur. This seemingly uncontrollable need to buy up as many modern items as possible when abroad was magnificently illustrated by Brazil's soccer World Cup–winning squad of 1994: on their return from the finals in the United States, the jet chartered to fly the players home was filled with eleven tons of electrical products.

Consumerism and fashion in Latin America are greatly inspired by such globalized phenomena as the importance of the shopping mall in the lives of the urban population and a fascination with European catwalks. However, as in other areas, Latin Americans appropriate these trends and make them their own, as witnessed, for example, by the more important role that food and entertainment play in shopping malls in Brazil than in North America and Europe.

Individuals often use fashion to identify themselves as being part of a particular social or ethnic group or from a particular region. In Brazil members of the pop nobility (musicians) from the state of Bahia, for example, often wear African-inspired outfits as a mark of their racial and cultural heritage, and young *gaúchos* (inhabitants of Brazil's southernmost states) are fond of wearing *alpargatas* (espadrilles), the traditional footwear of their southern region. Fashion and other lifestyle choices are greatly influenced by urban life, particularly by Latin America's megacities, such as Mexico City, Buenos Aires, Bogota, Rio de Janeiro, and São Paulo.

—*Stephanie Dennison*

See also: *Sport and Leisure:* Food; Soccer; *Cultural Icons:* Regional and Ethnic Types (The Gaúcho in Brazil)

Consumerism

Colombia. The huge urban centers in Colombia, such as Bogota, Cali, and Medellín among others, have over recent years attracted large numbers of internal migrants. Although figures are imprecise, Bogota's population was estimated at close to ten million in the year 2000. While many of these new arrivals live in poor conditions, cities such as Bogota have also seen an explosion of capital for certain sectors and the rise of consumer-driven recreational centers such as shopping malls, multiplexes, and theme parks.

The so-called Centro Internacional (International Center) of Bogota, which houses the major banking, actuarial, and management consultancy firms among others, is typified by immense skyscrapers, the majority of which were constructed during the boom of the mid-1980s to the mid-1990s, giving this part of the city what Raymond Leslie Williams has termed a "postmodern glitter and glaze" (1999, p. 130). Alongside these office blocks, in recent years several vast shopping malls, such as Metropolis and Unicentro, have emerged. Unicentro, with one shopping center in Bogota and another in Calí, is a huge mall and entertainment multiplex containing a myriad of shops—including smaller boutiques and ubiquitous national department stores such as Ley—game areas for children, an eight-screen cinema, a bowling alley, a casino, and several food outlets, including El Corral, a Colombian chain serving hamburgers.

In addition to shopping centers, the past two decades have seen the growth of such modern tourist attractions as the Parque Jaime Duque (Jaime Duque Park), which

Metropolis shopping center in Bogota, Colombia. (Courtesy of Edwin Moyano)

opened in 1983 in Tocancipá, near Bogota. This theme park includes both cultural events geared toward children and rides such as Fantasía las Mil y Una Noches (1,001 Nights Fantasy), bumper cars, a carousel, a mini-train, go-carts, the Palacio de Cristal (Hall of Mirrors), and a monorail. Other similar parks within Bogota itself include Camelot, Mundo Aventura (Adventure World), and the new Salitre Mágico (Magical Salitre; Salitre is the district in Bogota where the park is located), all of which attract large numbers of visitors, mostly domestic tourists, each year.

Alongside these standard theme parks Bogota has recently developed hi-tech tourist attractions, such as Maloka. Maloka, according to its own publicity, is the biggest interactive center for science and technology in the whole of South America. It came about in 1989 as an initiative of the Asociación Colombiana para el Avance de la Ciencia (Colombian Association for the Advancement of Science). An immense visitor and attraction center, Maloka was designed by a group of scientists, designers, and educators. Spread over several floors, it has a series of interactive games; a wide-screen cinema; a music, water, and light display; and a variety of different scientific exhibits covering subjects such as the human being, biodiversity, the city, and telecommunications. The name "Maloka" is a play on the indigenous Amazonian word *maloca*, meaning dwelling place or meeting place, while

Camelot theme park, Colombia. (Courtesy of Edwin Moyano)

also conveying the notion of a place for transmitting knowledge.

—*Claire Taylor*

Bibliography

Gilbert, Alan. 1994. *The Latin American City.* London: Latin American Bureau.

Harding, Colin. 1995. *Colombia: A Guide to the People, Politics, and Culture.* London: Latin American Bureau.

Pérgolis, Juan Carlos. 1998. *Bogotá fragmentada: Cultura y espacio urbano a fines del siglo XX.* Bogota: TM Editores.

Williams, Raymond Leslie. 1999. *Culture and Customs of Colombia.* Westport, CT: Greenwood.

Brazil. Brazilians from many different walks of life are known for their remarkable capacity for consumption. The expression *"meu sonho de consumo,"* which roughly translates as "my dream purchase," is frequently used in Brazil. It is perhaps *not* a coincidence that Brazil's advertising agencies are renowned the world over for their sophisticated ad campaigns. Brazilians crave the latest goods, both national and especially imported goods, and those with the economic means to do so will use the Internet and take advantage of cut-rate flights to the United States in their desire to shop for the latest products. For those less well off, *camelôs,* or street vendors, many of whom work illegal pitches and sell fake or illegal items (without a license in public venues), offer a cheaper alternative to buying in shops. *Camelôs* buy their wares from *sacolões* (literally, "large bags"), vendors who make regular bus trips to the tax-free and fake-goods shopping haven of Paraguay and bring back huge bags full of goods to sell at home.

Most state capitals have at least one large modern shopping mall, known as *shoppings.* There are 253 malls in total in Brazil, with the largest number found in the state of São Paulo (91). Consumers' preference for *shoppings* is understandable, given their free parking, air-conditioning, and, most important, increased safety. Shopping malls are popular spaces for dining out, and the fare on offer is not always limited to fast-food outlets such as McDonald's or the homegrown burger chain Bob's. Like their counterparts in Europe and the United States, they often house cinemas (1,038 in total) and nightclubs, and some even have ice rinks and ten-pin bowling alleys. The Shopping Eldorado in São Paulo is home to an amusement park: the Parque da Mônica, based on Brazil's most popular children's comic books.

Many states also have at least one large theme park or water park. For example, Rio's Wet 'n' Wild is a new addition to the international water park chain, also found in Mexico. São Paulo has a number of large and very popular parks, including the country's first and still best theme park, Playcenter, built in 1973. Another favorite park, Beto Carrero World in Santa Catarina, is inspired and run by the popular rodeo performer of the same name.

One of the most striking examples of Brazilians' fascination with U.S. lifestyle and with imitating it as a marker of success is the beachfront neighborhood known as Barra da Tijuca, to the west of Rio de Janeiro. Expanding rapidly since the early 1980s, Barra is known as the rather soulless home of the *emergentes,* Rio's nouveaux riches. The layout of the neighborhood, the names of commercial complexes (New York City Center, Downtown, São Conrado Fashion Mall), and the activities being offered (extra-large shopping centers, Pizza Hut, Hard Rock Café, power walking on the promenade, and so on) remind both its fans and its critics more of Miami than of a Brazilian city.

—*Stephanie Dennison*

See also: *Popular Literature:* Comic Books

Bibliography

Allen, Roger M. 1999. "Cultural Imperialism at Its Most Fashionable." Pp. 447–453 in *The Brazil Reader: History, Culture, Politics*, edited by Robert M. Levine and John J. Crocitti. Durham, NC, and London: Duke University Press.

Banck, Geert A. 1994. "Mass Consumption and Urban Contest in Brazil: Some Reflections on Lifestyle and Class." *Bulletin of Latin American Research* 13, no. 1: 45–60.

Beto Carrero World Website. http://www.betocarrero.com.br (consulted 13 March 2004).

Brazilian Association of Shopping Centers Website. http://www.abrasce.com.br (consulted 13 March 2004).

Parque da Mônica Website. http://www.monica.com.br/parques (consulted 13 March 2004).

Playcenter Website. http://www.playcenter.com.br (consulted 13 March 2004).

Argentina. Any discussion of consumerism in Argentina has to recognize the sheer dominance of the capital, Buenos Aires, over the rest of the country. Buenos Aires is by far the biggest of Argentina's cities and is home to most of the country's middle-class population, which is surprisingly large in Latin American terms. Buenos Aires, perhaps better than any other Latin American city, meets the needs of the modern consumer, providing exclusive boutiques, shopping centers, theme parks, multiplexes and recreational spaces, social life, and so on.

Argentine consumers enjoy their shopping malls as much as any other consumers in the West: the number of retail centers grew from four in 1988 to fifty-two in 2002. Most shopping malls are situated in the capital and surrounding districts, such as the important Galerías Pacífico, on the once trendy but now slightly faded downtown Calle Florida, and the Alto Palermo Shopping Center in one of the elegant middle-class neighborhoods of Buenos Aires. The Patio Bullrich shopping center and the surrounding streets in the exclusive Recoleta neighborhood are the destination of shoppers looking for more upmarket fashions and purchases, while consumers with limited buying power rely on cheap imports from China that have been swamping the Argentine market of late, which are sold in shops in more distant and less fashionable areas of the city.

Buenos Aires and other large cities in Argentina follow the trends seen elsewhere in the world of building cinema multiplexes, often within shopping centers and generally in middle-class neighborhoods. Buenos Aires and surrounding areas also have their fair share of modern theme parks, such as the Showcenter, the Parque de Diversiones Spadalandia, and Parque de la Costa.

As in other countries in Latin America, such as Brazil, those who can afford it will often invest in a second home away from the bustle and stress of the city, where most of the population lives. These retreats range from small apartments in the rural suburbs, to beach houses in the popular Mar del Plata or chalets in the ski resort of Bariloche, to *estancias*, huge farms in the countryside, to which the truly wealthy traditionally disappear for the whole of the summer.

—*Stephanie Dennison*

See also: *Sport and Leisure:* Fashion (Argentina)

Bibliography

Argentine Association of Shopping Centers Website. http://www.casc.org.ar (consulted 13 March 2004).

Parque de la Costa Website. http://www.parquedelacosta.com.ar (consulted 13 March 2004).

Showcenter Website. http://www.showcenter.com.ar (consulted 13 March 2004).

Spalandia Website. http://www.spadalandia.com.ar (consulted 13 March 2004).

Mexico. Although a substantial proportion of the Mexican population does not even participate in the market economy and although even larger numbers of Mexicans find themselves suffering from the downside of global capitalism, exploited in their labor in *maquiladoras* (large-scale sweatshops owned by foreign companies) and bombarded in their scant leisure time by images of products they can ill afford, over the last couple of decades, particularly during the presidential administration of Carlos Salinas de Gortari (1988–1994), a consumerist lifestyle on a scale comparable to that of the United States has become very much a reality in Mexico's largest urban centers, for those who can afford it.

Mexico City, Guadalajara, and Monterrey all boast a substantial number of upscale shopping malls, complete with department stores (such as Liverpool and the Palacio de Hierro), banks, travel agencies, bars, restaurants (transnational fast-food chains, Mexican chains such as Sanborn's, and more upmarket, individualized options), and leisure facilities such as multiplex cinemas. The Centro Santa Fe, on the western edge of Mexico City, is hailed by the guidebooks as being the biggest mall of its kind in Latin America (although the award should probably go to the five-story, five-hundred-outlet-strong Centro Sambil in Caracas, Venezuela). Opened in 1993, the Santa Fe mall boasts 285 different shops and fourteen movie theaters. It prides itself on offering a safe shopping environment: once patrons enter its doors, they no longer see any trace of the inequalities in wealth distribution so typical of Latin America. Shoppers can feel as if they are in Houston or Los Angeles, with only a few postmodern architectural reminders of their Latin American location (the odd frieze, mural, or pyramid-shaped fountain, for example). The city of Guadalajara is dominated by two huge shopping malls: the Plaza Tapatía in the old downtown area, near the cathedral, and the Plaza del Sol on the southwest side of the city. Whereas the latter can boast that it was the first big out-of-town shopping mall of its kind to be built in Latin America (it was constructed from scratch in only nine months in 1969) and that it is home to countless transnational companies, the former actually marries old and new architecture in innovative ways and helps keep the old heart of the town alive.

Other key neighborhoods in these cities also cater to the consumerist lifestyle in a less "enclosed" manner. In Mexico City some of the most upscale hotels, restaurants, and designer outlets, including internationally renowned venues such as Habita and the newly opened W Hotel, are found in the streets of Polanco. The neighborhood has even become synonymous with the concept of Mexican consumerism—the so-called *reinas de Polanco* (queens of Polanco) are those women who can afford to live the consumerist lifestyle. Writer Guadalupe Loaeza has immortalized these women and their lives in her books on the subject of consumerism in Mexico, such as

Las reinas de Polanco (1988) and *Compro, luego existo* (*I Buy, Therefore I Am*, 1992). Although she is critical of this kind of lifestyle, the loving detail with which she reconstructs the lives and daily concerns of such women does detract from her critical edge.

In addition to urban consumerism, since the 1970s Mexico has vigorously promoted its tourist industry to a national market. Key locations like Cancún, Zihuatanejo, and La Paz have been developed to offer the same sorts of amenities as are available in the big cities to those seeking to indulge in Mexican beach tourism. Furthermore, on the outskirts of such locations, Disney-style adventure parks, spas, water parks, safari parks for animals both imported and indigenous to the Americas, behind-the-scenes moviemaking parks, and even eco-theme parks, such as Xcaret near Cancún, have all sprung up in response to the need for entertainment at the beach in addition to shopping opportunities. Nevertheless, aware of the dangers of runaway consumerism, the Mexican government now runs a federal program (PROFECO) to warn consumers of the dangers of debt. It was under the auspices of this program that Loaeza's latest novel, *Debo, luego sufro* (*I Am in Debt, Therefore I Suffer*, 2000), was published.

—*Thea Pitman*

See also: *Travel and Tourism:* Beach Tourism

Bibliography

Gilbert, Alan. 1994. *The Latin American City.* London: Latin America Bureau.

Loaeza, Guadalupe. 1988. *Las reinas de Polanco.* Mexico City: Cal y Arena.

———. 1992. *Compro, luego existo.* Mexico City: Alianza Editorial.

———. 2000. *Debo, luego sufro.* Mexico City: Planeta.

Puchet Angel, Martin, and Lionello F. Punzo. 2001. *Mexico beyond NAFTA.* London: Routledge.

Roux, Caroline. 2003. "The Whimsy of W." *London Guardian*, 6 December, "Travel" section.

Fashion

Brazil. Brazilian fashion is inspired in great part by the *carioca* (Rio de Janeiro) way of life, which is itself influenced by high temperatures all year round and the importance of beach culture. Clothes are thus designed both to keep the wearer cool and to reveal as much as possible of tanned, fit bodies. In terms of beachwear, although some trends, such as sarongs and Capri pants, come and go, both surfwear and the famous *fio dental*, or "dental floss" bikini, with its two tiny triangles covering the typically small Brazilian breasts and its ultra-revealing panties (Brazilian men are widely reputed to be fond of rear ends), seem to be here to stay. Bikini and beach accessory designers such as Rosa Chá, Salinas, and Bum Bum, associated with Ipanema, Rio's fashionable beachfront neighborhood, are starting to make inroads into the international fashion market. Brazil's footwear industry has long been exporting cheap leather shoes en masse. Now Constança Basto, a designer relatively new to the footwear market, is taking more exclusive Brazilian shoe design to the United States: she already has two stores in New York, in Soho and on the Upper East Side. And remarkably, Havaianas, Brazil's most popular brand of cheap rubber flip-flops, are currently highly sought-after items in Europe and the United States.

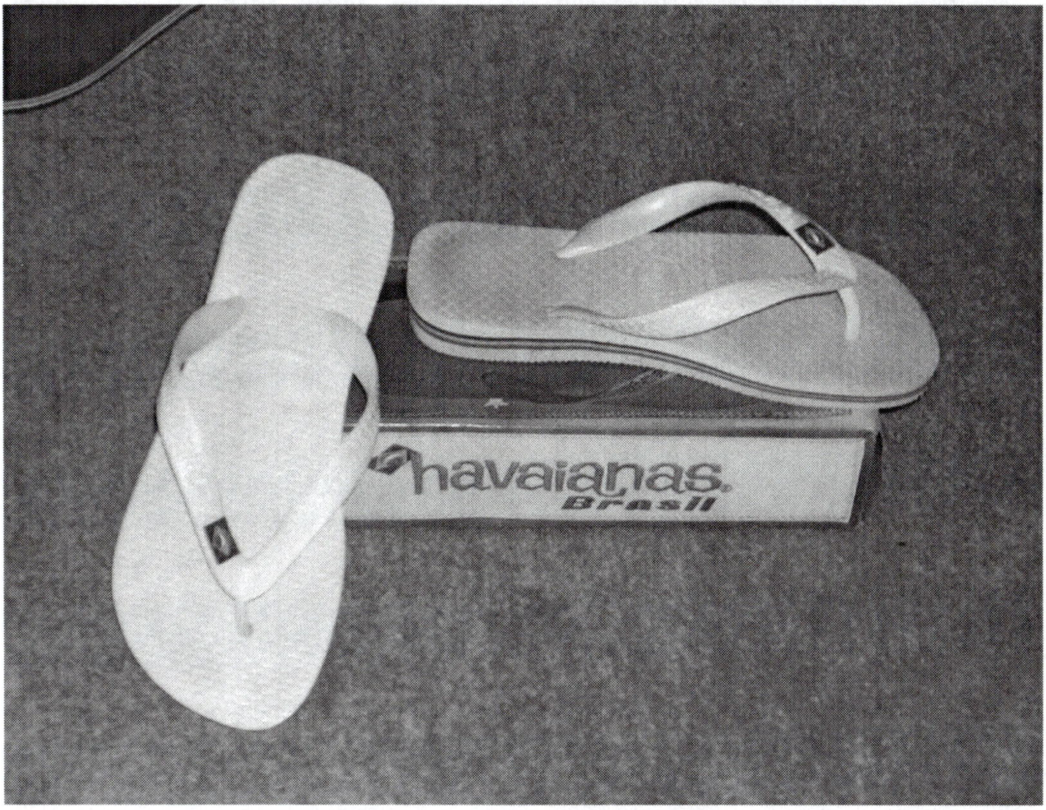

The ubiquitous Havaianas, cheap Brazilian footwear that is now a high-fashion item both at home and abroad. (Courtesy of Alex Nield)

Although a number of international high-street chains can be found in Brazil's cities, such as Benetton and the increasingly popular Spanish chain Zara, young urban Brazilians often prefer their own (regional) chains, such as Company, Cantão, and Chocolate in Rio de Janeiro, and domestic labels such as Osklen and Ellus. For those who cannot afford to buy ready-made clothing, cheap labor and inexpensive cloth mean that one can dress more economically either by paying a seamstress or by convincing a family member to make an outfit. In terms of business wear, *paulistas* (the inhabitants of São Paulo) believe they dress more elegantly than their *carioca* counterparts, given the fact that (beach-less) São Paulo is a more work-oriented city. Brazil's only Armani store is in São Paulo rather than Rio. São Paulo has recently been stealing the fashion limelight in Brazil thanks to the success of the annual São Paulo Fashion Week. The world domination of Brazilian supermodel Gisele Bundchen (1980–) has not done the Brazilian fashion industry any harm either.

A number of talented homegrown designers have emerged in Brazil in the last few years, including the husband-and-wife team Glória Coelho and Ronaldo Fraga, whose precocious twelve-year-old son recently produced a fashion collection for São Paulo Fashion Week. Other important designers are Reinaldo Lourenço, Lino

Vilaventura, André Lima, Fause Haten, and Alexandre Herchcovitch. High-society women of a certain age put their trust in such established haute couture names as Mara Mac of the Mariazinha label and Andréa Saleto, but many prefer to dress in French brands, such as Chanel and Yves Saint Laurent, often purchased on shopping trips to Europe and the United States.

Because pedestrians will often be relieved of expensive-looking jewelry and athletic shoes by opportunistic thieves, young people going out socially tend to dress casually and discreetly. All over Brazil, a mock-hippie dress code seems to exist for the left-wing student contingent: tie-dye T-shirts, a rejection of labels, natural leather sandals, bags bought at the local hippie market or on a backpacking trip to the northeast, and, in the case of young men, long hair and beards à la Che Guevara.

—*Stephanie Dennison*

See also: *Cultural Icons:* Political Icons (Che Guevara)

Bibliography

"Big in Brazil—from Plastic Surgery to Sex Motels: Your Guide to the Hottest Country on Earth." 2004. *Sunday Times* (London) *Style Magazine*, 11 April.

Kalil, Glória. 2003. *Chic: Um guia básico de moda e estilo.* São Paulo: Senac.

Rodrigues, Iesa. 2001. *30 estilistas: A moda do Rio.* Rio de Janeiro: Senac.

Santa Catarina Fashion Website. http://www.santamoda.com.br (consulted 14 March 2004).

Argentina. The stereotype of the Buenos Aires elite is one of impeccable imitation of European tastes and fashions, betraying centuries-old cultural links to the aristocratic traditions of the Old World. According to the same stereotype, *porteños* (people from Buenos Aires) are polo-playing, English-speaking, French-dressing conservatives with carefully coiffured hair. The stereotype denies the existence, for example, of youth culture, with its budding club scene and attendant "alternative" music and dress codes, and of the mass of the population, predominantly poor and living in tenements often carefully removed from view of the fashionable areas of the city. Nevertheless, the stereotype does seem to hold true for a sizable part of the population. Mature women who cannot claim links with the Old World are still conservative in their dress. Whereas middle-aged lower-middle- and working-class women can frequently be seen in tight jeans and skimpy tops in Brazil, for example, many in Argentina continue to mimic the Jackie Kennedy–esque elegance of Evita Perón (1919–1952). Evita, during her time as wife of populist president Juan Perón (1895–1974) and role model to the poor, was dressed by local designers Paula Naletoff and Henriette.

The well-heeled of Buenos Aires are very fond of foreign labels, from Armani and Louis Vuitton to Chanel, and in most cases they can buy what they need in Argentina. When they cannot find what they are looking for at home, they often travel to the United States, but with European rather than U.S. labels in their sights. Although a number of homegrown fashion chains exist that cater to a younger clientele, such as Paula Cahen D'Anvers and Vitamina, younger and older alike prefer European styles of dress, meaning that many commentators find it difficult to speak of an Argentine fashion, certainly one comparable, say, to Brazil's distinctive style. That said, there are a number of successful fashion houses in Argentina, including the ultra-trendy Martín Churba, Gino Bogani, and Roberto Piazza.

—*Stephanie Dennison*

See also: *Cultural Icons:* Political Icons (Evita)

Bibliography

Gina Bogani Website. http://www.ginobogani.com.ar (consulted 14 March 2004).
Roberto Piazza Website. http://www.robertopiazza.com.ar (consulted 14 March 2004).
Saulquin, Susana. 1991. *La moda en la Argentina.* Buenos Aires: Emecé.

Mexico. Mexico is known throughout the world for the colorful and varied traditional dress of its numerous indigenous communities. These images are promoted by the government and the tourist industry as icons of the Republic's distinctive cultural history. Nevertheless, few present-day urban Mexicans of any social class aspire to copy such dress (despite the endorsement earlier in the century of the artist Frida Kahlo), and even in areas where traditional dress still prevails there is a clear tendency among the younger generations to adopt the ubiquitous Western jeans and T-shirt, reverting to traditional dress only for special occasions if at all.

In the twentieth century, North American fashions have become more popular than those of Spain (influential from the time of the Conquest until the early nineteenth century) or France (influential in the latter half of the nineteenth century) across all strata of society in Mexico. There are a number of reasons for this. The inroads made by U.S. film and television have promoted U.S. dress codes as the norm, and the ever-increasing number of backpacking tourists in the far-flung corners of the Republic—tourists who are only too willing to exchange a T-shirt for a locally produced artifact—has given those traditionally excluded from the market economy access to Western clothing. Furthermore, the relatively recent appearance of *maquiladoras*, the sweatshops and factories producing cheap fashion items for U.S. and European markets by taking advantage of the pitifully low labor costs in Mexico, has also increased the demand for similar products in Mexico itself, either via legitimate channels or via the black market in seconds.

Despite the facts that the Mexican clothing industry is much more geared to the *maquila* (assembly) of imported designs and that little space is afforded to designers from the national community (certainly this is the view of those currently trying to work as fashion designers in Mexico), a concept of Latin American haute couture has been fostered across the continent in the last decade by such events as the Miami Fashion Week and, specifically in Mexico, by the Expo-Fashion Mexicana. Reputable fashion design schools are now open in both Mexico City and Guadalajara. Perhaps the only market for homegrown haute couture is the urban middle and upper classes, the so-called *reinas de Polanco* (literally, the "queens of Polanco," who patronize and often reside in an upper-class shopping area in Mexico City), who have the disposable income and leisure time to spend on such luxuries. However, the existence of such fashions does also demonstrate the concern of those working in the industry in Mexico to offer creative alternatives, often inflected with a certain national spirit, to the hegemony of U.S. fashions.

Three Mexican designers have stood out in the last ten years: Armando Mafud, Héctor Terrones, and Sarah Bustani. Mafud, the eldest of the three, deliberately creates clothing that makes a statement about Mexico in its use of color and motifs (much of his work is inspired by the paintings of artists such as Diego Rivera, Rufino Tamayo, and Rodolfo Morales) or in its cut (copying the traditional *huipiles*, or smocks, and wraparound skirts of the women of the Tehuantepec Peninsula, for example). The overall effect is a conscious nod to the deliberately nationalist image of painter Frida Kahlo. Terrones, like Mafud, opts for designs that lie somewhere between art and fashion, taking inspiration from historical models (medieval and Victorian in his case), yet he does not aspire to capture anything specifically Mexican in his work, instead seeking to respond to international trends in haute couture and to provide "practical solutions for special occasions" (Hofman n.d.) such as weddings (although he does also have a ready-to-wear line). Bustani, perhaps the most accessible and most contemporary of the three designers, designs clothes for teenagers and young adults, making great use of modern synthetic fabrics such as Lycra. Her clothes are designed to be easy to wear (but still stylish) and affordable. They are inspired by her appreciation of film and television and by her visits to high schools both in Mexico and abroad to see what young people actually want to wear. In her designs for women, she focuses on making comfortable clothes specifically for the physique of Mexican women. Thus, she bases her fashions on the needs and aspirations of her target market rather than seeking to impose a sense of "Mexican" fashion on Mexicans or on the international community. Bustani has had remarkable success in her career so far; she had opened seventeen of her own shops across the Mexican Republic by 2000 and has sales outlets in Spain, Latin America, and the United States. She also dresses Latin pop and soap stars, for example Thalía. Finally, the most recent and most promising names on the Mexican fashion circuit are those of sisters Julia and Renata Franco, whose low-budget casual line, Julia Y Renata, was a runaway success at the 2002 Mexican Fashion Fair.

—*Thea Pitman*

See also: *Popular Music:* Transnational Pop Icons; *Visual Arts and Architecture:* Art (Frida Kahlo; Diego Rivera)

Bibliography

Gillespie, Judi. 2000. "Sarah Bustani: Mexico's Sun Goddess." *Lifewise*, 2 June. http://www.canoe.ca/LifewiseMirrors Friday00/0602_sarah.html (consulted 10 November 2003).

Hofman, Nina. n.d. "Héctor Terrones." www.terra.com/especiales/lamoda/moda_en_miami/hector_terrones/hector_terrones.html. (consulted 10 November 2003).

Loaeza, Guadalupe. 1988. *Las reinas de Polanco.* Mexico City: Cal y Arena.

———. 1992. *Compro, luego existo.* Mexico City: Alianza Editorial.

Takahasi, Masako. 2003. *Mexican Textiles.* Introduction by Tony Cohan. San Francisco: Chronicle Books.

Indigenous Dress and Its Influences. The question of dress in Latin American countries with a strong indigenous presence is indeed vexed. European and other outside interference in native dress is as old as colonialism itself, particularly in hotter climes where indigenous people were encouraged, at considerable detriment to their health, to cover up. Spanish colonizers in more temperate zones also Europeanized

Aymara women drink beer at a wedding celebration on the main Floating Island on Lake Titicaca, c. 1997. (Craig Lovell/Corbis)

indigenous dress, but as in many areas of pre-Columbian organization, they were happy to continue the practice of dressing according to geographical or ethnic origin. This "traditional" dress can still be seen in many areas of Latin and Central America today, although inevitably it is under threat.

Any influence by indigenous dress on European styles has been demonstrated far more among European and North American tourists than among the Latin American white or *mestizo* populations, which are still at pains to distance themselves from stigmatized native customs. Ironically, these foreign visitors are the ones who take the keenest interest in indigenous textiles, whether for academic research, for business, or simply as souvenirs. This interest at least helps such practices to survive, but there is inevitably a downside, as traditional motifs are abandoned in favor of what locals imagine, correctly or otherwise, tourists will want to buy. Another destructive practice is that of cutting up woven items so they can be included as decorative panels in leather bags and satchels.

Traditional indigenous dress has been losing ground over recent decades to cheap mass-produced clothing originating particularly in the United States. It is common to see men in baseball caps and bomber jackets in Andean cities or even in the Andean countryside. Women, however, have remained closer to their ethnic heritage, guardians both of native language and of dress styles. Indigenous dress is, of course, not a static phenomenon, as is evidenced by Bolivian Aymara women's adoption of the British bowler hat during colonial times. Much has been made of the adoption of jeans and other stock items from Western culture, but little has been said about the reverse: Latin American native styles can be seen particularly among younger tourists and travelers in the region, where local communities have turned to making clothing that uses their own materials but that is adapted to outsiders' needs and tastes. The growth of "ethnic" shops in European and North American cities has also brought an awareness of the beauty of indigenous aesthetics, reinforced by widespread sympathy for the plight of threatened cultures and peoples.

There are thus indications that pride in indigenous dress is not irrevocably waning. In Ecuador native peoples have stubbornly refused to submit to modern society's demands that they conform. Native men serving in the nation's military are now not even required to cut off their braids, known as *shimba.* In Guatemala legislation passed in 1999 to protect indigenous dress has won international praise, although many areas of provision for native welfare are lacking.

Some enterprises exist to promote and conserve indigenous weaving traditions, such as ASUR (Anthropologists of the Southern Andes), run by the Chilean anthropologist Verónica Cereceda in Sucre, Bolivia. Other "fair trade" groups, such as Crossroads Trade, deal directly with weavers and artisans, encouraging them to maintain ecologically viable practices and ancient styles and selling the finished articles in the United States.

—Keith Richards

See also: *Language:* Indigenous Languages

Bibliography

Healy, Kevin. 2001. *Llamas, Weavings, and Organic Chocolate: Multicultural Grassroots Development in the Andes and Amazon of Bolivia.* Notre Dame, IN: University of Notre Dame Press.

Jackson, Jean E., and Kay B. Warren, eds. 2003. *Indigenous Movements, Self-Representation, and the State in Latin America.* Austin: University of Texas Press.

"Minorities at Risk: Indigenous Peoples of Guatemala." n.d. http://www.cidcm.umd.edu/inscr/mar/data/indguat.htm (consulted 10 December 2003).

Sieder, Rachel, ed. 2002. *Multiculturalism in Latin America: Indigenous Rights, Diversity, and Democracy.* Basingstoke, Hampshire, UK: Houndmills.

Food

Food and drink is a key theme in any discussion of popular culture in Latin America, for it lies at the heart of so many other popular cultural practices, from the spiritual (the all-important consumption of tea in the Santo Daime religion, for example) to the profane (sociologist Gilberto Freyre has written extensively on the link between food and sex in Brazil, for instance). It is also one of the main ways in which many Latin American countries are identified by those from outside. The average American's or Briton's knowledge of Mexico is largely based on his or her experience of eating Mexican food, either at a local restaurant or, increasingly, purchased ready-made in supermarkets.

Given the strong link between the local environment and the development of traditional cuisine, food in Latin America cannot always be easily divided into nations and regions within nations. There is more in common, for example, between the highland cooking of, say, Peru and Ecuador than between regional cuisines within national boundaries. The traditional food of the *gaúcho* of southern Brazil (*churrasco,* for example) has more in common with the cuisine of Uruguay and Argentina than it does with food from the northeast of Brazil. Similarities can be drawn between the traditional dish of Brazil, *feijoada*, and food found in other regions with a slave-holding past, including the southern United States.

It is worth considering the products that have crossed in both directions between Latin America and Europe or Asia. For example, from the Andes, Central America, and Mexico came the potato and maize; from the Old World came coffee, rice, sugar, and such livestock as sheep, pigs, and cattle. Wine production, especially in Chile, is a prime example of a product being imported into Latin America, developed there, and successfully exported back to the Old World. As well as being clearly influenced by indigenous peoples and Africans brought to the subcontinent as slaves, Latin American cuisine has been greatly affected by the arrival of immigrant groups from Asia and Europe in the nineteenth and twentieth centuries, as witnessed, for example, in Peru's own brand of Chinese cuisine and the popularity of Italian cooking and restaurants in Argentina and Brazil.

Without doubt, the Latin American cuisine that is best known outside of the region is Mexican. It is a common quip that the main type of homesickness Mexicans traveling abroad experience is for their national cuisine, and even non-Mexicans perceive Mexican food to be as distinctive and delectable a national cuisine as that of China, Italy, or India. Today, Mexican salsa has even overtaken ketchup as the most popular condiment on the dining tables of the United States. Yet what is currently recognized as typical Mexican food is the product of over five centuries of cross-cultural exchange, and that is still an ongoing process.

—*Stephanie Dennison, Thea Pitman, and Keith Richards*

See also: *Cultural Icons:* Regional and Ethnic Types (The Gaúcho in Brazil); *Popular Religion and Festivals:* Santo Daime

Indigenous, African, and Immigrant Influences (the Andean Countries). The rich culinary tradition of the Andean countries is the product of over five centuries of demographic flux and cultural interaction. An already long-established pre-Columbian indigenous cuisine has been augmented by European, African, and Asian influences. These elements are not only readily discernible to the eye and palate but are often evident from the very names of the dishes. However, there are considerable regional differences among coast, mountains, and jungle, three distinct environments that, in cultural terms, largely supersede nationality. All these regions, naturally, base their cuisine on local produce: in coastal areas, fish and rice; in the mountains, maize and potato; in the Amazon basin, yucca, palm, cassava, manioc, rice, and fish as well as elements less readily adapted by the Europeans, such as larvae, peccary meat, and drinks made from fermented vegetable juices.

Despite this interchange of foodstuffs between the Andean countries and Europe, certain dishes have changed little since before the Conquest. A prime example is *pachamanka*, whose Quechua name means earth (*pacha*) oven (*manka*), in which heated stones are placed at the bottom of a pit, followed by layers of meat, potatoes, sweet potato, maize, and other vegetables. The *cuy* (guinea pig) is a source of protein in the region and also serves medicinal purposes. An important dish in the Bolivian Andes is *chairo*, a soup made using the black potato known as *chuño*, which is naturally freeze-dried by exposing it to the fierce extremes of temperature found at the high elevations of the *altiplano*, or high plain. In the Andes, cereals such as *quinua* (quinoa) and maize have long been of huge importance to the human diet.

Given the massive differences in topography and demographic patterns, the cuisines of western Latin America vary considerably. Unlike Peru, Bolivia, and Ecuador, where the first Europeans were met by relative abundance and an established cuisine, Chile had an early colonial history characterized by hunger and frustration as the newcomers gradually came to terms with the inhospitable nature of their surroundings and the indigenous cultures they encountered. In Colombia it is perhaps the African influence that was felt most strongly, and that influence is evidenced by *arepas* and other forms of pancakes as well as sauces, and by the use of yams and plantains.

Ceviche, a dish common to most national cuisines along the Pacific seaboard from Chile to Mexico, is white fish or shellfish quickly marinated in lime juice and served with yucca and sweet potato. It can also be adapted as a vegetarian dish. Ceviche has its origins in pre-Columbian times, when it was prepared using *chicha* (maize-based liquid or beverage). It was transformed by the advent of citrus fruits brought by the Spaniards, followed by the influence upon fish preparation exerted by the Japanese, who crossed the Pacific in great numbers to settle in the late nineteenth and early twentieth centuries.

The Asian influence is represented mainly in the Peruvian brand of Chinese cuisine known as *chifa*, also popular in Chile, Ecuador, Bolivia, and elsewhere. Such dishes as *wan ton*, noodles, and fried rice are served in a way not much different from the methods traditional in China. The wok first appeared in Peru in the mid-nineteenth century, and garlic soon kept company with ginger and soy sauce in many *chifa* dishes. By the early twentieth century most comfortably off Peruvian households boasted a Chinese chef. A dish that reflects the Chinese influence is *lomo saltado*, a sautéed beef dish cooked with soy, tomato, and onion and served with fried potatoes.

Drinks reflect a similar range of social and historical processes. *Chicha*, made from maize and popular throughout the region, is a pre-Columbian recipe made during Incan times by the Acllakuna, or chosen Virgins of the Sun, for strictly controlled consumption. Today it is widely available both as a soft drink (usually made from purple maize and known as *chicha morada*) and as an alcoholic drink (called *chicha jora*). Another maize-based beverage, ideal for warming the body against the bitter Andean cold, is *api*, a nonalcoholic drink on sale at highland market stalls.

European settlement brought the grapevine, first to the Ica desert, which had an irrigation infrastructure already put in place by the Incas. Peruvian wine production was decimated as the result of a plague in the nineteenth century, and instead high-quality red wines began to appear in Chile, northern Argentina, and southern Bolivia. Another product of the vine is *pisco*, a variant of grappa also originating in Peru and developed largely by the Italians in that country. Italians have also been influential in developing the chocolate and ice cream industries in Peru, with the prominent D'Onofrio company (bought out in the 1990s by Nestlé) and the soft drink company Salvietti.

The other important European influence in the Andean countries, affecting above all the production of beer, is that of Germany. Breweries as far afield as the Andwanter in Validivia, Chile; the Paceña in La Paz; and the Alemana on the outskirts of Caracas, Venezuela, are all testaments to the quality of this contribution by German immigrants.

A noteworthy aspect of the study of gastronomy in the Andean countries is the exploitation of food and drink to illustrate broader social, demographic, ecological, political, and even ideological themes. The work of Isabel Álvarez, a Peruvian sociologist, chef, and restaurant owner, investigates myriad aspects of her country's history and cultural identity through its cuisine, suggesting the maintenance of a rich regional variety as a means of resisting the standardizing effects of globalization. In an Amazonian context, the U.S.-based Bolivian poet and cultural theorist Nicomedes Suárez Araúz has adapted a collection of recipes left by his mother into a set of striking and universally recognizable metaphors for the continuing destruction and consumption of his native rain forest.

—Keith Richards

Bibliography

Álvarez, Isabel. 1997. *Huellas y sabores del Perú.* Lima: Universidad de San Martín de Porres.

Pereira-Salas, Eugenio. 1943. *Apuntes para la historia de la cocina chilena.* Santiago, Chile: Editorial Universitaria.

Peruvian Cookery Website. http://www.yanuq.com (consulted 15 November 2003).

Suárez Araúz, Nicomedes. 2002. *Edible Amazonia: Twenty-One Poems from God's Amazonian Recipe Book.* Fayetteville, NY: Bitter Oleander.

Van Aken, Norman. 2003. *New World Cuisine: Latin American and Caribbean Cuisine.* New York: Ecco.

Mexican Food. Essentially, Mexican food is a mixture of Spanish products and traditions with indigenous ones. The indigenous contribution consists of maize, beans, tomatoes, cocoa, and, above all, a large variety of chili peppers (a predominantly vegetarian diet), together with the tradition of accompanying and serving foodstuffs with corn tortillas. The Spaniards brought wheat, cows (and hence dairy products), pigs, sheep, chickens, sugar, and a whole range of spices stemming from the Arab influence in the Iberian Peninsula. They also brought with them the art of baking (with wheat flour) and a preference for thick stews and sauces. The combination of the two produced such national dishes as *mole de guajolote* (indigenous turkey served with a thick sauce combining the flavors of a traditional, Arab-influenced Spanish stew with indigenous smoky-flavored chili peppers and cocoa). Even today, it is rumored that immigration officials ask interviewees what *mole de guajolote* is as a quick proof of Mexican identity!

Yet what is considered "Mexican" today was not always considered to be so. Independence in the early nineteenth century brought with it a concern to identify national characteristics in all aspects of life. In Mexican cookery, this national characteristic was found in the use of chili peppers at a time when European, especially French, cookery had moved away from spicy foods. Yet such more clearly indigenous dishes as pozole (a kind of thick stew with boiled corn) and *atole* (a corn-based drink), together with tortillas and other corn-based *antojitos* (snacks) such as tacos, quesadillas, *sopes*, gorditas, and tamales, no matter how mixed-origin they were in their ingredients (using pork fat or cheese, for example), were considered inferior and even immoral up until the time of the Mexican Revolution (1910–1920). It was the post-Revolutionary reevaluation of the indigenous contribution to Mexican identity that confirmed such dishes as an essential part of contemporary Mexican national cuisine—see, for example, the menus of fiestas thrown by Frida Kahlo and Diego Rivera in *Frida's Fiestas* (Rivera Marín and Colle Corcuera 1994)—together with a growing tradition of cookery books published by women writers who chose not to follow the standard divisions between acceptable food of Spanish origin and unacceptable indigenous cookery (Pilcher 1997). (Interestingly, as Pilcher notes, cookery has been one of the few areas where Mexican women have traditionally been most free to imagine a distinctive national identity for themselves.) Changes in lifestyle in urban areas (longer commutes to work) have also meant that Mexicans now have an entrenched restaurant culture that caters to all wallets: from itinerant taco vendors on street corners, to down-home eateries serving *comida corrida* (set lunches), to middle- and even high-class restaurants that specialize in national dishes or in the distinctive variations that stem from the different regions of the Republic, such as the Yucatan peninsula. This tradition of eating out has helped cement ideas concerning what constitutes Mexican national cuisine.

Mexican cuisine continues to evolve, assimilating influences from new immigrant groups (hence the growing preference for the meat for tacos to be cooked on an upright spit, kebab-style; tacos made this way are known as *tacos al pastor*, or *tacos árabes*, when served with a kind of pita bread) or even forcing concessions from the ubiquitous multinational fast-food chains (McDonald's now sells a McMuffin *à la mexicana* in the Republic). Some snobbery is still found in Mexico with respect to Mexican cuisine: many among the upper classes still prefer the less spicy, more prestigious cuisine of France, for example. Nevertheless, in the last few years a *nueva cocina mexicana* (Mexican nouvelle cuisine) movement has come about that uses the more humble and idiosyncratic indigenous products, such as *huitlacoche* (a fungus that grows on maize in the rainy season and that is cooked with fresh Italian pasta), to create dishes that will tempt and surprise even the most refined palates. Furthermore, a number of restaurants specialize in cooking specifically pre-Columbian food, again making acceptable some of the Republic's more unusual and wonderful foodstuffs, such as *chapulines* (grasshoppers) and *gusanitos* (worms, traditionally those that live in and off the maguey cactus and that can be found in the bottom of bottles of mezcal and tequila). Finally, Mexican national dishes such as *chiles en nogada* (green bell peppers covered in walnut sauce and decorated with pomegranate seeds to reflect the colors of the national flag) have also had a boost in popularity since the publication in 1989 of post-Boom writer Laura Esquivel's magical-realist international bestseller *Like Water for Chocolate*, and the even more popular film of the book made in 1992.

—*Thea Pitman*

See also: *Popular Literature:* The Post-Boom; *Visual Arts and Architecture:* Art (Frida Kahlo; Diego Rivera)

Bibliography

Esquivel, Laura. 1993. *Like Water for Chocolate: A Novel in Monthly Instalments with Recipes, Romances, and Home Remedies.* London: Black Swan.

Kennedy, Diana. 2000. *The Essential Cuisines of Mexico.* New York: Potter.

Pilcher, Jeffrey M. 1997. "Cuisine." Pp. 385–389 in *Encyclopedia of Mexico*, vol. 1, edited by Michael S. Werner. Chicago: Fitzroy Dearborn.

———. 1998. *Qué vivan los tamales: Food and the Making of the Mexican Identity.* Albuquerque: University of New Mexico Press.

Quintana, Patricia. 1986. *The Taste of Mexico.* New York: Stewart, Tabori and Chang.

Rivera Marín, Guadalupe, and Marie-Pierre Colle Corcuera. 1994. *Frida's Fiestas: Recipes and Reminiscences of Life with Frida Kahlo.* New York: Potter.

Brazilian Food. A country as vast as Brazil naturally has lots of regional specialties, many of which are linked historically to particular ethnic or immigrant groups or to the local environment. The staples of Brazilian cuisine are rice, beans, and manioc (the meal of a root vegetable also known as cassava, contributed by indigenous tribes), and some of the most traditional Brazilian dishes are adaptations of Portuguese or African foods. Two Portuguese dishes popular in Brazil are *bacalhau* (imported dried, salted codfish) and *cozido* (a meat and vegetable stew). *Feijoada* (a stew made of black beans with a variety of dried, salted, or smoked meats) is the equivalent of soul food in the United States and is considered Brazil's "national dish." It was created by African slaves using the scraps of meat discarded by their white masters in colonial times. *Feijoada* for lunch on Saturdays has become something of an institution in Rio de Janeiro, where it is served with white rice, finely shredded kale, and *farofa* (manioc root meal toasted with butter). It is frequently accompanied by the ubiquitous *caipirinha*, a cocktail made from *cachaça* (sugarcane alcohol), limes, and sugar.

In colonial times Afro-Brazilian slave women worked as cooks for their masters, and thus many of their culinary practices and influences became central to Brazilian cuisine. New ingredients, such as *dendê* palm oil and okra, also arrived in Brazil on the trans-Atlantic slave ships. The African influence is most apparent in the state of Bahia, particularly in the city of Salvador, the main port of entry for African slaves. Two common ingredients of the local specialties are coconut milk and *dendê* palm oil. Some of the most popular dishes of this region include *vatapá* (fresh and dried shrimp, fish, ground raw peanuts, coconut milk, *dendê* oil, and seasonings thickened with bread to form a creamy texture), *moqueca* (fish, shrimp, crab, or a mixture of seafood in a *dendê* oil and coconut milk sauce), *caruru* (a gumbo of shrimp and okra with *dendê* oil), and *acarajé* (a patty made of ground beans fried in *dendê* oil and filled with *vatapá*, dried shrimp, and hot pepper). *Acarajé* is commonly sold on the streets of Salvador by *baianas* (literally, "Bahian women," always of Afro-Brazilian origin), who wear the traditional dress of a white lace blouse and turban. This outfit is closely linked to the costumes worn by the priestesses of the Afro-Brazilian religion *Candomblé*, and Carmen Miranda adopted a stylized version of it for her screen roles in Hollywood.

Bahian woman prepares *acarajé*.
(Jan Butchofsky-Houser/Corbis)

The *churrasco*, or barbecue, is popular all over Brazil, but its origins lie in the southern region, where the *gaúchos*, or cowboys, traditionally roasted meat over an open fire. In the Amazon region the native Indian influence is naturally most prevalent, and the rivers produce a great variety of edible fish, including various members of the piranha family. *Tucupi* is a common ingredient, often served with duck (*pato no tucupi*). It is made from manioc leaves and has a slightly numbing effect on the tongue. Amazonian fruits, such as *acerola* and *cupuaçú*, form the basis of an exotic range of desserts, ice creams, and juices in the towns and cities of the states of Amazonas and Pará. In the arid interior of the northeast, dried salted beef (known as *carne seca* or *carne de sol*) is a local favorite. Tapioca (the starch produced from the manioc root when it is ground into meal) is widely eaten in the form of *beijus*, similar to tortillas and usually stuffed with shredded coconut, or in *cuscuz*, a stiff pudding made with coconut milk. The state of Minas Gerais, with its cooler climate, has a celebrated local cuisine, based on pork, vegetables (especially *couve*, or spring greens), and *tutu*, a kind of refried bean cooked with manioc flour and used as a thick sauce.

The contributions of various immigrant communities to national cuisine are in evidence in most large towns and cities in Brazil. The city of Belém, at the mouth of the Amazon River, for example, has several Japanese restaurants, the legacy of a Japanese colony founded over fifty years ago in the interior of the northern state of Pará. Nowhere is the eclectic mix of eating establishments more apparent than in the city of São Paulo. The influx of migrant labor to work on the coffee plantations of the surrounding state at the turn of the nineteenth and twentieth centuries has led to the creation of one of the most cosmopolitan cuisines in the world. The city's restaurants rival those of New York for their sheer variety and quality. They range from Japanese establishments in the district of Liberdade (and more recently their Korean neighbors) to Italian trattorias and Middle Eastern fast-food chains. German immigrants who settled in the south of Brazil in the nineteenth century also brought with them their culinary traditions and skills, such as the production of sausages, cheeses, and specialty breads and biscuits. The city of Blumenau, in the southern state of Santa Catarina and home to an annual Oktoberfest, has several German restaurants, and the nearby city of Pomerode, which arguably has the best claim to being the most "German" city in Brazil, every year hosts a celebration of local industry, culture, and, not least, food.

—Lisa Shaw

See also: *Cultural Icons:* Latin Americans in Hollywood (Carmen Miranda); Regional and Ethnic Types (The Gaúcho in Brazil); *Popular Religion and Festivals: Candomblé*

Bibliography

Botafogo, Dolores. 1993. *The Art of Brazilian Cookery.* New York: Hippocrene Books.

Idone, Christopher. 1995. *Brazil: A Cook's Tour.* New York: Potter.

Ortiz, Elisabeth Lambert. 1992. *A Little Brazilian Cookbook.* Belfast, Northern Ireland: Appletree.

5

Popular Theater and Performance

In the cultural arenas of Latin American theater and performance the impact of German dramatist Bertolt Brecht and his informal, modernizing approaches is clear, as is the political climate in which are developed and staged the various plays and acts dealt with in this chapter. For example, Brazil's well-known Brecht-inspired dramatist and creator of the Theater of the Oppressed, Augusto Boal, has his counterparts in Chile's José R Morales, Colombia's Enrique Buenaventura (a practitioner of so-called *Nuevo Teatro*, or New Theater), and Alan Bolt, a Sandinista from Nicaragua who is involved in the communitarian theater movement. This chapter reveals the extent to which Latin American theater has been politically committed throughout times of dictatorship and beyond.

But Latin America also has a very strong music-hall tradition that continues to influence the stage and screen in Brazil, Mexico, and Argentina. Such traditions are little known outside their countries of origin, given that international audiences tend to be more interested in avant-garde and politically motivated Latin American theater and performance. For example, the work of Nelson Rodrigues, one of Brazil's most prolific playwrights of the twentieth century, was inspired by the *teatro de revista*, or Brazilian music-hall tradition. Rodrigues's work has enjoyed a revival since the early 1990s. As a result, his plays dominate both amateur and professional productions to such an extent that it is currently difficult for any new work to be staged in Brazil.

In addition to the productions discussed in this chapter, Latin America inevitably contains examples of real performance creativity that do not fit neatly into a "scene," for example the avant-garde circus troupe from Buenos Aires, De la Guarda, whose high-energy circus act *Villa Villa*, performed to a trendy drum and bass soundtrack, has wowed audiences over the last few years at home and in London, Mexico City, and New York.

—*Stephanie Dennison*

Bibliography
Weiss, J. 1993. *Latin American Popular Theater.* Albuquerque: University of New Mexico Press.

Theater of the Oppressed

The Theater of the Oppressed, the creation of Brazilian theater practitioner Augusto Boal (1931–), is highly influential in experimental theater groups throughout the world. Boal developed his Theater of the Oppressed in 1974, during the heady days of the Brazilian dictatorship. The very title of this new theatrical style was bound to create problems with the censors in Brazil, as were Boal's leftist political credentials, for which he had already been imprisoned and tortured for three months in 1972. On his release from prison he went into self-imposed exile in Argentina, Peru, Portugal, and Paris until the late 1980s, and therefore the Theater of the Oppressed was devised outside of Brazil but as a result of Brazilian oppression.

Boal is closely associated with the educator Paulo Freire, a fellow Brazilian, particularly with regard to his use of consciousness-raising techniques. Boal's motivation behind developing new approaches to the theater was to set up a dialogue with the audience and to encourage a sense of empowerment among people on the margins of traditional decision-making processes. So in a performance based on Boal's techniques, the clear divisions between stage and audience, performers and spectators, are replaced by a free-flowing interaction between the two. Workshops replace plays, and the traditional middle-class audience is replaced by marginalized groups. Boal believed that while some people make theater, others *are* theater.

Workshops usually begin by explaining the background of the Theater of the Oppressed to those taking part. This is followed by game playing that is normally very physical. There are over two hundred possible games listed in Boal's seminal work *Games for Actors and Non-Actors* (2002). The purpose of these games is to heighten participants' senses, de-mechanize the body, develop relationships and trust, and have a good time. The workshop then proceeds with exercises. The exercise most associated with the Theater of the Oppressed is "forum theater," whereby actors play out a situation describing some kind of oppression that the audience can relate to, and at the end the audience is asked to intervene and offer alternative solutions or actions for the oppressed character. The workshop usually ends with a lively debate involving all participants.

Such is the impact of Boal's method that over twenty books have been written on the subject and official Theater of the Oppressed centers can be found in seventy countries. The first center was set up in Paris, where Boal's work is more popular than anywhere else in the world, including Brazil. Recent Theater of the Oppressed projects in the United States and the United Kingdom have involved working with the homeless, and in Brazil, Boal and his proponents work with groups in prisons, the MST (Landless People's Movement), maids, the unemployed, and so on. Most recently Boal has turned his attention to reworking more conventional theatrical genres, such as a version in 2002 of Verdi's *La Traviata* set to samba music, which Boal called a "*sambópera.*"

—*Stephanie Dennison*

See also: *Popular Music:* Samba; *Popular Social Movements and Politics:* MST

Bibliography

Boal, Augusto. 1989. *Theatre of the Oppressed.* London: Pluto.
———. 1994. *The Rainbow of Desire: The Boal Method of Theatre and Therapy.* London and New York: Routledge.
———. 1998. *Legislative Theatre: Using Performance to Make Politics.* London and New York: Routledge.
———. 2001. *Hamlet and the Baker's Son: My Life in Theatre and Politics.* London and New York: Routledge.
———. 2002. *Games for Actors and Non-Actors.* London and New York: Routledge.
Brown, Ray. 2002. "Bums off Seats." *London Guardian,* 24 July.
Cardboard Citizens—The Homeless People's Theatre Group Official Website. http://www.cardboardcitizens.co.uk (consulted 1 August 2003).
Theater of the Oppressed Center—Rio de Janeiro. Website. http://www.ctorio.com.br (consulted 1 August 2003).

Theater under Dictatorship

Chile

Late twentieth-century Chilean popular culture was indelibly marked by the experience of military dictatorship, beginning with the coup led by General Augusto Pinochet in 1973 that overthrew the socialist Popular Unity government of Salvador Allende and ended with a plebiscite in 1990. The blow of authoritarianism was all the heavier for having been inflicted upon a society that had known considerable civil liberty. The savagery of the military action taken against real or supposed Marxists, which included summary executions, disappearances, and forced exile, was followed by a period of extended terror as the regime sought to consolidate its position. The term "*apagón cultural,*" or cultural blackout, soon became the governing metaphor for the arts in Chile. For theater the situation was exacerbated by the fact that drama had long had connections with universities, which in turn were associated with radical politics of the Left. The most famous examples of this were the experimental groups founded at the University of Chile and the Catholic University in the early 1940s, during the Marxist coalition Frente Popular (Popular Front) government. These groups were temporarily closed and afterward were stringently controlled, allowed during the first years of military rule to stage little other than classics. During the 1960s playwrights produced by the university environment, such as Jorge Díaz, Sergio Vodánovic, and Egon Wolff, had criticized bourgeois society but presaged social changes feared by the middle classes rather than offering revolutionary alternatives.

Those who continued to work on the stage in Chile after 1973 found that expressing defiance to Pinochet's regime had to be a process of evolution and gradual advancement. Poor judgment could prove costly: a satire on the coup by Grupo Aleph, *Al principio existía la vida* (*And in the Beginning Was Life,*1974), was summarily repressed, and the group's members were jailed before being sent into exile. In contrast Grupo Ictus was sufficiently established and well known abroad to be tolerated, the government allowing its productions to continue as a demonstration to the outside world of the absence of repression.

A series of plays gradually emerged that avoided censorship by making their political content nonconfrontational or coded. José R. Morales's 1974 comment on consumerism, *Orfeu y el desodorante, o El úl-*

timo viaje a los infiernos (*Orpheus and the Deodorant, or The Last Journey to Hell*), was tolerated, but, perhaps due to its subtlety in an era of polarization, it made little impact. The watershed year 1976 saw considerable success for Marco Antonio de la Parra with *Lo crudo, lo cocido, y lo podrido* (*The Raw, the Cooked, and the Rotten*), a political allegory set in a moribund café whose clients are dying off along with their outmoded beliefs. In the same year Luis Rivano's *Te llamabas Rosicler* (*You Were Called Rosicler*) presented a similar image of decay, a house in a once aristocratic neighborhood whose inhabitants' attempts to restore it are doomed. *Pedro, Juan, y Diego* (*Tom, Dick, and Harry*, 1976), by Julio Benaventes and Grupo Ictus, was one of several plays that took up the theme of unemployment and its humiliating effects. *Tres Marías y una Rosa* (*Three Marias and one Rosa*, 1979), which Benaventes created along with the Taller de Investigación Teatral (Theater Research Workshop), gives a complementary viewpoint of women's experience. The play is set among makers of *arpilleras*, the famous patchwork tapestries depicting everyday scenes. The playwright Isidora Aguirre, who had begun to write socially critical plays well before the coup, continued to produce work that clearly allegorized the dictatorship, such as *Retablo de Yumbel* (*Yumbel Altarpiece*, 1987), a work that marked the discovery of a mass grave, dating from just after the coup, by establishing a parallel with Christian martyrdom.

Another group that evolved with the times, seeking a measure of success while avoiding overt censure, was Grupo Feria. Its 1977 production of *Hojas de Parra* (*Leaves from Parra's Book*), by José Manuel Salcedo and Jaime Vadell, attracted sizable audiences. The title plays on the surname of the poet Nicanor Parra (*parra* means "vine"), on whose work the piece is based. However, its central metaphor, a cemetery's encroachment upon a city, was too close to reality for some critics, and the marquee in which it was performed mysteriously burned down. Another Feria creation, *Una pena y un cariño* (*Sadness and Joy*, 1978), satirized the idyllic official image of Chile.

One of the most significant developments in theater in Chile resulting from the dictatorship was that of grassroots performance. A product and expression of popular movements throughout the country's poorer areas, this type of theater continues to respond to all manner of social and political challenges. The movement received a new impetus in the mid-1980s, especially outside the capital city, Santiago, with the political gains made against the dictatorship. Repression has given rise to a heightened creativity in grassroots communication, which has also had its effects on mainstream theater. Many people from established theater groups have collaborated with the grassroots movements, enabling a mutual influence to take place.

This process continues in current Chilean theater: the nation's ongoing debate still sets the option of reconciliation (collective amnesia for some) against that of a full and unblinking examination of the Pinochet legacy. A group of dramatists called La Academia Imaginaria (The Imaginary Academy), which seeks to maintain an atmosphere of inquiry into the country's history through theater, certainly favors the latter option.

—Keith Richards

Bibliography

Albuquerque, Severino João. 1991. *Violent Acts: A Study of Contemporary Latin American*

Theatre. Detroit: Wayne State University Press.
Boyle, Catherine M. 1992. *Chilean Theatre, 1973–1985: Marginality, Power, Selfhood.* London: Associated University Presses.
Ochsenius, Carlos. 1991. "Popular Theater and Popular Movements." Pp. 173–188 in *Popular Culture in Chile: Resistance and Survival*, edited by Kenneth Aman and Cristián Parker. Oxford: Westview.
Versenyi, Adam. 1998. "Social Critique and Theatrical Power in the Plays of Isidora Aguirre." Pp. 159–177 in *Latin American Women Dramatists: Theater, Texts, and Theories*, edited by Catherine Larson and Margarita Vargas. Bloomington: Indiana University Press.

Argentina

The period of military dictatorship in Argentina commonly known as the *Guerra Sucia* (Dirty War) began in 1976 and reached its squalid demise with defeat in the Falklands/Malvinas War of 1982. The Dirty War was an assault on all individuals, groups, and institutions that could be considered left-wing or liberal under practically any definition. Also known as the Process of National Reorganization (*el Proceso*), it was conceived as a complete restructuring of Argentine society that would eliminate all forms of resistance to the extreme Right and reestablish the Catholic Church's authority, male supremacy, and the most stringently conservative codes of behavior. Diana Taylor (1997) has argued that the military rule had its distinctly theatrical element, on the part of both the perpetrators and the civilian resistance. Within this ambiance the material potential for social comment in the theater increased just as the conditions for such content were severely diminished.

Considerably shorter than the dictatorship in Chile, the Argentine experience was nevertheless one of extraordinary brutality. An estimated 35,000 people were seized by the military during this time. Many of these "disappeared" (a verb that began, in this context, to be used transitively). This period, which revealed the profound divisions in Argentine society, at least saw a temporary détente in the realm of drama; the hostilities between realism and experimentation or between naturalism and the avant-garde were shelved as the theatrical response to dictatorship blossomed into *Teatro Abierto* (Open Theater). This movement was known not only for the audacity of its political and aesthetic stance but also for its role in uniting the above-mentioned tendencies. Despite its brevity (1981 to 1985), *Teatro Abierto* is still considered one of the most influential of Argentina's theatrical movements.

Argentina had long been accustomed to periods of authoritarian rule, and interference in artistic production was not uncommon even during spells of formal democracy. The country's theater had developed means of dealing with such conditions by anticipating and precluding right-wing backlashes. However, the first years of the *Proceso* were particularly severe. Some of the country's most established playwrights, such as Griselda Gambaro, Osvaldo Dragún, and Roberto Cossa, were excluded from the state-run theaters during this period. Gambaro, Eduardo Pavlovsky, and many others among the theatrical community were exiled. Some dramatists, such as Rodolfo Walsh and Fernando Urondo, were even "disappeared." Performances of plays considered subversive were often attacked and the theaters housing them were burned down. All these measures had long been employed, albeit more sparingly, but they intensified in 1976.

Controversial plays were treated particularly severely in 1976 and 1977. For instance, the premiere of Pavlovsky's *Telarañas* (*Spider-Webs*, 1976) was first postponed due to problems with the censor and then banned by decree. David Viñas's *Dorrego* (1974) was also banned, and neither of these plays would be performed until the end of military rule.

Dramatists were forced into indirect social comment, such as metaphorical explorations of the murkier areas of family life and personal relationships. Such ostensibly neutral themes nevertheless offered possibilities for political and social analogy. *Telarañas* was a prime example, with its image of domestic dictatorship and victimization within the nuclear family. Cossa's plays *La nona* (*Granny*, 1977) and *No hay que llorar* (*No Need to Cry*, 1979) both criticized the Argentine middle class through allegorical visions of the family, rendered dysfunctional by social circumstances that it had helped to create. *La nona*, with its grotesque central figure of the ancient grandmother whose voracious eating creates hunger all around her, was a particularly vivid depiction of unconsciously brutal inequality, entrenched and intractable.

Another thematic area fruitful for dramatists seeking to avoid censorship was that of games and rituals, often depicted in brutal excess of their normal conditions and rules. The title of Cossa's *Tute cabrero* (1981) is the name of the card game through which one of the three players, all workers at a factory, is to lose his job. *Juegos a la hora de siesta* (*Games during Nap Time*, 1977), by Roma Mahieu, examined childhood cruelty in an allegory of adult sadomasochism, suggesting that the oppressed had a responsibility to resist. Susana Torres Molina's *Extraño juguete* (*Strange Plaything*, 1977) uses a meta-theatrical device in the cathartic enactment of the characters' fantasies. The possibility of multiple interpretations and the self-contained nature of game and ritual meant these plays largely escaped the attention of the censors.

Playwrights also exercised self-censorship. This painful by-product of repression led many to question their own writing and the degree to which they had bowed to pressure. María Elena Walsh, in her influential article "Desventuras en el País-Jardín-de-Infantes" ("Misadventures in Kindergarten-Land," 1986), was one of many writers to lament the effects of this climate of terror upon national intellectual life, even after the transition to formal democracy.

The dictatorship gradually lost its grip on theater, as with society in general, during its final three years, with divided authorities now outwitted by the dramatists' facility in attacking the political situation with increasing force and subtlety. In July 1981, a little over halfway through the *Proceso* years, *Teatro Abierto* arose as a formal movement. Credit for resistance should be given not only to those involved in production but also to critics, such as Osvaldo Pellettieri and Jorge Dubatti, who not only interpreted plays but also helped playwrights, in tacit collusion against the authorities, to avoid censure.

The effects of the *Proceso* are still being felt and discussed in theater as in the other arts. The playwrights mentioned above continue to probe the causes and effects of dictatorship, but they also need to respond to Argentina's present-day condition: the catastrophic economic collapse in 2000–2001 and the comprehensive loss of faith in formal politics. These themes have been taken up not only by the more established Argentine theater but also by the fringe. *Circuito Off*, a Buenos Aires movement whose central figure is the theatrical director Ricardo Bartís, resists orthodox politics as nonrepresentative and rejects both state and corporate funding in its efforts to avoid being forced into a space contrived by political authority.

—*Keith Richards*

Bibliography

Graham-Jones, Jean. 2000. *Exorcising History: Argentine Theatre under Dictatorship.* London: Associated University Presses.

Larson, Catherine, and Margarita Vargas, eds. 1998. *Latin American Women Dramatists: Theater, Texts, and Theories.* Bloomington: Indiana University Press.

Taylor, Diana. 1996. "Rewriting the Classics: *Antígona furiosa* and the Madres de la Plaza de Mayo." Pp. 77–93 in *Perspectives on Contemporary Spanish American Theatre,* edited by Frank Dauster. London: Associated University Presses.

———. 1997. *Disappearing Acts.* Durham, NC, and London: Duke University Press.

Versényi, Adam. 1993. *Theatre in Latin America: Religion, Politics, and Culture from Cortés to the 1980s.* Cambridge: Cambridge University Press.

Popular Theater and Music Hall

Carpa

Carpa (literally "tent" theater) is a popular Mexican theatrical tradition based on vaudeville and improvisation. *Carpa* theaters flourished in the 1920s and 1930s in the working-class districts of Mexico City and many provincial cities, especially in the old Barrio Latino, a brothel district on the west side of the Mexican capital, an area that was demolished during urban renewals of the contemporary era. This form of popular theater was dedicated to representing the common people, and authorities viewed it with suspicion. They closed down many carpas in the 1940s and 1950s to make way for movie theaters.

The stock character of the *carpa,* as in Brazil's *teatro de revista,* was the country bumpkin who is bewildered by the big city but far wiser than the supposedly urbane people around him. In common with popular theater all over the world, the *carpa's* typical cast included city slickers, policemen, effeminate males, harlots, and shrews. A *carpa* show, known as a *tanda,* was very cheap to attend and consisted of four acts, including comic monologues, lewd songs and dances, acrobatic stunts, and romantic skits. Audience participation, in the form of applause, comments, and heckling, was very much part of the experience. The *carpa* relied on improvisation rather than scripts and thus on the skills of individual artists in bringing the stock characters to life.

The modern *carpa* is thought to have begun in the 1870s with temporary theaters set up for the holiday season beginning on the Day of the Dead (1 November) and continuing throughout Christmas, when pastoral plays were performed. The city council of Mexico City then began to issue permits, giving rise to circuses, novelty theaters, variety salons, and *jacalones* (literally "big shacks"). By 1922 these popular theaters had been given the name of *carpas.* The facilities were poor, such as unpredictable stage lights and uncomfortable seats for the audience. Only about one in ten *carpas* had toilets. Stagehands would hang the canvas big top from any available pole, including streetlights.

Performances relied on what has been called a carnivalesque aesthetics, which demanded that those on stage establish an immediate rapport with the poorly educated audience. The early shows were based on the medieval popular culture of feast days and marketplaces, but they already reflected elements of modern industrial society. A favorite theme was the culture clash between rural and urban society, often in the form of an encounter between a city slicker and a country bumpkin. The *carpa* highlighted the negative effects of modern life on the family, masculinity, and patriarchy.

The comic film star Cantinflas (Mario Moreno, 1911–1993) began his acting career in the *carpa* around 1930. In that year he began working regularly at the Carpa Sotelo in a suburb of Mexico City, and three years later he joined the Carpa Valentina, a troupe that belonged to Russian circus performers who had fled the chaos of the civil war in Russia in 1919. After he made the transition to the big screen, many less successful *carpa* performers accused Cantinflas of stealing their characters, costumes, mannerisms, and skits. His success at the box office ultimately dealt a fatal blow to the *carpa* theater.

—*Lisa Shaw*

See also: *Popular Theater and Performance:* Popular Theater and Music Hall (*Teatro de Revista*); *Popular Cinema:* Comedy Film (Cantinflas); *Popular Religion and Festivals:* Popular Festivals (Mexico)

Bibliography

Covarrubias, Miguel. 1938. "Slapstick and Venom: Politics, Tent Shows, and Comedians." *Theater Arts* 22 (August): 685–696.

Pilcher, Jeffrey M. 2001. *Cantinflas and the Chaos of Mexican Modernity.* Wilmington, DE: Scholarly Resources.

Teatro de Revista

Teatro de revista, Brazil's version of music-hall theater, had taken shape by the 1880s and continued to flourish between the 1920s and 1940s. This form of popular theater relied heavily on circus humor, sociopolitical critique, and musical numbers, and it was a particularly *carioca* (Rio de Janeiro–based) phenomenon. It is most closely associated with Artur Azevedo (1855–1908), the most prolific and highly regarded popular playwright of the late nineteenth century.

In the *teatro de revista*, sketches and jokes that hinged on saucy humor and satirical commentary, and an eclectic range of music ranging from Afro-Brazilian rhythms to imported genres like the fox-trot, took precedence over choreography, although the tradition gave center stage to scantily clad dancing girls. Carnival provided the *teatro de revista* with enduring subject matter and was often combined with political satire. From the second decade of the twentieth century onward, the *revista carnavalesca* (carnival revue) came into its own. The *revista carnavalesca* was launched a few months before Carnival each year, and in the 1930s it vied with the *chanchada* films as the mouthpiece for promoting the music destined for the annual celebration. The inversions so intrinsic to Carnival were reflected in the title of the 1915 *revista, De pernas pro ar* (*Topsy-Turvy*). Many future film stars, such as Oscarito and Carmen Miranda, established their acting careers in the *teatro de revista.*

The first of the *revistas de año* (revues of the year) premiered in 1859. At the end of each year, they provided good-humored commentary on political events and focused on daily life through a comic lens. Like the early *chanchadas* of the 1930s and 1940s, they referred to everyday problems with which the audience could identify, such as faulty telephone connections, the failings of public transport, and dirty streets. The revue *O Rio de Janeiro em 1877* (*Rio de Janeiro in 1877*), written by Artur Azevedo, poked fun at the stupidity of the police force and politicians. It also highlighted problems faced by ordinary people during the previous year, ranging from flooding in the then capital and the terrible drought that afflicted the northeast to the yellow fever epidemic that was a regular summer occurrence in the city.

Another dominant theme of these theatrical revues was the culture clash between rural and urban lifestyles, as symbolized by the arrival of an illiterate hick, known as the *caipira*, in the big city. In the *revista Abacaxi* (*Pineapple*, 1893), for example, the actor João Colás played a character referred to simply as "*o caipira do Ceará*," literally "the hick from Ceará," a drought-ridden state in northeastern Brazil. In *O meu boi morreu* (*My Ox Has Died*, 1916), an identical character from Ceará arrives in Rio and is overwhelmed by the marvels and pitfalls of city life; he is finally reassured that his rural existence, however humble, is infinitely preferable. This character became synonymous with the Jeca, who appeared in the eponymous revue *Jeca Tatu* (1919).

The stereotypes of the urban landscape that provided the stock characters of the *teatro de revista* ranged from the uneducated migrant to the indolent civil servant, from the wily *mulata* (mixed-race woman of African and white European descent) and wide-boy *malandro*, or spiv (similar to the term "zoot-suiter"), to the Portuguese immigrant. Furthermore, these revues often featured stylized, white-skinned *baianas* (the caricature of the Afro-Brazilian female street vendors of the city of Salvador), pretending to be black, which would become synonymous with Carmen Miranda's screen persona and later with the *chanchadas* of the 1950s. The male performers in these theatrical shows also often appeared in drag, such as in the revue *Silêncio, Rio!* (*Shut up, Rio!* 1941), in which five well-known female artists were impersonated by male stars.

—*Lisa Shaw*

See also: *Cultural Icons:* Latin Americans in Hollywood (Carmen Miranda); *Popular Cinema:* Comedy Film (*Chanchada*); *Popular Religion and Festivals:* Popular Festivals (Carnival in Brazil)

Bibliography

Cavalcanti de Paiva, Salvyano. 1991. *Viva o rebolado! Vida e morte do teatro de revista brasileiro.* Rio de Janeiro: Nova Fronteira.

Dennison, Stephanie, and Lisa Shaw. 2004. *Popular Cinema in Brazil.* Manchester, UK: Manchester University Press.

Süssekind, Flora. 1986. *As revistas de año e a invenção do Rio de Janeiro.* Rio de Janeiro: Nova Fronteira—Fundação Casa de Rui Barbosa.

Circus and Cabaret

Astrid Hadad (1954–)

The Lebanese-Mexican performance artist and cabaret singer Astrid Hadad undertook professional training in the 1970s first as an actress and subsequently as a singer. Nevertheless, she has rebelled against the solemnity of traditional theater and opera, preferring to focus her work on the most eclectic elements of Mexican popular culture, on ad-lib political satire, and on a revision of women's place in Mexican culture. Her performances demonstrate the influence of early twentieth-century German cabaret, early Mexican cinema, and the post-revolutionary Mexican *carpa* and the *teatro de re-*

Astrid Hadad performs at "La Bodega," Mexico City, August 2001. (Lynsey Addario/Corbis)

vista traditions (the latter a marginal practice in Mexico that blended conservative Spanish operetta with the remnants of the Mexican circus and with sexual license). Her shows are a breathtaking, disturbing, and highly entertaining form of postmodern cabaret. She has worked with other alternative Mexican actresses and singers, such as Jesusa Rodríguez (1955–), but in 1985 she went solo and subsequently formed her own group, Los Tarzanes (an old name used to denominate *pachucos*). Her records include *¡Ay!* (*Woe Is Me!* 1990), *Corazón sangrante* (*Bleeding Heart*, 1995), and *Pecadora* (*Sinner*, 2003).

In the early 1990s, Hadad's work resulted in the creation of a new style of popular music called "heavy nopal" (nopal is the iconic edible cactus that figures on the Mexican flag). Heavy nopal is an ironic reworking of the style and themes typical of the Mexican popular music known as ranchera. Hadad took as her inspiration the early twentieth-century ranchera singer Lucha Reyes (1908–1944). Reyes was the first woman to adopt the raw, belligerent style of singing that male ranchera singers used, and her sexuality also clearly lay beyond the bounds of officially sanctioned heterosexuality. Although this subversive edge had been eroded with time and Reyes had been assimilated into the official pantheon of heroes and heroines of Mexican popular culture, Hadad revived Reyes's repertoire and delivery with a view to reclaiming the singer for her own revisionist approach to official culture. Furthermore, Hadad upped the ante by performing traditional ranchera songs with costumes, props, and gestures that treated the songs' lyrics ironically. Purists of ranchera music were scandalized, calling her "*malinchista*" (a reference to Hernán Cortés's lover La Malinche, who is synonymous with betrayal in Mexico).

After the initial heavy nopal phase, Hadad moved on to a repertoire based on Cuban rumbas and *sones*, together with elements of traditional Spanish and Portuguese popular music. She has also moved from literal but ironic interpretations of traditional songs to irreverent adaptations of such lyrics intended to enhance her ironic approach and to incorporate references to contemporary popular culture and topical events such as the AIDS epidemic, the North American Free Trade Agreement (NAFTA), and the uses of the Internet in Mexico. Her "alternative" views on sexual preference are also increasingly apparent.

Hadad's work has been compared to that of fellow Mexican artist Frida Kahlo as well as to that of the Spanish film director Pedro Almodóvar. Although she denies any direct influence on her work by these artists, she, like Kahlo and Almodóvar, is producing work that has garnered a certain international reputation. Indeed, Hadad is more popular in the United States and Great Britain than in Mexico. This is perhaps due to her irreverent, even sacrilegious, attitude to official Mexican culture. For example, her use of the image of the Virgin of Guadalupe on her skirt in the early 1990s was censored on Mexican television. Nevertheless, heavy nopal has had some influence on young Mexican rock musicians, and Hadad continues to provide a healthy counterweight to the myopia of the regime.

—*Thea Pitman*

See also: *Popular Music:* Mariachi, Ranchera, Norteña, Tex-Mex; *Popular Theater and Performance:* Popular Theater and Music Hall (*Carpa*); *Cultural Icons:* Religious and Mythical Figures (La Malinche; Virgin of Guadalupe); *Visual Arts and Architecture:* Art (Frida Kahlo)

Bibliography

Alzate, Gastón. 1997. "Expandiendo los límites del teatro: Una entrevista con Astrid Hadad." *Latin American Theater Review* 30, no. 2: 153–163.

Constantino, Roselyn. 2000. "And She Wears It Well: Feminist and Cultural Debates in the Work of Astrid Hadad." Pp. 398–421 in *Latinas on Stage*, edited by Alicia Arrizón and Lillian Manzor. Berkeley: Third Woman Press.

Guillermoprieto, Alma. 1995. *The Heart That Bleeds: Latin America Now*. New York: Vintage.

Hadad, Astrid. n.d. "Astrid Hadad." Astrid Hadad Website. http://www.astridhadad.com (consulted 13 June 2003).

Guillermo Gómez-Peña (1955–)

The work of notorious contemporary Mexican/Chicano performance artist Guillermo Gómez-Peña has included such extreme acts as trying to crucify himself on a beach outside San Francisco one Easter to see the reaction of passersby (on the assumption that passersby would intervene and save him from death). The wider context of this work was an exploration of U.S. citizens' reactions to "Latino immigrants." He was within hours of dying by the time he was taken down from his cross.

Gómez-Peña's main aim in his performance art is to disturb people's preconceived ideas about racial and national identity and about self and other. Much of his work depends on the physical reality of the U.S.-Mexican border to give it coherence. Since 1992, however, the border has become a much more flexible metaphor that enables him to explore many of the more conceptual borders of the postmodern world. He often uses his own body and personal experiences as a source of inspiration and as a site for the incarnation of his performances. He was born and raised in Mexico City, although since 1978 he has lived and worked in the United States and now has dual nationality. Yet he fits neither national culture: he is too *pocho* (Anglicized) and too antinationalist for Mexican culture, and he is too Hispanic to blend into mainstream U.S. Anglo culture (he deliberately cultivates the look of a brown-skinned, illegal immigrant, complete with bushy mustache). Furthermore, since he is not really Chicano by birth he is not fully integrated into that cultural group either. He uses his experiences of not fitting into these various cultures as the subject of his art in order to criticize them. It is his intention to explode such stable, discrete concepts of national identity in favor of the much more fluid reality of life in the borderlands.

Gómez-Peña tends to work in collaboration with other performance artists, often Latino, such as the Chicano Roberto Sifuentes and the Cuban-American Coco Fusco. Activities include setting up "living dioramas" in museums, where they pose as postmodern "saints" in Plexiglas boxes for days on end. Museum visitors can confess their sins via a computer terminal and request that Gómez-Peña and colleagues perform various acts to exorcise the visitors' cross-racial fears and desires. He is also known for the videos of his performances, such as *Border Brujo* (1988, 1990), in which he plays the role of an extravagantly attired cross-cultural shaman who again offers to confront and exorcise racial fears. In the same performance he also incarnates a wide array of border personae such as the *pachuco*, the upper-class Latino, and the redneck to exemplify racial tensions. More recently he has also published a number of books to accompany or supplement his performances, for example the comic books *Friendly Cannibals* (1996) and *Codex Espangliensis* (2000), produced in conjunction with artist Enrique Chagoya, and *Dangerous Border Crossers* (2000), a genre-defying account of some of his performances, performance personae, and extra-performance autobiographical experiences. His work is undoubtedly both entertaining and effective in disturbing the audience. Gómez-Peña has met with increasing success in recent years and has taken his performances as far afield as Wales and Russia.

—*Thea Pitman*

Bibliography

Aldama, Frederick Luis. 1999. "The New Millennial Xicano: An Interview with Guillermo Gómez-Peña." *XCP: Cross-Cultural Poetics* 5: 7–11.

Drake, Jennifer. 2001. "The Theater of the New World (B)Orders: Performing Cultural Criticism with Coco Fusco, Guillermo Gómez-Peña, and Anna Deavere Smith." Pp. 159–173 in *Women of Color: Defining the Issues, Hearing the Voices*, edited by Diane Long Hoeveler and Janet K Boles. Westport, CT: Greenwood.

Fox, Claire F. 1996. "Mass Media, Site Specificity, and the U.S.-Mexico Border: Guillermo Gómez-Peña's *Border Brujo*." Pp. 228–243 in *The Ethnic Eye: Latino Media Arts*, edited by Chon A. Noriega and Ana M. López. Minneapolis: University of Minnesota Press.

Gómez-Peña, Guillermo. 2000. *Dangerous Border Crossers*. London: Routledge.

Gómez-Peña, Guillermo, Enrique Chagoya, and Felicia Rice. 2000. *Codex Espangliensis: From Columbus to the Border Patrol*. San Francisco: City Lights; Santa Cruz, CA: Moving Parts.

Coco Fusco (1960–)

Since the late 1980s the writer, performance artist, and academic Coco Fusco has produced a body of work that is at the same time accessible, experimental, and fiercely polemical. She can be considered a popular artist at least as regards the subject matter, intended audience, and beneficiaries of her work: her performances are usually staged in public spaces where they are more immediate, avoid the label "art," and achieve maximum impact. She often creates apparently absurd situations that nonetheless present an essential truth, creating public awareness of some inherently vicious treatment of those without formal rights or representation. Often the targets of her work are damaging and iniquitous cultural prejudices and stereotypes. As a U.S. citizen of Cuban origin, she is able to inform such performances with personal experience.

Perhaps her most famous piece of performance art is the 1992 *Two Undiscovered Amerindians Visit the West*, which Fusco cocreated with Guillermo Gómez-Peña and which was performed during the highly controversial celebrations marking the fifth centenary of Columbus's voyages to the Americas. It sought to lampoon the notion of European "discovery" of the Americas and the ethnographic exhibition of peoples during the colonial era. Fusco's and Gómez-Peña's three-day sojourns in a golden cage as inhabitants of Guatinau, a fictional island in the Gulf of Mexico, had unexpected consequences. First, even though the authors intended the piece to be transparently satirical, numerous members of the public believed the story was true. Second, the artists were criticized on moral grounds (chiefly that of misleading the public) by individuals either unable to comprehend the spirit of the performance or else disingenuously sidestepping its political implications.

Another collaboration with Gómez-Peña, *Mexarcane International* (1994–1995), was performed in shopping malls and presented a sham agency offering "ethnic talent for export." Again the performance was not announced as such, an omission intended to heighten the satire of the mall's sterile atmosphere: a safe (white) haven where the exotic may be sampled without risk. *Mexarcane International* was performed in Scotland, England, and Canada, but did not appear in the United States.

Stuff (1996), created by Fusco and the Mexican-American Nao Bustamante, deals with the mythology feeding the phenomena of sex tourism and cultural tourism through enactments of visits to the performers' countries of origin. Despite their obvious differences, Cuban prostitution, or *jineterismo*, and the Maya liberation struggle of the supporters of Zapatismo in Chiapas are shown as attractions linked by globalization and its attendant processing, in the Western mind, of the exotic. *Stuff* uses material collected from conversations with women in both Cuba and southern Mexico, and the show includes members of the audience brought on stage and given roles as foreign visitors, sampling foods and repeating lines of dialogue. *Stuff* flouts political correctness in exploring the dubiously patronizing motives behind New Age exoticism, bogus radicalism, and the rationalization of sex tourism.

Sudaca Enterprises (1997) was created and performed with Juan Pablo Ballester and María Elena Escalona during the ARCO international contemporary art fair in Madrid in 1997. The target of this performance was the hypocrisy of selling Latin American art at a time when people from the former Spanish colonies (*sudacas*, in derogatory Iberian Spanish slang) were subject to new, stringent immigration laws. In *Sudaca Enterprises* the participants, clad in Zapatista-style masks and Andean hats, were illicitly selling T-shirts with messages contrasting the prices of the artwork with the cost to a Latin American immigrant of entering and surviving in Spain.

Coco Fusco has demonstrated that her work is not driven merely by political ideology. A series of writings and performances focusing on Cuba, her mother's homeland, highlights some of the contradictions experienced by its people. She has developed links with Havana's best-known independent gallery, Espacio Aglutinador, where her performance *El evento suspendido* (The Suspended Event, 2000) marked her own experience of accidental exile from the island and solidarity with those unable to leave.

Dolores from 10 to 10 (2002), performed with Ricardo Domínguez in 2000, enacts the experience of a worker in a *maquiladora*, one of the many assembly plants situated just inside Mexico that allow U.S. companies to avoid high labor costs and other responsibilities. Shut in a room for twelve hours by her boss on suspicion of planning to start a union, the woman resisted efforts to force her to resign before taking the company to court. The situation of *maquila* workers was also the subject of the performance *ACCESS DENIED* in 1998.

The 2001 video *Els Segadors*, whose title is taken from a hymn to Catalonia, features inhabitants of Barcelona singing in "traditional" Catalan, coached in the language by a Cuban immigrant. This project aimed to expose the contradictions in Catalan nationalism, long oppressed under the regime of Francisco Franco but intolerant, in today's more prosperous climate, of the cultural diversity brought by immigration.

—*Keith Richards*

See also: *Popular Social Movements and Politics:* Zapatismo; *Popular Theater and Performance:* Circus and Cabaret (Guillermo Gómez-Peña); *Travel and Tourism:* Cultural Tourism; Sex Tourism

Bibliography
Fusco, Coco. 1995. *English Is Broken Here: Notes on Cultural Fusion in the Americas.* New York: New Press.
———, ed. 2000. *Corpus Delecti: Performance Art of the Americas.* London: Routledge.
———. 2001. *The Bodies That Were Not Ours: And Other Writings.* London: Routledge.

Circo-Teatro

Circo-teatro is a popular twentieth-century Brazilian "theater-circus" that grew out of the traditional circus (which originated in Renaissance Europe) in the second half of the nineteenth century, partly inspired by developments in the circus in Argentina at the same time. In most cases these small and inexpensively run circuses functioned like traveling variety shows; they offered clowns, magic acts, plenty of musical interludes, and one-act plays, often set to music. The inclusion of these plays in the circus program may have been inspired by the *entremez*, the tradition of short comedic plays set to music that had been brought over from Portugal to Brazil in the first half of the nineteenth century. The popularity of the *circo-teatro* was such that they were said to have dealt a fatal blow to the traditional theater outside of Brazil's large cities.

The *circo-teatro* kept diversifying throughout the twentieth century in order to survive competition from radio, cinema, and, later, television. Despite the infamous proliferation of television sets in Brazil, there were between 100 and 150 *circo-teatros* in the suburbs of São Paulo in 1980. By the 1980s the shows included dancing competitions, groups playing samba and northeastern music, lengthy interviews with contestants for prizes offered in between acts, and pop hits from television and radio. The guaranteed success of such a format was and is evident in the continued popularity of the weekend television staple in Brazil, the so-called *programa de auditório*, or variety show. The *programa de auditório* also has its roots in popular theater and the circus and was popularized on television by the legendary variety show host Chacrinha and media mogul Sílvio Santos, whose personal style of locution in turn influenced the *animadores*, or ringmasters, in the circuses.

Circus audiences were free to voice their opinions during the shows (talking loudly, booing and heckling actors depicting greedy landowners, and so on), which created a sense of community spectatorship. The audience could even influence the performances, as long as it did not show disrespect for the artists themselves. In the *circo-teatro* this sense of audience participation was reinforced on a practical level by the help offered by the local population, and children in particular, in setting up the circus tent. Most of the circus members came from poor neighborhoods similar to those where they perform. Those who were "discovered" in the circus and went on to become radio, television, and film stars often returned to their communities and made guest appearances in these small circuses, in much the same way that they would appear on Sílvio Santos's variety television program, for example.

One of the most significant elements of the circus in Brazil was the clown, who in the late nineteenth century played a pivotal role in the development of circus theatrics. The so-called *palhaço-ator*, or actor-clown, is regarded as unique to Brazil. These clowns were also responsible for increasing the importance of music in the circus, often by setting plays to music or singing slightly rude *modinhas*, the popular musical form of the time, presumably under pressure of competition from the increasingly popular *teatro de revista*, or music-hall theater, in cities such as Rio de Janeiro. A number of successful *palhaços-atores* at the turn of the century went on to have careers in the music industry, thus reinforcing the link among clowning, singing, and musicality. Eduardo Sebastião das Neves was one such *palhaço-ator* who found success as a musical performer. Like many singing clowns, he was black and he had *ginga*, or swing, considered essential in black entertainers for successful comedic performances. In the popular cinema, four such "clowns" who started out in the circus are Mazzaropi, who would also burst into song in his films; Oscarito and Grande Otelo, the well-known double act of the Atlântida *chanchadas*, both renowned for their facial expressions; and Mussum, the black member of the Trapalhões, who combines a background in music (samba) with humor based on facial expressions.

—*Stephanie Dennison*

See also: *Popular Music:* Samba; *Popular Theater and Performance:* Popular Theater and Music Hall (*Teatro de Revista*); *Mass Media:* Radio (Brazil); Television (Brazil); *Popular Cinema:* Comedy Film (*Chanchada*)

Bibliography

Dennison, Stephanie, and Lisa Shaw. 2004. *Popular Cinema in Brazil.* Manchester, UK: Manchester University Press.

Tinhorão, José Ramos. 2000. "Circo brasileiro: O local no universal." Pp. 193–214 in *Entre Europa e África: A invenção do carioca*, edited by Antonio Herculano Lopes. Rio de Janeiro: Topbooks/Edições Casa de Rui Barbosa.

Street Theater

Mexico

In the southern Mexican state of Chiapas the very existence of Mayan ethnicity and culture has long been under insidious threat from landowning concerns, tacitly supported by political authority. The theater group Lo'il Maxil (Monkey Business) was formed in 1985, two years after the founding of the Mayan cultural center of which it forms a part: Sna Jtz'ibajom (House of the Writer) in San Cristóbal de las Casas. Lo'il Maxil comprises members of communities speaking the indigenous Tzeltal and Tzotzil languages, although plays are performed only in Tzotzil and Spanish. The group aims at nothing less than salvaging Mayan cultural heritage in the area, redressing the erosion caused by centuries of oppression. Taking as a model the Chiapaneca poet and novelist Rosario Castellanos (1925–1974), who incorporated the indigenous oral tradition into her work and insisted upon its value, the group became a workshop for writers keen to develop their craft. Building up from small-scale grassroots publishing and needing to overcome initial suspicion of their intentions from all sides, Sna Jtz'ibajom mounted a literacy project in the early 1980s, funded by the Smithsonian Institution. It has become a well-respected institution supported by several major international bodies.

The group has a repertoire of twelve plays, some of which are available on video in Spanish, written and developed collectively by the group's members. Lo'il Maxil also benefits from North American collaboration: ten of its plays were directed by Ralph Lee of New York's Mettawee River Company, and Robert Laughlin acts as impresario in several essential areas. Diego Méndez Guzmán, current director of Sna Jtz'ibajom, is Mexico's first Mayan novelist and provided the basic idea for the play *Herencia fatal* (*Deadly Inheritance*, 1993). This is a true story of sibling jealousy over a disputed inheritance resulting in fratricide, a crime dealt with by the local community according to Mayan tradition, bypassing central authority. On a different note the comedy *¿A poco hay cimarrones?* (*Who Believes in Spooks?*, 1990) lampoons irrational fears by revisiting the Mayan legends that in colonial times grew up around the phenomenon of runaway African slaves, who were seen as supernatural beings. Other Lo'il Maxil productions are more directly political, such as *De todos para todos* (*From All for All*, 1994). Based on the Zapatista rebellion, this work has been performed for Mayan immigrants in the United States as well as on television in Mexico.

The growing international reputation of Lo'il Maxil led in 1995 to their involvement and participation in the John Sayles film *Men with Guns*, set in Central America in the 1980s at the height of the persecution of native peoples under the banner of anticommunism. Shot in Chiapas, this film owes its sense of authenticity to Sayles's insistence on using indigenous actors, as well as to the fact that such strife was and still is unresolved.

—Keith Richards

See also: *Popular Social Movements and Politics:* Zapatismo; *Language:* Indigenous Languages

Bibliography

Frischmann, Donald. 1995. "Contemporary Mayan Theater and Ethnic Conflict: The Recovery and (Re) Interpretation of History." Pp. 71–84 in *Imperialism and Theatre*, edited by Ellen Gainor. London: Routledge.

Laughlin, Robert. 1995. "*From All for All*: A Tzotzil-Tzeltal Tragicomedy." *American Anthropologist* 97, no. 3: 528–542.

Sna Jtz'ibajom, the House of the Mayan Writer Website. http://www.laneta.apc.org/snajtzibaj/theatre.htm (consulted 1 August 2003).

Steele, Cynthia. 1994. "'A Woman Fell into the River': Negotiating Female Subjects in Contemporary Mayan Theatre." Pp. 239–258 in *Negotiating Performance: Gender, Sexuality, and Theatricality in Latin/o America*, edited by Diana Taylor and Juan Villegas. Durham, NC, and London: Duke University Press.

The Andes

The Peruvian theater collective Yuyachkani Cultural Group was founded in 1971, and since then it has remained one of the most innovative and politically committed in the country. Its focus has remained upon native Andean culture and the Andean indigenous experience of twentieth-century social upheaval. This can be seen from the Quechua name (meaning "I am thinking" or "I am remembering"), which hints at the power of reflection and historical memory in the process of resistance. This identification is evident too from the group's aesthetic, that is, its use of dance, masks, and ritual, an eclecticism reflected in the title "Cultural Group." Despite its chosen subject matter, Yuyachkani has generally used humor as a common element in its repertoire.

The presentation of *Encuentro de zorros* (*Meeting of Foxes*, 1985) confirmed the group's tendency to see Peruvian nationhood as inevitably and inexorably multicultural. The piece was based on the posthumously published novel by José María Arguedas, *El zorro de arriba y el zorro de abajo* (*The Fox from Up Above and the*

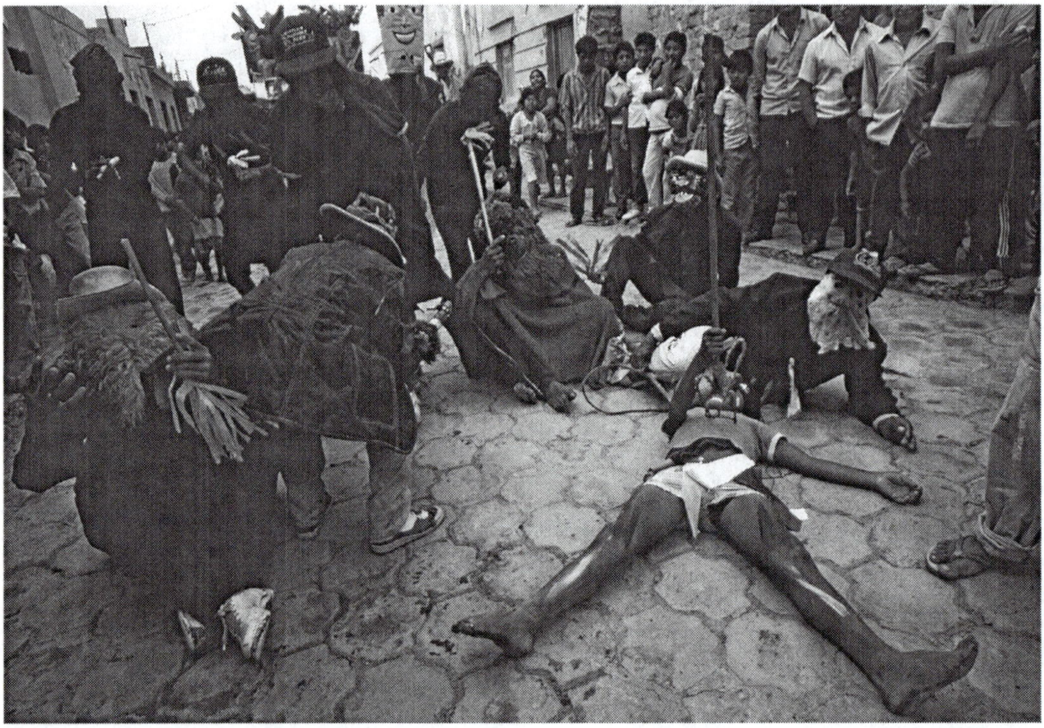

Dancers perform during an annual street festival in the small fishing village of Eten along Peru's northern coast, 30 July 1988. (Nathan Benn/Corbis)

Fox from Down Below, first published in 1971), which examines the extraordinary demographics of Peru in the 1960s and the massive migration from the rural Andes to the coastal cities.

Adiós Ayacucho (1990) was based on Julio Ortega's novel of the same name (which was translated as *Ayacucho, Goodbye*) and speaks for the inhabitants of the region most ravaged by Peru's political violence. Its protagonist, after being tortured and killed by soldiers, travels to Lima in search of the soul and body parts he has lost. The displacement and victimization of indigenous peasantry caught in the cross fire between the Peruvian military and the Maoist Shining Path guerrillas occurred again and again, and to some extent still occurs, in the Peruvian Andes.

Santiago (*St. James*, 2000) reflects the hemorrhaging population of many Andean areas as a result of unrest and economic decline. It depicts a long-neglected religious ceremony revived, in desperation, by the three remaining inhabitants of a remote village. *Antigone* (2000) is another development of a literary text, this time José Watanabe's transposition of the Sophocles play to an Andean context.

Yuyachkani has at times been criticized for softening or even abandoning its political stance; at others it has been charged with excessive militancy and pessimism. However, the group has never compromised its commitment to the culture from which it draws.

In Ecuador a number of groups perform theater that explores political themes, though not necessarily using Andean native tradition. Malayerba (Weed), founded in Quito in 1979, has a repertory of social allegory that includes *Pluma y la tempestad* (*Feather and the Storm*, 1997). This play adapts a rural tale to the context of a modern city, transforming the original woodland setting into a dangerous barrio. The play warns against disenchantment and cynicism and the tendency toward solitude and alienation in contemporary life. Another Ecuadorian group is Zero No Zero. Its iconoclastic director and writer is Peky Andino, whose *Ulises y la máquina de perdices* (*Ulysses and the Pheasant Machine* (1998) is an exercise in virtuoso wordplay in monologue.

The Bolivian group Teatro los Andes, based in Sucre, also reworks a Greek classic with implicit references to national politics. The group explores themes concerning Andean culture, such as the acceptance of death, in *Los abarcas del tiempo* (*The Sandals of Time*, 1995) and political repression in *Ubu en Bolivia* (1994), a transposition of the Alfred Jarry play *Ubu roi*.

—*Keith Richards*

See also: *Popular Social Movements and Politics:* Shining Path

Bibliography

Arguedas, José María. 2000. *The Fox from Up Above and the Fox from Down Below* (1971). Translated by Frances Horning Barraclough. Pittsburgh: University of Pittsburgh Press.

Muguercia, Magali. "Cuerpo y política en la dramaturgia de Yuyachkani." http://www.magarte.com/ensayos/cuerpo_politica_yuyachkani.html (consulted 4 September 2003).

Soberón, Santiago. 2001. "Treinta años de Yuyachkani." *Babab*, no. 10 (September). http://www.babab.com/no10/yuyachkani.htm (consulted 4 September 2003).

Teatro de Los Andes Website. http://www.utopos.org/LosAndes/andesp.htm (consulted 4 September 2003).

6

Travel and Tourism

Latin America continues to grow in popularity as a tourist destination for the American and British traveler, and perhaps one of the main reasons for this is the variety of holiday experiences that the region offers. These range from traditional beach tourism holidays, such as those found in the immensely popular Cancún resort in Mexico, to the trendy adventure tourism and gap-year travel undertaken predominantly by American and European students. But despite the steady growth in tourism to the region, a number of factors deter potential tourists. The fluctuation in value of local currency can affect tourists' interest in traveling to Latin America as well as Latin Americans' capacity to travel at home or abroad. In 1998, for example, when the Brazilian currency was strong, many Brazilians rushed to get a passport for the first time and travel to the United States and Europe. As a result of this trend, and of foreign travelers such as Argentines being scared off by comparably high prices in Brazil and choosing cheaper destinations, the domestic tourist market in Brazil suffered greatly. During the political and economic crisis in Argentina in 2000–2001, many tourists stayed away, afraid of high prices, difficulty in obtaining money within the country, and popular unrest.

A number of Central American countries, such as Nicaragua and El Salvador, continue to be no-go areas in the minds of prospective tourists, given their history of political turmoil. Others are avoided because of well-known terrorist organizations, such as Shining Path in Peru and the Zapatistas in the Chiapas region of Mexico—even though neither movement is a serious threat to tourists. In Colombia, however, domestic revolutionary groups such as FARC (Revolutionary Armed Forces of Colombia) and the ELN (National Liberation Army) pose a real threat to foreign visitors: the fact that 28 Americans have been kidnapped since 2000 explains the U.S. State Department's harsh warnings of the dangers posed by "narcoterrorist groups" in Colombia.

Although neither the State Department nor the British Foreign Office, at the time of this printing, has named any Latin American countries as no-go areas, their Websites do instruct their citizens to enter some regions only as part of organized tours (in particular, the border areas surrounding Colombia), and to proceed into others with care (Rio de Janeiro and Mexico City, for example). The State Department discourages all holiday and nonessential travel to a small number of destinations, including Haiti, the North Atlantic Autonomous Region (RAAN) in Nicaragua, the northern border areas of Ecuador and Paraguay, and a number of rural and border areas in Colombia. In these regions, travelers are warned, policing is often at a minimum and gangs of drug traffickers have been active.

The other no-go area for U.S. citizens is Cuba. Since the socialist revolution of 1959, fear of communism in their backyard has led the United States to enact a series of embargoes against Fidel Castro's government, which are still in place today with no signs of improved relations between the two nations for the foreseeable future. One of the results of this troubled relationship is that it is very difficult for U.S. citizens to travel to Cuba, at least for the pure and simple purpose of tourism.

—*Stephanie Dennison*

See also: *Popular Social Movements and Politics:* Castrismo; Shining Path; Zapatismo

Bibliography

The U.K. Foreign and Commonwealth Office official Website. www.fco.gov.uk (consulted 22 June 2004).

U.S. Department of State homepage. www.state.gov (consulted 22 June 2004).

Ecotourism

A relatively recent term, *ecotourism* describes tourism that is environmentally friendly, in terms of both the experience of the tourists who visit natural sites and the consumption of resources. In Latin America, ecotourism is flourishing, to differing degrees, in Costa Rica, Ecuador, and Brazil.

Costa Rica has the most developed ecotourism sector, primarily for two reasons. The country contains an estimated 500,000 plant and animal species, making it one of the most biodiverse countries in the world. Furthermore, Costa Rica's strategies for protecting and conserving its natural environment are well developed, with an estimated 27 percent of its landmass designated as national parks. As a result, tourism has become Costa Rica's main source of foreign income, surpassing even the banana trade by 1992.

One of the best-known and most frequently visited of Costa Rica's ecotourism sites is Monteverde Cloud Forest Reserve, situated in the Tilaran mountains of central Costa Rica. The term "cloud forest" refers to a rare type of tropical ecosystem that has nearly constant clouds and high humidity, which produce a rich and unique vegetation. Monteverde's popularity is due, on the one hand, to its rare and impressive animal and plant life, and on the other, to its relatively well-developed accommodations for tourists.

Ecuador is also well known for its biodiversity, and ecotourism is growing there, too. The main ecotourism destination in Ecuador is the famous archipelago of the Galapagos Islands, designated Galapagos National Park in 1959. On these remote islands, tourists can follow in the footsteps of naturalist Charles Darwin and glimpse species, such as giant tortoises and rare lizards, that have lived in virtual isolation for centuries. The number of visitors to the park is restricted; it currently stands at 25,000 per year.

Diver and barberfish, Galapagos Islands, March 1994. (Stephen Frink/Corbis)

Though the Galapagos Islands are Ecuador's most striking ecotourist attraction, mainland Ecuador has also been successful in developing ecotourism on a smaller scale. Kapawi Ecolodge, located in Ecuador's Amazonian region, is typical of many ecotourism projects. It accommodates visitors in huts built in traditional Achuar Indian style, making use of local, renewable materials such as twine to bind the roofs, and solar energy to provide both power and hot water. In this way, tourists have a chance to observe nature, while their impact, in terms of consumption of resources, is minimal—a key feature of ecotourism.

Brazil, the other country with a strong ecotourism sector based on the Amazonian region, is counted among the ten "megadiversity countries" in the world. It not only contains vast numbers of species, it also boasts one-third of the entire rainforest on the planet. The most popular ecotourism destination here is the Amazon, the rainforest that runs alongside much of the famous river and covers millions of square kilometers. Though the Amazonian region is the best known of Brazil's ecological sites, ecotourism has also recently taken root in the wetland ecosystem of Pantanal, located in southwest Brazil. Although small in comparison to the Amazon, the Pantanal hosts wildlife species such as caiman and capybara.

To prove its commitment to new forms of tourism, Brazil hosted the World Tourism Forum for Peace and Sustainable Development in 2003. During the event, President Luis Inácio Lula da Silva stated that the kind of tourists he wanted to encourage were pacifists and environmentalists. Ecotourism in Brazil rose 15 percent during 2003, compared with a 3 percent rise in tourism overall. Nevertheless, Lula has a battle on his hands if he wants to see more ecotourists in the country, since only 50,000 people visited the Amazon, Brazil's most attractive ecotourist destination, compared with the millions that flood to Rio de Janeiro in pursuit of beach tourism, and occasionally, sex tourism.

Ecotourism is a growing sector in several countries in Latin America. However, as a number of researchers have noted, ecotourism has its drawbacks. For instance, the limit that the Galapagos National Park Management Plan imposes on tourists each year is always exceeded, and the result is disturbance of the animal life and vegetation. Research on other locations has noted similar problems, as well as the erosion of paths due to the number of visitors. Nevertheless, ecotourism is an important development within tourism in Latin America and within these countries' economies.

—Claire Taylor and Stephanie Dennison

See also: *Travel and Tourism:* Beach Tourism; Sex Tourism

Bibliography

Damon, Thomas A., and Christopher Vaughan. 1995. "Ecotourism and Wildlife Conservation in Costa Rica: Potential for a Sustainable Partnership?" Pp. 211–216 in *Integrating People and Wildlife for a Sustainable Future*, edited by John A. Bissonette and Paul Krausman. Bethesda, MD: Wildlife Society.

Hamilton, Dominic. 2003. "Pocket-Sized Paradise." *Geographical: Royal Geographical Society Magazine* 75, no. 4: 96–101.

Menkhaus, Susan, and Douglas J. Lober. 1996. "International Ecotourism and the Valuation of Tropical Rainforests in Costa Rica." *Journal of Environmental Management* 47: 1–10.

Pearson, David L., and Les Beletsky. 2002. *Brazil: Amazon and Pantanal, The Ecotravelers' Wildlife Guide.* San Diego: Academic Press.

"Planeta: Global Journal of Practical Ecotourism." www.planeta.com (consulted 13 March 2004).

Stem, Caroline J., James P. Lassoie, David R. Lee, and David J. Deshler. 2003. "How 'Eco' Is Ecotourism? A Comparative Case Study of Ecotourism in Costa Rica." *Journal of Sustainable Tourism* 11, no. 4: 322–347.

Wallace, George N., and Susan M. Pierce. 1996. "An Evaluation of Ecotourism in Amazonas, Brazil." *Annals of Tourism Research* 23, no. 4: 843–873.

Weaver, David B. "Magnitude of Ecotourism in Costa Rica and Kenya." *Annals of Tourism Research* 26, no. 4: 792–816.

Sex Tourism

In this form of tourism, mostly concentrated around the Caribbean and Brazil, tourists travel abroad in order to engage in sex with locals, whether paid or in exchange for goods. The term has, in recent years, become synonymous for many with the procurement of child prostitutes abroad.

With cheaper charter flights available from the United States and Europe direct to many countries in Latin America, and with many traditional sex tourism destinations such as Thailand and the Philippines clamping down on illegal activities by foreign visitors, the sex tourist (more often than not, a male from the United States) is increasingly turning his attention to destinations such as Costa Rica and Brazil. In Costa Rica a network of hotels, bars, massage parlors, along with airport staff and taxi drivers, makes the procurement of sex relatively easy. Adult prostitution is legal, and paying a child for sex has only recently been made illegal, although it continues to be a common practice.

A host of Internet sites make the procurement of paid sex easy for foreign travelers. These sites rarely use the term "prostitution." Men are invited to meet "new friends," "special ladies," and "escorts." The friendliness, coy flirting, and perceived exoticism of the women, many of whom are of mixed race, along with the flattery they offer their new foreign "friends," make it easy for many tourists to indulge in prostitution in places like Brazil, even though they would not use the services of a prostitute back home. In Rio de Janeiro many of the beachfront bars, particularly those around a block known as Prado Júnior, are well-known meeting places for prostitutes and their tourist clients. There the working girls tend to sit in pairs and flirt with anyone who is interested, then strike up a conversation and arrange a rendezvous in a nearby hotel or apartment. Streetwalkers tend to come out only very late at night. At the far end of Copacabana, on the edge of the Ipanema district, potential customers run the risk of getting a surprise if they take one of the beautiful young "ladies" on display on street corners back to their hotel: they are the notorious *travestis*, Brazil's uncannily feminine-looking pre-op transvestites, popular with both hetero- and homosexual clients.

In 1994, ECPAT (End Child Prostitution, Child Pornography, and the Trafficking of Children for Sexual Purposes) estimated that 500,000 children in Brazil were involved in the sex trade. The domestic market for child prostitutes in Brazil is very large, and reports of outrageous abuses of children appear in the press almost daily. In the Amazon region, for example, an estimated 10,000 children work as prostitutes. Organized fishing trips from São Paulo to the Pantanal were recently exposed as a front for child sex tourist excursions, and a UNICEF study recently identified sixty-five lodgings in the Pantanal that are fronts for whorehouses. Ironically, the Pantanal and the Amazon, Brazil's two major ecotourism regions, are popular sex tourist destinations.

Cuba's relationship to the global sex tourism trade has been ambivalent over the years. In the 1950s, prior to the revolution, when tourism provided the second largest influx of hard currency to the island, Cuba was termed the "brothel of the Caribbean." The revolution aimed to eradicate prostitution and, along with it, sex tourism—and was largely successful for many years. But the collapse of the Soviet Union and the resultant loss of income for Cuba meant that the country had to look for new sources of foreign currency. From 1989 onward, the Cuban government turned once again to tourism as a source of income. Tourism has grown by roughly 20 percent per year. Figures from 1998 show an estimated 1.4 million tourists, the majority from Europe or Canada. However, the revival of tourism in Cuba is not without its problems. In addition to intensifying the societal divisions between Cubans and foreign tourists, tourism has led to a resurgence of the sex trade, since Cubans desperate for hard currency turn to prostitution to earn dollars.

Though exact data are hard to come by due to the unregulated nature of this business, researchers generally agree that by the 1990s Cuba had become one of the major sex tourism destinations, alongside established locations such as Thailand and the Philippines. Most prostitution within Cuba takes place around the tourist centers of Havana, Varadero, Santiago de Cuba, and Santa Lucia. The vast majority of sex tourists who visit Cuba are men, while the prostitutes are predominantly women or girls, although there are some male prostitutes.

O'Connell Davidson's research into sex tourism in Cuba provides one of the clearest studies of this phenomenon. She notes that the women and girls who work as prostitutes catering to tourists—known in Cuba as *jineteras* (literally, jockeys)—exchange sex not only for cash but also for goods, drinks, or meals. In looser arrangements, the woman or girl supplies not only sex, but a range of additional services: she serves as guide or translator, she provides lodging, and she cooks, in exchange for which the man pays for food, drinks, and luxury items such as cosmetics and clothing. But unlike some of the more established sex tourist destinations, Cuba has no network of brothels. Instead, the sex tourist in Cuba deals with individual prostitutes—a system that represents a financial saving for the client and, as a result, has encouraged the rise in sex tourism.

Despite the fact that it provides an influx of needed cash to some Latin American countries, sex tourism is clearly a problem. It not only contributes to the spread of HIV and AIDS, it encourages the exploitation of vulnerable women and girls, who earn meager sums of money. Furthermore, complex issues of race are implicated in the sex tourism trade—for example, maintaining the dangerous myth of the lascivious dark-skinned Latin woman. While tourism in general has therefore provided economic benefits for countries such as Cuba, the accompanying rise in sex tourism is of concern.

—*Claire Taylor and Stephanie Dennison*

See also: *Travel and Tourism:* Ecotourism

Bibliography

Clancy, Michael. 2002. "The Globalization of Sex Tourism and Cuba: A Commodity Chains Approach." *Studies in Comparative International Development* 36, no. 4: 63–88.

"EPCAT International." www.epcat.com (consulted 13 March 2004).

Fernandez, Nadine. 1999. "Back to the Future? Women, Race, and Tourism in Cuba." Pp. 81–89 in *Sun, Sex, and Gold: Tourism and Sex Work in the Caribbean*, edited by Kamala Kempadoo. Lanham, MD: Rowman & Littlefield.

Kempadoo, Kamala, and Jo Doezema, eds. 1998. *Global Sex Workers: Rights, Resistance and Redefinition.* New York: Routledge.

"Libertad Latina—Defending Latina and Indigenous Women's Rights." www.libertadlatina.org (consulted 13 March 2004).

O'Connell Davidson, Julia. 1996. "Sex Tourism in Cuba." *Race & Class* 38, no. 1: 39–48.
Patullo, Polly. 1996. *Last Resorts: The Cost of Tourism in the Caribbean.* London: Cassell.
Schwartz, Rosalie. 1997. *Pleasure Island: Tourism and Temptation in Cuba.* Lincoln: University of Nebraska Press.
Trafficking of Brazilian Prostitutes to Work Abroad—Argentina, Portugal, United States, and United Kingdom. Online brochure.
"UCSB's SexInfo—Sex Tourism." University of California at Santa Barbara. www.soc.ucsb.edu/sexinfo/ (consulted 13 March 2004).

Adventure Tourism and Gap-Year Travel

Latin America is fast becoming one of the top destinations for both adventure tourists and students taking a "gap year" between school and university.

Adventure tourism has been booming since the 1980s, most notably in the United States and Australia, largely as a reaction to the increasingly urban and sedentary nature of many people's lives in these countries. Given the proximity of Latin America to the United States, it is no surprise that many of the top adventure tourism destinations are found in that region. Three of the top ten scuba-diving destinations in the world, for example, are located in Mexico and Honduras.

Adventure tourism generally involves the practice of noncompetitive sports that involve some degree of risk—rafting, mountaineering, caving, and modes of travel that require physical effort and even privation (trekking, sailing, cycling). All this adventure is set against the backdrop of stunning landscapes and remote locations, previously the preserve of the ecotourist. The "adventure" lies in the innovative nature of the undertaking and the challenge it provides for individuals to break personal barriers or records. World-famous geographical features such as the Andes and the Amazon guarantee Latin America's popularity with adventure tourists.

Chile and Argentina are key destinations for the region's best mountaineering, trekking, and skiing, while boat trips up and down the Amazon and its tributaries are well-established routes for the adventure tourist. The highlands of Central America are a popular destination for cycling, mountain biking, and, at slightly lower elevations, whitewater rafting. Costa Rica also offers locations where zip-lining (zipping across the top of the jungle canopy on a wire, or flying fox) can be practiced. This concept of "adventure," however, does not include the results of political instability or poor hygiene, even though being kidnapped or catching dysentery might constitute an adventure and are the realities that still face the independent traveler in many parts of Latin America.

For young adults from English-speaking nations, the custom of taking a year off between school and university (the "gap year") has become popular in recent years. Although accurate statistics are hard to come by, it is estimated that around 25,000 gap-year travelers from the English-speaking world are traveling in Latin America at any one time.

Gap-year travelers tend to be more limited by tight budgets than adventure tourists but less limited by time constraints. Thus, although adventure tourism does feature substantially among the activities that attract gap-year travelers to Latin America, activities such as work (teaching English, volunteering for conservation work or com-

Patagonian Andes and Lake Pehoe in Torres del Paine National Park, 1995. (Pablo Corral Vega/ Corbis)

munity projects) and study (primarily language courses) also figure into their motivations, not to mention the rich cultural heritage and traditional tourist attractions that the region has to offer (museums, ancient ruins, beaches, national parks, and so on). Latin America is popular with this type of traveler because it combines so many different types of attractions in one place, and because it is generally an affordable destination for budget travelers, especially once they are off the beaten track.

The gap-year traveler tends to move around the region in an effort to experience the greatest diversity of attractions, even combining the visit to Latin America with a trip around the world. Most often, the gap-year traveler enters Latin America at Mexico's northern border and travels south through Central America and the west side of South America toward Patagonia and Tierra del Fuego in the far south of Argentina—or he or she undertakes the same journey in reverse. This route is used so often it has been nicknamed "The Gringo Trail." Other popular routes include La Ruta Maya (the Mayan Route) through southern Mexico, Guatemala, Belize, and Honduras and The Inca Trail in Peru. Both routes allow the traveler to focus on the pre-Columbian culture that these regions have to offer. Many gap-year travelers also plan their routes to coincide with key festivals, such as Carnival in Brazil or the Day of the Dead in Mexico.

—Thea Pitman

See also: *Popular Religion and Festivals:* Popular Festivals (Carnival in Brazil; Mexico)

Bibliography

Gifford, Nigel, and Richard Madden. 2004. *The Adventurous Traveller: The One-Stop Guide to Travel with a Challenge*. London: Robinson.

Hall, Colin Michael. 1992. "Adventure, Sport and Health Tourism." Pp. 141–158 in *Special Interest Tourism*, edited by Betty Weiler and Colin Michael Hall. London: Belhaven Press.

Hindle, Charlotte, et al. 2003. *The Gap Year Book*. Hawthorn, Australia: Lonely Planet.

Lumsdon, Les, and Jonathan Swift. 2001. *Tourism in Latin America*. London: Continuum.

Plomin, Joe. 2001. "Gap Year Popularity Soars." *London Guardian*, 13 September. www.education.gardian.co.uk/print/0%2C3858%2C4256380-108229%2C00.html (consulted 22 April 2004).

Tabata, Raymond S. 1992. "Scuba Diving Holidays." Pp. 171–184 in *Special Interest Tourism*, edited by Betty Weiler and Colin Michael Hall. London: Belhaven Press.

Beach Tourism

A common type of tourism within Latin America, particularly in those countries situated in the Caribbean or having a Caribbean coast. Beach tourism, which includes several subcategories, usually relates to holidays taken in hotels or all-inclusive resorts, frequently involving minimal contact with the host community.

Cuba remains one of the principal destinations for beach tourism within Latin America, and what are frequently termed "sun and sand" holidays dominate there. Cuba had a strong tourist industry in the early to mid-twentieth century, with its heyday in the 1950s, but after the Cuban Revolution, foreign tourism declined precipitously. In the late 1980s and early 1990s, though, as a result of the collapse of the Soviet Union and the loss of its substantial economic support to Cuba, there have been concerted efforts in Cuba to expand the tourism industry. According to Lumsdon and Swift, this expansion has entailed a change in government policy: Cuba has had to make alliances with capitalist tourism enterprises. They note that Cubanacan, the official government tourism organization, has engaged in joint ventures with a variety of multinational hotel companies, including Grupo Sol from Spain and Golden Tulip International. Today, Cuba's principal beach tourism destination is the major resort of Varadero, although there are over fourteen kilometers of beaches to the east of the capital, Havana, and a variety of other resorts, including the Isla de la Juventud (Island of Youth) and the islet Cayo Largo del Sur.

Among the Latin American countries that rely on tourism as a source of foreign income, the Dominican Republic is a leader. With a population of a mere 7.3 million, it welcomes 2.2 million tourists per year. As early as the 1960s, the country had set up its ministry of tourism. Tourism development initially came from local investors, although by the late 1970s and early 1980s, foreign companies such as Radisson, Sheraton, and Club Med began to invest in Dominican tourism.

One of the main developments in beach tourism in the Dominican Republic in recent years—as in several other Caribbean countries—has been the creation of so-called all-inclusive resorts. For a sojourn at one of these resorts, the tourist pays one price to the travel agent that covers all costs—accommodation, meals, drinks, and leisure activities. These types of resorts are becoming increasingly common throughout the main beach tourism destinations in Latin America; in the Dominican Republic

The northwest coast of the Dominican Republic at Playa Sosua with hotels in the background, 2003. (Danny Lehman/Corbis)

such resorts can be found in locations such as Boca Chica, Playa Dorada, and Puerto Plata, among others. Though such all-inclusive deals are marketed as advantageous for the tourist, providing one set price for the holiday, they reduce the amount tourists spend in local markets, since they no longer spend money outside the resort. As a result, these resorts have been dubbed "enclave resorts." The bulk of the profits goes to the multinationals that own the resorts rather than remaining in the country itself.

But beach tourism in the Dominican Republic is far from homogenous. K. J. Meyer-arendt and colleagues have provided a typology of the Dominican Republic's coastal resorts, identifying five types of beach tourism ranging from the "urban *balneario*" ("seaside resort"), the "domestic destination resort," the "integrated domestic/international destination resort," and the "interactive enclave resort" to the "self-contained enclave resort."

Of all the developing countries, Mexico tops the list in revenue earned from tourism over the last twenty-five years, with tourism now the country's second largest employer. Mexico's beach tourism provision is found both along its extensive Pacific coastline and throughout the Gulf of Mexico and its Caribbean coastline. The established beach resorts in Mexico will be familiar names to many—places such as Acapulco and Puerto Vallarta on the central Pacific Coast. By the late 1980s, however, Cancún, a resort in Mexico's Yucatan peninsula, had surpassed all other sites in Mexico to become the single largest tourist destination in the country, attracting an estimated four million tourists per year.

The statue of Christ the Redeemer that towers over Rio de Janeiro, Brazil, and attracts hundreds of thousands of tourists each year. (Courtesy of Alex Nield)

In Brazil, despite the growing popularity of beaches on the country's unspoiled and relatively safe northeastern coast, and despite the new flights from the United States and Europe to northeastern cities such as Salvador, Recife, and Fortaleza and southern cities in and around Florianópolis, Rio de Janeiro remains Brazil's most popular beach tourism destination. Like Havana, Rio de Janeiro is a name that has been associated with glamorous and exotic holidays since the first half of the twentieth century. The city's most famous beaches are Copacabana and Ipanema, and it is to these *bairros* (neighborhoods) that most tourists head. (*Bairros* has become somewhat of a misnomer for these areas, since one million people live in Copacabana alone.)

Rio has the advantage of offering beach and urban tourism simultaneously, with its downtown colonial architecture, important national and tourist museums (including the Fine Arts Museum and the Carmen Miranda Museum), and some of the most famous scenery in the world (including Sugarloaf Mountain, with its dramatic cable-car ride to the summit, and the 30-meter-high Christ statue, built in 1931 atop Corcovado Mountain, both offering breathtaking views of the city).

However, the well-publicized incidents of tourist muggings in Rio de Janeiro, together with the city's association with sex tourism, have resulted in the growth of all-inclusive resorts that are removed from the city. These range from the sophisticated Club Med resorts down the coast from Rio and near Salvador in the northeast, to the cut-price package deals, to specially built resorts offered by the British travel agency Going Places.

Although Cuba, Mexico, the Dominican Republic, and Brazil are the leaders in beach tourism in Latin America, other countries such as Venezuela have a smaller but growing beach tourism sector. Venezuela has an extensive coastline along the Atlantic Ocean and the Caribbean Sea, with a variety of resorts, the majority of which are located to the west of the capital, Caracas. In addition to these mainland resorts, Isla Margarita, situated in the Caribbean Sea off the north coast of Venezuela, is an increasingly popular beach resort.

—*Claire Taylor and Stephanie Dennison*

See also: *Travel and Tourism:* Beach Tourism; Sex Tourism; *Cultural Icons:* Latin Americans in Hollywood (Carmen Miranda)

Bibliography

Clancy, Michael J. 1999. "Tourism and Development: Evidence from Mexico." *Annals of Tourism Research* 26, no. 1: 1–20.

Freitag, Tilman G. 1994. "Enclave Tourism Development: For Whom the Benefits Roll?" *Annals of Tourism Research* 21, no. 3: 538–554.

Lumsdon, Les, and Jonathan Swift. 2002. *Tourism in Latin America.* London: Continuum, pp. 84–98.

Martin de Holan, Pablo, and Nelson Phillips. 1997. "Sun, Sand, and Hard Currency: Tourism in Cuba." *Annals of Tourism Research* 24, no 4: 777–795.

Meyerarendt, K. J., R. A. Sambrook, and B. M. Kermath. 1992. "Seaside Resorts in the Dominican Republic: A Typology." *Journal of Geography* 91, no. 5 (Sept.–Oct.): 219–225.

Urban Tourism

Urban tourism is not a popular kind of tourism in Latin America. For most foreign tourists, large cities function primarily as gateways to the more exotic, ethnic, and exciting destinations, and tourists generally avoid spending time in the cities, worried about the dangers to their health and personal safety. Generally the tourists who visit cities in their own right are international and national business travelers, and nationals visiting friends and relatives. Nevertheless, a few big cities constitute attractions to tourists in themselves, despite checkered histories of crime and pollution. Factors that influence a city's appeal to tourists include its cultural life (museums, galleries, festivals); its social life (restaurants, café culture, nightlife); its architecture, monuments, parks, and public spaces; the shopping opportunities it affords the visitor; and its proximity to other tourist attractions (volcanoes, beaches, pyramids).

Buenos Aires ranks as one of the most attractive urban destinations in Latin America, despite its less-than-ideal location as a gateway city for the rest of Argentina. Indeed, trips to *estancias* (ranches) in the flat and seemingly endless *pampas* (grasslands) surrounding the city constitute the most touted local excursions. Other highlights—Patagonia, the Andes, and even the Iguazú Falls—are all too far off to visit easily. Another popular day trip—a ferry ride across the River Plate to Uruguay—takes tourists out of Argentina altogether. Nevertheless, the city scores highly for its cultural and social life, its architecture and parks, and its tourist facilities, and it is considered relatively safe in terms of street crime and pollution.

Though the city has no pre-Columbian archeology to offer, it has some colonial architecture and a vast array of nineteenth-century French-style buildings. The city used to be nicknamed "the Paris of the South," and it is this elegant and refined ambience that the local authorities market to the tourist. Tourists concentrate on the sights of the downtown area, the *microcentro*, and the upper- and middle-class *barrios* to the north. In these areas are a number of excellent museums and art galleries, including the *Museo Nacional de Bellas Artes* (National Fine Arts Museum) and the *Malba-Colección Constantini* (the Buenos Aires Museum of Latin American Art), which opened in 2001 and contains the largest and most important collection of Latin American art anywhere in the continent.

Despite the city's outstanding museums and galleries, tango and the bohemian café culture in which it thrives are the major draw of the city for foreign tourists, particularly the working-class *barrios* of San Telmo and La Boca in the south of the city. San Telmo is known for its *tanguerías*, cafés furnished with faded elegance, where visitors and locals alike go to hear and see tango performed. The antique shops of San Telmo are another popular attraction, along with the Sunday flea market in the central square, brimming with even more antiques and street entertainment. La Boca is the name given to the port area founded by poor Italian immigrants in the nineteenth century, the home of Argentina's largest soccer club, Boca Juniors, and their stadium, La Bombonera.

Finally, Buenos Aires also attracts tourists who are captivated by the mystique of cultural icon Evita Perón—"pilgrimages" organized by the local authorities and commercial enterprises include trips to the Casa Rosada (presidential palace), to the Museo Evita in the *barrio* of Palermo, and to her grave in Recoleta cemetery. (Similar tours also follow the footsteps of other local cultural icons such as tango singer Carlos Gardel and Jorge Luis Borges, poet, short-story writer, and leading figure in the so-called Boom in Latin American literature.

Although the "beaches and pyramids" model is now the focus of Mexico's tourism promotion, Mexico City was the nation's star tourist attraction until the 1940s. It still attracts tourists interested in culture and history, though crime and pollution are sources of concern for visitors to Mexico City today. The city was built on top of pre-Columbian ruins—the excavated foundations of the Aztec Templo Mayor (Great Temple) lie just to one side of the Metropolitan Cathedral and next to the Palacio Nacional (National Palace) in the Historical Center of the city. It also has a wealth of beautifully preserved colonial buildings in both the Historical Center and many of the outlying districts (former villages), such as Coyoacán and San Angel, now incorporated into the conurbation of the Federal District, as the city is known locally.

Mexico City also houses some of the most important museums and art galleries in the whole of Latin America. In the huge Museo Nacional de Antropología (National Anthropology Museum) in Chapultepec Park, for example, cultural artifacts from around the republic are on permanent display, leaving only replicas in their places of origin. Other key cultural sites include the (Modern Art Museum) Museo de Arte Moderno and the murals painted by the great

Mexican muralists Diego Rivera, David Alfaro Siqueiros, and José Clemente Orozco in public buildings around the city, such as the Palacio de Bellas Artes (the city opera house) and the Museo de las Culturas Populares (Museum of Popular Culture) in Coyoacán. Even the tourist who views Mexico City as primarily a gateway to more tranquil parts of the country often visits at least some of these features.

Furthermore, in terms of contemporary popular culture, the city is home to the shrine of the Virgin of Guadalupe, Mexico's patron saint, and tourists can join with the thousands of pilgrims who come to pay homage to the Virgin on 12 December every year. The Plaza Garibaldi is the most renowned place in Mexico to see mariachis performing their music. Huge arts and crafts markets dot the city, and a vibrant restaurant culture caters to all budgets and palates. The city is also strategically located for visiting the great pyramids at Teotihuacán and the archaeological site of Tula to the north, and the striking volcanoes Popocatépetl and Iztaccíhuatl to the south.

In recent years, the governments of both Argentina and Mexico have also invested substantially in improving the infrastructure and attractions of both cities in order to preserve their places in the urban tourism market.

—Thea Pitman and Stephanie Dennison

See also: *Popular Music:* Mariachi, Ranchera, Norteña, Tex-Mex; Tango; *Sport and Leisure:* Soccer; Food (Mexican Food); *Cultural Icons:* Political Icons (Evita); Legends of Popular Music and Film (Carlos Gardel); Religious and Mythical Figures (Virgin of Guadalupe); *Popular Literature:* The Boom; *Visual Arts and Architecture:* Art (José Clemente Orozco; Diego Rivera; David Alfaro Siqueiros)

Bibliography

Caistor, Nick. 2000. *Mexico City: A Cultural and Literary Companion.* Oxford: Signal Books.

Garasa, Delfín Leocadio. 1987. *La otra Buenos Aires: Paseos literarios por barrios y calles de la ciudad.* Buenos Aires: Sudamericana-Planeta.

Lumsdon, Les, and Jonathan Swift. 2001. *Tourism in Latin America.* London: Continuum.

Saragoza, Alex M. 1997. "Tourism." Pp. 1413–1416 in *Encyclopedia of Mexico*, vol. 2, edited by Michale S. Werner. Chicago: Fitzroy Dearborn.

Wilson, Jason. 1999. *Buenos Aires: A Cultural and Literary Companion.* Oxford: Signal Books.

Cultural Tourism

The term covers a wide range of activities, including visits to heritage attractions (archaeological sites and old buildings, museums and art galleries) and trips to see indigenous peoples in their "native" environment and to experience their way of life, traditional festivities, and rituals. Cultural tourism means sampling the contemporary popular culture in the broadest sense—everything that has been written about in the other chapters of this book: carnival, tango, tequila, and so on.

Cultural tourism has been the most enduring form of tourism practiced in Latin America, if not the most popular. Independent leisure travelers to the region in the early twentieth century (that is, the pioneers of contemporary tourism) were typically attracted by the mystique of the indigenous cultures of the Latin American nations. Latin American nations, in turn, capitalized on their cultural attractions in order to profit from tourist revenues. In Mexico beginning in the 1920s, for example, coincident with the flourishing cultural nationalism of the post-revolutionary era, the government promoted Mexican folklore and colonial architecture to attract tourists from the United States and Europe.

In the 1970s, Latin American nations shifted the focus of their tourism promotion to their natural attractions, particularly their beaches, but cultural tourism remains on the itineraries of even the most deckchair-bound tourist. A typical image of Mexico in tourist literature is that of the archeological ruins at Tulúm, perched on the edge of cliffs overlooking the white sands and azure seas of the Caribbean—visitors can thus effortlessly combine the Mayan heritage with the leisure of the beach. Indeed, the current trend in Latin America is for tourists to take holidays that combine several specialized types of tourism—ecotourism, adventure travel, and cultural tourism—with the traditional beach package. As a result, cultural tourism has increasingly become part of tourists' motivations for visiting Latin America since the 1960s.

Latin American nations offer cultural tourists a chance to explore a wide variety of cultural heritages. The countries that most actively promote their pre-Columbian cultures are Mexico and Peru, the crucible of Aztec and Mayan civilizations in the first case, and of the Inca Empire in the second. The Mexican government has invested heavily in making its pre-Columbian heritage accessible to tourists since the 1920s, sponsoring extensive excavations and rehabilitation of key sites, improvements to roads and facilities at such sites, and construction of museums. Much of this work has been coordinated by the INAH (Instituto Nacional de Antropología e Historia, the National Institute of Anthropology and History) since its founding in 1938. Key sites include the enormous pyramids at Teotihuacán; the numerous Mayan pyramids of the Yucatan peninsula and the southeast, such as Chichén Itzá and Palenque; as well as the Museo Nacional de Antropología in Mexico City, which houses many of the most famous pre-Columbian artifacts from across the nation, such as the huge statue of the goddess Coatlícue and the Piedra de Sol (Sun Stone), or Aztec Calendar.

For the Peruvian tourist board (FOPTUR), Machu Picchu, the "lost city" of the Incas perched on a mountaintop in the Andes, constitutes a tourist attraction par excellence. Rediscovered in 1911, the ruins have been a popular attraction since the 1950s. Currently they are the most important tourist destination in Peru, attracting up to 300,000 visitors a year. Peru also successfully promotes its pre-Incan heritage, particularly the mysterious Nazca Lines, huge earthworks depicting animals and other symbols that can only properly be viewed from the air and whose construction remains a mystery. Other countries active in the promotion of their pre-Columbian heritage include Guatemala (Mayan ruins) and Chile (the Moaias or giant heads of Easter Island).

Although it is a less important draw for visitors than pre-Columbian culture, colonial culture is also successfully exploited as a tourist attraction by many Latin American countries. Colonial culture comprises architecture and artifacts that date from the time of the Spanish Conquest (the very late fifteenth and the sixteenth century) to the Era of Independence (the early nineteenth century). The Mexican tourist industry actively promotes such cities as

Machu Picchu, Peru, 2000. (Jim Erickson/Corbis)

Guanajuato, San Miguel de Allende, and Zacatecas on the basis of their colonial architecture rather than their proximity to any ruins, beaches, or other tourist attractions. Countries with less to offer in archeological sites emphasize their colonial heritage in their promotional literature. Paraguay promotes its seven *misiones* (missionary settlements).

Although pre-Columbian and colonial cultural attractions are a long-established wing of the tourism industry in Latin America, national tourist boards have only recently grasped the attractiveness to the international tourist of the real live Mayans living in the shadow of the grand pyramids built by their ancestors. The ethnographic dimension of cultural tourism is currently an area that is expanding rapidly. The attraction of real live Mayans lies behind current marketing strategies for La Ruta Maya (the Mayan Route), a tourist itinerary that encompasses southern Mexico, Guatemala, Belize, and Honduras. The governments of the Latin American nations that have the greatest concentrations of indigenous communities are now actively involved in preserving the folkloric charm of traditional festivals, dances, and rituals for the tourist's gaze—this is the focus of officially sponsored tourist enterprises in the states of Puno in Peru and Oaxaca in Mexico. For the tourist who wishes to engage more fully with the real political situations of indigenous communities, tours are also run by nongovernmental organizations and local indigenous groups themselves. The Zapatistas of southern Mexico, for example, have organized *Zapaturs* since the mid-1990s, taking tourists to isolated rebel communities and even into prisons where Zapatistas were being held.

The attraction of contemporary popular culture (of a less indigenous and often urban variety) is also a major focus of cultural tourism. For example, Buenos Aires markets itself as the home of tango, whereas Carnival in Rio de Janeiro is a key date on many tourists' itineraries (the four days preceding Ash Wednesday). Even typical food is part of the cultural attraction of some nations, particularly Mexico and Argentina. Furthermore, all the above forms of cultural tourism (the historical, the ethnographic, and the popular cultural) can be found coexisting dynamically across Latin America to produce a particularly attractive product to the tourist.

Despite the value of cultural tourism to Latin America, serious dangers accompany its unregulated expansion. Many archaeological sites have been irreparably damaged by too many visitors, and the effect of tourists on indigenous communities could either fossilize their traditional way of life in an unnatural way or mold it to fit foreign conceptions of what indigenous traditions should look like. Though most governments have now taken some measures to curb the damaging effects of cultural tourism (and thus protect their revenues), the dangers still persist, particularly with regard to the lives of indigenous peoples. However, evidence suggests that a balance is being established between the demands of the tourist market for souvenirs and the traditions of the indigenous producers. For example, textiles are being produced in the traditional way but then made into items that Westerners will find useful, such as the ubiquitous Guatemalan purses. García Canclini also notes the success of the potters of Ocumichu in Michoacán state, Mexico, in adapting their traditional iconography to incorporate images and themes that tourists might like to see represented. Thus indigenous communities may benefit from the revenues of tourism without wholly sacrificing their cultural identity and traditions.

—*Thea Pitman*

See also: *Popular Music:* Tango; *Popular Social Movements and Politics:* Zapatismo; *Sport and Leisure:* Food; *Popular Religion and Festivals:* Popular Festivals (Carnival in Brazil)

Bibliography

Cooper Alarcón, Daniel. 1997. *The Aztec Palimpsest: Mexico in the Modern Imagination.* Tucson: University of Arizona Press.

García Canclini, Néstor. 1995. *Hybrid Cultures: Strategies for Entering and Leaving Modernity.* Trans. by Christopher L. Chiappari and Silvia L. López. Minneapolis: University of Minnesota Press.

Lumsdon, Les, and Jonathan Swift. 2001. *Tourism in Latin America.* London: Continuum.

Moreno, J. M., and M. A. Littrell. 1996. "Marketing Culture to Tourists: Interpreting and Translating Textile Traditions in Antigua, Guatemala." Pp. 138–144 in *Tourism and Culture*, edited by M. Robinson, N. Evans, and P. Callaghan. Newcastle-upon-Tyne: University of Northumbria Press.

Van den Berghe, P. 1995. "Marketing Mayas: Ethnic Tourism Promotion in Mexico." *Annals of Tourism Research* 22, no. 3: 568–588.

Zeppel, Heather, and Colin Michael Hall. 1992. "Arts and Heritage Tourism." Pp. 47–68 in *Special Interest Tourism*, edited by Betty Weiler and Colin Michael Hall. London: Belhaven Press.

7

Popular Literature

This chapter highlights a number of fictional works that have made an impact on domestic markets in Latin America. Internationally, the region is perhaps best known for the so-called Boom novels, but the range of literary forms in Latin America goes beyond the more traditional genres of the novel, the poem, and the play. The chapter discusses some of the more popular of these alternative forms, such as comic books and *literatura de cordel* (chapbooks), and their successors, the *fotonovela.* Also worthy of mention is the so-called *testimonio* or testimonial literature of the region, which is currently enjoying a high profile abroad. The most famous example is Rigoberta Menchú's 1983 work, *Me llamo Rigoberta Menchú y así me nació la conciencia* (literally: My name is Rigoberta Menchú and this is how I developed a conscience), translated in 1984 as *I, Rigoberta Menchú: An Indian Woman in Guatemala.* The work of Menchú, a Nobel peace prize winner, partly inspired the infamous canon debates of the 1980s, when works of "fiction" such as hers were replacing those of Cervantes, for instance, in university courses, much to the chagrin of academic traditionalists.

Popular literature is an area of Latin American culture where considerable cultural cross-fertilization takes place; the most obvious example is the large number of fictional works that have been transformed into television serials and films. The work of Chico Buarque is an interesting case in point. A singer-songwriter associated with the Brazilian protest music of the period of dictatorship, Buarque has also written plays, musicals, and two best-selling novels. His first novel, *Estorvo* (*Turbulence*, 1991), was transformed into a feature film by Ruy Guerra in 1998. But it is not just traditional literary forms that have been given the celluloid treatment: comic strips, particularly in Brazil, have proved successful at the box office, such as Miguel Paiva's comic detective character *Ed Mort* (1997). The Argentine Quino, one of Latin America's best-known cartoonists internationally, produced a series of short films in the 1980s for the ICAIC (The Cuban Film Institute) called "Quinoscopios." The new wave of television comedians in Brazil, such as the team who produce and star in *Casseta e planeta urgente!*, have clearly been influenced stylistically and in terms of humor by their own roots in comic strips.

—*Stephanie Dennison*

See also: *Popular Music:* Brazilian Protest Music

The Boom

The Boom is a term for the explosive growth in the popularity of Latin American fiction that took place during the 1960s. The Boom was not restricted to a local or even Latin American readership, but signified an international profile and a worldwide reputation. It was centered on a group of talented male writers that included the Colombian Gabriel García Márquez (born 1928), the Argentine Julio Cortázar (1914–1984), the Peruvian Mario Vargas Llosa (born 1936), and the Mexican Carlos Fuentes (born 1928). Critics have also linked to this literary phenomenon the Chilean José Donoso (1924–1996) and the Cubans Guillermo Cabrera Infante (born 1929) and Alejo Carpentier (1904–1980), among others. Critics generally agree that three main impulses were responsible for the phenomenon of the Boom: the political circumstances of the period, especially the Cuban Revolution; the unprecedented quality of writing occurring at the time; and the key role played by the rise of publishing houses, both in Latin America and in Spain.

The Boom writers were a cosmopolitan group, in terms of both their life experiences and the universal appeal of their writing. They enjoyed considerable publishing success as their works were read around the world. Several of them also resided abroad: Cortázar lived for thirty years in Paris; García Márquez spent periods in Europe; Vargas Llosa lived in Europe for more than twenty years; while Fuentes lives what has been described as a "nomadic" lifestyle, never remaining fixed within any one country.

Critics have debated the defining characteristics of Boom writing at length, and the synopsis provided by Donald Shaw gives a good indication of their work. Shaw suggests that Boom novels tend to subordinate reality to mystification; they tend to emphasize the ambiguous and the irrational and to abandon the linear, logical structure typical of the realist novel. They also tend to subvert the notion of chronological time and to replace the omniscient third-person narrator with multiple or ambiguous narrators. The Boom writers all engage in experimentation with fiction, although the emphasis differs within the work of each writer.

The Colombian author Gabriel García Márquez is the most popular author of Latin American literature, and his 1967 work *Cien años de soledad* (*One Hundred Years of Solitude*) universalized the concept of magical realism broadly understood as a mode of writing in which improbable, fantastical occurrences are narrated in a dead-pan, realistic style. Much of the success of García Márquez's novel can be attributed to the fact that it skillfully blends a depiction of local color with a manipulation of worldwide myths in its examination of a variety of themes including the family, the advent of modernity, and the concept of fate. Set in the mythical town of Macondo, the novel follows the rise and fall of the Buendía family, and the story can be read as both a national and pan-Latin-American allegory. In the story of the Buendía family, García Márquez combined a high level of literary achievement with popular appeal, and *Cien años de soledad* remains one of the bestsellers within literature written in Spanish. In 1982 García Márquez was awarded the Nobel Prize for literature, an indication of both the quality of his work and the impact of his fiction on an international stage.

After García Márquez, Vargas Llosa is perhaps the best known of the Boom writers, for both his literary and his political careers. Vargas Llosa's fiction combines an analysis of Latin American history with his own life experiences and those of Peruvians in general. One of his most famous works is the 1963 novel *La ciudad y los perros* (literally, *The City and the Dogs*, although it was published in English translation as *The Time of the Hero*). The book is a harsh condemnation of the Peruvian military, specifically the Leoncio Prado military school, and it gained him international attention as thousands of copies of the book were burned in protest on the patio of the military school that he criticized. Following this, Vargas Llosa's second novel, *La casa verde* (*The Green House*), published in 1965, was a highly complex play of what critics have termed "telescoped dialogs," in which what initially appears to be one conversation taking place in the present in fact has several previous conversations interwoven within it; his third novel, *Conversación en La Catedral* (*Conversation in the Cathedral*) is considered his masterpiece. The title of this 1970 work indicates the subversion Vargas Llosa undertakes within the novel: though the title apparently refers to a cathedral, the reader learns that "The Cathedral" is in fact the name of a bar.

Carlos Fuentes is Mexico's most commercially successful writer. One of the most prolific of the Boom writers, he has received many prizes for his fictional works. *La muerte de Artemio Cruz* (*The Death of Artemio Cruz*, 1962) is considered Fuentes's first major novel and a milestone in the development of the Latin American Boom. In this novel, Fuentes explores the legacy of the Mexican Revolution and engages in innovative literary techniques, such as the extensive use of flashbacks and the reworking of history that exemplify his conviction that politics and writing go together. His other works of particular note include *Zona sagrada* (*Holy Place*, 1967) and *Cambio de piel* (*A Change of Skin*, 1967), as well as a respected study of the Boom novels entitled *La nueva novela hispanoamericana* (*The New Spanish-American Novel*, 1969).

The Argentine Julio Cortázar is perhaps the most cosmopolitan of the group. Born in 1914 in Brussels, where his father was an attaché at the embassy, Cortázar spent much of his life living abroad and in Paris from 1951 onward. Cortázar's most important contribution to the Boom and to Latin American literature as a whole was his 1963 novel, *Rayuela* (*Hopscotch*), in which he draws on a variety of influences including surrealism to produce a truly original work of fiction. True to its title, *Rayuela* functions as a type of hopscotch, in that the reader is offered the choice of skipping onto the optional "capítulos prescindibles" ("dispensable chapters") in addition to reading the linear story, thus providing multiple ways of reading the novel and subverting the traditional novelistic structure. Later works of note by Cortázar include *62 modelo para armar* (*62, a Model Kit*) of 1968, which follows on from *Rayuela*, and *Libro de Manuel* (*A Manual for Manuel*) of 1973, which engages with Latin American political reality.

Although the Boom is strongly associated with the Spanish-speaking countries of Latin America, popular Brazilian writers of the period are occasionally included in anthologies of Boom writers, as much by a kind of token gesture toward Brazilian writers as by the features they share with their Spanish-American counterparts. One such writer is Jorge Amado (1912–2001), one of Latin America's most prolific literary exports and closely associated with the international view of Brazil as a cultural and sexual melting pot.

Amado was born in northeastern Brazil and wrote his first novel when he was nineteen. His most critically acclaimed novel is *Terras do sem fim* (*The Violent Lands*, 1942). The novel describes the creation of the town of Itabuna in the heartland of Bahia's cacao lands. Amado's father was a cacao planter, so while he is critical of the exploitation by landowners of the landless indentured workers who sacrificed so much for the economic good of the nation, he admires self-made men like his father, whose ruthless instinct for survival and capacity to forge new communities are praised in the book.

Most critics agree that a change in Amado's writing occurred around 1958, with the publication of *Gabriela, cravo e canela* (*Gabriela, Clove and Cinnamon*). In this novel, the depiction of colorful, exotic locations and characters, particularly the lascivious dark-skinned Bahian woman, takes precedence over sociopolitical discussion and critique. *Gabriela*, which sold over 800,000 copies, is one of Amado's most commercially successful novels. A remarkable seventy-six editions were printed in Brazil from 1958 to 1984. Amado's novels are read predominantly by Brazilians in the southern states of the country, so his work has had considerable impact on how northeastern culture is perceived in other parts of Brazil. Amado's fascination with popular culture—for example, the magical qualities associated with popular religions such as *Candomblé* in *Dona flor e seus dois maridos* (*Dona Flor and Her Two Husbands*, 1966) and *Tenda dos milagres* (*Tent of Miracles*, 1969)—has resulted in his work being labeled magical realist.

Several significant films have been based on this second phase of Amado's writing, including the box-office success *Dona Flor e seus dois maridos* (*Dona Flor and Her Two Husbands*, 1976), *Tenda dos milagres* (*Tent of Miracles*, 1977), *Gabriela* (1983), and most recently *Tieta do Agreste* (*Tieta*, 1996). The latter two works were also very successfully adapted as *telenovelas* (televized soap operas) in the early 1970s and late 1980s respectively. In the United States *Dona Flor* was made into a film entitled *Kiss Me Goodbye* (1982), starring Sally Field and James Caan.

From the 1970s onward, Amado's work has been the target of considerable criticism from feminist academics such as Walnice Nogueira Galvão and Daphne Patai, who condemn his 1972 novel *Teresa Batista cansada de guerra* (*Teresa Batista Home from the Wars*) for its voyeuristic depictions of sexual abuse. Others have drawn attention to the naïveté of his attitude to race relations in Brazil. In Amado's obituary in the *Guardian*, Branford and Treece wrote that his work was "a dish which all too easily corresponded to official Brazilian and international expectations of a prepackaged, stereotypical image of an exotic third world culture able to dance, sing and love its way out of misery." But Amado had defended himself from earlier accusations of sexism and racial stereotyping by stating: "I consider myself more of a journalist than a novelist because I do not add anything to my writing about the people of Bahia that does not already exist in their lives. I simply transfer the reality of their lives to a literary plane and recreate the ambience of Bahia, and that is all."

In 1961 Amado was voted into the ranks of the "immortals" of the Brazilian Academy of Letters, and in 1999 he was nominated for the Nobel Prize for literature. His contribution to Brazilian letters is also recognized in the Casa de Jorge Amado, an important center of Afro-Brazilian culture in the city of Salvador, Bahia.

—*Claire Taylor and Stephanie Dennison*

See also: *Mass Media:* Telenovela; *Popular Cinema:* The Brazilian Film Industry (Box-Office Successes and Contemporary Film in Brazil); *Popular Religion and Festivals: Candomblé*

Bibliography

Armstrong, Piers. 1999. *Third World Literary Fortunes: Brazilian Culture and Its International Reception.* Lewisburg: Bucknell University Press.

Branford, Sue, and David Treece. 2001. "Obituary: Jorge Amado." *London Guardian*, 9 August.

King, John, ed. 1987. *Modern Latin American Fiction: A Survey.* London: Faber.

Lindstrom, Naomi. 1994. *Twentieth-Century Spanish American Fiction.* Austin: University of Texas Press.

Martin, Gerald. 1989. *Journeys through the Labyrinth: Latin American Fiction in the Twentieth Century.* London: Verso.

Patai, Daphne. 1983. "Jorge Amado: Morals and Marvels." Pp. 111–140 in *Myth and Ideology in Contemporary Brazilian Fiction.* London: Associated Presses.

Shaw, Donald L. 2002. *A Companion to Modern Spanish American Fiction.* Woodbridge: Tamesis.

Swanson, Philip, ed. 1990. *Landmarks in Modern Latin American Fiction.* London: Routledge.

The Post-Boom

By the start of the 1970s, the Boom was waning, and a new generation of Latin American writers, designated "post-Boom," was calling for changes to the concept of fiction. One of the features of this new type of writing was its attempt to bridge the divide between "high" and "low" culture by introducing a variety of popular cultural features into the novel form. As critics have noted, post-Boom works employ a more reader-friendly technique, rely more on humor, and frequently integrate mass media and popular cultural forms into their writing.

The Argentine Manuel Puig (1932–1990) was one of the first writers to successfully integrate into the novel a variety of traditionally popular forms, including tango, bolero, detective fiction, popular romance, and Hollywood B-movies. Although his earlier works are contemporaneous with those of the Boom writers, Puig is generally seen as the instigator of the post-Boom, and his incorporation of popular, "low" culture into the novel format challenged the notion of "high" literature. Significantly, Puig does not merely make reference to popular culture in his novels; he adopts several of its stylistic features into the telling of the story. For example, Puig titled his 1969 novel *Boquitas pintadas* (literally, "painted mouths," although released in English translation as *Heartbreak Tango*) and subtitled it *folletín* (serialized novel). He structured the novel to give it the appearance of a serialized romance and

Chilean writer Isabel Allende, 1994. (Ed Kashi/Corbis)

used lines from popular tango lyrics as epigraphs to the novel. In common with the rest of Puig's works, this novel was highly accessible to a popular readership and sold in large numbers. The majority of Puig's work continues this integration of popular discourses into the novel format. His most famous novel, *El beso de la mujer araña* (*Kiss of the Spider Woman*, 1976), along with its cinematic adaptation by Héctor Babenco in 1985, gave Puig a high profile and international recognition.

Another key figure in the post-Boom is the Chilean writer Isabel Allende (born 1942), one of the first female Latin American writers to win worldwide recognition and popularity. Sales of her work equal those of García Márquez, and her first and most famous novel, *La casa de los espíritus* (*The House of the Spirits*, 1982) was an international bestseller. In this novel, Allende blends magical elements with a plot dealing with Chile's social and political situation in the twentieth century, focusing on the female lineage of the del Valle family. Similarities have often been noted between this work and García Márquez's *Cien años de soledad*, and Allende's novel is often read as a copy of, or a critical parody of, García Márquez's earlier work. A more overt manipulation of popular cultural forms comes in Allende's 1987 novel *Eva Luna*. Here she takes up the format of the *telenovela*, as the narrative of the protagonist Eva merges with the soap opera script she is writing.

Following on the heels of Allende's most famous work was the resounding international success of the first novel by Mexican author Laura Esquivel (born 1950), *Como agua para chocolate: Novela de entregas mensuales, con recetas, amores y remedios caseros* (*Like Water for Chocolate*, 1989). According to the most recent tally, over 4.5 million copies of the book have been printed worldwide. The novel is a popular romance, depicting the passion of the protagonist, Tita, for her true love, Pedro. But Esquivel also integrates another popular cultural form: the recipe book. Each chapter opens not with an introductory paragraph but with a recipe and its *manera de hacerse* (instructions). Moreover, as the title of the novel indicates, this work also takes the form of the *novela por entregas* (serialized fiction). Each chapter ends with *continuará* ("to be continued"), the traditional "cliff-hanger" of this type of popular fiction. Coming soon after the novel was the 1992 film version, *Como agua para chocolate*, directed and produced by Alfonso Arau, itself a box-office hit. Esquivel's later works have failed to achieve the same runaway success as her first novel, although her second novel, *La ley del amor* (*The Law of Love*, 1995), attempts a further crossing of literary boundaries with the inclusion of popular music on CD and drawings alongside the written word.

—*Claire Taylor*

See also: *Popular Music:* Bolero; Tango; *Popular Literature:* The Boom; *Mass Media:* Telenovela

Bibliography

Lindstrom, Naomi. 1994. *Twentieth-Century Spanish American Fiction.* Austin: University of Texas Press.

Shaw, Donald L. 1998. *The Post-Boom in Spanish American Fiction.* Albany: State University of New York Press.

———. 2002. *A Companion to Modern Spanish American Fiction.* Woodbridge: Tamesis.

Swanson, Philip. 1985. *The New Novel in Latin America: Politics and Popular Culture after the Boom.* Manchester: Manchester University Press.

"New-Age" Fiction—Paulo Coelho

Paul Coelho is a literary phenomenon whose fable-like novels have been translated into over fifty languages for a readership that spans 150 countries. Born into a middle-class family in Brazil and best known for his novel *O alquimista* (*The Alchemist*, 1988), which sold over 27 million copies worldwide, Paulo Coelho (1947–) is the bestselling Latin American writer of all time. His work is characterized by a spiritual dimension and encourages contemplation and self-discovery. He counts Madonna, Julia Roberts, and Sinéad O'Connor among his self-confessed fans.

The Alchemist sold more copies than any other book in the history of Brazilian letters and even made it into the *Guinness Book of Records.* In May 1993, HarperCollins published 50,000 copies of the novel, the largest-ever initial print run of a Brazilian book in the United States. In 2002 the Portuguese literary review *Jornal de Letras* declared that *The Alchemist* had sold more copies than any other book written in Portuguese in the entire history of the language. A film version of the book starring British actor Jeremy Irons is currently being planned in Hollywood.

Coelho's latest book, *Onze minutos* (*Eleven Minutes*), published by HarperCollins in the USA and Canada in 2004 and in the United Kingdom the previous year, is billed as an odyssey of self-discovery and an exploration of the nature of sex and love. It tells the story of Maria, who, after a chance encounter in Rio de Janeiro, travels to Geneva, where she dreams of finding fame and fortune yet ends up working the streets as a prostitute. On 25 July, 2002, Paulo Coelho was elected to the prestigious Academia Brasileira de Letras (Brazilian Academy of Letters), the aim of which is to safeguard the language and culture of Brazil. This was a significant event, since his work has been dismissed by many literary critics. His loyal fans greeted the

Brazilian writer Paulo Coelho looks on as his fans reach for his autograph after a press conference in Kiev, 15 September 2004. (Mykhailo Markiv/Reuters/Corbis)

news with widespread enthusiasm and delight, and Coelho became the focus of media attention throughout Brazil.

At the age of seven, Coelho entered the Jesuit school of São Ignácio in Rio de Janeiro but soon came to hate the obligatory nature of religious practice. It was there that he discovered his true vocation—he won his first literary prize in a school poetry competition. His sister, Sonia, tells of how she won an essay prize by entering a composition that her brother had relegated to a wastepaper bin. His father, Pedro, an engineer, wanted his son to follow in his footsteps professionally, which caused the young Paulo to rebel against his family. His father interpreted his rebellion as a sign of mental illness, and when Paulo was seventeen his father twice had him committed to a psychiatric hospital, where he underwent several sessions of electric shock therapy. Soon afterward, Paulo joined a theater group and began working as a journalist. Viewing the theater as a hotbed of immorality, his parents had him committed to a hospital for a third time. His experiences in this period of his life provided the inspiration for his novel *Veronika decide morrer* (*Veronika Decides to Die*).

According to Coelho: "*Veronika Decides to Die* was published in Brazil in 1998. By September I had received more than 1,200 e-mails and letters describing similar experiences. In October some of the subjects he discussed in the book—depression, panic attacks, suicide—were addressed at a conference that went on to have national repercussions. On January 22 of the following year, Senator Eduardo Suplicy read out some extracts from my book at a plenary session [in Congress] and managed to get approval for a law that had been doing the rounds of the Brazilian Congress for ten years—a law prohibiting arbitrary hospitalization."

In the 1960s, despite the fact that Brazil was ruled by a repressive military regime, established in 1964, the hippie movement took root there, and Coelho lived the alternative lifestyle to the full, growing his hair long, making a point of never carrying his identity card, and taking drugs. He started a magazine, but only two issues were ever published.

Coelho also became half of a songwriting partnership with Brazilian singer Raul Seixas. He wrote the lyrics to more than sixty songs produced by the duo up to 1976. In 1973 they both became members of the "Alternative Society," an organization that opposed capitalist ideology, defended the individual's right to do as he or she pleased, and practiced black magic. Coelho later described these experiences in his book *As valkírias* (*The Valkyries*, 1992). During this period Coelho and Seixas began publishing a series of comic strips that called for greater individual freedom. Considered subversive by the military dictatorship, they were both arrested; Coelho, deemed to be the "brains" behind the creative partnership, was detained for several days. Upon his release he was re-arrested while walking down the street and taken to a military torture center, where he remained for several days. Coelho recounts that he escaped death by telling his torturers that he was insane and had already been admitted to mental hospitals three times. He began to physically harm himself in front of his captors, and in the end they stopped torturing him and let him go.

Coelho then pursued a more conventional life, going on to work for the record companies Polygram and CBS. In 1977 he moved to London with his then wife and began writing, without much success. In 1979, after they separated, he met up with an old friend, Christina Oiticica, whom he later married and with whom he still lives. The couple traveled to Europe and visited the former concentration camp in Dachau, Germany. Coelho claims that there he had a vision in which a man appeared to him, a man whom he actually met later in a café in Amsterdam. This man, whose identity Coelho has never revealed, suggested that he should return to Catholicism, so he then began to study the symbolic language of Christianity. The man also advised Coelho to walk the medieval pilgrims' route known as the "Road to Santiago," between France and Spain. In 1987, a year after completing that pilgrimage, Coelho wrote his first book, *O diário de um mago* (*The Pilgrimage*), which recounted his experiences during the trip and his discovery that extraordinary things happen in the lives of ordinary people. In 1988 he wrote another, very different book, *The Alchemist*, which eventually went to the top of the bestseller lists, along with *The Pilgrimage*.

—*Lisa Shaw*

Bibliography:

Coelho, Paulo. 2000. *The Pilgrimage*. San Franscisco: HarperSanFrancisco.

———. 2001. *Veronika Decides to Die*. New York: Perennial.

———. 2003. *The Alchemist: A Fable about Following Your Dream*. San Francisco: HarperSanFrancisco.

———. 2003. *Warrior of the Light: A Manual*. New York: HarperCollins.

———. 2004. *Eleven Minutes.* New York: HarperCollins.

Paulo Coelho Official Website. www.paulocoelho.com (consulted 1 August 2003).

Science Fiction

Although not immediately associated with Latin America, this genre has been growing in force throughout the twentieth century, and the writings of Latin American authors have revitalized the paradigms coming from European and U.S. writing. On the whole, Latin American science fiction is generally seen as "soft" rather than "hard"—that is, it deals more with philosophical possibilities than with physics.

The work of the Argentine writer Jorge Luis Borges (1899–1986) has often been described as one of the forerunners of science fiction in Latin America. Though his well-known short stories, written over several years and brought together in the collection *Ficciones* (*Fictions*, 1944), do not classify as "hard" science fiction, since no spaceships or intergalactic battles appear in these tales, they nevertheless disrupt a variety of philosophical and scientific norms. His experiments with time, space, and parallel existence in stories in these collections, such as "El jardín de senderos que se bifurcan" ("The Garden of Forking Paths," 1944) and "Tlön, Uqbar, Orbis Tertius" (1944, the title of which is the name of an imaginary universe and its regions), as well as in the longer 1949 work *El aleph* (*The Aleph*), are evidence of Borges's affinities with the science fiction tradition.

Borges's groundwork in experimental fiction inspired an array of writers to take up the challenge of proposing alternative worlds and technologically enhanced realities. In Borges's native Argentina, his friend Adolfo Bioy Casares (1914–1999) was another key exponent of early science fiction. Bioy Casares's novela *La invención de Morel* (*The Invention of Morel*, 1941) is an overt response to H. G. Wells's famous novel *The Island of Dr. Moreau* (1896). It describes a simulation machine invented by the scientist Morel, and ultimately reveals that the inhabitants of the island are merely holograms produced by the machine.

Writing in the science fiction vein can also be found in some of the short stories of Julio Cortázar (1914–1984) and his compatriot Eduardo Goligorsky (born 1931), particularly in Goligorsky's short stories in the collection *Memorias del futuro* (*Memories of the Future*, 1966). It also occurs, notably, in the novels and short stories of Angélica Gorodischer (born 1928), who, some would argue, is Argentina's only committed female science fiction writer. Gorodischer's works, such as her 1967 novel *Opus 2* and her 1979 short story collection *Trafalgar*, include a variety of science fiction scenarios such as intergalactic travels and the disruption of timescales. More recently, Argentine writer Ricardo Piglia (born 1941) has continued this tendency toward the futuristic with the publication of his novel *La ciudad ausente* (*The Absent City*, 1992), set in 2004–2005 and described by Avelar as a "futurist/cyberpunk detective story."

Though science fiction in the Southern Cone (the countries in the south of Latin America, comprising Argentina, Brazil, Chile, Paraguay, and Uruguay) is dominated by Argentina, the case for a Chilean science fiction is made by critic Remi-Maure, who details a variety of works in this genre. Remi-Maure dates the start of

Chilean science fiction as 1959, with the publication of Hugo Correa's (born 1926) now classic novel *Los altísimos* (*The Highest*), although he sees Chile's "golden age" of science fiction as lasting only until the mid-1970s.

In Colombia, two of the best-known names in the science fiction genre are Antonio Mora Vélez (b. 1942) and René Rebetéz (b. 1933). Rebetéz's 1996 collection of short stories, *Ellos lo llaman amanecer y otros relatos* (*They Call It Dawn, and Other Tales*), provides a good introduction to his work and includes a brief opening essay on science fiction as a genre. Mora Vélez is considered one of the pioneers of science fiction in Colombia and has written both fiction, such as his 1982 collection of short stories, *El juicio de los dioses* (*The Judgement of the Gods*), and critical essays on science fiction, such as *Ciencia ficción: El humanismo de hoy* (*Science Fiction: The Humanism of Today*, 1996).

In recent years the genre of science fiction has witnessed a transformation at the hands of women writers. In particular, the Mexicans Carmen Boullosa (b. 1954) and Laura Esquivel (b. 1950), the latter more famous for her novel *Como agua para chocolate* (*Like Water for Chocolate*), have experimented with this genre. Esquivel's *La ley del amor* (*The Law of Love*, 1995), billed as a "*novela multimedia*," engages with some of science fiction's conventions to produce a parodic take on the genre, while Boullosa's *Cielos de la tierra* (*Heavens of the Earth*, 1997) is a more pessimistic account of the futuristic destruction of bodily integrity.

At the close of the twentieth century, one of the most interesting developments in science fiction in Latin America was the use of new technologies to create new forms of fiction. Juan B. Gutiérrez's *Condiciones extremas* (*Extreme Conditions*, 1998) is described as an example of "hyperfiction," a work that includes both the written word and images within a hypertext. The story, which revolves around three protagonists, Índigo Cavalera, Miranda Macedonia, and Equinoccio Deunamor, starts out in the year 2090, and, like many other science fiction works, involves time travel as the characters move backward and forward in time to change the course of events. Structurally, the work is organized into numerous short chapters, each containing generally two hyperlinks, one to the following chapter and the other to the previous chapter. In this way, the story still remains conventionally linear, but the reader has the option to revisit previous chapters, a strategy that mimics the characters' revisiting of the past. The work was initially available in book and CD-ROM format, and is now freely available on the

Mexican writer Laura Esquivel, 2001. (James Leynse/Corbis)

Internet and can be read at http://www.condicionesextremas.com.

Overall, the observations that Pérez and Pérez offer about Argentine science fiction can be applied to science fiction throughout Latin America. They note that it is used for satirical purposes within Latin America; they also note that this genre, because it reaches a wide readership, can be used to attract readers and then engage them in political or philosophical debates.

—*Claire Taylor*

See also: *Mass Media:* The Internet

Bibliography

Avelar, Idelber. 1999. *The Untimely Present.* Durham: Duke University Press.

Fernández Delgado, Miguel Ángel. 1996. "A Brief History of Continuity and Change in Mexican Science Fiction." *The New York Review of Science Fiction* 9, no. 3: 18–19.

Kreksch, Ingrid. 1997. "Reality Transfigured: The Latin American Situation as Reflected in Its Science Fiction." Pp. 173–182 in *Political Science Fiction*, edited by Donald M. Hassler and Clyde Wilcox. Columbia: University of South Carolina Press.

Pajares Tosca, Susana. 2001. "*Condiciones Extremas:* Digital Science Fiction from Colombia." *Hispanic Issues* 22: 270–287.

Pérez, Janet, and Genaro J. Pérez. 1987. "Foreword: Hispanic Science Fiction/Fantasy and the Thriller." *Monographic Review/Revista Monográfica* 3: 1–2.

Remi-Maure. 1984. "Science Fiction in Chile." *Science Fiction Studies* 11: 181–189.

Comic Books

Mexico

Mexican comic books, or *historietas*, are a booming mass cultural phenomenon. Millions of copies are published every week and are sold (or frequently resold secondhand) on street stands throughout Mexico and beyond. Many are marketed simultaneously in other Latin American countries such as Colombia and Venezuela. Individual weekly titles can have print runs of up to a million copies. Since most cost less than fifty cents new, they are accessible to even the poorest sectors of society, and with their combination of images and words, their colloquial language, and their simple grammar, they cater to those who are poorly educated. Indeed, comic books are one of the few sources of accessible reading matter for the poor and semiliterate sectors of society and, as such, they not only offer entertainment but also play a crucial role in the dissemination of information and ideology. On a superficial level, they tell stories of action and adventure, love and sex (there is a substantial market for X-rated *historietas*). Nevertheless, most include some form of social comment, and some are frankly didactic, telling tales of Mexican history and fostering a sense of national identity.

Comic books are a post-revolutionary phenomenon, having made their first appearance in the early 1930s. As Rubenstein notes, these early comics, by commenting on contemporary issues, helped guide Mexicans through the turbulent post-revolutionary era with its modernization and urbanization. However, the contemporary, risqué approach to life that characterized these comics did not go unchallenged by conservative, often devoutly Catholic forces, who tried to have them banned outright in the early 1940s. They did not succeed, but in 1944 the government began censoring the most outrageous publications. Although this had little impact on the comics themselves (because of the censors' limited ability to enforce their own rulings), it was successful in limiting the dissemination in Mexico of U.S. comic books considered racist toward Mexicans (for example, in their stories of the Wild West). Thus the national market was protected.

Many Mexican comic book series and/or comic book characters have lasted for decades. For example, the comic *Pepín* ran for fifteen years from 1936, and at its most popular it was published eight times a week and sold over a million copies per edition. The word *pepín* even entered Mexican Spanish as a synonym for comic books. This kind of long-running comic book molded itself somewhat to changes in contemporary society, but generally mixed topical references into more eternal story lines. Other comic books appeared at specific moments in history and pursued specific agendas. Such is the case of the 1970s comic *Torbellino* (*Whirlwind*), written by Orlando Ortiz and drawn by Antonio Cardoso. This comic responded to the more open political environment provoked by the 1968 massacre of students at Tlatelolco Square in Mexico City and was much more pointedly critical of the Mexican establishment than previous publications had been. It also attracted a heterogeneous audience for its weekly installments, appealing to middle-class students and the poor. This was due to the quality of the text and drawings as well as the social content. Today, although the market for comic books in general has declined since the 1990s, probably because of the influence of television, this kind of *historieta de arte* (art-house comic book), which presents social critique alongside a highly eclectic, creative sampling of visual and textual sources, is still thriving in the work of Edgar Clément (*Operación Bolívar*) and Enrique Chagoya, who works in conjunction with Guillermo Gómez-Peña.

—*Thea Pitman*

See also: *Popular Theater and Performance:* Circus and Cabaret (Guillermo Gómez-Peña)

Bibliography

Hinds, Harold E., and Charles M. Tatum. 1992. *Not Just for Children: The Mexican Comic Book in the Late 1960s and 70s.* Westport, CT: Greenwood Press.

Palacios, Julia Emilia. 1986. "*Torbellino:* Toward an Alternative Comic Book." *Studies in Latin American Popular Culture* 5: 186–195.

Rubenstein, Anne. 1998. *Bad Language, Naked Ladies and Other Threats to the Nation: A Political History of Comic Books in Mexico.* Durham, NC: Duke University Press.

Argentina

Comic books in Argentina are dominated by the internationally known *Mafalda*, the creation of Quino (Joaquín Salvador Lavado), a fine arts graduate born in 1932 in Mendoza. *Mafalda* was devised in 1963 to promote a new line of kitchen equipment that was never in fact marketed. Quino then took his finished comic strip to the *Primera plana* newspaper in 1964 and by 1966 he had published the first of many *Mafalda* annuals. The strip was published in Italy in 1968 and in 1970 in Spain, where the Franco government insisted that the publishers make clear that it was for adults only. By 1971 the strip had already been translated into seven languages.

The central, eponymous character in *Mafalda* is a young middle-class girl from Buenos Aires who thinks and speaks like a worldly-wise adult, much like Charles M. Schulz's *Peanuts* characters, which were Quino's main inspiration. Most of the short strips in which Mafalda appears make ironic comments on Argentine society and national idiosyncrasies. Quino has a good ear for the affected way that the capital's bourgeoisie speaks, and his strips include a certain amount of inevitable stereotyping. Quino's strip was popular in Argentina because it offered the population a humorous opportunity for self-recognition in a market dominated by U.S. comics. In fact, the reason *Mafaldo* traveled so successfully throughout Latin America, David William Foster writes, is that most of Latin Americans also see the Argentines as idiosyncratic.

Quino stopped producing the *Mafalda* strip in 1973 and moved to Italy in 1976. Although he was not censored by the Argentine dictatorship, he had grown tired of the constant criticism of his work: the Left thought he was too tame and the Right thought he was too critical of national characteristics. Since that time, *Mafalda* has made occasional reappearances as part of public information campaigns, as, for example, in a 1977 UNICEF publicity exercise. The strip, which had become a television series as early as 1965, was adapted for the big screen in 1982.

A more recent comic strip craze in Argentina is *Boogie, el aceitoso* (*Boogie the Greaser*). Unlike Mafalda, Boogie is a thoroughly unpleasant, mean-spirited individual. An Argentine based in New York, Boogie earns his living in a number of distasteful professions: mercenary, bodyguard, hit man. One reason that has been suggested for the strip's popularity is that the Argentine bourgeoisie can identify with Boogie's contempt for minority groups in New York (blacks, feminists, Jews, liberals, gays, and Asians), his sidestepping of the law, and his ignoring the rules of the system. Despite his meanness of spirit and violence, Boogie poses no threat to his readers at home, since the milieu in which he gives vent to his prejudices is the United States. He also helps to explode the myths associated with the Colossus of the North. *Boogie* is the product of satirical cartoonist Roberto Fontanarrosa, who enjoyed success earlier in his career with *Inodoro Pereyra*, about a backward and rather indolent gaucho type.

—Stephanie Dennison

See also: *Cultural Icons:* Regional and Ethnic Types (The Gaucho in Argentina and Uruguay)

Bibliography

Evora, José Antonio. 2000. "Quinoscopios." P. 1229 in *Encyclopedia of Contemporary Latin American and Caribbean Cultures*, vol. 3, edited by Dan Balderston, Mike González, and Ana M. López. London: Routledge.

Fernández L'Hoeste, Hector D. 1998. "From Mafalda to Boogie: The City in Argentine Humor." Pp. 81–106 in *Imagination Beyond Nation: Latin American Popular Culture*, edited by Eva P. Bueno and Terry Caesar. Pittsburgh: University of Pittsburgh Press.

Foster, David William. 1989. *From Mafalda to the Supermachos: Latin American Graphic Humor as Popular Culture.* Boulder, CO, and London: Lynne Rienner.

Peiretti, Rodrigo. 2000. "Mafalda." Pp. 890–891 in *Encyclopedia of Contemporary Latin American and Caribbean Cultures*, vol. 2, edited by Dan Balderston, Mike González, and Ana M. López. London: Routledge.

Brazil

Along with the United States and Japan, Brazil is one of the world's three largest markets for comics, known in Brazil as *histórias em quadrinhos* or *gibis.* Most of Brazil's commercially successful comics are imported, with the notable exception of *A Turma da Mônica*, the creation of Maurício de Sousa. Sousa was born in 1935 in São Paulo. He began publishing his famous comic strip in the daily broadsheets in the late 1950s, and by 1970 *A Turma da Mônica* was a very popular comic book. Sousa soon set up his own production company, and now Maurício de Sousa Produções owns not only a successful publisher of comics but also amusement parks based on Monica and her gang and the fourth largest animation studio in the world.

The toothy main character, Mônica, was based on one of Sousa's daughters, as was one of her gang, Magali. Other well-known members of Mônica's gang (there are 300 in all) are Cebolinha ("scallion"), who has a speech impediment, Cascão, who smells bad, and Chico Bento, the country bumpkin. Such is *A Turma da Mônica*'s success within the children's market that these homegrown comics outsell Disney titles.

The teenage comic market was dominated until recently by the Brazilian version of the anarchic U.S. comic *Mad*, which was also rewritten and published in Argentina, Mexico, and Puerto Rico. Although the comic is no longer published, the style of humor of *Mad*, established in Brazil by the well-known satirical cartoonist Ota in 1974, has been influential in homegrown underground comics and the alternative comedy scene on Brazilian television.

Domestic comic production has been influenced by cinema and television: for example, in the 1960s and 1970s the notorious horror film director Mojica Marins produced his own popular comics based on his film character Zé do Caixão (Coffin Joe), while the Trapalhões comedy quartet, at the height of their popularity in the 1970s and 1980s, appeared in a series of children's comics.

During the dictatorship a number of satirical cartoonists rose to fame through the politically committed and oft-censored magazine *Pasquim*, including the much admired Henfil and Ziraldo: the latter has achieved success recently within the children's market with the comic strip *O menino maluquinho* (The Nutty Boy). With the loosening of censorship laws in the late 1970s, the content of comic strips became more sexual than political, and most young cartoonists were obliged to work for hardcore "adult comics" such as those produced in the 1980s by Editora Gafipar. This generation, still influential today, was inspired graphically by Japanese comics and pop art.

As comics once again become trendy among Brazil's young urban bourgeoisie, new cartoonists and comics have begun to appear. The Editora Fluminense series, for example, deals with Brazilian historical themes such as the slave leader Zumbi dos Palmares (2002), illustrated by the talented Allan Alex.

—*Stephanie Dennison*

See also: *Popular Cinema:* The Brazilian Film Industry (Box-Office Successes and Contemporary Film in Brazil); Coffin Joe

Bibliography

"Brazilian comic-book encyclopedia." www.gibindex.com. (consulted 1 August 2003).

Moya, Alvaro de. 1988. "Comics in Brazil." *Studies in Latin American Popular Culture* 6: 227–239.

Rinka, Marcie D. 2000. "Comics." Pp. 387–388 in *Encyclopedia of Contemporary Latin American and Caribbean Cultures*, vol. 1, edited by Dan Balderston, Mike González, and Ana M. López. London: Routledge.

Literatura de Cordel

Cheaply produced chapbooks popular in the northeast of Brazil, these publications

Brazilian chapbook (*literatura de cordel*) on the life of the infamous social bandit Lampião, illustrated using traditional woodcut techniques. (Courtesy of Mark Dineen; photo by Alex Nield)

are also known as *folhetos. Literatura de cordel*, which literally means "literature on a string," in reference to the way the loose sheets are tied together and displayed on stands at rural markets, can be traced as far back as the sixteenth century. In the Iberian Peninsula, popular verse, inspired by the epic poetry in vogue among the nobility, began to be transcribed at that time, and the trend was taken to the New World by Spanish and Portuguese colonists. The popular poetic tradition took root particularly among Brazil's rural population, perhaps because these verses were written to be recited aloud or sung and therefore were accessible to the country's large illiterate population. They were also written in a way that reflected the popular speech of the rural poor, with their own colloquialisms and flexible attitude to grammatical rules. From the early twentieth century onward, professional *cordel* writers or *folheteiros* would travel the interior selling their printed poetry. They read their work aloud in marketplaces but omit the ending of their stories in order to entice literate representatives of small communities to buy them.

In the late nineteenth century, these stories began to be sold in the form of chapbooks. At first they dealt with themes common to the *Romanceiro* or medieval poetic tradition that inspired them, such as tales of knights, symbolic battles between good and evil, and Christian parables. But by the mid-twentieth century, at the height of their popularity, themes in the chapbooks had broadened to include popular history, anecdotes about modern life, and critical commentary. Many chapbooks told of the adventures of Lampião, the legendary *cangaceiro* or social bandit who terrorized the lawless northeastern interior in the first decades of the twentieth century. Padre Cícero (1844–1934), one of many messianic priests from the northeast, also features widely in the chapbooks from this time.

From the 1940s onward, the tradition traveled along with the northeasterners who headed south to cities such as São Paulo in search of work. At this point, chapbooks began to incorporate themes connected to the experiences of urban life, such as strikes and safety at work. They reputedly played an important role in the consciousness-raising of the *Ligas Camponesas* or Peasant Leagues of the 1950s, which demanded land reform and better treatment of landless workers. One of the most popular stories incorporated into *cordel* literature was the suicide of the populist president Getúlio Vargas in 1954, bringing *cordel* readers and listeners in touch with the goings-on of central government.

With the spread of radio and television and the decline of open-air markets, the relationship between *literatura de cordel* and the public changed. Remote communities no longer relied on the chapbooks as a source of contact with the outside world. Since the early 1960s, scholars have ceased treating them with disdain, and today *cordel* literature is popular with an educated middle-class readership for its folk curiosity and its monetary value: like comics, many older chapbooks change hands for considerable sums of money. Large comic-book publishers have also reinvented the genre, selling neatly packaged printed versions with colorful covers. The few genuine *folheteiros* that remain frequently rely on contracts from advertising agencies and the propaganda machines of politicians.

—*Stephanie Dennison*

See also: *Popular Religion and Festivals:* Popular Catholicism (Brazil)

Bibliography

Dineen, Mark. 1996. *Listening to the People's Voice: Erudite and Popular Literature in North East Brazil.* London: Kegan Paul International.

Slater, Candace. 1982. *Stories on a String: The Brazilian Literatura de Cordel.* Los Angeles: University of California Press.

Fotonovela

Literally, a "photonovel," that is, a story consisting primarily of still photographs with balloon captions or brief written legends, widely read in much of Latin America and predominantly targeted at a female readership. The *fotonovela* arose out of the romance fiction market. Originally it was associated with the Spanish author Corin Tellado, a prolific writer of romance fiction whose work was published not only in the form of traditional novels and magazine serials, but also as *fotonovela*. Tellado's writing perhaps equates most closely to Harlequin romances in the United States, or to Mills and Boon in the United Kingdom. The *fotonovela* continues this tradition of romantic fiction, although it provides the story in a new format: that of photographic images accompanied by thought or speech bubbles, or brief written glosses. Given that it relies on minimal text and leaves much of the action to be explained by visual cues, it offers easy access to a readership with lower levels of literacy. As late as the end of the 1980s, it was noted that more people read *fotonovelas* than read daily newspapers in many countries of Latin America.

Although the *fotonovela* had its roots in the Spanish tradition of romantic fiction and was initially produced in Spain for distribution in Latin America, a flourishing national *fotonovela* industry quickly established itself in Brazil, Mexico, and Argentina. Some differences can be seen among the products of these three countries: Brazil and Argentina produced a more "literary" type of fiction, while the Mexican *fotonovela* took its inspiration from the *historieta* or comic books. In Argentina the *fotonovela* had gone into decline by the 1970s, while in Mexico it maintained its popularity and became a major force within the area of popular literature.

In terms of theme, the *fotonovela* initially concentrated on romantic love. A typically sentimental and melodramatic scenario would involve the heroine triumphing over circumstances to gain the heart of the wealthy hero. Usually the heroine was poor but virtuous, and these stories tended to convey a chaste romantic ideal. This early type of *fotonovela* has been termed the *fotonovela rosa* ("pink *fotonovela*"); the term *rosa* refers to the concept of the *novela rosa* or romantic novel. This type of *fotonovela*, according to Butler Flora, spans the period from the 1950s to the 1970s.

Though the early *fotonovelas* were sentimental, romantic, and stereotypical, over time they began to incorporate more modern plots and characters. Butler Flora notes that the heroes of the *fotonovela* gradually descended in social class, becoming middle- and even working-class in their origin. This led to an increase in the *fotonovela*'s popularity, as readers were able to identify more readily with the situation of the protagonists. Thus, the *fotonovela* branched out into different forms, moving in the course of the 1970s from the initial *fotonovela rosa* to what Butler Flora has called the *fotonovela suave* ("soft *fotonovela*"), in which the implausible romance stories of the earlier versions are toned down, namely, more realistic.

The *fotonovela* underwent another change at the end of the 1970s, when the *fotonovela roja* ("red *fotonovela*") emerged. These later works broke with the tradition of idealized romantic situations and instead dealt with the harshness of daily life, including issues such as social deprivation, prostitution, rape, money problems, and drug addiction. The characters were frequently poor, and as the plots became more realistic, the visual aspect of the *fotonovela* changed: the models used in the photographs are darker, their clothes less elaborate, and the setting often a poorer part of town. Today this "red" version of the *fotonovela* sells much better than the romantic "soft" and "pink" versions.

Though these works were most popular in Mexico, readership was widespread throughout Latin America. Chile saw increased sales of *fotonovelas* during the Popular Unity government of Salvador Allende from 1970 to 1973. Though most of these *fotonovelas* were produced in Spain, a new format was introduced by Quimantú, Chile's state publishing company. In Argentina, *fotonovela* production ended in the 1970s, but the demand for these works continued and readership remained relatively high. During this time many Argentine companies moved their production to Colombia, where costs were cheaper. In Colombia, the *fotonovela* also had a wide national readership. By the 1980s, however, the majority of the *fotonovelas* on sale there were from Mexico, though many had been "Colombianized" by the replacement of some of the more obvious Mexicanisms with Colombian expressions, and by the changing of location—for instance, the Mexican resort of Acapulco became the Colombian town of Cartagena.

While these works are aimed predominantly at a female readership, the recent growth of a further subgenre, what Butler Flora terms the *fotonovela picaresca* ("picaresque *fotonovela*"), is aimed at the adolescent male and is sexually explicit, frequently centering on the story of a young man whose sexual powers drive women to the heights of passion. This relatively new incarnation of the *fotonovela*, though seen by some as conservative and sexist in its content, is an example of the adaptation of the genre to different readerships and an attempt to corner the male market.

—*Claire Taylor*

See also: *Popular Literature:* Comic Books

Bibliography

Butler Flora, Cornelia. 1973. "The Passive Female and Social Change: A Cross-Cultural Comparison of Women's Magazine Fiction." Pp. 59–85 in *Female and Male in Latin America: Essays*, edited by Ann Pescatello. Pittsburgh: University of Pittsburgh Press.

———. 1980. "Women in Latin American Fotonovelas: From Cinderella to Mata Hari." *Women's Studies International Quarterly* 3, no. 1: 95–104.

———. 1982. "The *Fotonovela* in America." *Studies in Latin American Popular Culture* 1: 15–26.

———. 1989. "The Political Economy of *Fotonovela* Production in Latin America." *Studies in Latin American Popular Culture* 8: 215–230.

Franco, Jean. 1986. "The Incorporation of Women: A Comparison of North American and Mexican Popular Narrative." Pp. 119–138 in *Studies in Entertainment: Critical Approaches to Mass Culture*, edited by Tania Modleski. Bloomington: Indiana University Press.

Oral "Literature" in Mexico and Guatemala

Though the term "oral literature" is to a certain extent an oxymoron, it is the term closest to describing the oral folktales, legends, and myths of pre-Hispanic cultures within Mesoamerica.

The forerunner of modern-day oral literature is the *Popul Vuh*, also known as the Maya Bible, which contains a series of creation myths, stories of gods and heroes, and some historical records. Although this work was originally written down in the Quiché language, it was nevertheless produced after the Conquest. The Quiché original is now lost, with only a Spanish translation made by a priest during the eighteenth century remaining. In addition to this important Mayan source, several books of this period were discovered in Yucatan, which have come to be known collectively as the books of *Chilam Balam.* These, too, were written down after the Conquest.

In more modern times, attempts have been made to record current popular myths, legends, and stories in written form. Key in this enterprise within Mexico has been the collection of works published by the Instituto Nacional Indigenista (National Indigenist Institute) during the 1990s and edited by Carlos Montemayor. These works, forming the series *Letras Mayas Contemporáneas* (Contemporary Mayan Letters), are a collection of tales, poems, and indigenous beliefs, and are published in parallel text with the original language accompanied by a Spanish translation. Frequently, these works took their impetus from a series of workshops held within indigenous communities during which the members of these communities were encouraged to relate their stories and record them in written form. The texts are available in an inexpensive paperback format, with the intention of disseminating them to a wide readership and preserving them for posterity.

In addition, Speck's *Zapotec Oral Literature* brings together in a single collection several tales from the oral literature of the Zapotecs living southwest of Oaxaca City, translated into both Spanish and English. The book contains thirteen folktales and a chapter of Zapotec proverbs, and along with the translations, includes the original

Zapotec text, with the stated aim of making the tales accessible to the Zapotec people. Speck's book forms part of a series, *Folklore Texts in Mexican Indian Languages*, that attempts to record and recuperate a variety of oral tales in different native languages.

Dennis Tedlock's book, *Breath on the Mirror*, represents a similar project in Guatemala. It brings together in English translation a series of Mayan myths and tales as they are told today, mostly by the Quiché Maya in the highlands of Guatemala. The book includes several transcriptions of tales told orally and recorded by tape recorder, with the resulting text including a variety of features to indicate changes in pace, emphasis, and tone of voice. These features, such as the use of bold type to indicate a loud voice, or spaced-out typing to indicate words that are pronounced slowly, are an attempt to bring the reader as close as possible to the way these tales were told and to convey their oral, popular nature.

—Claire Taylor

See also: *Language:* Indigenous Languages

Bibliography

Brotherston, Gordon. 1992. *Book of the Fourth World: Reading the Native Americas through Their Literature.* Cambridge: Cambridge University Press.

Burns, Allan. 1982. *An Epoch of Miracles: Oral Literature of the Yucatán Maya.* Austin: University of Texas Press.

Speck, Charles H. 1998. *Zapotec Oral Literature: El folklore de San Lorenzo Texmelucan.* Dallas, TX: Summer Institute of Linguistics.

Tedlock, Dennis. 1993. *Breath on the Mirror: Mythic Voices and Visions of the Living Maya.* Albuquerque: University of New Mexico Press.

Testimonio

Literally "testimony," *testimonio* is a growing genre of Latin American writing that attempts to convey a first-person, frequently oral account through the written word. Often associated with the voice of the masses, *testimonio* aims to give voice to those whose voices are traditionally excluded from the written word and the literary canon.

Testimonio as a form of writing has several key features. First, it is an account told by a first-person narrator who was an eyewitness or real protagonist in the events described. In this way, *testimonio* differs from the novel in that it is based on real-life events and derives its impact from what has been termed the "truth effect" (Beverley, p. 74). *Testimonio* does not exist in isolation as a work of literature but is inextricably linked to the social conditions that produced it and a part of social practice in itself.

Second, the voice of the narrator, that of one individual, is also seen as representative of an entire social class, frequently the lower classes or oppressed social groups. Thus the most famous of *testimonios*, that of the Guatemalan Rigoberta Menchú, deals with Menchú's experience of violence and oppression, but is expressly set out in terms of the collective. Menchú's memorable opening paragraph includes the lines "it's not only my life, it's also the testimony of my people. . . . My story is the story of all poor Guatemalans" (p. 1). This opening makes clear that her book is much more than a personal story or autobiography.

A third issue that has raised much debate regarding *testimonio* is its challenge to the conventions of authorship. Since the

Guatemalan Nobel Peace Laureate Rigoberta Menchu Tum (left) with Brazilian singer and Minister of Culture Gilberto Gil (background) in Barcelona, 14 May 2004. (Victor Fraile/Reuters/Corbis)

testimonio is an attempt at transcribing an oral, first-person account told by an illiterate subject, what is recounted orally must be subsequently transcribed and edited by a writer. Thus, rather than the standard, single author as source of the text, this type of writing is a form of cooperative authorship between narrator and transcriber, and the term "author" is replaced with "compiler" (Beverley, p. 77). Thus *Testimonio* challenges the conventions of bourgeois literature with its reliance on the notion of the elite author as the source of the text; it has been described by Sklodowska as a type of "'solidarity pact' forged between intellectuals and the common people" (p. 103). At the same time, this relationship between the narrator and the compiler has engendered considerable debate, in terms of the tensions involved in the conveying of the experiences of an illiterate, rural, usually indigenous subject through an educated, frequently metropolitan, and white compiler.

Though the rise of the *testimonio* began in the 1960s, it gained prominence in the 1980s and 1990s and is still a growing genre today. In addition to Menchú's seminal account, other recent figures associated with the *testimonio* include the Mexican writer and intellectual Elena Poniatowska, who has brought out several works based on testimonial accounts narrated to her, and the Colombian journalist Alonso J. Salazar, known for his publication of accounts by gang members in Medellín. Thus *testimonio* is proving to be an important force within Latin American writing, giving voice to popular sectors of society.

—*Claire Taylor*

See also: *Language:* Parlache

Bibliography

Beverley, John. 1993. *Against Literature.* Minneapolis: University of Minnesota Press.

Latin American Perspectives. 1991. Special Issue, *Voices of the Voiceless in Testimonial Literature* 70 & 71 (Summer and Fall).

Menchú, Rigoberta, with Elisabeth Burgos-Debray. 1984. *I, Rigoberta Menchú: An Indian Woman in Guatemala,* translated by Ann White. London: Verso (originally published in Spanish, 1983).

Randall, Margaret. 1985. *Testimonios: A Guide to Oral History.* Toronto: Participatory Research Group.

Sklodowska, Elzbieta. 2003. "Latin American Literatures." Pp. 86–106 in *The Companion to Latin American Studies,* edited by Philip Swanson. London: Arnold.

8

Cultural Icons

The image of Latin America and its people as seen from abroad has tended to focus on photogenic individuals, ranging from the political figures of Che Guevara and Eva Perón (Evita) to movie stars Carmen Miranda and, more recently, Salma Hayek. Their faces have reached iconic status, largely thanks to the power of cinema and television screens. These household names have in many cases given rise to often one-dimensional archetypes, such as that of the fiery, hot-blooded Latina.

Throughout the twentieth century Hollywood depicted Latin America and its people through a series of clichés and stock types. The cinema sanitized the racial makeup of Latinos by foregrounding white-skinned stars and relegating those with darker coloring to minor roles as extras. During both world wars, however, the Hollywood images of Latinos improved as a direct consequence of political events and commercial considerations. During World War II in particular, the United States began to exercise greater care in its portrayal of its Latin American neighbors in an effort to unite the hemisphere against the threat posed by the Axis powers.

It is only in the last few years that major changes have taken place in the representation of Latin American identity on screen. U.S. film producers have finally awakened to the fact that Hispanics are the "majority minority" community in the United States today. What is now referred to as "Latino power" in Hollywood has become such an issue that the casting of a non-Latino in the role of a Latin American would now be considered tantamount to casting a white actor in blackface as an African American. But just a few years ago this was not the case. In 1996 Italian-Americans with unconvincing Latino accents were cast in Baz Luhrmann's *Romeo + Juliet*, and Madonna played Eva Perón in *Evita* (1996). In the forties and fifties the Mexican actor Anthony Quinn was cast only in subordinate ethnic roles; today it is fashionable to look Latino. Light brown skin and a curvaceous physique are portrayed on screen as beautiful, epitomized by the phenomenally successful singer and actor Jennifer Lopez, the first Latina ever to earn a salary in excess of $1 million for a screen role.

In the United States today, Chicano (Mexican-American) identity draws heavily on iconic figures and myths from that community's shared popular culture. The hybrid nature of Chicano identity, to which concepts such as *mestizaje*, transculturation, and the conceptualization of the border are central, is reflected in such figures as *La Llorona* (literally, "The Weeping Woman"), who on migration to North America has come to symbolize the poor migrant or "wetback." Likewise, *el pachuco*, or disenchanted Mexican-American youth, personifies the mythical hybrid essence of Chicano identity. Despite some ongoing ambivalence about the meaning of *el pachuco* for Chicanos (for some, the word is still synonymous with gang violence and sacrificial, self-destructive urges), in Chicano films such as Luis Valdez's *Zoot Suit* (1981) this figure is nevertheless a potent representation of the community's place in U.S. society.

—*Lisa Shaw and Thea Pitman*

See also: *Introduction*

Latin Americans in Hollywood

Historically, Hollywood has portrayed Latin Americans via recurrent stereotypes. In the first decades of sound cinema, female actors with Latin American backgrounds were obliged to take screen roles as fiery temptresses (Lupe Vélez, Carmen Miranda) or virginal, aristocratic *señoritas* (Dolores Del Río). Males were typically cast as Latin lovers (Ramon Novarro, César Romero). Such clichéd and unflattering depictions of Latino identity, which hinge on a mythical sexuality, have resurfaced in recent years with male stars like the Spaniard Antonio Banderas and the Cuban-born Andy García often typecast as smoldering Romeos. Latina actors still have to struggle against a reemergence of the spitfire stereotype.

In the 1930s and 1940s, major films featured Latino and Latina stars with clearly identifiable Hispanic names (Ramon Novarro, Ricardo Montalban, Lupe Vélez, Carmen Miranda, Dolores Del Río), and these actors played a variety of roles. Today it is difficult to find their equivalent among female actors. Even in films with Latino settings and characters, such as *The House of the Spirits* (1993), *The Perez Family* (1995), *Evita* (1996), and *The Mask of Zorro* (1998), the lead female roles are given to established non-Latina stars, reflecting the overwhelming importance of commercial considerations over "authenticity." Contemporary Hollywood film has toned down but not eliminated the Latin lover stock type for male actors, and the Latino bandits that featured widely in early Westerns have been transformed into urban equivalents in films about the Latino community that are increasingly being set in crime-ridden and often violent inner-city contexts. However, alternative filmmakers from the Latino community in the United States have produced creative responses to issues of exclusion, discrimination, and stereotyping.

The exclusion of Latinos from leading roles in mainstream films has been challenged recently by the hit movie *Frida* (2002), produced by Mexican-born Salma Hayek, who also starred in the leading role as avant-garde artist Frida Kahlo. Although some have criticized the choice of non-Latino actors for some of the major parts in this film, such as that of Ashley Judd to play the Italian-born Mexican photogra-

Hollywood's Latino heartthrob, Andy Garcia. (Miramax/The Kobal Collection)

pher Tina Modotti, Hayek herself is being hailed as the first Mexican Hollywood star since Dolores Del Río. There seems to have been a slow awakening in recent years to the fact that 47 percent of the population of Los Angeles is Hispanic (including 5 million Mexicans). Two major films have been released that contain a significant portion of spoken Spanish (*Before Night Falls* [2000] and *Traffic* [2000]). In both cases a

Ricardo Montalban in 1953, one of many successful Latinos in Hollywood. (Eric Carpenter/MGM/The Kobal Collection)

Spanish speaker not native to the country being portrayed made every effort to imitate a local accent. Both the Spaniard Javier Bardem, as a Cuban in *Before Night Falls*, and Puerto Rican American Benicio del Toro, as a Mexican in *Traffic* (who won the Oscar for best actor for his performance), were entirely convincing. The producers of both films knew how many Cubans and Mexicans would be part of the audience for these films in the United States and realized that they could not be fooled. Just a few years earlier, the filmmakers would not have paid such attention to detail—in 1998 the Welsh actress Catherine Zeta Jones was cast as a Mexican in *The Mask of Zorro*.

From the early days of cinema, Latino actors were divided into two groups, in accordance with their perceived color and class. Those with European "looks" became major actors (Dolores Del Río, Carmen Miranda, Raul Roulien, César Romero), and those with darker coloring were destined to play small parts as bandits or work as "native" extras. When a character with darker pigmentation was called for, brownface makeup was applied.

Myrtle Gonzalez, a native Mexican Californian and the daughter of a Los Angeles grocer, was Hollywood's first Latin star. She starred in more than forty silent movies between 1911 and 1917. Dolores Del Río is often referred to as "the first Latina superstar," and her fellow Mexican Lupe Vélez became synonymous with the fire-spitting vamp. Katy Jurado made the journey from Mexico City to Hollywood in 1951 and starred in the critically acclaimed Western *High Noon* (1952) as a strong Latina character who had been the mistress of both leading men but was also the feisty owner of the local saloon. In Mexican films she usually played the role of glamour girl or wealthy socialite, whereas in U.S. films she was cast as a sultry Mexican beauty, Indian squaw, or long-suffering matriarch. Ricardo Montalban and Fernando Lamas both starred as romantic leads in Hollywood films from the 1950s. Montalban was instrumental in forming the organization Nosotros (meaning "us" in Spanish) in 1969, which seeks to improve opportunities for Latinos in the U.S. media.

Others have forged their careers on the big screen by turning their backs on their Hispanic identities. Rita Hayworth, born to an Irish mother and Spanish father, began her career as Margarita Carmen Cansino, playing Mexican señoritas. By anglicizing her name, raising her hairline off her face through electrolysis, and dying her hair auburn, she went on to become the "all-American girl," favorite pinup of the 1940s, and the eponymous heroine of a movie called *The Strawberry Blonde* (1941). Similarly, Raquel Welch, born into an Anglo-Bolivian family in Chicago as Raquel Tejada, has become a movie icon whose ethnic roots are not emphasized, or even well known, from the roles she has chosen.

In the period just before and during the Second World War, large portions of the European economy were closed to Hollywood's products, so the Latin American market for movies became increasingly important. At the same time, the U.S. State Department was concerned about hemispheric unity in the face of the fascist threat in Europe. The United States implemented its so-called Good Neighbor Policy in 1933, aimed at achieving greater understanding and cooperation between North and South America. Film was central in fostering a spirit of Pan-Americanism. The year 1933 saw the release of RKO's *Flying Down to Rio*, starring Brazilian Raul Roulien and Mexican Dolores Del Río (playing Belinha Rezende, a member of Brazil's white-skinned elite). This musical, like others that followed in its wake, aimed to create an impression of Latin identity that would be acceptable to both North and Latin American audiences while loosely enacting the diplomatic gestures toward Latin Americans required by the new foreign policy. However, in *Flying Down to Rio*, Brazilian/Latin American women are once again synonymous with powers of seduction and lasciviousness. When Belinha first dances with her handsome Anglo suitor, one of her blonde female companions from the United States complains, "What have the South Americans got below the Equator that we haven't?"

To more effectively implement the "Good Neighbor Policy," the U.S. government established the Office of the Coordinator of Inter-American Affairs (CIAA) in 1940. Headed by Nelson Rockefeller, the CIAA sponsored newsreels and documentaries for Latin American distribution and encouraged the Hollywood studios to make films with Latin American themes. Between 1939 and 1947, Hollywood films featuring Latin American stars, music, locations, and stories flooded U.S. and international markets. By 1943, thirty films with Latin American themes or locales had been released and twenty-five more were in production; by 1945 eighty-four films with Latin American subjects had been produced. The CIAA's motion picture section, directed by John Hay Whitney, aimed to ensure that North Americans developed a better understanding of Latin America and to avoid causing offense to the neighbors to the south. When the war began, Hollywood's Production Code Administration (PCA) played a key role as "watchdog," ensuring that no negative images of Latin Americans reached the screen. A Cuban-raised Latin American specialist, Addison Durland, was hired as part of the PCA staff in 1941 to monitor Hollywood's depiction of Latin America and its people and to avoid the kind of errors that had previously been committed, such as depicting Brazil as a Spanish-speaking country.

—Lisa Shaw

See also: *Cultural Icons:* Latin Americans in Hollywood (Dolores Del Río; Salma Hayek; Carmen Miranda; Lupe Vélez); *Visual Arts and Architecture:* Art (Frida Kahlo); Photography (Tina Modotti)

Bibliography

García Berumen, Frank Javier. 1995. *The Chicano/Hispanic Image in American Film.* New York: Vantage Press.

Mexican beauty and Hollywood star Dolores Del Río. (Ernest Bachrach/RKO/The Kobal Collection)

Richard, Alfred Charles Jr. 1993. *Censorship and Hollywood's Hispanic Image: An Interpretive Filmography, 1936–1955.* Westport, CT, and London: Greenwood Press.

Ríos-Bustamante, Antonio José. 1991. *Latinos in Hollywood.* Encino, CA: Floricanto Press.

Rodríguez, Clara E. 1998. *Latin Looks: Images of Latinas and Latinos in the U.S. Media.* Boulder, CO, and Oxford: Westview.

Dolores Del Río (1905–1983)

Mexican film star and legendary, glamorous beauty who became famous as the face of the sophisticated Latina in Hollywood. Born into a wealthy family in Durango, Mexico, on 3 August 1905 (according to some accounts 1901), she died on 11 April 1983.

Del Río arrived in Hollywood with her lawyer husband in 1925, and her career spanned the silent and early sound eras. In 1928 she signed an exceptional contract with United Artists to make seven films at 100,000 dollars apiece, her fee reportedly including six months' paid holiday per year. Between 1925 and 1942 she participated in twenty-eight North American feature films. Although considered "exotic," she appeared in a variety of films and roles, and she was not restricted to playing the part of Latinas even though she was undeniably Latin American. Above all she played ethnically ambiguous characters with a potent sexuality and a penchant for white, blond leading men. These included South Seas princesses, Indian maidens, Latin American *señoritas* (not only Mexicans—in RKO's *Flying Down to Rio* she played an upper-class Brazilian), and a range of other beauties with an aristocratic air. Her status as a great Hollywood star was undeniable and evidenced by the fact that the Pullman company named three of its sleeper carriages in her honor: "Del Río," "Dolores," and "Ramona" (the latter is the title of one of her movies).

In 1943, when opportunities began to dry up in the United States, Del Río returned to Mexico to dedicate herself to the cinema and theater of her homeland, where she had become a focus for national pride. There she went on to star in several box-office successes, such as *Flor Silvestre* (*Wild Flower*, 1943) and *María Candelaria* (1944), where she played an uneducated, barefoot Indian girl, totally transforming her screen image.

Del Río divorced her first husband in 1928, and two years later married Cedric Gibbons, the well-known artistic director of MGM, a union that transported her into the Hollywood jet set. By 1941 she was involved in a controversial relationship with Orson Welles, who, after directing *Citizen*

Kane (1941), was Hollywood's man of the moment. She attended the film's premiere on the arm of her lover. They had been planning to marry, but while Del Río was waiting for her divorce to come through, Welles found another Hispanic beauty to take her place—Margarita Carmen Cansino, better known as Rita Hayworth.

—Lisa Shaw

See also: *Cultural Icons:* Latin Americans in Hollywood; *Popular Cinema:* Melodrama

Bibliography

López, Ana M. 1993. "Are All Latins from Manhattan?: Hollywood, Ethnography and Cultural Colonialism." Pp. 67–80 in *Mediating Two Worlds: Cinematic Encounters in the Americas*, edited by John King, Ana M. López, and Manuel Alvarado. London: BFI Publishing.

Monsiváis, Carlos. 1997. "Dolores del Río: The Face as Institution." Pp. 71–87 in *Mexican Postcards*, edited and translated by John Kraniauskas. London and New York: Verso.

Lupe Vélez (1908–1944)

Mexican film star who became synonymous with the comic role of the hot-blooded, thickly accented, "fire-spitting vamp" in Hollywood movies of the 1930s, such as *Hot Pepper* (1933) and *Strictly Dynamite* (1934). Born in San Luis Potosí, Mexico, on 6 July 1908, her first major role was opposite Douglas Fairbanks in the silent movie *The Gaucho* (1928). A star of the silent screen by the end of the 1920s, she successfully made the transition to sound films in the 1930s as a result of her husky, almost "cartoon-like" voice. Her career was consolidated in 1939 when she began starring in the so-called Mexican Spitfire series. She made eight films in this series before committing suicide at the height of her fame and success on 12 December 1944, when she was five months' pregnant out of wedlock.

Vélez's screen persona was the antithesis of that of her compatriot, Dolores Del Río. Together the pair personified the dualistic stereotypical Hollywood depiction of Latin American women as either earthy spitfires or cool *señoritas*. Unlike Del Río, Vélez's position in Hollywood was defined by her potent ethnicity and aggressive sexuality rather than her acting ability. Vélez is sometimes compared unfavorably with Del Río, but she had impressive comic skills, shown off to perfection in RKO's Mexican Spitfire series with her portrayal of the fiery, funny, and streetwise Carmelita, who often outwitted other women to "get the guy" in the end. On and off screen, she, like Del Río, was paired off with and married North American men.

—Lisa Shaw

See also: *Cultural Icons:* Latin Americans in Hollywood (Dolores Del Río)

Bibliography

López, Ana M. 1993. "Are All Latins from Manhattan?: Hollywood, Ethnography and Cultural Colonialism." Pp. 67–80 in *Mediating Two Worlds: Cinematic Encounters in the Americas*, edited by John King, Ana M. López, and Manuel Alvarado. London: BFI Publishing.

Rodríguez, Clara E. 1998. *Latin Looks: Images of Latinas and Latinos in the U.S. Media.* Boulder, CO, and Oxford: Westview.

Carmen Miranda (1909–1955)

Singer and film star who came to embody Latin American music and identity in Hollywood films of the 1940s and 1950s. Born in Portugal in 1909, Miranda's parents emigrated to Brazil when she was a small child. She died in 1955, aged forty-six.

The "Brazilian Bombshell," Carmen Miranda, 1939. (Bettmann/Corbis)

Miranda's career in Brazil as a singer of samba was established in the 1920s and 1930s, when she recorded gramophone records, performed regularly on the radio stations of Rio de Janeiro, and was featured in many of the first sound films or *chanchadas* made in Brazil. "Discovered" in 1939 by U.S. show business impresario Lee Schubert, Miranda was taken to Broadway and subsequently to Hollywood, where she became the highest-paid female star, best known for her performances in the Twentieth Century Fox "Good Neighbor" musicals of the early 1940s, such as *That Night in Rio* (1941) and Busby Berkeley's *The Gang's All Here* (1943). She also became known for her flamboyant costumes, and particularly her fruit-laden turbans. Since the 1960s she has become something of an international icon among gay men and transvestites, not least for a carnival group in Rio named after her. Her characteristic tutti-frutti hats and necklaces, frilly sleeves, and multicolored skirts are easily parodied.

Within the context of the so-called Good Neighbor Policy toward the Latin American subcontinent, Miranda's success in the international arena as the epitome of Latino identity hinged on her acquiescence in diluting samba for the Anglo-Saxon palate. For this reason she has remained a polemical figure in Brazil, as was eloquently conveyed in Helena Solberg's biopic *Carmen Miranda: Bananas Is My Business* (1994). This film highlighted Miranda's iconic status among the ordinary people of Brazil, despite the fact that elite intellectuals criticized her for being a passive tool of North American cultural imperialism.

President Getúlio Vargas of Brazil, in power between 1930 and 1945, was a great fan of Miranda, and he saw her 1939 trip to the United States as a public relations coup for his nation. For her part, Miranda took her role as Brazil's "goodwill ambassador" quite seriously, and the ultimate good neighbor was later drafted into the service of the Allied armed forces. Newsreel footage of her arrival in New York declared that the Depression was over when Miranda came to town. For American audiences she would remain the archetypal Latina bimbo. (In her first interview in the United States she famously claimed to know only the following words of English: money and men.) When she returned to Brazil some eighteen months later, the Vargas regime's DIP (Press and Propaganda Department) held an official reception in her honor, and the masses clamored to greet her. This warm welcome could not have differed more from the frosty reception she received from the elite audience at her homecoming show at the Urca casino, organized by Brazil's first lady, Darcy Vargas.

Carmen Miranda soon returned to the United States and to a contract with Twentieth Century Fox, and her immense popularity ensured that she was the studio's greatest asset. Consequently, Fox insisted that she play stereotypical roles in similar musicals, which reproduced the image of the exaggerated and caricatured Latina, despite her desire to play more varied roles. In *Carmen Miranda: Bananas Is My Business*, Helena Solberg comments on Miranda's poignant attempts to reaffirm her own Brazilian identity, often by merely speaking a few words of Portuguese in a film, and by poking fun at her poor English. Solberg also focuses on the inconsistencies and paradoxes in Miranda's screen image; her outfits and the music she danced to (samba) were symbols of black Brazil, yet she was the daughter of white Portuguese immigrants. She was the most potent symbol of Latin America in the Hollywood musical, yet was fiercely attacked back in Brazil for acquiescing to this cultural stereotyping. She became the highest-paid woman in the United States, and although she acknowledged her debt of gratitude to her iconic status, singing "I make my money with bananas" and stating "bananas is my business," she was clearly uneasy in the cultural straitjacket she had been forced to wear.

Her attempts to free herself from her image are reflected in her decision to buy herself out of her contract with Twentieth Century Fox, and the fact that in her first movie with another studio, *Copacabana* of 1947 with Groucho Marx, she appears for the first time as a blonde. Nevertheless, fragments of her old caricature were retained in this film, in which she played both the role of the blonde Mademoiselle Fifi and that of the archetypal Latin temptress, a Brazilian singer named Carmen Navarro. In the context of a postwar America, where the neighbors to the south of the border ceased to be a pressing concern, Miranda was destined to become merely a novelty act, particularly on television.

By the mid-1930s Miranda was relatively well established as a singer in Brazil. In 1936, she was one of the many Brazilian radio stars to appear in the film *Alô, alô, carnaval!* (*Hello, Hello, Carnival!*), often called the first example of the *chanchada* musical genre. Though successful in Brazil, the film achieved no critical or popular attention when shown in the United States. In 1939 she made her final film in Brazil, *Banana da terra* (*Banana of the Land*), set on the fictitious Pacific island of Bananolândia. It was in this film that Miranda first appeared dressed as a *baiana*, in a stylized version of the costume worn by the Afro-Brazilian street vendors of the city of Salvador in the state of Bahia, which transformed the baskets of fruit that these women carried on their heads into an exuberant, edible turban.

In the 1940s the image of Carmen Miranda became central to both Hollywood's "Good Neighbor" films and Pan-Americanism itself. She made nine films with Twentieth Century Fox between 1940 and 1946 and was also a key figure in advertising campaigns of the time, promoting clothing based on her own exotic style for Saks Fifth Avenue, along with various beauty products.

—*Lisa Shaw*

See also: *Popular Music:* Samba; *Mass Media:* Radio (Brazil); *Popular Cinema:* Comedy Film (*Chanchada*)

Bibliography

Augusto, Sérgio. 1995. "Hollywood Looks at Brazil: From Carmen Miranda to *Moonraker*." Pp. 351–361 in *Brazilian Cinema*, edited by Randal Johnson and Robert Stam. New York: Columbia University Press.

Gil-Montero, Martha. 1989. *Brazilian Bombshell: The Biography of Carmen Miranda*. New York: Donald I. Fine.

López, Ana M. 1993. "Are All Latins from Manhattan?: Hollywood, Ethnography and Cultural Colonialism." Pp. 67–80 in *Mediating Two Worlds: Cinematic Encounters in the Americas*, edited by John King, Ana M. López, and Manuel Alvarado. London: BFI Publishing.

Salma Hayek (1966–)

Actor born in southeast Mexico to a father of Lebanese origin and a Mexican mother, often referred to as the first Mexican Hollywood star since Dolores Del Río. She began her career in *telenovelas* or soap operas on Mexican television in the late 1980s, then moved to Hollywood, where she played several minor roles before receiving critical acclaim for her work in *Desperado* (1995) alongside the Spaniard Antonio Banderas. She then returned to Mexico to film *El Callejón de los Milagros* (*Midaq Alley*, 1995), for which she was nominated for an Ariel, the Mexican equivalent of the Oscar. She was the creative force behind the latest film based on the life of Mexican artist Frida Kahlo, coproducing and starring in the title role of *Frida* (2002).

In the late 1980s, Hayek was perhaps Mexico's biggest television star. She appeared in soap operas such as *Un nuevo amanecer* (*A New Dawn*, 1988) and *Teresa* (1989). When she arrived in Los Angeles, however, she found that it was hard to carve out an acting career. She once said:

Mexican actress and Hollywood star Salma Hayek. (Mitchell Gerber/Corbis)

"Being Mexican was considered so uncool. People in Hollywood only know Mexicans as maids." She has espoused the Latino cause in the United States, running through the streets of Washington, D.C., wearing a wedding dress in 2002 to protest domestic violence. In an interview with *Latina* magazine in October 2002 she tackled the subject of the marginalization of Latino actors in Hollywood, saying: "You can't wait for things to change, so I don't wait; I try to create jobs for myself and for other Latins and tell our stories. That's the best we can do."

It took Hayek eight years to get her beloved Frida Kahlo project off the ground, fighting off fierce competition from Madonna, who had long been campaigning to play the role. Since then she has directed the television film *The Maldonado*

Miracle (2003) and has starred in the Roberto Rodriguez movie *Once Upon a Time in Mexico* (2003).

There is evidence that Hayek is sometimes stereotyped as the fiery Mexican, following in the footsteps of Lupe Vélez. As recently as 22 July 2003, the admittedly low-brow *National Enquirer* described Hayek as "the 5-foot-2 spitfire."

—*Lisa Shaw*

See also: *Cultural Icons:* Latin Americans in Hollywood (Dolores Del Río; Lupe Vélez); *Mass Media:* Telenovelas (Mexico); *Visual Arts and Architecture:* Art (Frida Kahlo)

Bibliography

Duncan, Patricia J. 1999. *Salma Hayek.* New York: St. Martin's Press.

Menard, Valerie. 1999. *Salma Hayek: A Real-Life Reader Biography.* Elkton, MD: Mitchell Lane.

Scott, Kieran. 2001. *Salma Hayek: Latinos in the Limelight.* Broomall, PA: Chelsea House.

Walt Disney's Latino Cartoon Characters

The animated character of Joe Carioca (Zé Carioca in Brazil), a Brazilian parrot, starred in two feature-length films in the 1940s, *Saludos Amigos* (RKO-Disney, 1943) and *The Three Caballeros* (RKO-Disney, 1945). *Saludos Amigos* also featured Pedro, a "baby" Chilean airplane that transported mail between Chile and Argentina; Goofy dressed as an Argentine gaucho; and Donald Duck as a U.S. tourist visiting the Andes. In *The Three Caballeros*, Joe Carioca starred alongside Donald Duck, a Uruguayan flying donkey called Burrito, and a Mexican bird named Panchito.

These cartoon representations of Latin American identity were central to Hollywood's depiction of the subcontinent in the political context of the U.S. "Good Neighbor Policy" toward its neighbors to the south. On returning from his fact-finding trip to South America in 1941, Disney was keen to emphasize that attention to authentic detail would be a principal feature of his "Good Neighbor" projects.

Saludos Amigos was a combination of a travelogue that documented a trip carried out by Disney and his creative team to Latin America and an animated cartoon. The latter was divided into four discrete shorts, the first set in Bolivia, the second in Chile, the third in Argentina, and the fourth in Brazil. The first short begins with Donald Duck arriving in Lake Titicaca, suffering from altitude sickness and encountering a friendly indigenous boy and his llama. The second shows Pedro the plane transporting the mail over the Andes between the cities of Santiago in Chile and Mendoza in Argentina when his "papa" (the official mail plane) falls ill. The third segment is set in Argentina, with location shots of sophisticated Buenos Aires and an animated sequence set in the rural pampas. In the final sequence, entitled "Aquarela do Brasil" ("Watercolor of Brazil"), the streetwise, cigar-smoking Joe Carioca introduces Donald Duck to the wonders of Rio de Janeiro, more specifically samba, *cachaça* (sugarcane brandy), and the nightspots of the Urca casino and Copacabana. Disney's Brazil combines natural and exotic treasures with cosmopolitan sophistication, and the foreign tourist (Donald) is made most welcome. The documentary footage that precedes this fourth animated segment opens with picture-postcard shots of Rio, as Disney narrates: "This time we planned to stay a little longer and get a better look at some of the famous sights, such as Sugarloaf overlooking the bay, and Copacabana beach, the playground of Rio, and Corcovado overlooking Rio itself. This is the kind of city that always appeals to artists, picturesque little outdoor cafes, colorful mosaic sidewalks."

The Three Caballeros mixed live action with animation and was viewed in the motion picture press as a remarkable technical achievement. Aurora Miranda, Carmen Miranda's younger sister, appears dancing alongside Joe Carioca. Beautiful young girls such as Miranda, the Mexican singer Dora Luz, and dancer Carmen Molina feature prominently in this Technicolor visit by Donald Duck to Mexico and Brazil. In Mexico, Donald flirts with Luz and Molina on the beaches of Acapulco and later visits Mexico City. The Brazilian section is authenticated by the incorporation of songs by the Brazilian samba composer Ari Barroso ("Bahia" and "Os quindins de Yayá"—"Missy's Coconut Cakes"). Promotional material for the picture describes it as "a miracle-world of rhythm and fun!" (*Variety*, 3 January, 1945), an epithet that encapsulates Disney's view of Latin America. In this film the spectator visits Bahia (Salvador), not Rio, but the two cities are barely distinguishable and the choice of Bahia would appear to stem, in part at least, from the themes of Barroso's two songs, one of which is a hyperbolic anthem to Salvador, the other a tribute to the Afro-Brazilian food sellers of the city (represented on screen by the very white Aurora Miranda in the traditional dress of the Afro-Brazilian *baiana* street vendors).

In both *Saludos Amigos* and *The Three Caballeros*, Brazil and its "representative," Joe Carioca, epitomize, more than any other nation depicted, the essence of Hollywood's vision of Latin America in the 1940s as a source of pure spectacle, rhythmic exuberance, and carnal spontaneity.

—*Lisa Shaw*

See also: *Popular Music:* Samba; *Sport and Leisure:* Food (Brazilian Food); *Cultural Icons:* Latin Americans in Hollywood (Carmen Miranda); Regional and Ethnic Types (The Gaucho in Argentina and Uruguay)

Bibliography

Burton-Carvajal, Julianne. 1994. "'Surprise Package': Looking Southward with Disney." Pp. 131–147 in *Disney Discourse: Producing the Magic Kingdom*, edited by Eric Smoodin. New York and London: Routledge.

Conde, Maite, and Lisa Shaw. In press. "Brazil through Hollywood's Gaze: From the Silent Screen to the Good Neighbor Policy Era." In *Latin American Cinema: Essays on Modernity, Gender and National Identity.* Jefferson, NC: McFarland.

Political Icons

Evita (1919–1952)

The affectionate nickname of Eva Duarte de Perón, the one-time actress of lowly origin who rose to a position of considerable power within Argentine society and whose political life was tragically cut short by cancer.

Eva María Duarte Ibarguren was born in Los Toldos, in the province of Buenos Aires, the illegitimate child of a failed landowner. According to popular mythology, Eva from an early age was determined to drag herself out of the penury into which she had been born. At age fifteen she seduced a tango singer and convinced him to take her with him to the Argentine capital, where she embarked on a series of romances. She survived financially by taking small parts in theatrical and radio productions. Some of her biographers have

Argentina's former first lady Eva Perón, better known as Evita, gives an election speech at a mass labor meeting, Buenos Aires, 1951. (Bettmann/Corbis)

suggested that when acting work was thin on the ground, Eva turned to prostitution.

Eva's fortunes took a turn for the better when she met and married Colonel Juan Domingo Perón, the minister for labor, in 1945. Perón became president of the Republic in 1946 on a populist ticket and was reelected in 1951. Eva's role in Perón's government was to offer a softer, more humane face to what was ultimately an authoritarian regime. Taking the role of first lady far beyond its traditional limits of dutiful support and companionship, Eva became directly involved in her husband's welfare policies, heading the charity foundation Fundación Eva Perón, which was responsible for the distribution of vast quantities of foodstuffs and material goods, including cookers, bicycles, and toys.

Eva Perón's supporters (a wide majority of the population at the time) viewed her with great affection because, as they saw it, her welfare work helped bring the so-called *descamisados* (literally "the shirtless" poor, partly made up of Argentina's previously invisible mixed-race peasants) to the center of political discussion. She also provided a strong role model for many of the women (the new breed of female factory worker, for example) who had been granted suffrage under Perón's government and who felt included in political culture for the first time. Her enemies, the conservative elite and radical Left, accused her and her husband of the worst excesses of populist politics and "clientelism."

Evita's perceived generosity was not the only reason for her remarkable popularity.

She was a highly charismatic figure whose stage presence and melodramatic speeches captivated the masses. Through her charity work and the time she took to visit and talk to the poor, she successfully projected messages of hope and empathy to the Argentine people, whom she frequently described as her family. In 1951 she was matron of honor at the wedding ceremony of 1,608 couples. The love for Evita was so powerful that she was likened to the caring Virgin. Many believed that she was capable of miraculous acts. On her death, tens of thousands of letters were sent to the Vatican attributing miracles to her and demanding that she be canonized. When Evita was diagnosed with cancer, many of her fans made ambitious promises to God to have her restored to good health. Also, large numbers of people attempted to make the headlines, in the hope that they would be in her thoughts when she passed on, for example, the tango dancer who danced for 127 hours with 127 different partners.

The official mourning of Evita's death lasted for four days. Juan Perón set to building a mausoleum in which to display her embalmed body, but in 1955 the military regime buried her in a Milanese cemetery to prevent her grave from becoming a symbol of resistance. It was not until 1976 that Eva Perón was finally accepted by the Argentine elite, when she was laid to rest in Recoleta, the Buenos Aires cemetery for the rich and powerful.

Evita still enjoys iconic status in Argentina, similar to that of the tragic figure of Princess Diana in the United Kingdom. Like Diana, she was a trendsetter. Young people would copy her attire, in particular her penchant for wearing flared skirts and strappy shoes, as well as her hair swept back in plaited chignons. To this day, the trend set by Evita for peroxide-blond hair continues in Argentina among upper-class women in northern Buenos Aires, those working at the grassroots political level, and among the wives of governors.

During her lifetime Eva Perón enjoyed a high profile throughout much of the Spanish-speaking world, but it was not until the 1970s that she became known to a wider, English-speaking public, when lyricist Tim Rice, having heard a radio broadcast on Eva Perón in his car, decided to transform the story of her life into a musical. With music by Andrew Lloyd Webber, *Evita* the musical premiered in London's West End at the Prince Edward Theatre in 1978 and enjoyed a run of over 2,900 performances. It hit Broadway in 1979, where it ran for 1,567 performances and garnered seven Tony awards. Since then it has been staged in twenty-eight countries in fourteen different languages, making it one of the most successful musicals of all time. The show, which questions Eva's morality in earlier years and emphasizes her ruthlessness in acquiring an important husband, was banned in the Philippines because of alleged parallels between the life of Eva Perón and President Marcos's wife, Imelda.

In 1996 a film version of the musical was released. Alan Parker's practically dialogue-free movie was a bold attempt at a modern reworking of the musical form. Starring Madonna in the title role (another love/hate figure with iconic status), with Antonio Banderas playing Che, the everyman character, it was shot on location in Argentina, sparking controversy among Evita's many fans for its seemingly irreverent treatment of their heroine. Despite the film's hype, *Evita* the movie received a lukewarm reception by critics and the public.

—Stephanie Dennison

See also: *Popular Music:* Tango; *Popular Social Movements and Politics:* Peronismo

Bibliography

Auyero, Javier. 2000. *Poor People's Politics: Peronist Survival Networks and the Legacy of Evita.* Durham: Duke University Press.

Evita (video recording). 1996. Directed by Alan Parker.

Fraser, Nicholas, and Marysa Navarro. 1996. *Evita: The Real Lives of Eva Perón.* London: André Deutsch.

Martínez, Tomás Eloy. 2002. "Saint Evita." Pp. 296–303 in *The Argentina Reader: History, Culture, Politics,* edited by Gabriela Nouzeilles and Graciela Montaldo. Durham and London: Duke University Press.

Perón, Eva. 1953. *My Mission in Life.* New York: Vantage.

Che Guevara (1928–1967)

The most romantic and photogenic of all Latin American revolutionaries, Ernesto "Che" Guevara has, ever since his death, been associated primarily with a single image. The famous picture of Che, gazing into the distance from beneath the star on his beret, became the single most potent element of his iconic status in the 1960s and early 1970s. Since then, images of him in the West have become increasingly divorced from his political and historical context and, ironically, have been exploited as a radical-chic commercial icon. In Latin America, however, awareness of the value of Guevara's thought and example has largely been maintained.

Ernesto Guevara Lynch de la Serna was born into a comfortable but politically active family and spent his childhood in the Argentine city of Córdoba. He showed few early signs of the political activity to come and appeared destined for a medical career. Journeys into deprived areas of Argentina (1949) and into Chile, Peru, and Colombia (the famous motorcycle trip in 1951–1952) brought him to an increasingly militant position and the renunciation of a comfortable bourgeois existence. Having completed his studies, he was in Guatemala in 1954 during the CIA-led overthrow of the Arbenz government. By now a hardened foe of U.S. imperialism, he traveled to Mexico and his fateful encounter with Fidel Castro.

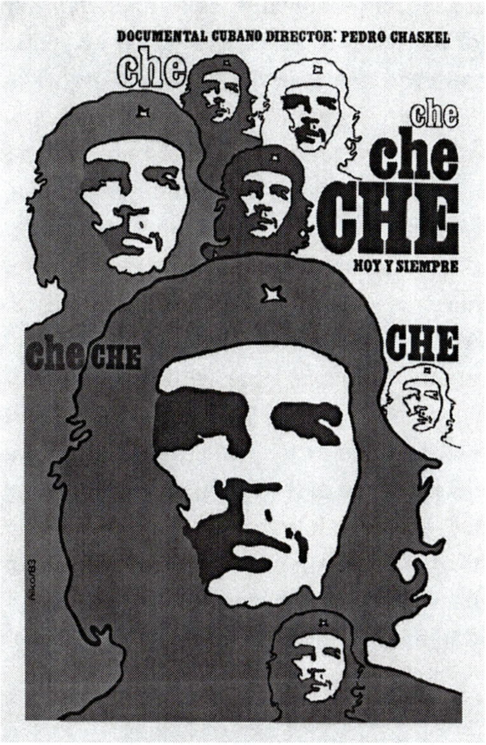

Che, Hoy y Siempre movie poster (1983). (Swim Ink/Corbis)

After the success of the armed struggle in the Cuban Sierra Maestra mountains, during which he rose to second in command, Guevara's writings and actions compounded his immense popularity and identification with the Cuban Revolution. Granted Cuban citizenship, he coined the notion of a new humanity, which had to arise from the socialist experiment in order for the latter to make any sense. Idealistic and even anarchic, he was in many ways the antithesis to Fidel Castro's pragmatism, and the two tendencies could not coexist indefinitely. After briefly filling an ambassadorial role, he criticized the Soviet Union in 1965 as an accomplice of imperialism and was sidelined from formal politics. Progressively less involved with Cuban internal affairs and more with revolutionary activity elsewhere, Che went to Africa and took part in efforts to end the Belgian colonial presence in the Congo. After returning to Cuba for training, he embarked upon the ill-advised incursion into eastern Bolivia that was to prove his downfall.

Many of the peasants he had hoped would support and even join the cause proved to be mistrustful, susceptible to government propaganda demonizing foreign Communists. Having expected to find the same degree of political awareness in the sparsely populated east as in the militant mining areas of western Bolivia, Guevara's forces were left hopelessly depleted and outflanked, and their leader was finally shot dead without trial on express instructions from Washington in December 1967.

As a grisly postscript, Che's hands were severed from his corpse by the military for reasons of identification. Having been hidden in a house in La Paz, they were eventually smuggled to Cuba for burial. Publication of the diaries of Guevara's motorcycle journey through South America in 1950–1951 was greeted by attempts to discredit him through an anachronistic application of 1990s "political correctness." However, this book brought to light the self-abnegation and identification with the Latin American poor that characterized Guevara. A new film of the book, *The Motorcycle Diaries* (2004), directed by the Brazilian Walter Salles and featuring Mexican actor Gael García Bernal as Che, may further enhance the Argentine revolutionary's reputation.

—*Keith Richards*

See also: *Popular Social Movements and Politics:* Castrismo

Bibliography

Anderson, Jon Lee. 1997. *Che Guevara: A Revolutionary Life.* New York: Grove Press.

Guevara, Ernesto. 1995. *The Motorcycle Diaries: A Journey around South America.* London: Verso.

James, Daniel, ed. 2000. *The Complete Bolivian Diaries of Che Guevara and Other Captured Documents.* New York: Cooper Square Press.

Suárez Salazar, Luis, ed. 2001. *Che Guevara and the Latin American Revolutionary Movements.* New York: Ocean Press.

Regional and Ethnic Types

The Gaucho in Argentina and Uruguay

A figure that has long held a central place in the national imaginations of both Argentina and Uruguay. From the eighteenth to twentieth centuries, metropolitan views of this "cowboy of the pampas" were transformed from initial contempt to grudging admiration to an eventual nostalgia for the loss of a way of life seen as quintessentially Argentine or Uruguayan.

The origins of the gaucho are unclear, and debate on the subject is divided into "Hispanist" and "Americanist" schools. These hold that the gaucho's crucial formative factors are, respectively, the Arabic-Iberian influence crystallized in Andalusia, and the frontier experience of the New

World. What is beyond doubt is that these people were the result of a cultural and ethnic mixture (*mestizaje* in Spanish) discernible from their speech, accoutrements, and lifestyle. An example is the hunting instrument known as the *boleadora;* of indigenous origin, it consists of stone balls strung together and thrown to entwine the legs of a running animal. The gaucho's music also took native and African forms and blended them with Spanish verse patterns, resulting most notably in the *milonga* song form that would later metamorphose into the tango. Even the etymology of the term "gaucho," a possible corruption of the Quechua *guacho* (orphan), suggests an indigenous element.

A crucial dimension of gaucho life was their almost uncanny empathy with their horses and understanding of their natural environment, the vast *pampa* or open plains. This is conceded even by some of those people least sympathetic to gaucho existence, particularly the writer (and later statesman) Domingo Faustino Sarmiento (1811–1888). Even though his project for the Argentine nation was the elimination of such apparent obstacles to progress, Sarmiento records his awe at the feats of gaucho trackers in his seminal *Civilization and Barbarism.* This work, written while he was in exile in Chile in the 1840s, set out the positivist dichotomy that would prove to be the gaucho's death-knell: "civilization," synonymous with private capital and modernization, and "barbarism," the brush with which all non-Europeans would be tarred. Ironically, much of Sarmiento's work was done for him by his bitterest enemy, the tyrant Juan Manuel de Rosas (1793–1877). The frontier wars waged by Rosas in the 1820s, pitting mostly press-ganged gauchos and Negroes against indigenous populations in order to win control of the *pampa,* did much to eliminate all these "undesirable" elements.

Sarmiento's eventual return and election as president in 1868 meant that such ideas could be fully implemented. One of the most eloquent voices of opposition to Sarmiento's brutal "civilizing" project came in literary form. José Hernández's epic poem *El Gaucho Martín Fierro* (1872) is still hugely popular in Argentina. The finest example of the *gauchesco* poetic genre that drew on the speech, song, and mythology of the *pampa,* it has been the source of numerous adaptations and imitations. The success of the first part, *La Ida* or outward journey, seems due to the transparency and fallibility of the protagonist, a gaucho enlisted in the wars, and his predicament. Torn from his family, he deserts and then kills a man in a duel, becoming a pariah. The less convincing *Vuelta,* or return (1879), sees the gaucho rehabilitated, Fernández having partly accepted the new social climate.

The passing of the gaucho into folklore represents the abandonment of a kind of primeval innocence and adoption of the new rationalism that entered the region along with British commercial interests after the industrial revolution. The theme has often been revisited, albeit more obliquely, in the work of Jorge Luis Borges.

—*Keith Richards*

See also: *Popular Music:* Tango; *Popular Literature:* Science Fiction; *Language:* Indigenous Languages

Bibliography

Fuente, Ariel Eugenio de la. 2000. "Facundo and Chacho in Songs and Stories: Oral Culture and the Representations of Caudillos in the Nineteenth-Century Argentine

Interior." *Hispanic American Historical Review*, 80, no. 3: 503–535.

Lynch, John. 2000. *Massacre in the Pampas, 1872: Britain and Argentina in the Age of Migration.* Norman: University of Oklahoma Press.

Rivas Rojas, Raquel. 1998. "The 'Gaucho' and the 'Llanero': Settling Scores with the Past." *Travesía: Journal of Latin American Cultural Studies* 7, no. 2 (November): 185–201.

Slatta, Richard W. 1983. *Gauchos and the Vanishing Frontier.* London: University of Nebraska Press.

The Gaúcho in Brazil

Traditional mixed-race inhabitant of the *pampas* of Brazil's southernmost state, Rio Grande do Sul, and now a term used to describe Brazilians of any ethnic origin who hail from the south of the country.

The press that the Brazilian *gaúcho* received was never as bad as that of gauchos elsewhere in the Southern Cone. In Brazil, the brunt of the criticism from Brazil's white, sophisticated elite was aimed not at the *gaúchos* of the south, but at the mixed-race, landless poor of the northeastern states (the *caboclos*), famously portrayed by Euclides da Cunha in *Rebellion in the Backlands* and later by Colombian Boom novelist Gabriel García Márquez in *The War of the End of the World.*

Like his Argentine and Uruguayan counterparts, the Brazilian *gaúcho* as a social type has clearly defined (and widely mimicked) characteristics. He is associated with eating barbecued meat (*churrasco*) and drinking green tea (*chimarrão* or *mate*). According to social etiquette, *chimarrão* is consumed informally by groups of *gaúchos* in a *cuia* or small wooden basin and is sucked through a heavy metal straw or *bomba*. The *cuia* is drained before being refilled with hot water and passed on to the next drinker. The origins of drinking hot, green tea can be traced back to the sixteenth century, when Spanish soldiers borrowed its use from Guarani Indians as a much-needed hangover cure. *Gaúchos* strongly deny both the unhygienic aspect of the method of consuming this communal beverage and its alleged carcinogenic properties.

In addition to their own style of music and dance (for example, the fandango with its Hispanic roots) and speech that is peppered with phrases borrowed from their Spanish-speaking neighbors, Brazilian *gaúchos* have their own traditional attire, which relates to their cattle-herding past: black boots or espadrilles, neck scarf, and cowboy hat. The Turkish-style pants or *bombachas* that they wear were inherited from English soldiers, who reportedly brought them from the Ottoman Empire as spoils of war and dumped them in Paraguay during the War of the Triple Alliance (1865–1870).

The stereotypical *gaúcho* man is one who refuses to mince his words, and who is notoriously sexist and racist. He was brilliantly portrayed by comic writer Luis Fernando Veríssimo in *O analista de Bagé* (*The Analyst from Bagé*), which imagines the kind of politically incorrect advice that would be dished out by a psychoanalyst from the *pampas.*

In the 1940s, when rural workers poured into the towns and cities on the southern coast in search of jobs in the blossoming industrial sector, a *gaúcho* traditionalist movement began, with the purpose of combating the influence of culture from Rio de Janeiro and North America. This *Movimento Tradicionalista Gaúcho* claims to be the largest popular cultural organization in the Western world. The *35 Centros de*

Tradições Gaúchas or 35 Centers of Gaúcho Traditions were set up at this time as a space to celebrate *gaúcho* culture. There are now over 1,500 such centers in the state of Rio Grande do Sul, as well as large numbers in the two other southern states of Santa Catarina and Paraná. They can also be found as far afield as Paraguay and Boston. Critics of the movement argue that poor *gaúcho* peasants, on whom the modern cultural stereotype is based, were excluded from participating in the movement because of the costly joining fee. They also argue that at meetings the traditionalists take pride in dressing up in the clothes of these poor cowboys, but they adhere to the ideology of the rural elite. Such organizations are frequently seen from outside Rio Grande do Sul as being potentially politically conservative, separatist, and socially exclusive.

—*Stephanie Dennison*

See also: *Popular Literature:* The Boom

Bibliography

Oliven, Ruben George. 1996. *Tradition Matters: Modern Gaúcho Identity in Brazil.* New York: Columbia University Press.

Veríssimo, Erico. 1951. *Time and the Wind,* vol. 1. Translated by. L. L. Barrett. New York: Macmillan.

El Pachuco

Although the *pachuco* was the early twentieth-century predecessor of the contemporary Chicano *vato loco* or gang member (literally, a "crazy guy"), the image has not disappeared from contemporary popular culture. Since the Chicano movement of the 1960s the *pachuco* has become an icon of Chicano "national" identity.

The figure of the *pachuco* first became visible in the 1930s and 1940s in the rundown Mexican-American barrios of U.S. cities, particularly in the Southwest. The term *pachuco* is most probably a slang term for a resident of El Paso. *Pachucos* distinguished themselves as alienated youths who did not identify with the cultural values of their Mexican or Mexican-American parents or with those of their new Anglo-American cultural context. Instead, they created a whole subculture for themselves, with a particular form of slang (*Caló*) and a distinctive, exaggerated fashion sense, epitomized by the zoot suit. This consisted of very baggy trousers with tightly tapered bottoms, and a long jacket with padded shoulders. Typically *pachucos* also wore a long watch chain, slicked back hair, and a fedora hat. Even their gait was an exaggerated lope, with their shoulders pulled back and their hands deep in their pockets. What they were doing with this image was appropriating and exaggerating eclectic aspects of mainstream U.S. culture. In other, less visible respects, particularly in their perceived alienation, they could be seen as exaggerating facets of Mexican identity.

In wartime USA, the *pachuco* was demonized by the Anglo-American press, aggressively pursued by Anglo-American youths (in the Zoot Suit Riots of 1943, for example), and shunned by the more conservative, assimilationist factions of the Mexican-American community. Nevertheless, he laid the cornerstone for contemporary Chicano identity as a hybrid of two different cultures that seeks to create a third, distinctive culture for itself. Over the course of time this negative, hostile image has been sanitized and reappropriated by both mainstream U.S. and Mexican culture (see, for example, the fashions worn by The Fonz in the television series *Happy*

Days or the characters in the blockbuster movie *Grease* [1977] in the United States, and the film comedies of Tin Tan in Mexico). The figure of the *pachuco* continues to be a powerful embodiment of the Chicano community's place in U.S. society.

—*Thea Pitman*

See also: *Language:* Chicano Spanish; *Popular Cinema:* Comedy Film (Tin Tan)

Bibliography

Babcock, Granger. 1995. "Looking for a Third Space: El Pachuco and Chicano Nationalism in Luis Valdez's *Zoot Suit.*" Pp. 215–225 in *Staging Cultural Difference: Cultural Pluralism in American Theatre and Drama*, edited by Marc Maufort. New York: Lang.

Sánchez, Rosaura. 1994. *Chicano Discourse: Socio-historic Perspectives.* Houston, TX: Arte Público Press.

Sánchez-Tranquilino, Marcos, and John Tagg. 1992. "The Pachuco's Flayed Hide: Mobility, Identity, and Buenas Garras." Pp. 556–570 in *Cultural Studies*, edited by Lawrence Grossberg, Cary Nelson, and Paula A. Treichler. London: Routledge.

Webb, Simon. 1998. "Masculinities at the Margins: Representations of the Malandro and the Pachuco." Pp. 227–264 in *Imagination beyond Nation: Latin American Popular Culture*, edited by Eva P. Bueno and Terry Caesar. Pittsburgh, PA: University of Pittsburgh Press.

Legends of Popular Music and Film

Carlos Gardel (1890–1935)

Argentine singer and film star who died tragically in a plane crash in 1935 at the age of forty-five but is even now, nearly seventy years after his death, still a household name in Argentina, across Latin America, and beyond.

Carlos Gardel, Argentine tango singer, movie star, and heartthrob. (Bettmann/Corbis)

Gardel's exact origins are something of a mystery. He was probably born Charles Gardès in Toulouse, France, in 1890, the illegitimate son of a French woman; Gardel's preferred version of the story has him born in Uruguay (or occasionally Argentina). But regardless of his exact place of birth, he grew up in the poor *barrios* or districts of Buenos Aires, where he started to make a living as a folk singer before he became the supreme icon of the new, rather risqué tango songs in the 1920s and 1930s. Some of his most famous hits include "Volver" ("Return") and "Mi Buenos Aires querido" ("My Lovely Buenos Aires").

By the late 1920s, after achieving success in Argentina and in other parts of South America, Gardel became a hit in Europe, especially France, and later in the United States as well. In fact, most of the films that he would star in during the latter half of his career were made by either French or, more often, U.S. companies. Films such as *El día que me quieras* (*When You Fall in Love with Me*, 1935) were largely vehicles for Gardel's songs—a tango equivalent of the immensely popular Hollywood musicals of the day. Another factor in Gardel's international presence was that his songs suffered at the hands of the censors in Argentina in the early 1930s, and he left his "homeland" for a kind of self-imposed exile in Europe and the United States in 1933. His body was later returned for his funeral—an event of immense public interest—in late 1935.

While Gardel's debonair appearance and appealing, husky voice (he had a bullet lodged in his lung for much of his life) may partially account for his massive appeal to the Argentine public, it was the lyrics and vocabulary of the tango-songs, penned by songwriters such as Alfredo Le Pera for Gardel, that made him the icon of popular Argentine identity. Gardel was a poor boy, probably an immigrant, as were so many Argentines, and he expressed their feelings and concerns in their language, *lunfardo*, the working-class slang of Buenos Aires. Furthermore, the character that he projected in his songs exemplified perfectly the psychology of the *porteño* (Buenos Aires) working-class male: he was macho, loyal, materially successful, and haughty—often something of a *malevo* (a bad guy) but also alienated and vulnerable in some senses, particularly where women were concerned.

Gardel was not only enormously successful with the Argentine working classes, whom he represented. Despite the censorship of Gardel's work, tangos—particularly the music—have been appropriated by successive populist leaders, most notably Juan Domingo Perón, in an attempt to harness the people's support. Several state-sponsored films were made about Gardel during Perón's regime. Today, tangos and Gardel himself are seen by both the Argentine people and their successive governments as the purest expression of their national identity.

—*Thea Pitman*

See also: *Popular Music:* Tango; *Popular Social Movements and Politics:* Peronismo; *Language:* Lunfardo

Bibliography

Castro, Donald. 1991. *The Argentine Tango as Social History, 1880–1955: The Soul of the People.* Lewiston/Queenston/Lampeter: Edwin Mellen Press.

———. 1998. "Carlos Gardel and the Argentine Tango: The Lyric of Social Irresponsibility and Male Inadequacy." Pp. 63–78 in *The Passion of Music and Dance: Body, Gender and Sexuality,* edited by William Washabaugh. Oxford: Berg.

Collier, Simon. 1986. *The Life, Music and Times of Carlos Gardel.* Pittsburgh, PA: University of Pittsburgh Press.

Pedro Infante (1917–1957)

Mexican singer and film star who, nearly fifty years after his death, remains one of the nation's most enduring icons and idols, along with other famous names from the "golden age" of Mexican cinema, such as María Felix and Jorge Negrete.

Infante was born in 1917 into humble surroundings in the northern Mexican state of Sinaloa, where he quickly developed an interest in the kind of popular music played by mariachis and *ranchera* singers. Set on trying his luck in the big city, he moved to Mexico City in his early twenties and started making a living as a radio actor and performer of popular music in the con-

Lupita Infante (right), daughter of Pedro Infante, and Amparito, the president of the Pedro Infante fan club, stand next to the star's grave to mark the 47th anniversary of his death in Mexico City. (Daniel Aguilar/ Reuters/Corbis)

cert halls of the day. He rapidly became a big hit. In the period from 1943 until his death in 1957, he is reputed to have recorded over 200 albums. One of his most famous numbers is the bolero "Amorcito Corazón" ("Little Darling"), and his *ranchera* inflection of boleros in general is still a popular approach to the genre in Mexico.

At almost the same time that his career as a singer took off, Infante started to act in films, and over the course of his movie career he appeared in sixty films, starring in up to five different feature films in the course of any one year. Some of his most famous films include *Los tres García* (*The Three García Cousins*, 1946), *Nosotros los pobres* (*We Poor People*, 1947), *Angelitos negros* (*Little Black Angels*, 1948), and *La vida no vale nada* (*Life Is Cheap*, 1954). Many of the films that he starred in fall within the bounds of the *comedia ranchera* genre, a very popular type of "golden-age" Mexican film that blends comedy, often with an amorous theme, with the setting of the northern Mexican ranches, one of the most iconic locations of a sense of Mexican national identity in the post-revolutionary era. Later in his career, Infante would appear in films with more urban locations, helping to create the myth of modern Mexico City. He met an untimely end in 1957 when the plane that he was flying crashed on the Yucatan peninsula. Ironically, at the time of his death, he was preparing to make a film based on the theme of air travel entitled *Ando volando bajo* (*Flying Low*).

By the time of his death, Infante had become an icon of national proportions in Mexico—so much so that the day of his death was declared a national day of mourning across the Republic. His success was due not only to his good looks and his particular style of singing, but also to the fact that, as an actor, he frequently played the part of the poor boy he had once been, and despite his fame and fortune, he still remained very much one of the people. Furthermore, through his songs and film roles he epitomized the macho Mexican male that lies at the heart of the traditional, popular concept of Mexican identity. Like Carlos Gardel in Argentina, Infante became the most visible icon of Mexican identity and was co-opted by the state into representing this role after his death. Infante's iconic status has not diminished with time.

In Mexico today, young stars such as Luis Miguel still record hits with old Infante songs and, in popularity contests, Infante is still likely to win hands down against these younger heartthrobs.

Infante's success has not only been limited to Mexico. In his lifetime, he toured both North and South America and received prizes and awards in many countries. At the time of his death, he was also on the cusp of breaking into the U.S. film industry. Even today, he remains an icon of Mexico in the international arena.

—Thea Pitman

See also: *Popular Music:* Bolero; Mariachi, Ranchera, Norteña, Tex-Mex; *Cultural Icons:* Legends of Popular Music and Film (Carlos Gardel); *Popular Cinema:* Melodrama; The Mexican Film Industry

Bibliography

Fein, Seth. 1997. "Pedro Infante." Pp. 702–704 in *Encyclopedia of Mexico*, vol. 1, edited by Michael S. Werner. Chicago: Fitzroy Dearborn.

Mora, Carl J. 1989. *The Mexican Cinema: Reflections of a Society, 1896–1988.* Berkeley: University of California Press, pp. 157–174 (passim).

Rojas, Raymundo Eli. 2002. "It's Been 40 Years." www.geocities.com/Broadway/ 2626/ pedro.html (consulted 1 July 2003).

Wilson, Rita Lynn, and Xicotencatl Fernández. 2001. "Pedro Infante." www.lonestar.utsa .edu/rlwilson/PedroInfante.html (search on Pedro Infante) (consulted 1 July 2003).

Religious and Mythical Figures

Virgin of Guadalupe

Mexico's patron saint, Guadalupe, is said to have appeared to an indigenous peasant named Juan Diego on 9 December 1531 at

Mexico's revered Virgin of Guadalupe. (Mireille Vautier/The Art Archive)

the village of Teyepac near what is now Mexico City. Legend tells that she ordered the man to have the local bishop Zumarraga build a church upon the site and provided proof when Diego's story was questioned. What is beyond doubt is that Guadalupe has become a source of comfort and sustenance for the poorest of Mexicans, and indeed she is now recognized throughout Latin America.

The extraordinary persuasiveness of the image surely has much to do with its heterogeneity. Even the original document describing the apparition, produced by an interpreter since Diego spoke no Spanish and Zumarraga no Nahuatl, is of uncertain veracity; the perpetual bugbear of mutual incomprehension, rife in most stories of conquest in the Americas, also leaves its mark here. There is also a Nahuatl-language document published in 1649 and of unknown authorship.

Similarly the religious origins of the Virgin have been traced to many sources other than Christian. The Aztec goddess Tonantzin, also a virgin mother, has been associated with Guadalupe, as has Quetzalcóatl, the winged serpent. For Gloria Anzaldúa, she is derived from Coatlalopeuh, one of several Mesoamerican goddesses associated with creation and fertility, in turn an aspect of the figure of Tonantzin. Anzaldúa points out that for Chicanos, Guadalupe is one of three mothers alongside the symbolic traitor, *La Malinche*, and *La Llorona*, the weeping mother forlornly seeking her lost children. The three are seen as complementary aspects of a complete figure.

A further possible interpretation of the Virgin of Guadalupe's origin is that soon after the devastation wrought by the Spanish Conquest, indigenous peoples were in dire need of some form of moral sustenance. At the same time the Catholic Church would have been eager to find a means with which to convert and claim this spiritually disenfranchised people. Guadalupe, much as occurred in other Spanish colonies at key moments in the process of acculturation and consolidation of empire, proved an invaluable tool of empire as well as a source of solace for the dispossessed. Guadalupe is thus a classic example of transculturation and *mestizaje* (cultural mixing) in Mexico and throughout Latin America.

—*Keith Richards*

See also: *Introduction; Cultural Icons:* Religious and Mythical Figures (*La Llorona; La Malinche*); *Language:* Indigenous Languages

Bibliography

Anzaldúa, Gloria. 1996. "Coatlalopeuh, She Who Has Dominion over Serpents." Pp. 52–55 in *Goddess of the Americas: Writings on the Virgin of Guadalupe*, edited by Ana Castillo. New York: Riverhead Books.

Lafaye, Jacques. 1976. *Quetzalcoatl and Guadalupe: The Formation of Mexican National Consciousness, 1531–1813.* Chicago: University of Chicago Press.

Poole, Stafford. 1995. *Our Lady of Guadalupe: The Origins and Sources of a Mexican National Symbol, 1531–1797.* Tuscon: University of Arizona Press.

Rodríguez, Jeanette. 1994. *Our Lady of Guadalupe: Faith and Empowerment among Mexican-American Women.* Austin: University of Texas Press.

La Malinche

A quasi-mythical figure distilled from the traumatic conquest of Mexico by Spaniards led by Hernán Cortés, *La Malinche* is as much fictional as historical. She is in some ways typical of a select group (selected as much by chance as by choice) of indigenous people enlisted to assist the Spanish effort during the era of Conquest. Felipillo in Peru, to cite just one other famous example, was tutored in Spanish and used as an interpreter. Such figures were invaluable in forging alliances with outlying peoples colonized by the dominant Aztec and Incas. These peoples joined forces with the Spaniards in the belief that they would rid themselves of oppression. Felipillo, whose testimony was manipulated by Pizarro's men to justify executing the Inca Atawallpa, is despised by native Andean peoples as a symbol of collusion with the invaders. *La Malinche*, too, represents the "translator-traitor," though with crucial differences associated with her gender and nationality.

Little is known for certain about her origins, but it seems indisputable that she was from a noble indigenous family in the Tabasco region of Mexico. Whether she was initially stolen or given away is unknown, but she doubtless became a token passed between powerful masters until she was given to Cortés's men as part of a gift of twenty women. When her linguistic skills came to light, she was swiftly accorded far higher status than that of concubine, though she did become the lover of Cortés and bore at least one child by him. However, her knowledge of several indigenous languages, from both central and southern Mexico, was what made her invaluable to the invaders. She was able to speak to the envoys of Moctezuma, and even to the emperor himself, in a highly specialized and recondite form of Nahuatl. This, according to Frances Karttunen, leaves no question as to her noble ancestry.

The shifting focus on her personality and role is reflected by the mutations of her name. Baptized "Marina" by the Spaniards when they received her as a gift in 1519, she became known by natives as "Malintzin" through an adaptation to indigenous phonetics and conventions, which in turn was to be re-hispanicized into "Malinche." The respectful "doña Marina" used by chroniclers such as Bernal Díaz del Castillo reflects the status she enjoyed among the Spaniards. Similarly, the Nahuatl suffix "-tzin" in Malintzin points to her high esteem in the eyes of contemporary fellow natives. The denigration of her name seems to have come about following Mexico's independence from Spain, the consequent search for an independent identity, and the need for scapegoats to exorcise the sense of national humiliation.

Writers and artists in the twentieth century have been keen to review the adoring image presented by Bernal Díaz. Perhaps the most famous is Octavio Paz, who made *La Malinche* the focus of his chapter "Los hijos de la chingada" ("Sons of the Sexually Abused") in his seminal essay on the Mexican national psyche, *El laberinto de la soledad* (*The Labyrinth of Solitude*, 1950). In exploring her image as mother of mixed-race Mexico, Paz identifies a *mestizo* sense of abandonment and humiliation as the product of a violation. This gels with the central tenet of Mexican machismo that, in the final analysis, everything can be blamed upon women. It is a notion enshrined in countless popular songs and in the unflattering 1926 depiction of *La Malinche* with Cortés above the body of a murdered native, painted by José Clemente Orozco (1883–1949). The surrealist-influenced painting *El sueño de la Malinche* (*Malinche's Dream*, 1939) by Antonio Ruiz (1892–1964) offers a more circumspect view, with the sleeping woman seen against cracks in the walls resembling lightning and thunderclouds, her bedclothes turned into a landscape with, at the highest point, a Christian church. Ruiz appears to suggest that she was an unconscious harbinger of traumatic changes in her country, a view that may gain further currency in forthcoming years.

—*Keith Richards*

See also: *Language:* Indigenous Languages; *Visual Arts and Architecture:* Art (José Clemente Orozco)

Bibliography

Cypess, Sandra Messinger. 1991. *La Malinche in Mexican Literature: From History to Myth.* Austin: University of Texas Press.

Díaz del Castillo, Bernal. 1632 (1995). *True History of the Conquest of New Spain.* London: Penguin.
Karttunen, Frances. 1997. "Rethinking Malinche." Pp. 291–312 in *Indian Women of Early Mexico,* edited by Susan Schroeder, Stephanie Wood, and Robert Haskett. Norman: University of Oklahoma Press.
Paz, Octavio. 1950 (1990). *The Labyrinth of Solitude.* London: Penguin.

La Llorona

Literally "The Weeping Woman," *La Llorona* is an extremely popular figure in Mexican and Chicano folklore, though the tale is told throughout Latin America. There are several variants to the story, but in all versions *La Llorona* is the ghost of a woman who cries at night near lakes and rivers for her child or children whom she has drowned. The different versions of the tale focus on the reasons she might have killed her own children before taking her own life—through jealousy and anger over their father's infidelities, his heartless rejection of her, her inferior social class or racial group, or her callous desire to obtain a new lover. One version exonerates her completely by suggesting that her own father drowned her illegitimate baby (possibly the fruit of a virgin birth) and that she died from overwhelming grief.

La Llorona is the equivalent of the "bogey woman" for Mexican and Chicano children. Although she is more often heard than seen, she is imagined as dressed in black, with long gleaming fingernails, and either a horse's head or an empty space in place of her face. Parents tell small children the story to warn them off staying out late at night. For older girls, the story warns of the dangers of falling for dashing young men with no intention of marrying them. In the case of young men, *La Llorona* is depicted as a siren figure who will lure them into danger and an uncertain fate. Nevertheless, in contemporary times, the "fright value" of the tale has largely been supplanted by the association of *La Llorona* with other familiar figures from the pantheon of Halloween ghosts, now popular in Mexico as well as the United States.

The origins of the tale are unclear. Some critics have found pre-Columbian echoes in the story, although empirical proof suggests that it was first told in the late nineteenth century and that it is more clearly associated with European folkloric tradition. More recently, some critics have been tempted to find a resonance of the story of *La Malinche* in that of *La Llorona,* in that both are bad women who betray their people/children. *La Llorona* has also enjoyed a surge in "popularity" in contemporary Chicano culture, perhaps because of the potential for betrayal that the Chicano community faces as they try to balance Mexican and Anglo-American cultures. Or, perhaps, because her mourning along the banks of a river reminds Chicanos of the experiences of so many "wetbacks" who lose their own lives, and those of their children, trying to cross the Río Grande/Bravo. Indeed, in these newer interpretations of her story, she ceases to be associated with evil and selfish behavior, and emphasis is placed, instead, on her grief and pain. Finally, some of the contemporary interpretations of her story also seek to draw parallels between her and other bad mother figures from world folklore, such as Medea.

—*Thea Pitman*

See also: *Cultural Icons:* Religious and Mythical Figures (*La Malinche*)

Bibliography

Anaya, Rudolfo. 1984. *The Legend of La Llorona.* Berkeley, CA: Tonatiuh/Quinto Sol Press.

Arora, Shirley L. 1997. "La Llorona." Pp. 753–754 in *Encyclopedia of Mexico*, vol. 1, edited by Michael S. Werner. Chicago: Fitzroy Dearborn.

del Castillo, Adelaida R., ed. 1990. *Between Borders: Essays on Mexican/Chicana History.* Encino, CA: Floricanto Press.

Hayes, Joe. 1987. *La Llorona: The Weeping Woman.* El Paso, TX: Cinco Puntos Press.

Signs crowd the main street in Salta, Argentina, 1994. (Paolo Ragazzini/Corbis)

9

Language

Spanish is the official language of all Spain's former colonies in Latin America. In Brazil the Portuguese arrived with their language in 1500 and they, too, left a permanent linguistic legacy. The European colonizers were keen to impose their respective languages on the indigenous peoples that they encountered in the New World. But indigenous languages did not die out. In the Andes today, for example, the Quechua and Aymara languages are still widely spoken, as is Guaraní in Paraguay and Nahuatl in Mexico.

The Spanish and Portuguese spoken in Latin America today understandably differ from their European counterparts; they evolved independently and were influenced by indigenous languages, the speech of African slaves, and later the languages brought by different immigrant groups, ranging from the Italians to the Japanese. As a consequence, there are many significant differences in the Spanish spoken in the different Latin American countries. In Argentina, *lunfardo* is a combination of Spanish and elements of various European languages brought over by immigrants toward the end of the nineteenth century. In Cuba, the impact of languages and dialects brought by African slaves is evident, particularly in vocabulary relating to Afro-Cuban culture. The same is true of Brazilian Portuguese, where terms such as *Candomblé*, *Umbanda*, *caçula* (the youngest sibling in a family), and *capoeira* have clear African origins.

The Spanish and Portuguese languages share many similarities, since both derive from Latin and have been influenced by Arabic. These similarities have led native speakers of each to communicate with each other in a pragmatic, invented tongue, referred to humorously in Brazil as "portunhol"—literally a mixture of Portuguese (*português*) and Spanish (*espanhol*).

In general, Portuguese stays closer to the Latin than Spanish does. The Latin verb *fabulare* (to speak) became *falar* in Portuguese but *hablar* in Spanish. Similarly, the Latin verb *facere* (to do) became *fazer* in Portuguese but *hacer* in Spanish. Other basic differences have a similar pattern, making it easier for native speakers of one language to adapt to the

Nobel Prize–winning author Gabriel García Márquez, with a copy of his most famous book, *One Hundred Years of Solitude.* (Isabel Steva Hernandez/Colita/Corbis)

other. Words beginning with "ll" in Spanish, for example, tend to begin with "ch" in Portuguese: *llave* and *chave* (key), *lleno* and *cheio* (full), *llorar* and *chorar* (to cry), *llover* and *chover* (to rain), and so on.

Spanish and Portuguese are significantly different, of course, at the level of syntax, pronunciation, and vocabulary, so nonnative speakers must proceed with caution to avoid upsetting their foreign neighbors. For example, in spite of their similarity, the adjectives *embaraçado/a* ("embarrassed" in Portuguese) and *embarazado/a* ("pregnant" in Spanish) should not be confused. (This example was used in a recent advertising campaign in Brazil promoting Spanish language courses.) Perhaps for this reason increasing numbers of Brazilians have begun to study Spanish, and Spanish-speaking Latin Americans have enrolled in Portuguese courses. This trend has been fuelled by the creation of the MERCOSUR (known as the MERCOSUL in Portuguese) in 1991, a free-trade area embracing Brazil, Argentina, Paraguay, and Uruguay.

The Colombian writer Gabriel García Márquez once wrote: "We writers of Latin America and the Caribbean must recognize, with hand on heart, that reality is a better writer than we are. Our destiny, and perhaps our glory, is to try to imitate it with humility, to the best of our ability." His comment points out the fundamental sense in Latin America that Spanish is an alien tongue that, as he goes on to assert, is inadequate to describe the region's natural and

Business signs in Spanish near the Mexican border, El Paso, Texas, in the 1980s. (Owen Franken/Corbis)

cultural phenomena. This sense of adapting an alien language to a new milieu was compounded by a concerted program on the part of Latin American intellectuals to control the teaching and development of the language to make it serve the purposes of nation building and the creation of identity. As Castilian Spanish, enshrined by Antonio de Nebrija's grammar of 1492, became the linguistic cement of the Castile-Aragon nation, so it was conceived as a homogenizing factor in the colonies–turned–independent states.

One common misconception about Latin American Spanish should be quickly dispelled: the notion that it differs so dramatically from country to country, or from European Spanish, as to make communication impossible. In fact, variations are never so great as to hinder communication, and Latin Americans and Spaniards have no more problems with mutual intelligibility than the British and North Americans. It is undeniable that words derived from Latin are more diverse in the Iberian Peninsula. Nevertheless, Latin American Spanish, just like its Iberian counterpart, is notorious for (or blessed with) a great regional variety that stems from various factors. One of these lies in Latin America's history of conquest and colonization, as settlers from different provinces of Spain generally established themselves in particular regions of the New World: for example, Galicians went to Cuba, Andalusians to Argentina.

The exact origin of the language taken originally to the Americas is still a matter of heated debate among linguists, who are divided into two main camps: those who argue for the Andalusian influence, and those who maintain the legacy of Castile. Numerous phonological similarities support the Andalusian thesis, most notably the *seseo*, or lack of the lisping sound ("c" and "z" are pronounced [s] in both Latin America and Andalusia). The argument for Castilian is more historically and politically based, emphasizing the far greater prestige of this dialect that had come to embody Spanish power; the phonological differences can be attributed to mutations occurring over the span of 500 years. Others have noted the discrepancy between highland and lowland Spanish in Latin America, the former resembling Castilian and the latter Andalusian. This can be explained by the fact that most sedentary pre-Columbian civilizations were based in highland areas, and these were conquered mainly by

A sign in Spanish advertising a furniture store for the benefit of the Cuban community in Miami, Florida, 1963. (Bettmann/Corbis)

Castilians, while Andalusians came later to farm the lowlands.

Another factor is the introduction of African slaves to many areas, particularly those where large plantations were common. In Cuba and Brazil, the slaves' influence on language was considerable in lexical terms. The Yoruba language is still spoken in Cuba, chiefly in connection with the Afro-Cuban religious practice of *Santería.* In Latin America, Africans were allowed to maintain aspects of their languages and cultural practices. As a result, African influence is particularly notable in the Caribbean and coastal South America, though not in the Central American countries with a Caribbean coastline (Panama, Costa Rica, Nicaragua, Honduras, and Belize), where the black populations tend to be English-speaking or bilingual in English and Spanish.

Finally, it is important to take into account various forms of linguistic regionalism, whether caused by natural topographical barriers between distant communities or by local rivalries and conflicts. Natural features such as the Andean mountain chain and the Amazonian rainforest made communication far more difficult than in the relatively homogenous topography of North America. For instance, Chile, crammed between the twin barriers of the Andes and the Pacific, has the only dialect in the region limited to a single country. The tradition of large landholdings in Spain also contributed to the concentration of land in the hands of small groups in Latin America. This tradition created oligarchies and concentrations of power in regional centers that became divisive and corrosive, provoking wars and social unrest, particularly in Central America, and led to the maintenance of linguistic differences.

The conditions existing in Latin America and the nature of Iberian colonialism meant that contact between languages and cultures would continue to occur. In North America, by contrast, American English was exposed to much less intense contact with other languages, and due to the U.S. policy of systematically acculturating African slaves, did not come into contact with African languages. The enrichment of the English language resulting from contact with Spanish is noticeable mostly in certain border areas with Mexico, New York, and Miami, though this situation is changing at a precipitous rate due to Latino immigration to all areas. Conversely, Latin American Spanish is increasingly influenced by proximity (real or virtual) to English.

In contrast to North America, language contact in Latin America is kaleidoscopic, even without taking into account the indigenous languages. Spanish in Uruguay, for instance, is affected by the Portuguese of neighboring Brazil. The River Plate area generally is conditioned by Italian, since large numbers of Italian immigrants settled there. All kinds of minor influences add to the diversity of Latin American Spanish due to the presence in the region of immigrants from parts of the Old World other than Spain, mostly Europe and Asia. Numerous Germans have settled in Chile and other Southern Cone countries since the mid-nineteenth century, as well as Yugoslavs, Arabs, Scandinavians, French, and British. The Paraguayan capital Asunción is home to a thriving Korean population, while coastal Peru, São Paulo, and the Santa Cruz area of Bolivia have significant Japanese communities. Parts of Patagonia were until fairly recently Welsh-speaking, and Mennonites from Germany and Central Europe have settled in the Chaco region of central South America, an extensive lowland plain that extends into Paraguay, Bolivia, and Argentina.

—*Lisa Shaw and Keith Richards*

See also: *Sport and Leisure: Capoeira*; *Popular Literature:* The Boom; *Popular Religion and Festivals: Candomblé*; *Santería; Umbanda*

Bibliography

García Márquez, Gabriel. 1991. "Something Else about Literature and Reality." Pp. 119–121 in *Notas de Prensa 1980–1984*. Madrid: Mondadori.

Penny, Ralph J. 2000. *Variation and Change in Spanish*. Cambridge: Cambridge University Press.

Scavnicky, Gary E. A., ed. 1980. *Dialectología hispanoamericana: Estudios actuales*. Washington, DC: Georgetown University Press.

Silva-Corvalán, Carmen. 1995. *Spanish in Four Continents: Studies in Language Contact and Bilingualism*. Washington, DC: Georgetown University Press.

Valle, José del, and Luis Gabriel-Stheeman. 2002. *The Battle over Spanish between 1800 and 2000: Language Ideologies and Hispanic Intellectuals.* London: Routledge.

Regional Differences in Latin American Spanish

Certain pronunciation traits belonging to specific regions are reasonably easy to recognize to an ear trained in Spanish. The River Plate area (Uruguay and greater Buenos Aires) has a distinctive rendering of the "ll" as a /sh/ sound, as well as the cadence borrowed from Italian. Caribbean Spanish is notable for the aspiration or deletion of the final "s," and pronunciation of "n" at the ends of words as in the English "ng". A feature of Andean speech is the limited enunciation of vowel sounds, which are apt to be confused (making "e" and "i," "o" and "u" largely interchangeable) due to the three-vowel systems used by native languages. Chileans usually pronounce "b" as "v," an inversion of general practice in Spanish, and they assibilate rather than roll the "r" as in English. Standard Mexican Spanish, as spoken by educated middle-class Mexicans, differs from Castilian Spanish mainly in terms of pronunciation and vocabulary, although there are a few grammatical differences, too. Today there are still over fifty different indigenous languages, such as Nahuatl, Maya, and Tzeltal, that are spoken in Mexico, and Mexican Spanish has been greatly enriched by borrowings from these languages.

Another feature of some areas is the so-called *voseo*, or use of the *vos* pronoun, which has its own verb conjugations and is found in the River Plate area, southern Bolivia, and some areas of Central America, as well as in parts of Colombia. In common with several other Latin American countries, parts of Colombia use the *voseo* form of address in place of the standard *tuteo* (using the informal *tú* pronoun). Not as widespread as in Argentina, for example, *voseo* usage in Colombia is mostly restricted to the regions of Antioquia, Chocó, and Caldas in the west of the country. Also of interest is the fact that in the Andean region of Boyacá, the third-person term *su merced* (literally, "your grace"), now archaic in Spain and elsewhere in Latin America, is still in common usage both as a term of respect and as a familiar term among friends or family members, frequently shortened to *sumercé.* In Colombia, *usted*, the formal form of address in Spain and much of Latin America, is imbued with much wider meaning and is used as an affectionate term of address between friends and family members throughout the country. In Mexico the use of *vos* occurs predominantly in the south of the country, in rural areas, and *vos* is often used today by indigenous people when they speak in Spanish. Traditionally, *vos* was the personal pronoun used by Mexicans of Spanish descent when they spoke to their indigenous servants, with *tú* and *usted* reserved for use only within their own racial group. *Usted* ("you," polite, singular) is also used much more frequently in Mexico than in Spain, and *vosotros* ("you," familiar, plural) is not used at all—even groups of friends are referred to as *ustedes* ("you," polite, plural).

Other grammatical differences between Mexican Spanish and Castilian include the preference in the former for the preterite tense over the perfect tense and the concept of the preposition *hasta* as intrinsically negative, meaning "not until." Thus a Mexican would say *¿Qué hiciste esta* *mañana?* (What did you do this morning?) rather than the more standard Castilian *¿Qué has hecho esta mañana?* (What have you done this morning?), and for a Mexican *Abrimos hasta las diez* means "We don't open until 10 o'clock (in the morning)," rather than "We stay open until 10 (at night)," which is what a Spaniard would take it to mean. This last example can lead to some frustrating experiences.

Vocabulary can present problems for the speaker unaware of specific usage and can lead to embarrassment, particularly in the case of apparently innocent words with regional sexual connotations, such as *coger* (normally meaning to pick up) in Argentina, Mexico, and elsewhere, and *tirarse* (generally to leap or dive) in Peru. There are also some curiously diverse regional meanings of ostensibly specific words, for example *guagua*, which in Cuba and the Canary Islands means a bus, in the Andes a baby, and in Chile a jug.

Indigenous words that have been incorporated into Latin American Spanish include *aguacate* (avocado pear) from the Nahuatl word *ahuacatl*, and *chocolate* from the Maya words *chokol* (hot) and *atl* (water), referring to the way chocolate is typically drunk mixed with hot water in Mexico. Even the Mexican spelling of the word *México* with an "x" (rather than the "j" of Castilian Spanish [*Méjico*]) is a nod to the Mexica (Aztec) origins of the country (although, of course, the use of the letter "x" actually stems from archaic Castilian spelling preferences, since the Mexica used an ideographic rather than alphabetic form of writing).

—*Keith Richards, Thea Pitman, and Claire Taylor*

See also: *Language:* Indigenous Languages

Bibliography

Bjarkman, Peter C., and Robert Matthew Hammond, eds. 1989. *American Spanish Pronunciation: Theoretical and Applied Perspectives.* Washington, DC: Georgetown University Press.

Cotton, Eleanor Greet, and John M. Sharp. 1988. *Spanish in the Americas.* Washington, DC: Georgetown University Press.

Lloyd, Paul M. 1987. *From Latin to Spanish: Historical Phonology and Morphology of the Spanish Language.* Philadelphia: American Philosophical Society.

López Morales, Humberto. 1971. *Estudios sobre el español de Cuba.* Long Island City, NY: Las Americas.

Santamaría, Francisco de, ed. 1991. *Diccionario de Mejicanismos.* Mexico City: Porrúa.

Brazilian Portuguese

The relationship between Brazilian Portuguese and the language of Portugal could be described as similar to that between U.S. English and the language of Great Britain. A Brazilian would certainly understand a European Portuguese speaker, and vice versa, but each would instantly recognize the distinctive accent of the other. In addition, there are some important differences between the two varieties of the language in terms of vocabulary, spelling, and syntax.

With regard to phonetics, the letter "r" is usually pronounced as [x] in Brazil, whereas speakers of European Portuguese have the option of this pronunciation, or [rr]. The Brazilian "o" is more open than in Portugal, and there is some variation in the quality of the oral vowels "a" and "e." When the letter "s" comes before certain consonants, Brazilians produce a more sibilant sound, while the Portuguese pronounce it /sh/.

Some basic differences in vocabulary between Brazilian and European Portuguese often catch the foreign traveler off guard. Brazilians call breakfast *o café da manhã* (literally "morning coffee"), whereas the Portuguese opt for *o pequeno almoço* (literally "small lunch," like the French). In Brazil a train is an anglicized *trem*, while in Portugal it is a *comboio*. Brazilians call the bathroom *o banheiro*, but the Portuguese call it *a casa de banho* (literally, "the house of the bath"). In Brazil a fruit juice is a *suco* and a menu a *cardápio*, but they are a *sumo* and an *ementa* respectively in Portugal. Not only nouns but also verbs differ, with the Brazilian *pegar* replacing the Portuguese *apanhar* (to catch). The verb to put, *pôr*, is often rendered colloquially as *botar* in Brazil. Speakers of European Portuguese need to take care when in Brazil, since several everyday terms used in Portugal have quite different meanings. Confusingly, the noun *rapariga* is the standard term for a girl in Portugal, but in Brazil it can mean a prostitute. The noun *bicha* in Portugal means a line or a queue, whereas in Brazil it is a slang term for a homosexual.

In spite of efforts to standardize the spelling of Brazilian and European Portuguese, significant orthographic differences continue to exist. In Portugal a choice exists between "oi" or "ou" in words such as *toiro/touro* (bull) and *loiro/louro* (blond), but Brazilians almost always prefer the "ou" spelling and accompanying pronunciation. Whereas the letters "c" and "p" are written but not pronounced in nouns such as *acção* (action) and *baptismo* (baptism) in European Portuguese, in Brazil they are neither pronounced nor written, giving *ação* and *batismo*. Brazilian Portuguese reduces the double "mm" and "nn" of certain words such as *comummente* (commonly) and *connosco* (with us), giving *comumente* and *conosco*.

The major difference between Brazilian and European Portuguese in terms of syntax concerns forms of address. Whereas the Portuguese address their loved ones and friends with the *tu* pronoun, which takes a second-person singular verb ending, Brazilians rarely use this form, except in certain regions, replacing it with the third-person singular form *você*, which has a more neutral function in Portugal. Another notable difference is that in Portugal the possessive adjective is preceded by the definite article, giving *o meu carro* (my car, but literally "the my car," and so on), while in Brazil the definite article is often omitted in such cases, giving simply *meu carro*.

Indigenous languages have made their impact on the vocabulary of Brazilian Portuguese, as have various African tongues brought over to the New World by slaves. The Portuguese missionaries used the language of the Tupi Indians of the Amazon and coastal areas as a lingua franca in the sixteenth century. From then on, Tupi became quite widely spoken in the interior by African slaves, the Portuguese, and those of mixed race. The Tupi heritage is particularly prevalent in the names of plants, animals, and places. *Tapioca* and *jacaré* (alligator) are two well-known examples. The linguistic influence of African slaves is most apparent in Brazil's northeast. Again, in terms of vocabulary, this legacy is strongest in areas most closely linked to the cultural practices of the slaves, such as *Candomblé*, samba, and the martial art/dance *capoeira*, the names and associated terminology of which are clearly of African origin.

Not only do students of Brazilian Portuguese have to be aware of the language's marked differences from so-called continental or European Portuguese, they also have to deal with the seemingly enormous gap that exists between spoken and written language in Brazil. For example, in (informal) written Portuguese, Brazilians often prefer to place object pronouns before the verb (as in Spanish), while in Portugal in most instances these will be placed after the verb and attached by a hyphen. Thus, "you saw them" is rendered *você os viu* in Brazil but *você viu-os* in Portugal. However, in spoken language, Brazilians from nearly all walks of life will often replace the object pronoun with a subject pronoun (giving *você viu eles*, for example). This practice is much more widespread than, say, the use of phrases deemed "incorrect" within certain English-speaking communities, such as "you was" rather than "you were." Brazil also has its share of "incorrect" grammar usage, even within the flexible tenets of spoken language, which are often region-specific. For example, the second-person singular verb form (*tu*) is as good as redundant in Brazilian Portuguese, but *gaúchos* from the south of the country, a wide number of *nordestinos* or northeasterners, and streetwise urban young people can often be heard using the second-person singular subject pronoun *tu* with third-person singular verb forms, for example: *Tu* (instead of *você*) *foi ao cinema?*, meaning "Did you go to the cinema?"

The main regional differences in Brazilian Portuguese have to do with vocabulary and pronunciation, and the sources of these differences can generally be found in the distinct communities that settled in the country. For example, it is said that the *paulista* (São Paulo) accent and intonation were influenced by the massive wave of Italian immigration to the city in the late nineteenth and early twentieth centuries. *Cariocas* (people from Rio de Janeiro) like to promote the belief that their pronunciation of the letter "r" at the end of words (coda *r*) came about from the impact of French culture in and around Rio de Janeiro from the seventeenth century onward (the French-sounding [x]). In the city of São Paulo, coda *r* is pronounced [r], as in Spanish. In the interior of the state of São Paulo, and in parts of the states of Minas Gerais, Mato Grosso, Mato Grosso do Sul, and Goiás, coda *r* is pronounced as in Standard American English. To many Brazilians, this pronunciation sounds provincial and is associated with the speech of the *caipira* or hillbilly. In much of the northeast, coda *r* is simply not pronounced at all. Although the *carioca* accent is now regarded as standard in Brazil, the exaggerated final *r* ([x]) is often toned down by TV presenters, for example, who prefer the more neutral São Paulo pronunciation. Likewise, the *cariocas'* pronunciation of coda *s* (/sh/), rendering *festas* or parties as "feshtash," as in European Portuguese pronunciation, is regarded by some as rather affected.

Brazilians, much more so than the Portuguese, who often prefer to create Portuguese equivalents of new and/or popular foreign words, have incorporated a large number of English terms into their language, sometimes with altered spelling to aid pronunciation. Words relating to information technology are often borrowed from English, such as *Internet* and *mouse* (the Portuguese often prefer *rede* and *rato*, the literal translations of these terms). Words are sometimes borrowed from English and used in slightly "incorrect" ways, such as the noun *shopping*, meaning "shopping mall," and *happy end*, meaning "a happy ending to a film."

In 1998 the *Comunidade dos Países de Língua Portuguesa* (the Commonwealth of Portuguese-speaking Countries) unanimously agreed to reform the spelling of their language. The new Orthographic Code, drawn up by prestigious grammarians from Portugal and Brazil, is currently awaiting ratification by national governments. The code proposes certain linguistic standardizations designed to facilitate communication among member countries, potentially doing away, for example, with the current need/preference for distinct translations of bestsellers and film subtitles for both the Portuguese and Brazilian markets. Detractors of the reform argue that the present difficulties experienced by Portuguese speakers on both sides of the Atlantic with each other's language have much more to do with unfamiliar vocabulary and semantics than with trivial differences in orthography, such as the *trema* (dierisis), currently used only in Brazilian Portuguese (for example, in the verb *agüentar*, meaning "to put up with"), and silent consonants in European Portuguese (e.g., *facto*, meaning "fact" would, under the new proposals, become *fato*, in line with Brazilian orthography).

—*Stephanie Dennison and Lisa Shaw*

See also: *Popular Music:* Samba; *Sport and Leisure: Capoeira*; *Cultural Icons:* Regional and Ethnic Types (The Gaúcho in Brazil); *Language:* Indigenous Languages; *Popular Religion and Festivals: Candomblé*

Bibliography

Doyle, Terry, ed. 1995. *Discovering Portuguese: An Introduction to the Language and People.* London: BBC Books.

Giangola, James P. 2001. *The Pronunciation of Brazilian Portuguese.* Munich: Lincom Europa.

Martinez, Ron. 2003. *How to Say Anything in Portuguese.* Rio de Janeiro: Campus.

Lunfardo

A linguistic phenomenon that is often associated with the underworld of Buenos Aires. This speech may, depending on the observer's outlook, be termed a dialect of Spanish, a vernacular, or simply slang. The term *lunfardo* refers both to the idiom and to its speakers, traditionally the marginalized immigrants to Argentina, specifically the wave that entered the country during the final decades of the nineteenth century, many of whom were from Italy. *Lunfardo* contains words from a wide range of languages and cultures, including Brazilian Portuguese (*bondi*—bus) and Polish (*papirusa*—beautiful woman), and some taken from Spanish dialects, such as the gypsy *Caló* and the eighteenth-century thieves' cant known as *germanía.* Words such as *pibe* (kid, mate), *cana* (police), and *guita* (cash) have become popular in an area far beyond Buenos Aires and can now be found in the dictionary of the *Real Academia Española*, Spain's Royal Academy.

The metropolis of Buenos Aires saw massive immigration from Europe in the latter half of the nineteenth century, mostly from Italy, France, Great Britain, Ireland, and a second wave from Spain. Some of the early immigrants were *golosinas* or "swallows," migrant workers who crossed the Atlantic every year to work in the harvests of both Argentina and Europe. However, factors such as European investment, Argentine prosperity, and the country's desire to find a place within the First World—an aim it largely achieved in the nineteenth century—made it an increasingly attractive destination for migrants. Between the mid-nineteenth century and the beginning of the First World War in 1914, the population of Buenos Aires swelled from some 90,000 to over 1.5 million. Just as far-reaching was the change in the nature of that populace; instead of so-called *criollos* of Spanish descent, it came to feature a bewildering array of cultures and languages that included, in addition to those nationalities mentioned above, Arabs, Basques, Dutch, Germans, Jews, Poles, Russians, Yugoslavs, and Welsh.

Some 38 percent of the newcomers to Argentina during the latter decades of the nineteenth century were Italian, and their mark on Argentine Spanish would prove indelible. As well as the unmistakable cadence brought in by the so-called *tanos*, they introduced numerous words that derive from marginalized forms of Italian, such as *gergo* and *furbesco* (from the Italian *furbo*, meaning "cunning"), as well as regional dialects from Genoa, Naples, and Milan. *Lunfardo* also incorporated elements of German *Gaunersprach* and English (Cockney) slang; it was influenced by European languages spoken by those émigrés who, as in the United States, had to overcome prejudice and achieve social status. The figure of the *lunfardo*, for many a synonym for "thief," has also been associated with that of the *compadrito*, a young man from the outskirts who imitates the fierce independence of the urbanized gaucho or *compadre*.

The combination of mass immigration from various countries and the traditionally independent and self-reliant nature of the *porteño* (native of Buenos Aires), which was honed by decades of neglect by the Spanish Crown, resulted in a city characterized by its own peculiar use of Spanish. Although *lunfardo* acts as a way of excluding outsiders, preventing discourse and content from being overheard, it has as much to do with creating a sense of belonging and identity as it does with hoodwinking the police, many of whom are today adequately versed in the idiom.

Whatever the true categorization of *lunfardo*, its elevation to the status of language is a matter of some controversy. Some argue that its speakers simply use the structure and syntax of Spanish but replace nouns and verbs with their own terms. Nonetheless, the Academia Porteña del Lunfardo (Buenos Aires Academy of Lunfardo) was founded in 1962 to encourage formal study, and *lunfardo* continues to evolve as some words are discarded, some are invented and adopted, and others change meaning.

Lunfardo made its way into mainstream culture and earned a degree of acceptance in wider society through its association with the tango. But here again, opinions differ. Scholars such as Donald Castro hold the two to be brothers, while José Gobello sees them as products of entirely different traditions (the tango of essentially African origin and *lunfardo* as European). For Gobello, *lunfardo* words were simply used to flavor the tango rather than being an essential ingredient of the lyrics. Moreover, the use of *lunfardo* is inconsistent among lyricists, with some of the finest never straying from largely mainstream Spanish. Little *lunfardo* has been used in literature, even in writing that deals with the social margins of Buenos Aires. But this speech form is featured in the dialogue of contemporary Argentine films, such as *Pizza, birra, faso* (*Pizza, Beer, Smokes*, 1996), a gritty tale of street life in the capital city directed by two of Argentina's up-and-coming young filmmakers, Bruno Stagnaro and Adrián Caetano.

—*Keith Richards*

See also: *Popular Music:* Tango; *Cultural Icons:* Regional and Ethnic Types (The Gaucho in Argentina and Uruguay); *Language:* Brazilian Portuguese; Chicano Spanish; *Popular Cinema:* The Film Industry and Box-Office Successes in Argentina

Bibliography

Borges, Jorge Luis, and José Edmundo Clemente. 1963. *El lenguaje de Buenos Aires.* Buenos Aires: Emece Editores.
Castro, Donald S. 1991. *The Argentine Tango as Social History, 1880–1955: The Soul of the People.* Lewiston: Edwin Mellen Press.
Gobello, José. 1996. *Aproximación al lunfardo.* Buenos Aires: EDUCA.
Vélez, Wanda A. *South American Immigration: Argentina.* www.yale.edu/ynhti/curriculum/units/1990/1/90.01.06.x.html#c (consulted 13 March 2004).

Parlache

A term used to refer to the popular street slang of the city of Medellín, Colombia, spoken primarily by the young. *Parlache* was first spoken in the 1980s in the slum areas of the city, and then its use extended to other sectors. The language itself is formed through transformations of existing Spanish words. Some of the predominant transformations include the addition of phonemes, giving, for example, *sisas* in place of *sí* ("yes"), or conversely the suppression of phonemes giving *ñero* instead of *compañero* ("mate"). Also prevalent is the use of syllabic inversion, where a common word such as *calle* ("street") becomes *lleca* and *frío* ("cold") becomes *ofri.*

Why this particular form of speech arose in Medellín rather than in another urban center in Colombia is due to a range of social factors, including violence, drug culture, and the accompanying social crisis that Medellín, more than any other city in Colombia, has suffered. As a result of this dramatic shift in social circumstances, language, too, has evolved to reflect new social hierarchies. In *parlache,* a high proportion of the words refer to violence. Although this dialect began in the poor neighborhoods of the city, its use has extended not only to other social groups, but it has also appeared in press headlines, in *telenovelas* (soap operas), and in other television programs. One example of *parlache* in context can be found in Alonso J. Salazar's book *No nacimos pa' semilla: La cultura de las bandas juveniles en Medellín* (1990, published in English translation as *Born to Die in Medellín* in 1992), a collection of eyewitness reports and first-person testimonies by members of the groups of hired killers that operate in Medellín. The book includes a glossary of common *parlache* terms.

—*Claire Taylor*

See also: *Popular Literature:* Testimonio; *Mass Media:* Telenovela (Colombia)

Bibliography

Castañeda, Luz Stella, and José Ignacio Henao. 2000. "El *parlache*: Historias de la ciudad." Pp. 509–542 in *Literatura y cultura: Narrativa colombiana del siglo xx,* vol. 3, *Hibridez, alteridades,* edited by María Mercedes Jaramillo, Betty Osorio, and Ángela Inés Robledo. Bogotá: Ministerio de Cultura.
Lipski, John M. 1994. *Latin American Spanish.* London: Longman.

Montes Giraldo, José Joaquín. 1985. *Estudios sobre el español de Colombia.* Bogotá: Instituto Caro y Cuervo.

Salazar, Alonso J. 1990. *No nacimos pa' semilla: La cultura de las bandas juveniles en Medellín.* Bogotá: CINEP.

———. 1992. *Born to Die in Medellín.* Trans. by Nick Caistor. London: Latin America Bureau.

Chicano Spanish

The variety of Spanish spoken by the Chicano (U.S. Mexican-American) community is notable for its combination of Spanish and English. Monolingual English or Spanish speakers often refer to it disparagingly as "Spanglish." Nevertheless, it is a vibrant and creative "language" spoken by an ever-expanding community of Chicanos (18 million in 1995, to reach an estimated 70 million by 2050) and an important means of self-identification. It should not be dismissed as a substandard form of Spanish—it is a variety of Spanish as worthy of attention and acceptance as Mexican or Argentine Spanish.

Chicano Spanish constitutes an identifiable dialect; there is no single "standard" form. Instead, there are many different varieties, shaped by the precise region that the speaker comes from, his or her age, class, and so on. But most varieties will include the following phenomena to some degree: standard Mexican Spanish, popular Mexican Spanish, loan words from English transformed to fit Spanish grammar, code-switching between English and Spanish (where the speaker moves from one grammatical code to another rather than transforming words in one language to fit the grammar of the other), and the use of slang words and expressions (known as *pachuquismos* or *Caló*).

The term "standard Mexican Spanish" refers to the language used by educated middle-class Mexicans, which is almost identical in terms of grammar to standard Castilian Spanish, even though it includes a large number of regionally specific words, often derived from indigenous Mesoamerican languages. "Popular Mexican Spanish" is the term used to refer to the language (lexicon and grammatical variants) used by uneducated or poorly educated people of Mexican origin. The strong presence of elements of popular Mexican speech in Chicano Spanish contributes significantly to the fact that the latter is considered a working-class dialect and looked down upon by speakers of standard Spanish. Differences may also be noted between the popular Mexican Spanish spoken in the *barrios* of a city such as Los Angeles and the popular Mexican Spanish spoken in rural locations where, until recently, most Chicanos lived and worked. To give just one example, popular Mexican Spanish declines some very common verbs in slightly different ways than standard Spanish: *fuiste* ("you went") is typically pronounced and written as *fuistes* in popular urban Spanish and *juites* or *fuites* in popular rural Mexican Spanish.

The incorporation of loan words from English is evident in most varieties of Spanish spoken today. Nevertheless, the frequency with which they appear in Chicano Spanish is notable and makes this an idiosyncratic feature of the dialect. Such loan words include the verb *guachar* or *huachar*—a regular Spanish "ar" verb derived from the English verb "to watch," the feminine noun *birria* from the English "beer," and the literal translation of the English "high school" as *la escuela alta* (rather than *el colegio*). Code-switching can happen at many different levels: in a conversation one person might speak in Spanish while the other replies in English. This might correspond to the speakers' slightly different cultural backgrounds and competencies in the two languages. Age may also be a significant factor. However, more complex and creative versions of code-switching are typical within a single Chicano speaker's utterances—the changing of codes in this kind of example does not betray a speaker's linguistic limitations so much as offer a way of asserting the intrinsic hybridity of Chicano identity and the Chicano's refusal to assimilate to the dominance of any one code. Code-switching of this type is evident in the following sentence, quoted by Sánchez: *Sabe, carnal, we don't think that we're bravotes* ("You know, man, we don't think that we're real tough"). Much has been made of the issue of code-switching in Chicano literature and the arts, such as in the work of Gloria Anzaldúa or Guillermo Gómez-Peña, pushing its usage well beyond what is found in typical Chicano discourse.

Pachuquismos (idiosyncratic terms used by the *pachucos* of the 1940s), and now *Caló* (slang used by the *vatos locos* or crazy guys, the contemporary descendants of the *pachucos*), also play a defining role in the makeup of Chicano Spanish. These terms are a mixture of Mexican slang, underworld and prison slang from both sides of the border, Spanish gypsy slang (*Caló* means gypsy dialect in Castilian Spanish), and a kind of rhyming slang that the speaker can invent as he goes along. With respect to the latter phenomenon, where the context makes the speaker's meaning clear, a key word can be swapped for any other one that starts with the same letter. Thus *Ahí nos vidrios* is the *Caló* version of *Ahí nos vemos* ("See you later"). Other popular examples are *simón* for *sí*, *nel* for *no*, and *¿Qué pasión?* for *¿Qué pasó?* ("What happened?"). While these *Caló* terms are not as frequent in the dialect as an outsider might think, a mere sprinkling of key interjections such as *ése* ("man") and *carnal* ("brother") can give an otherwise standard Spanish utterance a Chicano feel. Indeed, these terms are usually used by urban male youths (rather than other members of the Chicano community) for the purposes of performance rather than the communication of information: above all, they identify the speaker as part of a social group. One of the best examples of Chicano Spanish (with plenty of *Caló*) is Miguel Méndez's novel *Peregrinos de Aztlán* (*Pilgrims in Aztlán*, 1974). Other examples can be found in Chicano films such as Luis Valdez's *Zoot Suit* (1981) and Allison Anders's *Mi vida loca (My Crazy Life*, 1994).

—Thea Pitman

See also: *Popular Theater and Performance:* Circus and Cabaret (Guillermo Gómez-Peña); *Cultural Icons:* Regional and Ethnic Types (El Pachuco); *Language:* Regional Differences in Latin American Spanish

Bibliography

Anzaldúa, Gloria. 1987. *Borderlands/La Frontera: The New Mestiza.* San Francisco: Aunt Lute Books.

Camarena, Salvador. 1996. "Mexicanos más allá de las fronteras." *Reforma*, 16 June, p. 12A.

Galván, Roberto A., and Richard V. Teschner. 1995. *The Dictionary of Chicano Spanish/*

El diccionario del español chicano. Lincolnwood, IL: NCT Publishing Group.
Polkinhorn, Harry, Alfredo Velasco, and Malcolm Lambert, eds. 1986. *El libro de Caló: The Dictionary of Chicano Slang.* Mountain View, CA: Floricanto Press.
Sánchez, Rosaura. 1994. *Chicano Discourse: Socio-historic Perspectives.* Houston, TX: Arte Público Press.
Stavans, Ilan. 2003. *The Making of a New American Language.* New York: Rayo.

Palenquero

Thought to be one of only three remaining Spanish-based Creole languages in the world, *palenquero* includes elements of the Bantu language brought to the New World by African slaves. It is spoken in Palenque de San Basilio, a small, remote community in the province of Bolívar in northern Colombia close to the Caribbean coast. Runaway African slaves established this community, and it is estimated that the current number of *palenquero* speakers is three to four thousand.

As well as some differences in pronunciation from Spanish, *palenquero* has very interesting features in terms of its grammar. Gender is simply nonexistent; all adjectives are related to the masculine in Spanish. Plurals are formed by adding the particle "ma" before the noun, and the endings of verbs do not change according to person. Instead, subject pronouns are used, some of which will be familiar to the Spanish speaker (e.g., *yo* for "I"), while others, such as *enú* and *ané* for "they," will not, since they are Bantu in origin.

—*Claire Taylor*

Bibliography

Lipski, John M. 1994. *Latin American Spanish.* London: Longman.
MacKenzie, Ian. 2001. *A Linguistic Introduction to Spanish.* Munich: Lincom Europa.
Montes Giraldo, José Joaquín. 1985. *Estudios sobre el español de Colombia.* Bogotá: Instituto Caro y Cuervo.

Mexican Slang

Mexican Spanish is famed throughout the Spanish-speaking world for its vibrant vulgarity. Indeed, in one popular Latin American film, illegal immigrants passing through Mexico on their way north from other parts of the subcontinent are advised to learn to swear in Mexican Spanish to avoid arousing the attention of immigration officers. Since the 1950s, however, two major sources of influence have enriched this vein of Mexican Spanish: the creative blending of Spanish and English that occurs in the speech of Chicanos and the juvenile slang of *La Onda*, the Mexican version of the "hippie generation."

The term *madre* (mother) is most revealing of Mexican psychology. While motherhood is greatly esteemed (the Virgin of Guadalupe is the prime example of veneration of the mother figure), the rape of indigenous Mexican women by invading Spaniards at the time of the Conquest, and the dubious complicity of *La Malinche* with Hernán Cortés, mean that motherhood is also associated with violence and betrayal. As the symbolic mother of the mixed-race Mexican nation, the treacherous *La Malinche*, who acted as interpreter for the Spanish colonizing forces, is a particularly problematic mother figure. Thus *madre* has become a prime term of abuse. *Me vale madre* means "I don't give a damn" (literally, "It is worth 'mother'" i.e., nothing to me) and *partirle la madre a alguien* is "to beat someone up" (literally, "to break someone's mother"). Interestingly, *padre* (father) has become a positive term in comparison with *madre*, and the common expression *¡Qué padre!* means "Wow!" or "Great!". *Chingar* ("to f—," or more precisely "to rape") is also a specifically Mexican term, stemming again from the rape of indigenous Mexican women in colonial times. Together, *madre* and *chingar* provide the most Mexican of insults: *¡Chinga (a) tu madre!* (literally, "Go f— your mother!," but really the equivalent of "F— you!"). *La chingada* means a woman who has been raped and appears in some very common insults such as *¡Vete a la chingada!* (Go to hell!) and *¡Hijo de la chingada!* (Son of a bitch!).

Over the course of the last fifty years, Mexican slang has been enriched by Chicano slang or *Caló*, so that terms such as *nel*, *simón*, and *¿Qué pasión?* are all very common among the urban youth of Mexico. In fact, the peak of the influence of Chicano slang on Mexican Spanish coincided with the rise of *La Onda*. The youths who were involved in this hippie movement looked to Chicano slang for inspiration and borrowed extensively from it. The term *La Onda* means "The Wave" or "The Vibe" and is, in itself, one of the key slang terms to originate with this movement. Even today the expression *¿Qué onda?* (What's up?) and the description of a person as being *de buena onda* (good-natured) or *de mala onda* (bad-natured) is commonly heard in the mouths of most Mexicans. Young *onderos* (hippies) also had a preference for using syllabic inversion to breathe life back into hackneyed words and expressions. Thus the expression *Me vale madre* can be *Me vale drema* in the mouth of an *ondero*. One of the writers who has most notoriously captured the variety and vulgarity of Mexican slang from the 1960s is the Boom writer Carlos Fuentes, whose *Cambio de piel* (*Change of Skin*, 1967) and *La región más transparente* (*Where the Air Is Clear*, 1968) are excellent examples.

—*Thea Pitman*

See also: *Popular Music:* Contemporary Urban Music; *Popular Literature:* The Boom; *Cultural Icons:* Religious and Mythical Figures (*La Malinche; Virgin of Guadalupe*); *Language:* Chicano Spanish

Bibliography

Glantz, Margo, ed. 1994. "Onda y escritura: Jóvenes de 20 a 33." Pp. 212–243 in *Esguince de cintura* by Margo Glantz. Mexico City: Consejo Nacional para la Cultura y las Artes.

Jones-Reid, M. F., Charlene Lopez, and L. H. Robinson. 1992. *Mexican Slang Plus Graffiti*. San Diego, CA: Sunbelt Publications.

Lonely Planet: Mexican Spanish Phrasebook. 2003. London: Lonely Planet Publications.

Paz, Octavio. 1996. *The Labyrinth of Solitude*. Translated by Lysander Kemp, Yara Milos, and Rachel Phillips Belash. Harmondsworth: Penguin.

Indigenous Languages

There is far more linguistic diversity in Latin America than is generally believed. The Ethnologue.com Website lists 295 indigenous languages for Mexico alone, 288 of which are living and 7 extinct. However, many of these are limited in terms of geographical extension and number of speakers, and some are in an apparently irreversible state of decline. Fifty-two are spoken by fewer than 1,000 people. Peru has 106 living languages and Colombia 78 (but only 500,000 speakers of American Indian languages out of a population of over 4 million). Guatemala has 54 living tongues, Venezuela 40, Bolivia 37, and Argentina 25. These figures include certain languages brought by immigrants from Asia and Europe, and some of those listed are not confined within national boundaries but are spoken in two or more countries. Nevertheless, considering the decimation suffered by native cultures and populations, this linguistic variety is impressive. According to AILLA.org (The Archive of the Indigenous Languages of Latin America), there are 550 to 700 distinct indigenous tongues in the region. The diversity in Latin America compared with Europe is startling: 56 language groups compared with 2 European ones, plus 73 with no known relative (in Europe only Basque fits this category).

These numbers should not, however, be taken as a sign that all is well, because many languages are on the brink of inevitable extinction. For instance, according to estimates made in 1986, the Boruca language of Costa Rica was spoken by a mere 5 women out of an ethnic group of 1,000. Much of this linguistic erosion has to do with the hegemony of Spanish, the official language in all the former colonies of Spain, and the effects of mass urban migration and its consequent destruction of communities. Many indigenous peoples are ashamed of their own mother tongue and reluctant to consign their children to marginalization, as they see it, by teaching them an idiom stigmatized as backward. White or mixed-race Latin Americans often refer to indigenous languages as "dialects," thus minimizing their importance and status. This attitude displays a lack of awareness of the arbitrary and often politically founded distinction between the two categories. It evokes the oft-quoted Yiddish maxim attributed to Max Weinstein: "A language is a dialect with an army and navy." Some national and foreign institutions and organizations are attempting to remedy this situation through bilingual education programs and campaigns to teach the value of preserving linguistic heritage and identity.

Indigenous languages have naturally exerted the greatest influence on Spanish in those countries where native populations, cultures, and civilizations were strongest and managed to survive the Conquest reasonably intact. Peru, Bolivia, and Paraguay are nations particularly affected by the survival of native populations and languages. Although no native culture survived this holocaust in pristine condition, some native peoples managed to stay vigorous and numerous enough that they were impossible to ignore in a modern national context. The interplay of indigenous languages with Spanish is intense in many areas of Latin America, and mutual influences abound. Interchange between languages is naturally strongest among bilinguals but can affect all social strata to varying degrees, depending on the status (which may be merely historical or symbolic) of the language in the nation as a whole or at a regional level.

Quechua, the most widely spoken of Amerindian languages, has 8 million speakers spread across Ecuador, Peru, Colombia, Bolivia, Chile, and Argentina, and an estimated forty-six dialects (or languages within a linguistic family, again depending on one's definition). *Runasimi*, to use the correct indigenous name, was the lingua franca of the Inca civilization, spoken throughout Inca territory. Marginalized today, Quechua was once itself the language of expansion and hegemony as the Incas sent populations out from the Cuzco region to acculturate far-flung communities. Not surprisingly, it is in Peru where Quechua has the highest profile and has inflected Spanish most deeply. Although it is still largely despised in Peru's coastal cities, Quechua has made its mark, due primarily to the number of native speakers who migrated from the mountains during the economic and political crises of the 1980s and 1990s. But even before this demographic shift, Quechua loan words were notable in all social strata, where autochthonous culinary terms like *cancha* (roasted maize), *choclo* (corn cob), and *chichi* (maize wine) have long been present in Peruvian Spanish. In certain areas of the Andes, knowledge of Quechua is prestigious, particularly in the Cuzco region, which was once the Inca capital and which chauvinistically boasts that its dialect is the true version.

In Mexico, too, several languages have survived from great pre-Columbian civilizations. Nahuatl was spoken and spread by the Aztecs. Today it embraces some twenty-six dialects and is still widely spoken by around a million people, mostly in central Mexico. Ironically the language was spread further still after the Conquest, when the Spanish rulers used Aztec officials and messengers to contact and settle lands previously beyond their boundaries. Many Nahuatl loan words appear in Mexican Spanish and modern English (chocolate, tomato, coyote, for example). The Mixteco language has fifty dialects and is spoken mostly in the region of Oaxaca. The Maya language family spreads through most of the northern section of the Central American isthmus. Traditional and largely segregated social structures, such as those that provoked the Zapatista rebellion in the southern Mexican state of Chiapas since the mid-1990s, have meant that Maya languages have less contact with Spanish than many other Amerindian idioms. Yucatec Maya has the most speakers; they inhabit the Yucatan peninsula, Belize, and northeastern Guatemala. Highland Guatemala is home to the Quiché group, probably the closest to classic Maya; the famous Maya text *Popol Vuh* was written in this language. Chorti Maya is spoken in parts of Honduras and El Salvador.

In Paraguay the situation is unique, since proficiency in the Guaraní language is practically a national badge of honor. Here Spanish and Guaraní are habitually interspersed during speech in a very complex practice known as Jopara, another form of speech that defies categorization. For some observers Jopara constitutes the third language of Paraguay and the true national tongue, though strict linguistic taxonomy would class it as a combination of two languages in which both sets of grammar and syntax are kept intact and separate yet are complementary. Nonetheless, Paraguayan linguistic practice is not an entirely smooth and idyllic blend. As Shaw N. Gynan has shown, there are monolingual tendencies, particularly among those who speak mainly Spanish and wish to curb Jopara and Guaraní use.

Aymara is the dominant language in the Bolivian cities of Oruro and La Paz. It is also common around the Peruvian shores of Lake Titicaca, where the main urban centers are Puno and Juliaca, and in some areas of northern Chile. Spanish in these areas is greatly affected by Aymara with regard to syntax and the use of temporal adverbs and adverbial phrases (such as *siem-*

pre [always] and the pluperfect tense *había sido*). There the verb often comes at the end of even very long sentences. Numerous words are taken directly from Aymara and used as slang: *macurca*, for example, is the muscular pain following exercise; *chaki* is a hangover; *k'encha* is bad luck, a jinx; *kara*, a term actually meaning physically or culturally stripped bare, is applied to white people and those of mixed race.

In Brazil, where an estimated 280,000 native Indians live today, the majority in the Amazon Basin, some 160 different indigenous languages are still spoken. If you include those that are usually classed as dialects, the number increases to almost 200. With the exception of ten isolated languages that are unrelated to any other, this huge variety of languages can be divided into fourteen groups. Four major linguistic groups spread across large areas that cross over into other Spanish-speaking countries: Macro-Tupi, Macro-Jê, Aruak, and Karib. Ten linguistic groups are territorially more compact and are almost all from the periphery of the Amazon Basin, encompassing a smaller number of languages: Arawá, Txapakúra, Pano, Guaykuru, Nambikwára, Mura, Katukina, Yanomami, Tukano, and Maku families. Today, according to the Brazilian constitution, teaching in indigenous areas must be bilingual.

—Keith Richards and Lisa Shaw

See also: *Popular Social Movements and Politics:* Zapatismo

Bibliography

Cotton, Eleanor Greet, and John M. Sharp. 1988. *Spanish in the Americas.* Washington, DC: Georgetown University Press.

Dixon, R.M.W. 2004. *Jarawara Language of Southern Amazonia.* Oxford: Oxford University Press.

Gynan, Shaw N. 2003. "Social Psychological Dimensions of Paraguayan Bilingualism: Attitudes toward Standard Guaraní and Spanish." www.inst.at/kulturen/2003/06sprachen/sektion_muhr_gynan.htm (consulted 13 March 2004).

Klee, Carol, and Luis A. Ramos-Garcia, eds. 1991. *Sociolinguistics of the Spanish-speaking World: Iberia, Latin America, United States.* Tempe, AZ: Bilingual Press/Editorial Bilingue.

Mar-Molinero, Clare. 2000. *The Politics of Language in the Spanish-speaking World: From Colonisation to Globalisation.* London: Routledge.

Stoler, Ann Laura. 1995. *Race and the Education of Desire: Foucault's History of Sexuality and the Colonial Order of Things.* Durham: Duke University Press, 1995.

www.ethnologue.com//web.asp (consulted 13 March 2004).

10

Mass Media

The presence of the mass media in Latin America has led to a loss of cultural memory in terms of traditional forms of popular culture, according to some. But the mass media and the urban-based culture industry have also facilitated the preservation of rural cultures in the face of mass migration to the cities.

At the beginning of the 1990s the majority of television viewers in the subcontinent were still involved in some form of pre-capitalist cultural activity, such as popular religious festivals. Thus it is essential to study the cultural context in order to understand the reception of the mass media in Latin America, where the press, radio, television, and most recently the Internet are points of contact between contradictory ways of remembering and interpreting realities.

The omnipresent *telenovela* or soap opera, for example, may feature rural settings or deal explicitly with the plight of rural-urban migrants, and at the same time, it may also offer viewers a glimpse of a sophisticated, bourgeois lifestyle. However, its melodramatic tone can be interpreted by those on the margins of society as parodic and even grotesque.

In the 1970s, discussion of the media in Latin America centered on the concept of cultural dependency: the countries of the subcontinent suffered the effects of neo-imperial colonization, especially from the United States, via the television in particular. Since then more emphasis has quite rightly been given to the reception of ideological messages and the potential for subversive or at least culturally specific "readings." Furthermore, it has become clear that Latin American *telenovelas* are not simply imitations of foreign models but are rooted in longstanding cultural traditions, such as popular theater and the *folletín* or serialized fiction published in newspapers in the nineteenth and early twentieth centuries.

Though television programming in Latin America is dominated by the *telenovela*, the so-called reality shows have recently begun to vie with soap operas for TV audiences in many countries, reflecting global trends in media entertainment. Considerable profit can be derived from these programs, which demand minimal investment in terms of money or intellectual or artistic creativity. Reality television, with pretensions to social documentary, is exemplified by the Peruvian show *Laura de América* (*Laura from the Americas*), which presents a supposedly real-life "protagonist" who suffers from a psychological condition resulting from ill-treatment, infidelity, abandonment, or some other misfortune. This individual is confronted with the wrongdoer in a studio "chat" not entirely unlike those featured on U.S. television celebrity Jerry Springer's show, and what ensues is a similarly scabrous round of recriminations and insults that may culminate in physical violence and even police intervention. Another similarity with the Jerry Springer show emanates from the inevitable suspicion that the stories told have been staged or at least deliberately exaggerated. One of the most successful exponents of this increasingly popular "genre" is the Argentine show *Entre Moria y vos* (*Between You and Moria*), hosted by celebrity Moria Casan, which exhibits a cynical pseudo-humanitarianism in its use of a gallery of social and medical unfortunates.

Telenovela production in Latin America started out as the adaptation of radio dramas, mostly originating from Cuba, into a format for the screen. The *telenovela* is by far the most popular television genre in Latin America. Unlike its U.S. or U.K. counterparts, the Latin American series does not continue indefinitely but has a defined end; it usually runs five or six days per week over the course of three to six months. A classic early example, frequently cited in studies of the genre, is the black-and-white Peruvian production of 1965, *Simplemente María* (*Simply María*). It consisted of 448 episodes and told essentially a rags-to-riches tale. This *telenovela* was very successful at the time, with such an effect on the viewing public that, for the episode of María's wedding, a crowd of about 10,000 people gathered outside the church, bearing gifts for the bride and groom. In addition to its popularity within Peru, *Simplemente María* has had a wide influence on other Latin American countries, and critics have noted that the basic plot of this *telenovela* has been repeated in countless others, including the Venezuelan smash hit of 1986, *Cristal*.

"Latin American" soap operas have also begun to sell in U.S. markets. Though companies in the U.S. have traditionally restricted themselves to the broadcasting of *telenovelas* produced in Mexico, Colombia, Venezuela, or elsewhere, U.S. production companies have recently moved into the market with *telenovelas* such as *María, María* and *Dos mundos* (the aptly titled *Two Worlds*), which are made in Miami for Latino audiences. Whether these Miami-based productions will prove as popular as their Mexican or Colombian counterparts remains to be seen; what is certain is that the *telenovela* itself, one of the most prominent Latin American cultural forms, will continue to run and run.

Radio has long been a crucial means of communication in Latin America, particularly in countries with poor infrastructure and severe topographical challenges. The introduction in the 1960s of the transistor radio, in particular, brought distant communities into contact with cities as never before, opening them up to all kinds of influences. With the advent of the radio, political messages, religious broadcasts, advertising, music, and educational transmissions have penetrated into previously inaccessible national interiors. Radio has also provided a means of bypassing the perennial problem of illiteracy. In Brazil, for example, *cantadores* or rural poets, whose traditional role was to disseminate information in rural communities, have in recent years used the radio to create a nationwide communication network.

In the mid- to late nineteenth century the press was instrumental in assisting the transition to modernity in Latin America; in the twentieth century, however, it became almost synonymous with censorship and the suppression of freedom of speech. The question of press censorship in Latin America almost inevitably brings forth images of the elimination (or "disappearance" in official government-speak) of journalists and the closure of newspapers, particularly those that took a stand against the brutal military dictatorships of the 1970s. Though this view is undeniably valid, it is incomplete. Not only those countries normally associated with severe repression of dissent are guilty of stifling or strangling press freedom. As well as Argentina, Chile, Uruguay, and Paraguay, to name the most notorious of Southern Cone dictatorships in Spanish America; the military dictatorship in Brazil (1964–1985); and Fidel Castro's rule in Cuba, it is possible to cite as an example the long period of government in Mexico of the PRI (*Partido Revolucionario Institucional* or Institutional Revolutionary Party), during which numerous journalists were killed. Freedom of the press also implies, in most Latin American countries, freedom for certain sectors of urban society to publish versions of events that will be read by a relative minority of literate citizens, again mostly in the cities. It is important to recognize that the violation of press freedoms is not confined to the Left or Right, dictatorship or "democracy," and that legal limitations on public information and debate stem from centuries of restriction. These limitations are generally passed off as imperatives for the protection of citizens from the perceived enemy of the moment—internal rebellion, military threat from a neighboring state, or the infiltration of an ideological menace.

It is argued in many quarters that, due to the institutional weaknesses of many Latin American countries, the responsibility of the press in safeguarding social justice is all the more onerous. This task is complicated, however, by the question of ownership; many of the longest-established papers remain in the hands of oligarchic families whose economic interests in the industrial and agricultural sectors mean they have little enthusiasm for reform. Generally speaking, due to the low literacy rates in many Latin American countries and the capital required to start up and maintain a newspaper, the press was the most conservative of the mass media during the nineteenth and early twentieth centuries. In addition, another reactionary element has recently arrived on the scene: the so-called *prensa amarilla* (literally, "yellow press"), with its sensationalism, lurid headlines, and avoidance of all but the most basic political or social content. On the other hand, a number of Latin America's finest novelists have also practiced journalism, including Gabriel García Márquez.

With the increase in access to the Internet, the many Latin Americans living outside their countries of origin can easily keep abreast of events back home by reading online newspapers and viewing online news programs (Brazil's *Globonews*, for example). The increasing numbers of people with access to satellite and cable television are now served by a dedicated news channel, CNN en Español (CNN in Spanish), aimed not only at the millions of Spanish speakers in the United States, but also at those living in Latin America. Just as the radio once played an important role in creating unity in rural and underpopulated nations, new technologies are now helping to create a notion of a Hispanic community throughout the Americas and beyond.

—Lisa Shaw, Claire Taylor, and Keith Richards

See also: *Popular Social Movements and Politics:* Castrismo; *Popular Literature:* The Boom

Television

Brazil

In Brazil, television is dominated today by the privately owned giant media conglomerate Rede Globe. It includes twenty radio stations and the second largest newspaper in Brazil, and until recently was headed by the media mogul Roberto Marinho (1904–2003). His TV Globo station was launched in 1964, and today Rede Globo is the world's fourth largest commercial network.

The television industry in Brazil started as a speculative venture in the 1950s, launched by businessmen looking for new sources of profit. During the military dictatorship (1964–1985), television gradually came to play a political role in an attempt to unite a huge country, to foster a sense of national identity, and to impose economic and political control. Recently the so-called reality shows have risen in popularity. Many of them focus on daily events in poor, crime-ridden areas of big cities, such as *Na rota do crime* (*In the Route of Crime*), which was broadcast by the Manchete channel from 1996 to 1997.

Sílvio Santos (born Senor Abravanel) is one of the most influential media figures in Brazil. He is the owner of the commercial television network based in São Paulo, SBT, and a popular variety show host. Xuxa, the alter ego of Maria da Graça Meneghel, has become the most famous television phenomenon in Brazil. This media icon and recording star—and former girlfriend of soccer star Pelé—reached the height of her stardom as the hostess of a children's television show in the late 1980s and early 1990s. In 1991 she became the first Latin American to appear on the *Forbes* list of the world's highest-paid entertainers.

The first commercial television station in Brazil was TV Tupi, which broadcast for the first time on 18 September 1950. By the end of the 1950s the cities of Rio de Janeiro and São Paulo were home to six television stations between them. In 1960 two programs were transmitted that attracted very large audiences and sparked a rush to buy advertising airtime, namely the inauguration ceremony of the new capital city, Brasilia, and more bizarrely, a performance of Shakespeare's *Hamlet*, recorded on videotape. In the 1960s the number of TV stations grew to a total of sixteen, spread across Brazil and located in the country's state capitals. Under the military dictatorship the television industry grew rapidly.

From the outset TV Globo endeavored to produce 60 percent of its own programs and today produces virtually all of them. TV Globo's success was founded on the sale of advertising time and a policy of buying up smaller, bankrupt TV stations, such as TV Paulista in 1966 and TV Excelsior in 1969. Enjoying the political support of the military regime and the financial and technical support of the U.S. media group

Brazilian singer, actress, and television phenomenon Xuxa. (Neal Preston/ Corbis)

Time-Life, TV Globo had the monopoly of the audience share by the 1970s and produced the most *telenovelas* (soap operas). Since the 1970s, Globo has exported its *telenovelas*, and to date Brazilian soap operas and miniseries have been sold to some 130 countries throughout the world. Cable and satellite television became widespread in Brazil in the 1990s, laying down a challenge to national networks like Globo, but only as yet among the wealthier minority of the population.

Xuxa hosted her first children's television program in 1983 and went on to launch the hugely successful *Xou* (pronounced "Show") *da Xuxa* in 1986, broadcast on TV Globo for five hours a day, six days a week. Mass audiences of all ages tuned in to watch the program, which provided a vision of a make-believe Brazil ruled by this self-styled "*Rainha dos Baixinhos*" ("The Queen of Kids"). As a tall, blue-eyed blonde and former model, Xuxa's appeal extended to adult men, who desired her, and adult women, who wanted to be like her. In 1997 Xuxa's Internet homepage called her an "authentic national institution," and a 1996 poll published in the respected *Veja* magazine ranked her tenth on a list of Brazil's most powerful people. Critics have commented on the more controversial aspects of Xuxa's star persona:

- She projects a white ideal of beauty in a country with the second largest population of African descent in the world.
- Through her relentless merchandising she transmits a consumer-led version of modernity in a nation where the majority live on or below the poverty line.
- Although she is ostensibly a children's entertainer, her screen image and spin-off clothing lines for children have an erotic dimension.
- In the largest Catholic country in the world, pseudo-religious imagery has been used to market her. Xuxa shared the stage in her *Xou da Xuxa*, for example, with an oversized sculpture of herself alongside a copy of Rio de Janeiro's most famous landmark, the Christ the Redeemer statue, and she discussed "miracles" that supposedly occurred on her show. There was even a rumor that a Xuxa doll, one of the many products that she endorses, had wept blood.

Perhaps in partial response to these criticisms or to tap into an expanding market, in the late 1990s Xuxa made conscious attempts to incorporate elements of black culture into her show *Xuxa* by including in the regular cast a nonwhite hip-hop group called You Can Dance and a mixed-race female singer called Bom Bom.

The trend for reality television in Brazil began in the early 1990s, with the SBT channel's series *Aqui, agora* (*Here and Now*), in which reporters and cameramen with handheld cameras visited *favelas* (shantytowns) and other poor neighborhoods in Brazil's cities, bringing to the screen private conflicts such as domestic violence, rape, and robbery. *Here and Now*'s format, which attracted adult male viewers in particular, served as inspiration for other programs, such as TV Record's *Cidade alerta* (*Warning for the City*) and CNT/Gazeta's *190 urgente!* (*190 Emergency!*), both of which first aired in 1996. More recently, Brazil has seen the rising popularity of reality game shows, such as *Big Brother Brasil*, broadcast by Globo, and the very similar *Casa dos artistas* (*Artists' House*), shown by rival station SBT, headed by media mogul and ultrapopular television presenter Sílvio Santos. Santos famously started out as a street trader before making the move to television via the radio. He made his name as the presenter of *programas de auditório*, or variety shows, which have their roots in Brazil's *teatro de revista*, circus and radio shows, and are the weekend television staple in Brazil.

—Lisa Shaw

See also: *Popular Theater and Performance:* Popular Theater and Music Hall (Teatro de Revista); Circus and Cabaret (Circo-Teatro); *Mass Media:* The Internet; Radio (Brazil); Telenovela (Brazil); *Visual Arts and Architecture:* Architecture and Landscape Design (*Favelas*)

Bibliography

da Rocha, Francisco Jacob Pimenta. 1995. "The Decision Is Yours: TV Globo's Search for a Brazilian God." *Travesía: Journal of Latin American Cultural Studies* 4: 51–63.

Mattelart, Michele, and Armand Mattelart. 1990. *The Carnival of Images: Brazilian Television Fiction.* Westport, CT: Greenwood Press.

Simpson, Amelia. 1993. *Xuxa: The Mega-Marketing of Gender, Race and Modernity.* Philadelphia: Temple University Press.

Sinclair, John. 1999. *Latin American Television: A Global View.* Oxford: Oxford University Press.

Skidmore, Thomas E., ed. 1993. *Television, Politics and the Transition to Democracy in Latin America.* Baltimore and London: Johns Hopkins University Press.

Mexico

Historically, the growth of television in Mexico was closely linked to its relationship with the state. Mexico's most powerful television company, Televisa, was a private monopoly that maintained a noticeably pro-government stance during the reign of the PRI (*Partido Revolucionario Institucional*—Institutional Revolutionary Party) and dominated broadcasting in Mexico.

Though the most notable Mexican television output is the *telenovela*, Televisa has also been successful in the area of children's programs, in particular those associated with the performer Chesperito (literally, "little Shakespeare"). From the early 1970s, Chesperito had a sketch show with a variety of characters, from which sprang his two most enduring creations, *El chavo del 8* (*The Kid from Number 8*) and *El chapulín colorado* (*The Coloured Grasshopper*). *El chavo*, a tale about a little boy who gets into scrapes, became a hugely popular children's television program sold all over Latin America and is still being shown in repeats today. An indication of its enduring popularity is the pop song version of the theme tune, which was released in 2002. *El chapulín colorado* is the story of a superhero dressed in red as a grasshopper, who has a series of comical catchphrases and fights villains.

With the loosening of the PRI's influence in public life beginning in the 1990s, Mexican television began to change. Channel Thirteen, previously a state-run channel, was privatized and became Televisión Azteca (Aztec Television), now transmitting on Channels 7 and 13. Televisión Azteca's output is mostly aimed at a popular market, with programs such as *El rival más débil* (a Mexican version of *The Weakest Link*), and *Estrellas de novela* (*Soap Stars*), a reality show in which contestants compete over several weeks to become soap stars. Televisa has continued with much the same formula for years, although its ubiquitous newsreader, Jacobo Zabludovsky, recently retired from its long-running news program *24 horas* (*24 Hours*). Amongst Televisa's most popular shows are a Mexican version of *Big Brother*, and game shows such as *100 mexicanos dijeron* (*One Hundred Mexicans Said*), in which contestants win money by answering correctly questions put to the general public.

A relatively new player on the scene is CNI Canal Cuarenta (Channel 40), which began operating in 1995 and currently reaches 5 million homes, mostly in Mexico City and other major urban areas. This relatively small channel has yet to make its mark but could prove an important factor in opening up Mexico's television markets. Another important corporation is Channel 11, the channel belonging to the IPN (*Instituto Politécnico Nacional*—National Polytechnic Institute), which has been running for several decades. One of the most interesting programs made by this station is *Aquí nos tocó vivir* (*We Ended up Living Here*), a program that has run for some twenty-five years, hosted by Cristina Pacheco, in which Pacheco travels around Mexico to interview real people from different walks of life.

Mexican television is currently undergoing major changes, now that Televisa's hold is diminishing, although the standard fare of *telenovelas*, game shows, and sport still dominates ratings.

—*Claire Taylor*

See also: *Mass Media:* Telenovela (Mexico)

Bibliography

Saragoza, Alex M. 1997. "Television." Pp. 1397–1400 in *Encyclopedia of Mexico*, vol. 2, edited by Michael S. Werner. Chicago: Fitzroy Dearborn.

Sinclair, John. 1999. *Latin American Television: A Global View.* Oxford: Oxford University Press.

Thomas, Adam, and Simon Dyson, eds. 2001. *Latin American Television.* London: Informa Media Group.

Trejo Delarbre, Raúl. 1988. *Espacios de silencio: La televisión mexicana.* Mexico City: Nuestro Tiempo.

Argentina

Television made its entry into Argentine life in 1951 but did not become a social force until some years later, when TV sets became available at prices accessible to the general public. The existence of a cinematic infrastructure meant that, to a certain extent, Argentina already had the expertise and technical capacity to produce a good deal of its own programming rather than import massively. As in most parts of the world, Argentine television has reflected and to a degree influenced social events and trends. During the military dictatorship of the late 1970s the medium was coerced into playing a supportive role, strictly controlled and intimidated by the authorities. Television also played an important role in the 1989 presidential elections, though far less central than in other Latin American countries. Subsequently, Argentine television was transformed from a state-run enterprise with virtually no competition into an open, fiercely competitive environment.

Due primarily to the social and economic crisis into which the Argentine public has been plunged in recent years, the current brand of "entertainment" offered is escapist, averting its own and the viewer's gaze from everyday problems and concerns. One example is *Videomatch*, which has been running for almost thirteen years and whose presenter, the former sports journalist Marcelo Tinelli, has become one of Argentina's most popular TV personalities, maintaining a steady rise in ratings ever since the program's inception. *Videomatch* began life in 1990 as a routine sports show, but soon incorporated elements of humor, such as bloopers and *Candid Camera*–style setups, to define an idiosyncratic but hugely successful style and format. Another program in this category, which has broken all records for ratings, is *Hola Susana*, fronted by the former film star Susana Giménez. This is a phone-in game show in which the public takes part from home in "live" competitions for prizes consisting of sums of money or products provided by companies wishing to make their goods known to the general public.

Argentina also has its share of reality shows: for example, *El Gran Hermano* (*Big Brother*) and *El Bar* (*The Bar*). As with European or North American variations, the screen is inhabited by participants who not only attempt to win the set prize by being the only person not eliminated by public vote, but also have their sights set on a shortcut to fame of some kind. These shows are money-spinners for producers, who need make only a very limited outlay, with no fees for artists or

Popular Argentine television presenter Susana Giménez, flanked by soccer star Diego Maradona and Spanish singer Julio Iglesias, on her TV show in April 2004. (Rodrigo Nesplol/La Nacion/AP Photo)

celebrities. The potential earnings, on the other hand, are massive. Reminiscent of the U.S. dance marathons in the Great Depression, in which contestants suffered all manner of indignity in their quest for remuneration or recognition, reality television is by now ubiquitous on the menu of globalized television.

Sport is another television favorite, soccer in particular. Argentina is one of the world's most fanatical nations when it comes to soccer. In many households, Sundays are reserved for a televised match.

News programs are known for their exploitation of the lowest common denominator, evident in a generally sensationalist tone calculated to echo the *prensa amarilla* ("yellow" or gutter press) in maximizing potential ratings. Reports thus tend to dispense with the analysis of important themes, preferring to offer readily digestible interpretations replete with sound bites. Emphasis is also placed on show business gossip and similar trivia, some of which is positively malicious in its pursuit of the juiciest scandal.

—*Keith Richards*

See also: *Mass Media:* The Press (Argentina); Telenovela (Argentina)

Bibliography

Ford, Aníbal, Jorge B. Rivera, and Eduardo Romano. 1984. *Medios de comunicación y cultura popular.* Buenos Aires: Editorial Legasa.

Galperín, Hernán. 2002. "Transforming Televisión in Argentina: Market Development and Policy Reform in the 1990s." Pp. 22–37 in *Latin Politics, Global Media,* edited by Elizabeth Fox and Silvio R. Waisbord. Austin: University of Texas Press.

Pierce, Robert N., and John Spicer Nichols. 1979. *Keeping the Flame: Media and*

Government in Latin America. New York: Hastings House.

Sinclair, John. 1999. *Latin American Television: A Global View.* Oxford: Oxford University Press.

Sinclair, John, Elizabeth Jacka, and Stuart Cunningham. 1996. *New Patterns in Global Television: Peripheral Vision.* Oxford: Oxford University Press.

Zuleta-Puceiro, Enrique. 1993. "The Argentine Case: Television in the 1989 Presidential Election Campaign." Pp. 55–81 in *Television, Politics, and the Transition to Democracy in Latin America,* edited by Thomas E. Skidmore. Washington, DC: Woodrow Wilson Center Press; Baltimore: Johns Hopkins University Press.

Telenovela

Brazil

Serialized soap operas known as *telenovelas,* or simply as *novelas,* have dominated television production and ratings in Brazil for the last thirty-five years. They are screened six days a week, chiefly in prime time, for four to five hours per day, for six to seven consecutive months. They play a central social role in the lives of the majority of the population, particularly the illiterate and semiliterate poor, in a country where there is one television set for every 4.5 inhabitants. First broadcast in the early to mid-1950s, early examples of Brazilian *telenovelas* frequently imported scripts from Mexico, Cuba, and Argentina. Ivani Ribeiro and Janete Clair were among the first Brazilian authors of *telenovelas.* The social routine of watching several *telenovelas* every night was established between 1968 and 1974, the most repressive period of the military regime (1964–1985), as people tended to keep off the streets after dark. Today Brazil's more than 110 million television viewers (out of a population of some 170 million) with their 32 million television sets represent a huge market for commercial advertising, and the *telenovelas* are an unrivalled vehicle for reaching them.

The first daily *telenovela,* entitled *25499 Ocupado* (*25499 Line Busy*), aired in Brazil in July 1963 on TV Excelsior. In May 1964, TV Excelsior transmitted *A moça que veio de longe* (*The Girl Who Came from Far Away*), a love story between a rich man's son and the maid of the house. It attracted large audiences and was the first soap opera broadcast in the primetime 8 p.m. slot in Brazil. In September 1964, TV Tupi launched *O direito de nascer* (*The Right to Be Born*), an adaptation of a *radionovela* by the Cuban writer Felix Caignet, which established the success of the daily soap opera. In this initial phase of production, the target audience for the soaps was middle-class housewives, the vast majority of whom owned television sets. In the mid-1960s each of the four major TV networks in Brazil was showing three to four *telenovelas* every day, but by the beginning of the 1970s, TV Globo's *novelas* were far and away the market leaders.

The first realistic *telenovela* is considered to have been *Beto Rockfeller,* broadcast on TV Tupi in 1968. With mass migration to the cities, tales of the urban life of ordinary Brazilians on television screens offered migrants ideas about how to negotiate their new existence, just as the *chanchada* films had done earlier. (In the 1980s many soap operas took their lead explicitly from the *chanchada* film comedies of the 1940s and 1950s.) Janete Clair's major success, *Selva de pedra* (*Stone Jungle*) (1972–1973), a love story between two migrants newly arrived in the city, became the most popular Brazilian *telenovela* of all time.

TV Globo diversified the genre in the 1970s, broadening its appeal and target audience by combining the melodrama and the emotional extravagance of the earlier soap operas with a more modern approach. Throughout the 1970s, Globo dominated production, creating some "alternative" soap operas that relied on social satire, such as *Gabriela*, based on the novel *Gabriela, cravo e canela* (*Gabriela, Clove and Cinnamon*) by Jorge Amado. TV Globo was the first producer in Brazil to realize the potential of incorporating more daring and up-to-date themes into their soap operas. It also consciously allocated specific kinds of *telenovelas* to given time slots. The 6 p.m. soap was initially targeted at teenagers, housewives, and domestic staff, and tended to be an adaptation of a work of Romantic literature. But since 1982, Globo has oriented this slot toward young people. The 7 p.m. soap, too, has traditionally been aimed at teenagers and housewives—but also at working women who by this time have returned home. Its programming continues to be characterized by light story lines, with an element of romance and humor, such as the 1983 comedy *Guerra dos sexos* (*Battle of the Sexes*). The 8 p.m. *novela* is aimed at the family unit as a whole, including husbands who have by now returned from work. Its plots have tended to focus on daily life, family problems, or wider issues. Finally, the 10 p.m. slot has traditionally been set aside for more experimental story lines. In 1973 the *telenovela O bem-amado* (*The Beloved*), the first to be screened in color, established the 10 p.m. *novela* as a specific subgenre and was also the first Brazilian soap opera to be sold to other Latin American countries. In recent years this time slot has been increasingly occupied by another televisual fiction genre, the miniseries: it consists of between ten and twenty episodes in total, and is aimed at a more high-brow audience, often in the form of a literary adaptation.

In the late 1980s and throughout the 1990s the 8 p.m. *novelas* contained political subtexts and dealt with contemporary issues, ranging from corruption and nepotism to the demise of the Catholic Church and the enforced celibacy of priests. *Roque Santeiro*, consisting of 209 episodes aired between 1985 and 1986, was the first *telenovela* of this kind. Similarly, *O rei do gado* (*The Cattle King*, 1996–1997) dealt with the controversial issue of land reform.

The distinctions between the fictional world of the soap opera and the real lives of its stars and their fans have become blurred on occasion. On 27 December 1992, Daniella Perez, one of the main actors in the 8 p.m. soap *De corpo e alma* (*Of Body and Soul*), was murdered in the middle of the night in Rio de Janeiro. As rumors of the tragedy spread, the soap's fans were confused about whether it was true or whether it was a leaked story line of how Daniella's character in the soap, the heroine Yasmin, had been killed off. It transpired that the prime suspect in the case was Daniella's co-star in *Of Body and Soul*, Guilherme de Padua. A rally was held in a soccer stadium in São Paulo, attended by 70,000 people, to demand that he be brought to trial. After Daniella's mother, Glória Perez, a creator of *telenovelas* herself, presented a petition of 1.3 million signatures, a minute's silence was held, which ended with the playing of the musical theme associated with the character of Yasmin in the soap. Four years later, in 1997, Padua and his real-life wife were finally imprisoned for this crime.

—*Lisa Shaw*

See also: *Popular Literature:* The Boom; *Mass Media:* Radio (Brazil); Television (Brazil); *Popular Cinema:* Comedy Film (*Chanchada*); Melodrama

Bibliography

da Rocha, Francisco Jacob Pimenta. 1995. "The Decision Is Yours: TV Globo's Search for a Brazilian God." *Travesía: Journal of Latin American Cultural Studies* 4: 51–63.

Fox, Elizabeth. 1997. *Latin American Broadcasting: From Tango to Telenovela.* Luton, UK: University of Luton Press.

Hamburger, Esther. 2003. "Politics of Representation: Television in a São Paulo *Favela.*" *Framework* 44, no. 1: 104–115.

López, Ana M. 1995. "Our Welcomed Guests: *Telenovelas* in Latin America." Pp. 256–275 in *To Be Continued . . . : Soap Operas around the World*, edited by Robert. C. Allen. New York: Routledge.

Mattelart, Michele, and Armand Mattelart. 1990. *The Carnival of Images: Brazilian Television Fiction.* Westport, CT: Greenwood Press.

Skidmore, Thomas E., ed. 1993. *Television, Politics and the Transition to Democracy in Latin America.* Baltimore and London: Johns Hopkins University Press.

Straubhaar, Joseph D. 1982. "The Development of the *Telenovela* as the Pre-eminent Form of Popular Culture in Brazil." *Studies in Latin American Popular Culture* 1: 138–186.

Mexico

With over forty years of *telenovela* production, Mexico is the dominant player within the Spanish-language market. Within Mexico itself, the leading figure is undoubtedly Televisa, a multimedia conglomerate whose market dominance is largely due to its capacity to handle all aspects of media production. (When the title songs from Brazil's Globo soap operas become hits, for example, they are released under the Fonovisa label, Televisa's musical wing.) Nevertheless, a smaller competitor, TV Azteca, has recently entered the market and attempted to deviate from the standard fare churned out by Televisa.

The standard Mexican *telenovela* is highly sentimental and emotional, featuring often improbable characters in improbable situations dealing with universal issues such as love, betrayal, and revenge. In her classification of national variants of *telenovelas*, Ana López sees Mexican ones, as exemplified by Televisa's productions, as characterized by their weepiness, Manichean characterizations, and lack of historical references. One example of this Mexican format is the 1979 Televisa production *Los ricos también lloran* (*The Rich Cry Too*), directed by Rafael Banquells, with the theme tune "Aprendí a llorar" ("I Learnt to Cry") sung by the leading actress, Verónica Castro. Castro played the lead role of Mariana Villareal in this rather improbable story of mistaken identities and unknown parentage, a plot that continues to be repeated in different formats in a host of *telenovelas* around Latin America. *The Rich Cry Too* became Mexico's greatest *telenovela* hit, selling not only to the Spanish-language market but also to a variety of countries, including Russia, where it was reputedly watched by two-thirds of Moscow's population.

—*Claire Taylor*

See also: *Mass Media:* Television (Mexico)

Bibliography

Fox, Elizabeth. 1997. *Latin American Broadcasting: From Tango to Telenovela.* Luton, UK: University of Luton Press.

Fox, Elizabeth, and Silvio Waisbord, eds. 2002. *Latin Politics, Global Media.* Austin: University of Texas Press.

López, Ana M. 1995. "Our Welcomed Guests: *Telenovelas* in Latin America." Pp. 256–275 in

Filming a scene from one of the daily episodes of the Mexican *telenovela* (soap opera) entitled *Infierno en el Paraíso* (*Hell in Paradise*), produced by Televisa. (Keith Dannemiller/Corbis)

To Be Continued . . . : Soap Operas around the World, edited by Robert C. Allen. New York: Routledge.

Mato, Daniel. 2002. "Miami in the Transnationalization of the *Telenovela* Industry: On Territoriality and Globalization." *Travesía: Journal of Latin American Cultural Studies* 11, no. 2: 195–212.

Singhal, Arvind, and Everett M. Rogers. 1999. *Entertainment Education: A Communication Strategy for Social Change*. Mahwah, NJ: Lawrence Erlbaum Associates.

Skidmore, Thomas E., ed. 1993. *Television, Politics and the Transition to Democracy in Latin America*. Baltimore and London: Johns Hopkins University Press.

Colombia

If the Mexican market is characterized by the repetition of generic plots, Colombian *telenovelas* offer a product closer to the "Brazilian model," with specific cultural references (frequently regional) and a mixture of melodrama and comedy. Notable within this trend are *telenovelas* that express the way of life of a specific region and focus on its geography, landscapes, produce, culture, and music. The 1994 production *Café con aroma de mujer* (*Coffee with a Scent of Woman*) is typical of this strand of *telenovela*. Directed by Pepe Sánchez, it became a hit not only in Colombia but also in the rest of Latin America and among Latino audiences in the United States. Though based on the typical melodramatic rags-to-riches plot, this *telenovela* is more culturally specific than its Mexican counterparts, detailing the life of Gaviota, a worker in Colombia's coffee-growing region. It includes such details as the customs of coffee harvest and the nature of the work, along with portraits of the local people and environment.

Another example of this regionalist trend is the 1991 Caracol production *Escalona*, which incorporates musical forms and uses music as a form of narration—both typical features of the Colombian *telenovela*. In this *Escalona*, based on the life of the *vallenato* composer Rafael Escalona, the lead actor, Carlos Vives, sings Escalona's works in the course of the episodes.

Perhaps the most striking hit among Colombia's recent *telenovelas* is the 2001 production *Betty la fea* (*Ugly Betty*), which was watched by some 28 million viewers in Colombia when it came out, about 70 percent of the population. In addition to its success in Colombia, this soap opera took the rest of the Spanish-language market by storm, with more than 80 million viewers in Latin America and in the United States.

—Claire Taylor

See also: *Popular Music:* Vallenato; *Mass Media:* Telenovela (Brazil); *Popular Cinema:* Melodrama

Bibliography

Fox, Elizabeth. 1997. *Latin American Broadcasting: From Tango to Telenovela.* Luton, UK: University of Luton Press.

Hodgson, Martin. 2000. "Ugly Betty Woos Colombian Viewers Night after Night." *The Guardian*, 18 September.

López, Ana M. 1995. "Our Welcomed Guests: *Telenovelas* in Latin America." Pp. 256–275 in *To Be Continued . . . : Soap Operas around the World*, edited by Robert C. Allen. New York: Routledge.

Venezuela

Today the major companies involved in the production of *telenovelas* in Venezuela are Venevisión and Radio Caracas Televisión (RCTV), along with RCTV's subsidiary, Coral de Venezuela. RCTV's *Cristal* (1986) was the first truly successful Venezuelan *telenovela* export; popular across Latin America, it also won an audience share of 80 percent in Spain and was rerun several times. This *telenovela*, too, reworks the rags-to-riches theme in the life of Cristal, a young woman brought up in an orphanage who achieves success and becomes a model. Also popular was Coral's *Kassandra* (1992), which reworked another familiar plot, the tale of babies switched at birth and the ensuing mistaken identities and problems. This series gained a huge audience in Venezuela and throughout Latin America—and even proved to be a hit in Eastern Europe.

Meanwhile, one of the most interesting Venezuelan *telenovelas* in recent years was the 1992 RCTV production *Por estas calles* (*In These Streets*), which marked a move toward social commentary. Its 250 episodes told the life story of a corrupt ruler and were seen by many as a comment on the situation in Venezuela at the time (the Venezuelan president Carlos Andrés Pérez left office two years later due to a corruption scandal).

—Claire Taylor

Bibliography

Fox, Elizabeth. 1997. *Latin American Broadcasting: From Tango to Telenovela.* Luton, UK: University of Luton Press.

Fox, Elizabeth, and Silvio Waisbord, eds. 2002. *Latin Politics, Global Media.* Austin: University of Texas Press.

López, Ana M. 1995. "Our Welcomed Guests: *Telenovelas* in Latin America." Pp. 256–275 in *To Be Continued . . . : Soap Operas around the World*, edited by Robert C. Allen. New York: Routledge.

Argentina

Argentina has been producing *telenovelas* since the early 1950s. During the Perón era, these products of state-owned television, with their populist glorification of an acquiescent working class, were generally tepid, timid love stories. Visually, the staid likes of *Amor en mesa de saldos* (*Love in the Sales*, 1952) and *Como te quiero, Ana* (*How I Love You, Ana*, 1953) provide a striking contrast to the fare available on Argentine television in the early years of the twenty-first century. However, the condescending spirit with which they approach their audience has not changed.

The first years of television broadcasting coincided with Argentina's most prosperous times, and the nation was able to build enviable print, radio, and cinema industries during the early decades of the twentieth century. As a result, Argentina, which was already serializing stories with remarkable success in newspapers, magazines, and on radio, became one of the first Latin American countries to exploit the possibilities of television serials, which gave rise to the *telenovela*. The stultifying effects of these serializations on the public psyche are recorded in several of the novels of Manuel Puig, such as *Boquitas pintadas* (*Heartbreak Tango*, first published in 1969).

Argentina today is the Latin American country with the highest incidence of cable subscribers. It is also one of the countries with the least state control of television, a legacy of the privatization programs of Presidents Alfonsín in the early 1980s and in particular Menem in the late 1980s and 1990s. One result of this media globalization is a renewed conservatism, but now with infinitely greater attention given to heightening the glamour and sex appeal of TV stars at the expense of any concern with external conditions and events, or any sense of cultural or geographical grounding. Nonetheless, Argentine soap operas are hugely marketable: the country's networks sell widely, not only across Latin America but as far afield as Asia and Eastern Europe.

—*Keith Richards*

See also: *Popular Social Movements and Politics:* Peronismo; *Popular Literature:* The Post-Boom; *Mass Media:* Television (Argentina)

Bibliography

Fox, Elizabeth. 1997. *Latin American Broadcasting: From Tango to Telenovela.* Luton, UK: University of Luton Press.

Fox, Elizabeth, and Silvio Waisbord, eds. 2002. *Latin Politics, Global Media.* Austin: University of Texas Press.

López, Ana M. 1995. "Our Welcomed Guests: *Telenovelas* in Latin America." Pp. 256–275 in *To Be Continued . . . : Soap Operas around the World*, edited by Robert C. Allen. New York: Routledge.

Puig, Manuel. 1992. *Heartbreak Tango.* New York: Vintage.

———. 2000. *Boquitas Pintadas.* Barcelona: Seix Barral.

Radio

Cuba and the Andes

In Cuba and in the Andean countries, radio has proved instrumental in providing entertainment and information while conveying political messages and maintaining levels of social awareness in remote rural areas. Of course, the prevailing political climate in these two areas is as different as the cultural and ethnic makeup of their inhabitants. In Cuba radio has been an important mouthpiece of Fidel Castro's revolution, bolstering revolutionary values and complementing the literacy campaigns that began in 1959; in the Andes radio has largely been linked to programs of bilingual education in areas where the indigenous languages, principally Aymara and Quechua, are threatened by the encroachment of Spanish. The medium has also been used for some time by religious groups of various kinds, by nongovernmental organizations (NGOs) anxious to raise awareness in order to minimize ecological and other problems, and by government agencies wishing to educate rural dwellers in avoiding dangers from disease or natural phenomena. Radio is also a medium that can be used from outside national borders by foreign groups with a variety of intentions.

The *radionovela* or radio soap opera (a forerunner of the *telenovela* in many countries) has had a long history of success in Latin America, above all in the boom of the 1930s and 1940s when the genre was fresh and public appetite sharp. Since the 1970s, however, there has been a different approach to the genre that intends to be both entertaining and didactic. A series of *radionovelas* promoted mainly by governments and NGOs seeks to raise not only a sense of the value of linguistic and cultural heritage but also an awareness of historical roots.

Cuba in 1959 had the highest private ownership of radio and television receivers in Latin America and a considerable broadcasting infrastructure to match. But this was true only in urban centers. The poor and uneducated rural populations that were unattractive as targets for commercial, advertisement-funded broadcasting were excluded. Radio, then, was an important means of consolidating the power base of the Revolution among the rural social sectors that had supported Castro's guerrilla forces. Ever since that time radio has been used to serve government interests and to enable official positions and pronouncements to reach every corner of the island. Though not enormous in size, Cuba's terrain presents logistical difficulties, particularly in the mountainous eastern province of Oriente. The importance of radio during the early years lay in the ease with which it could reach outlying populations with little opportunity to learn to read.

Surprisingly, the role of radio in Cuba became even more important during the "Special Period" following the fall of the Berlin Wall than it was during the years immediately following the overthrow of Fulgencio Batista's dictatorship. Since the successful literacy campaigns of the early 1960s, the main hindrance to the distribution of the Communist Party daily newspaper, *Granma*, and other organs is the scarcity of paper, which must be imported at great cost. But given Fidel Castro's style of leadership, with his legendary penchant and gift for long and impassioned speeches, the prevalence of radio as a vehicle is hardly surprising. Radio stations in Cuba are, without exception, run or monitored by the state along lines prescribed by the party. The three networks are Radio Havana, which broadcasts international news and comment; Radio Reloj, which deals in more general programming as well as current affairs; and Radio Oriente, which caters to the eastern end of the island.

An example of the use of *radionovela* in Cuba can be seen in the station Radio Cadena Agramonte, based in Camagüey, which offers period dramas and historical adventures for both children and young people. A more didactic content can be seen in the *testimonio* genre, which offers eyewitness accounts of events leading up to the Revolution, with a particular focus on the Camagüey region.

Another important player in the drama of Cuban radio is one that broadcasts from offshore. The Florida-based station Radio Martí, supported by the U.S. government, largely owes its existence to the political muscle of the Miami Cuban exile community. In the seemingly endless war of words between Havana and Miami, the very name Radio Martí is characteristic of the conflicting interpretations of a common heritage. The station is named after José Martí (1853–1895), the Cuban poet and patriot whose political stance and declarations are claimed as the exclusive property of both the political Right and Left. However, Martí's position, favorable to the United States until around 1890, became increasingly hostile to Cuba's as U.S. foreign policy became ever more domineering. To the mortification of Miami hard-liners, the Clinton administration severely cut government funding to Radio Martí, a situation that George W. Bush's Republicans have yet to redress.

In the Andes, radio made rare incursions until the revolutionary years of 1952 in Bolivia and 1968 in Peru, because the potential audience, like the Cuban countryside, was of little importance to the dominant commercial interests. With the triumph of the Bolivian MNR (*Movimiento Nacional Revolucionario* or Revolutionary National Movement) in 1952, numerous radio stations grew up in order to inform and influence the hitherto ignored peasantry and underrepresented miners. In Peru, the 1968 coup by General Juan Velasco Alvarado brought the nationalization of media interests and a similar campaign to educate and politicize the rural indigenous population. Velasco favored education in indigenous languages and argued for their value at a time when this was inconceivable as an official position. In Peru and Bolivia, as in other Latin American countries where state media have attempted to compete with foreign commercial interests, a strong motive has been safeguarding the integrity of national culture against the threat of it being swamped by "Western" culture (Velasco famously banned U.S. and European rock and pop music during his spell in power).

Apart from these aims, radio in the Andes has assumed the supplementary role of protecting indigenous culture from the erosive effects of the city and the metropolis. Radio stations have sprung up that broadcast entirely in Aymara or Quechua, with the intention of providing Indian communities with a means of hearing their languages in a context other than that of their immediate surroundings. An example of the use of radio to bolster a sense of cultural and linguistic worth in the face of the insidious threat of encroachment is the Jesuit station ACLO. Based in Sucre, in the southern Bolivian Andes, ACLO (*Acción Loyola*, a reference to the founder of the Jesuits) broadcasts programs that seek to raise awareness on all possible levels: the station teaches correct agricultural practices, health care, and political consciousness as well as providing news, music (including an annual provincial music festival), and other programs aimed at preserving cultural self-esteem.

Radio has had a strong political role to play in the Andean countries, largely because of the ease with which transistor radio sets can be bought and carried. Radio stations were of particular importance during the various miners' strikes in Bolivia. The vicious dictatorship of Luis García Meza in the early 1980s made radio stations a prime target for repression and forced them to broadcast news reports drawn up by the regime.

Projecting a sense of historical identity is the intention of the group ALER, based in Quito, Ecuador. The Asociación Latinoamericana de Educación Radiofónica (Latin American Radio Educators) produces programs to be broadcast in a variety of areas. Among their *radionovelas* is *Taky Ongoy* (*Dance of Sickness*), which dramatizes a sixteenth-century indigenous campaign of ritual resistance to Spanish occupation. The movement intended to revive the sacred figurines or *huacas* that would in turn restore indigenous self-rule. Another ALER production dramatizes the experiences of sixteenth-century indigenous chronicler Guaman Poma de Ayala, who set out to inform the King of Spain of his representatives' abuse of power. Yet another tells the story of Santa Rosa de Lima, patron saint of the Americas.

Ecuador, which has a history of benign media legislation interspersed with periods of authoritarianism, hosted the 1960 conference on education in the mass media, from which sprang the influential International Center for Higher Journalism Studies for Latin America (CIESPAL).

Among foreign broadcasters operating in the Andes and other inaccessible areas of Latin America is Radio Netherlands, which provides *radionovelas* aimed at promoting health awareness, avoiding AIDS, and dealing with other threats. The importance of radio is also acknowledged by the COMSALUD health awareness project, launched in 2001 and run by the Panamerican Health Organization in conjunction with UNESCO, US-AID, and other bodies. The project uses *radionovelas* along with other media in its bid to reach the widest possible public. The BBC's broadcasts, *Voice of America*, and formerly Radio Moscow are radio sources used by populations facing severe media restriction due to authoritarian rule.

A great deal of research must be carried out in order to determine the full impact of these and other campaigns designed to bring development projects into the everyday lives of undereducated people in both rural and urban areas. The role of radio broadcasting on the Internet is another area in which constant change is occurring but which has been little studied to date.

—*Keith Richards*

See also: *Popular Social Movements and Politics:* Castrismo; *Language:* Indigenous Languages; *Mass Media:* The Internet; Telenovela

Bibliography

Alisky, Marvin. 1981. *Latin American Media: Guidance and Censorship.* Ames: Iowa State University Press.

Davies, Catherine. 2000. "Surviving (on) the Soup of Signs: Postmodernism, Politics and Culture in Cuba." Pp. 74–92 in *Cultural Politics in Latin America,* edited by Anny Brooksbank-Jones and Ronaldo Munck. New York: St. Martin's Press.

Rivadeneira Prada, Raúl. 1988. "Bolivian Television: When Reality Surpasses Fiction." Pp. 164–170 in *Media and Politics in Latin America: The Struggle for Democracy,* edited by Elizabeth Fox. London: Sage.

Brazil

Radio took root in Brazil in the 1920s but really took off in the 1930s, under President Getúlio Vargas (1930–1945), who harnessed the nascent medium to spread his nationalist ideology to the country's far-flung population. From the 1930s to the late 1950s, radio variety shows known as *programas de auditório* (literally, auditorium programs) vied with the *chanchada* films as the principal source of mass entertainment, and the demise of both came only with the consolidation of the television in Brazil in the 1960s. These eclectic live-audience variety shows established a tradition of popular entertainment that today finds its legacy in the television shows of the likes of Sílvio Santos. Brazilian *telenovelas* also owe a debt to the *radionovelas* or radio soap operas that enthralled audiences in the 1940s.

Under President Vargas, the *Hora do Brasil* (*Hour of Brazil*) show was broadcast daily between 8 p.m. and 9 p.m. by all radio stations and was designed to foster social and political unity. In a country where over half the adult population was illiterate in 1940, the radio was the perfect tool for spreading the regime's patriotic message. After 1939, Vargas tightened censorship restrictions on all media. In 1940 alone, 108 radio programs were banned, and all radio stations had to broadcast news items supplied to them by the regime's official press agency. In 1940 the government took charge of the Rádio Nacional station, founded in 1936, which proceeded to dominate the airwaves, monopolizing the Brazilian audience. Nevertheless, the growth of radio continued unabated: in 1940 there were 80 radio stations in Brazil, and by 1944 this figure had risen to 110.

The *programas de auditório* combined comic interludes and magic acts with musical performances and prize competitions. Recorded in front of a live audience and aired on weekend afternoons, these variety shows featured a varied musical repertoire. They also energetically fostered notions of stardom, encouraging audience members to swear allegiance to their favorite female singer, whether Emilinha Borba, Marlene, or Ângela Maria, who competed to be crowned the "queen of radio" on a yearly basis.

In the Vargas era, radio stations transmitted plays in the evenings, known generically as *rádio-teatro* or radio-theater, which later developed into the highly popular *radionovela* or radio soap opera, the forerunner of the *telenovela*. From 1941 onward, with the airing of *Em busca da felicidade* (*In Search of Happiness*), written by the Cuban Leandro Blanco, Rádio Nacional gradually began to devote more and more airtime to soap operas. By 1945, radio-theater made up 14.3 percent of Rádio Nacional's programming, slightly more than variety shows.

In 1968 the first FM stations were established in Brazil, and in 1977 the Rádio Cidade FM station was founded in Rio de Janeiro, which went on to enjoy the largest audience share throughout the 1980s. In 1990 the Rádio Bandeirantes station, set up in São Paulo in 1954, created the first national satellite radio network, and in 1995 the Catholic Church launched Igreja-Sat, the biggest station in the country today. By 1997, 90.3 percent of Brazilian households owned a radio set, as opposed to 84.9 percent in 1992. In the twenty-first century, interest is growing in virtual radio stations linked to Internet Websites.

—*Lisa Shaw*

See also: *Mass Media:* The Internet; Telenovela (Brazil); Television (Brazil); *Popular Cinema:* Comedy Film (*Chanchada*)

Bibliography
McCann, Bryan. 1999. "The Invention of Tradition on Brazilian Radio." Pp. 474–482 in *The Brazil Reader: History, Culture, Politics*, edited by Robert M. Levine and John J. Crocitti. London: Latin America Bureau.
———. 2004. *Hello, Hello, Brazil: Popular Music in the Making of Modern Brazil.* Durham and London: Duke University Press.

The Press

A number of international organizations of various political hues monitor press freedom in Latin America. *Pulso del periodismo* (*Pulse of Journalism*) is a bilingual journal and Website published by Florida International University's Media Center of the School of Journalism and Mass Communication. The Freedom Forum, though sponsored by the U.S. government, declares itself nonpartisan and recently sponsored the Latin American Journalism Project (*Proyecto de Periodismo Latinoamericano*) to train journalists in the region. Another organization, the Foundation for New Latin American Journalism (*Fundación Para un Nuevo Periodismo Latinoamericano*, or FNPI), was founded by Nobel prize-winning novelist Gabriel García Márquez and runs workshops and seminars from its base in Cartagena, Colombia. García Márquez views his time as a reporter with the Bogotá daily *El espectador* (*The Spectator*) as crucial in his development as a writer. Among many other Latin American novelists who have practiced some form of journalism are the Peruvian Mario Vargas Llosa, Rómulo Betancourt in Venezuela, and Marcelo Quiroga Santa Cruz in Bolivia.

Catching up on current events, Colombia, 1996. (Jeremy Horner/Corbis)

Despite the continuing threats to independent journalism, many well-respected, if politically conservative, newspapers operate in Latin America. These include the Argentine *Clarín*, the newspaper with the highest circulation in the Spanish-speaking world; the Peruvian daily *El comercio; El mercurio* in Chile; Venezuela's *El universal;* and *El tiempo* in Colombia. Newspapers with a more politically defiant stance include the Nicaraguan *La prensa*, with its resistance to the brutal Somoza regime, and the Mexican daily *Excelsior.*

—Keith Richards

See also: *Popular Literature:* The Boom

Bibliography
Alisky, Marvin. 1981. *Latin American Media: Guidance and Censorship.* Ames: Iowa State University Press.

Fox, Elizabeth, ed. 1988. *Media and Politics in Latin America: The Struggle for Democracy.* London: Sage.
Freedom Forum. http://www.Freedomforum.org (consulted 17 March 2003).
Fundación Nuevo Periodismo Iberoamericano. http://www.fnpi.org/ (consulted 17 March 2003).
Pulso del Periodismo. http://www.pulso.org/English/index.htm (consulted 17 March 2003).
Waisbord, Silvio. 2000. *Watchdog Journalism in South America: News, Accountability and Democracy.* New York: Columbia University Press.

Chile

The press in Chile has been conditioned by the political upheaval that, in the early 1970s, broke a half century of political stability. During this period the country had established a sophisticated mass media, heterogeneous in the sense of its political representation and sponsorship. This state of affairs, in which a free press was only one of many democratic institutions, was gradually eroded as the country became politically polarized during the late 1960s and early 1970s, and when the government of Salvador Allende was overthrown in 1973. The dictatorship of General Augusto Pinochet, which followed and lasted until 1990, silenced the pro-Allende press. It also began a concerted campaign through the secret police of DINA (Directorate of National Intelligence) to infiltrate and manipulate the journalistic community, eventually imposing rigid controls on the press and all other media.

Chile is well known for having been the first Latin American country to adopt and apply free-market economics during this time. The imposition of neoliberalism became closely identified with Pinochet and with the right-wing newspaper *El mercurio*, which never wavered in its support for him or for these economic policies. Despite the removal of Pinochet in a plebiscite in 1990, and the country's formal return to democracy in 1991, Chile still witnesses the intermittent yet persistent harassment of writers and journalists. Censorship in Chile today has much to do with the innate conservatism of the nation's middle classes and the ideological protection of its neoliberal economic project.

—*Keith Richards*

See also: *Popular Theater nd Performance:* Theater under Dictatorship (Chile)

Bibliography

Alisky, Marvin. 1981. *Latin American Media: Guidance and Censorship.* Ames: Iowa State University Press.
Catalán, Carlos. 1988. "Mass Media and the Collapse of a Democratic Tradition in Chile." Pp. 45–55 in *Media and Politics in Latin America: The Struggle for Democracy,* edited by Elizabeth Fox. London: Sage.
Hojman, David E. 1997. "*El Mercurio*'s Editorial Page ('La Semana Económica') and Policy Making in Today's Chile." Pp. 171–185 in *Ideologies and Ideologues in Latin America,* edited by Will Fowler. Westport, CT, and London: Greenwood Press.

Cuba

In Cuba the only national daily newspaper is the chief organ of the Communist Party. *Granma* (named after the ship that took Fidel Castro's revolutionaries from Mexico to Cuba in 1956) offers national and international news but little breadth of opinion. *Juventud rebelde* (*Rebel Youth*), which appears from Wednesdays to Sundays, is the mouthpiece of the party's youth movement, and the weekly *Trabajadores* (*Workers*) is the voice of the trade unions. The country's cultural magazines, such as *Bo-*

Reading the news in Cuba, 1 September 1994. (Caron Philippe/Corbis Sygma)

hemia and *Revolución y cultura* (*Revolution and Culture*), are more independent. The Cuban authorities neither deny nor make any apology for their control over the nation's press and media, arguing that it is essential for the maintenance of public security in the face of more than forty years of economic embargo and sabotage by the United States. Whatever one's chosen interpretation, Fidel Castro appears regularly in lists of enemies of the free press published by foreign journalists' associations.

—*Keith Richards*

See also: *Popular Social Movements and Politics:* Castrismo

Bibliography

Alisky, Marvin. 1981. *Latin American Media: Guidance and Censorship.* Ames: Iowa State University Press.

Fox, Elizabeth, ed. 1988. *Media and Politics in Latin America: The Struggle for Democracy.* London: Sage.

Argentina

Between 1976 and 1982, Argentina was stricken by the Dirty War, a concerted attack upon certain sectors of society that was conceived as a restructuring of the nation along ultraconservative lines. It was responsible for the disappearance of an estimated 30,000 citizens for alleged subversion. Press censorship was one of the military regime's political tools. Today the country faces problems of censorship of an informal kind: the harassment of journalists investigating the country's financial corruption and searching for explanations for its economic collapse in the early twenty-first century. *Periodistas*, the Website of the Buenos Aires–based Association for the Defense of Independent Journalism, continues to record a high incidence of threats and physical aggression against investigative journalists.

—*Keith Richards*

See also: *Popular Social Movements and Politics:* Las Madres de la Plaza de Mayo

Bibliography

Alisky, Marvin. 1981. *Latin American Media: Guidance and Censorship.* Ames: Iowa State University Press.

Fox, Elizabeth, ed. 1988. *Media and Politics in Latin America: The Struggle for Democracy.* London: Sage.

Waisbord, Silvio. 2000. *Watchdog Journalism in South America: News, Accountability and Democracy.* New York: Columbia University Press.

Peru

Under the revolutionary military government led by General Juan Velasco, the period between 1968 and 1975 saw the nationalization of numerous industries in Peru, including the eventual expropriation of newspapers, which were to be handed over to cooperatives formed by employees. However, the government's restrictions on the press and media, followed by a radical restructuring in the ownership and administration of newspapers, led to a hemorrhaging of support for Velasco's regime from those newspapers and sectors that had previously lent it. This well-intentioned experiment involving newspapers cooperatively owned by their employees would eventually founder, partly due to this lack of media backing for the government and the initiative.

Peru in the 1990s saw press restriction of a different kind with the populist presidency of Alberto Fujimori, whose virtual war on the country's press culminated in the deportation of Baruch Ivcher, the Israeli-born owner of a television station, among other journalists. Fujimori's rule was supported by the shadowy figure of Vladimiro Montesinos, through whom the president maintained a grip on the movements of several potential opponents of his regime. Fujimori, who was ousted in 2001, made regular appearances in the New York–based Committee for the Protection of Journalists' annual list of the Ten Worst Enemies of the Press.

The *prensa amarilla*, or low-brow, sensationalist "yellow press," has been described less as a journalistic phenomenon than as a cultural entity at the margins of the press. In Peru, papers such as *Ajá* (*Ah-ha!*) and *El chino* (*The Chinaman*, a common nickname for the ethnically Japanese Fujimori) have been seen as a cynical extension of the *chicha* culture belonging to recent immigrants to Lima and other cities. Such barely literate and undereducated communities, generally marginalized inhabitants of outlying shantytowns, are easily distracted from the social realities that affect them. Through the anecdotal subject matter and hysterical tone of the sensationalist press, they are even further disconnected from a society that disowns them, alienated from all aspects of the political process. Of course such press is by no means confined either to Peru or to Latin America.

—*Keith Richards*

See also: *Visual Arts and Architecture:* Architecture and Landscape Design (*Pueblos Jóvenes*)

Bibliography

Alisky, Marvin. 1981. *Latin American Media: Guidance and Censorship.* Ames: Iowa State University Press.

Fox, Elizabeth, ed. 1988. *Media and Politics in Latin America: The Struggle for Democracy.* London: Sage.

Brazil

In June 2000, Brazil had a total of 465 different daily newspapers, but only nine of these sold more than 100,000 copies a day. Seven of these top-sellers were based along the Rio de Janeiro–São Paulo axis, with the remaining two located in the city of Porto Alegre, state capital of Rio Grande do Sul. The *Folha de São Paulo* has the largest circulation in Brazil today, followed by *O Estado de São Paulo*, the Rio-based *O Globo*, and *Extra*. On 12 May 1995, the *Folha de São Paulo* sold a record 1,613,872 copies, largely thanks to the free historical atlas that came with the newspaper that day. The success of that edition started a trend for free gifts, such as CDs, videocassettes, and encyclopaedias, in an effort to boost sales. In May 1995 the *Jornal do Brasil*, based in Rio de Janeiro, launched the first online newspaper in Brazil, the *JB Online*. Since then all the other major titles have followed suit.

Approximately 40 percent of the Brazilian population read a newspaper on a daily basis, a quarter of whom are between the ages of twenty and twenty-nine. In order to attract readers from lower income brackets, cheaper newspapers have been launched in recent years, such as *Agora São Paulo*, which soon after its appearance in March 1999 became the eighth most popular newspaper in Brazil.

After the coup of 1964 and the ensuing installation of the military regime, various opposition publications emerged, such as the newspapers *O pasquim* (1969), *Opinião* (1972), *Movimento* (1975), *Em tempo* (1977), and *O lampião da esquina* (1978). During the military regime (1964–1985) the restrictions imposed on the press grew, particularly after the so-called AI-5 of 1968, a series of laws that signaled harsh repression of free speech and personal freedoms. Strict prior censorship of the press was imposed, and as a result many newspapers were raided, wrecked, or closed down by the police. With the process of political *abertura* or opening in the early 1980s, it was the *Folha de São Paulo* newspaper that led the "Diretas Já" campaign for direct democratic elections in 1984.

In spite of the fact that some 1,600 different magazine titles are on sale in Brazil's newspaper kiosks, Brazilians buy only two magazines per year on average. The Abril group is the most dominant magazine publisher, counting the top-selling current affairs magazine *Veja* (launched in 1968) among its titles, as well as the successful women's magazine *Claudia*, the celebrity magazine *Caras*, and *Playboy*. The Globo group lies in second place with respect to the number of regular publications, which include *Época*, another important current affairs magazine, alongside *Veja* and *Istoé*, the latter owned by the Três publishing house.

More than 20 percent of the magazine market in Brazil is represented by smaller-scale publications for a more specific readership, such as *Raça*, which is targeted at the black population, and *CD-Rom*, which, as its name suggests, deals with information technology. Comic books, publications dedicated to the lives of TV and film stars, children's magazines and cookery magazines are also popular. It has been estimated that over half the readers of magazines in Brazil are women, and that the majority of them are between twenty and twenty-nine years of age.

—*Lisa Shaw*

See also: *Mass Media*: Television (Brazil)

Bibliography

Alisky, Marvin. 1981. *Latin American Media: Guidance and Censorship.* Ames: Iowa State University Press.
Fox, Elizabeth, ed. 1988. *Media and Politics in Latin America: The Struggle for Democracy.* London: Sage.
Smith, Anne-Marie. 1997. *A Forced Agreement: Press Acquiescence to Censorship in Brazil.* Pittsburgh: University of Pittsburgh Press.
Waisbord, Silvio. 2000. *Watchdog Journalism in South America: News, Accountability and Democracy.* New York: Columbia University Press.

Venezuela and Paraguay

During the current presidency of Hugo Chávez in Venezuela, the press is almost unanimously hostile to a government that nonetheless has a considerable popular mandate. Venezuelan newspaper owners belong to social sectors for whom the revolutionary position of Chávez, and his political ties with Cuba, override any reformist intention he may have. Chávez has withstood powerful challenges to his authority, including a national strike in late 2002, after which he decided upon restrictions on press freedom. The end of Alfredo Stroessner's dictatorship (1954–1989) in Paraguay did not by any means spell an immediate return to freedom of information. As late as 2001, legislation was being passed to impede access to official data or material relating to pending court cases.

—*Keith Richards*

See also: *Popular Social Movements and Politics:* Chavismo

Bibliography

Alisky, Marvin. 1981. *Latin American Media: Guidance and Censorship.* Ames: Iowa State University Press.
Fox, Elizabeth, ed. 1988. *Media and Politics in Latin America: The Struggle for Democracy.* London: Sage.

The Internet

Mexico was the first Latin American country to connect to the fully interactive Internet, with the rest of Latin America following close behind. Today, all Latin American countries are connected. But the Internet is still a relatively new phenomenon; most of the networks were established only in recent years.

Recent estimates suggest that use of the Internet in Latin America increased by over 100 percent in the two years from 1997 to 1999. Nonetheless, this market remains much smaller than that of the United States or Europe, with Latin American users making up only 3.2 percent of the total of worldwide Internet users in 1999. Figures for the end of the year 2002 are in the range of 25 million in terms of narrow-band subscribers, while predicted usage for 2004 is 60.6 million, with Argentina, Brazil, and Mexico accounting for 65 percent of the total population of Internet users in Latin America.

Researchers like Ricardo Gómez have asked whether there is anything specifically "Latin American" about the way the Internet is used in these countries, raising issues such as surfing patterns, designs, and links. Though many of these issues are still being investigated today, Gómez highlights as the most salient difference the cost of the equipment and Internet connections, arguing that since costs tend to be higher in Latin America than in the more developed regions, cost itself can prove a significant obstacle. However, despite these and other, mainly superficial, differ-

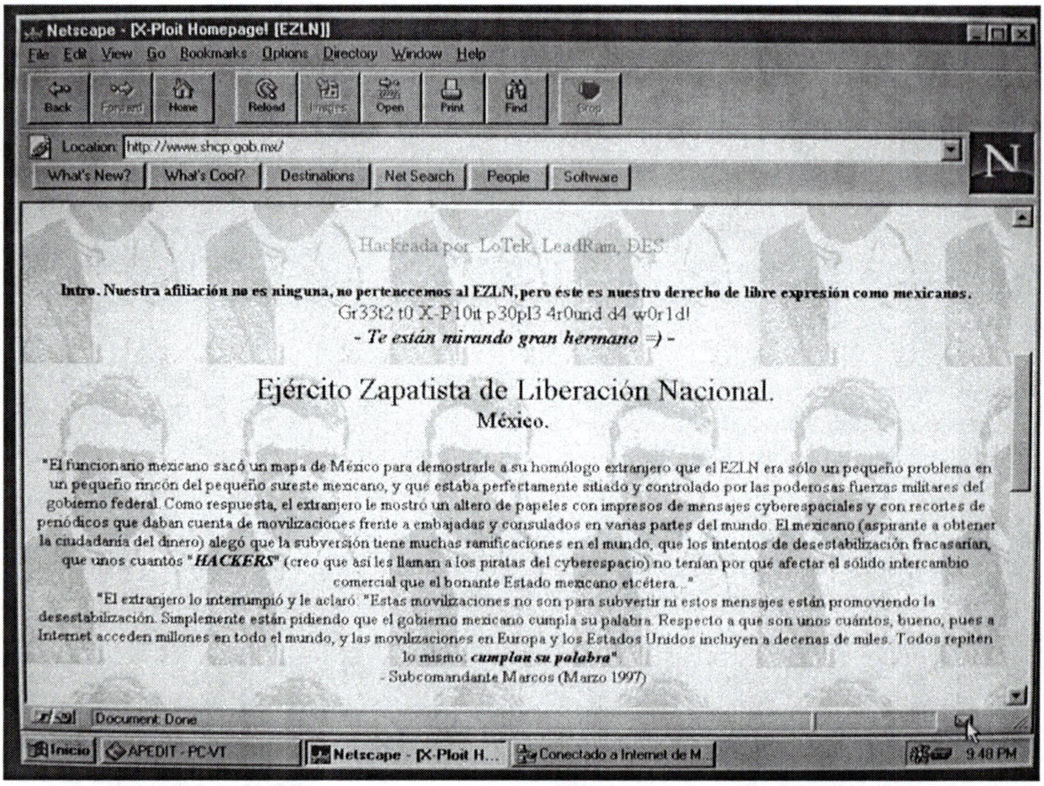

The Internet has been used to great effect by the Zapatistas in southern Mexico. Here a computer screen displays a March 1997 communiqué from the movement's leader, Subcomandante Marcos. (Roverto Velazquez/AP Photo)

ences, Gómez and others conclude that there is little that is specifically Latin American in current Internet trends in the subcontinent, since what tends to be formed is a "global village" rather than a national or pan–Latin American identity.

That said, there are instances of this global village being used in a notably national and indeed local way. One of the most striking examples is that of the struggles of the Zapatistas in Mexico. A popular, grassroots movement, the *Ejército Zapatista de Liberación Nacional* (EZLN), led by Subcomandante Marcos, brought their demands to the world stage by means of the Internet. According to Ronfeldt and Martínez, word of the Zapatista insurrection first spread via this new medium, and they quote Mexico's foreign minister, José Angel Gurria, as describing the current unrest in the Chiapas region of Mexico as a "war on the Internet" (p. 380). This electronic war takes the form of a variety of e-mail networks distributing Zapatista information and campaigns, and an ever-growing range of affiliated Websites. Crucial to this has been the inclusion of Marcos's revolutionary speeches on the Websites, often translated, thus spreading what began as local oral presentations to a worldwide audience. In this way, the presence of the Zapatistas on the Web indicates the transgression of traditional social and political frameworks. Originally restricted geographically to Chiapas in southeast Mexico, the Zapatistas have made use of modern technology to increase their political weight and have integrated these new methods into their old-style guerrilla tactics. Although the Zapatistas's access to conventional media has been limited, with the Mexican state controlling much media coverage, the Zapatistas and their supporters have been able to circumvent restrictions through recourse to "cyber communication."

A further use of the Internet in Latin America is in the realm of education. Distance education in its more traditional forms is already established in Latin America, due to difficult terrain and the geographical remoteness of many areas from centers of education. A leading player within this growing market is the Instituto Tecnológico y de Estudios Superiores de Monterrey, known as Tec de Monterrey, in Mexico, which offers within its "Virtual University" a variety of continuing education, social, and postgraduate courses ranging from business administration to engineering and humanities. Also related to the area of education are recent developments in museum and national heritage preservation by means of the Internet. The Diego Rivera Virtual Museum offers a wide selection of his murals for viewing, while Colombia's Museo del Oro (Gold Museum) has an extensive Website that includes an "interactive room" with a variety of activities related to the different exhibits of the museum.

Though there is a tendency to use the Internet simply as an add-on to existing educational structures, projects are currently in progress that attempt to use this new technology in a more dynamic fashion. These include a project of the National University of Quilmes, Argentina, that attempts to create a new *habitus* within the citizen, encouraging new forms of perceiving, acting, and participating in society by means of innovative use of information technology. Similarly, the project *Comunidad Virtual Mística*, developed by the Fundación Redes de Desarrollo of the Dominican Republic, aims to create a "cyberculture" based on solidarity and democratic participation.

Other innovative uses of the Internet in Latin America include the publication of novels in electronic form. One of the first such works was Peruvian Jaime Bayly's novel *Los amigos que perdí* (*The Friends I Lost*), which appeared first as an online work before being published in print form in 2000. The Website http://eltiempo.terra.com.co/libros/noticias/index.html now has a selection of *libros virtuales* (virtual books) with free chapters available online. In addition to novels, the world of print has been revolutionized by the introduction of Web-based versions of national newspapers, such as *O Globo* and *Folha de São Paulo* of Brazil; *El tiempo* and *El espectador* of Colombia; *La nación* of Argentina; and *La jornada*, *El universal*, and *El heraldo* of Mexico. The availability of these newspapers on the Web has allowed the many millions of Latin American immigrants in the United States, Europe, and elsewhere immediate access to their country's news, thereby forming a virtual community of Latin Americans.

—*Claire Taylor*

See also: *Popular Social Movements and Politics:* Zapatismo; *Mass Media:* The Press; *Visual Arts and Architecture:* Art (Diego Rivera)

Bibliography

Diego Rivera Virtual Museum. http://www.diegorivera.com (consulted 17 March 2003).

Gómez, Ricardo. 2000. "The Hall of Mirrors: The Internet in Latin America." *Current History* 99, no. 634. http://www.idrc.ca/pan/pubhall_e.htm (consulted June 2003).

Hahn, Saul. 1999. "Case Studies on Developments of the Internet in Latin America: Unexpected Results." *Bulletin of the American Society for Information Science* 25, no. 5. http://www.asis.org/Bulletin/Jun-99/case_studies_on_developments_o.html (consulted June 2003).

Holloway, John, and Eloína Peláez, eds. 1998. *Zapatista! Reinventing Revolution in Mexico.* London: Pluto Press.

Rodríguez-Alvez, Fernando. 1999 (June). "Present and Future of the Internet in Latin America." *Trends in Latin American Networking.* http://lanic.utexas.edu/project/tilan/reports/Present&Future.html (consulted 17 March 2003).

Ronfeldt, David, and Armando Martínez. 1997. "A Comment on the Zapatista 'Netwar'." Pp. 369–391 in *In Athena's Camp: Preparing for Conflict in the Information Age*, edited by John Arquilla and David Ronfeldt. Santa Monica, CA: Rand.

11

Popular Cinema

Latin American cinema is often thought of abroad as comprising films that can be defined as art-house and/or politically committed, particularly as a result of the highbrow *auteurist* movements of the 1960s and 1970s, such as the Brazilian *cinema novo* (new cinema), Cuba's *cine imperfecto* (imperfect cinema), Argentina's Third Cinema, and so on. The truth is that few films of these genres made any impact with audiences at home, despite their populist pretensions. As this section will reveal, when Latin American audiences were not watching the same Hollywood-produced films popular throughout the world in the modern era, they went to the cinema to see homegrown comedies, musicals, and melodramas. Though much has been written on Latin America's art-house cinematic production, the existence of these popular genres is not always acknowledged, even in national film histories.

Popular films made in Latin America, like those produced elsewhere, traditionally have not traveled or translated well. They fall into the category of what have been described as "unexportable films," too insignificant to be appreciated by spectators outside a given popular cultural arena. Today, however, many commercially successful films are hits both inside and outside Latin America, particularly those from Mexico, Brazil, and Cuba. Consider, for example, the impact made in the United States and the United Kingdom by Cuba's *Fresa e chocolate* (*Strawberry and Chocolate*, 1993) and *Guantanamera* (1994), Brazil's *Central do Brasil* (*Central Station*, 1998) and *Cidade de Deus* (*City of God*, 2002), and Mexico's *Amores perros* (*Love's a Bitch*, 2000) and *Y tu mamá también* (*And Your Mother Too*, 2001).

—Stephanie Dennison

The Mexican Film Industry

With the advent of sound in films in the early 1930s, the state began to play a central role in the film industry in Mexico. The "golden age" of the industry occurred between 1940 and 1954, when Mexican cinema became the most important in Latin America. Government support for the industry continued until the end of the 1970s, when it was largely replaced by the involvement of the Televisa television company in filmmaking. The 1990s witnessed the virtual collapse of the industry during a period of wider economic crisis, but as the decade drew to a close, a series of new production companies emerged. Since then production figures have risen steadily, and a number of talented first-time directors have emerged from Mexico City's two film schools.

In the 1930s a centralized, nationalized industry coexisted with private enterprise in the form of a variety of small production companies. The government of President Cárdenas (1930–1940) took a very active part in the development of the cinema industry, introducing a protectionist policy for domestic film production, which included tax exemptions for local producers and a screen quota for Mexican films. In 1934 the government guaranteed a loan to finance the building of the first modern film studio in Mexico City. This policy of state support continued under the administration of President Avila Camacho (1941–1946). The National Film Bank, which was created in 1942 as a private institution, received considerable backing from the government, and supported the creation of several distribution companies. Mexico received continuous support from the United States during World War II, and by 1943 its film industry had established itself as the most important in Latin America. From 1945, however, domestic production was marked by thematic repetition and a decline in artistic creativity, due to some extent to closed-shop union policies that prevented fresh talent from entering the industry.

In the 1960s and 1970s the Mexican government continued to participate in the production, distribution, and exhibition of locally made films, chiefly by lending its support to local entrepreneurs. In 1970 the National Film Bank began to take on the role of director-producer, due to a growing lack of interest among independent producers. During the presidency of Luis Echeverría Alvarez (1970–1976) the state became more involved with film production and Mexican cinema experienced one of its fabled periods of renaissance, during which a number of important directors emerged, including Jorge Fons, Arturo Ripstein, and Felipe Cazals. In 1975 the state bought the America studios, Mexico's second most important after the state-owned Churubusco. In 1979 the National Film Bank was dissolved as a consequence of the new political climate that coincided with the government of President José López Portillo (1976–1982), which favored encouraging independent film producers. This decision also reflected the increasing involvement of Televisa, the giant private television company, in the production of films starring personalities from TV shows and signaled a period of relatively high production figures and low production values.

With the economic crisis of 1994, the Mexican film industry ground to a halt, as the production companies that had dominated the box office since the 1930s went out of business. Film production fell to an all-time low; only eleven feature films were produced in 1998, the smallest number since the early 1930s. Toward the end of the 1990s, however, new production companies like Altavista, Argos, and Titan helped to revive the industry. In 2000 twenty-eight feature films were produced in Mexico, and production figures continue to rise, though some of Mexico's most accomplished directors, such as Alfonso

Cuarón, Alejandro González Iñárritu, and Guillermo del Toro, have crossed the border into the United States in search of bigger budgets.

The Mexican Film Institute (IMCINE), established in 1983, is responsible for film policy, coproduction, exhibition, and distribution, and continues to be a major source of film financing. A significant percentage of recent films have been directed by young graduates of Mexico City's two film schools, the CUEC (University Center for Film Studies) and the CCC (Center for the Study of Filmmaking).

—Lisa Shaw

See also: *Popular Cinema:* Box-Office Successes and Contemporary Film in Mexico; Comedy Film (Cantinflas; Tin Tan); Youth Movies, Cinema, and Music

Bibliography

Hershfield, Joanne, and David Maciel. 1999. *Mexico's Cinema: A Century of Film and Filmmakers.* Wilmington, DE: SR Books.

Mora, Carl J. 1982. *Mexican Cinema: Reflections of a Society, 1896–1988.* Berkeley: University of California Press.

Noble, Andrea. Forthcoming. *Mexican National Cinema.* London: Routledge.

Paranaguá, Paulo Antonio. 1995. *Mexican Cinema.* London: British Film Institute.

Schnitman, Jorge A. 1884. *Film Industries in Latin America: Dependency and Development.* Norwood, NJ: Ablex.

Box-Office Successes and Contemporary Film in Mexico

In the 1930s and 1940s, film melodramas, particularly on the theme of the Mexican Revolution, proved to be the most popular genre at the box office. Comedy films, such as those starring Cantinflas and Tin Tan, delighted audiences from the late 1930s up until the 1960s, and comedy remains a popular genre to this day, often poking fun at incompetent political leaders and the foibles of Mexican society. But Mexican box-office hits since the mid-1990s have favored a more serious tone and have often featured unflattering portraits of the nation, such as Alejandro González Iñárritu's graphic *Amores perros* (*Love's a Bitch,* 2000).

Alfonso Arau's 1992 hit film *Como agua para chocolate* (*Like Water for Chocolate*) was an unprecedented success, both at home and abroad. To date, this love story, based on the novel of the same name by Laura Esquivel, Arau's former wife, is the highest-grossing foreign film ever released in the United States, and in global box-office terms it is the most successful film ever in the history of Mexican cinema. *Like Water for Chocolate,* a film that celebrates a rather stereotypical vision of Mexican identity, enjoyed both mass-market appeal and critical acclaim, winning eleven Ariel awards, the Mexican equivalent of the Oscars.

A wave of artistically ambitious and commercially successful films followed the crisis in the Mexican film industry in the mid- to late 1990s, such as Antonio Serrano's comedy *Sexo, pudor y lágrimas* (*Sex, Shame and Tears,* 1998). Outshining *The Phantom Menace* at the box office, its reception proved that domestic films could attract a large middle-class audience, who were increasingly drawn to the country's modern, multiplex cinemas. This audience also flocked to see the disintegration of family life among the middle classes in Benjamin Cann's *Cronica de un desayuno* (*Chronicle of a Breakfast,* 1999).

In 2000, Mexican films represented 17 percent of the nation's box-office takings. Among them, *Love's a Bitch* was the top domestic earner, also well received in Europe and the United States. The political satire *La ley de Herodes* (*Herod's Law*), also released in 2000, depicted the PRI (*Partido Revolucionario Institucional* or Institutional Revolutionary Party, the political party that had ruled Mexico for over seventy years), exposing the corruption and dishonesty of politicians. This comedy proved very popular with a wide audience. The 2001 Guadalajara Film Festival showcased a series of urban dramas about disenchanted youth, such as Gerard Tort's *De la calle* (*Streeters*), which explores the violence and degradation experienced by the marginalized young on Mexico City's streets. More recently, Carlos Carrera's *El crimen del padre Amaro* (*The Crime of Father Amaro*, 2002), nominated for an Oscar for best foreign-language film in 2003, has provoked intense controversy for its anticlerical subject matter. The twenty-first century has seen the emergence of a group of talented women filmmakers, such as Marcela Arteaga (*Recuerdos* [*Memories*]), Eva López Sánchez (*Francisca*), and Maria Novaro (*Sin dejar huella* [*Without a Trace*]).

Surprisingly, Mexican films are often received less enthusiastically by the Mexican press than by the press in the United States or Europe. Arturo Ripstein's work is a case in point. With the exception of his *El coronel no tiene a quien le escriba* (*No One Writes to the Colonel*, 1999), his work fails to attract domestic audiences. More surprisingly, *Love's a Bitch* received most of its negative reviews in Mexico.

—*Lisa Shaw*

See also: *Popular Cinema:* Comedy Film (Cantinflas; Tin Tan); Melodrama; The Mexican Film Industry; Youth Movies, Cinema, and Music

Bibliography

Foster, William David. 2002. *Mexico City in Contemporary Mexican Cinema.* Austin: University of Texas Press.
Mora, Carl J. 1982. *Mexican Cinema: Reflections of a Society, 1896–1988.* Berkeley: University of California Press.
Noble, Andrea. Forthcoming. *Mexican National Cinema.* London: Routledge.
Tsao, Leonardo García. 2001. "After the Breakthrough of *Amores Perros*, What's Next for Mexican Cinema." *Film Comment*, July–August 2001.

The Brazilian Film Industry

By 1912 a brief boom in Brazilian silent film production came to an abrupt end as the North American film industry, by then an international concern, encountered no protectionist legislation in Brazil. It was not until the sound era of the 1930s that a Brazilian film industry began to develop, fostered by President Getúlio Vargas (1930–1945), who considered film an important facet of his regime's powerful propaganda machine. The Vargas regime viewed cinema as an instrument of national unity that could engender a sense of *brasilidade* or "Brazilianness." In the 1940s and 1950s there were two attempts at creating a studio system in Brazil. The Rio-based Atlântida studios, founded in 1941, achieved a prolific output of low-budget box-office successes throughout the 1940s and 1950s by producing popular musical comedies. The Vera Cruz studios, set up in 1949 by a group of São Paulo industrialists, modeled themselves on the MGM studios in Hollywood. The 1970s represented a high point in the production and distribution of Brazilian films, largely due to government support from Embrafilme, the official film agency. With the withdrawal of state support, the film industry virtually ground to a halt in 1990, but the situation was rectified in 1993 by the introduction of the Audio-visual Law. Recently extended until 2006, this legislation gives businesses a reduction on their income tax bill in return for investing in audiovisual projects. It has undeniably contributed to the rebirth of Brazilian cinema.

Atlântida set out to establish a national cinema industry and to reach a level of production comparable to that achieved in the United States. This studio also initially aimed to represent real life on screen and to introduce an element of social commentary into its films, but it soon bowed to commercial pressures. To satisfy the mass market, the Atlântida studio started to channel its efforts into musical comedies known as *chanchadas*.

The Vera Cruz studio imitated Hollywood in everything except financial success. In its attempt to create a "classy" cinema with glossy production values, Vera Cruz completely ignored the tastes, interests, and life experiences of the Brazilian people. The studio produced eighteen feature-length films before going bankrupt in 1954. The most famous was *O Cangaceiro* (*The Bandit*, 1953), directed by Lima Barreto and produced by Alberto Cavalcânti; it won two prizes at the Cannes film festival and was distributed in twenty-two countries.

Influenced by Italian neorealism and the Brazilian left-wing regionalist literary movement of the 1930s and 1940s, the *auteurs* of the *cinema novo* (literally, "new cinema") movement of the 1960s sought to transform society through film. To challenge what they considered the vacuous, derivative, and industrially produced *chanchada* films, they sought to apply a new critical and modernist vision of the nation, and to find a new cinematic language that better reflected Brazilian reality. Although the *cinema novo* did not inspire the Brazilian cinema-going public at the time, films such as Nelson Pereira dos Santos's *Vidas secas* (*Barren Lives*, 1962) and Glauber Rocha's *Deus e o diabo na terra do sol* (*Black God, White Devil*, 1964) did help to put Brazilian cinema on the world cinematic map and have helped to increase its international dissemination and popularity with art-house audiences ever since.

In 1961 the Executive Group of the Film Industry (GEICINE) was set up by developmentalist president Juscelino Kubitschek (1956–1961) to foster film production in Brazil. But GEICINE failed to increase the number of films made in Brazil at an otherwise productive time for the nation. It was incorporated in 1966 into the National Film Institute (INC), which had been set up by the military dictatorship installed in 1964 in order to protect the country from the perceived threat of socialism and anarchy.

Both the INC and, after 1969, Embrafilme, the state promotion, distribution, and later, film financing agency, sought to lend legitimacy to the authoritarian regime. These state institutions co-opted cineastes and influenced the direction of Brazilian cinema. Their influence is evident in films such as Carlos Coimbra's *Independência ou morte* (*Independence or Death*, 1972), the government-approved historical epic about the declaration of Brazilian independence in 1822. Many *cinema novo* directors enjoyed a surprisingly close relationship with Embrafilme in the 1970s. They were happy to support a cultural agency of the government in exchange for its backing against a greater enemy: an invading foreign cinema.

On average, seventy national films were released each year during the first half of the 1970s, nearly double the output of the previous five years. This figure rose again in the second half of the 1970s, peaking at 104 in 1979. The number of spectators paying to see national films also rose over the decade, with an average of over 50 million tickets sold per year from 1975 onward. The number of days that Brazilian movie theaters were obliged to show Brazilian films increased from 63 days in 1969 to 112 days in 1975.

A severe debt crisis, the closure of thousands of cinema theaters, and the arrival of video took their toll on national cinema as the dictatorship came to an end in the mid-1980s. In 1990 Brazil's first elected president in almost three decades, Fernando Collor de Mello (later impeached on corruption charges), dealt the fatal blow when he abolished all state support for the arts. Not until 1995 would national cinema reemerge. By then, the 1993 Audio-visual Law had begun to make an impact on production, helping to foster the *retomada* or renaissance of Brazilian cinema. The law is designed to encourage filmmakers and producers to rely less on the state for financial support and to foster productive relationships with the private sector. A law that allowed foreign film distributors to invest up to 70 percent of their taxes in Brazilian film also proved useful. Despite these financial initiatives, private sources of funding are still the most important in Brazilian filmmaking. For example, the smash hit *Cidade de Deus* (*City of God*, 2002) had a budget of 8.2 million *reais* (around $3 million at the time), and only 15 percent of that budget came from Laws of Incentive. A consequence of this trend in financing, inevitably, is that contemporary producers and directors cannot afford to disregard commercial questions when developing film projects.

—*Stephanie Dennison*

See also: *Popular Cinema:* Box-Office Successes and Contemporary Film in Brazil; Coffin Joe; Comedy Film (*Chanchada*); Youth Movies, Cinema, and Music

Bibliography

Dennison, Stephanie, and Lisa Shaw. 2004. *Popular Cinema in Brazil.* Manchester: Manchester University Press.

Johnson, Randal. 1987. *The Film Industry in Brazil: Culture and the State.* Pittsburgh: University of Pittsburgh Press.

King, John. 1990. *Magical Reels: A History of Cinema in Latin America.* London: Verso.

Box-Office Successes and Contemporary Film in Brazil

In the postwar era, until the consolidation of television in the late 1950s, popular Brazilian cinema was dominated by a comedic genre known as the *chanchada.* Popularized by the likes of Carmen Miranda, the *chanchada* grew out of films designed to promote carnival music, especially samba, in the 1930s. Elsewhere, Amácio Mazzaropi produced and starred in a series of films in the 1950s, 1960s, and 1970s as Jeca, the country bumpkin from the state of São Paulo who, like the characters played by Cantinflas in popular Mexican cinema, struggled to come to terms with the nation's newfound modernity. Like the *chanchada*, Mazzaropi's films appealed in particular to the oppressed and marginalized rural poor who moved in droves to the cities of Rio de Janeiro and São Paulo in search of work from the 1940s onward.

The roots of both the *chanchada* and Mazzaropi's comedy and performance style

Still from the popular Brazilian comedy *O Trapalhões no planalto dos macacos* (*The Trapalhão on the Plateau of the Apes*, 1976). (Courtesy of the Film Archive of the Museu de Arte Moderna, Rio de Janeiro)

can be found in the Brazilian music-hall tradition (*teatro de revista*) and in the traveling theaters and circuses that were still popular in the interior of the country until the 1980s. Like the *chanchada* films from the 1950s, Mazzaropi's films often took inspiration from the film and television successes of the time. His most popular film, *Jeca contra o capeta* (*Jeca versus the Devil*, 1976), was very loosely based on *The Exorcist.* The Trapalhões, which roughly translates as "the morons," were a four-man version of the Three Stooges. They too produced their own films and took inspiration from Hollywood trends—for example, their 1976 version of *Planet of the Apes* (*Os Trapalhões no planalto dos macacos*). Fourteen of the twenty-five top-grossing Brazilian films between 1970 and 1984 were Trapalhões movies, and even though two of the four Trapalhões died in the 1990s, the two remaining stars continue to this day to make commercially successful films. Reruns of their popular TV series still attract large audiences, particularly among children. Other children's television entertainers have dominated the film charts in the 1980s and 1990s, such as Xuxa, who stars, for example, in *Super Xuxa contra o baixo astral (Super Xuxa against the Bad Vibes*, 1988), *Popstar* (2000), and *Xuxa e os duendes I & II* (*Xuxa and the Elves I & II*, 2001 and 2002).

Alongside the Mazzaropi and the Trapalhões series, *pornochanchadas* (soft-core porn comedies) dominated cinema production during the 1970s, until the advent of hard-core toward the end of the decade. Morally conservative in terms of their message (often in an attempt to dodge the censors), they sold the (mostly unfulfilled) promise of sex through innuendo in film titles and taglines. Examples include the film *Eu dou o que ela gosta* (*I Give Her What She Wants,* 1975), with a tagline that translates roughly as "And what she wants isn't for softies!" Many of these films parodied U.S. box-office successes such as *Jaws* and *Grease* (*Bacalhau*, 1975, and *Nos tempos da vaselina*, 1979, respectively). *Pornochanchada* is an ill-defined pejorative term that critics applied mainly to the cheap productions coming out of São Paulo's red-light district. Therefore successful (and more expensive) erotic films made by respected directors, such as Bruno Barreto's record-breaking *Dona Flor e seus dois maridos* (*Dona Flor and Her Two Husbands*, 1976), avoided the label, even though they shared many of the *pornochanchada*'s features.

Dona Flor was supported by a major advertising campaign on Brazilian television and released at the height of the film boom, when filmmakers could rely on considerable support from the state in terms of financing and distribution through Embrafilme, and before the rapid closure of movie theaters and the expansion of the video market in the 1980s. With over twelve million viewers in Brazil, *Dona Flor* is considered the most successful national film of all time. Based on the eponymous best-selling novel by Jorge Amado (published in 1966), it stars Sônia Braga, one of the most popular and sought-after actresses in Brazil at the time. Braga plays Flor, whose roguish but very sexy husband, Vadinho, drops dead during carnival. She remarries, this time to a decent and honest but rather boring pharmacist—but she dreams of the lovemaking she once enjoyed with Vadinho. She seeks out an *Umbanda* priestess and summons back her first husband, naked and visible only to her, so that she can enjoy the qualities that both men have to offer her. National hardcore pornographic production, which dominated the film charts in Brazil, met its demise in the late 1980s.

The Brazilian cinema industry was said to have been reborn in 1995. The film most associated with this rebirth or *retomada* is Carla Camurati's 1995 hit *Carlota Joaquina, princesa do Brazil* (*Carlota Joaquina, Princess of Brazil*), a comedy based on the life of the sex-mad Spanish wife of King John VI of Portugal. The following year the Oscar-nominated *O quatrilho* by Fábio Barreto, which deals with the lives of an Italian immigrant community in the south of Brazil at the turn of the last century, attracted well over one million spectators to cinemas in Brazil. Three more recent films sealed the success of the *retomada* with the cinema-going public and proved that Brazilian cinema was once again a force to be reckoned with on the international screen: Walter Salles's *Central do Brasil* (*Central Station*, 1998), Fernando Meirelles's *Cidade de Deus* (*City of God*, 2002), and Hector Babenco's *Carandiru* (2003).

Central Station, a hit both at home and abroad, is a touching tale, beautifully filmed by Walter Carvalho, of a journey made by a frustrated spinster, played by Academy Award nominee Fernanda Montenegro, and a young orphaned child from the dangerous city of Rio de Janeiro, through the breathtaking landscape of Brazil's *sertão* or backlands, to the northeast of the country. According to the director, over seven million people have seen the film worldwide.

City of God, based on the best-selling novel of the same name by Paulo Lins, is an exhilarating depiction of twenty or so years in the life of a Rio de Janeiro *favela* or slum through the eyes of one resident who manages to grow up surrounded by drug-dealing, gang-warfare, and extreme poverty. It stars a mostly amateur cast made up of *favela* inhabitants, in many cases, and marks a significant departure, in terms of directorial and acting style, from the TV-influenced fare that has dominated the film charts of late (for example, *Orfeu*). Meirelles's film, nominated for a Golden Globe and four Academy Awards and distributed in Europe and the United States, was seen by over 3 million people in Brazil, making it the most successful film since the *retomada*—until *Carandiru* was released. This film, about a real-life riot and massacre in the notorious Carandiru prison in São Paulo, attracted more than 4.5 million spectators in Brazil in its first two months of exhibition. Like *City of God*, it forms part of a recent trend in Brazil for films that graphically represent violence, deprivation, and alienation.

—*Stephanie Dennison*

See also: *Popular Music:* Samba; *Popular Theater:* Popular Theater and Music Hall (Teatro de Revista); *Popular Literature:* The Boom; *Cultural Icons:* Latin Americans in Hollywood (Carmen Miranda); *Mass Media:* Television (Brazil); *Popular Cinema:* The Brazilian Film Industry; Coffin Joe; Comedy Film (*Chanchada*); Youth Movies, Cinema, and Music; *Popular Religion and Festivals: Umbanda; Visual Arts and Architecture:* Architecture and Landscape Design (*Favelas*)

Bibliography

Dennison, Stephanie. 2000. "A Meeting of Two Worlds: Recent Trends in Brazilian Cinema." *Journal of Iberian and Latin American Studies* 6, no. 2: 131–144.

Dennison, Stephanie, and Lisa Shaw. 2004. *Popular Cinema in Brazil.* Manchester: Manchester University Press.

Johnson, Randal. 1984. "Popular Cinema in Brazil." *Studies in Latin American Popular Culture* 3: 89–94.

Nagib, Lúcia, ed. 2003. *The New Brazilian Cinema.* London and New York: I. B. Tauris.

The Film Industry and Box-Office Successes in Argentina

Argentina, whose economic heyday coincided with the birth of cinema, was able to boast one of the first film industries in Latin America worthy of the name. Its first star following the advent of sound films in the 1930s was the singer Carlos Gardel. The "golden age" of cinema in Argentina was the decade preceding the Second World War, during which most Latin American countries avidly consumed Argentine films like Lucas Demare's *Guerra Gaucha* (*Gaucho War*, 1942) and Luis Saslavsky's *La casa del recuerdo* (*The House of Memory*, 1945). During the socially traumatic period between the late 1960s and the end of the Dirty War in 1982, an important thematic trend in Argentine film was the overt confrontation with military authority and imperialism typified by Fernando Solanas and Octavio Getino's *La hora de los hornos* (*The Hour of the Furnaces*, 1968) and the work of Fernando Birri. In recent years, and in spite of economic difficulties, a new generation of young, independent Argentine filmmakers has begun to make its mark at international film festivals.

During the Second World War, Argentine cinema suffered as a result of the nation's tacitly pro-German stance, which meant film stock from the United States was rerouted to Mexico. Its partial revival in the Peronist postwar years saw an even more deliberate attempt to create an essentially national cinema that would also raise the country's cultural standing abroad. This era's outstanding contributor was Leopoldo Torre Nilsson, whose *La mano en la trampa* (*The Hand in the Trap*, 1961) exemplified the auteurist aesthetic with which, building upon the work of his father, Leopoldo Torres Ríos, he made a reputation in Europe as well as at home.

In addition to the work of Solanas, Getino, and Birri, other films made openly during the period from the end of the 1960s to the early 1980s explored the darkest corners of the national psyche by taking the form of thrillers that duped the censors. A prime example is Adolfo Aristaraín's *Tiempo de revancha* (*Time for Revenge*, 1981), a thriller that implicitly depicted a country riddled with corruption. Since the 1980s, Argentine film has, like most other cinemas of the region, sought to make itself commercially viable without turning its back on the social reality from which it springs. A controversial example is the work of Eliseo Subiela, whose *Hombre mirando al sudeste* (*Man Facing Southeast*, 1986) takes a characteristically oblique and poetic look at the effects of the Dirty War. Another film that takes a similar approach is Alejandro Agresti's *Boda secreta* (*Secret Wedding*, 1990). The economic crisis of the early twenty-first century and its accompanying corruption have been the background themes for films like Marcelo Piñeyro's *Caballos salvajes* (*Wild Horses*, 1995) and Fabián Bielinsky's *Nueve reinas* (*Nine Queens*, 2000).

The films of the "New Independent Argentine Cinema," though made with very low budgets, have enjoyed considerable commercial success as well as critical acclaim both at home and abroad. Up-and-coming directors such as Lucrecia Martel, Pablo Reyero, Daniel Burman, and Pablo Trapero, who emerged in the first half of the 1990s from Argentina's film schools, are creating a new, gritty, urban style of filmmaking.

—Keith Richards

See also: *Popular Social Movements and Politics:* Peronismo; *Cultural Icons:* Legends of Popular Music and Film (Carlos Gardel); *Popular Cinema:* Youth Movies, Cinema, and Music

Bibliography

Falicov, Tamara L. 2003. "*Los Hijos de Menem:* The New Independent Argentine Cinema, 1995–1999." *Framework: The Journal of Cinema and Media* 44, no. 1: 49–63.

King, John, and Nissa Torrents, eds. 1988. *The Garden of Forking Paths: Argentine Cinema.* London: British Film Institute.

Schnitman, Jorge. 1984. *Film Industries in Latin America: Dependency and Development.* Norwood, NJ: Ablex.

The Film Industry and Box-Office Successes in Cuba

In Cuba, where film was a sporadic and largely elitist pursuit until the Revolution, film production began in earnest in 1959, with the creation of ICAIC (Cuban Institute of Cinematic Arts and Industries). The ICAIC placed considerable emphasis on documentary films and those geared didactically toward raising awareness of social issues. The emergence of the "Imperfect Cinema" aesthetic of two of ICAIC's founding members, Julio García Espinosa and Tomás Gutiérrez Alea, was influential in alerting viewers to the need for a more critical and less passive view of film—not as a replica of reality but as an artifice. The finest example of this tendency is Gutiérrez Alea's *Memorias del subdesarrollo* (*Memories of Underdevelopment*, 1968), although the same director went on to make numerous successful films in a more accessible vein, including *Guantanamera* (1994). During the "Special Period" since 1990, Cuban cinema has inclined increasingly toward entertainment, eschewing its more revolutionary approach, to the distaste of many.

A watershed for ICAIC was a film by Daniel Díaz-Torres that openly questioned Cuba's loss of revolutionary direction, namely *Alicia en el pueblo de Maravillas* (*Alice in Wondertown*, 1990), which was withdrawn from public exhibition by authorities concerned with its potentially destructive effect upon morale, then eventually reinstated. The ribald farce *Un paraíso bajo las estrellas* (*A Paradise beneath the Stars*, 1999), by Gerardo Chijona, proved as successful as it was controversial, facing charges at home of pandering to a foreign tourist's view of the island.

—*Keith Richards*

Bibliography

Chanan, Michael. 1985. *The Cuban Image: Cinema and Cultural Politics in Cuba.* London: British Film Institute.

———. 2003. "Interior Dialogue in the Work of T. G. Alea." *Framework: The Journal of Cinema and Media* 44, no. 1: 11–21.

Schnitman, Jorge. 1984. *Film Industries in Latin America: Dependency and Development.* Norwood, NJ: Ablex.

Other Regional Cycles, Booms, and Notable Successes

In the shadows of Latin America's big cinemas—those of Mexico, Brazil, and Argentina, along with Cuba, Chile, and Venezuela—are numerous marginal national cinemas for whom the production of a feature film is an event of considerable importance. Regardless of its quality, such a film is likely to attract a sizeable audience through sheer novelty value. If it is also well made and a faithful portrait of national reality, then it will occasionally exceed the box-office performance of Hollywood blockbusters. But this kind of success is rare. Ambitious projects often fail for a variety of reasons, including the filmmakers' shortcomings and failure to understand their intended audience and its expectations. An element shared by all these productions is the difficulty involved in completing them mostly or entirely with only national funding. Only one of the films discussed below is a coproduction.

Cinema in Ecuador had long been a minority pursuit when Camilo Luzuriaga's film *Entre Marx y una mujer desnuda* (*Between Marx and a Naked Woman*) was released in 1996 to an enthusiastic reception both at home and elsewhere. It was based on the 1974 novel by Jorge Enrique Adoum, which tells of a writer's battle with his own blocks, self-doubts, and misgivings with the genre, exacerbated by the context of political struggle against military dictatorship. Luzuriaga's film is painstakingly constructed to convey the spirit of Adoum's fractured narrative, with its passages of self-interrogation and its indictment of Ecuador's social stagnation. Luzuriaga's first film, *La Tigra* (*The Tigress*, 1990), based on a 1930 story by another writer from Ecuador, José de la Cuadra, met with a tepid response despite its clear linear narrative. The success enjoyed by *Entre Marx,* despite its relative inaccessibility, vindicates the faith placed in a discerning public who appreciated the film's high standards of direction, script, acting, and photography, as well as the

Still from the Ecuadorian film *Entre Marx y una mujer desnuda* (*Between Marx and a Naked Woman*, 1995), directed by Camilo Luzuriaga. (Courtesy of Camilo Luzuriaga; photo by Olivier Auverlau)

score by Diego Luzuriaga, brother of the director.

Bolivia has a relatively rich cinematic history, for example in the vein of militant film, claiming rights for Andean indigenous peoples, particularly by the Ukamau group and its outstanding figure, Jorge Sanjinés. However, the success in 1995 of *Cuestión de fe* (*A Matter of Faith*), by the debut director Marcos Loayza, broke the mold. This is a tale not of resistance to oppression but of coexistence with a social environment that is necessarily imperfect. Loayza's picaresque comedy tells of an alcoholic *santero*, maker of religious images, who is forced to sculpt a Virgin and transport her to the hometown of a notorious drug baron. His attempts to comply, in a journey from La Paz through the semitropical Yungas region alongside two equally flawed friends, makes for a buddy/road movie in the context of Bolivia's propensity for syncretic religious beliefs combining native and Christian elements, all of which is comically juxtaposed with human fallibility.

Similar success was achieved in Paraguay, a country almost devoid of film history, with *Miss Ameriguá* (1994). Made by the Swedish-based Chilean Luis Vera, and reflecting his own country's experience of militarism, this film is a satirical look at the abuse of military authority in a small town when its annual beauty pageant features both the daughter of a certain Colonel Banderas and his mistress. Made partly with Swedish financial and technical assistance, *Miss Ameriguá* owes its success in Latin America, Europe, and North

America to a combination of political and social satire and absurdist humor with tragic and romantic elements.

The Dominican Republic can also boast an isolated film success in the bittersweet comedy *Nueba Yol* (the title is a Dominican slang term for New York, 1996), directed by Angel Muñiz. Its tale of escape from the economic doldrums of home to the promise of the United States struck a chord with a national audience all too familiar with the problems of migration. The tragic effects of migration were explored with less commercial success in Agliberto Meléndez's 1989 film *Un pasaje de ida* (*One-Way Ticket*). The public's identification with Balbuena, the earnest protagonist of *Nueba Yol*, was no doubt heightened by the fact that the role was played by popular merengue singer Luisito Martí. Emboldened by the film's success at home and abroad, Muñiz irreverently bucked numerical sequence by following up with *Nueba Yol 3: Bajo la nueva ley* (*New York 3: Under the New Laws*, 1998).

—*Keith Richards*

See also: *Popular Music:* Merengue

Bibliography

Crismon, Chaz. 2001. "Dominican Music and Film against Immigration to America." Stanford Undergraduate Research Opportunities Small Grant Research Paper. www.crismons.com/chaz/research/grants/small/paper.doc (consulted 15 March 2003).

King, Noel. "Film Culture in Paraguay: Interview with Hugo Gamarra Etcheverry." Senses of Cinema, Issue 24. www.Sensesofcinema/com/contents/02/21/etcheverry_interview.html (consulted 15 March 2003).

Richards, Keith. 1998. "*Cuestión de fe* in the Context of Recent Bolivian Cinema." Pp. 145–154 in *Changing Reels: Latin American Cinema against the Odds*, edited by Rob Rix and Roberto Rodríguez-Saona. Leeds: Leeds Iberian Papers.

Cantinflas, the Mexican comic film star, 1961. (Hulton-Deutsch Collection/Corbis)

Comedy Film

Cantinflas

The stage name of the very popular Mexican comic actor Mario Moreno (1911–1993), Cantinflas has often been compared to Charlie Chaplin, since both humorously represented the underdog in a constant battle with the modern, industrialized world. Cantinflas was well known for his peculiar brand of linguistic acrobatics or double-talk, which jumbled up multiple conversations, relied on a Mexican tradition of sophisticated puns or *albures*, and alternated between forms of deference and defiance. He sought to mock society's middle classes and the elite by drawing them into his topsy-turvy celluloid world and highlighting the artificial nature of the distinctions within Mexico's social hierarchy. In 1939 Cantinflas established his own production company, Posa Films, which became an associate of Columbia Pictures, and he enjoyed widespread success throughout the Spanish-speaking world.

Moreno's career began humbly in the improvised *carpa* (tent) theater, the Mexican equivalent of vaudeville, in around 1930, where he played the stock character of the *pelado* or *peladito*, the country bumpkin bewildered by his encounter with the big city. Moreno would later become synonymous with the *peladito* on screen, in films such as the box-office smash *Ahí está el detalle* (*That's the Point*, 1940), the title of which would become his catchphrase, and *Gran Hotel* (*Grand Hotel*, 1944), which addressed one of the principal social concerns of the 1940s: mass migration to Mexico City. These comic movies generated laughter among popular audiences all over the country, thus helping Mexicans to imagine a national community during a decade in flux. Cantinflas also articulated an ambivalent masculinity in his films, and his frequent transgressions of gender roles on screen formed part of his strategy to turn the world upside down.

Moreno went on to parody labor bosses on screen, yet, ironically, became a union leader for film workers in the late 1940s and early 1950s. From about 1950, however, Moreno's films, which relied more and more on repetitive scripts, began to voice support for the right-wing government's program of industrialization, and by the 1960s Cantinflas had started to become a parody of his former self. This erstwhile champion of popular identity adopted an increasingly reactionary stance in relation to the common people. From a transgressive symbol of a diverse society who embodied the mixed-race underclass, Moreno became little more than a children's entertainer in holiday matinees.

Although Moreno was awarded a Golden Globe for best comic actor in 1957 for the role of Passepartout in the Hollywood movie *Around the World in 80 Days* (1956), his success in the United States was mixed. But recognition of his impact on popular consciousness in the Hispanic world came in 1992, when the Royal Academy of the Spanish Language decided to add to its dictionary the verb *cantinflear*, meaning to talk a lot without saying anything.

—*Lisa Shaw*

See also: *Popular Theater and Performance:* Popular Theater and Music Hall (*Carpa*)

Bibliography

Monsiváis, Carlos. 1997. "Cantinflas: That's the Point!" Pp. 88–105 in *Mexican Postcards*, edited by Carlos Monsiváis. London and New York: Verso.

Pilcher, Jeffrey M. 2001. *Cantinflas and the Chaos of Mexican Modernity.* Wilmington, DE: SR Books.

Tin Tan

Stage name of Germán Valdés (1915–1973), a popular Mexican film star between 1945 and 1960 who initially embodied the borderland figure of the *pachuco* or Mexican American with his bewildering "Spanglish" dialect and trademark zoot suit, a symbol of popular modernity in itself. Tin Tan starred in a host of comedy films that appealed directly to the urban masses, in which he was progressively forced into the role of Cantinflas imitator, since the Mexican government clamped down on his use of English as part of its nationalism drive. Today Tin Tan's films are shown on television and continue to amuse younger generations, and he is an enduring personification of the urban vitality of a bygone age.

Born in Mexico City in 1915, Valdés grew up in the bordertown of Ciudad Juárez, where he began his show business career performing comic impersonations of famous stars on the radio. He toured Mexico and the southwestern United States as part of ventriloquist Paco Miller's company. After his return to Mexico City in 1943, Valdés starred in his first film, *El hijo disobediente* (*The Disobedient Son*, 1945), a film that showcased his use of borderland slang and his irreverent musical impersonations, such as his parody of Jorge Negrete as a drunken mariachi. (Tin Tan often performed *rancheras* or boleros in his films, in a characteristically exaggerated style.)

Shortly after the release of *The Disobedient Son*, Tin Tan was instructed by the government to cease speaking "Spanglish," alleging that it corrupted the speech of Mexico's youth. His most famous movie, and his most subversive, was *El rey del barrio* (*The King of the Neighborhood*, 1949), in which he ridiculed government corruption. Gradually, an exploitative film industry forced Tin Tan to become more a Mexico City *pelado*, like Cantinflas, than a borderland *pachuco*, suppressing the latter's radical humor and Valdés's outstanding comic talents. Nevertheless, his modern style of humor paved the way for a whole generation of television comedians.

—*Lisa Shaw*

See also: *Popular Music:* Bolero; Mariachi, Ranchera, Norteña, Tex-Mex; *Cultural Icons:* Regional and Ethnic Types (El Pachuco); *Language:* Chicano Spanish; *Popular Cinema:* The Mexican Film Industry (Box-Office Successes and Contemporary Film in Mexico); Comedy Film (Cantinflas)

Bibliography

Monsiváis, Carlos. 1997. "Tin Tan: The Pachuco." Pp. 106–118 in *Mexican Postcards*, edited by Carlos Monsiváis. London and New York: Verso.

Chanchada

A type of musical comedy that dominated Brazilian film production from the 1930s to the end of the 1950s and enjoyed unrivalled box-office success. Originally designed as a vehicle to promote carnival music, especially samba, in advance of the annual celebrations, the *chanchada* of the 1930s featured established stars from the radio and record industry, such as the well-known samba singer Carmen Miranda.

The Atlântida studio, established in Rio de Janeiro in 1941, developed the genre, drawing on the talents of a team of actors with experience in popular theater (the *teatro de revista*) and the circus. Naturally favored by the semiliterate or illiterate masses over subtitled imports, and deliberately appealing to rural-urban migrants, the *chanchada* played on the audience's feelings of alienation in the big city and encouraged them to identify with the characters and predicaments presented on screen. Toward the end of the 1940s the *chanchadas* lost their close associations with carnival music, but their formulaic plots increasingly took their inspiration from the hierarchical inversions intrinsic to the Carnival celebrations. Typically they featured cases of mistaken identity, wherein a marginalized member of the lower classes is catapulted into the realms of high society by a twist of fate. The widespread appeal of the low-budget *chanchadas* endured throughout the 1950s and only came to an end with the consolidation of television in Brazil at the end of that decade.

Journalists and film critics coined the term *chanchada* in the 1930s as a scathing label for the highly derivative, light musical comedies that were often modeled on Hollywood movies of the same era. Eventually this designation became the accepted way of referring to increasingly polished productions, particularly those of the Atlântida studio, some of which were not even musicals.

The *chanchada* evolved out of a tradition of documentary films that used Rio's Carnival as their subject matter, and the genre was born in 1935 when the Rio-based Cinédia studio launched the famous musical *Alô, alô, Brasil!* (*Hello, Hello, Brazil!*). Cinédia realized that films featuring songs destined for the annual Carnival parades held huge commercial potential. *Hello, Hello, Brazil!* set the trend for using radio artists to sing and dance in front of the cameras and to perform the most popular songs of the moment in the run-up to Carnival. This film was made up of a series of loosely connected scenes created with the sole intention of allowing the up-and-coming star Carmen Miranda, her sister Aurora, and a host of other popular composers to sing a selection of hit carnival songs. The inhabitants of the big cities, who had begun to swarm into the radio studios to watch live performances and talent contests, now provided a ready-made viewing public for these musical films. The follow-up to this film, *Alô, alô, carnaval!* (*Hello, Hello, Carnival!*), premiered in January 1936 and remained in exhibition for the whole month, a record in that era.

The Atlântida studio produced a series of low-budget but highly successful *chanchadas* in the 1940s and 1950s. These relied on ingenuous slapstick humor and appealed to both children and adults. The films also included numerous music and dance sequences, invariably featuring scantily clad dancing girls in a conscious attempt to lure men to movie theaters along with the rest of their families. The *chanchadas* starred popular comic actors, such as Oscarito and Grande Otelo, who appeared as a double act in over ten Atlântida productions, all filmed against the clock. In October the most likely hits of the Carnival to be held in February of the following year were chosen, the script was ready by November, and filming took place in December. Little thought was given to the plot, which tended to follow a tried and trusted formula. The main objective of the studios was commercial gain.

In the 1950s, Atlântida produced a number of more sophisticated *chanchadas* that parodied Hollywood films, yet also gently mocked the limitations of the Brazilian cinema industry. These playful spoofs included *Matar ou correr* (*Kill or Run*, 1954), a self-confessed parody of *High Noon* (entitled *Matar ou morrer* or *Kill or Die* in Brazil). Similarly, Atlântida's *Nem Sansão nem Dalila* (*Neither Samson nor Delilah*, 1954) satirized Cecil B. DeMille's biblical epic *Samson and Delilah.*

The *chanchada* genre has had an undeniable influence on subsequent cinematic movements and styles in Brazil. Carla Camurati's box-office hit *Carlota Joaquina*,

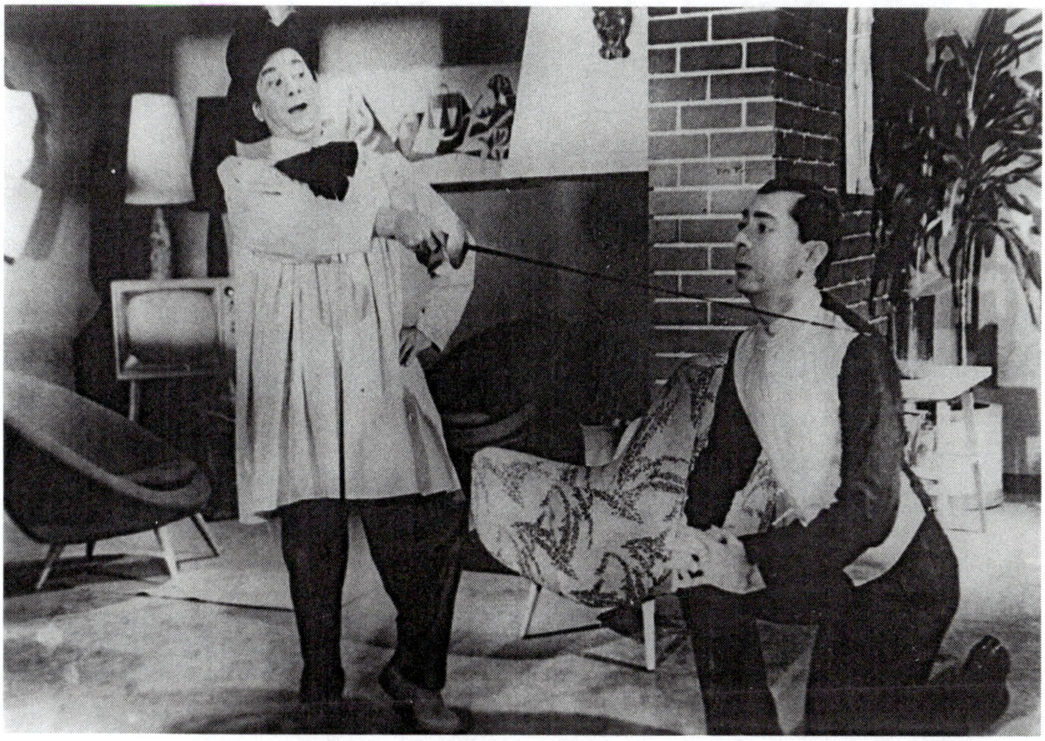

A film still advertising the Brazilian *chanchada Pintando o sete* (*Painting the Town Red*, 1959), starring Oscarito (left). (Courtesy of Atlântida Cinematográfica)

Princess of Brazil (1995), a comic spin on the life story of the Spanish wife of King John VI of Portugal, who fled to the colony of Brazil in 1808 to escape the invading forces of Napoleon, recalls various key features of the *chanchada* tradition: irreverent humor directed at the elite and carnivalesque interludes of music and dance. In the same vein, the musical comedy *For all: O trampolim da vitória* (*For All: The Springboard to Victory*, 1998) includes characters directly inspired by the stock types of the *chanchada*, particularly the comic antiheroes played by Oscarito.

—Lisa Shaw

See also: *Popular Music:* Samba; *Popular Theater and Performance:* Popular Theater and Music Hall (*Teatro de Revista*); *Cultural Icons:* Latin Americans in Hollywood (Carmen Miranda); *Mass Media:* Radio (Brazil); Television (Brazil); *Popular Cinema:* The Brazilian Film Industry (Box-Office Successes and Contemporary Film in Brazil)

Bibliography

Dennison, Stephanie, and Lisa Shaw. 2004. *Popular Cinema in Brazil.* Manchester: Manchester University Press.

Stam, Robert. 1997. *Tropical Multiculturalism: A Comparative History of Race in Brazilian Cinema and Culture.* Durham, NC, and London: Duke University Press.

Stam, Robert, and João Luiz Vieira. 1985. "Parody and Marginality: The Case of Brazilian Cinema." *Framework: The Journal of Cinema and Media* 28: 20–49.

Vieira, João Luiz. 1995. "From *High Noon* to *Jaws:* Carnival and Parody in Brazilian

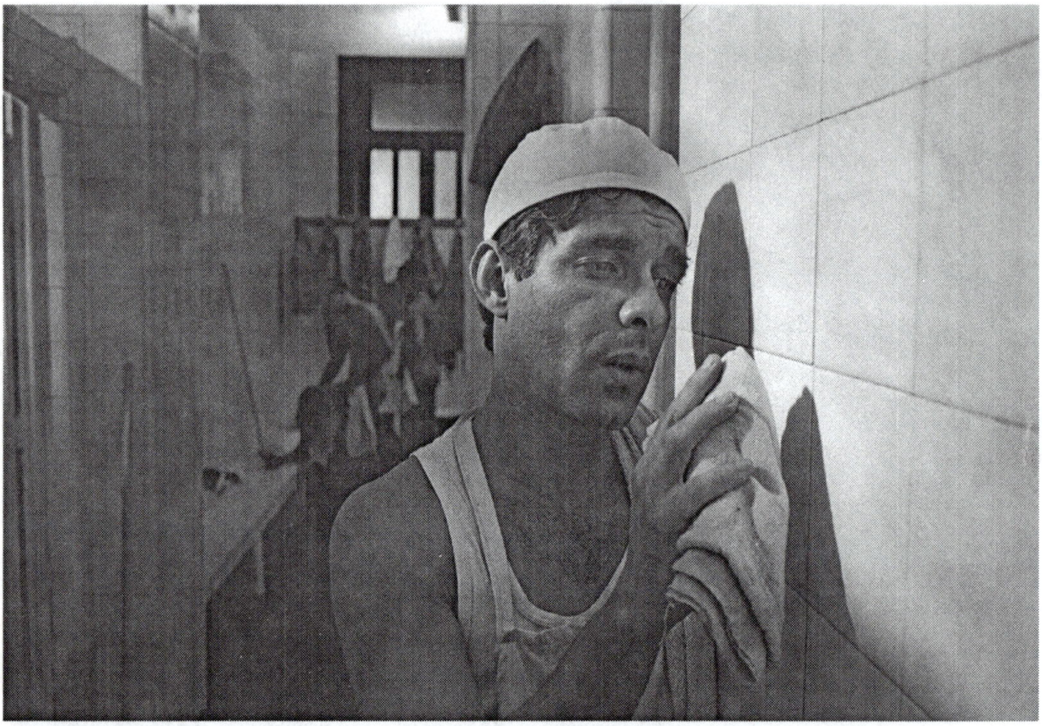

Luiz Carlos Tourinho in the role of Sandoval in a modern take on the *chanchada* genre, *O Trampolim da vitória* (*For All*, 1998). (Courtesy of Luiz Carlos Lacerda; photograph by Zeca Guimarães)

Cinema." Pp. 256–269 in *Brazilian Cinema*, edited by Randal Johnson and Robert Stam. New York: Columbia University Press.

Melodrama

A genre with its roots in eighteenth-century European drama, readily transferred to the big screen in Hollywood, and most closely associated, in the context of Latin American culture, with Mexican cinema. Most popular Mexican films from the 1930s and 1940s could be described as melodramas. As Julianne Burton-Carvajal has pointed out, it is especially in Mexico that melodrama insists on asserting itself as a metagenre, one that subsumes and hybridizes with other generic categories. These films of the "golden age" (1940–1954) made Mexican films the most popular in the Spanish-speaking markets.

Melodrama is closely linked to depictions of family and private life. Most melodramas use music for dramatic and emotional emphasis, frequently resort to the device of plot reversal, and rely heavily on fatalism and human powerlessness in the face of implacable destiny. Melodrama became a popular stylistic choice among Mexican directors from 1917 onward, superseding comedies and documentaries about the Revolution, because U.S. and French film melodramas were very popular with the Mexican public at the time.

Like the *chanchada* in Brazil, melodrama in Latin American cinema was regarded by many in the 1930s, 1940s, and

1950s as an imitation of Hollywood and thus a symptom of cultural colonization by the United States. More recently, however, critics such as Carlos Monsiváis have argued that the excessive nature of Latin American melodrama, such as its lack of emotional limits, presented a challenge to hegemonic Hollywood cinema and ensured the commercial survival of national cinemas in the subcontinent. Argentine cinema in the 1930s, for example, was dominated by the tango melodrama, inspired by the melodramatic lyrics of the national musical form. It could also be argued that the growth and domination of *telenovelas* (soap operas), clearly stylistically inspired by the excess of Latin American melodrama, have ensured that national television production in countries such as Brazil can compete with international programming.

Two basic types of melodrama developed in Mexico between 1930 and 1960: family melodramas (those dealing with issues of love, sexuality, and parenting) and epic melodramas (those that reworked national history, especially those depicting the Mexican Revolution). Melodrama made stars of a number of actors and actresses, who tended to become typecast within the genre. For example, within the family melodrama sub-genre, maternal melodramas were particularly popular; they frequently starred Sara García, the screen's archetypal good mother in films such as *Madre adorada* (*Beloved Mother*, 1948). María Félix, on the other hand, played characters who suffered internally and were tragic and lonely figures (see, for example, *La devoradora* [*The Devourer*, 1946]). Meanwhile, Dolores Del Río regularly played women who had morally erred but who were later redeemed by motherhood. Pedro Armendáriz was equally typecast as the macho Mexican, particularly in epic melodramas such as *Flor Silvestre* (*Wild Flower*, 1943) and *Enamorada* (*Girl in Love*, 1946). Later, actor and singer Pedro Infante, one of Mexico's biggest male stars of the "golden age," would become associated with *caberetera* (brothel) melodramas, in which he would often express heightened emotions by bursting into song, for example in *Angelitos negros* (*Little Black Angels*, 1948). The *caberetera* melodramas were very popular in the 1940s and 1950s, at a time when audiences would be hard-pressed to find such regular depictions of prostitution on the big screen elsewhere in the world. Take, for example, Emilio (El Indio) Fernández's *Salón Mexico* (1948), in which a cabaret dancer and prostitute called Mercedes (Marga López) humiliates herself nightly to keep her unsuspecting little sister at boarding school.

The melodramatic genre involves the exploitation of sentimentalism and the manipulation of viewers' reactions. This is clearly evident in the work of Mexico's filmmaker of excess, Ismael Rodríguez, famous for his exaggerated sets and scenarios and overly dramatic direction. In *Nosotros los pobres* (*We the Poor*, 1948), a paralytic mother is beaten up by a drug-addict neighbor for money. Meanwhile, honest carpenter Pepe el Toro (Pedro Infante) is falsely accused of murder and in prison pokes out the real murderer's eye with a stick. The film's plot then follows the one-eyed man as he seeks revenge. The various story lines of the film's sequel, *Ustedes los ricos* (*You the Rich*, 1948), continue in the same excessive vein.

The "New Latin American Cinema" movement of the 1960s helped discredit the melodrama and bring its domination to an end in the 1960s. However, a number of more recent Latin American films can be said to have been inspired stylistically by the genre, such as Argentina's *La historia oficial* (*The Official Story,* 1985) and Mexico's *Como agua para chocolate* (*Like Water for Chocolate,* 1992). The importance of the genre in the context of Latin American cinema was recently recognized by Brazilian director Nelson Pereira dos Santos, who, when approached by the British Film Institute to make a movie to commemorate the first one hundred years of cinema, produced *Cinema de lágrimas* (*Cinema of Tears,* 1995), a kind of filmic anthology of the best of Mexican melodrama.

—*Stephanie Dennison*

See also: *Popular Music:* Tango; *Cultural Icons:* Latin Americans in Hollywood (Dolores Del Río); Legends of Popular Music and Film (Pedro Infante); *Mass Media:* Telenovela; *Popular Cinema:* The Mexican Film Industry (Box-Office Successes and Contemporary Film in Mexico); Comedy Film (*Chanchada*)

Bibliography

Burton-Carvajal, Julianne. 1997. "Mexican Melodramas of Patriarchy: Specificity of a Transcultural Form." Pp. 186–234 in *Framing Latin American Cinema: Contemporary Critical Perspectives,* edited by Ann Marie Stock. Minneapolis: University of Minnesota Press.

García, Gustavo. 1995. "Melodrama: The Passion Machine." Pp. 153–162 in *Mexican Cinema,* edited by Paulo Antonio Paranaguá. London: British Film Institute.

López, Ana M. 1993. "Tears and Desire: Women and Melodrama in the 'Old' Mexican Cinema." Pp. 147–163 in *Mediating Two Worlds: Cinematic Encounters in the Americas,* edited by John King, Ana M. López, and Manuel Alvarado. London: British Film Institute.

Mexican Horror Films

When the Mexican film industry experienced a slump in the early 1950s, bringing to an end its "golden age," many producers turned to low-cost genre films destined for a working-class audience as a way of riding out the crisis. These genre films include "chili (as an alternative to 'spaghetti') Westerns;" the comedies of Cantinflas, Tin Tan, and others; films that exploited a modicum of "artistic nudity;" wrestling films; and horror films. These last two genres—wrestling and horror films—produced countless box-office hits during the 1950s and 1960s, and their popularity went hand in hand throughout the period.

Actor-turned-producer Abel Salazar was instrumental in the development of the horror film genre in Mexico. His intention was to emulate the kind of success achieved in Great Britain and the United States in the 1930s and 1940s by producers such as Hammer and Universal. Nevertheless, while these Mexican horror films clearly imitated earlier, foreign productions, they did not simply transpose the standard plots and themes to a Mexican setting, swapping Dracula's castle for a Mexican hacienda. The genre was adapted to the tastes of its Mexican audience, plundering "the worst and the best of Mexico's popular imagination," as one critic has observed. Indeed, Mexican culture clearly offered attractions for the genre: pre-Columbian civilizations such as the Aztecs and the Maya and their artifacts (mummies, masks, and more) were good additions or alternatives to the standard horror film's plot, setting, cast, and imagery. So too were aspects of popular Mexican religion (shamanism, the cult of the dead), festivals (*papier-mâché* life-size figures), and folklore (*La Llorona,* the crying woman). Recurrent protagonists include vampires, mummies, witches, waxworks, and robots/cyborgs.

The film that inaugurated the Mexican boom in horror was *El vampiro* (*The Vampire*, 1957), produced by Salazar and directed by Fernando Méndez. Its success, due in part to the quality of the acting and other technical features, was built on in the following decade, when at least twenty films on the theme of vampirism were produced by Salazar and others.

What characterizes Mexican horror films, apart from their hybrid blend of gothic horror and Mexican popular culture, is their taste for "excess" and their generic hybridity. Directors such as Méndez and Chano Urueta had both worked in the industry during its heyday and had known greater artistic freedom; both were ambivalent about having to make horror films in order to survive. In response, these directors tend to subvert the genre by overloading it with extravagant special effects, exaggerating its artificiality, and refusing to let it rest within its traditional generic boundaries. In Urueta's *El barón del terror* (*The Brainiac*, 1961), for example, the monster of the title and the comet on which he arrives on earth are far from realistic. In Urueta's *El espejo de la bruja* (*The Witch's Mirror*, 1960) the imagery and special effects produce results that are almost surreal. In other instances, such as Rafael Baledón's *La maldición de la Llorona* (*The Curse of the Crying Woman*, 1961), a degree of self-consciousness and hybridization is evident as the film "quotes" from a number of earlier Mexican horror films.

In terms of the hybridization of genres, the most important blend comes in the fusion of horror films with the wrestling films that had become popular in the early 1950s. Masked wrestling by both men and women, known as *lucha libre*, became a popular sport in Mexico in the 1930s. By the 1950s it began to be televised and then incorporated into the plots of countless films, many of which featured the silver-masked superhero El Santo, both a successful wrestler in the ring and a popular comic book character. Over fifty films featuring El Santo were produced, and once the varieties of terrestrial adversaries had been exhausted, the producers turned to those of horror films. From the late 1950s, El Santo was pitted against enemies such as vampire women and waxwork monsters. The most famous of these crossover wrestling-horror films is *Santo contra las mujeres vampiro* (*Santo versus the Vampire Women*, 1962), directed by Alfonso Corona Blake.

By the early 1970s the attraction of wrestling-horror films was waning and the Mexican government, which by then had largely nationalized the film industry, was not interested in funding further horror productions. Sex was briefly added to the generic mixture in films such as René Cardona's *El vampiro y el sexo* (*Sex and the Vampire*, 1968), which also featured El Santo, but this did not rescue the genre's ratings. Forced to be independent through lack of government funding, the one significant director of horror films from the 1970s, Juan López Moctezuma, made films such as *Alucarda* (1975) that display both independence of thought and aesthetic innovation. Nevertheless, his films were highly personal statements and not great hits at the box office.

In more recent years, the horror film genre has attracted the interest of another innovative director, Guillermo del Toro. Unlike López Moctezuma, del Toro works

Still from Mexican director Guillermo del Toro's cult horror movie, *Cronos* (1992). (Iguana/Ventana/IMCINE/The Kobal Collection)

with genre films because of their ability to attract a mass audience, and he has succeeded in doing so. Del Toro's internationally acclaimed *Cronos* (1992) is a vampire story set in contemporary Mexico City, yet he protests that it should not be seen as "a Mexican, Catholic vampire movie with mariachis"—it is more than just a Mexican version of a foreign genre model. Like the best of its 1960s forerunners, it is a hybrid product, both in terms of genre (wrestling and El Santo are both present in small doses) and in terms of its deliberate flaunting of the boundaries of national cinema. This is an ironic, revisionist, transnational vampire film. Other innovative recent incursions into the horror film genre include Eduardo Soto-Falcón's short film *Dhampira* (2001). The current climate seems receptive to the ongoing exploration of horror-related themes, particularly those including hybrid figures such as the cyborg-vampire.

Some of the early Mexican horror films have become cult classics, both in Mexico and abroad. *The Vampire* became a cult movie in Mexico in the late 1960s and early 1970s. *Santo versus the Vampire Women* achieved cult film status in Europe in the early 1960s as a result of the positive reviews of horror film enthusiasts. Most of these Mexican horror films were sold to U.S. producers, who had them dubbed into English and shown on U.S. TV in the 1960s (El Santo became Samson in the U.S. versions). The same films were then rediscovered on video many years later by the same U.S. audiences and hailed as cult classics. Many are still available today, digitally remastered for DVD.

—*Thea Pitman*

See also: *Popular Music:* Mariachi, Ranchera, Norteña, Tex-Mex; *Sport and Leisure:* Sport (*Lucha Libre*); *Popular Literature:* Comic Books; *Cultural Icons:* Religious and Mythical Figures (*La Llorona*); *Popular Cinema:* Comedy Film (Cantinflas; Tin Tan); The Mexican Film Industry

Bibliography

Kantaris, Geoffrey. 1998. "Between Dolls, Vampires, and Cyborgs: Recursive Bodies in Mexican Urban Cinema." www.cus.ac.uk/~egk10/notes/Vampires-Cyborgs.htm (consulted 6 December 2002).

La Vega Alfaro, Eduardo de. 1999. "The Decline of the Golden Age and the Making of the Crisis." Pp. 165–191 in *Mexico's Cinema: A Century of Film and Filmmakers*, edited by Joanne Hershfield and David R. Maciel. Wilmington, DE: Scholarly Resources Books.

Schneider, Steven Jay, ed. 2002. *Fear without Frontiers: Horror Cinema across the Globe.* Godalming: FAB Press.

Stock, Ann Marie. 1999. "Authentically Mexican?: *Mi querido Tom Mix* and *Cronos* Reframe Critical Questions." Pp. 267–286 in *Mexico's Cinema: A Century of Film and Filmmakers*, edited by Joanne Hershfield and David R. Maciel. Wilmington, DE: Scholarly Resources Books.

Tombs, Pete, and Andy Starke, dirs. 2001. "Mexican Horror Movies." Documentary included on DVD of *The Vampire* (*El vampiro*) (1957), directed by Fernando Méndez. Mondo Macabro/Boum Productions (includes interviews with David Wilt and Ignacio Durán).

Wilt, David. 2003. "The Films of El Santo." www.wam.umd.edu/~dwilt/santo.html (consulted 6 March 2003).

Coffin Joe

José Mojica Marins, aka Zé do Caixão (Coffin Joe), Brazil's foremost horror director and actor, made a series of popular horror films in the 1960s and 1970s. Marins was born in 1936 and brought up in a working-class, Spanish immigrant community in the city of São Paulo. He started filming when he was a teenager, making little more than home movies with friends and no budget. Marins never learned to look after his money and was constantly broke, so even at the very height of his career his films were characterized by their very low budgets. In fact, it is a miracle that the films were made at all.

Marins first metamorphosed into Coffin Joe in 1963. He apparently dreamed one night of a horrific gravedigger with long fingernails, dressed in a black cape and a top hat. He woke up the next morning desperate to re-create the excitement, fear, and dramatic tension of his dream. He decided to make his first horror film, and after abandoning his search to find a leading man, Marins's alter ego, Zé do Caixão, was born.

Marins has been described as Brazil's first genuinely multimedia performer: during his heyday in the 1960s, the character Zé do Caixão was associated with films, television programs, radio presentations, gramophone records, advertising (for soap and food), public appearances, and Marins's personal favorite, a range of horror comic books. The extent to which

Marins was inspired in his filmmaking by horror comics is clearly visible in his editing technique, his use of close-ups, dialogue to camera, narration off-camera, and the rather expressionist look of his films.

Coffin Joe's first outing was in *À meia-noite levarei sua alma* (*At Midnight I'll Take Your Soul*, 1964). Set in an unnamed town in the interior of the state of São Paulo, the local gravedigger, Zé do Caixão, is obsessed with finding a woman who will give him the perfect son. First, he kills his barren wife, Lenita, by tying her up and letting loose on her body a poisonous spider. Then he turns his attention to his best friend's fiancée, Terezinha. He drowns his best friend in a bathtub, then rapes Terezinha with a cry of "You're going to give me the child I've always wanted." Terezinha hangs herself as a result of the rape, and a gypsy rightly predicts that on All Souls Day, at midnight, the spirit of all the people that Zé has killed will return to seek their revenge.

The film made a lasting impression on the public because of one particularly blasphemous scene in which Coffin Joe tucks into a leg of lamb on Good Friday while laughing at an Easter procession passing by his house. Here was a director making, for the first time, a Brazilian horror film, with Brazilian concerns (the blasphemy scene would not have shocked Anglo-Saxon audiences as much) and a very Brazilian backdrop. For example, Zé do Caixão established in this film his trademark cursing: audiences were delighted to be sent away with a curse such as "May you wander through eternity feeling the pain of a roasted suckling pig!" Also, Zé do Caixão looks out for children and old people in his films, with a sentimentality that is perfectly acceptable to Brazilian audiences.

Zé do Caixão's second cinematic outing, *Esta noite encarnarei no teu cadáver* (*This Night I Will Possess Your Corpse*, 1967), picks up where the story line of his previous film left off. Having survived an attack by the spirits of those he had murdered in *At Midnight I'll Take Your Soul*, Zé continues both his search for the perfect woman to bear him a child and his murderous ways. At the end of this film, he is drowned in a lake where he has dumped the bodies of his childbearing rejects.

Marins had hoped to release his film as soon as it was ready in 1966, in order to make the most of the positive publicity and box-office success of *At Midnight I'll Take Your Soul*. The censors, however, had other ideas. As was the case with all of Marins's feature films, lengthy negotiations took place between the producer and the censors, resulting in the film being drastically cut. In this film Coffin Joe was even obliged to undergo a major personality transformation—to recognize the existence and power of God at the end of the film—thus losing much of his carnivalesque grotesqueness. Film critics were horrified by such interference in the creative process on the part of the censors, and Marins, who until then had viewed such negotiation as a necessary evil of filmmaking, saw the potential commercial advantage in declaring his outrage at such acts of censorship. He learned to promote his films by using newspapers to express controversial views, thus keeping the censors forever on his back.

The character Zé do Caixão appeared in only four more fiction films between 1968 and 1983: *O estranho mundo de Zé do Caixão* (*The Strange World of Coffin Joe*, 1968); *Ritual dos Sádicos*, renamed *O despertar da besta* (*The Awakening of the*

Beast, produced in 1969 but seized by the censor and not released until 1983); *O exorcismo negro* (*Black Exorcism of Coffin Joe*, 1974), and *Delírios de um anormal* (*Hallucinations of a Deranged Mind*, 1978). Meanwhile Marins continued, as he had always done, to make other usually violent and sexually daring feature films (almost thirty between 1958 and 1986). In the 1970s and 1980s he followed the path of many an independent filmmaker in São Paulo: to make ends meet, he produced both soft- and hard-core porn films. Coffin Joe entered a second phase of popularity in 1993, when Mike Vraney of Something Weird, a U.S. distributor of horror videos, discovered his films and marketed them for an English-speaking audience, provoking an overdue reappraisal of his work by the press and public back home.

—*Stephanie Dennison*

See also: *Popular Literature:* Comic Books; *Popular Cinema:* The Brazilian Film Industry (Box-Office Successes and Contemporary Film in Brazil)

Bibliography

Coffin Joe: The Strange World of José Mojica Marins. 2001. Documentary film, directed by André Barcinski and Ivan Finotti.

Dennison, Stephanie, and Lisa Shaw. 2004. *Popular Cinema in Brazil.* Manchester: Manchester University Press.

Youth Movies, Cinema, and Music

In the late 1980s and early 1990s, Latin American cinema began to sense its commercial possibilities, identifying its potential audience as mainly young people. At the same time, it managed to retain the perspective, prevalent in the 1960s and 1970s, that film has a social responsibility to educate and inform. Several recent productions, for example, have managed to combine their visual project with a lucrative music soundtrack: the Mexican films *Amores perros* (*Love's a Bitch*, 2000) and *Y tu mamá también* (*And Your Mother Too*, 2001), and the Argentine *Caballos salvajes* (*Wild Horses*, 1995). The trend is also visible in music documentaries such as German director Wim Wenders's *Buena Vista Social Club* (1999) and the Spanish filmmaker Fernando Trueba's homage to Latin Jazz, *Calle 54* (*54th Street*, 1993).

The phenomenon of Alejandro González Iñárritu's *Love's a Bitch*, both as a cinematic portrayal of Mexico City and as a remarkable critical and commercial success, offers insight into questions of cultural globalization, the dimensions of Latin American postmodernity, and the continuing redefinition of national cinemas in the region. *Love's a Bitch* won prizes for best film at no less than thirteen international festivals across the Americas and Europe (including the critics' special prize at Cannes). Though González Iñárritu was not truly a debut director—he had already made a number of short films and commercials—*Love's a Bitch* was his first feature. In addition to his audiovisual training, he was helped by his previous experience as a disc jockey. The soundtrack for *Love's a Bitch* includes Mexican hip-hop (Control Machete), rock (Café Tacuba), and pop (Julieta Villegas), as well as older and more internationally familiar artists such as The Hollies.

The script by Guillermo Arriaga presents a cross section of the Mexican capital without appearing contrived, and provides a setting within which violence is a kind of currency that permeates social and personal transactions. Also noteworthy is the

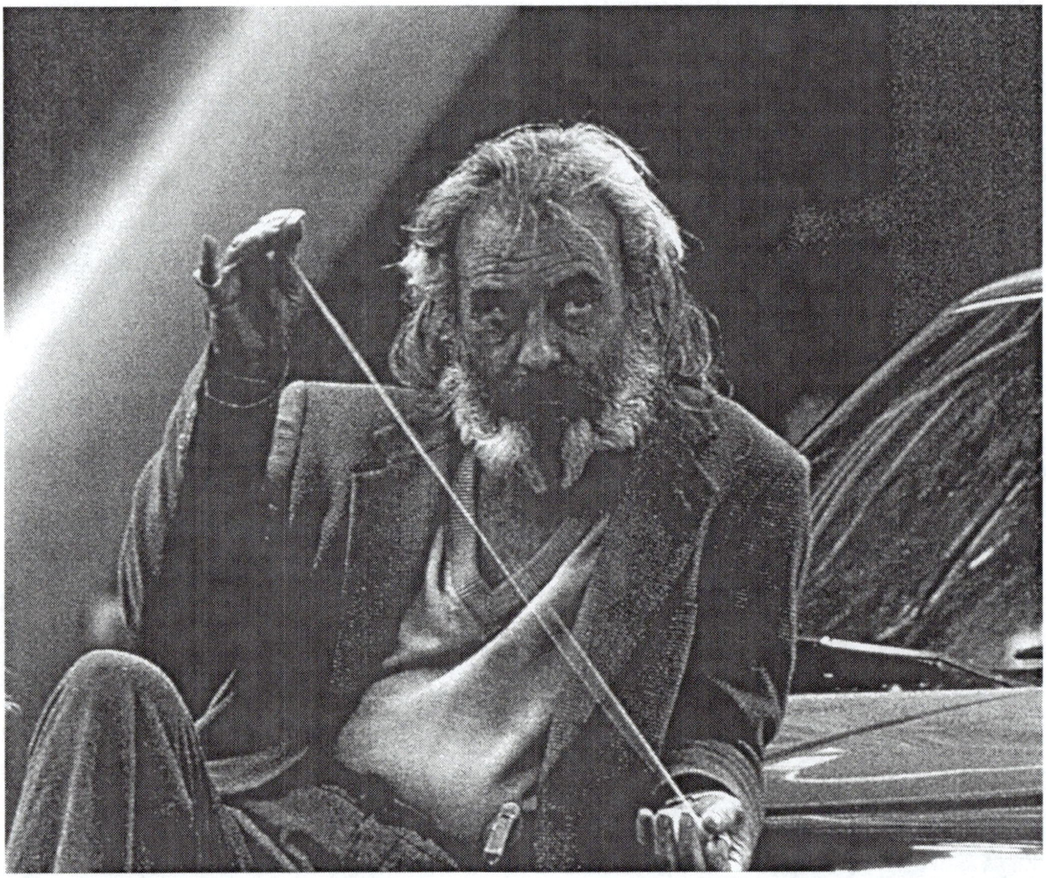

Emilio Echevarría in a scene from the Mexican film *Amores perros* (*Love's a Bitch*, 2001), directed by Alejandro González Iñárritu. (Courtesy of Lions Gate Films, Inc. via Getty Images)

film's use of the cityscape, avoiding references to landmarks or picturesque folklore. Instead the city is portrayed from ground level, with an insider's familiarity. Iñárritu shuns panoramic views in order to present characters from various economic and social backgrounds on the same level.

A comparable film, in terms of its impact, is Alfonso Cuarón's *Y tú mama también* (*And Your Mother Too*). It followed the lead of its Mexican predecessor, *Como agua para chocolate* (*Like Water for Chocolate*, 1992), by going on general release in the United States and Great Britain. Unlike the earlier film, though, *And Your Mother Too* and *Love's a Bitch* eschew any picturesque folkloric vision of Mexico. Mainly spoken in robust *Chilango* (Mexico City slang), these films address themes close to the heart of the nation's younger population yet are still important to older viewers. They are made with the youth market in mind, but also with an eye to the global market: *And Your Mother Too* was also accompanied by an eclectic soundtrack album featuring popular music from Latin America, the United Kingdom, and the United States—Mexican rock music, pop, hip-hop, and *rancheras* as well as music by Brian Eno and Frank Zappa. The

A scene from the Mexican box-office hit *Y tu mamá también* (*And Your Mother Too*, 2002), directed by Alfonso Cuarón and starring young heartthrob Gael García Bernal. (Anhelo Prod./IFC Films/The Kobal Collection)

film's cheerfully lurid bilingual Website offers a glossary of *Chilango* slang. Unlike *Love's a Bitch*, which featured hitherto practically unknown actors, Cuarón's film used some Mexican actors of recent fame, such as Gael García Bernal from *Love's a Bitch*, Diego Luna from *Un dulce olor a muerte* (*The Sweet Smell of Death*), and the alluring Spanish actress Maribel Verdú.

Despite the popularity of *And Your Mother Too*, it has many detractors. It was panned from a wide range of viewpoints by several criteria. Clearly the controversies (gratuitous sexual content, an unflattering depiction of Mexican society, dubious verisimilitude, and overly robust language) have also contributed to the film's success. Whatever one's judgment of *And Your Mother Too*, the film is undeniably persuasive and provocative in its portrayal of Mexico and of Mexico City's youth. No matter how irreverent, irresponsible, hedonistic, and hypocritical its protagonists, Tenoch and Julio, may be, the public is invited not only to laugh at them, but also to share something of their jaundiced view. Cuarón's film is an unsentimental and ultimately unsettling view of class, gender, and ethnicity in Mexico.

Marcelo Piñeyro's *Wild Horses* exploits the vein of anti-establishment feeling that existed in Argentina even before the economic disaster of 2002. In doing so it unites two profoundly different generations: the older generation, personified by the amateur bank robber (played by Héctor Alterio), represents a political consciousness that Leonardo Sbaraglia's yuppie banker would never share but for the events that subsequently bring them together. This film's loosely rebellious tone and its somewhat escapist "feel-good" element are heightened by the Argentine rock soundtrack, which includes songs by Andrés Calamaro and Los Abuelos de la Nada (The Grandfathers of Oblivion).

Although Brazil has used popular music to promote films (and vice versa) since the carnival movies of the 1930s that evolved into the *chanchada* genre, it is only since the *retomada* or rebirth of the film industry in the mid-1990s that producers have rediscovered the advantages of choosing salable soundtracks to accompany movies, particularly those films likely to appeal to a younger audience. The same mutually beneficial system can be seen in the relationship between music and *telenovelas* in Brazil, where each soap opera normally generates two chart-topping compilation albums, one with "national" singles used as incidental music in the TV series, and one featuring international hits.

An example of this latest tendency in Brazilian cinema is Paulo Caldas and Lírio Ferreira's *Baile perfumado* (*Perfumed Ball*, 1997), set in the northeastern *sertão* or backlands. This film deals with the real-life adventures of immigrant Benjamim Abraão, a Middle Eastern journalist who traveled through the backlands in the 1930s and eventually found and filmed the notorious *cangaceiro* or bandit Lampião and his gang. Images of the popular heroes are accompanied by the latest critically acclaimed urban sound from the state of Pernambuco (particularly from the cities of Recife and Olinda), known as *mangue beat*, performed by Fred Zero Quatro (Fred Zero Four) and Chico Science e Nação Zumbi (Chico Science and the Zumbi Nation).

More recently, trendy director Beto Brant's *O invasor* (*The Trespasser*, 2001) starred Paulo Miklos, bass guitarist and one of the many vocalists of the very popular 1980s rock band Titãs (Titans), as a low-life hired assassin who gradually worms his way into São Paulo's upper-middle classes through his relationship with a reckless poor-little-rich-girl. The soundtrack uses music from São Paulo's thriving underground hip-hop scene, and the film includes appearances by rappers (including the late Sabotage) little known outside of the poor suburbs of São Paulo.

Eu, tu, eles (*Me, You, Them*, 2000), which appeared in the wake of the highly successful *Central Station*, demonstrated once again that audiences, even international ones, were fascinated by tales from the Brazilian *sertão*. The film tells the story, based loosely on fact, of a rural worker (Maria Marlene da Silva Sabóia) from the northeastern state of Ceará (transferred to Bahia in the film) who lived with three men as if they were all her husbands. Maria (renamed Darlene in the film) is played by Regina Casé, a household name in Brazil. *Me, You, Them* boasts one of the most successful film soundtracks of recent years, picking up on a trend in southern Brazilian cities for the ultradanceable *forró*, a generic term for northeastern music. Reworked and performed by Gilberto Gil, former co-leader of the Tropicália movement in Brazilian popular music, the soundtrack includes old standards by Luiz Gonzaga such as "Asa Branca" ("White Wing"), considered to be the anthem of the northeast.

Directed by *cinema novo* veteran Carlos (Cacá) Diegues, *Orfeu* (*Orpheus*) was by far the most popular Brazilian film at the box office in 1999, partly because Toni Garrido, the pinup lead singer of popular reggae band Cidade Negra (Black City), played the title role (Garrido is also a part-time television presenter whose credits include the Brazilian version of *Fame Academy*, *Fama*, produced by TV Globo in 2003). *Orfeu* is a remake of French director Marcel Camus's Cannes- and Oscar-winning film *Orfeu negro* (*Black Orpheus*, 1959), itself based on a verse-play, *Orfeu da Conceição* (1953, staged 1956), by poet and songwriter Vinícius de Moraes, a pioneer of bossa nova. In his play Vinícius sought to transpose the Hellenic myth of Orpheus (the godlike man with a gift for music who falls madly in love with Eurydice, only to be destroyed by her in the end) to the world of black culture—in particular, Rio's *favelas* during Carnival time. Though the original film version helped bring bossa nova and samba to the attention of an international audience, it was criticized for idealizing the life of *favela* or slum inhabitants.

In the remake, Toni Garrido plays a samba composer for the local "samba school" or neighborhood carnival group (the fictitious Unidos da Carioca). The vibrant images of the school participating in Rio's annual Carnival parade were achieved by placing the chief actors in the real-life 1998 musical entry of Unidos do Viradouro, a Niterói-based samba school, who used Caetano Veloso's specially prepared samba for that year's competition.

Orfeu aimed at box-office success by adhering to what is often described as the *padrão global de qualidade*, the glossy production values associated with the Globo television network, one of the world's biggest exporters of soap operas. The movie was coproduced by Globo Filmes, the film production wing of the Globo media empire. The acting style is straight from the Globo soap opera textbook, as are many of the actors in the film, such as Patrícia França, who plays Eurydice.

The musical backdrop to the *favela* portrayed in *Orfeu* is Brazilian hip-hop rather than samba, played to accompany the local radio announcements that blare out of loudspeakers on every corner. In this the film recognizes that today most young working-class people listen to hip-hop and other forms of Brazilian urban music rather than samba, which is often only heard in the preparation for and during Carnival. Even Orfeu's composition for the Carnival parade daringly incorporates a rap halfway through, performed in the film by Orfeu himself and written by popular rapper Gabriel o Pensador. The soundtrack to *Orfeu* thus includes bossa nova, rap, and samba. The hit single from the film, "Sou você" ("I Am You"), was composed by Caetano Veloso and performed by the film's lead actor, Toni Garrido.

—Keith Richards and Stephanie Dennison

See also: *Popular Music:* Bossa Nova; Contemporary Urban Music; Mariachi, Ranchera, Norteña, Tex-Mex; Samba; Tropicália; *Language:* Mexican Slang; *Mass Media:* Telenovela; Television (Brazil); *Popular Cinema:* Box-Office Successes and Contemporary Film in Brazil; Box-Office Successes and Contemporary Film in Mexico; Comedy Film (*Chanchada*); The Film Industry and Box-Office Successes in Argentina; *Popular Religion and Festivals:* Popular Festivals (Carnival in Brazil); *Visual Arts and Architecture:* Architecture and Landscape Design (*Favelas*)

Bibliography

Dennison, Stephanie. 2000. "A Meeting of Two Worlds: Recent Trends in Brazilian Cinema."

Journal of Iberian and Latin American Studies 6, no. 2: 131–144.
Dennison, Stephanie, and Lisa Shaw. 2004. *Popular Cinema in Brazil.* Manchester: Manchester University Press.
Review of the film *Amores perros* on the Website of the BBC. www.bbc.co.uk/films (consulted March 2003).
Website of Canal Trece, Argentina. www.artear.com.ar/cine/caballos/ (consulted March 2003).

12

Popular Religion and Festivals

The introduction of Roman Catholicism to the New World was part of the colonizing policy of both the Spanish and the Portuguese, but on Latin American soil Christian beliefs and practices came into contact with those of the native Amerindian peoples, and later with those brought by enslaved Africans and their descendants. Latin American Catholicism has consequently absorbed elements of pre-Columbian religious beliefs and practices, giving rise to what is known as "popular" or "folk" Catholicism. Popular Catholicism has blended elements of different religions, yet it is still a recognizable mutation of traditional Roman Catholicism. In Mexico, for example, Catholic saints are matched up with pre-Columbian deities, as are Christian festivals with indigenous ones. Similarly, popular religion in the Andean countries must be understood in its historical and cultural context, since it is heavily influenced by the experience of conquest and the persistence of indigenous beliefs under a Christian guise.

In recent years, Catholicism in Latin America has also become synonymous with Liberation Theology, with its commitment to social change and improvement of the lot of marginal sectors. This radical theology was announced at Medellín, Colombia, in 1968 with a formal declaration of the Church's identification with the poor. The doctrine's complexity and diversity make it difficult to define, but the influence of Marxism is apparent, along with that of pioneering social reformers and educators such as the Brazilian Paulo Freire. Liberation Theology's most famous advocate is the Peruvian priest Gustavo Gutiérrez, whose humble origins sharpened his awareness of social problems. Gutiérrez was responsible for setting up the Bartolomé de las Casas center for theological research, named after another famous reforming churchman and situated in one of Lima's poorest districts. Liberation Theology essentially holds that salvation can occur in this life, and that it is not God's will that people suffer while awaiting redemption in the hereafter.

More recently Latin America has been marked by the growth of New Protestantism. Among the theories attempting to explain why Latin Americans are willing to abandon their traditional Catholicism (not just official Roman Catholicism, but more often popular Catholicism) in favor of evangelical churches is the notion that Protestantism and indigenous religions are similar. For example, both Protestantism, particularly Pentecostalism, and indigenous Mesoamerican religions allow for the possibility of direct communion with God and/or "possession" by spirits—in contrast to the more mediated versions of communion advocated by the Catholic Church.

The religious and mythological landscape of Latin America is undeniably rich. In Brazil and Cuba, African slaves forced to worship the Christian God and the saints preserved their own belief systems by drawing direct associations between Catholic icons and their own deities. This practice gave rise to *Candomblé* in Brazil and *Santería* in Cuba, both of which are sometimes referred to as syncretic religions. Religious faiths such as *Bahá'í*, and *Santo Daime* and *Umbanda* in Brazil, today continue to appeal to large numbers of people, who are drawn to the alternative approach and perspectives on life that they offer. Alongside organized religions, both within and outside the mainstream, many of the region's poorer inhabitants also maintain strong beliefs in pagan rituals, particularly those linked to healing. All strata of society unite annually to celebrate local and national festivals, such as Carnival in the run-up to Lent—particularly important in Brazil—and the Day of the Dead in Mexico.

—Lisa Shaw and Thea Pitman

Popular Catholicism

Mexico and Central America

A number of factors have affected the emergence of popular Catholicism in Mexico and Central America over the five centuries since the Conquest. These include, on the one hand, a substantial number of similarities between the pre-Columbian religions of Mesoamerica and Catholicism (similar symbols and concepts, parallels between gods and saints, and the existence of similar social structures based on hierarchy and wealth redistribution), and the willingness of the early missionaries to accept the use of such "metaphors" from the old religions to help indigenous peoples assimilate Catholic doctrine. On the other hand, a tradition of accepting the gods of conquering civilizations already existed in pre-Columbian society, along with a willingness to accept conversion to Christianity in exchange for some protection by the Church from the states that governed indigenous groups, and some respect for the latter's traditional self-image. The syncretic nature of the religious practices of these new converts did not go unnoticed or unpunished by the guardians of the faith, but by then the existence of popular Catholicism was a *fait accompli.*

In more recent times, it has become evident that popular Catholicism is also the preserve of women, both indigenous and white. Whereas the Catholic Church itself is very much a male-dominated institution, Mexican and Central American women have taken an active role in the more private world of popular Catholicism—in the imparting of beliefs and practices from one generation to the next, and in the veneration of saints on altars in their own homes, for example. Mexican women in particular have also found strength and identity in the role model that is the Virgin of Guadalupe, the *mestiza* (brown or mixed-race) virgin who is a popular Mexican adaptation of the Virgin Mary.

Contemporary popular Catholicism is most easily identified by a number of practices: dependency on a complex network of social support known as *compadrazgo* (kinship relations defined by the choice of godparents for different events in a person's life), the veneration of often uncanonized *santos* (saints) with a consequent lessening of emphasis on God, and the expression of such veneration in many annual *fiestas* (processions and dramatizations of biblical stories and historical events), in the construction of altars in private homes and on street corners, and in the painting of *retablos* (votive offerings) to thank saints for their help in times of need. To outsiders, the practices of popular Catholicism seem colorful and entertaining, and they constitute a substantial tourist attraction across the region. In recent years, the pre-Columbian elements of popular Catholic practices have been emphasized to lend weight to the reevaluation of the pre-Columbian contribution to Mexican and Central American cultures. This shift in emphasis is also highly attractive to tourists.

—*Thea Pitman*

See also: *Cultural Icons:* Religious and Mythical Figures (Virgin of Guadalupe); *Popular Religion and Festivals:* Indigenous Religious and Cultural Practices (Guatemala; Mexico); New Protestantism (Mexico and Central America); Popular Festivals (Mexico); Popular Medicine and Healing (Mexico and Central America); *Visual Arts and Architecture:* Art (Religious Folk Art)

Bibliography

Carrasco, Pedro. 1976. *El catolicismo popular de los tarascos.* Mexico City: SEP/Setentas.

Espin, Orlando O., and Roberto S. Goizueta. 1997. *The Faith of the People: Theological Reflections on Popular Catholicism.* Maryknoll, NY: Orbis Books.

Green, Duncan. 1997. "Thy Kingdom Come: The Church." Pp. 201–215 in *Faces of Latin America*, by Duncan Green. London: Latin America Bureau.

Ingham, John M. 1986. *Mary, Michael, and Lucifer: Folk Catholicism in Central Mexico.* Austin: University of Texas Press.

Rowe, William, and Vivian Schelling. 1991. *Memory and Modernity: Popular Culture in Latin America.* London: Verso, pp. 68–74.

Stracke, Claire T., and J. Richard Stracke. 1997. "Popular Catholicism." Pp. 1130–1134 in *Encyclopedia of Mexico*, vol. 2, edited by Michael S. Werner. Chicago: Fitzroy Dearborn.

The Andean Countries

The relationship between the Church and the lower classes in the Andean countries has always been contradictory, if not paradoxical—the result of a Spanish tradition of anticlericalism apparent even among the devout. Even as early as the sixteenth century, faith in God and contempt for ecclesiastical authorities were not mutually exclusive. Moreover, as Jeffrey Klaiber has shown in the Peruvian context, cleric support for despotic regimes has not always precluded popular support for the Church, even at times of popular rebellion. It is almost inconceivable that even the most extremist rebellion should include the kind of violent anticlerical retribution seen, for example, in the Spanish Civil War. Klaiber sees the Catholic faith as the only element shared by all social classes and ethnic groups in the Andes. An explanation for this unifying role can be found in the transcultural nature of Andean religiosity and in the reconciliatory movements within liberal sectors of the Church.

The expression of the integration of Christianity into indigenous belief systems can be clearly seen in colonial churches throughout the Andes and elsewhere in

Latin America, decorated largely by indigenous hands and according to native aesthetics. The Catholic Church during the colonial era learned the pragmatic value of tolerance and the incorporation of potentially troublesome popular movements. This sort of pragmatism is visible also in the absorption of native festivals into the Christian calendar, and more recently in the acceptance of unofficial saints, elevated to this status by popular belief. An example of this phenomenon is Sarita Colonia, a girl from the Andean town of Huaráz who migrated to Lima, where she died in 1926. Several miracles are attributed to Sarita, who is believed to be the patron saint of the urban migrants. Saints can also be created to placate marginal social sectors: this was arguably the case with another Peruvian, the black saint Martín de Porras, who was canonized in 1962 with the title Patron of Interracial and Social Justice. Other important figures in popular Andean religiosity are the Virgins that have appeared throughout the region, such as the Virgen del Agua Santa (Virgin of the Holy Waters) in Baños, Ecuador. One of many reputedly miraculous Christian apparitions in pre-Columbian sacred sites, the Virgin is credited with having saved many lives, is the object of pilgrimage, and is habitually showered with gifts.

—*Keith Richards*

See also: *Popular Religion and Festivals:* Indigenous Religious and Cultural Practices (The Andean Countries); Popular Medicine and Healing (The Andean Countries)

Bibliography

Candelaria, Michael R. 1990. *Popular Religion and Liberation: The Dilemma of Liberation Theology.* Albany: State University of New York Press.

Klaiber, Jeffrey L. 1977. *Religion and Revolution in Peru, 1824–1976.* London: Notre Dame.

Muskus, Eddy José. 2002. *The Origins and Early Development of Liberation Theology in Latin America: With Particular Reference to Gustavo Gutiérrez.* Carlisle: Paternoster Press.

Sobrino, Jon. 2001. *Christ the Liberator: A View from the Victims.* Maryknoll, NY: Orbis Books.

Venezuela

Popular Catholicism in Venezuela is intrinsically linked to Liberation Theology, a doctrine that conceives of action vital to the promotion of social justice and sees the everyday experience of the people as a source of valid religious values. In Venezuela, from the late 1950s onward, a growing interest developed within the official Catholic Church in working with popular sectors of society. Small, independent groups of clergy and activists set up a number of initiatives directed at the poor.

Though these movements had only limited impact in Venezuela, they paved the way for important pastoral work and offered free schooling or training, among other activities. By the late 1960s, as Levine notes, some religious congregations began to articulate a "liberationist position," and members went to "live with the people," got involved in barrio or community organizations, and came face-to-face with poverty and inequality.

Similar groups sprang up around the country. Not all of these groups survived, but two important initiatives from this period have not only lasted, but have played a major role in popular religion in Venezuela. The first of these is the Centro Gumilla, a Jesuit center for research and social action that was founded in 1969; it has two bases, one in Caracas, the other in Barquisimeto. The center produces a wide range of publications directed at the working class and rural poor, including a pamphlet series that has essays on such topics as educational reform, agriculture, Liberation Theology, and contemporary reworkings of Bible stories. These publications reveal a profound respect for popular culture and link religion with the experiences of real social groups.

The second initiative, CESAP (Centro al Servicio de la Acción Popular or Center for Popular Action), was founded in 1974 and offers courses to popular organizations. Each of its three regional centers runs courses, operates a lending library service, and runs a series of outreach programs on topics such as nutrition and literacy. Again, this center produces numerous pamphlets for group discussion and grassroots participation, and its stated goal is replacing capitalism with a just, participatory, and classless society.

Alongside these two important centers are a variety of popular religious organizations throughout Venezuela. There are differences among the forms of popular Catholicism in Venezuela, but there are common features as well, such as the emphasis on Bible study in which the local people are seen as active interpreters of biblical texts, and the importance of collective action. In this way, these and similar religious groups within Venezuela can be defined as "popular Catholicism" in that they attempt to return the Church to the people and to start out from the beliefs and experiences of the masses.

—*Claire Taylor*

See also: *Popular Religion and Festivals:* New Protestantism (Venezuela)

Bibliography

Berryman, Phillip. 1984. *When Theology Listens to the Poor.* San Francisco: Harper and Row.

Cleary, Edward, ed. 1990. *Born of the Poor: The Latin American Church since Medellín.* Notre Dame: University of Notre Dame Press.

Gutiérrez, Gustavo. 1973. *A Theology of Liberation.* Maryknoll: Orbis Books.

Levine, Daniel H. 1992. *Popular Voices in Latin American Catholicism.* Princeton, NJ: Princeton University Press.

Brazil

Within popular Catholicism in Brazil, homegrown saints are particularly important. The country has also witnessed the emergence of many millenarian cults, the most famous of which was that led by the ragged lay preacher Antônio Conselheiro ("the Counselor"), who settled thousands of his followers on an abandoned ranch called Canudos in 1893. Having refused to recognize the rule of the new Republican government established in 1889, the community was eventually brutally wiped out by the federal army. More recently, popular Catholicism has become closely interwoven with Liberation Theology (as is popular Catholicism in Venezuela and other parts of the subcontinent). In Brazil this radical doctrine became closely identified with the Franciscan Leonardo Boff, and Dom Paulo Evaristo Arns, the bishop of São Paulo archdiocese during the violent years of the military dictatorship established in 1964. Their evangelical concept was to allow people to liberate themselves from the socioeconomic injustices at the root of Brazilian society as part of a general liberation from sin.

In the state of Bahia the people show their devotion to the patron saint of the state, Nosso Senhor do Bonfim (Our Lord of the Good End), a manifestation of Jesus. The basilica that takes his name is situated on a hill overlooking the city of Salvador and facing the sea. People flock there from miles around to seek cures for their ills. Street vendors outside sell wristbands, narrow colored ribbons that bear the saint's name, as talismans to bring good luck. It is believed that he will grant three wishes during the three-time knotting of the ribbon, provided that the person making the wishes wears it until it drops off. A ritual cleansing of the church's steps takes place every year, a popular Catholic festival that is traditionally held on the Thursday before the third Sunday in January. This popular religious outpouring is given the tacit acquiescence of the Catholic Church, whose resident priest schedules a nine-day series of masses (*novenas*) during this period. Followers of *Candomblé* and *Umbanda* also participate in this street festival.

The national shrine of Nossa Senhora da Aparecida (Our Lady of Aparecida) is located two hours away by bus from the city of São Paulo. The construction of the present-day shrine, on the site of an earlier chapel, was begun in 1940 and only finished in 1990. According to legend, in the eighteenth century a group of fishermen, about to return home with only a few fish after an unsuccessful trip, found a wooden statue in the image of the *senhora* in their nets, whereupon they obtained a more abundant catch than ever before. With the permission of the Church they then built a small chapel to enshrine this statue of Our Lady of Aparecida. The fact that the image is black suggests that the poor were appropriating in their own way the devotion to the Immaculate Conception then being promoted in the Iberian Peninsula. An estimated six million Brazilians visit this shrine every year.

In the arid and poor northeast, several major religious figures have emerged on the margins of the Catholic Church, such as Padre (Father) Cícero, who opposed the transition of Brazil from monarchy to republic at the end of the nineteenth century. He remains the focus of pilgrimage even today, as depicted in Walter Salles's award-winning movie, *Central Station* (1998). Padre Cícero's image can still be seen in many of the homes of the poor in the northeast.

Liberation theologians introduced a system of "base community" pastoral work into the Catholic Church in the 1960s, for example in the shantytowns (*favelas*) of Brazil's big cities. In the heyday of these base communities, at the end of the 1970s, it appeared as if a new Church were being born, with an emphasis on lay leadership and consciousness-raising. In São Paulo, for example, the base communities were part of the so-called Operation Periphery. This program, launched by Archbishop Arns and his collaborators, sent people and resources to the poor outskirts of the city where new neighborhoods were being erected. Priests and nuns helped these communities with practical issues and encouraged them to make their own decisions, including interpretations of the Bible based on their own life experiences.

The progressive Catholic Church in Brazil in the 1980s showed considerable courage in defending the lives and cultures of indigenous communities and the rural and urban poor against both the state and powerful groups who were prepared to use extreme violence to protect their vested interests.

But Church leaders in Rome, and even in some parts of Brazil, watched the Liberation Theology movement with growing alarm. For them it represented a trend

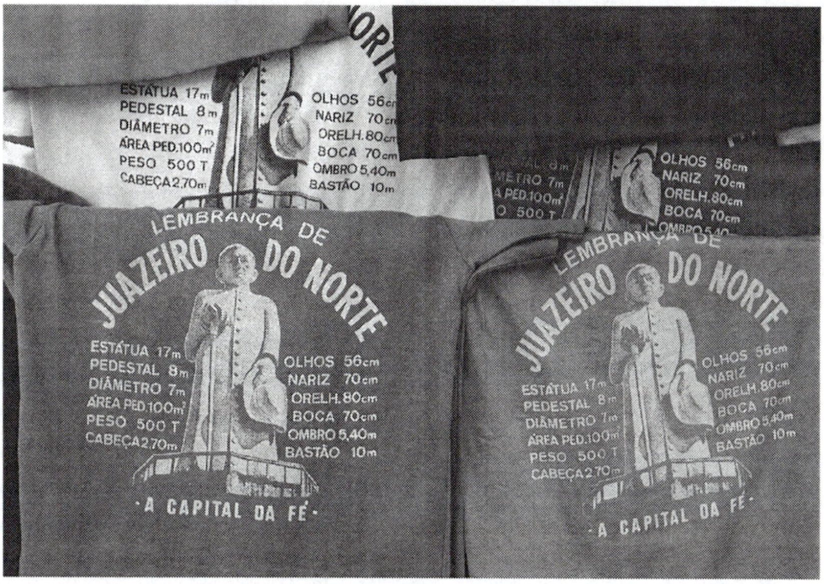

T-shirts featuring an image of Padre Cícero are sold in Juazeiro do Norte, the town that the priest founded in the 1920s. (Stephanie Maze/Corbis)

away from Church orthodoxy toward a materiality considered inappropriate. As bishops have retired or left the Church in Brazil and in other Latin American countries, Pope John Paul II, in office since 1978, has replaced them with orthodox clergy who do not espouse the ideals of social reform or Marxist economic analysis. Although the movement was thus brought to a halt, it did not fail. Hundreds of people who were schooled in its ideologies have gone on to advocate a range of socially just causes.

—Lisa Shaw

See also: *Popular Social Movements and Politics:* Base Communities in Brazil; *Popular Cinema:* The Brazilian Film Industry (Box-Office Successes and Contemporary Film in Brazil); *Popular Religion and Festivals: Candomblé*; New Protestantism (Brazil); Popular Catholicism (Venezuela); Popular Medicine and Healing (Brazil); *Umbanda*; *Visual Arts and Architecture:* Architecture and Landscape Design (*Favelas*)

Bibliography

Boff, Leonardo, and Clodvis Boff. 1994. *Introducing Liberation Theology.* New York: Hyperion Books.

Burdick, John. 1993. *Looking for God in Brazil: The Progressive Catholic Church in Urban Brazil's Religious Arena.* Berkeley: University of California Press.

da Cunha, Euclides. 1944. *Rebellion in the Backlands.* Translated by Samuel Putnam. Chicago: University of Chicago Press.

Gutiérrez, Gustavo. 1988. *A Theology of Liberation: History, Politics and Salvation.* Maryknoll: Orbis Books.

Nagle, Robin. 1999. "Liberation Theology's Rise and Fall." Pp. 462–467 in *The Brazil Reader: History, Culture, Politics*, edited by Robert M. Levine and John J. Crocitti. London: Latin America Bureau.

Silverstein, Leni. 1995. "The Celebration of Our Lord of the Good End: Changing State, Church, and Afro-Brazilian Relations in Bahia." Pp. 134–151 in *The Brazilian Puzzle: Culture on the Borderlands of the Western World*, edited by David J. Hess and Roberto DaMatta. New York: Columbia University Press.

Santería

One of many religions of the African diaspora in Latin America brought across the Atlantic with the slave trade, all of which combine elements of African worship with the Catholic faith. *Santería,* although best known in its Cuban manifestation, also exists under the same name in Puerto Rico, Venezuela, and Mexico. A similar phenomenon in Haiti and the southern United States is the unjustly demonized vaudun, or voodoo. Brazil has its *Candomblé,* Uruguay its *Candombe,* and Trinidad its *orisha.* The common feature of all these religions is their preservation of beliefs deriving mostly from the Central West African Yoruba culture that continues to exist in present-day Nigeria, Congo, and Benin.

When they were brought to the Spanish and Portuguese colonies in the New World, slaves were transported in groups that generally remained more or less intact after arrival, a policy that permitted them to retain elements of the African cultures they left behind. In contrast, the British colonies separated slaves who might have language or customs in common, thus systematically erasing cultural roots in order to better acculturate and control them. The result of the Iberian approach is a visible continuation of African cultural and religious practices in Latin America, a phenomenon rarely seen in North America or the British Caribbean.

Santería was not brought to Cuba in a single demographic wave; the first consignments of slaves arrived in the mid-sixteenth century, and the height of the slave trade occurred more than two centuries later, in the late eighteenth and early nineteenth centuries. This continual wave of forced migration from Africa allowed Afro-Cuban cultural practices to maintain a relationship to the mother continent while evolving into something specific to the island.

In *Santería* and similar religions, African and European elements coexist, originating in the religious instruction with which colonial masters were supposed to "repay" those they had displaced and dispossessed. However, Africans, like indigenous peoples in the Americas, were wary of discarding their religious heritage and unreservedly adopting Christianity. They needed to preserve their own spiritual traditions and appease their ancestral gods as well as the Christian deity, while maintaining the appearance of obedience to their masters. They fulfilled this need through dual worship: the African pantheon, multiple and multifaceted, was paralleled with the Christian system of saints. Thus each Yoruba deity, known as an *orisha,* would be "paired" with the saint who most closely resembled his or her physical attributes, spheres of influence, or preoccupations. This phenomenon is often described with the contentious term "syncretism" but can also be seen as a simultaneous and parallel observance of discrete cultural codes.

The *Santería* system, also known in Cuba as *La Regla de Ocha* or Rule of Ocha, is not merely a duplicitous practice aimed at hoodwinking religious authority. Nor is it simply a product of the trauma or cultural crisis created by the experience of slavery. The identification of *orishas* with saints does reveal certain similarities between African and European worship, since the *Santería* figures have spheres of influence similar to the Christian ones. For Fernando Ortiz, the original scholar of Afro-Cuban culture, the complexity and richness of Yoruba mythology are comparable to those of ancient Greece. Ortiz

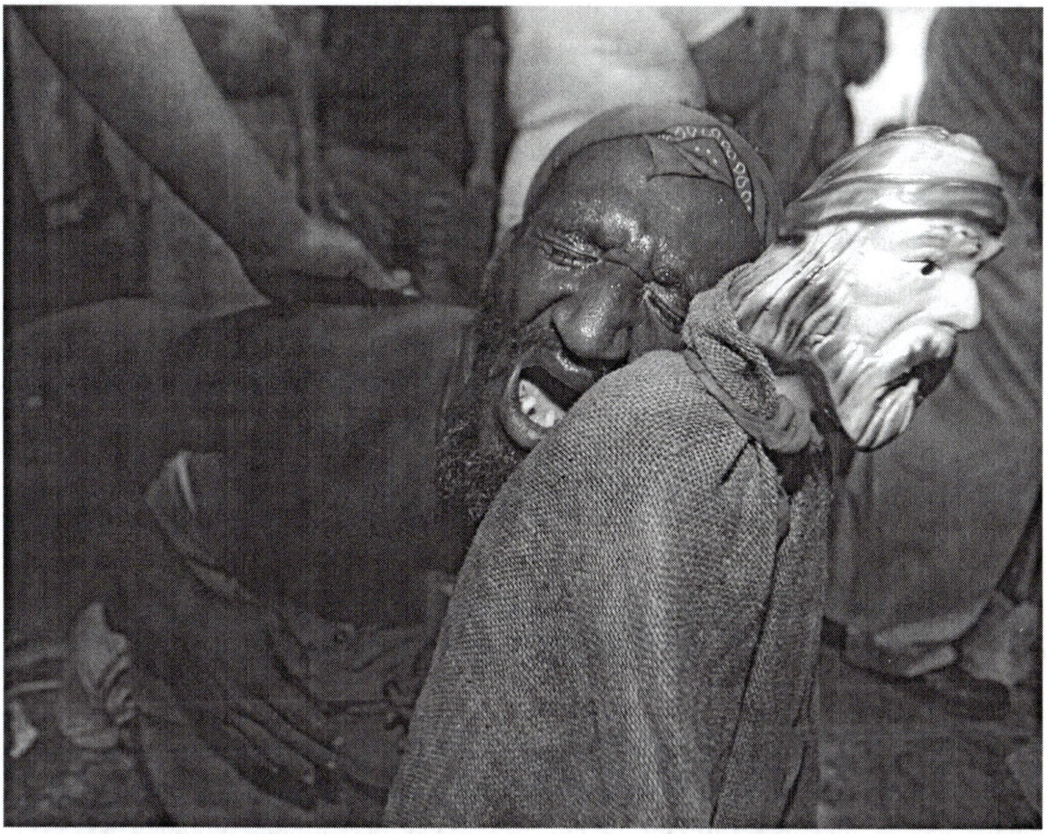

A Cuban worshipper weeps over the icon of St. Lazarus, who is both a Catholic saint and an important deity in the Afro-Cuban religion *Santería*. (Reuters/Corbis)

coined the crucial term "transculturation" to describe the interaction and reciprocal influence between cultures, irrespective of political and social power. *Santería* is a prime example of this phenomenon.

The Yoruba creator god Olodumare is the almighty in the *Santería* pantheon, from whom *aché* or cosmic energy originates. The *orishas* are his emissaries, and their exploits, strengths, and frailties parallel the human world, as did those of the Greek gods. Moreover, the divine and mortal worlds are linked by the figure of Elegguá, the messenger and intermediary who opens paths, and the prankster who teaches moral lessons with levity. Identified with St. Anthony as his Catholic manifestation, Elegguá is the figure evoked first in all ceremonies, as he alone permits communication. Yemayá, the archetypal maternal figure who controls the sea and the moon, is the figure most closely identified with women's lives and exclusively female concerns. Like all the *orishas*, she is an ambivalent figure with moods just like those of human beings: she nurtures but can also be implacable and merciless when riled. She is paired with Our Lady of Regla, patron saint of the port of Havana. Several of the *orishas* are of indeterminate gender and may change sex according to circumstance. Changó, one of the fundamental *or-*

ishas, is identified with a female saint (Barbara) despite his association with traditionally masculine roles as a warrior, drinker, womanizer, and daredevil. His brother Oggún (St. Peter), still worshipped widely in West Africa, represents telluric energy and governs all activities involving the use of iron. Another androgynous god, Obbatalá (Our Lady of Mercy), represents truth, peace, and justice. The severe female god Oyá (St. Teresa) reigns over death, wind, and lightning, and cares for the dead. She is closely associated with Changó, who occasionally disguises himself as Oyá. Ochún (Our Lady of Charity) is the counterpart of Changó, displaying all the characteristics considered essentially feminine.

There are now some thirty *orishas* in Cuban *Santería*, pared down from the original Yoruba pantheon, which numbered hundreds of deities. Others have arisen from non-Yoruba sources, including Bantu culture and Catholicism. All are considered ancestors who have become divine, indicating the fundamental role of family and lineage in *Santería*.

Music and dance are crucial elements of *Santería* worship, facilitating the evocation of *orishas* and their possession of worshippers. Drumming sessions, known as *bembe* in the Lucumi language, are held to evoke an *orisha* with his or her own particular rhythms. The possessed are familiar with the deity's habits and are able involuntarily to reproduce them. The sacred *batá* drum, brought out only in sunlight, is indispensable to these rituals. The other musical element is singing, particularly by the *akpwon*, who knows the prayers for all the *orishas* and is able to lead a session of followers. There is a close link among musicians, dancers, and the lead singer, who are conceived of as a whole and whose contributions combine as one single expression.

Another important part of *Santería* practice is divination, performed either with *obi* (coconuts split into four parts), by means of seashells in a system known as *diloggún*, or using a complex set of configurations called the *Tablero de Ifá*. The *babalaos* or *santeros*, high priests who originally introduced these systems, are the prominent figures in the divination process. Central figures in the *Santería* hierarchy, they oversee all other ceremonies and initiations. Sacrifice or propitiation (*ebó*) is also essential, and each *orisha* has preferred foods or animal sacrifices. There are also colors associated with each one, seen in the necklaces or *elekes* worn by followers.

The fact that it has survived discrimination and occasional persecution throughout Cuban history is a testament to its persuasive force. Today *Santería* has been accepted, though in diluted forms, even among the nation's white population. It is also evident in some of the mainstream culture emanating from the island: in the 1992 novel *Dreaming in Cuban* by the Cuban-American writer Cristina García, numerous white characters are influenced by a *santero*'s advice and predictions. An example in music is the jazz pianist Omar Sosa's 2001 album *Sentir* (*Feeling*), and in film, Tomás Gutiérrez Alea's *Guantanamera* (1994). *Santería* is still practiced by new generations of Cubans. Although the original Yoruba elements are fading, the survival of this Afro-Cuban religion, and the music associated with it, appears assured.

—*Keith Richards*

See also: *Introduction; Popular Cinema:* The Film Industry and Box-Office Successes in

Cuba; *Popular Religion and Festivals: Candomblé*

Bibliography

Atwood Mason, Michael. 2002. *Living Santería: Rituals and Experiences in an Afro-Cuban Religion.* Washington, DC: Smithsonian Institute.

Barnet, Miguel. 2001. *Afro-Cuban Religions.* Princeton, NJ: Markus Wiener.

González Wippler, Migene. 1999. *Santería: Mis experiencias en la religión.* St. Paul, MN: Llewellyn.

Candomblé

An Afro-Brazilian religion that originated among the slaves taken from the Dahomey and Yoruba regions of what is today southwest Nigeria, *Candomblé* first emerged as a religious practice in around 1830. Today it is practiced mainly in the city of Salvador in the state of Bahia. Its most important deity or god, known as an *orixá*, is Oxalá. This religion shares its origins with *Santería*, the Afro-Cuban religion.

Candomblé began as an expression of resistance to slavery. The African slaves brought to Brazil belonged to a variety of different religious belief systems, but their Portuguese masters forced them to convert to Christianity upon arrival in the colony. In order to preserve their beliefs, the slaves made associations between their own religious figures and icons and the Catholic God and saints that they were obliged to worship—or to seem to worship. This system of associations gave rise to what is often referred to polemically as a syncretic belief system that combines elements of Catholicism and African religious practices. Oxalá, for example, is considered to be the equivalent of the Christian God, and the sea goddess, Iemanjá (sometimes written Yemanjá), is directly associated with the Virgin Mary. The iconography of *Candomblé* today directly reflects this idea of syncretism or at least parallel association. The *orixá* Oxossi, for example, is associated with St. George and is depicted as a hunter connected with the forest. Iemanjá is depicted with both the face of the Virgin Mary and the body of a mermaid. Iansã (or Yansan) is syncretized with St. Barbara and associated with the color red.

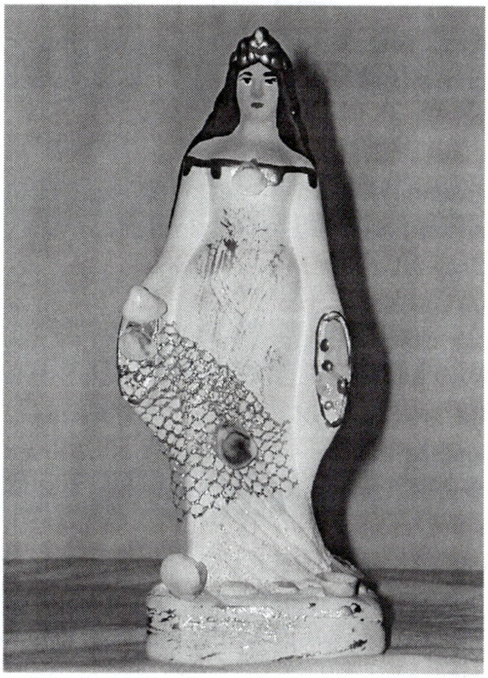

A statue of Iemanjá, the *Candomblé* and *Umbanda* deity who combines elements of both the Virgin Mary and a mermaid. (Courtesy of Alex Nield)

Each *orixá* has his or her own special day (equivalent to the saints' days of Catholicism), on which he or she is honored and appeased. Each is associated with a particular color, symbol, song, dance, and type of food, all of which feature in the ceremony held on that day. Oxossi's preferred foods are boiled yellow corn mixed with coconut, yams, and black beans, and his color is turquoise blue. Iansã's favorite food is a fried cake of ground black-eyed peas (*acarajé*) and cooked okra cut into circles (*caruru*). Each follower of *Candomblé* has his or her own personal *orixá* who appears to him or her every week and to whom he or she must pay tribute on a weekly basis. Exú is the messenger of the *orixás*, the means of making contact with them. It is believed that he sometimes makes mischief and so must be appeased before the deities will come to earth. His favorite food is *farofa* (roast manioc flour) and a glass of water or *cachaça* (a kind of rum made from sugarcane).

The place of worship is called a *terreiro*, and the religious leaders are known as *pais-de-santo* or *mães-de-santo* (literally fathers or mothers of the saints). It is the *mães-de-santo* or priestesses who hold the positions of greater power and prestige. They are ordained in a ceremony that involves shaving their heads and smearing them with the blood of hens or goats. Chicken feathers are then stuck to their foreheads. This ceremony is accompanied by the beating of *atabaque* drums and chanting in African languages. The priestesses dance frenetically until the new *mãe-de-santo* falls into a trance. Spirit possession or a trancelike state is the crucial mechanism of *Candomblé*. In the public ceremonies, called *toques*, animals are often sacrificed (Iansã's preferred sacrifices, for example, are nanny goat, hen, and guinea fowl). Songs are sung in Nagô, the Yoruban language, from which terms are taken to describe the different hierarchical positions within this religion. As each *orixá* or deity is honored in a ceremony, his followers (known as *filhas-* or *filhos-de-santo*, literally daughters or sons of the saints) fall into a trance as their particular *orixá* enters their body. When the followers are possessed by the spirit of the *orixá*, they retire, returning to the central area of the *terreiro* wearing the clothes and adornments associated with their deity.

Candomblé provides a closed, alternative society with its own hierarchy, and thus appeals to the marginalized poor, largely of mixed race. The priestesses preserve the oral history of the Afro-Brazilian community by reciting the names of their ancestors and those of other worshippers, and describing how their forebears were transported to Brazil in slave ships. This information is passed on to newly ordained priestesses to ensure that cultural memory is preserved.

—*Lisa Shaw*

See also: *Sport and Leisure:* Food (Brazilian Food); *Language:* Brazilian Portuguese; *Popular Religion and Festivals: Santería*

Bibliography

Afonjá, Ilé Axé Opô. 1999. "*Iansã* Is Not Saint Barbara." Pp. 408–410 in *The Brazil Reader: History, Culture, Politics*, edited by Robert M. Levine and John J. Crocitti. London: Latin America Bureau.

Rowe, William, and Vivian Schelling. 1991. *Memory and Modernity: Popular Culture in Latin America.* New York and London: Verso.

Silverstein, Leni. 1995. "The Celebration of Our Lord of the Good End: Changing State, Church, and Afro-Brazilian Relations in Bahia." Pp. 134–151 in *The Brazilian Puzzle: Culture on the Borderlands of the Western World*, edited by David J. Hess and Roberto DaMatta. New York: Columbia University Press.

Umbanda

A Brazilian religion that combines elements of European Spiritism (founded by Allan Kardec, 1804–1869) and Catholicism, together with Afro-Brazilian and Amerindian religious beliefs. It is sometimes referred to as *macumba*. Today people practice *Umbanda* to cure illnesses and solve personal problems. For this reason it has been called a form of psychotherapy for the poor. *Umbanda* emerged in the early twentieth century in urban Brazil and is often called the only truly Brazilian religion.

There are dozens of different sects of *Umbanda*, and each is independent within this religion. Followers meet in centers, each known as a *centro* (center), *tenda* (tent), *cabana* (hut), or *terreiro* (yard). Each center is associated with a particular saint, such as Caboclo (an Amerindian spirit) or Pai or Vovó (literally, father or granny, the spirits of African slaves). Caboclo is worshipped with candles, Pai likes cigars, and Vovó smokes a pipe (or at least the mediums who make contact with them do). The possession of mediums by the spirits is the central mechanism of *Umbanda*. The mediums use alcohol and tobacco to aid spirit possession. Followers believe in reincarnation and seek separation of the spirit from the body. *Umbanda* shares some of its terminology (although not always with the same meanings) and icons with *Candomblé*, such as Iemanjá, an amalgam of the Virgin Mary and a mermaid, and Oxalá. The good spirits are known as *orixás* and the evil spirits are called *exús*.

In the 1930s the processes of urbanization and industrialization were beginning to take hold in Brazil under the presidency of Getúlio Vargas (1930–1945). It was a time of great social upheaval, particularly for former Afro-Brazilian slaves and their descendants, who after the abolition of slavery in 1888 moved en masse to the cities, particularly the then federal capital, Rio de Janeiro, in search of work. Finding a belief system of their own became very important for the marginalized and displaced Afro-Brazilians.

In the 1920s and 1930s, *Umbanda* was persecuted by the state, which feared gatherings of disenchanted Afro-Brazilians. It was only given official status in the 1940s, principally to attenuate any threat it posed for inciting racial tensions. The first *Umbanda* congress took place in 1941, and it is said that the religion took its name from the sacred Sanskrit word *Aum-Bandha*, meaning "the divine principle" or "the limit of the unlimited."

—*Lisa Shaw*

See also: *Popular Religion and Festivals: Candomblé*

Bibliography

Brown, Diana Degroat. 1994. *Umbanda: Religion and Politics in Urban Brazil.* New York: Columbia University Press.

Goodman, Felicitas D., Jeannette H. Henney, and Esther Pressel. 1982. *Trance, Healing and Hallucination: Three Field Studies in Religious Experiences.* Huntington, NY: R. E. Krieger.

Indigenous Religious and Cultural Practices

The Andean Countries

As in most areas of Latin America with a deeply rooted native culture and dense population, the Spanish colonizers were able to make only limited inroads into indigenous religion in the Andes. The strength of belief in autochthonous deities was severely tested by the ravages of Conquest and disease in the early sixteenth century, but there followed in 1564 a movement known as Taki Onqoy, or "Dance of Sickness." It invoked regional deities or *wakas* in challenging both the spiritual and political authority of the Europeans. Taki Onqoy aimed to end Spanish rule through a combination of ritual and direct action, by invoking the old gods and mobilizing them against the invader. Its eventual suppression was followed by the first campaigns to wipe out idolatry: these had only limited success but required the Spaniards to understand certain characteristics of the Andean religion they sought to replace.

The result of this shared experience, in which Andeans and Spaniards not only engaged in confrontation but were ultimately obliged to reach some consensus, is the kind of ritual in which both belief systems are honored simultaneously. Variously seen as syncretic, transcultural, or hybrid, such rituals often take place in sites held sacred by indigenous tradition. The Catholic Church traditionally reports an apparition, at or near an indigenous holy site, of a Christian saint, the Virgin, or Christ himself, thus allowing the Church to influence, though by no means transform, the preexisting indigenous event held there.

A prime example of this phenomenon is *Qoyllur Rit'i* ("snow star" in Quechua), held annually at Sinakara in the Ocongate region of southern Peru near Cuzco. The site, some 4,700 meters above sea level and even now difficult to reach, is below the snowcapped peak of Ausangate, an *Apu* or object of ancestral worship. It is believed that, in the late eighteenth century, the infant Christ appeared to an indigenous boy and eventually left behind an image on a stone. A church built to house this image is visited only during the festival, in early June. As Michael Sallnow has shown, the appearance of these "miraculous shrines" constituted a phase of consolidation in the imposition of Christianity and served to link the native worship of natural phenomena with the introduced Christian features and sacred elements. It is also likely that, as often occurred, the "miracle" came at an opportune moment. The great Andean rebellions of the 1780s (Tupac Amaru II in southern Peru and Tupac Katari in the La Paz region) had barely ended, the repression of indigenous culture had been institutionalized, and the reconciliation of the two religious systems might have been seen as politically expedient. The original nature and function of *Qoyllur Rit'i* is, however, still visible. It coincides with the rise of the Pleiades in the southern skies, a fine moment to propitiate deities able to influence harvests.

Visually, however, *Qoyllur Rit'i* is unmistakably an indigenous Andean festival: pilgrims arrive from villages in traditional dress as well as in guises assumed for the event itself, such as *chunchos* (Amazonian peoples) and *ukukus* (bears). The *ukukus*, always personified by young men, have a variety of roles. They police the event, mocking any miscreants in a Quechua delivered in falsetto. They also spend the night on the snowcap, in the morning bringing down the ice. This ice, which is considered sacred, is taken into Cuzco and shared amongst the faithful there. *Qoyllur Rit'i* is today a massive pilgrimage, constantly changing in nature according to the circumstances, and is adopted by white Peruvians as well as natives and those of mixed race, not to mention the increasing number of tourists. It is a prime example of syncretic religious practices in the Andes.

—*Keith Richards*

See also: *Introduction; Language:* Indigenous Languages; *Popular Religion and Festivals:* Popular Catholicism (The Andean Countries); Popular Medicine and Healing (The Andean Countries)

Bibliography

Fleet, Michael. 2001. "Religion in Latin America." Pp. 295–320 in *Understanding Contemporary Latin America*, edited by Richard S. Hillman. Boulder, CO: Lynne Rienner.

MacCormack, Sabine. 1991. *Religion in the Andes: Vision and Imagination in Early Colonial Peru.* Princeton, NJ, and Oxford: Princeton University Press.

Mills, Kenneth. 1997. *Idolatry and Its Enemies: Colonial Andean Religion and Extirpation, 1640–1750.* Princeton, NJ, and Oxford: Princeton University Press.

Sallnow, Michael. 1988. *Pilgrims of the Andes: Regional Cults in Cuzco.* Washington, DC: Smithsonian Institution Press.

Mexico

The cultural and religious practices of the ancient civilizations of Mexico, in particular the Mexica (or Aztecs) and the Maya, are well documented. It is common knowledge, for example, that these peoples undertook vast civil engineering projects to construct ceremonial centers, some still visible today in the form of pyramids; that they had ideographic writing systems and recorded their own history; and that they had advanced knowledge of astronomy and mathematics (the Maya are credited with the invention of the concept of zero, or rather the "place-value" numerical system we use today). They were polytheistic (worshipped many gods); they believed in preprogrammed cyclical transformation and renewal on a social and individual level, and hence viewed death as less of an end than a new beginning; they believed that all things, including rocks, were animate beings that had souls; and most, as has been widely reported, conducted sacrificial rituals that included the offering up of anything from corncobs to small children.

In the five centuries since the Conquest, despite decimation by war and disease, forced conversions to Christianity and Western cultural values, and the gradual process of *mestizaje* (racial mixing between Spaniards and indigenous peoples), there are still millions of indigenous people living in Mexico, divided into over thirty different ethnic groups defined by factors such as territory, culture, and language. Many indigenous people still do not speak Spanish fluently and many still continue religious practices that predate the Conquest. Nevertheless, almost all indigenous groups have, by now, been influenced by Catholicism, and indigenous cultural and religious practices are best perceived through the prism of the colonizers' culture and religion. In some Catholic churches, such as that in San Juan Chamula, Chiapas, all the pews have been removed, and the local Tzotziles kneel on pine needles strewn on the floor, light candles and incense, pray to their *santos*, sleep, eat, and drink. Today, they even use Coca-Cola to burp out evil spirits. Catholic priests are used only to provide the odd service; otherwise, the practices of these Tzotziles are almost entirely pre-Columbian in nature. The rituals and beliefs of faith healers (*curanderos*) are also infused with elements of Catholic iconography, but those forms of faith healing that aim to cure spiritual rather than physical ailments are perhaps where indigenous religion is at its purest.

Curanderos also tend to respect the traditional calendrical systems of the ancient civilizations and organize rituals to coincide with them.

Despite the gradual merging of cultures, many indigenous groups are making a concerted effort to preserve their cultural identity by recording their beliefs, their oral history, and their traditional ways of working (agricultural methods or patterns of weaving, for example). By working with institutions such as the Instituto Nacional Indigenista (National Indigenist Institute) they protect their right to be different; in extreme cases, such as the Zapatistas in Chiapas, they rise up in arms. A few groups have had less contact than others with Spanish culture (often because of the difficult access to their territories) and continue to live and work as their ancestors did. Such is the case of the Lacandón group in southern Chiapas. This very small group of people has never been Christianized and continues to practice essentially the religion of the ancient Maya.

—Thea Pitman

See also: *Introduction; Popular Social Movements and Politics:* Zapatismo; *Language:* Indigenous Languages; *Popular Religion and Festivals:* Indigenous Religious and Cultural Practices (Guatemala); New Protestantism (Mexico and Central America); Popular Catholicism (Mexico and Central America); Popular Festivals (Mexico); Popular Medicine and Healing (Mexico and Central America); *Visual Arts and Architecture:* Art (Religious Folk Art)

Bibliography

Benítez, Fernando. 1989. *Los indios de México: Antología.* Mexico City: Era.

Bonfil Batalla, Guillermo. 1996. *México profundo: Reclaiming a Civilization.* Austin: University of Texas Press.

Carrasco, David. 1990. *Religions of Mesoamerica.* San Francisco: Harper and Row.

Green, Duncan. 1997. "Race against Time: Indigenous Peoples." Pp. 183–200 in *Faces of Latin America,* by Duncan Green. London: Latin America Bureau.

Sullivan, Lawrence E., ed. 2002. *Native Religions and Cultures of Central and South America: Anthropology of the Sacred.* New York: Continuum.

Wauchope, Robert, ed. 1969. *Handbook of Middle American Indians.* 16 vols. Austin: University of Texas Press.

Guatemala

Within Guatemala, a country where an estimated 56 percent of the population are *mestizo* (of mixed Amerindian and Spanish origin) and 44 percent are predominantly Amerindian, indigenous religions are widely practiced. Guatemala's Indians are the modern-day descendants of the great Mayan civilizations, and their communities are for the most part concentrated in the western highlands. However, what may be termed Guatemala's "indigenous community" is very diverse. At least twenty different Mayan languages are spoken, and the various communities range in size from some groups with fewer than 5,000 members to others with up to 80,000.

Until the mid-twentieth century many Mayan communities remained outside the scope of the Catholic Church in terms of religion. Instead, a dual system has arisen, whereby a local Catholic church exists alongside a parallel system of "shaman-diviners" outside the Church who help out the people with their concerns over crops, health, and personal problems.

As a whole, Mayan religious and cultural practices are centered on the principle of living in tune with nature and a spiritual connection to the land. A variety of rituals are performed, the most important of which are those related to the sowing and cultivation of maize, rituals that have existed since the time of the ancient Maya. These rituals involve a night vigil before the day of sowing the seed and a ritual at the moment of harvest to thank the land for providing the crop. Other rituals include that of "house feeding," a ceremony that takes place when a house has just been built. Friends, relatives, and other villagers are invited to a meal that is presided over by the *pasawink*, or elder of the village.

Interestingly, within these popular practices are frequent syncretic elements that combine indigenous traditions with the symbols of Catholicism. Siebers notes that the cross, for instance, is frequently used in indigenous communities during the ritual of the sowing of the maize, and that this has a dual meaning: on the one hand, the cross refers to the Christian cross and Christ's death; on the other, it represents the concept of the four corners of the universe within Mayan belief, and also the spirit of the maize. In this way, the indigenous groups integrate different religious elements and practices into their lives and culture.

The percentage of Guatemalans who consider themselves followers of indigenous religion is very low: according to U.S. government statistics, only 1 percent of the population describe themselves as practitioners of traditional Mayan religions, with the majority describing themselves as Roman Catholics. However, many elements of Mayan religion have been incorporated into popular Catholicism within Guatemala. Wilson, who carried out extensive research with Mayas in the province of Alta Verapaz, found that the traditional Mayan rituals of fertility and healing are once again gaining in popularity. He describes how this ethnic revivalist movement was led by Catholic lay activists, who encouraged a renovation of the "earth cult" in an attempt to create a new ethnic identity. In this way, just as popular indigenous practices contain elements of Christian symbolism, so too has the Catholicism practiced in Guatemala taken on a variety of elements from indigenous beliefs and rituals.

—*Claire Taylor*

See also: *Language:* Indigenous Languages; *Popular Religion and Festivals:* Popular Catholicism (Mexico and Central America); Popular Medicine and Healing (Mexico and Central America)

Bibliography

Marzal, Manuel M., Eugenio Maurer, Xavier Albó, and Bartomeu Melia. 1996. *The Indian Face of God in Latin America.* New York: Orbis.

Siebers, Hans. 1996. "Popular Culture and Development: Religion, Tradition and Modernity among the Q'eqchi'es of Guatemala." *Latin American Studies* 76: 137–158.

Smith, Carol A., ed. 1990. *Guatemalan Indians and the State: 1540 to 1988.* Austin: University of Texas Press.

Wilson, Richard. 1995. *Maya Resurgence in Guatemala: Q'eqchi' Experience.* Norman: University of Oklahoma Press.

Popular Medicine and Healing

Brazil

In Brazil, *curandeiros* (healers) and *benzedeiras* (blessers) are ritual healers who treat various illnesses and problems such as infertility, poverty, and unemployment. They employ a mixture of Catholic symbols and prayers and a special relationship with the supernatural. This is traditionally a female domain, since the majority of problems they deal with are related to the family. *Pajés* (medicine men) are local spirit healers that are consulted by people all over Brazil who do not have access to medical services. Such forms of alternative medicine, which are typically offered free of charge, are naturally very attractive to the poor.

Over the last hundred years or so the hierarchy of the Roman Catholic Church has condemned these practices as pagan traditions and actively sought to suppress them. However, the *benzedeiras* consider themselves an essential part of popular Catholicism in Brazil, and they use prayers and psalms from the Bible to cure many ailments and predicaments. When a person is "cured," he or she has to give gifts to the healer, and a relationship of dependence and obligation is established. These healers have to be obeyed exactly, and their authority over many of their clients is not unlike that of a shaman, an alternative source of power to the Church that is open only to the initiated in the community. Any person with a special *dom* or gift, Spiritist or Catholic, can become a healer. In many ways these practices offer an alternative religious vocation to women, who are denied access to the priesthood and marginalized by the male-dominated medical profession.

The beliefs of the *pajés* are allegedly based on those of the indigenous tribes of Brazil and center on the spirits of dead Indians. These spirits are believed to work mischief and to introduce objects into a person's body to cause illness. The *pajé* has the power to discover what these objects are and how to remove them. Tobacco smoke is used to induce a trance or is blown on the *pajé*'s hands before he passes them over the sufferer. Massages and baths are also given to remove the influence of the spirits. These rituals are very similar to those used in *Umbanda.* The *pajé* can also traditionally perform harmful actions if a client requests this: for example, an egg buried underneath the hammock of one's enemy will, they believe, cause him or her to go blind.

—*Lisa Shaw*

See also: *Popular Religion and Festivals:* Popular Catholicism (Brazil); *Umbanda*

Bibliography

Van den Hoogen, Lisette. 1988. "Benzedeiras within the Catholic Tradition of Minas Gerais." Pp. 177–193 in *Social Change in Contemporary Brazil,* edited by Geert Banck and Kees Koonings. Amsterdam: Centre for Latin American Research and Documentation.

The Andean Countries

The Andean region has a rich and varied tradition in healing. Like most areas of indigenous culture in the Americas, it was repressed by European colonizers quick to associate the unknown with devil-worship. However, since the 1980s official attitudes have changed. In 1984 Bolivia became the first Latin American country to officially accept indigenous medical practices, which in any case are often the only recourse for remote or impoverished communities.

A particularly famous example of Andean medicine is that of the Kallawaya people who live to the north of La Paz. They are renowned herbalists who reputedly treated the Inca nobility and have long been itinerant healers; their practice was institutionalized in 1987. Today they are well enough respected and established to be the subject of tourist excursions. Other famous communities of healers can be found in Catacaos, near Piura in coastal Peru, Iluman in Ecuador, and among the Kogi of the Colombian Sierra Nevada.

The role of coca in Andean society is controversial due to the leaf's use as a narcotic since the early twentieth century. However, coca use in both diagnosis and healing is an ancestral practice. It is also used in divining, an activity not divorced in the Andean mind from medicine; diagnosis often focuses on the spiritual condition of the patient. Moreover, coca is an important social component that reinforces community relationships and identity. North American and European attempts to suppress coca have contributed to a widespread distrust of Western medicine, giving rise to numerous modern myths no doubt also inspired by rumors of rogue organ transplants and the practice of herbal and gene piracy.

Another widespread Andean practice, if less controversial, involves the use of *cuy*, or guinea pigs, in diagnosis. Here coca is often consumed by the doctor to aid his concentration. Then the animal is rubbed over the patient's body before being opened and its organs examined. A diagnosis of the patient is then made. Such practices must be seen as elements of an overall cosmology and of a complex system of interactions between humanity and the natural environment. Traditional medicine is also crucial in the maintenance of trade and reciprocity between neighboring regions.

—*Keith Richards*

See also: *Popular Religion and Festivals:* Indigenous Religious and Cultural Practices (The Andean Countries); Popular Catholicism (The Andean Countries)

Bibliography

Allen, Catherine. 1988. *The Hold Life Has: Coca and Cultural Identity in an Andean Community.* London: Smithsonian Institution Press.

Koss-Chioino, Joan, Thomas Leatherman, and Christine Greenway, eds. 2002. *Medical Pluralism in the Andes.* London: Routledge.

Morales, Edmundo. 1995. *The Guinea Pig: Healing, Food and Ritual in the Andes.* Tucson: University of Arizona Press.

Revista Medica. www.revistamedica.8m.com/histomed130.htm (consulted September 2003).

Ventura i Oller, Montserrat. 2001. "Chamanismo y redes de intercambio en el Ecuador contemporáneo." *Revista GeoNotas* 5, no. 2. Online journal attached to the Website of the Department of Geography, State University of Maringá. www.dge.uem.br//geonotas/vol5–2/ventura.shtml (consulted September 2003).

Mexico and Central America

Popular medicine in Mesoamerica covers a wide range of practices, some of which deal with the curing of identifiable physical ailments and conditions, such as a broken leg or pregnancy. Others concern culturally specific, often emotional ailments such as *susto* (fright) and *mal de ojo* (the effects of the evil eye), or are of a more spiritual order such as the loss of one's soul, moral dilemmas, or those ailments thought to be caused by the ill effects of sorcery. In all cases the approach is far more holistic than that offered by traditional Western medicine, and almost all cures combine practical solutions (medicinal infusions, etc.) with prayer, ritual, and psychological support. Rituals involve such activities as the sacrifice of chickens and other small animals, the use of incense, blowing or spraying the patient's body with liquids, and passing objects such as eggs and plants over the body.

Practitioners who deal with a wide range of ailments, especially those pertaining to the spirit, are referred to by the overlapping terms of *curanderos/as* (curers, faith healers), *chamanes* (shamans), and/or *brujos/as* (witch doctors). Many other terms used to designate *curanderos* are specific to certain regions and ethnic groups, such as *sukias* in Nicaragua and *h'men* in the Mayan Yucatan. Many of these healers, specifically shamans, invoke the supernatural world via trancelike states (often provoked by the ingestion of hallucinogenic drugs such as *peyote* or magic mushrooms) and then journey into the supernatural realm with the aid of a "spirit helper," who often takes the form of an animal such as a coyote.

Curanderos may be either male or female, although across Mesoamerica there is a tendency for purely spiritual healing to be done by men (with this position go social prestige, civic authority, and even special dress codes and artifacts), and for the forms of physical healing done with medicinal plants and prayers, especially those associated with gynecological issues and childbirth, to be the preserve of women. Most *curanderos* assume their role as a hereditary duty after a long apprenticeship. However, many female *curanderas* begin their healing activities on the death of or abandonment by their husband in order to make a living and have a valued place in their community.

Since the time of the Conquest indigenous *curanderos* have experienced persecution for their beliefs and practices. Even in the twentieth century, state health-care workers across the region were at pains to eradicate *curanderismo* in favor of Western medical science. Nevertheless, *curanderos* are an essential part of the makeup of most Mesoamerican indigenous communities, closely entwined with popular Catholicism. In rural regions they easily outnumber state health-care workers. Furthermore, the relationship of trust between patient and *curandero* is much greater than that between patient and health-care worker, and this promotes the use of *curanderos* and even their ability to provide effective cures (faith alone can help heal). Even among the urban *mestizo* (mixed-race) populations of the region, *curanderismo* has not been totally supplanted by Western medicine. For example, *limpias* or *barriadas* (ritual cleansings) are still popular, cheap, and easy.

In more recent years, the countries of Central America have attempted to utilize the knowledge of *curanderos* and to license them as practitioners rather than outlaw the practice altogether. Indigenous *parteras* (midwives) have been legalized in El Salvador, and *curanderos* may obtain licenses in Guatemala. Furthermore, health-care workers have been encouraged to cooperate with *parteras* and *curanderos* so that their healing integrates elements of Western medicine and so that, in certain cases, patients can be referred to state health-care workers when their complaints fall beyond the realms of the faith healers.

—*Thea Pitman*

See also: *Popular Religion and Festivals:* Indigenous Religious and Cultural Practices (Guatemala; Mexico); Popular Catholicism (Mexico and Central America); Popular Festivals (Mexico)

Bibliography

Castañeda, Carlos. 1968. *The Teachings of Don Juan: A Yaqui Way of Knowledge.* Berkeley: University of California Press.

Dow, James W. 1986. *The Shaman's Touch: Otomí Indian Symbolic Healing.* Salt Lake City: University of Utah Press.
Huber, Brad R., and Alan R. Sandstrom, eds. 2001. *Mesoamerican Healers.* Austin: University of Texas Press.
Rowe, William, and Vivian Schelling. 1991. *Memory and Modernity: Popular Culture in Latin America.* London: Verso, pp. 68–74.
Trotter, Robert T., II, and Juan Antonio Chavira. 1981. *Curanderismo: Mexican-American Folk Healing.* Athens: University of Georgia Press.

Santo Daime

A religious cult founded in the Amazon at the turn of the twentieth century, based on the ritual, communal consumption of an infusion of herbs. *Santo Daime* was made popular from the 1980s onward by the large number of Brazilian celebrities who have adhered to its doctrines.

The inspiration for *Santo Daime* (or the Eclectic Cult of Fluid Universal Light, to give it its formal title) came from Mestre Raimundo Irineu Serra (otherwise known as *Rei* or King Juramidã), a rubber tapper and son of black slaves who learned about the healing properties of Amazonian plants from Peruvian Indians. It is said that on drinking for the first time one particularly potent mixture, *ayahuasca,* a blend of the *jagube* liana (*Banesteriopsis caapi*) and the *rainha* leaf (*Psicotrya viridis*) that supposedly has been around since the days of the Incas, Serra received a visitation from the Virgin Mary. Thereafter, every time he consumed the tea (which he named *Santo Daime*), he would receive prayers that later would form the basis of the cult's worship.

Having started out as little more than a backwoods shaman, Serra would go on to establish a church and community in the rainforest where followers would live together in harmony with each other and with nature, combining periods of work, silence, and meditation with the drinking of tea on set feast days. These days consist of twelve hours of chanting and dancing to the rhythm of maracas around a six-pointed star, with the express purpose of becoming closer to God and learning about oneself.

The notions of fraternity, community spirit, and love of nature, so dear to the movement, along with the speedy arrival at a state of transcendence afforded by the *Santo Daime* tea itself, drew the attention of Brazilian hippies in the 1970s, who took Serra's teachings, and his drink, to other parts of the country. In the 1980s, government investigations concluded that there was nothing untoward taking place within the Church and that followers of *Santo Daime* were not drug addicts. A number of critics of *Santo Daime* have argued that governments have continued to turn a blind eye to the drug-taking in these communities because they can count on the support of the powerful environmental lobby, of a number of senators representing the northern states, and even of some Catholic bishops.

Several high-profile stars from television and the music industry became involved with the movement in the 1980s, such as the popular composer Peninha, singer-songwriter Ney Matogrosso, actress Maitê Proença, and most significantly, the *telenovela* (soap opera) superstar Lucélia Santos, who temporarily gave up her television and film career to live in one of the Church's remote communities.

The espousal of values such as the protection of vegetation, along with the

Church's charity work to aid the environment, has recently attracted people from all over the world, both New Age ecotourists and people seeking alternative systems of belief, to the headquarters in Céu do Mapiá in Amazonas state. As well as having established a number of churches throughout Brazil (most in rural areas traditionally associated with Brazil's hippie population), *Santo Daime* has traveled to Europe and the United States where, according to the movement's official Website, there are ten churches. With the exception of Spain, where the use of the infusion in recognized religious rituals has recently been made legal, followers abroad are obliged to celebrate in secret, and transporters of *Santo Daime* tea to locations outside Brazil have been given prison sentences for drug trafficking.

—*Stephanie Dennison*

See also: *Travel and Tourism:* Ecotourism; *Mass Media:* Telenovela (Brazil)

Bibliography

Official Santo Daime Website. www.santodaime.org (consulted September 2003).

Bahá'í

A faith that was founded in 1844 along universalist principles by the Bahá'u'lláh, the title of the Persian mystic Mirzá Husayn Ali (1817–1892). It first made its mark on Latin America in the late 1930s, in Mexico and Central America, entering most of South America a few years later. Today it is the third most popular organized religion in many Latin American countries after Catholicism and Protestantism. The appeal of this religion, with its accent on global unity, lies in its rejection of discrimination on grounds of ethnicity, gender, or social background.

Bahá'í, which has neither dogma nor priesthood, proposes a noncentralized faith in which all creeds can converge and share both differences and similarities. The emphasis upon unity is manifested in the faith's temples, which are circular, intimating the deliberate exclusion of any geographical focal point or place of origin such as Mecca or Jerusalem. This philosophy is applied in practical terms in communities with differing faiths: *Bahá'í* meetings begin with prayers from members of all religions represented.

Bahá'í is clearly attractive to those seeking an alternative atmosphere, social as well as spiritual, in societies with entrenched chauvinist attitudes and where discrimination on the basis of gender, ethnicity, or beliefs is all but institutionalized (the advancement of women is a notably high priority in all *Bahá'í* literature). In Bolivia, where a high proportion of followers are from indigenous communities, *Bahá'í* works to implement social benefits, raising funds for projects such as educational facilities, without the apparent self-promotion and paternalism associated with more entrenched religions. The results are apparent both at grassroots and central levels: in remote villages, where the possibility of extending local education into high school has been achieved, and in a city like Santa Cruz, where the influential *Bahá'í*-inspired Nur University runs a program to train teachers to serve the entire Andean region.

Radio has also been a successful tool for *Bahá'í*, raising its profile in Latin America while facilitating communication among rural communities. The world's first *Bahá'í* radio station, in the Otavalo region of Ecuador, was set up as a means of enabling contact between members but eventually took on a far broader role. The realization of the potential of indigenous communities, within the context of the modern nation, became central to its aims, and the station has enjoyed considerable success. Conserving Andean cultural traditions has been one of its main achievements, though it also promotes numerous social projects.

Bahá'í has formal associations with the United Nations and with many nongovernmental organizations such as UNIDA (*Unidad en Diversidad*, or Unity in Diversity), a group that responds to the political crisis in Argentina via training programs aimed at providing models for participatory development and the fortification of civil society.

Of the estimated 7 million or so *Bahá'í* followers worldwide, there are an estimated 57,000 members in Brazil and 300,000 in Bolivia. Of the seven worldwide *Bahá'í* temples, one is in Latin America (Panama) and a second is currently under construction in Chile.

—*Keith Richards*

See also: *Mass Media:* Radio (Cuba and the Andes)

Bibliography

Bahá'í Official Website. www.bahai.org (consulted September 2003).

Hein, Kurt John. 1988. *Radio Bahá'í Ecuador: A Bahá'í Development Project.* Oxford: George Ronald.

Lamb, Artemus. 1995. *The Beginnings of the Bahá'í Faith in Latin America: Some Remembrances.* http://www.bahai-library.org/books/latinamerica.lamb.html (consulted September 2003).

New Protestantism

Mexico and Central America

The Protestant faith, particularly the newer branches (as opposed to traditional Anglicanism or Lutheranism), has witnessed a boom in popularity in Mexico and Central America since the 1970s, both in rural areas and in poor neighborhoods in urban areas, and in particular among the substantial indigenous populations of these countries (i.e., the poorest sectors of society). Statistics show that growth has been particularly large in Honduras and Guatemala since the mid-1980s (7 percent and 6 percent respectively of the populations of these countries converted to Protestantism over the period 1985–1995). Mexico, the most populous country in Central America, has the highest number of Protestants, around 5.5 million in 1995, despite a slower rate of growth of the Protestant community.

Unlike the original split in Europe between the Catholic and Protestant Churches, the split in Mexico and Central America was not based on a clash over doctrine. Much of the "new" Protestantism in the region is evangelical in nature, and hence sets itself up in opposition to all other religions, including other branches of Protestantism.

Community health workers in Chiapas, southern Mexico, have noted that indigenous women prefer a religion that allows them to use contraception, and that in general, women find that the Protestant Church offers them a more active role than that available to them in the male-dominated Catholic Church. It has been argued that indigenous communities also use Protestantism as a way of showing their dissent from the impositions of the

Catholic-oriented nation-states by which they are governed. Other theorists suggest that concerted missionary activity from abroad, the experience of rapid modernization, and/or large-scale demographic change (migration to big cities or to other countries), coupled with the dismemberment of traditional social structures and cultural practices, have created a spiritual gap that Protestantism has filled.

One of the most compelling explanations put forward is that economic change, and in particular the advance of the market economy into parts of the world where people have previously been unaffected by its logic, is the root cause of the surge in popularity of New Protestantism in the region. In traditional, indigenous communities—in the highlands of Guatemala, for example—a "cargo system" is still in place. This system, intimately related to the Catholic calendar, is a way of redistributing wealth for the benefit of the whole community by designating individual community members to be in charge of organizing and financing specific festivals. However, this practice stands in direct opposition to the concept of a market economy where the individual seeks to make and retain profits for the benefit of his/her own family. Protestantism, with its concept of a "work ethic," provides the religious background to support the logic of the market economy and is hence making dramatic in-roads in parts of the region where the market economy is not yet fully in place. Nevertheless, such widespread conversions to Protestantism have not gone unopposed, and there is substantial disharmony recorded in the indigenous communities of Chiapas, Mexico, for example, between breakaway Protestant groups and those members of the same indigenous group who have chosen to remain Catholics.

—Thea Pitman

See also: *Popular Social Movements and Politics:* Zapatismo; *Popular Religion and Festivals:* New Protestantism (Brazil; Venezuela); Popular Catholicism (Mexico and Central America)

Bibliography

Dow, James W., and Alan R. Sandstrom, eds. 2001. *Holy Saints and Fiery Preachers: The Anthropology of Protestantism in Mexico and Central America.* Westport, CT: Praeger.

Fleet, Michael. 1997. "Religion in Latin America." Pp. 295–320 in *Understanding Contemporary Latin America,* edited by Richard S. Hillman. Boulder, CO: Lynne Rienner.

Green, Duncan. 1997. "Thy Kingdom Come: The Church." Pp. 201–215 in *Faces of Latin America,* by Duncan Green. London: Latin America Bureau.

Martin, David. 1990. *Tongues of Fire: The Explosion of Protestantism in Latin America.* Oxford: Blackwell.

Stoll, David. 1990. *Is Latin America Turning Protestant?: The Politics of Evangelical Growth.* Berkeley: University of California Press.

Venezuela

The evangelical presence in Venezuela's capital city, Caracas, is low-key in comparison with Brazil's main cities, but the systematic promotion of New Protestantism is actively under way. The best-known evangelical phenomenon in Caracas is the independent Las Acacias Pentecostal Church.

In the 1990s, about half of Venezuela's 325,000 Protestants could be found in six churches: Assemblies of God, Light of the World, OVICE (Venezuelan Organization of Evangelical Christian Churches), Peniel, the National Baptist Convention, and the Presbyterian Church. The first two churches are

Pentecostal, and the second two are of the Free Church tradition.

With the exception of the Baptists and the Presbyterians, the mainstream Protestant churches have had relatively little presence in Venezuela. A survey carried out in 1992 found that the 231 Protestant churches in Caracas had a total membership of 31,000 people, which represented just over 1 percent of the 3 million people in the area surveyed. As low as this figure is, it is important to remember that Catholic practice is on the decline. It has been estimated that 6 percent of the inhabitants of Caracas attend mass on any given Sunday and that this percentage falls to just 2 or 3 percent in poorer areas.

The history of Protestantism in Venezuela dates from the early nineteenth century, when itinerant Bible salesmen passed through the country. The first congregations in Caracas were established in the 1870s. For decades, however, missionaries were attracted more to rural areas, and virtually no Protestant congregations were founded in the capital city until the 1940s and 1950s. Many of these first-generation church leaders were still active in the 1990s.

—*Lisa Shaw*

See also: *Popular Religion and Festivals:* New Protestantism (Brazil; Mexico and Central America)

Bibliography

Berryman, Phillip. 1996. *Religion in the Megacity: Catholic and Protestant Portraits from Latin America.* London: Latin America Bureau.

Brazil

The following Protestant Churches are now represented in many Brazilian cities: the Baptist Church, the Assemblies of God, the Christian Congregation, the Foursquare Gospel Church (which now has more followers in Brazil than in the United States, where it originated), Brazil for Christ, God Is Love, and the Universal Church of the Kingdom of God. For many Brazilians, the Universal Church epitomizes the new brand of Pentecostalism, with "services" akin to television shows and a heavy emphasis on financial contributions from the "audience." Members of other churches worry about the effect of the Universal Church on the image of the Protestant community as a whole. A common misconception holds that the growth of Protestantism is fostered and funded from abroad, but it is the Brazilian churches that are expanding the fastest.

The rapid rise of evangelical Protestantism in Brazil can be explained in part by the failure of Liberation Theology to provide spiritual solace for the impoverished masses. Following the Vatican's decision, taken in 1989, to carve up the archdiocese of São Paulo arbitrarily, the poor central districts of the city were increasingly neglected by the Catholic Church, allowing the evangelicals to gain a foothold.

Like Brazil for Christ and God Is Love, the Universal Church of the Kingdom of God, established in 1977, revolves around its founder, Edir Macedo. By 1990 the organization had 700 churches and claimed to have 500,000 members. In that year it bought a television station in São Paulo for 45 million U.S. dollars. Macedo obviously appealed to mass audiences. One morning in September 1990 he drew 150,000 people to a stadium in Rio de Janeiro and then caught a plane to São Paulo, where he addressed a crowd of 50,000. Like soccer fans, many of them carried banners, includ-

Edir Macedo, the infamous founder of Brazil's Universal Church of the Kingdom of God. (Ted Soqui/Corbis Sygma)

ing one that read: "Pele, the king of soccer, has gone, and Jesus, the king of kings, has arrived." There have been reports of bizarre and disturbing events at these gatherings. On one occasion, for example, Macedo promised to cure people's eyesight. Hundreds of pairs of spectacles were handed over to him, which he promptly trampled on.

—*Lisa Shaw*

See also: *Popular Religion and Festivals:* New Protestantism (Mexico and Central America; Venezuela); Popular Catholicism (Brazil)

Bibliography

Berryman, Phillip. 1996. *Religion in the Megacity: Catholic and Protestant Portraits from Latin America.* London: Latin America Bureau.

Popular Festivals

Colombia

One of the most important popular festivals within the Andean region of Colombia is the *Aguinaldo Boyacense,* the period of celebration held in the Boyacá region in the last few days before Christmas. The *Carnaval de Barranquilla* (Barranquilla Carnival), which takes place in the city of Barranquilla on the northern coast of Colombia, traces its roots back over several centuries. It has links with the black slave celebrations that took place in nearby Cartagena de Indias in colonial times. While *Semana Santa,* or Holy Week, is important throughout Colombia, the place that is most famous for this celebration is Popayán in the southwestern part of Colombia.

The Aguinaldo Boyacense festival lasts from 16 to 23 December each year. Games for children and a variety of sporting events or competitions, such as tennis, cycling, and chess, are held throughout the day and into the night. The afternoon activities are dominated by the *novena* or religious service; in the early evening the main attractions are the processions, which often include decorated *carrozas* (carnival floats). The *carrozas* are created by a variety of local entities, including schools, churches, local companies, and the police force, and prizes are awarded for the best float. Finally, once the processions are over, a lively, open-air concert is held in the main square, the Plaza Bolívar. Every night at least three bands perform into the small hours, playing salsa, *vallenato,* or even *car-*

Women in costume dance in the street during carnival, Barranquilla, Colombia, 1994. (Jeremy Horner/Corbis)

ranguera, the local folk music of the Boyacá region. The concert usually includes at least one big national name, such as Los Tupamaros, who performed there in 2002.

From the mid- to late nineteenth century the Carnaval de Barranquilla proper started to take shape. Now the carnival takes place over four days, starting on Saturday and ending the day before Ash Wednesday. Over the four days, a variety of events are staged: on the opening Saturday is the *Batalla de flores* (Battle of the Flowers), an event that memorializes the civil war that Colombia endured between 1899 and 1903, the *Guerra de Mil Días* (War of a Thousand Days), and that functions as a tribute to peace. During this event, a large procession makes its way through the city, with carnival queens, dancers, and floats, all decorated with flowers. Sunday is taken up with the *Gran Parada* (Big Parade), which concentrates on folk, indigenous, and black forms of music and dance, including *cumbia*, *mapalé*, and *son*. On the Monday, the *Festival de Orquestas* (Festival of Bands) takes place, during which national and international bands play salsa and the obligatory *vallenato* to crowds in the Romelio Martínez stadium. The last day of the carnival is dominated by the tradition known as the *Muerte de Joselito* (Death of Joselito). Legend has it that Joselito was a coachman who drank so much that he fell asleep in his coach; to tease him, the carnival-goers decided to put him in a coffin and carry him to the cemetery, amid great wailing and mourning. Every year this prank is reenacted, with the crowd carrying a coffin and crying over "Joselito" as they process through the streets.

Holy Week in Popayán is marked by solemn processions throughout the week, as well as the *Festival de Música Religiosa* (Festival of Religious Music), which attracts choirs and orchestras from all over the world. The celebrations consist of six processions: one during the day on Palm Sunday to represent Christ's triumphal arrival in Jerusalem, and five at night, from Tuesday to Thursday, which represent the passion, death, and burial of Christ. The final procession takes place on Saturday to celebrate Christ's resurrection. During these processions, images carried on platforms are decorated with candles and a different color of flowers each day, leading up to the final celebration on Saturday, in which multicolored flowers symbolize joy at the resurrection.

—*Claire Taylor*

See also: *Popular Music:* Cumbia; Salsa; Vallenato; *Popular Religion and Festivals:* Popular Festivals (Carnival in Brazil; Mexico)

Bibliography

Harding, Colin. 1995. *Colombia: A Guide to the People, Politics and Culture.* London: Latin America Bureau.

Samper Martínez, Diego. 1994. *Carnaval caribe: Exploración del carnaval de Barranquilla Colombia.* Quito: Andes Editores.

Williams, Raymond L. 1999. *Culture and Customs of Colombia.* Westport: Greenwood Press.

Mexico

Mexico celebrates a huge variety of *fiestas populares* (popular festivals) that attract visitors from all over the world. Its carnival is the third biggest in the world, after those of Rio de Janeiro and New Orleans. Many of the festivals are based on the events of the Roman Catholic calendar (saints' days, *posadas* or pre-Christmas processions, Easter week celebrations, and reenactments of the crucifixion), though some may have been superimposed over older pre-Columbian festival days and ritual practices. Others are purely civic celebrations designed to reaffirm a sense of national pride (for example, *El Grito de Independencia* or Independence Day and *El Día de la Raza* or Mexico Day). Still others, which celebrate the culture or the artifacts of a particular place, have been developed by the Mexican government and the tourist industry as a way of promoting trade and tourism (for example, the Silver Fair in Taxco). The concept of the *fiesta popular* really applies only to the first category of festival mentioned. Nevertheless, in contemporary Mexico many of the traditional, popular *fiestas* based on the Roman Catholic calendar have incorporated elements of the more urban-based civic and commercial festivals. This is part of the process of encroaching national and global (capitalist) culture, studied in detail by Néstor García Canclini.

Undoubtedly the most important and the most idiosyncratic of Mexico's popular festivals is *El Día de los Muertos* (The Day of the Dead). The festival dates back to colonial times, although some critics see it as a prime example of the blending of indigenous culture with Spanish Catholic culture (the Mexica are known to have venerated their dead in similar ways using similar iconography). This festival has developed spectacularly since the 1960s and is now an essential part of Mexico's national identity.

Typical skeleton figures used to celebrate Mexico's popular festival the Day of the Dead. (Danny Lehman/Corbis)

The festival of the Day of the Dead stretches over two days, on 1 and 2 November of every year, which correspond to All Saints' Day and All Souls' Day in the Roman Catholic calendar. Traditionally, the departed souls of small children are honored on the first of the two days, and those of adults on the second, and it is usually the second of the two days that is the more exuberant day of the festival. The basic festival consists of several masses. However, *ofrendas* (offerings of food, drink, and other symbolic items for the dead) constructed in people's homes and the candlelit vigil at the graveside of departed relatives on the night of 1 November are the readily identifiable symbols of the festival today. In the run-up to the festival, the *ofrendas* become ubiquitous, more in public places than in private homes, and a vast amount of merchandise is available in shops and markets to decorate *ofrendas*, the graves themselves, or simply to offer as gifts to friends. These items include *pan de muertos* (loaves of bread decorated with crossed bones, which are also made of bread), *calaveras* (skulls made out of sugar or chocolate and brightly decorated), and all sorts of arts and crafts that play on the theme of death. (In recent years, products associated with Halloween have appeared for sale beside them as the two festivals have begun to merge.) Although the death of relatives is still a cause for great sadness among Mexicans, the humor brought to the fore in this festival is remarkable and helps shape the popular view that Mexicans treat death lightly.

—*Thea Pitman*

A reveler shows off his Internet costume during the Rio de Janeiro Carnival in 2000. (Antonio Scorza/AFP/Getty Images)

See also: *Popular Religion and Festivals:* Popular Catholicism (Mexico and Central America); Popular Festivals (Carnival in Brazil; Colombia)

Bibliography

Canclini, Néstor García. 1993. "*Fiesta* and History: To Celebrate, to Remember, to Sell." Pp. 87–104 in *Transforming Modernity: Popular Culture in Mexico*, edited by Néstor García Canclini and translated by Lidia Lozano. Austin: University of Texas Press.

Carmichael, Elizabeth, and Chloë Sayer. 1991. *The Skeleton at the Feast: The Day of the Dead in Mexico.* London: British Museum.

Nutini, Hugo G. 1988. "Pre-Hispanic Component of the Syncretic Cult of the Dead in Mesoamerica." *Ethnology* 27, no. 1: 57–78.

Rosoff Beimler, Rosalind. 1998. *The Days of the Dead/Los días de muertos.* Photography by John Greenleigh. San Francisco: Pomegranate.

Carnival in Brazil

Some form of pre-Lenten celebration (like Mardi Gras in New Orleans) has existed in Brazil since the mid-sixteenth century, after the arrival of the Portuguese in 1500. Today this annual event, held seven weeks before Easter, is most widely associated with the city of Rio de Janeiro, where the so-called *escolas de samba* ("samba schools"), or neighborhood carnival associations, take part in a lavish parade that is screened by satellite all over the world. *Carnaval* is celebrated all over Brazil for four days, from Saturday to Tuesday. Not every city has a street carnival, however; some prefer well-behaved indoor balls.

The musical accompaniment to the carnival processions in Rio de Janeiro is percussion-based samba, provided by a 300-piece drum section or *bateria* from each "samba school." The *marcha carnavalesca* or carnival march provides an alternative rhythm in Rio, favored for indoor balls and by the *bandas*, groups consisting of brass and drums, that pass through Rio's streets with crowds following behind them.

The official celebrations in Rio are held in the purpose-built *Sambódromo* (Sambadrome). Each *escola*'s parade must have a theme or *enredo*, which might be historical or political, or linked to a particular individual. The *carnavalesco*, a kind of art director within each *escola de samba*, chooses the theme, and in June of the previous year the *escola*'s composers begin writing sambas on this theme. The best songs are chosen by the directors of the "school," and around September the rehearsals begin in the headquarters of each organization. On a given night, usually at the end of October, the members choose the winning samba. For the parade, the "school" is divided into units called *alas*, or wings. Each *ala* wears a different costume relating to a specific aspect of the theme. The bigger *escolas* have over sixty *alas*, each containing eighty or so members. Two *alas* are compulsory: one is the *ala das baianas*, older women dressed in the attire of the Afro-Brazilian street vendors of Salvador da Bahia, who wear turbans and long lace dresses (this costume harks back to the Bahian women who first practiced *Candomblé* in Rio, personified by Carmen Miranda in Hollywood); and the *comissão de frente* (literally, front commission), who open the parade by walking or dancing slowly. The main samba dancers are called *passistas*, the most important of whom are the *porta-bandeira* (the flag-bearer, always a woman, who carries the *escola*'s flag) and the *mestre-sala* (master of ceremonies), a man. In between the *alas* come the ornately decorated floats—the *carros alegóricos*—that take around six months to build. On top of the floats stand the *destaques*, men and women wearing either very expensive and elaborate costumes or next to nothing. Another aspect of the city's festivities are the *blocos de empolgação*, great masses of people wearing the same costume that parade in one solid block and dance energetically. The *bloco* called *Cacique de Ramos*, for example, always dress up like Indians, and *Bafo da Onça* (*Jaguar's Breath*) consists of 6,000 to 7,000 members. They dance to the *samba de bloco* played by the *bateria* at the close of the carnival parade in the Sambadrome.

Today Salvador da Bahia in Brazil's northeast vies with Rio to create the most popular carnival in Brazil. Each year an estimated 2 million people crowd into Salvador's narrow streets to dance, sing, and party to the music of the *blocos afro* (Afro-Brazilian carnival groups), *afoxés* (carnival groups that perform music and dance based on *Candomblé* rituals), and *trios elétricos* (musicians playing electrified instruments on top of decorated trucks). In the northeastern states of Bahia, Ceará, and Pernambuco, *frevo*, a fast, syncopated version of the *marcha*, is the main carnival music. In Recife, and Fortaleza in Ceará state, the *maracatu*, an Afro-Brazilian processional dance, is performed during Carnival. Participants sing and dance to a heavy, slow, almost trance-inducing rhythm.

Carnival has its roots in pre-Christian festivities held by the ancient Greeks, Romans, and others. In spite of their pagan origins these festivities were assimilated into the traditions of Roman Catholic countries of Europe. The early carnivals in Brazil were based on a popular festival known as *entrudo*, a tradition that originated in the Azores and became popular in Portugal in the fifteenth and sixteenth centuries. Associated with riotous antics and pranks, the *entrudo* was outlawed in Brazil in 1853 and finally died out at the beginning of the 1900s. In the first years of the twentieth century, three separate carnivals were held in Rio de Janeiro: that of the poor, largely Afro-Brazilian population in the central Praça Onze district of the city; that of the middle classes in the Avenida Central (now the Avenida Rio Branco); and that of the wealthy, white elite, which centered on lavish masked balls. By the 1920s the annual event had become associated with two musical rhythms, the carnival march (*marcha* or *marchinha*), of bourgeois origin and inspired by Portuguese marches that were brought to Brazil with music hall *(teatro de revista)*, and the samba, believed to have grown out of the percussion-based *batuques* and *lundus* performed by African slaves on rural plantations.

The first *escola de samba*, named *Deixa Falar* (*Let Them Talk*), was founded in 1928 in the Rio district of Estácio de Sá by a group of Afro-Brazilian samba composers. The term "samba school" is said to have been an ironic reference to the school across the street from where this marginalized group used to meet. A kind of neighborhood club, *Deixa Falar* was dedicated to making music (samba) and parading during Carnival. It was only in 1935, during the presidency of Getúlio Vargas (1930–1945), that the *escolas de samba* were no longer repressed as manifestations of Afro-Brazilian culture, and their carnival parades were officially recognized. Today Rio's main *escolas de samba* are still associated with particular areas of the city, often one of the hillside shantytowns (*favelas*), and include Mangueira, Portela, and Salgueiro.

—Lisa Shaw

See also: *Popular Music:* Samba; *Popular Theater and Performance:* Popular Theater and Music Hall (*Teatro de Revista*); *Cultural Icons:* Latin Americans in Hollywood (Carmen Miranda); *Popular Cinema:* Youth Movies, Cinema, and Music; *Popular Religion and Festivals: Candomblé*; Popular Festivals (Colombia; Mexico); *Visual Arts and Architecture:* Architecture and Landscape Design (*Favelas*)

Bibliography

Guillermoprieto, Alma. 1991. *Samba.* New York: Vintage Books.

McGowan, Chris, and Ricardo Pessanha. 1998. *The Brazilian Sound: Samba, Bossa Nova and the Popular Music of Brazil.* Philadelphia: Temple University Press.

Teissl, Helmut. 2000. *Carnival in Rio.* New York: Abbeville Press.

13

Visual Arts and Architecture

Art

Until relatively recently the art of twentieth-century Latin America was dismissed by European and North American critics as a pale imitation of the mainstream modernism of the United States and Western Europe. Such critics argued that Latin American art was intrinsically hybrid, an eclectic and sometimes incompatible mix of traditions and styles. Although there is no question that the majority of the most acclaimed artists from Latin America studied abroad or at least participated in wider aesthetic movements, today it is precisely this hybrid quality that is seen as one of the great features of painting and other forms of visual culture produced in Latin America. The racial and ethnic diversity of the region, where Amerindian tribes still coexist with the descendants of Spanish or Portuguese colonizers, of African slaves, and of European, Middle Eastern, or Far Eastern immigrants, has contributed to the vitality and originality of artistic production. Ideas from abroad have been assimilated but creatively adapted to the New World context, breathing new life into established artistic styles. Cubism, for example, influenced many Latin American artists, not least the Cuban Wifredo Lam and the Brazilian Tarsila do Amaral. They adapted the new European style to their local environments, combining it with indigenous sources.

The visual arts in Latin America have related more closely to their sociopolitical context than their European or North American counterparts have traditionally done. The association between the literary avant-garde and visual artists, an association that began in the 1920s when Latin American modernism first formally emerged in the arts as a whole, has tended to raise artists' awareness of social and political problems. This social commitment was reflected in particular in the Mexican muralism of the 1920s and 1930s, still sometimes considered the only "authentic" Latin American art of the twentieth century. Marxist theory has had a powerful influence on artists and their work in many Latin American countries. For example, the Mexican muralist David Alfaro Siqueiros, who served as secretary of the Communist Party of Mexico, combined his artistic career with trade union activities. His political activities resulted in his imprisonment and subsequent exile.

Certain Latin American governments have also been instrumental in commissioning works of art and, notably, for drawing on the talents of avant-garde and potentially controversial artists to carry out major government and other official projects. After the Mexican Revolution (1910–1920), the Mexican government invited three mural painters, Diego Rivera, José Clemente Orozco, and David Alfaro Siqueiros, to decorate a number of government buildings to inspire a sense of national identity. Likewise, in Brazil the highly nationalistic regime of Getúlio Vargas (1930–1945) called upon the services of the muralist Cândido Portinari to similar ends.

Like writers, artists enjoy a privileged position within the consciousness of Latin American nations, where political institutions have traditionally proved ineffectual at forging a sense of belonging to a wider community. Artists and other intellectuals enjoy a status and credibility rarely afforded their overseas counterparts. This celebrity status sometimes extends beyond Latin America, as in the cases of Mexican painters Diego Rivera and Frida Kahlo.

Many Latin American artists of the twentieth century, including, for example, Frida Kahlo, drew inspiration from the rich tradition of religious folk art, which survives all over Latin America and increasingly caters to the tourist market. Women painters, in particular, including the Chicana artist Carmen Lomas Garza, have used this personal, naïve form of self-expression to convey women's concerns in art, as an alternative to the visual idioms preferred and prized by the male-dominated art world.

—*Lisa Shaw*

Bibliography

Ades, Dawn. 1989. *Art in Latin America: The Modern Era, 1820–1980*. London: Hayward Gallery.

Lucie-Smith, Edward. 1993. *Latin American Art of the 20th Century*. London: Thames and Hudson.

José Clemente Orozco (1883–1949)

The Mexican artist José Clemente Orozco, a native of the state of Jalisco, is best known for his giant murals in the expressionist style. He is closely associated with Diego Rivera and David Alfaro Siqueiros. His most impressive works can be found in the state capital, Guadalajara. Orozco is perhaps the least overtly political of the three Mexican muralists, and his later work often seems politically ambiguous. Most of his early work can be found in Mexico City, where he painted murals between 1922 and 1927. He then spent seven years in the United States, but it was on his return to Mexico that his artistic powers reached their peak, in the late 1930s and 1940s.

Like Rivera and Siqueiros, Orozco's chief patron was the state, and most of his important works were created to decorate public buildings, such as the Palacio de Gobierno (Government Palace) and the university in Guadalajara. His murals on the Palacio de Gobierno depict the Mexican people's oppression and struggle for liberty, from pre-Conquest Eden to post-revolutionary emancipation. Orozco's murals decorate the chapel ceiling of the nearby Hospicio Cabañas, a former orphanage. These more spiritual works depict the Spanish conquistadors as the Horsemen of the Apocalypse, trampling the indigenous peoples of Mexico underfoot. In Mexico City, Orozco's work can be found on the

Detail of a mural depicting scenes from Mexican history by José Clemente Orozco that decorates the Palacio de Gobierno (Government Palace) in the city of Guadalajara. (Courtesy of Lisa Shaw)

main staircase and around the first floor of the main patio of the Colegio de San Idelfonso (also called the Escuela Nacional Preparatoria, or ENP). In spite of his enthusiasm for the Mexican Revolution (1910–1920), as elsewhere, these works reflect his doubts about its prospects, and they caricature modern Mexico almost as brutally as they do the nation prior to the Revolution.

Orozco's time in the United States gave rise to the mural *Mankind's Struggle*, painted in 1930 for the New School for Social Research in New York City. His North American murals also include *Prometheus*, painted between 1932 and 1934 for Frary Hall at Pomona College, and the acclaimed work *Epic of American Civilization* (1932–1934), for the Baker Library at Dartmouth College. The latter work, composed of twenty-four individual panels or scenes and covering approximately 3,200 square feet, depicts the history of the Americas from the migration of the Aztecs into Central America to the development of modern industrialized society. Orozco's work in the United States challenged traditional conservative views, attacking hypocrisy, greed, and oppression, and often proved highly controversial.

Born in Zapotlán (now Ciudad Guzmán), as a child Orozco moved to Guadalajara, and later to Mexico City, where he was influenced by the renowned folk artist José Guadalupe Posada. Much of his work is fresco painting, executed directly on wet plaster.

—Lisa Shaw

See also: *Visual Arts and Architecture:* Art (Diego Rivera; David Alfaro Siqueiros)

Bibliography

Ades, Dawn, ed. 2002. *José Clemente Orozco in the United States, 1927–1934.* New York: Norton.

Cruz, Barbara C. 1998. *José Clemente Orozco: Mexican Artist.* Berkeley Heights, NJ: Enslow.

Orozco, José Clemente. 2001. *José Clemente Orozco.* Mineola, NY: Dover.

Diego Rivera (1886–1957)

Diego Rivera was the most famous and arguably the greatest of the three renowned Mexican mural artists (along with José Clemente Orozco and David Alfaro Siqueiros). The husband of artist Frida Kahlo, Rivera interpreted Mexican history and particularly the Mexican Revolution (1910–1920) through the medium of huge murals principally created to decorate public buildings in Mexico City. He was largely responsible for bringing Mexican art to the attention of international audiences.

Greatly influenced by the Mexican Revolution and its Russian counterpart (1917), Rivera believed that art should help empower the working classes to understand their histories. He believed that art should be accessible to everyone, not isolated in museums and galleries. To this end he traveled to Italy to study early Renaissance fresco painting. In 1921 a new cultural program was introduced in Mexico to take art to the masses, and the government commissioned Rivera, along with Orozco and Siqueiros, to paint a series of frescoes for public buildings across the country. Many of Rivera's early murals are deceptively simple, even naïve, and give technique less importance than the themes: Mexican history, the oppression of the indigenous peoples, and post-revolutionary society. Like Siqueiros, however, he took a scientific view of his work, continually experimenting with the new techniques that emerged with industrialization.

Rivera's most ambitious project, a series of epic murals based on Mexican history for the Palacio Nacional (National Palace) in Mexico City, remained unfinished owing to his death on 25 November 1957. Begun in 1929, these murals epitomize Rivera's style and are among his greatest works. Around the walls of the main staircase the vast panorama of Mexican history combines brutal imagery with attention to detail. The main section depicts the Spanish Conquest, subjugation of the native inhabitants, war, Inquisition, invasion, Independence, and the Mexican Revolution. The depiction of post-revolutionary Mexico and the future features Karl Marx pointing the way forward for the workers. Frida Kahlo and her sister Cristina are also depicted.

By the 1930s Rivera's fame had spread to North America and beyond, and his work was exhibited in New York. From 1930 to 1931 he carried out two commissions in San Francisco, the murals *Allegory of California,* for the Stock Exchange building, and *The Making of a Fresco,* for the California School of Fine Arts. He returned to the city in 1940 to execute the mural *Pan American Unity* for the Golden Gate International Exposition. He was also asked to paint large murals for the Detroit Art Institute and the mural *Man at the Crossroads* (1934) for the Rockefeller Center in New York City. *Man at the Crossroads,* however, proved highly controversial because one of the figures depicted in it resembled Lenin, and the work was thus considered by some as representing anti-capitalist ideology. As a re-

Detail of one of the epic murals by Diego Rivera that adorn the Palacio Nacional (National Palace) in Mexico City, depicting Mexican history. (Courtesy of Lisa Shaw)

sult, the Rockefeller Center destroyed this mural and replaced it with one by another artist. However, Rivera later reproduced it for the Palacio de Bellas Artes (Museum of Fine Arts) in Mexico City.

Born in the city of Guanajuato, Rivera moved to Mexico City in 1892, where he studied traditional European artistic styles in the San Carlos Academy from the age of ten. He also learned his trade in the workshop of folk artist José Guadalupe Posada, as did Orozco. By the age of sixteen Rivera had emerged as an accomplished painter with a distinctly Mexican style. In 1907 he traveled to Spain to study the work of artists such as Goya and El Greco in the Prado art museum in Madrid. From there he moved to Paris, where he absorbed the latest trends, most importantly cubism. In a 1949 interview he is quoted as saying, "I've never believed in God, but I believe in Picasso" (The Virtual Diego Rivera Web Museum, http://www.diegorivera.com). While in exile in Paris, he and Siqueiros planned a popular, native style of art to express the new society that was emerging in Mexico.

Rivera was a member of the Communist Party from 1923 until 1930 and then again from 1954 until his death. He was not only a renowned artist but also a political activist who incited debate in Mexico, the United States, and the former Soviet Union.

From the end of the 1930s onward, Rivera painted landscapes and portraits. These later paintings, with indigenous subjects and a social realist style, such as *Nude with Calla Lilies* (1944) and *The*

Flower Seller (1949), are frequently reproduced on postcards and posters today.

—*Lisa Shaw*

See also: *Visual Arts and Architecture:* Art (Frida Kahlo; José Clemente Orozco; David Alfaro Siqueiros)

Bibliography

Hamill, Pete. 2002. *Diego Rivera.* New York: Abrams.

Marnham, Patrick, and Elise Goodman. 2000. *Dreaming with His Eyes Open: A Life of Diego Rivera.* Berkeley and Los Angeles: University of California Press.

Portrait of an Artist: The Frescoes of Diego Rivera (1986). 2002. Home Vision Entertainment (video).

Rivera, Diego. 1992. *My Art, My Life: An Autobiography.* Mineola, NY: Dover.

Rochfort, Desmond. 1998. *Mexican Muralists: Orozco, Rivera, Siqueiros.* San Francisco: Chronicle Books.

The Virtual Diego Rivera Web Museum. http://www.diegorivera.com (consulted September 2003).

David Alfaro Siqueiros (1896–1974)

The career of Mexican mural painter David Alfaro Siqueiros was more erratic than those of his fellow muralists and compatriots, Diego Rivera and José Clemente Orozco, because of his interest in politics. His life was marked by a series of dramatic events, such as imprisonment and exile, and his personal legend became intrinsically linked to the powerful and often brutal artistic images he created. He took part in the first mural campaign commissioned by the Mexican government in 1922. His most famous work is Mexico City's Polyforum Cultural Siqueiros, a building that he designed and decorated and that houses what is allegedly the world's largest mural (about 4,500 square meters), *The March of Humanity on Earth and towards the Cosmos* (1964–1971), painted by Siqueiros.

Siqueiros studied art at the San Carlos Academy in Mexico City and went to Europe on a government grant in 1919. There he made contact with Diego Rivera and in 1921 launched from Barcelona his "Manifesto to the Artists of America," the tone of which owed much to the futurist manifestos of the period before World War I. In it he declared, "Let us live our marvelous dynamic age!" and "Let us love the modern machine that provokes unexpected plastic emotions." More significantly, he recommended a return to indigenous sources, but combined with a modernist aesthetic. His manifesto continued:

> Let us, for our part, go back to the work of the ancient inhabitants of our valleys, the Indian painters and sculptors (Mayas, Aztecs, Incas, etc.). . . . They demonstrate a fundamental knowledge of nature that can serve as a point of departure for us. Let us absorb their synthetic energy, but avoid those lamentable archaeological reconstructions ("Indianism," "Primitivism," "Americanism") which are so in vogue here today but which are only short-lived fashions. (Lucie-Smith 1993, 62–63)

On his return to Mexico in 1922 he worked alongside Rivera and Orozco on large murals at the Escuela Nacional Preparatoria in the Mexican capital, and his work there, like Orozco's, was interrupted by the student protests of 1924. Siqueiros's mural remained unfinished, and he completed his first mural in his homeland only after his return from the Spanish Civil War (1936–1939). Entitled *Portrait of the Bourgeoisie* (1939–1940), it adorned the headquarters of the Electricians' Union in Mexico City. With its twisted perspective and dramatic tone, it is characteristic of his flamboyant, unrestrained style. While in prison in Mexico at the beginning of the 1930s, Siqueiros produced some of his best work, namely a series of paintings that were small and simple but monumental in design; they clearly show the influence of the fresco painters he had studied in Europe. Most of his major mural projects were executed during the last thirty years of his life, ironically when muralism was beginning to face challenges from other styles and ideas.

Siqueiros fought in the civil wars in Mexico and became involved in trade union organization. He was one of the leading activists in the Union of Technical Workers, Painters, and Sculptors, and he edited its journal, *El Machete.* By the mid-1920s his political and trade union interests occupied almost all his time and energy. He served as secretary of the Communist Party of Mexico and as president of the National Federation of Mineworkers. Most of his activities were centered on the northern Mexican state of Jalisco, but in 1930 he took part in a prohibited May Day march in Mexico City; as a result, he was imprisoned for a year. He fought on the side of the Republicans in the Spanish Civil War, and upon his return to Mexico he led an unsuccessful attempt to assassinate the exiled Leon Trotsky. Once again he was forced into exile, returning in 1944. From 1962 to 1964 he served another, and final, period of imprisonment in Mexico.

In 1932 Siqueiros fled Mexico for the United States, becoming a teacher at the Chouinard School of Art in California. There he began to experiment with new techniques, such as the use of photographic projectors and spray painting, which would prove to be highly influential on subsequent generations. Later, in New York, he went on to run an experimental group for young painters, one of whom was Jackson Pollock.

—Lisa Shaw

See also: *Visual Arts and Architecture:* Art (José Clemente Orozco; Diego Rivera)

Bibliography

Lucie-Smith, Edward. 1993. *Latin American Art of the 20th Century.* London: Thames and Hudson.

Rochfort, Desmond. 1998. *Mexican Muralists: Orozco, Rivera, Siqueiros.* San Francisco: Chronicle Books.

Rodriguez, Antonio. 1992. *David Alfaro Siqueiros: Pintura Mural.* Mexico City: Bancomext.

Siqueiros: Artist and Warrior (1998). 2002. Home Vision Entertainment (video).

Stein, Philip, and Ann Warren, eds. 1994. *Siqueiros: His Life and Works.* New York: International.

White, D. Anthony. 1994. *Siqueiros: A Biography.* Mountain View, CA: Floricanto.

Cândido Portinari (1903–1962)

Cândido Portinari, a Brazilian painter of Italian descent, enjoyed critical acclaim both at home and abroad and is best known for his large murals, including those at the Ministry of Education building in Rio de Janeiro and at the United Nations building in New York. As his career developed, he became increasingly distanced from homegrown subject matter rather than closer to it. Although his style as a muralist initially owed much to his Mexican counterpart Diego Rivera, putting across a political message was always less important to Portinari than creating a pleasing decorative effect. Nevertheless, he was an active member of the Brazilian Communist Party;

he ran for party deputy in 1945 and as the party's candidate for senator in 1947. Some of his later work, created in collaboration with the acclaimed Brazilian modernist architect Oscar Niemeyer, consists of wall decorations made of ceramic tiles known in Portuguese as *azulejos*, which were traditionally used in Brazilian colonial architecture.

Portinari was born on a coffee plantation near Brodósqui, a town in the state of São Paulo. A child of poor Italian immigrants, he left school with only a primary-school education. At the age of fifteen he went to Rio de Janeiro to study painting and enrolled in the Escola Nacional de Belas Artes (National School of Fine Arts). In 1928 he was awarded a foreign travel and study prize and went to Paris, where he lived for a year in 1930. Homesick, Portinari decided that when he returned to his country in 1931, he would concentrate on depicting the Brazilian people in his work, embracing an experimental, antiacademic, modernist approach.

In 1936 Portinari painted murals for the Highways Monument located on the Rio de Janeiro–São Paulo highway and began work on frescoes for the new Ministry of Education building in Rio de Janeiro, completed in 1944. These works epitomize Portinari's art, evidencing his adoption of social themes, which was to be the hallmark of all his later work. In 1943 he created eight panels known as the Biblical Series, reflecting the impact of World War II and strongly influenced by Pablo Picasso's *Guernica*. In 1944, invited by Niemeyer, he began decorative work for the Pampulha architectural complex in Belo Horizonte, in the state of Minas Gerais, creating the murals *St. Francis* and *The Stations of the Cross* (1944) for the local church. The rise of Nazism and fascism and the horrors of the war in Europe reinforced the social and tragic aspects of his work, inspiring the series entitled *Migrants* and the *Brodósqui Children*, both of which were painted from 1944 to 1946. In 1949 he produced the impressive mural *Tiradentes*, which recounts the story of the trial and execution of the eponymous Brazilian hero who fought for independence against Portuguese colonial domination in the eighteenth century. For this work Portinari was awarded the gold medal by the committee of the International Peace Prize in Warsaw, Poland, in 1950.

Recognition abroad came for the first time in 1935, when Portinari won second honorable mention at the Carnegie Institute's International Exhibition in Pittsburgh with a large canvas entitled *Coffee* (1935), depicting with dignity poor migrant workers and the descendants of African slaves toiling in the Brazilian coffee fields. In the late 1930s Portinari's prestige in the United States was consolidated. In 1939 he painted three large panels for the Brazilian pavilion at the New York World's Fair. In the same year, New York's Museum of Modern Art (MOMA) purchased his canvas *The Shantytown* (1939). In 1940 he took part in an exhibition of Latin American art at New York's Riverside Museum, and he put on successful one-man shows at Detroit's Institute of Arts and New York's MOMA. In December 1940 the University of Chicago published the first book on the painter, *Portinari: His Life and Art*, with an introduction by the artist Rockwell Kent and a large number of reproductions of Portinari's work. In 1941 he painted four large murals on Latin American historical themes for the Library of Congress's Hispanic Foundation, in Washington, D.C. In 1946 he returned to Paris to

Detail of a painting by Candido Portinari. (Time Life Pictures/Getty Images)

hold his first exhibition in Europe, at the Galerie Charpentier. The exhibition was highly successful and earned Portinari the Légion d'Honneur award. In 1947 he exhibited at Salón Peuser in Buenos Aires and at Comisión Nacional de Bellas Artes (National Fine Arts Museum) in Montevideo. In 1948 he sought political asylum in Uruguay, where he produced the panel *The First Mass in Brazil* (1948), commissioned by a Brazilian bank, Banco Boavista. In 1952 he began studies for the panels *War* and *Peace*, which the Brazilian government offered to the new headquarters of the United Nations. Completed in 1956, the panels—measuring about fourteen meters by ten meters each, the largest ever made by Portinari—decorate the entrance hall of the United Nations building in New York. In 1955 Portinari was awarded the gold medal for best painter of the year by New York's International Fine Arts Council. In 1956, invited by the Israeli government, he traveled to Israel, where he exhibited at several museums and made drawings inspired by his contact with the then recently founded country, which were later exhibited in Bologna, Lima, Buenos Aires, and Rio de Janeiro. In the late 1950s Portinari held a number of exhibitions abroad, and in 1958 he was the only Brazilian artist represented at the "50 Ans d'Art Moderne" exhibition at Brussel's Palais des Beaux Arts (Museum of Fine Arts). In 1959 he exhibited his paintings at New York's Wildenstein Gallery, and together with other great Latin American artists, such as José Clemente Orozco and Diego Rivera, he participated in the Collection of Inter-American Art at the Museo de Bellas Artes (Museum of Fine Arts) in Caracas, Venezuela. Portinari died on 6 February 1962 while preparing an exhibition of about two hundred of his works that had been proposed by the city of Milan. It is said that he was poisoned by the cumulative effect of the toxins in the paints he used throughout his life.

—*Lisa Shaw*

See also: *Visual Arts and Architecture:* Architecture and Landscape Design (Oscar Niemeyer); Art (José Clemente Orozco; Diego Rivera)

Bibliography

Bento, Antonio. 2003. *Portinari.* Rio de Janeiro: Leo Christiano Editorial.

Fabris, Annateresa. 1990. *Portinari: Pintor social.* São Paulo: Edusp.

———. 1996. *Cândido Portinari.* São Paulo: Edusp.

Lucie-Smith, Edward. 1993. *Latin American Art of the 20th Century.* London: Thames and Hudson.

Projeto Portinari Official Website. http://www.portinari.org.br (consulted 30 September 2003).

Frida Kahlo (1907–1954)

Frida Kahlo is probably the best known of all Latin American women artists. Her work has made a major contribution to Mexican art, and her striking images have made her one of the most prominent Latin American artists worldwide. Born Magdalena Carmen Frida Kahlo y Calderón, she was the daughter of Matilde Calderón and the prominent photographer Guillermo Kahlo. She gained an insight into the artistic world from her father during her childhood and went on to paint some two hundred works between the mid-1920s and her death in 1954. Kahlo's paintings are frequently marked by images of pain and illness, strongly influenced by two major incidents in her life: a serious bout of polio, which she contracted at age seven, and a traffic accident at age eighteen, in which she suffered horrific injuries. It was when convalescing from this latter incident that Kahlo first began to paint, and several of her self-portraits address pain and bodily mutilation; many also depict her tumultuous relationship with the muralist Diego Rivera, to whom she was married twice, once in 1929 and again in 1940.

Kahlo's work challenges the representation of the female body in art, refusing to offer the female body as an object of beauty and consumption. For example, in *The Broken Column* (1944) Kahlo paints herself with nails stuck in her flesh and with her torso split open to reveal a crumbling and shattered architectural column inside. In *My Birth* (1932) she subverts the traditional nativity scene: the mother's head is covered, suggesting death, while the baby's head appears grotesquely large and has the trademark Kahlo bushy eyebrows.

Arguably the best known of Kahlo's paintings is *The Two Fridas*, painted in the autumn of 1939, in which (as in several of her other works) she appears in dual form. One Frida is depicted in European dress; the other wears the traditional Tehuana costume that Diego Rivera is said to have preferred her to wear. The two figures represent, according to Kahlo, the woman Rivera loved and the one he no longer loved. In this painting, done during the period when she and Rivera were divorcing, the female body is again shown mutilated—the hearts of both of the Fridas are removed, depicting emotional pain.

Although Kahlo is most famous for these very personal paintings, others combine the

Married Mexican artists Diego Rivera and Frida Kahlo (1907–1954) read and work in a studio. Kahlo's self-portrait, *The Two Fridas* (1939), hangs in the background among other works. (Hulton Archive/Getty Images)

focus on the self with a wider examination of issues of nationality. For example, in the 1932 work *Self Portrait on the Border Line between Mexico and the United States*, painted while the artist was on a trip to the United States, Kahlo located herself in the center of the picture, standing on the border stone separating Mexico from the United States, with the two countries depicted on either side of her. The Mexican side is replete with images relating to that country's pre-Columbian heritage, such as the temples shown in the background and fertility idols in the middle ground. In contrast, the side of the painting representing the United States has a series of motifs depicting that nation's industrial status, such as skyscrapers and smoke emanating from four chimneys. Thus, this painting, titled a self-portrait, at the same time presents the contrasting cultures and lifestyles of the neighboring countries and has a wider significance beyond the purely personal.

—*Claire Taylor*

See also: *Cultural Icons:* Latin Americans in Hollywood (Salma Hayek); *Visual Arts and Architecture:* Art (Diego Rivera)

Bibliography

Alcántara, Isabel, and Sandra Egnolff. 1999. *Frida Kahlo and Diego Rivera.* London: Prestel.

Billeter, Erika, ed. 1993. *The Blue House: The World of Frida Kahlo.* Seattle: University of Washington Press.

Herrera, Hayden. 1992. *Frida Kahlo: The Paintings.* London: Bloomsbury.

Turner, Robyn. 1993. *Frida Kahlo.* Boston: Little, Brown.

Zamora, Martha. 1990. *Frida Kahlo: The Brush of Anguish.* London: Art Data.

Tarsila do Amaral (1886–1973)

Tarsila do Amaral, the most influential female Brazilian painter, was closely associated with the modernist movement in Brazilian arts, which officially began in 1922. Amaral (or Tarsila, as she is always referred to in Brazil) combined cubist techniques acquired in Europe with visual themes that were typical of her homeland. Her best-known works fall into two distinct phases: the *pau-brasil* (brazilwood) phase and her anthropophagist, or cannibalistic, period.

After studying in Europe, Amaral returned to Brazil in 1922 and joined the group of artists and intellectuals who made up the modernist movement. Although she did not participate in the important Modern Art Week event held at São Paulo's Municipal Theater in February 1922, when she was still in Paris, Amaral was at the heart of this iconoclastic artistic movement. She became one of the so-called group of five, along with fellow female painter Anita Malfatti and writers Oswald de Andrade, Mário de Andrade, and Menotti del Picchia.

Amaral was greatly influenced by cubism and studied with the great cubist masters Albert Gleizes and Fernand Léger upon her return to Europe in 1923. There, she mixed with other modernist intellectuals and forged a close friendship with the French-Swiss poet Blaise Cendrars. Her second visit to Europe was brief but decisive. In April 1923 she wrote to her family in Brazil: "I feel myself ever more Brazilian. I want to be the painter of my country" (Tarsila do Amaral Official Website, http://www.tarsiladoamaral.com.br). In December of that year she returned to Brazil and, accompanied by Cendrars and Oswald de Andrade, began to explore the rich popular culture, colonial architecture, and landscapes of her homeland. Thus began a new phase in her painting, known as the brazilwood phase for its use of typically Brazilian colors and themes, which combined local naïve art with cubism. Some of her most famous works from this period include *The Black Woman* (1923) and *Fruit Seller* (1925).

The second and most creative period in Amaral's artistic career, known as the anthropophagist, or cannibalistic, phase, took its name from the literary manifesto *Antropófago*, published by Oswald de Andrade in 1928. In January of that year Amaral had given her most famous work, *Abaporu* (1928, the title literally meaning "man who eats" in the indigenous Tupi-Guarani language of Brazil), as a birthday present to Oswald, whom she had married in 1926. The painting shows a single monstrous figure with huge hands and feet and an enormous head. The simplified landscape is reduced to a single oversized cactus and a large sun. The underlying idea of the anthropophagy movement was that Brazilian artists should devour foreign influences, digest them thoroughly, and turn them into something new, just as some cannibalistic tribes had done more literally in the early colonial period. In *Abaporu* Amaral assimilated the surrealist aesthetic and the influence of Fernand Léger's reclining women subjects, combining them with an intrinsically Brazilian theme. Her canvas *Factory Workers* (1933), which vividly captures the racial and ethnic mix of Brazil's workforce, signaled the beginning of social painting in Brazil.

Amaral was born into a very wealthy family from the state of São Paulo. She studied art at the Colégio Sion in the city of São Paulo and subsequently in Barcelona, Spain, where she painted her first picture, at the age of sixteen, entitled *Sacred Heart of Jesus* (1902). In 1906 she married for the first time, but in 1916 she separated from her husband and the father of her only daughter, Dulce. She then began studying sculpture in São Paulo. In 1920 she left Brazil for Europe to study in the Académie Julian in Paris and in the workshop of the conservative painter Émile Renard. In 1922 she had her first canvas accepted by the Official Salon of French Artists. In 1926 she exhibited her work in Paris to great acclaim. In 1929 she had her first solo exhibition in Brazil. In the 1950s she returned to the brazilwood theme in her work. In 1963 her work was honored at the seventh biennial art exhibition of São Paulo, and the following year at the thirty-second Venice biennial exhibition.

—*Lisa Shaw*

See also: *Language:* Indigenous Languages

Bibliography

Ades, Dawn. 1989. *Art in Latin America: The Modern Era, 1820–1980.* London: Hayward Gallery.

Gotlib, Nádia Battella. 1997. *Tarsila do Amaral: A Modernista.* São Paulo: Senac.

Lucie-Smith, Edward. 1993. *Latin American Art of the 20th Century.* London: Thames and Hudson.

Tarsila do Amaral Official Website. http://www.tarsiladoamaral.com.br (consulted 19 September 2003).

Fernando Botero (1932–)

The work of Fernando Botero, perhaps the contemporary Latin American artist who is most popular internationally, is regularly reprinted on posters, calendars, and greeting cards. In fact, his imagery, with its smooth lines and bold colors, its faux-naïf style, and its characteristically inflated figures, is more instantly recognizable than the name of the artist himself. Nevertheless, despite its massive popularity with the consumers of greeting cards, Botero's work is not simply decorative. Instead, perhaps confusingly, it plays with questions of artistic lineage and political message.

Botero was born in Medellín, Colombia, and after a brief stint as a trainee bullfighter, he started work as an illustrator for a local newspaper at age sixteen. His early work—drawings and watercolors—betrayed the influence of the great Mexican muralist tradition and was particularly reminiscent of the work of José Clemente Orozco. However, by the mid-1950s, those Latin American artists who did not wish to follow the predominant trend toward abstract art also began to find the muralist tradition too limiting. In search of inspiration, some turned to the repertoire of classical art, combining it with the "distorting" techniques of such European avant-garde

Fernando Botero's *The Presidential Family* (1967). (AFP/Getty Images)

movements as cubism. In 1952 Botero himself traveled to Europe, where he studied the work of the great masters in Madrid and Florence and also became familiar with the work of cubists such as Pablo Picasso and Georges Braque. By the late 1950s Botero had also incorporated abstract expressionism into his work, although without, of course, losing his focus on figurative art. Rather, abstract expressionism's spirit of revolt against tradition stimulated his interest. Botero's first sale to a major international gallery (*Mona Lisa at Age Twelve*, 1959) held the conflicting currents of classicism and revolt against tradition in a fine balance.

By the mid-1960s Botero had developed a distinctive style of his own, combining classical compositions (often "quotations" of well-known works of art) with a distorting technique frequently referred to by his critics as "gigantism" in which objects, particularly people, appear inflated like balloons or cartoon characters. Botero has always claimed that his aim is to be "sensually provocative" rather than satirical, although some satirical impact is inevitable. This technique was already apparent in his early preference for the rotund forms of certain musical instruments, such as the lute, and again in his distortion of the Mona Lisa's head in *Mona Lisa at Age Twelve.* Nevertheless, from the mid-1960s onward Botero moved away from the rough, painterly approach of his earlier, more avant-garde work, and the influence of the Old Masters was apparent in the types of paint and brushstrokes he began to use. Despite the potentially comic effect of his work, egg tempera and smooth, meticulous strokes make it seem much more traditional and hence, his less generous critics assume, less rebellious or politically incisive.

Another reason Botero has not found favor with art critics is his choice of subjects. He has cited Diego Rivera as the artist who showed other, younger Latin American painters how to create "independent," *mestizo* (mixed-race) Latin American art through his combination of heterogeneous influences. However, Botero's choice to produce "quotations" of the works of the Old Masters and other, more recent European painters often seems to suggest that he has turned his back on his own cultural tradition. Certainly, he paints neither indigenous subjects nor even images that reflect the harsher realities of Latin American life (although recently he has started to produce a series of paintings that depict the lives and times of infamous Colombian drug barons, such as Pablo Escobar). Furthermore, when he does opt to paint a scene depicting life in Latin America, his choice of subjects (politicians, prostitutes, or bureaucrats), together with his style of gigantism, suggests that he is adopting an ironic, detached, even frivolous attitude toward his own culture. However, Botero's irreverent, highly self-conscious paraphrases of the work of the Old Masters rework Spanish and Italian Renaissance painting in ways that call into question the ideals, styles, and values of the Enlightenment and the validity of the imposition of that culture upon Latin America.

—*Thea Pitman*

See also: *Visual Arts and Architecture:* Art (José Clemente Orozco; Diego Rivera)

Bibliography

Ades, Dawn. 1989. *Art in Latin America: The Modern Era, 1820–1980.* London: Hayward Gallery.

Baddeley, Oriana, and Valerie Fraser. 1989. *Drawing the Line: Art and Cultural Identity in Contemporary Latin America.* London: Verso.

Lucie-Smith, Edward. 1997. *Latin American Art of the 20th Century.* London: Thames and Hudson.

Spies, Werner, ed. 1992. *Fernando Botero: Paintings and Drawings.* Munich: Prestel.

Wifredo Lam (1902–1982)

Wifredo Lam is the most famous Cuban painter of the twentieth century and the first Latin American artist to express the African component of Latin American culture as the predominant focus of his work. Lam was also strongly associated with the international artistic and literary movements of cubism, surrealism, and négri-

Wifredo Lam's *The Jungle* (1943). (The Museum of Modern Art/Licensed by SCALA/Art Resource, NY)

tude, balancing the different demands of these movements in his work.

Lam was the son of a Chinese immigrant father and an Afro-Cuban mother. He grew up in the working-class, mulatto sector of Cuban society, experiencing the popular culture of this society at first hand. His godmother was a practitioner of *Santería* (the syncretic Cuban religion that combines West African religious practices and beliefs with those of Roman Catholicism). His artistic training was very traditional: he started painting still lifes and landscapes at the Escuela de Bellas Artes (School of Fine Arts) in Havana, and in 1923 he made the inevitable journey to Europe to study strict academic rigor. Nevertheless, he was soon inspired by the artists of the European avant-garde, and even his work of the 1920s showed signs of cubist influence. By the late 1930s Lam had become a close friend of Pablo Picasso's, and soon after, he joined André Breton's group of surrealist artists and writers.

Both cubists and surrealists were interested in African and other "primitive" art forms, and Lam benefited from this interest in so-called exotic black culture to discover his own ethnocultural roots. This was evident in the geometric style of painting he now adopted. Lam's work was given a further push in the direction of black culture when, fleeing the Nazi invasion of Paris in 1941 and on his way back to Cuba after nearly twenty years' absence, he was detained in Martinique. There he made the acquaintance of the Martinican black poet (and one of the main exponents of the négritude movement) Aimé Césaire. The négritude movement had originated in Paris in the 1930s, stimulated perhaps by the cubist and surrealist interest in African culture, but it aimed to go beyond such artists' exoticist, de-historicized interest in black culture to express an awareness of black social reality (the history of slavery and discrimination) and to celebrate the difference of the black experience. After this key encounter, Lam started to depict elements of Afro-Cuban culture in works that clearly conveyed a political message. His work, nevertheless, continued to use the styles of cubism and surrealism as the medium for such messages.

Lam's most famous work, *The Jungle* (1942–1944), a huge mural-like piece that took him over two years to paint, caused a scandal when it was first exhibited because of the supposed ferocity and overtly sexual nature of the imagery, which offended bourgeois ideas of good taste. It depicts four polymorphic figures (combining human and animal body parts in grotesque and chaotic forms) that blend seamlessly with a background of sugarcane and tobacco leaves and brandish masks and scissors. The composition as a whole seems to suggest a *Santería* ritual in which participants become possessed by certain deities: a person in a state of possession is referred to as being *el caballo* (the horse), hence the frequent equestrian imagery in the painting. Furthermore, the jungle of the painting's title does not refer to any real location but, rather, to the *Santería* term for the site where a religious ritual takes place. Thus, the painting clearly incorporates a particularly defiant version of Afro-Cuban culture as its theme. But in the presence of sugarcane and tobacco leaves, a reference is also made to the history of slavery and the Afro-Cuban's typical place of enslavement: the tobacco and sugarcane plantations. The image therefore combines references to both servitude and resistance, via the visual idioms and thematic predilections of both cubism and surrealism.

After a trip to Haiti in 1945–1946 in the company of Breton, Lam's work lost the colorful exuberance of his initial rediscovery of Cuba, developing a darker, more violent tone, expressed in browns, blacks, grays, and white. His later work from the 1950s until his death gradually became even more abstract and monochromatic. References to Afro-Cuban cultural practices such as *Santería* and its *orishas* (deities) can still be spotted in this work, but these never form a coherent narrative support to the image.

—*Thea Pitman*

See also: *Popular Religion and Festivals: Santería*

Bibliography

Fletcher, Valerie. 1992. *Crosscurrents of Modernism: Four Latin American Pioneers (Diego Rivera, Joaquín Torres-García, Wifredo Lam, Matta)*. Englewood Cliffs, NJ: Prentice Hall.

Herzberg, Julia P. 1996. "Rereading Lam." Pp. 149–169 in *Santería Aesthetics in Contemporary Latin American Art*, edited by Arturo Lindsay. Washington, DC: Smithsonian Institution Press.

Mosquera, Gerardo. 1995. "Modernism from Afro-America: Wifredo Lam." Pp. 121–132 in *Beyond the Fantastic: Contemporary Art Criticism from Latin America*, edited by Gerardo Mosquera. London: Institute of International Visual Arts.

Poupeye, Veerle. 1998. *Caribbean Art*. London: Thames and Hudson.

Hélio Oiticica (1937–1980)

The Brazilian experimental artist Hélio Oiticica is perhaps best remembered for his installation *Tropicália*, exhibited in 1967, which gave its name to the eponymous movement within Brazilian popular music. Oiticica was a leading figure in the Brazilian art movements Grupo Frente (Front Group, 1954–1956) and neo-concretism (1959–1961).

Oiticica's work rebelled against the traditional values of the art world and formed part of the cultural explosion that occurred in Brazil in the middle to late 1950s and 1960s. He coined a series of terms to refer to his artworks, including *bólides* (bolides, sometimes translated as fireballs or nuclei), *parangolés* (not literally translatable, but encompassing cape and tent forms), and *penetráveis* (penetrables). *Bólides* were initially objects containing color as a mass, in the form of pigment, earth, dust, liquid, or even cloth, and thought of as forming a kind of energy center. Later *bólide* became the term Oiticica used for a container in a very broad sense. Such containers were envisaged as a means of focusing perceptions when looked at, entered, occupied, or worn. *Bólides* were given titles that referred to the materials that they were made of, such as the *Bólide Caixa* (Box Bolide) series, the *Bólide Vidro* (Glass Bolide) series, and the *Bólide Cama* (Bed Bolide) series, all created between 1963 and 1968. These works were numbered sequentially. He called these structures "*Transobjetos*" (Transobjects) in his text entitled "Bólides," written on 29 October 1963. In 1964 he created his first three *parangolés*, composed of tents, banners, and flags. The fourth was the first to incorporate a cape, which would become a central element of this type of work. In 1965 at the Museum of Modern Art in Rio de Janeiro, Oiticica staged "Parangolé Inauguration," a public demonstration involving capes, tents, and flags and the participation of a group of his friends from the Mangueira samba school. The photographer Desdémone Bardin recorded the event. Oiticica's so-called penetrables were pieces of installation art, the most famous of which were PN_2 and PN_3 (1967), better known as *Tropicália*, which explored the stereotypical representation of Brazil as a tropical paradise. The work consists of two structures, the two penetrables, made of wood and brightly colored printed fabric, which are reminiscent of Brazil's *favelas* (shantytowns). Sand and pebble paths and tropical plants circle the structures, and live parrots flutter about in a large cage. The main penetrable invites the participants into a dark, labyrinthine passage, at the end of which is a functioning television.

In 1969 a one-man show of Oiticica's work was held at the Whitechapel Gallery in London, and he was invited to be artist in residence at the University of Sussex, England. In 1970 his work was exhibited at the Museum of Modern Art in New York.

Oiticica was associated with the wider cultural movement known as Tropicália, which was spearheaded by popular song. In 1968 he and other artists demonstrated against the military regime in the chic Rio de Janeiro district of Ipanema. They displayed a banner stating "*Seja marginal, seja herói*" (Be a marginal, be a hero); the slogan was later incorporated into a show by the singer-songwriter Caetano Veloso that was subsequently banned by the police.

In 1973 Oiticica created the concept known as quasi cinema and began to work with filmmakers and to produce slides, such as the series "Helena inventa Angela Maria" (Helena invents Angela Maria, 1975). In this set of slides he evoked the famous Brazilian singer of the 1950s Angela Maria. He participated in Brazilian cinema in the late 1960s, acting in the film *O câncer* (*Cancer*, 1968) by iconoclastic filmmaker Glauber Rocha. His work also featured in the documentary films *Arte pública* (*Public Art*, 1968) by Sirito and *Apocalipopótese* (*Apocalypopothesis*, 1968) by Raimundo Amado and Leonardo Bartucci. In 1975, when in New York, he acted in Andreas Valentin's film *One Night on Gay Street*, and in 1979 he appeared in *O segredo da múmia* (*The Secret of the Mummy*) by Brazilian filmmaker Ivan Cardoso.

Oiticica began studying painting at the Museum of Modern Art in Rio de Janeiro in 1954. On 31 March of that year he produced his first written text on the subject of the plastic arts, and he went on to write a diary of his reflections on art. His early work was displayed at the second, third, and fourth exhibitions of the so-called Grupo Frente during 1955 and 1956. He went on to show his work at the first national exhibition of concrete art at the Museum of Modern Art in São Paulo and participated in the exhibition of contemporary Brazilian painting in Montevideo, Uruguay, in 1956. The following year he took part in the fourth biennial art exhibition of São Paulo.

—Lisa Shaw

See also: *Popular Music:* Samba; Tropicália; *Visual Arts and Architecture:* Architecture and Landscape Design (*Favelas*)

Bibliography

Basualdo, Carlos, ed. 2002. *Hélio Oiticica: Quasi-cinemas.* Ostfildern, Germany: Hatje Cantz.

Favaretto, Celso. 1992. *A invenção de Hélio Oiticica.* São Paulo: Edusp.

Oiticica, Hélio. 1997. *Hélio Oiticica.* Rio de Janeiro: Centro de Arte Hélio Oiticica.

Chicano Muralism

Chicano muralism, a vibrant popular art movement, emerged in the late 1960s, coinciding with the rising awareness of Chicano identity and rights promoted by the cultural and nationalist Chicano movement.

Chicano muralists often sought to express the Chicano spirit formally through an eclectic mixture of visual idioms taken from fine art and from popular culture, thus representing the hybrid nature of Mexican American culture. Thematically, the Chicano muralists chose to focus on the positive depiction of Chicanos and of icons of Chicano culture—such as Aztec gods, the *pachuco* (the early twentieth-century predecessor of the contemporary Chicano gang member), the Virgin of Guadalupe, *La Llorona* (literally, the crying woman)—and on relevant social issues such as racism, poverty, and bilingual education. The muralists attempted to raise awareness of Chicano culture and social problems by communicating directly with their target audience, an audience that did not necessarily have the linguistic skills, leisure time, or disposable income to enable it to absorb this information in any other format. Indeed, even for the artists and activists themselves, this kind of community art (together with agitprop theater troupes and poetry readings) was not only the best but also one of the only means available to communicate with their audience, since Chicano issues were not being dealt with fairly in the mainstream U.S. media. Furthermore, murals were often painted by groups of people and regularly involved the help of local community members, so their creation strengthened a sense of solidarity.

In the movement's heyday in the 1970s there were three main groups of muralists. Los Four and Asco were the most prominent. Los Four was made up of Carlos Almaraz, Gilbert Sanchez Lujan, Roberto de la Rocha, and Frank Romero. These muralists had trained in art school and took a rather theoretical, didactic approach to mural art. The influence of the work of the three great artists of Mexican muralism, José Clemente Orozco, Diego Rivera, and David Alfaro Siqueiros, is clear in their approach to their art and even in their ironic, bilingual choice of name for their group.

Asco (Disgust) was made up of Gronk (Glugio Gronk Nicandro), Willie Herron, Patssi Valdez, and Harry Gamboa Jr. and represented the visions and issues of urban Chicano youth. The influences on this group were more eclectic, including mainstream U.S. popular culture (Walt Disney cartoons, advertising, and the like) and the iconography of barrio gangs (for example, their *pachuco*-related fashions and their graffiti art). Herron's *The Wall That Cracked Open* (1972), which combines preexisting barrio graffiti with a mural exploiting an actual crack in the wall to illustrate

Chicano mural in Westlake, Los Angeles, 2003. (David McNew/Getty Images)

the theme of gang violence, is one of the most impressive and identifiable images of Chicano mural art.

A third group, Las Mujeres Muralistas (Chicana Women Muralists), based in San Francisco, had as its core members Graciela Carrillo, Consuelo Mendez, Irene Perez, and Patricia Rodriguez, although virtually every Chicana artist of the epoch was associated with it at one point or another. The group was formed in the mid-1970s with the aim of representing women's issues, otherwise largely ignored by the male-dominated mainstream Chicano art movement. The influence of Frida Kahlo and of Mexican folk art in general is frequently apparent in the works of these artists.

The Chicano muralist movement, despite being a popular, alternative art movement, still needed support in order to finance mural paintings, to broker deals over where murals could be painted, and even to commission particular murals. This support generally came from the Chicano community's own resources: the most significant source of this support was and still is the Social and Public Art Resource Center (SPARC). One of the most ambitious projects sponsored by SPARC was *The Great Wall of Los Angeles*, which is over half a mile long and was worked on by more than 450 people over a period of five years (1978–1983). Significantly, over time SPARC's commissions have broadened the thematic range of Chicano muralism to encompass issues that affect many minority groups in the United States, and *The Great Wall* achieves just this, retelling the history of a wide variety of minority groups in California.

Although today there is greater official acceptance of the Chicano muralists by the Anglo art world and although many former muralists have moved away from muralism proper into the space of the gallery, murals continue to be painted in Chicano neighborhoods across the United States and continue to have an impact. Most recently, one of David Alfaro Siqueiros's controversial Los Angeles murals, *Tropical America* (1932), which had been totally whitewashed over by 1938, has been in part repainted and in part adapted and updated where it was originally located. Although this new mural, *Homage to Siqueiros* (1998), won prizes in the Chicano community, it received no recognition by the mainstream Anglo media, thus proving the ongoing subversive potential of the Chicano muralist movement.

—*Thea Pitman*

Examples of Mexican religious folk art. (Karen Huntt/Corbis)

See also: *Cultural Icons:* Regional and Ethnic Types (El Pachuco); Religious and Mythical Figures (*La Llorona*;Virgin of Guadalupe); *Language:* Chicano Spanish; *Visual Arts and Architecture:* Art (Frida Kahlo; José Clemente Orozco; Religious Folk Art; Diego Rivera; David Alfaro Siqueiros)

Bibliography

Benvidez, Max. 2002. "Chicano Art: Culture, Myth, and Sensibility." Pp. 10–21 in *Chicano Visions: American Painters on the Verge*, edited by Cheech Marin. Boston: Bulfinch.

Cockcroft, Eva, John Pitman Weber, and James Cockcroft. 1998. *Toward a People's Art: The Contemporary Mural Movement.* Albuquerque: University of New Mexico Press.

Cockcroft, James D., and Jane Canning. 2000. *Latino Visions: Contemporary Chicano, Puerto Rican, and Cuban American Artists.* Danbury, CT: F. Watts.

Keller, Gary D. 2002. *Contemporary Chicano and Chicana Art: Artists, Work, Culture, and Education.* Tempe, AZ: Bilingual Press.

Religious Folk Art

In Latin America the production of artifacts for religious devotion existed before the arrival of Christopher Columbus (1492) and of the Portuguese in Brazil (1500). However, since the time of the Conquest, when Roman Catholicism was first brought to the region, there has been a need to produce large quantities of artifacts for use in specifically Catholic religious devotions. It was cheaper and more convenient in most cases to produce these objects locally, copying them from Spanish and other European models, than to import them from Spain or Portugal. Furthermore, over time, the craft was passed on to local indigenous or *mestizo* (mixed-race) producers rather than being kept in the hands of recently arrived, trained artists from Europe. The resulting tradition of religious folk art still exists today. European models are inflected by indigenous Latin American preferences (for dark-skinned saints with indigenous facial features, for example) and are further transformed by the varying degrees of artistic training received by the local artisans. The Virgin of Guadalupe, the national patroness of Mexico, is clearly *mestiza* (of mixed race) in the depictions made of her, and she is one of the most popular images in Mexican religious folk art.

Within the field of religious folk art, there are paintings (*retablos* and *ex-votos*), carvings (*santos* or *bultos*), *milagros* (diminutively small metal casts of body parts), *nichos* (reliquaries), and crosses. Strictly speaking, *retablos* are images of saints, the Virgin, or Christ, painted by artisans and meant to be displayed on altars in homes. *Ex-votos*, or votive offerings, are depictions, accompanied by narratives, of moments when individuals have prayed to a saint or the Virgin for intercession on their behalf. They are painted as an expression of gratitude for that successful intercession. *Ex-votos* are meant for public display in the church where the particular saint's image is housed, and they may be painted by the individual in question or commissioned from a local artisan. In practice, however, the terms *retablo* and *ex-voto* are used interchangeably to indicate items in this second category, which is by far the most important in terms of religious folk art.

These images were traditionally painted on wood, canvas, silver, or copper, but since the nineteenth-century explosion in tin mining in Latin America, they have typically been painted on thin sheets of tin (a durable, nonrusting material to which paint adheres well). Few examples of earlier *retablos* painted on other media survive, and even old tin *retablos* are collector's items today. (Artists Frida Kahlo and Diego Rivera amassed a vast personal collection in the 1930s.) New *retablos* are rarely made, perhaps reflecting the present lull in fervent Catholic belief or an unwillingness to spend money on this expensive form of gratitude, given the affordability of mass-produced images available at every church's gates. However, fake "old" *retablos* are still painted for sale to tourists, and thus the art form does still survive.

Santos (usually fairly small carvings of saints), or *bultos* (literally "lumps" or "bundles") as they are also known, also have a long tradition in Latin America. They were typically fashioned out of wood, sealed, and then painted, and were meant for display on altars or in small chapels in private homes. In the Caribbean, in particular, these carvings have traditionally been thought to have a life of their own, being offered food and drink and spoken to like any other member of the family. Unlike the *retablo* tradition, the *santo* tradition has managed to survive in contemporary Latin America, despite the availability of mass-produced religious "dolls." In Puerto Rico there is even a biennial exhibition of contemporary *santos*, and in the southwestern United States some Chicano *santeros* (makers of *santos*) still work full-time at their craft.

—*Thea Pitman*

See also: *Cultural Icons:* Religious and Mythical Figures (Virgin of Guadalupe); *Popular Religion and Festivals:* Popular Catholicism (Mexico and Central America); *Visual Arts and Architecture:* Art (Frida Kahlo; Diego Rivera)

Bibliography

Cockcroft, James D., and Jane Canning. 2000. *Latino Visions: Contemporary Chicano,*

Puerto Rican, and Cuban American Artists. Danbury, CT: F. Watts.

Egan, Martha. 1991. *Milagros: Votive Offerings from the Americas.* Introduction by Marion Oettinger Jr. Santa Fe: Museum of New Mexico Press.

Giffords, Gloria. K. 2001. *Mexican Folk Retablos.* Albuquerque: University of New Mexico Press.

Contemporary and Folk Art in Brazil

Influenced in part by the Brazilian modernists of the first half of the twentieth century and by the social, racial, and geographical disparities present in Brazil, contemporary gallery artists continue to be fascinated with the juxtaposition of the archaic and the modern, themes of everyday violence, cultural imperialism, rituals of mass culture, the exploration of new materials, and the importance of sensuality in Brazilian society. Brazil also continues to have a rich tradition of folk art, such as clay figures, the woodblock prints that illustrate chapbooks (*literatura de cordel*), and artifacts associated with the Afro-Brazilian religion *Candomblé.* Such folk art is produced chiefly in the poor northeastern section of the country by craftsmen of humble origin with little formal training.

Particularly in Brazil's larger cities, works of art can be exhibited and viewed at a surprisingly large number of venues, often for free. Many are financed by state-run or mixed-ownership companies, such as the Centro Cultural Banco do Brasil in Rio de Janeiro. Over eleven million people visited the art and culture exhibition that was held in 2000 in São Paulo and that later toured throughout Brazil and abroad to commemorate the five-hundredth anniversary of the "discovery" of Brazil by the Portuguese. The contemporary art scene in Brazil is thriving. A number of talented figurative and abstract artists are making their mark at home and abroad, including Siron Franco (1947–) with his ecologically correct paintings, the abstract artist Iberê Camargo (1914–1995), and the British-based Ana Maria Pacheco (1943–), whose striking work has been likened to the paintings of the internationally renowned Paula Rego. But despite the buoyant scene and the promotion of access to canonical artworks, the popularity of art in Brazil is debatable. A new generation of artists who are fascinated by popular culture and who, like many contemporary artists, are keen to experiment with new materials and technologies stand a chance of gaining greater access to the public at large. For example, Arthur Omar, who made his mark on the Brazilian cultural scene in the 1970s as a documentary/experimental filmmaker as well as a composer and photographer, has recently garnered plenty of publicity in the Brazilian art world with his innovative use of video technology. His highly ironic 1997 video installation *MASSAKER!*, exhibited in the Casa das Rosas in São Paulo, depicted Michael Jackson's 1996 arrival at the Morro Dona Marta, one of Rio's largest *favelas*, "and other kinds of massacres," according to the video itself. (Jackson was famously given safe passage through the *favela* in order to film a music video by the notorious drug dealer Marcinho VP.) The projected images of the installation were to be watched on exercise bicycles. Omar's more recent work has been exhibited in important modern art museums abroad, including the Reina Sofia Museum in Madrid and the Museum of Modern Art (MOMA) in New York.

As in many countries in Latin America, since the 1970s both the artistic intelligentsia and urban-based consumers have

Clay figures traditionally produced in the rural hinterland of Brazil's northeast. (Courtesy of Alex Nield)

appropriated the once-mocked examples of popular or folk art. One of the most familiar expressions of popular art is the work produced by the clay modeler Vitalino Pereira dos Santos (1909–1963), known as Mestre Vitalino, from the northeastern state of Pernambuco, and by those artists who have been inspired by him. The clay figures produced by Mestre Vitalino were initially criticized for their technical crudeness, but the expressiveness and extreme economy of the pieces have since been acknowledged. The figures deal with everyday themes with both humor and respect. The best-known figures are those dealing with bourgeois professionals, for example doctors and dentists, and their patients, often in amusing and rather grotesque situations or poses, such as a gynecological examination or a dentist pressing his foot against a patient's chest in order to help extract a tooth. Some depict the *retirantes* (poor migrant workers) heading east toward the coast in search of work, cow-herders, Lampião and other *cangaceiros* (social bandits), the old Iberian tradition of personifying animals to parody undesirable human traits, and so on. In Alto do Moura in Pernambuco, a small group of craftsmen and craftswomen, including Mestre Vitalino's children and grandchildren, carry on his work (as do untold imitators throughout the northeastern hinterland), creating figures destined for the cheap end of the souvenir trade. Recent changes in the production of the figures include the use of industrially produced paints and the inclusion of new themes. The work therefore is similar to *literatura de cordel* (chapbooks) in that its creators reveal a gift for communicating their community's view of the world. To some extent, the artists serve as the guardians of local memory and knowledge.

Folheteiros, the writers of *literatura de cordel*, took up printmaking in the 1940s, and a veritable school of chapbook illustrators grew up as a result. The covers of chapbooks, traditionally black-and-white *xilogravuras*, or woodblock prints, gradually became larger and incorporated color, and from the 1970s onward the more talented artists began to exhibit their work in galleries. Two such printmakers are José Francisco Borges (1935–) and Dila (José Soares da Silva, 1937–), both born into poverty in Pernambuco.

Another example of modern tourist "curio chic" from northeastern Brazil is the paraphernalia relating to the Afro-Brazilian religion *Candomblé*. Mestre Didi (1917–), the most celebrated Afro-Brazilian sculptor and craftsman, is a high priest in *Candomblé* in the state of Bahia and is therefore regarded as an unquestionably "authentic" producer of popular art. The pieces he produces are inspired by his faith and are used in religious celebrations, and they are thus of interest from both functional and aesthetic perspectives. The paintings of Rita Loureiro (1952–), from the state of Amazonas, depict expressions of rural popular culture, such as the *festas juninas*, or June popular religious festivals. Her style has been widely imitated, and once again the souvenir market provides a useful outlet for this work. The paintings depict lush green land, dark blue starry skies, and brightly painted matchstick-style people and animals in the middle ground going about their business, suggesting a harmony among the different elements of the natural world.

—*Stephanie Dennison*

See also: *Popular Literature: Literatura de Cordel; Popular Religion and Festivals: Candomblé; Visual Arts and Architecture:* Architecture and Landscape Design (*Favelas*)

Bibliography

Armstrong, Elizabeth, and Zamudio Taylor. 2000. *UltraBaroque: Aspects of Post–Latin American Art.* San Diego, CA: Museum of Contemporary Art.

Tribe, Tania Costa, ed. 2001. *Heroes and Artists: Popular Art and the Brazilian Imagination.* Cambridge: BrazilConnects and Fitzwilliam Museum.

Architecture and Landscape Design

Latin American architecture incorporates ideas from abroad, but often with a distinctive twist. For example, the Swiss-born French architect Charles-Edouard Le Corbusier has had considerable influence on such architects as the Mexican Juan O'Gorman and the Brazilians Lucio Costa and Oscar Niemeyer. In Brazil, the modernist architectural aesthetic was modified on Latin American soil in order to both reflect and function more effectively within the tropical setting.

The wave of architectural innovation between the 1930s and 1980s in Latin America had its chief expression in those countries with the greatest economic muscle and, in terms of social modernization, with the most to prove, namely Mexico, Brazil, and

Venezuela, resulting in the monumental efforts of Carlos Raúl Villanueva in Caracas; Pedro Ramírez Vásquez, Juan O'Gorman, and former partners Abraham Zabludowsky and Teodoro González de León in Mexico City; and Lucio Costa and Oscar Niemeyer in Brasília. The work of Costa and Niemeyer has entered the international architectural canon. Furthermore, innovative constructions have been created in the Chilean capital by Cristián de Groote and Mathias Klotz and in the Colombian capital by Rogelio Saltona. The Andean countries have shown less tendency toward architectural auteurs, and new developments there often take on the characteristics of an anonymous, internationalized modernity.

Colonial architecture in the national heritage site of Villa de Leyva, Colombia. (Courtesy of Claire Taylor)

Meanwhile, the architectural heritage of many Latin American cities faces a series of pressing dilemmas. The dichotomy between conservation and modernization is proving irreconcilable: on the one hand, the colonial heart is ripped out of many urban centers like Lima and La Paz to make way for unscrupulously utilitarian and aesthetically indefensible new structures. On the other hand, UNESCO grants have helped preserve certain smaller cities, such as Potosí and Sucre in Bolivia, the Ecuadorian capital Quito and the center of Cuenca, and Cartagena de Indias and Santa Cruz de Mompox in Colombia. UNESCO funds are also earmarked to preserve the old district of the Chilean port of Valparaíso. Protected Peruvian sites include the Incan remains of Machu Picchu, the unique mix of Incan and Spanish colonial architecture at Cuzco, and Arequipa, the white baroque city built of volcanic stone in the south of the country. Other designated heritage sites include the center of Lima, once the City of Kings and head of a Viceroyalty, though much damage has already been done there. Meanwhile, La Paz, the administrative capital of Bolivia, steadily loses what little remains of its architectural past.

The proud colonial legacy of many Latin American cities has been threatened for some time by a number of factors. Paramount among these is the inexorable advance of the motor vehicle, with its concomitant destruction of urban communities for the purpose of road building. The utilitarian nature of much architecture from the 1960s and 1970s (a reflection of a trend that occurred slightly earlier in Europe) also produced a crass attitude toward the notion of patrimony, as many city centers were wrecked to make way for ill-considered brutal "developments." Another factor has been the encroachment of rural migrant populations into urban areas, where they have settled and have begun to create distinct architectural features unencumbered by European traditions and sensibilities, such as in the *favelas* in Brazil and the *pueblos jóvenes* (young towns) in Peru.

Groups of concerned architects, both local and foreign, are making an effort to alleviate the devastation and urban chaos. In Havana the international conference The Havana Project (December 1994–January 1995) examined ways to restore the city's former glory while responding to its current needs. Looking to the Future, a similar event held in 2000 involving architects from Bolivia and the Netherlands, looked at solutions for the difficulties experienced by La Paz in an era of rapid change and demographic explosion. The colonial center of Lima is similarly under threat, although under the guidance of Mayor Alberto Andrade in the 1990s, serious efforts were made to restore and protect the old streets with their famous carved wooden balconies. In the outskirts of the Peruvian capital, though, a very different architectural prospect emerged: a swath of shantytowns has grown up that in the early 1980s still consisted mostly of shacks made of wicker panels, often without even a roof. Families improved their dwelling as best they could, acquiring bricks, mortar, and other materials as they saved, and gradually making their houses more secure and habitable. These euphemistically named *pueblos jóvenes* thus gradually acquire permanency and respectability. A case in point is Villa el Salvador, which lies to the south of Lima on the road to Ica and Arequipa. Within a few decades this settlement evolved from a pitiful collection of shacks into an impressively well-coordinated suburb, benefiting from the "informal" economy that is the locals' only viable source of income.

Although drastic improvements have been made in the infrastructure of *favela* communities in Brazil since the 1980s, on the initiative of nongovernmental organizations and local inhabitants as well as the state, these poor neighborhoods are increasingly coming under threat because of drug-related gang violence. The evolution of these communities and the dangers their inhabitants encounter on a daily basis were eloquently conveyed in the film *Cidade de Deus* (*City of God*, 2002). Despite the dangers, some *favela* dwellers (known as *favelados*) prefer to take their chances in the *favela* rather than move far away from their place of work and social life to a *conjunto habitacional*, the equivalent of the housing projects in the United States or of council housing estates in the United Kingdom, where there is no guarantee that the same violent elements will not eventually install themselves. *Cidade de Deus* depicted this dilemma well: the 1960s housing project of the same name drew residents from a number of different *favelas* near the center to the then isolated West Zone of Rio de Janeiro. As so often happens with such housing schemes, the residents of this new community were out of sight and were left to fend for themselves. Without their old community ties and with wholly inadequate schooling, policing, and transportation into the city center, lawlessness ensued, and self-declared gangster leaders were quick to occupy the power vacuum. Although Cidade de Deus is not officially recognized as a *favela*, such are the conditions in which residents live that most *cariocas* (the inhabitants of Rio de Janeiro) would not hesitate to give the place this label.

Perhaps the least known yet one of the most original aspects of architectural projects in Latin America is innovative garden design, most closely associated with the Brazilian Roberto Burle Marx. During the presidency of Juscelino Kubitschek (1956–

1961), Burle Marx, along with modernist architects Lucio Costa and Oscar Niemeyer, was given free reign to design the new federal capital, Brasília. Architectural projects in Brazil today still include a focus on landscape gardening. Similarly, in the northern Andes, topiary—particularly designs that reflect the natural world or pre-Columbian life—is used to enhance public spaces for the benefit of the local population and tourists alike.

—Keith Richards, Lisa Shaw, and Stephanie Dennison

See also: *Popular Cinema:* The Brazilian Film Industry (Box-Office Successes and Contemporary Film in Brazil)

Bibliography

Bayón, Damián. 1998. "Architecture, c. 1920–c. 1980." Pp. 369–392 in *A Cultural History of Latin America: Literature, Music, and the Visual Arts in the 19th and 20th Centuries,* edited by Leslie Bethell. Cambridge: Cambridge University Press.

Low, Setha M., ed. 1999. *Theorizing the City: The New Urban Anthropology Reader.* New Brunswick, NJ: Rutgers University Press.

Modern Architecture in Mexico

Since the end of the Mexican Revolution in 1920, a huge number of architectural projects have been commissioned by successive Mexican governments in order to embody the spirit of the new revolutionary nation. These buildings tend to be modernist in inspiration, often taking their lead from the work of the Swiss-born French architect Charles-Edouard Le Corbusier, and tend to project an image of Mexico as a modern nation in the full sway of "international style." Nevertheless, many of the most successful buildings combine modernism and an interest in new technologies with recognition of Mexican traditional architecture and iconography from the precolonial period. More specifically, in order to express a sense of Mexican national identity, such projects combine terracing with pyramidal constructions or integrate traditional building materials, such as the volcanic stone *tezontle,* with concrete.

One of the most interesting and complex architects of the early post-revolutionary period was Juan O'Gorman (1905–1982), whose contributions to the University City on the south side of Mexico City are his most famous landmarks. His early work of the 1930s, such as the house he designed for Frida Kahlo and Diego Rivera in San Angel (now a suburb, then a village, south of Mexico City), is exemplary of minimalism (two cubes—one blue, one pink—linked by a bridge). However, his University Library of the 1950s overuses pre-Columbian monumental references (the whole building is covered in an Aztec-style mosaic), which combine awkwardly with the functionalism of the building. Perhaps the most successful building in the modernist style to incorporate references to pre-Columbian architecture is Pedro Ramírez Vásquez's Anthropology Museum, built from 1963 to 1965 in Mexico City's Chapultepec Park. In this structure, terracing is used to great effect, usefully guiding the visitor around the museum and providing a visual link with the context of the artifacts exhibited. In the 1970s and 1980s, former partners Abraham Zabludowsky and Teodoro González de León won a significant number of competitions to design impressive public buildings in Mexico, including the National Auditorium in Chapultepec Park, built in an officially endorsed modernist, monumentalist style.

Anthropology Museum, Mexico City. (Danny Lehman/Corbis)

The work of Luis Barragán (1902–1989), though no less influential than that of his contemporary O'Gorman, was conducted largely in the domain of private construction. Barragán's main contribution to Mexican architecture is his use of color in conjunction with a modernist style of construction. His choice of bold colors—ochre, cerise pink, intense sky blue—is both very modern and very Mexican. Although his work takes cues from the decoration of colonial haciendas, it manages to do so without reminding Mexicans of a period of their history that in the post-revolutionary era they were eager to forget. Barragán's work is mainly hidden away from the public eye behind the high fences of such luxurious suburbs of Mexico City as the Pedregal de San Angel, a suburb that Barragán was instrumental in designing from scratch. However, his collaboration with Mathias Goeritz on the Satélite Towers—five huge, purely decorative, brightly colored concrete towers that mark the entrance to the Satélite city district to the north of Mexico City—remains a startling reminder of the impact of his work on the face of the city. Barragán's main disciple is Juan Legorreta, who, even though he is criticized for playing with color at the expense of attention to detail in construction or even functionality, is still one of Mexico's internationally best-known and most identifiably "Mexican" architects.

In contemporary Mexico, the taste for buildings that make great use of the latest technologies in building design, often imported from abroad, continues, although now usually without reference to the nation's specific geographical and historical context. Since the late 1980s the scene has been dominated by commissions for buildings from private, often transnational, corporations rather than from the Mexican state, hence perhaps lessening interest in the expression of "Mexicanness" and even, on occasion, leading to indulgence in postmodernist eclecticism. Nevertheless, some conversions of buildings in the old downtown area of Mexico City show signs of a continued dialogue between the old and the new in Mexican architecture.

—*Thea Pitman*

See also: *Visual Arts and Architecture:* Art (Frida Kahlo; Diego Rivera)

Bibliography

Bayón, Damián. 1998. "Architecture, c. 1920–c. 1980." Pp. 369–392 in *A Cultural History of Latin America: Literature, Music, and the Visual Arts in the 19th and 20th Centuries,* edited by Leslie Bethell. Cambridge: Cambridge University Press.

Burian, Edward R., ed. 1997. *Modernity and the Architecture of Mexico.* Austin: University of Texas Press.

Ingersoll, Richard. 1996. "A Silent Reproach: Observations on Recent Mexican Architecture." Pp. 6–16 in *Mexico 90's: Una arquitectura contemporánea/A Contemporary Architecture,* edited by Miquel Adrià. Mexico City: Ediciones GG.

Mutlow, John V. 2004. *The New Architecture of Mexico.* Victoria, Australia: Images.

Lucio Costa (1902–1998)

The Brazilian architect and urban planner Lucio Costa is best remembered for designing the layout of the purpose-built capital city, Brasília, inaugurated in 1960. One of the most significant examples of postwar city planning, Brasília put Brazilian architecture and urban planning on the international map, despite criticism that it was excessively functional. Closely associated with the rise of modernism in Brazilian architecture, Costa worked alongside Oscar Niemeyer on various projects.

In 1957 Costa was chosen from among other contenders to design the so-called pilot plan, or layout, for Brasília. Costa's fundamental idea for the city was unfashionably formal, based on two axes crossing each other at right angles in the sign of a cross. Brasília's site, on a high plateau in central Brazil, is a triangle of land sloping southeastward down to an artificial lake. One axis of the cross, the so-called monumental axis, runs down to the lake and contains the national and municipal centers; the other curves around the contour of a hill and contains the residential districts. Where the axes cross is the central district of large shops, hotels, banks, cinemas, restaurants, and other important buildings, such as the national theater. Traffic is provided for by six-lane highways along the monumental axis and a complex of local and express highways along the residential axis.

Costa was born in Toulon, France, to Brazilian parents. His father was Admiral Joaquim Ribeiro da Costa. He studied at the Royal Grammar School in Newcastle upon Tyne, England, and in Montreux, Switzerland. After returning to Brazil in 1917 he studied painting and architecture at the Escola Nacional de Belas Artes (National School of Fine Arts) in Rio de Janeiro, graduating in 1924. In 1930 he was appointed director of this prestigious art school and set about introducing important changes to its curriculum, most importantly the study of the emerging modernist aesthetic. From 1930 to 1932 Costa established a highly fruitful partnership with the Russian architect Gregori Warchavchik, who introduced modernism to Brazil.

In 1936 Costa persuaded the Swiss-born French architect Charles-Edouard Le Corbusier to visit Brazil in order to contribute to the plans for the new headquarters of the Ministry of Education in Rio. The decision to invite Le Corbusier to sketch out the first lines of the new ministry design was an act of protest against the plans of Archimedes Memória, whose art deco–style building had won the formal contest held to find the lead architect for the project. Costa's bold decision to override the result gave Brazilian modernist architecture the official seal of approval.

In 1938 Costa was involved, along with Oscar Niemeyer, in the design of the Brazilian Pavilion for the New York World's Fair of the following year. This building combined Brazilian architectural expression with the ideas of Le Corbusier. Its slender pillars, known as *pilotis*, and ramps, inner courtyards, and terraces with tropical gardens were characteristic of the Brazilian modernist style. In 1948 Costa created two projects that would prove to be paradigmatic for architects throughout Brazil: the Parque Guinle residential complex in the city of Rio de Janeiro and the Hotel do Park São Clemente in the mountain city of Nova Friburgo in the state of Rio de Janeiro. Costa played an important role in Brazil's Institute of National Historical and Artistic Heritage (IPHAN), becoming a pioneer in the protection of the urban and natural environment.

Costa enjoyed international recognition, and in 1960 he was appointed to an honorary position at Harvard University. Four years later he was asked to lead a project to restore the city of Florence, Italy, which had suffered flood damage. In 1976 he was invited to submit plans for the construction of the new capital city of Nigeria, Abuja, a project that was never carried out.

—Lisa Shaw

See also: *Visual Arts and Architecture:* Architecture and Landscape Design (Oscar Niemeyer)

Bibliography

Cavalcanti, Lauro. 2003. *When Brazil Was Modern: A Guide to Architecture, 1928–1960.* New York: Princeton Architectural Press.

Costa, Lucio. 1995. *Lucio Costa: Registro de uma vivência.* São Paulo: Empresa das Artes.

———. 1998. *Lucio Costa: Documentos de trabalho.* Rio de Janeiro: MEC/IPHAN.

Deckker, Zilah Quezado. 2000. *Brazil Built: The Architecture of the Modern Movement in Brazil.* London and New York: Routledge.

Oscar Niemeyer (1907–)

Oscar Niemeyer was the most influential Brazilian architect of the twentieth century. His works include the major monumental and government buildings in the capital, Brasília, and the new Museum of Contemporary Art in Niterói in Rio de Janeiro state. Niemeyer's work epitomizes the modernist style, inspired by the Swiss-born French architect Charles-Edouard Le Corbusier. It is characterized by its graceful curved forms and its use of concrete structures. Niemeyer began his career in the office of Lucio Costa in 1934 after graduating from the National School of Fine Art in Rio de Janeiro. He replaced Costa in the group that worked on Le Corbusier's design for the headquarters of the Ministry of Education in Rio de Janeiro, built between 1936 and 1945.

The purpose-built capital city, Brasília, inaugurated in 1960, will remain a lasting tes-

Oscar Niemeyer's MAC (Museum of Contemporary Art), Niterói, Brazil. (Courtesy of Alex Nield)

tament to Niemeyer's vision and skill in creating strikingly simple forms. The city's critics refer to the rather timeworn "space-age" quality of the architecture, which was considered futuristic when the city was built, but the most successful buildings combine function and structure to great effect. The concave and convex domes of the National Congress and the graceful columns (*pilotis*) of the Alvorada and Planalto Palaces and the Supreme Court are highly original features and reflect the architect's utopian goals. Niemeyer also designed the city's cathedral, and because of his position as architectural adviser for the new capital, his influence and authority extended throughout the area of the original city plan.

Beyond Brasília, Niemeyer was responsible for the following critically acclaimed constructions: Rio's cathedral and Sambadrome (the open-air auditorium where the annual Carnival parade is held); the Pampulha architectural complex, which includes the Church of St. Francis of Assisi (decorated by Cândido Portinari), in the city of Belo Horizonte in Minas Gerais; and the stunning Museum of Contemporary Art in Niterói, opened in 1996 and initially nicknamed "the flying saucer" by locals but now regularly cited as one of the most beautiful examples of contemporary architecture. Further afield, his works include the Museum of Modern Art in Caracas, the headquarters of the Communist

Party in Paris, the head office of Editora Mondatori in Milan, and Constantine University in Algeria.

Niemeyer's signature techniques are the use of reinforced concrete to form curves or a shell and the exploitation of the aesthetic possibilities of the straight line. He has used such features in the construction of factories, skyscrapers, exhibition centers, residential areas, theaters, places of worship, head office buildings for public- and private-sector companies, universities, recreational clubs, and hospitals, among others.

Niemeyer has won many international prizes in recognition of his contribution to world architecture, such as the Gold Medal of the American Institute of Architecture (1970), a UNESCO prize (1980), the prestigious Pritzker architectural prize (1988), an award from the Catalan College of Architects in Barcelona (1990), and the Gold Medal from the Royal Institute of British Architects (1998). Closer to home, in 1989 he was honored by the Rio de Janeiro samba school Unidos de Lucas, which based the theme of its Carnival parade that year on his architectural designs.

When the military dictatorship came to power in Brazil in 1964, Niemeyer, a committed Communist, was forced into exile in France. In the late 1960s he resumed his career in Brazil, teaching at the University of Rio de Janeiro and working in private practice.

—Lisa Shaw

See also: *Popular Music:* Samba; *Popular Religion and Festivals:* Popular Festivals (Carnival in Brazil); *Visual Arts and Architecture:* Architecture and Landscape Design (Lucio Costa); Art (Cândido Portinari)

Bibliography

Fundação Oscar Niemeyer Official Website. http://www.niemeyer.org.br (consulted 15 December 2003).

Museum of Contemporary Art of Niterói Official Website. http://www.macniteroi.com (consulted 15 December 2003).

Niemeyer, Oscar. 2000. *Curves of Time: Oscar Niemeyer Memoirs.* London: Phaidon.

Salvaing, Matthieu. 2002. *Oscar Niemeyer.* Paris and London: Assouline.

Sharp, Dennis. 1991. *The Illustrated Encyclopedia of Architects and Architecture.* New York: Quatro.

Underwood, David Kendrick. 1994. *Oscar Niemeyer and Brazilian Free-Form Modernism.* New York: George Braziller.

Pueblos Jóvenes

Pueblos jóvenes (young towns) is a term used to refer to unofficial urban settlements in Peru. The majority of Peru's *pueblos jóvenes* are grouped around its main cities. Lima, the capital, and the cities of Arequipa and Trujillo contain most of these settlements, with Lima having the greatest concentration. These communities started as a result of the mass migration of rural dwellers to Peru's main cities in the mid-twentieth century.

As Skidmore and Smith note, by the late 1960s, an estimated 750,000 rural migrants were living in the Lima area alone, and the majority of these were housed in squatter shantytowns. According to recent estimates (Ghersi 1997, p. 103), by the 1990s roughly half of Lima's population of eight million lived in these informal settlements. The *pueblos jóvenes* frequently lack one or more of such basic services as water, sewerage, public lighting, and roads.

Although these settlements originally sprang up in an independent and unsystematic way, the Peruvian government came to realize that buying a house by traditional means was beyond the resources of most Peruvians. By the late 1960s the then military government had decided that rather than quashing such illegal settlements it would encourage them to seek official recognition, and in 1968 it introduced the term *pueblos jóvenes* to replace the more informal *barriadas* (shantytowns). Although this did grant status to these developments, successive governments have been unable to keep up with their rapid growth, and many are still lacking essential services.

The dwellings within *pueblos jóvenes* are usually constructed over a long period of time, with improvements and amendments being made gradually. Homes are usually built by family members and friends rather than by established construction companies, and they are usually initially built of temporary materials such as wicker panels, to be replaced later by bricks and mortar.

The phenomenon of *pueblos jóvenes* has been instrumental in transforming traditional class relations in Peru. Whereas historically the underprivileged were not property owners, the rise of these informal constructions has provided a way for those at the bottom of the economic ladder to own their own homes.

—*Claire Taylor*

Bibliography

Batley, Richard. 1980. *Access to Urban Services: Studies of Squatter Settlement Improvement in Lima and Caracas.* Birmingham, UK: University of Birmingham.

Ghersi, Enrique. 1997. "The Informal Economy in Latin America." *Cato Journal: An Interdisciplinary Journal of Public Policy Analysis* 17, no. 1: 99–108.

Paerregaard, Karsten. 1997. *Linking Separate Worlds: Urban Migrants and Rural Lives in Peru.* Oxford: Berg.

Skidmore, Thomas E., and Peter H. Smith, eds. 1992. "Peru: Soldiers, Oligarchs, and Indians." Pp. 185–220 in *Modern Latin America.* Oxford: Oxford University Press.

Favelas

The *favelas*—Brazilian shantytowns or slum dwellings, particularly associated with the picturesque hillsides of Rio de Janeiro—were first set up in the early twentieth century and still exist on inhospitable land in Rio de Janeiro and other large cities, such as the land alongside major roads and rivers in São Paulo and on swampland in the northeastern city of Recife. These shantytowns serve as homes for the millions of migrant workers who pour into these cities from the northeastern countryside and other poor rural areas.

The origin of the *favelas* can be traced to the beginning of the twentieth century in Rio de Janeiro, then the Brazilian capital, when, in an attempt to "civilize" the city in the style of Baron Georges-Eugène Haussmann's reforms of downtown Paris, Mayor Pereira Passos ordered the *cortiços*, or overcrowded and unsanitary tenement buildings of the city center, to be pulled down. This so-called *bota-abaixo* left a large number of the city's poorer residents with no choice but to set up makeshift homes on the steep hillsides (*morros*) that dot Rio's landscape, the only spaces left on which to build near the center and places of work. The *favelas* that they constructed on the *morros* were originally groups of wooden shacks (*barracos*) made of abandoned planks of wood and other basic materials left over from the *bota-abaixo*, erected on unclaimed or illegally occupied land.

The term *favela* (literally, "beanstalk") is said to have been brought to Rio de Janeiro by soldiers returning from the battle of Canudos (1897) in the northeastern state of Bahia. One of the first *favelas* in Rio was built on land covered in beanstalks, similar to a settlement called Favela in the state of Bahia, where many were posted during the war. In Rio de Janeiro the term *morro* is commonly used to refer to these communities today.

The modern official definition of a *favela* is a collection of at least fifty-one makeshift homes made with the most basic materials (cheap bricks and mortar have now replaced stucco and wood) on unoccupied land and having sparse access to public services such as sanitation, electricity, and transportation. According to the year 2000 census, there are 3,905 *favelas* in Brazil, and these are predominantly found in large cities: one in five *cariocas* (residents of Rio de Janeiro) lives in such a home. In the modern middle-class imagination the term *favela* describes frightening, crime-ridden, no-go areas (unless one wants to buy cocaine) that cannot be reached by public transport.

Many of the old problems encountered by the *favelados* (*favela* dwellers) of the first half of the twentieth century continue, such as the stigma associated with living in such a place and its resultant social exclusion; the risk of landslides, especially during the rainy season, in *favelas* built on hillsides; and health risks in slums that have yet to be provided with such basic sanitation services as running water and sewerage. But in many ways the lives of *favelados* have improved: gradually public services are reaching the slums via a number of initiatives set up by state and federal governments, such as Rio's *Favela-Bairro* (*Favela*-Neighborhood) project. This is the biggest informal settlement upgrading program in Latin America, which since the early 1990s has sought to transform squatter settlements into recognized *bairros* (neighborhoods) by integrating them into the city's municipal infrastructure. The project includes the important work of regularizing land titles: problems over ownership of the land on which residents' homes are built are one of the reasons *favelas* have been (and in many instances continue to be) lawless. Shantytown community groups have also been instrumental in attempting to improve the quality of life of the local population.

Access to consumer goods has also improved: most *favelados* possess a refrigerator and a television set, for example. Residents of Rio de Janeiro's Rocinha, the largest slum in Latin America and home to 150,000 Brazilians, deny that their community is a *favela*. Public services have been set up in Rocinha, which is one of the oldest hillside settlements and is literally a stone's throw away from some of Brazil's most exclusive condominiums in the São Conrado district of the city. As a result, residents (or rather the fortunate and financially better-off ones who live at the bottom of the hill and often pay more rent than *cariocas* living in apartments in decent neighborhoods) have access to a range of services destined for Rio's wealthiest class. There is a considerable difference between the two- and sometimes three-story, brightly painted homes that cover the Rocinha hillside and the "cardboard cities" to be found underneath viaducts, for example, or the dilapidated wooden shacks with corrugated iron roofs built randomly alongside main thoroughfares. The latter, especially those that line the routes from the airports into city centers and the wealthy South Zones of Rio and São Paulo, have long been a headache for municipal governments. The billboards frequently placed in front of these

View of Rocinha, Rio de Janeiro. (Courtesy of Deborah Dwek)

makeshift dwellings to hide them from view have ironically been converted into housing for the truly desperate.

The quality of life has not improved overall for *favelados*. In recent decades, the gap between rich and poor in Brazil's cities has widened, and since the early 1980s many *favelados* have been facing a new and dangerous challenge: residents are now living in the shadow of gangland violence. Organized criminal gangs, with names such as Comando Vermelho (Red Command) and Terceiro Comando (Third Command), have taken control of many *favelas* in Brazil's large cities. *Favelas* make the perfect space in which to hide out, given their confused, labyrinthine streets and houses that all look the same (in some *favelas*, the gangs force residents to paint their homes the same color to confuse the police). Police regularly invade the *favelas* in search of criminals, and innocent residents are frequently caught in the crossfire that invariably ensues. In April 2004 the American School in Rio de Janeiro had to be closed until further notice because it was located in the middle of a three-way battle waged by rival drug gangs and police. This turf war over cocaine distribution points, which swept down from the Rocinha slum and involved a rival gang from Vidigal, a neighboring *favela*, claimed fifteen lives in just one week. As the fighting threatened to engulf the wealthy district of São Conrado, plans were floated to seal off Rocinha inside a security fence.

Of the 3,000 deaths that occur every year in Rio de Janeiro, most take place in the *favelas.* The internal space of the *favela* community is no longer used for leisure or recreation as it once was, with the exception of churchgoing, particularly attendance at the new Protestant (*evangélico*) churches that allegedly have come to dominate the *favelas* because of their tolerance of the drug traffickers.

Many police officers reputedly collaborate with the gangland bosses, as portrayed vividly in the box-office smash *Cidade de Deus* (*City of God*, 2002). Owners of the few commercial outlets found in most *favelas*, such as *botequins* (little bars) and the odd grocery store, depend on protection from the gangs that rule the slums. The violence, intimidation, and summary justice meted out by drug traffickers have produced a culture of silence within the *favelas.* As a result, even if the police were effectual, residents would be loath to call upon their help. With an estimated 100,000 members of drug gangs in possession of 65,000 firearms, it is unclear what the poorly paid and badly equipped police could do anyway. Political leaders struggle with the issue of police occupations of *favelas*, which tend to produce untold turmoil for residents and only a temporary lull in cocaine trafficking. That said, the Brazilian army occupied Rio's *favelas* for one week in 1992 during the international Earth Summit (Rio-Eco '92), and most *cariocas*, including many *favelados*, reportedly felt safe in their home city for the first time.

The extent to which drug culture is turning *favelas* in cities like Rio de Janeiro into unimaginably dangerous places was brought home to *cariocas* in 2002 with the sadistic murder of Tim Lopes, a well-known undercover TV investigator. Residents of the Favela da Grota asked Lopes to help do something about the daily violence in their community at the hands of the drug bosses. Lopes, who had worked on a number of high-profile stories about corruption and drug culture in Rio, entered the *favela* with nothing more than a hidden camera. He is said to have lost his life at the hand of the notorious drug baron Elias Maluco (Elias the Mad): he was tortured and executed, and his body was set on fire and dumped.

Despite the dangers, or perhaps because of them, *favelas* are a source of great curiosity to outsiders. *Favela* tours are becoming increasingly popular in tourist cities such as Rio de Janeiro, where safe passage by Jeep through the shantytown is guaranteed by the gangland bosses at a cost to the organizers. It is also possible to visit a *favela* during the run-up to Carnival by attending a practice session of a samba school, many of the more traditional of which, such as Mangueira and Salgueiro in Rio, are based in hillside slums.

—*Stephanie Dennison*

See also: *Popular Music:* Samba; *Popular Social Movements and Politics:* Base Communities in Brazil; *Travel and Tourism:* Ecotourism; *Popular Cinema:* The Brazilian Film Industry (Box-Office Successes and Contemporary Film in Brazil); *Popular Religion and Festivals:* New Protestantism (Brazil); Popular Festivals (Carnival in Brazil)

Bibliography

Almanaque Abril: Brasil 2003. São Paulo: Abril.

Bellos, Alex. 2002. "Brutal Death Sours Cup Joy." *Observer*, London, 7 July.

Gamini, Gabriella. 2004. "Rio's Rich Caught in Crossfire of Drug Gang War." *Times*, London, 17 April.

Marins, Paulo César Garcez. 1998. "Habitação e vizinhança: Limites da privacidade no surgimento das metrópoles brasileiras." Pp. 132–214 in *História da vida privada no*

An example of popular architecture in El Alto, Bolivia. This style is often scorned as part of a process of *cholificación* (deriving from the contemptuous *cholo*, an Andean term connoting indigenous origin and partial acculturation). (Courtesy of Keith Richards)

Brasil, vol. 3, edited by Nicolau Sevcenko. São Paulo: Companhia das Letras.

Perlman, Janice E. *Marginality: From Myth to Reality in the Favelas of Rio de Janeiro, 1969–2002.* www.idpm.man.ac.uk/cprc/Conference/conferencespapers/Perlman02.04.03.pdf (consulted March 2004).

Zaluar, Alba. 1998. "Para não dizer que não falei de samba: Os enigmas da violência no Brasil." Pp. 245–318 in *História da vida privada no Brasil*, vol. 4, edited by Lilia Moritz Schwarcz. São Paulo: Companhia das Letras.

Popular Architecture in Bolivia

A recognizable style of building is beginning to emerge in La Paz and in the city of El Alto, situated on the high plateau immediately above La Paz. This type of popular architecture, created by members of Aymara-speaking groups, is often scorned as part of a process of *cholificación* (deriving from the contemptuous *cholo*, an Andean term connoting indigenous origin and partial acculturation).

In the 1980s El Alto was a community of some 20,000 people, but currently it is home to around one million inhabitants. Building here had to begin from scratch, with very little in the way of a guiding tradition (this tendency is also evident in La Paz itself). The steep, narrow streets of the old city are undergoing a barrage of "modernization" as older adobe buildings are allowed to deteriorate and are eventually replaced by perfunctory brick dwellings,

Popular architecture in El Alto, Bolivia. (Courtesy of Keith Richards)

allowing the possibility for family expansion, which is accommodated by building upward. Those who can afford it eventually decorate the houses with abstract designs in a variety of colors. The members of Aymara-speaking groups who are largely responsible for these transformations belong to a nouveau riche, marginalized bourgeoisie, hugely successful in bringing consumer goods to these new markets through contraband from Chilean ports and through uncannily efficient commercial pirating.

The defiant political attitude demonstrated by Aymara speakers can also be seen as a reflection of a cultural position: the demolition of colonial and republican buildings, ostensibly to make space for new construction, has been seen as a response to centuries of oppression by the Spanish-speaking elite. The same might be said of the destruction of government buildings and other manifestations of privilege during the political unrest of February and October 2003.

The inhabitants of El Alto and those looking in from the outside hold markedly different attitudes toward the phenomena of urban migration and informal transformation of the cityscape. Groups of concerned architects, both local and foreign, are making efforts to alleviate such tensions. The architect Carlos Villagómez has criticized other Bolivian architects for being too paternalistic, saying their middle-class viewpoints conditioned by periods of European study leave them in a poor position to understand the concerns of Aymara migrants.

In 2003 Villagómez founded the Fundación de Estética Andina (FEA, Foundation for Andean Aesthetics), aimed at providing lasting and inclusive solutions to the problems of La Paz and El Alto. The acronym "FEA" spells the Spanish word for "ugly," yet although this might suggest more elitist sneering from the educated classes, Villagómez is himself at pains to emphasize his part-Aymara heritage. The foundation, which organizes numerous outdoor events intended to raise questions of the use of public space for the widest possible audience, takes *chola* architecture as a fait accompli that can be incorporated into Bolivia's broader cultural life and turned into a coherent aesthetic.

—*Keith Richards*

See also: *Language:* Indigenous Languages

Bibliography

Flores Troche, Northon. 2002. *Mirando al futuro/Looking to the Future.* The Hague: Prince Claus Fund for Culture and Development.

Low, Setha M., ed. 1999. *Theorizing the City: The New Urban Anthropology Reader.* New Brunswick, NJ: Rutgers University Press.

———. 2000. *On the Plaza: The Politics of Public Space and Culture.* Austin: University of Texas Press.

Villagómez, Carlos. 2004. *La Paz ha muerto.* La Paz: Plural.

Villanueva, Paulina, ed. 2000. *Carlos Raúl Villanueva.* New York: Princeton Architectural Press.

Roberto Burle Marx (1909–1994)

Brazilian landscape designer Roberto Burle Marx worked alongside architects Lucio Costa and Oscar Niemeyer to create some of the most striking examples of the modernist aesthetic in Brazil. He is perhaps best known for the tropical gardens that relieve the architectural austerity of the pragmatically designed capital city, Brasília, for which he planned the layout and selection of plant varieties to add a vivid green backdrop to the otherwise dry, yellow landscape of the local savanna vegetation.

Burle Marx worked with Costa and Niemeyer on the Ministry of Education building in Rio de Janeiro, which was begun in 1936 and is generally considered the first great monument to modern Brazilian architecture. He landscaped the building's broad esplanade, one of the many open spaces that are characteristic of this new style of architecture. The Costa–Niemeyer–Burle Marx team was then, in the 1940s, invited to create Pampulha Park in the city of Belo Horizonte in Minas Gerais state. Burle Marx's talents for landscape design were shown off to the full in this expansive recreational area, built around an artificial lake, which discreetly houses several public buildings, including an art museum and the Church of St. Francis of Assisi, designed by Niemeyer and decorated with murals by Cândido Portinari.

Burle Marx was born in São Paulo and moved to Rio de Janeiro as a small child. In 1928 he studied painting in Germany for a year. He spent a lot of time in Berlin's botanical gardens, where he came across Brazilian plants in the hothouses. His first landscape design was for an architectural project by Lucio Costa and Gregori Warchavchik in 1932.

In 1949 Burle Marx bought a large estate in Barra de Guaratiba, Rio de Janeiro, where he brought together a huge variety of plant species, which he had been collecting since early childhood. In an area of approximately 600,000 square meters he managed to create one of the most important collections of tropical and semitropical plants in the world, containing more than 3,500 different species. Today, the estate is also dedicated to research and teaching activities and houses Burle Marx's private library of approximately 3,000 titles. In 1985 he donated the estate's farm, and all of its archives, to Brazil's Institute of National Historical and Artistic Heritage (IPHAN).

In 1955 Burle Marx founded the company Burle Marx & Cia. Ltda., which carried out major landscape projects as well as the planning and maintenance of private and public gardens. Between 1965 and the year of his death, he worked alongside the architect Haruyoshi Ono, who is the company's current director.

—Lisa Shaw

See also: *Visual Arts and Architecture:* Architecture and Landscape Design (Lucio Costa; Oscar Niemeyer); Art (Cândido Portinari)

Bibliography

Burle Marx Official Website. http://www.burlemarx.com.br (consulted 15 December 2003).

Eliovson, Sima, and Roberto Burle Marx. 1991. *The Gardens of Roberto Burle Marx.* Portland, OR: Timber.

Montero, Marta Iris. 2001. *Roberto Burle Marx: The Lyrical Landscape.* Berkeley and Los Angeles: University of California Press.

Vaccarino, Rossana, ed. 2000. *Roberto Burle Marx: Landscapes Reflected, Landscape Views 3.* New York: Princeton Architectural Press.

Topiary in the Andes

The practice of topiary has become a common urban decorative feature in the northern Andes, particularly in the Peruvian city of Cajamarca and in Tulcán, capital of the northern Ecuadorian province of El Carchi on the border with Colombia. Near the

Topiary created by José Franco in the cemetery gardens, Tulcán, Ecuador. (Courtesy of Keith Richards)

cathedral on Cajamarca's central square, the Plaza de Armas, are examples that mainly take the form of animals and birds. At the Tulcán cemetery gardens created by José Franco in 1936, the style tends toward the abstract, with stylized zoomorphic shapes, pre-Columbian and Christian designs, as well as geometric forms, arches, and tunnels.

—Keith Richards

Bibliography

The Best of Ecuador Website. http://www.thebestofecuador.com/tulcan.htm (consulted 16 December 2003).

Ministry of Tourism, Ecuador, Website. http://www.vivecuador.com (consulted 16 December 2003).

Photography

Photographers working in Latin America have traditionally used their images to articulate social, political, and, more recently, environmental concerns. Today the Brazilian photographer Sebastião Salgado raises awareness about issues such as refugees and the impact of globalization on poor migrant workers, not just in Latin America. The vestiges of a rural way of life and of popular traditions have provided inspiration for the work of many, including Mariana Yampolsky and Graciela Iturbide. Iturbide's work explores a frequent motif in the arts of Latin America, that of the dualities of life in a region where the rural and the urban, or the third world and the first world, come into contact on a daily basis. Artistic influences from outside Latin America are also present in the region's photographic art, such as in the work of Manuel Álvarez Bravo, whose images bear the distinct imprint of a surrealist vision of the world.

—*Lisa Shaw*

Graciela Iturbide (1942–)

Graciela Iturbide is one of the leading contemporary Mexican photographers, and her work has gained international exposure and acclaim. It explores issues of Mexican identity, and her photographs illustrate the coexistence between indigenous, rural practices and aspects of modern consumer society that characterize contemporary Mexico.

Born in Mexico City, Iturbide studied during the early 1970s at the Centro Universitario de Estudios Cinematográficos (University Center for Cinematic Studies) at Mexico City's national university (UNAM) and also worked as an assistant to Manuel Álvarez Bravo in 1970 and 1971. Iturbide's work first appeared publicly in a joint exhibition with two other female photographers in 1975 in Mexico City, and from there the exhibition went to the Midtown Gallery in New York. After the success of this and of her subsequent solo exhibition in 1980, Iturbide's work was exhibited at the Pompidou Center in Paris in 1982, increasing her international exposure. Over the years her photographs have also been the subject of exhibitions in the United Kingdom, Japan, Argentina, and Brazil. She has been the recipient of various prizes, including a Guggenheim Fellowship in 1988 for her project *Festival and Death.*

The theme of Iturbide's photography is frequently village life in rural Mexico, evidencing her interest in the indigenous cultures of her country, particularly such popular local practices as celebrations, feast days, and carnivals. Examples of this theme can be seen in a series of photographs taken in La Mixteca, Oaxaca, during 1992 that take as their subject the practice of goat slaughter. The beautiful and moving images depict different instances within this tradition and portray animal alongside human, as in the photographs entitled "Before the Slaughter" and "The Sacrifice." In these works the focus is on the animals, with humans forming an accompaniment or backdrop; frequently it is the goats that are photographed in full view or close-up, with the human figure appearing only partially, in the form of shots from the waist down or of the feet only.

In the majority of Iturbide's other photographs, however, it is the human face and gestures that receive the most attention, as critics have noted. One of her most famous photographs of the human face is the particularly striking "Our Lady of the Iguanas" (1979). At first sight its female subject appears to be wearing an elaborate hat, but on closer inspection her headgear is revealed to be a cluster of iguanas. This work is one of a collection of photographs that

Iturbide took during a lengthy period in Juchitán, a Zapotec town in Oaxaca.

Another common feature of Iturbide's work is the juxtaposition of indigenous rural culture with modern consumer society. This juxtaposition is neatly illustrated by one of her best-known works, "Angel Woman" (1979), taken in the Sonora Desert. The woman who is the central figure in the foreground stands with arms spread in a semi-angelic pose and surrounded by a vast, unspoiled natural habitat, yet she carries a transistor radio in her hand. This photograph reveals the coexistence of traditional ways of life and accelerated modernity in contemporary Mexico. Another similar example of the combination of the rural with modern commercial features is "Keeper of the Roads" (1995), in which an old man seated in a rural landscape wears a modern brand of baseball boots.

—*Claire Taylor*

See also: *Popular Religion and Festivals:* Indigenous Religious and Cultural Practices (Mexico); *Visual Arts and Architecture:* Photography (Manuel Álvarez Bravo)

Bibliography

Ferrer, Elizabeth. 1993. "Manos Poderosas: The Photography of Graciela Iturbide." *Review: Latin American Literature and Arts* 47: 69–78.

Iturbide, Graciela. 1996. *Images of the Spirit.* Photographs by Graciela Iturbide, preface by Roberto Tejada, epilogue by Alfredo López Austin. New York: Aperture.

Kozloff, Max. 1999. "Images of the Spirit: Photographs by Graciela Iturbide." *Art in America* 87, no. 11: 122–127, 159.

Manuel Álvarez Bravo (1902–2002)

Mexico's best-known photographer, Manuel Álvarez Bravo made his name in the 1920s and is thought of as the founder of photographic art in his country. His artistic reputation was partly based on his association with Tina Modotti, a fellow pioneer whose life was closely entwined with that of Mexico. However, Álvarez Bravo developed his own aesthetic, and his work consistently displays a surrealist influence, an interest in capturing movement, and a delight in catching ordinary people in very unusual circumstances. He was a mentor for many budding photographers, either by example or, as in the case of his former assistant Graciela Iturbide, through instruction and direct influence.

During the period after the Mexican Revolution (1910–1920), artists in various media were forging a new, revitalized imagery befitting a revolutionized social reality. The legendary Italian photographer Tina Modotti, Edward Weston from the United States, and the German Hugo Brehme were but a few of the foreigners attracted to Mexico at a time when the muralists Diego Rivera, José Clemente Orozco, and David Alfaro Siqueiros were at their creative peak. Together with Álvarez Bravo, all loosely collaborated in founding an imaginary for the redefined Mexican nation based on an appreciation of what were seen as its essential characteristics. These comprised a reevaluation of indigenous culture, a celebration of harmonious human interaction with the natural surroundings, and an acceptance of the socialist ethos.

Álvarez Bravo's interest in photography did not develop until his early twenties, when he met and was influenced by Brehme. Modotti had an even more profound impact on him, specifically her depictions of Mexico in revolution and her interest in the country's cultural depth and diversity. Modotti encouraged the young

Álvarez Bravo to devote himself to the camera, and when she was expelled from Mexico in 1930, she urged him to carry on her work, photographing the murals and scenes from contemporary reality that had become her hallmark.

Like his compatriot, the poet Octavio Paz, Álvarez Bravo came under the influence of surrealism. An example of his surrealist vision can be seen in his juxtapositions of objects not normally associated with one another, giving them new meaning. The photograph "Two Pairs of Legs" (1928–1929) shows an image from an advertisement with well-clad male and female lower limbs emerging from the side of a building as if they were extensions of the windows just above. Another such image, in which the tawdry and homespun nature of the advertising that signaled Mexico's entry into capitalism creates an incongruous, surreal effect, is "Optical Parable" (1931), an ingenious take on a Mexico City optician's hand-painted shopfront.

A portrait of photographer Manuel Alvarez Bravo, Mexico, 1997. (Keith Dannemiller/ Corbis)

What Octavio Paz praised as Álvarez Bravo's "lens of revelations" (Paz 1997) was also admired by the great French photographer Henri Cartier-Bresson, himself renowned for having an uncanny eye and sense of timing. An example of Álvarez Bravo's vision is "Scale of Scales" (1931), which shows a doorway filled with objects ordered seemingly haphazardly but in a way that harmonizes the occupied and empty spaces. Light and darkness interact in Álvarez Bravo's work in a way that he likened to life and death: he saw the photographer's work as stealing images from oblivion. His fondness for capturing movement, usually with figures seen against blank backgrounds such as walls, streets, and deserts, also evokes this feeling of defiance of the passage of time. Other recurrent images are sensuous yet strangely unsettling nudes, and "ordinary" people caught in extraordinary situations. Although these images make some use of Mexico's rich popular traditions, they never descend into folkloric depictions of the picturesque, and above all they refuse to patronize their subjects or invite the viewer to pity them.

Álvarez Bravo portrayed many of Mexico's most renowned artists, such as Frida Kahlo, the above-mentioned muralist painters, and the novelist Juan Rulfo. Yet despite the widespread admiration for his work expressed by fellow artists in Mexico, he remained almost unknown abroad until the late 1930s, when he appeared in an exhibition of Mexican art set up by André Breton in Paris, and the early 1940s, when he began to exhibit in the United States. Further shows in France and the United States from the 1970s to 1990s confirmed his reputation internationally.

Unlike Modotti, Álvarez Bravo took little interest in ideology and shunned political gatherings, even in the militant 1920s and 1930s. Nonetheless, his identification with the lot of the ordinary people was always in evidence. Álvarez Bravo did not always convey this identification in a political context, as Modotti did in her shots of demonstrations, dignified workers, and socialist insignia. He preferred to work on the minutiae of everyday life, carefully avoiding the photogenic and picturesque. His famous photo "The Barber" (1924) is a prime example of this aesthetic, displaying a street barber whose only apparatus is the chair on which his client sits. Both men are viewed from behind, the barber's hunched stance hinting at a kind of menace as he looms over the young customer's exposed neck. Álvarez Bravo's only work with an arguably explicit social content is the image "Striking Worker, Assassinated, Oaxaca" (1934), which draws its political content from the title applied to this shot of a young man's head bleeding onto the ground.

—*Keith Richards*

See also: *Visual Arts and Architecture:* Art (Frida Kahlo; José Clemente Orozco; Diego Rivera; David Alfaro Siqueiros); Photography (Graciela Iturbide; Tina Modotti)

Bibliography

Hopkinson, Amanda. 2002. *Manuel Álvarez Bravo.* London: Phaidon.

Kaufman, Frederick. 1997. *Manuel Álvarez Bravo: Photographs and Memories.* New York: Aperture.

Kismaric, Susan. 1997. *Manuel Álvarez Bravo.* London and New York: Thames and Hudson; Museum of Modern Art.

Manuel Álvarez Bravo. 2001. Los Angeles: J. Paul Getty Museum.

Mraz, John. 1997. Review of Susan Kismaric, *Manuel Álvarez Bravo* (1997). *Estudios Interdisciplinarios de America Latina y el Caribe* 2 (July–December). http://www.tau.ac.il/eial/VIII_2/mraz.htm (consulted 10 December 2003).

Paz, Octavio. 1997. *Manuel Álvarez Bravo: Vintage Photos.* New York: Robert Miller Gallery.

Portal de las Artes Visuales, Venezuela, Website. http://www.portal.arts.ve/papeles/alvarezb/manuelalvarez1.htm (consulted 10 December 2003).

Tina Modotti (1896–1942)

Tina Modotti was one of the leading women photographers of the twentieth century in Mexico. Although not Mexican by birth, Modotti is best remembered for producing some of the most striking and emblematic images of the Mexican cultural renaissance of the first half of the twentieth century. Her photography evidenced her keen interest in the purity of form and the art of careful composition, but she was also deeply engaged in revolutionary politics in Mexico, and many of her works have a clearly defined political content. In addition to her own art, Modotti was involved significantly in documenting the Mexican muralist movement led by Diego Rivera, José Clemente Orozco, and David Alfaro Siqueiros. From the late 1920s onward she was engaged in producing a series of photographs of the murals, and her work enabled the muralists to gain greater prominence internationally, since her photographs were reproduced in magazines and journals worldwide.

Born Assunta Adelaida Luigia Modotti Mondini in Italy, Modotti was called Assuntina ("little Assunta") to distinguish her from her mother, who bore the same name;

this was quickly shortened to "Tina," which became the name she used throughout her life. By 1913 Modotti had left Italy for the United States, and while there she had a brief career in cinema, playing a series of supporting roles in silent movies. She also married the poet and painter Roubaix de L'Abrie Richey, and throughout 1921 she worked as a model for the famous photographer Edward Weston, with whom she had an affair. After her husband's death, Modotti and Weston moved to Mexico in 1923, and Weston encouraged Modotti to take up photography in her own right, initially as his apprentice. Modotti learned from Weston so-called pure formal values, which can be seen in the clean symmetrical shapes of some of her earlier works. Photographs such as "Sugar Cane" and "Glasses" (both 1925) depict recurring shapes and neat geometry in the symmetrical lines of the sugarcanes and the repeated circles of the glasses; notably, there is no human presence in these works.

A good example of Modotti's skill in combining formal composition with revolutionary content can be seen in her 1928 work "Peasant Workers Reading *El Machete.*" In this photograph, the peasant workers can be seen reading the radical newspaper *El Machete*, to which Modotti herself contributed, and at the same time the photograph maintains a pleasing formal symmetry in the repeated circles formed by their hats, shown in aerial view. Modotti also produced a series of compositions of arranged objects, each of which carries revolutionary meaning. These photographs are aesthetically striking and formally arranged; at the same time, the choice of subject matter—a guitar, an ammunition belt, maize, and a sickle—conveys a revolutionary theme. The guitar represents Mexican musical tradition, the ammunition belt is symbolic of the Mexican revolutionary, maize is the quintessential Mexican foodstuff, and the sickle is representative of farmwork but is also clearly a shorthand for communism. These photographs, by uniting elements of agriculture, music, and war, function as revolutionary icons and transmit a political message. In "Composition with Guitar, Ammunition Belt, and Sickle" (1927), for instance, there is a pleasing symmetry in the curved body of the guitar and the curved shape of sickle, but at the same time there is an obvious revolutionary theme.

In a further noteworthy series of photographs, taken in 1929 in Tehuantepec, Modotti focuses on the human form and its activities rather than on still-life compositions. Modotti concentrates on the women of Tehuantepec, depicting them raising children and undertaking a variety of chores, such as in "Women in the Marketplace" and "Mother with Baby in Tehuantepec." Although many of these photographs are less staged than Modotti's earlier work and have a more candid feel, several still show her characteristic style of careful composition.

Modotti maintained close friendships with the Mexican muralists and appears in one of Diego Rivera's most famous murals, *Distributing the Arms* (1928–1929), in the Ministry of Education building, Mexico City, in which she is depicted at far right, holding an ammunition belt. Toward the end of the 1920s life in Mexico for Modotti was becoming increasingly complicated because of her political activism, and she was eventually deported in 1930. She went to Europe, where she lived in several different countries, including Germany and Russia, but found the opportunities for

My Latest Lover! (1924) by photographer Tina Modotti. (Gelatin Silver Print, 9.2 x 4.4 cm; Center for Creative Photography)

photography not as favorable as those in Mexico, preferring to concentrate instead on direct political action. Modotti was finally able to return to Mexico in 1939, where she died in 1942.

—*Claire Taylor*

See also: *Visual Arts and Architecture:* Art (José Clemente Orozco; Diego Rivera; David Alfaro Siqueiros)

Bibliography

Armstrong, Carol. 2002. "This Photography Which Is Not One: In the Gray Zone with Tina Modotti." *October* 101: 19–52.

Hooks, Margaret. 1993. *Tina Modotti: Photographer and Revolutionary.* London: Pandora.

Lowe, Sarah M. 1995. *Tina Modotti: Photographs.* New York: Abrams.

Newman, Michael. 1983. "The Ribbon around the Bomb."*Art in America* 71, no. 4: 160–169.

Mariana Yampolsky (1925–2002)

The photographs of the well-known Mexican photographer Mariana Yampolsky typically record indigenous, rural, and popular traditions and evidence her commitment to social issues, but she also had a keen interest in photographing examples of popular architecture. In all cases, her photography aims to represent the customs and living conditions of the marginalized and to give value to popular forms of expression. Born in Chicago, Yampolsky became a Mexican citizen. She also worked as an engraver, illustrator of books, editor, and museum curator throughout her extensive artistic career.

After her childhood and studies in the United States, Yampolsky left for Mexico in 1944, part of a wave of artists who moved to Mexico inspired by the post-revolutionary climate. Yampolsky became the first woman member of the Taller de Gráfica Popular (Workshop for Popular Graphic Art), a cooperative project of painters and artists that had a strong commitment to social issues and was dedicated to the promotion of art for the people. In 1949 she was asked to produce a series of photographs of the members of this workshop, images that made up the book *The Workshop for Popular Graphic Art: A Record of Twelve Years of Collective Work.*

By 1959 Yampolsky had left the workshop and begun her photographic career in earnest. Her first major photographic project came in the 1960s, when she spent three years traveling around rural Mexico to remote locations, photographing traditional Mexican popular culture, such as festivals, ceremonies, dances, costumes, and folk art. These images formed the basis of the book *The Ephemeral and the Eternal of Mexican Popular Art* (1970). Much of Yampolsky's work has been published along with text by Mexican writer Elena Poniatowska, noted for her dedication to giving a voice to the marginalized by means of *testimonio*, or testimonial writing.

One of Yampolsky's most striking photographs is "The Blessing of the Corn" (1989), whose main feature is a thin cross that cuts a vertical line down the right side of the image and from which hang two cobs of corn. Set against a bare background of a cloudy sky, the corn, traditional symbol of Mexico, dominates the shot. Another work that captures the popular traditions of rural Mexico is "Day of the Dead, Mazahua" (1989), which conveys the Mexican tradition of the Day of the Dead, depicting a cross over a tombstone and women dressed in rural costume lining up with flowers. Similarly, "Crucifixion" (1991) presents a traditional religious ceremony with rural women standing before a reenactment of Christ upon the cross. Yet at the same time this photograph includes a modern car in the background, bringing the viewer abruptly back to the present day. A similar effect is produced by "Death Also Drinks Coffee" (1992), in which a participant in the Day of the Dead procession appears in mask and full costume, holding a coffee cup.

Another important body of Yampolsky's work can be seen in her 1993 book *Mazahua*, which focuses on the Mazahuan Indian women and their community and includes such photographs as "Mazahua School" and "Mazahua Women." In addition to her photographs focusing on the human subject and its rituals, Yampolsky has taken an interest in the depiction of Mexican architecture, as illustrated in her 1982 book *The House That Sings*, which comprises photographs of houses in rural Mexico, including pre-Hispanic buildings and popular architecture.

—*Claire Taylor*

See also: *Popular Literature:* Testimonio; *Popular Religion and Festivals:* Indigenous Religious and Cultural Practices (Mexico); Popular Festivals (Mexico)

Bibliography

Agosín, Marjorie. 1998. "Mariana Yampolsky: Reading the Gaze." Pp. 162–170 in *A Woman's Gaze: Latin American Women Artists*, edited by Marjorie Agosín. New York: White Pine.

Berler, Sandra. 1995. "Mariana Yampolsky: An Artistic Commitment." *Occasional Papers: Thomas J. Watson Jr. Institute for International Studies* 19: 29–42.

Yampolsky, Mariana. 1998. *The Edge of Time: Photographs of Mexico*. Foreword by Elena Poniatowska; introduction by Sandra Berler. Austin: University of Texas Press.

———. 1999. *Imagen memoria: Image—Memory*. Texts by Elizabeth Ferrer, Elena Poniatowska, and Francisco Reyes Palma. Mexico City: Conaculta.

Martín Chambi (1891–1973)

Martín Chambi, a Peruvian photographer of indigenous origin, made a major contribution to the *indigenista* (indigenist) movement that celebrated and interpreted native culture in Peru during the early decades of the twentieth century. Chambi was the first photographer to capture Machu Picchu, the so-called lost city of the Incas, after its "discovery" by Hiram Bingham in 1911. Chambi opened a studio in Cuzco in the early 1920s that produced many thousands of images that, quite apart from their undeniable aesthetic value, constitute fascinating social documents of the central Andean world in a period of crucial change.

Chambi was certainly a contributor to the ferment of ideas surrounding the *indigenista* movement, and indeed he largely embodied the notion of indigenous empowerment. He was born into a peasant family in the village of Coaza, near the *altiplano* (high plain) city of Puno on the banks of Lake Titicaca. Apprenticed to a photographer who worked for a British mining company in the area, in 1908 Chambi moved to Arequipa, where he worked at the Max T. Vargas Studio as an assistant. However, an indigenous person could not be successful in Arequipa, a city with too many pretensions linked to European lineage, and Chambi moved on to Sicuani, between Puno and Cuzco, to work independently. It was at this time that he began to do itinerant ethnographic work, traveling particularly in Canchis Province to record the area's rich heritage. He moved to Cuzco in 1924, attracted by its unparalleled history as both the former center of Inca civilization and a stunning colonial city built largely on existing pre-Columbian walls.

Although Chambi was the leading exponent of his art in southern Peru in the early twentieth century, it should nevertheless be remembered that numerous photographers were working in Cuzco at the same time. José Gabriel Gonzáles (1875–1952) and Avelino Ochoa (1900–1982) studied with and befriended Chambi; their eye for social themes allied with excellent technique was reminiscent of their master. Another artist, Juan Manuel Figueroa Aznar (1878–1951), provides an interesting point of comparison with Chambi because of their respective social and economic situations. Figueroa was connected by marriage to a wealthy landowning family and thus could comfortably indulge his passion for painting, keeping photography as an amusing sideline that sometimes influenced his work on canvas. By contrast, Chambi, of far more straitened means, knew that his future lay in faithfully pursuing his chosen path of commercial photography, which gave him the possibility of social stability if not advancement.

Chambi clearly aspired to a great deal more than merely making a living by painting family and individual portraits. He was fascinated by the cultural constitution of Cuzco and he undertook to portray the area in all its cultural manifestations. The Inca legacy is admirably represented, such as in his photographs of Machu Picchu. He took several further trips outside Cuzco to record the magnificent Inca ruins in sites such as Ollantaytambo, Tambo Machay, and Pisac. Perhaps most telling, however, are the images revealing the depth of inequality in Andean society in the early twentieth century; Chambi photographed fellow Indians, often alongside whites or in an alien urban environment, and captured their traditions, sadness, difficulties, and hopes.

Chambi achieved international recognition largely through the agency of Edward Ranney. The terrible earthquake of 1950, which claimed over 35,000 lives, was photographed by Chambi but effectively curtailed his career. The depression into which he sank upon viewing the devastation never truly left him, and he resolved never again to send his pictures out of Cuzco. His legacy was safeguarded by his son, Víctor Chambi, who fortunately undertook printing the glass slides containing some 18,000 images.

—Keith Richards

Bibliography

Benavente, Adelma. 1996. "Photography in Southern Peru, 1900–1930." Pp. 8–12 in *Peruvian Photography: Images from the Southern Andes, 1900–1945*, edited by Pauline Antrobus. Colchester, UK: University of Essex.

Facio, Sara, and José de Riva Agüero. 1985. *Martín Chambi: Fotografías del Perú.* Buenos Aires: La Azotea.

Levine, Robert. 1989. *Images of History: Nineteenth and Early Twentieth Century Latin American Photographs as Documents.* Durham and London: Duke University Press.

López Mondéjar, Publio, and Edward Ranney. 1993. *Martín Chambi: Photographs, 1920–1950.* Washington, DC: Smithsonian Institution Press.

Poole, Deborah. 1997. *Vision, Race, and Modernity: A Visual Economy of the Andean Image World.* Princeton: Princeton University Press.

Sebastião Salgado (1944–)

The internationally acclaimed Brazilian documentary photographer Sebastião Salgado is known for his powerful socially aware images of marginalized people, such as migrants, refugees, exploited workers, and landless peasants. Salgado has been awarded many major photographic prizes and awards in recognition of his accomplishments. He became internationally known in 1981, when he was the only professional photographer to document the assassination attempt on U.S. president Ronald Reagan. Salgado combines concerns for humanitarian issues with environmental work, such as a project to protect the remaining rainforest in the region where he was born. He said in an interview: "There is a direct relationship between poverty around the world and our destruction of the environment" (Sebastião Salgado Official Website, http://www.sebastiaosalgado.com.br).

Between 1977 and 1984 Salgado traveled through Latin America, walking to remote mountain villages to produce images for the book and exhibition entitled *Other Americas* (1986), which deals with peasant cultures and the cultural resistance of Indians and their descendants in Mexico and

Brazil. In the mid-1980s he worked for fifteen months with a French aid group in the drought-stricken Sahel region of Africa and created *Sahel: Man in Distress* (1986), a project on human dignity and endurance. From 1986 to 1992 he focused on *Workers* (1993), a documentary project on the topic of manual labor, shot in twenty-six countries. After *Terra: Struggle of the Landless* (1997), a project on the landless peasant movement in Brazil, Salgado published the photographic collection *Migrations: Humanity in Transition* and *The Children: Refugees and Migrants* (2000), on the plight of the displaced, refugees, and migrants in over forty different countries. He said in an interview: "I believe that the way the rich countries in the world live is the right way to live. Everybody has the right to healthcare, education, welfare, the right and the need to be a citizen. I believe that each human being on this planet must have the same rights" (Sebastião Salgado Official Website, www.sebastiaosalgado.com.br).

Salgado was born in 1944 in Aimorés, in the state of Minas Gerais, the sixth child and only boy in a family of eight children, the son of a cattle rancher. He studied economics in Brazil from 1964 to 1967 and graduated with a master's degree in economics in 1968 from the University of São Paulo and Vanderbilt University in the United States. In 1971 he completed his coursework for his PhD in economics at the University of Paris and worked as an economist for the International Coffee Organization until 1973. In 1973, after borrowing his wife Lélia's camera on a trip to Africa, he decided to pursue a career in photography and joined first the Sygma photo agency (1974–1975) and then the Gamma agency (1975–1979). In 1979 he was elected to membership in the international cooperative Magnum Photos and remained with that organization until 1994. From his base in Paris he covered news events such as wars in Angola and the Spanish Sahara and the taking of Israeli hostages in Entebbe, and he also started to pursue more personal and in-depth documentary projects. In 1994 Salgado founded his own press agency, Amazonas Images, which represents him and his work. He lives in Paris with his wife and collaborator Lélia Wanick Salgado, who has designed most of his books.

—*Lisa Shaw*

See also: *Popular Social Movements and Politics:* MST

Bibliography

Salgado, Sebastião. 1993. *Workers: An Archaeology of the Industrial Age.* New York: Aperture.

———. 1997. *Terra: Struggle of the Landless.* London: Phaidon.

———. 2000. *Migrations: Humanity in Transition.* New York: Aperture.

———. 2003. *The Children: Refugees and Migrants.* New York: Aperture.

Sebastião Salgado Official Website. http://www.sebastiaosalgado.com.br (consulted 15 December 2003).

Glossary

acculturation The one-way process of a native culture's absorption into a dominant culture. During the colonial period the dominant culture in Latin America was that of Spain or, in the case of Brazil, that of Portugal.

Amerindian A person belonging to one of the indigenous peoples of Latin America, or an adjective used to refer to such a person's culture.

Andean An adjective that literally refers to the Andes, a major mountain system of Latin America, but that is frequently also used to refer to the three countries where these mountains are primarily located, namely, Peru, Bolivia, and Ecuador.

Aztecs An indigenous Mexican people who established a great empire, centered in the valley of Mexico, that was overthrown by the Spanish conquistador Hernán Cortés and his followers in the early sixteenth century.

bairro Portuguese term meaning the same as barrio.

barrio Term for a district of a town or city in a Spanish-speaking country. The term is often used to refer to the poorer quarters of Latin American cities or to districts inhabited by Hispanics in the United States.

Bolívar, Simón (1783–1830) Latin American soldier and liberator who drove the Spanish from Venezuela, Colombia, Ecuador, and Peru. He is often referred to as the champion or hero of independence for Latin America.

carioca Someone or something from the city of Rio de Janeiro.

chanchada Low-budget but commercially successful popular musical comedies that dominated film production in Brazil between 1935 and 1960.

Chicano/a U.S. Mexican American.

chicha A type of drink and a style of music popular in the Andean countries, but also a broad cultural expression belonging to displaced Andean peoples attempting to come to terms with city life.

cholo/a Contemptuous Andean term connoting indigenous origin and partial acculturation.

clientelism The focusing of benefits on a political party's supporters rather than on society as a whole.

colonialism The policy pursued by European powers, such as Spain and Portugal, in Latin America of establishing overseas settlements and commercial interests. The terms "neocolonialism" and "cultural imperialism" are sometimes used to refer to the more recent phenomenon of independent nations, such as those of Latin America, being economically dependent on or politically influenced by more powerful nations, particularly, for example, the case of U.S. influence on Mexico.

Conquest The successful establishment of Spanish or, in the case of Brazil, Portuguese colonial domination in Latin America.

cultural imperialism *See* colonialism.

favela Brazilian term for shantytown or the poor district of a city.

globalization The process by which Western corporations and the capitalist ethos have taken root in developing nations, such as those of Latin America. This economic process, which has been occurring since the latter decades of the twentieth century, has also led to a perception that cultural distinctiveness between nations is being eroded.

***Guerra Sucia* (Dirty War)** The period of military dictatorship in Argentina that was established in 1976 and ended in 1982.

Hispanic Term referring to the Spanish-speaking world (sometimes also embracing Portugal and Brazil) in general and to U.S. residents of Latin American descent.

hybridity The process of cultural mixing resulting from the contact of two different cultures, social groups, or styles. In Latin America the contact between indigenous peoples or African slaves and the Spanish or Portuguese colonizers gave rise to a wealth of hybrid cultural forms, such as the popular religious practices of *Candomblé* in Brazil and *Santería* in Cuba.

Iberian Adjective used to refer to someone or something from the Iberian Peninsula of southwest Europe that encompasses modern-day Spain and Portugal.

Incas An indigenous Latin American people whose great empire, centered in Peru, lasted from approximately A.D. 1100 until the Spanish Conquest in the early 1530s.

indigenous Adjective referring to a people or culture native to a particular region, in preference to the term "Indian."

Latino/a A resident of North America who is of Latin American descent. The term tends to imply that the person concerned has been born or brought up in North America. It can also be used as an adjective to refer to the culture of this group of people.

Liberation Theology A belief that Christianity involves not only faith in the teachings of the Church but also a commitment to social and political change in societies where injustice, exploitation, or oppression exists. This doctrine is most closely associated with Latin America and particularly with the Peruvian priest Gustavo Gutiérrez, although its impact has been felt throughout the world. This radical theology first emerged with a formal declaration, given at Medellín, Colombia, in 1968, of the Catholic Church's identification with the poor.

lusophone Adjective referring in general to the Portuguese-speaking world.

magical realism A style of writing or painting most closely associated with Latin America that depicts images or scenes of surreal fantasy in a representational or realistic way.

Mayans An indigenous people from the area of Central America that roughly corresponds today to Belize, northern Guatemala, and Mexico's Yucatan peninsula. Their ancient culture was characterized by outstanding achievements in architecture and astronomy.

Mesoamerica Term used by archaeologists to describe the region that covers roughly central and southern Mexico, Guatemala, El Salvador, and parts of Honduras, Nicaragua, and Costa Rica.

mestizaje The process of interbreeding between peoples of different racial backgrounds, or cultural mixing, such as between indigenous or African and Spanish cultures in the New World. The term *mestizaje* is Spanish; the Portuguese noun *mestiçagem* has the same meanings.

mestizo/a* and *mestiço/a Adjectives, in Spanish and Portuguese respectively, referring to mixed-race origin. The terms can sometimes refer specifically to someone of indigenous and European descent.

Mixtecs An indigenous people from what we know today as Mexico.

modernism Modern tendencies or characteristics, often in relation to the arts and architecture, and in the case of Latin America most closely associated with the 1950s and 1960s. In Brazil the modernist literary movement emerged in 1922 from the Modern Art Week event held in São Paulo's Municipal Theater, which brought together writers, artists, musicians, and intellectuals.

mulato/a Someone of mixed black and white ancestry.

muralism An artistic movement of the first half of the twentieth century, with left-wing undercurrents. It is most closely associated with Mexican mural painters such as Diego Rivera but also made an impact in almost every other Latin American country.

neocolonialism *See* colonialism.

New World Term used by Europeans (the people of the Old World) to refer to the Americas once they understood that the continent was not physically connected to Asia, as had been previously believed.

Old World *See* New World.

pachuco Early twentieth-century predecessor of the contemporary Chicano gang member, who since the Chicano movement of the 1960s has become an icon of Chicano "national" identity.

paulista Someone or something from the São Paulo state.

porteño/a Someone or something from Buenos Aires.

postcolonial Adjective referring to the period following the establishment of independence in a former colony, such as those of Spain and Portugal in Latin America, or to any aspect of that period.

postmodern Adjective often used to refer to architecture or literature that reacts against earlier modernist principles; in

Latin America, postmodernism usually dates from the 1980s onward.

pre-Columbian Adjective used to refer to an aspect of Latin American culture or history that existed during, or had its origins in, the period before the arrival of Christopher Columbus in the Americas in 1492.

prensa amarilla Term used in Spanish-speaking countries in Latin America to refer to the low-brow, sensationalist, "gutter" press.

surrealism An artistic movement that emerged in the 1920s characterized by the juxtaposition of incongruous images in order to produce unconscious or dreamlike effects.

syncretism The process of blending of differing or contrasting elements, often resulting from two very different cultures coming into contact. The term "syncretic" is sometimes used to refer to religious practices—such as *Candomblé* in Brazil and *Santería* in Cuba—that mix together elements of Roman Catholicism, taken to Latin America by the Spanish and Portuguese, and the belief systems of African slaves.

telenovela A soap opera serialized on television.

transculturation The process by which cultures that come into contact are modified by each other. Unlike acculturation, transculturation is a two-way process.

Tropicália An avant-garde, countercultural artistic movement, also sometimes referred to as tropicalismo, that emerged at the end of the 1960s in Brazil. The movement found its chief expression in popular music, particularly the work of singer-songwriters Caetano Veloso and Gilberto Gil. Although the movement was short-lived, Tropicália had a profound impact on attitudes and cultural production.

Zapotecs An indigenous people of Central America inhabiting southern Mexico and chiefly the state of Oaxaca.

Bibliography

Journals

Latin American Theater Review. Lawrence: University of Kansas Press.

Studies in Latin American Popular Culture. Las Cruces: University of New Mexico Press.

Travesía: Journal of Latin American Cultural Studies. Oxford: Carfax Publishing.

Books and Articles

Aman, Kenneth, and Cristián Parker. 1991. *Popular Culture in Chile: Resistance and Survival*. Oxford: Westview.

Baddeley, Oriana, and Valerie Fraser. 1989. *Drawing the Line: Art and Cultural Identity in Contemporary Latin America*. London and New York: Verso.

Balderston, Dan, Mike Gonzalez, and Ana M. López, eds. 2000. *Encyclopedia of Contemporary Latin American and Caribbean Cultures*. Vols. 1–3. London: Routledge.

Bethell, Leslie, ed. 1998. *A Cultural History of Latin America: Literature, Music, and the Visual Arts in the 19th and 20th Centuries*. Cambridge and New York: Cambridge University Press.

Brooksbank-Jones, Anny, and Ronaldo Munck, eds. 2000. *Cultural Politics in Latin America*. New York: St. Martin's.

Bueno, Eva P., and Terry Caesar, eds. 1998. *Imagination beyond Nation: Latin American Popular Culture*. Pittsburgh, PA: University of Pittsburgh Press.

Clark, Walter Aaron, ed. 2002. *From Tejano to Tango: Latin American Popular Music*. New York: Routledge.

Del Sarto, Ana, Alicia Rios, and Abril Trigo, eds. 2004. *The Latin American Cultural Studies Reader*. Durham, NC, and London: Duke University Press.

Delgado, Celeste Fraser, and José Esteban Muñoz, eds. 1997. *Everynight Life: Culture and Dance in Latin/o America*. Durham, NC: Duke University Press.

Fairley, Jan. 2000. "Cuba-Son and Afro-Cuban Music: ¡Qué rico bailo yo!" Pp. 386–413 in *The Rough Guide to World Music*, vol. 2, *Latin and North America, Caribbean, India, Asia, and Pacific*, edited by Simon Broughton and Mark Ellingham. London: Rough Guides.

Fox, Elizabeth. 1997. *Latin American Broadcasting: From Tango to Telenovela*. Luton, UK: University of Luton Press.

Garretón Merino, Manuel Antonio. 2003. *Latin America in the Twenty-First*

Century: Toward a New Sociopolitical Matrix. Coral Gables, FL: North-South Center.

Gilbert, Alan. 1998. *The Latin American City.* London: Latin America Bureau.

Harding, Colin. 1995. *Colombia: A Guide to the People, Politics, and Culture.* London: Latin America Bureau.

Hillman, Richard S., ed. 2001. *Understanding Contemporary Latin America.* Boulder, CO: Lynne Rienner.

King, John. 1990. *Magical Reels: A History of Cinema in Latin America.* London and New York: Verso.

King, John, Ana M. López, and Manuel Alvarado, eds. 1993. *Mediating Two Worlds: Cinematic Encounters in the Americas.* London: British Film Institute.

Levine, Daniel H. 1992. *Popular Voices in Latin American Catholicism.* Princeton: Princeton University Press.

Lipski, John M. 1994. *Latin American Spanish.* London: Longman.

Lucie-Smith, Edward. 1993. *Latin American Art of the 20th Century.* London: Thames and Hudson.

Lumsdon, Les, and Jonathan Swift. 2002. *Tourism in Latin America.* London: Continuum.

Mar-Molinero, Clare. 2000. *The Politics of Language in the Spanish-Speaking World: From Colonisation to Globalisation.* London: Routledge.

McGowan, Chris, and Ricardo Pessanha. 1998. *The Brazilian Sound: Samba, Bossa Nova, and the Popular Music of Brazil.* Philadelphia: Temple University Press.

Nouzeilles, Gabriela, and Graciela Montaldo, eds. 2002. *The Argentina Reader: History, Culture, Politics.* Durham, NC, and London: Duke University Press.

Olsen, Dale A., and Daniel E. Sheehy, eds. 1998. *Garland Handbook of Latin American Music: South America, Mexico, Central America, and the Caribbean.* New York: Garland.

Peloso, Vincent C. 2003. *Work, Protest, and Identity in Twentieth-Century Latin America.* Wilmington, DE: Scholarly Resources.

Rowe, William, and Vivian Schelling. 1991. *Memory and Modernity: Popular Culture in Latin America.* London and New York: Verso.

Schechter, John M., ed. 1999. *Music in Latin American Culture: Regional Traditions.* New York: Schirmer Books.

Schelling, Vivian, ed. 2000. *Through the Kaleidoscope: The Experience of Modernity in Latin America.* London and New York: Verso.

Shaw, Donald L. 2002. *A Companion to Modern Spanish American Fiction.* Woodbridge, UK: Tamesis.

Sinclair, John. 1999. *Latin American Television: A Global View.* Oxford: Oxford University Press.

Skidmore, Thomas E., ed. 1993. *Television, Politics, and the Transition to Democracy in Latin America.* Baltimore and London: Johns Hopkins University Press.

Starn, Orin, Carlos Iván Degregori, and Robin Kirk, eds. 1995. *The Peru Reader: History, Culture, Politics.* Durham, NC, and London: Duke University Press.

Suárez Salazar, Luis, ed. 2001. *Che Guevara and the Latin American Revolutionary Movements.* New York: Ocean.

Swanson, Philip, ed. 2003. *The Companion to Latin American Studies.* London: Arnold.

Weiss, J. 1993. *Latin American Popular Theatre.* Albuquerque: University of New Mexico Press.

Werner, Michael S., ed. 1997. *Encyclopedia of Mexico.* Vols. 1 and 2. Chicago: Fitzroy Dearborn.

Index

Note: italic page numbers indicate pictures.

A

C

D

F

H

M

N

S

T

U

V

W

X

Y

Z

Contributors

Stephanie Dennison is lecturer in Portuguese and Brazilian Studies in the School of Modern Languages and Cultures at the University of Leeds, England, where she also codirects the master's program in World Cinemas. She is coauthor of *Popular Cinema in Brazil* (2004). She is also coeditor of *Latin American Cinema: Essays on Modernity, Gender and National Identity* (2005). She is currently working on a book on national identity in the Brazilian belle époque, a coedited book on world cinemas, and a coauthored book on Brazilian national cinema (with Lisa Shaw).

Thea Pitman is lecturer in Latin American Literature in the Department of Spanish and Portuguese, University of Leeds. She was awarded her PhD from University College, London, in 1999 for a thesis on Mexican travel writing and has a forthcoming book based on this research. She has also published three articles on aspects of Mexican travel writing, in *Journeys: Studies in Travel Writing*, and the *Bulletin of Spanish Studies*. Her research interests cover travel writing by Mexicans and other Latin Americans, travel writing by Latin American women writers, and Latin American popular culture.

Keith Richards has taught at several universities in Britain and the United States, and has published numerous articles on both Bolivian literature and culture and on Latin American cinema. His book *Lo imaginario mestizo* (*The Mestizo Imaginary*) was published in 1999, and three other books are currently in progress: a translation of Néstor Taboada Terán's novel *Manchay puytu* (to appear in English translation as *Music of Love and Death*), a critical bilingual anthology of short fiction from eastern Bolivia, and a study of contemporary literature and culture in that country.

Lisa Shaw is senior lecturer in Portuguese and Brazilian Studies at the University of Leeds, England. In the fall term of 1999 she was visiting professor in Brazilian Civilization and Popular Culture at the University of California, Los Angeles. She is author of *The Social History of the Brazilian Samba* (1999) and coauthor of *Popular Cinema in Brazil* (2004). She is also coeditor of the book *Latin American Cinema: Essays on Modernity, Gender and National Identity* (2005). She is currently working on a coauthored book with Stephanie Dennison on Brazilian national cinema.

Claire Taylor is lecturer in Hispanic Studies in the School of Modern Languages, University of Liverpool, England, where she teaches on a variety of topics related to Latin American culture and Hispanic cinema. Her main areas of research are contemporary Latin American women's writing, with particular emphasis on Colombian, Mexican, and Argentine authors; popular culture, with a particular interest in popular music and popular fiction; and Latin American film. She has published articles on a variety of women writers, and is author of the book *Bodies and Texts: Configurations of Identities in the Works of Griselda Gambaro, Albalucia Angel and Laura Esquivel* (MHRA, 2003).

CPSIA information can be obtained at www.ICGtesting.com
Printed in the USA
BVOW06*0203181214

379241BV00006B/77/P